Methods for Achieving Your Purpose   W9-CAP-325

The Bedford Reader centers on common ways of thinking and writing about all kinds of subjects, from everyday experiences to complex scientific theories. Whatever your purpose in writing, one or more of these ways of thinking—or methods of development—can help you discover and shape your ideas in individual paragraphs or entire papers.

The following list connects various purposes you may have for writing and the methods for achieving those purposes. The blue boxes along the right edge of the page correspond to tabs on later pages where each method is explained.

PURPOSE	METHOD
To tell a story about your subject, possibly to enlighten readers or to explain something to them	**Narration**
To help readers understand your subject through the evidence of their senses—sight, hearing, touch, smell, taste	**Description**
To explain your subject with instances that show readers its nature or character	**Example**
To explain or evaluate your subject by helping readers see the similarities and differences between it and another subject	**Comparison and Contrast**
To inform readers how to do something or how something works—how a sequence of actions leads to a particular result	**Process Analysis**
To explain a conclusion about your subject by showing readers the subject's parts or elements	**Division or Analysis**
To help readers see order in your subject by understanding the kinds or groups it can be sorted into	**Classification**
To tell readers the reasons for or consequences of your subject, explaining why or what if	**Cause and Effect**
To show readers the meaning of your subject—its boundaries and its distinctions from other subjects	**Definition**
To have readers consider your opinion about your subject or your proposal for it	**Argument and Persuasion**

THE BRIEF BEDFORD READER

Twelfth Edition

X. J. Kennedy

Dorothy M. Kennedy

Jane E. Aaron

Ellen Kuhl Repetto

BEDFORD/ST. MARTIN'S   BOSTON ◆ NEW YORK

For Bedford/St. Martin's

Publisher for Composition: Leasa Burton
Executive Editor: John E. Sullivan III
Publishing Services Coordinator: Elizabeth M. Schaaf
Senior Production Supervisor: Jennifer Peterson
Marketing Manager: Emily Rowin
Editorial Assistant: Rachel Greenhaus
Project Management: Lifland et al., Bookmakers
Copy Editor: Jane Hoover
Photo Researcher: Naomi Kornhauser
Text Design: Anna Palchik, Dorothy Bungert/EriBen Graphics, and Jean Hammond
Cover Design: Billy Boardman
Cover Art: Landscape #482 courtesy of Brian Hibbard, A Gallery Fine Art, Palm Desert, CA
Composition: Achorn International, Inc.
Printing and Binding: RR Donnelley and Sons

President, Bedford/St. Martin's: Denise B. Wydra
Editorial Director, English and Music: Karen S. Henry
Director of Marketing: Karen R. Soeltz
Production Director: Susan W. Brown
Director of Rights and Permissions: Hilary Newman

Manufactured in the United States of America.

1 2 3 4 5 6   17 16 15 14 13

For information, write: Bedford/St. Martin's, 75 Arlington Street, Boston, MA 02116
  (617-399-4000)

ISBN 978-1-4576-3696-7

PREFACE FOR INSTRUCTORS

"A writer" says Saul Bellow, "is a reader moved to emulate." In a nutshell the aim of *The Brief Bedford Reader* is to move students to be writers, through reading and emulating the good writing of others.

This twelfth edition pursues that aim both rhetorically and thematically. We present the rhetorical methods realistically, as we ourselves use them—as natural forms that assist invention and fruition and as flexible forms that mix easily for any purpose a writer may have. Further, we forge scores of thematic connections among selections, both to spark students' interest in reading and to show how different writers tackle similar subjects with unique results.

Filling in this outline is a wealth of features, new and enduring.

NEW FEATURES

ENGAGING NEW READINGS BY REMARKABLE WRITERS   As always, we have been engrossed in freshening the book's selections. In searching for works academic yet lively, we discovered exceptional rhetorical models that will, we trust, also compel students' interest. The seventeen new selections in the printed book include pieces by established favorites such as Sherman Alexie, Michael Chabon, and Meghan Daum as well as contemporary voices such as Junot Díaz, June Melby, and Dan Ariely. Three new contributions by exemplary college writers are part of the mix, ensuring that there is now at least one student model in every chapter.

EXCITING MULTIMEDIA DIMENSION   Glance through the table of contents, and you'll notice that *The Brief Bedford Reader* is more vibrant than ever. As before, each rhetorical chapter opens with a striking image—an ad, a photograph, a drawing—with accompanying text and questions to invite students' critical reading. For this edition we have dramatically extended this visual component with the e-Pages, an innovative Web platform that makes it easy to integrate relevant multimedia into the composition course.

For the first time, every chapter in Part Two of *The Brief Bedford Reader* includes at least one integrated media work: multimodal oral histories, audio essay, interactive graphic, video, and so forth. These twelve new selections promise to engage students with the rhetorical methods, showing how they work in materials we run across every day. For each one we provide introductory headnotes, a comprehension quiz, questions for analysis, and suggestions for writing to encourage close examination and to demonstrate that careful consumption of new media has become just as important as critical reading of words on a page.

Listed in the table of contents of the print book for ease of reference, the multimedia selections are housed at *bedfordstmartins.com/thebedfordreader*; students can access them for free with the purchase of a new book, or they can buy an access code online.

STUDENT-FRIENDLY GUIDES TO ACADEMIC READING AND WRITING At the request of instructors who use the book, *The Brief Bedford Reader* now does even more to guide students through drafting, revising, and editing their work for an academic audience, helping them move from initial idea to polished work.

- **A better reference.** The chapters on reading and writing in Part One and the introductions to the rhetorical methods in Part Two are simpler and clearer, with many explanations and suggestions distilled into bulleted lists and boxed guidelines so that students can easily follow and use the book's advice on their own.

- **A sharper discussion of critical reading.** Chapter 1 on reading now features a student's annotations on Nancy Mairs's "Disability" along with a more concise sample analysis of the essay. A new checklist for critical reading and two new boxed sets of questions help guide students as they analyze written and visual texts, and a new photograph, *Man Fishing by a Power Plant*, anchors a revised discussion of reading images critically.

- **New coverage of key writing topics.** Chapter 2 on writing expands the emphasis on the thesis, with tips on finding a focus and examples of weak and revised thesis statements. In addition, we now offer concrete suggestions for drafting the introduction, body, and conclusion of an essay, and we have annotated the examples of revised and edited drafts to highlight and explain the student writer's changes.

- **More help with writing from sources.** Chapter 3 on academic writing offers a stronger focus on the crucial skill of synthesizing ideas, from one text or many. A new section on avoiding plagiarism offers concrete advice for using the work of other writers ethically, followed by an expanded discussion of summary, paraphrase, and quotation, with clear examples of acceptable and unacceptable borrowing. Updated material on research emphasizes the benefits of using a library's Web site, includes boxed guidelines for evaluating sources, and offers several new models for documenting sources in MLA style. Both response writing and researched writing continue to be illustrated by an annotated student essay — written by the same student on related subjects — and seven additional examples of documented writing are spread throughout the book.

- **A new appendix on APA documentation.** The appendix offers a brief overview of the citation style, forty-seven models, and sample pages that demonstrate how researched writing looks in APA style.

TRADEMARK FEATURES

EXCELLENT SELECTIONS BY WELL-KNOWN AUTHORS   The print and multimedia selections in *The Brief Bedford Reader* vary in authorship, topic, even length and format. We offer clear and interesting models of the methods of development by noted writers such as Joan Didion, Brent Staples, Amy Tan, and E. B. White. Half the selections are by women, and a third touch on cultural diversity. They range in subject from family to science, from language to psychology, from food to politics.

EXTENSIVE THEMATIC CONNECTIONS   *The Brief Bedford Reader* provides substantial topics for class discussion and writing. A pair of essays in each rhetorical chapter addresses the same subject, from the ordinary (food) to the controversial (globalization). Four of those pairings are new, and the thoroughly refreshed chapter on argument now includes one essay pair and two new casebooks consisting of three selections apiece. At least one "Connections" writing topic after every selection suggests links to other selections in the book and in the e-Pages. And an alternate thematic table of contents arranges the book's selections under nearly four dozen topics (eleven new).

REALISTIC TREATMENT OF THE RHETORICAL METHODS   *The Brief Bedford Reader* treats the methods of development not as empty forms but as tools for inventing, for shaping, and, ultimately, for accomplishing a purpose.

- **Clear, practical chapter introductions** link the methods to the range of purposes they can serve and give step-by-step guidance for writing and revising in the method. (For quick reference, the purpose-method links also appear inside the front cover, where they are keyed to the marginal page tabs that appear in each chapter introduction.)

- **A "Focus" box in every rhetorical chapter** highlights an element of writing that is especially relevant to that method—for example, verbs in narration, concrete words in description, parallelism in comparison and contrast (new), and tone in argument and persuasion. To show these elements in context, most selections include a question about them.

- **Annotated examples** of a textbook passage and a college writing assignment end each chapter introduction to demonstrate academic applications of the methods across the disciplines.

- **An emphasis on mixing the methods** takes the realistic approach even further. We show how writers freely combine methods to achieve their purposes: Each rhetorical introduction discusses how that method might work with others, and at least one "Other Methods" question after every selection helps students analyze how methods work together. Most significantly, Part Three provides an anthology of works by well-known writers that specifically illustrate mixed methods. The headnotes for these selections point to where each method comes into play.

EMPHASIS ON GENRE   *The Brief Bedford Reader* is still the only rhetorical reader to show students how they can apply the methods to various genres of writing. Integrated discussions throughout Part One introduce students to the concept of genre and help them understand how purpose, audience, and convention affect a writer's choices. And in each rhetorical chapter in Part Two, an annotated sample of a student-written document—such as a case study, a field observation, or a lab report—demonstrates a specific application of method to genre, with brief guidelines for writing different kinds of projects. The new multimedia selections in the e-Pages extend this focus, showing additional genres—advertisements, cartoons, blogs, online comments, and so forth—at work in the real world.

UNIQUE COMMENTS BY WRITERS ON WRITING   After their essays, half of the book's writers offer comments on everything from grammar to revision to how they developed the particular piece we reprint. Besides providing rock-solid advice, these comments also prove that for the pros, too, writing is usually a challenge. For easy access, the "Writers on Writing" features are listed in the book's index under the topics they address. Look up *Revision*, for instance, and find that Junot Díaz, Annie Dillard, Dave Barry, and Russell Baker, among others, have something to say about this crucial stage of the writing process.

ABUNDANT EDITORIAL APPARATUS As always, we've surrounded the selections with a wealth of material designed to get students reading, thinking, and writing. To help structure students' critical approach to the selections, each one is preceded by a headnote on the author and one on the selection itself, which outlines the selection's cultural and historical contexts. Each selection is accompanied by an online reading quiz and followed by sets of questions on meaning, writing strategy, and language and at least five writing suggestions. One writing suggestion encourages students to explore their responses in their journals; another suggests how to develop the journal writing into an essay; and others emphasize critical writing, research, and connections among selections.

Besides the aids with every selection, the book also includes additional writing topics for every rhetorical chapter, a glossary ("Useful Terms") that defines key terms used in the book (all those printed in SMALL CAPITAL LETTERS), and an index that alphabetizes authors and titles and important topics (including the elements of composition and, as noted earlier, those covered in the "Writers on Writing" features).

EXTENSIVE INSTRUCTOR'S MANUAL Available online at *bedfordstmartins .com/thebedfordreader* or bound into the instructor's edition, *Notes and Resources for Teaching The Brief Bedford Reader* suggests ways to integrate journaling and collaboration into writing classes; ways to use the book's opening chapters on critical reading, the writing process, and academic writing; and tips on using visuals and multimedia selections in a writing course. In addition, *Notes and Resources* discusses every method, every selection (with possible answers to all questions), and every "Writers on Writing" feature.

TWO VERSIONS *The Brief Bedford Reader* has a sibling. A longer edition, *The Bedford Reader*, features sixty-seven selections (instead of the fifty in this book) and all of the digital selections in the e-Pages.

E-BOOK OPTION *The Brief Bedford Reader* is also available as a *Bedford e-Book to Go*, a customizable electronic edition that can be downloaded to a computer, tablet, or e-reader—for about half the cost of a print book. To order access cards for the *Bedford e-Book to Go* format, use ISBN 978-1-4576-6781-7. For details, visit *bedfordstmartins.com/thebedfordreader/formats*.

ACKNOWLEDGMENTS

Hundreds of teachers and students over the years have helped us shape *The Brief Bedford Reader*. For this edition, the following teachers offered insights from their experiences that encouraged worthy changes: Mary Jane

Atkins, Pierce College; Monique Bonfiglio, Westchester Community College; Ginny Buccelli, Contra Costa College; Steve Cirrone, Sacramento City College; Elizabeth Crews, Shorter University; Matthew Decker, Montgomery College; Christina Devlin, Montgomery College; Erin Ergenbright, Portland Community College; Robert Galin, University of New Mexico–Gallup Branch; John Hare, Montgomery College; Richard Follett, Los Angeles Pierce College; Andy Fried, SUNY Rockland Community College; Steve Gediman, Pierce College; Darrin Grinder, Northwest Nazarene University; Amy Handy, Austin Community College; Tara Hembrough, Southern Illinois University; Janet Henderson, Bergen Community College; Susan Herdzina, Santa Monica College; Barbara Hernandez, Napa Valley College; Pamela Hughes, Bergen Community College; Catherine Hutcheson, Troy University; Marlene Kawalick, SUNY Rockland Community College; Christopher Krietsch, Suffolk County Community College; Jill Kronstadt, Montgomery College; Rob Lively, Truckee Meadows Community College; Wendy Lym, Austin Community College; Debra Lee, Nash Community College; Deborah Mael, Newbury College; Nancy McGee, Macomb Community College; Mary McGlone, Suffolk County Community College; Kay Meyers, Oral Roberts University; Sheila Mulligan, Gettysburg College; Kimberly Murphy, Montgomery College; Kathy Quesenbury, Tarrant County College–Southeast; Dan Reade, Montgomery College; Pamela Reay, Phoenix College; Mae Sands, College of Central Florida; Danielle Santos, University of Massachusetts Lowell; Steven Schneider, SUNY Rockland Community College; Jim Schrantz, Tarrant County College–Trinity River; Pamela Stovall, University of New Mexico–Gallup; Christa Washington, Saint Augustine's College; Linda Weeks, Dyersburg State Community College; Page Whittenburg, Montgomery College; Cocoa Williams, Xavier University of Louisiana; Mitali Wong, Claflin University; Sue Wright, Austin Community College; and Connie Youngblood, Blinn College.

We are as ever deeply in debt to the creative people at and around Bedford/St. Martin's. Joan Feinberg, Denise Wydra, Steve Scipione, Maura Shea, and especially Karen Henry contributed insight and support. Our friend John Sullivan, assisted by Alyssa Demirjian and Rachel Greenhaus, suggested and directed the revisions and new features with imagination, intelligence, and patience. John Bostwick helped us look for new readings and update the author headnotes. Billy Boardman created the charming cover. Elizabeth Schaaf planned and oversaw the production of the book. And Jane Hoover helped to transform the raw manuscript into the book you hold.

ADDITIONAL RESOURCES FOR *THE BRIEF BEDFORD READER*

Bedford/St. Martin's offers resources and format choices that help you and your students get even more out of the book and your course. To learn more about or to order any of the following products, contact your Bedford/St. Martin's sales representative, e-mail sales support (*sales_support@bfwpub.com*), or visit *bedfordstmartins.com/readersguide/catalog*.

PORTFOLIOS   The flexible *Bedford e-Portfolio* lets students collect, select, and reflect on their coursework and personalize and share their e-portfolio with any audience. You can provide as much or as little structure as you see fit. Rubrics and learning outcomes can be aligned to student work, so you can gather reliable and useful assessment data. Every *Bedford e-Portfolio* comes pre-loaded with *Portfolio Keeping* and *Portfolio Teaching*, by Nedra Reynolds and Elizabeth Davis. *Bedford e-Portfolio* can be purchased separately or packaged with the book at a significant discount. An activation code is required. To order *Bedford e-Portfolio* with the print book, use ISBN 978-1-4576-7901-8. Visit *bedfordstmartins.com/eportfolio*.

PEER REVIEW   *Eli Review* lets you scaffold your assignments in a clearer, more effective way for students—making peer review more visible and teachable. *Eli Review* can be purchased separately or packaged with the book at a significant discount. An activation code is required. To order *Eli Review* with the print book, use ISBN 978-1-4576-7897-4. Visit *bedfordstmartins.com/eli*.

VALUE PACKAGES   Add value to your course by packaging one of the following resources with *The Brief Bedford Reader* at a significant discount. To learn more about package options, contact your Bedford/St. Martin's sales representative or visit *bedfordstmartins.com/thebedfordreader/catalog*.

- *EasyWriter*, **Fifth Edition, by Andrea Lunsford,** distills Andrea Lunsford's teaching and research into the essentials that today's writers need to make good choices in any rhetorical situation. To order *EasyWriter* packaged with *The Brief Bedford Reader*, use ISBN 978-1-4576-8382-4.

- *A Pocket Style Manual*, **Sixth Edition, by Diana Hacker and Nancy Sommers,** is a straightforward, inexpensive quick reference, with content flexible enough to suit the needs of writers in the humanities, social sciences, sciences, health professions, business, fine arts, education, and more. To order *A Pocket Style Manual* with *The Brief Bedford Reader,* use ISBN 978-1-4576-8383-1.

- *LearningCurve for Readers and Writers,* a Bedford/St. Martin's adaptive quizzing program, quickly learns what students already know and helps them practice what they don't yet understand. Game-like quizzing motivates students to engage with their course, and reporting tools help you discern your students' needs. An activation code is required. To order *LearningCurve* packaged with the print book, use ISBN 978-1-4576-7903-2. For details, visit *bedfordstmartins.com/englishlearning curve*.

- *Portfolio Keeping*, Third Edition, by Nedra Reynolds and Elizabeth Davis, provides all the information students need to use the portfolio method successfully in a writing course. *Portfolio Teaching*, a companion guide for instructors, provides the practical information you and your writing-program administrator need to use the portfolio method successfully in a writing course. To order *Portfolio Keeping* packaged with the print book, use ISBN 978-1-4576-7904-9.

RE:WRITING 2   The best collection of free writing resources on the Web, *Re:Writing 2* gives you and your students even more ways to think, watch, practice, and learn about writing concepts. Listen to Nancy Sommers on using a teacher's comments to revise. Try a logic puzzle. Consult our resources for writing centers. All free for the fun of trying it. Visit *bedfordstmartins.com/rewriting*.

INSTRUCTOR RESOURCES   Bedford/St. Martin's wants to make it easy for you to find the support you need—and to get it quickly.

- *TeachingCentral* (*bedfordstmartins.com/teachingcentral*) offers all of Bedford/St. Martin's print and online professional resources in one place. You'll find landmark reference works, sourcebooks on pedagogical issues, award-winning collections, and practical advice for the classroom—all free.

- *Bits* (*bedfordbits.com*) collects creative ideas for teaching a range of composition topics in an easily searchable blog format. A community of teachers—leading scholars, authors, and editors—discuss revision, research, grammar and style, technology, peer review, and much more.

- **Bedford Coursepacks** (*bedfordstmartins.com/coursepacks*) allow you to easily download digital materials from Bedford/St. Martin's for your course for the most common course management systems—*Black-board*, *Angel*, *Desire2Learn*, *Canvas*, *Moodle*, or *Sakai*.

CONTENTS

A writer with multiple sclerosis thinks she knows why the media carry so few images of
people like herself with disabilities: Viewers might conclude, correctly, that "there is
something ordinary about disability itself."

When college students suffer psychological problems — and the number who do is "staggering" — they seldom seek or receive the help they need. Drawing on sources, the student author of the response essay in Chapter 2 probes more deeply into the subject of psychological disability.

Visual image: *Proposal,* drawing by Demetri Martin

She didn't dare ring up a sale while that epic battle was on. A noted African American writer remembers from her early childhood the night when a people's fate hung on a pair of boxing gloves.

PAIRED
SELECTIONS

The writer recalls her teenage angst when the minister and his cute blond son attended her family's Christmas Eve dinner, an elaborate Chinese feast.

Playing football, throwing snowballs, and being chased: For this writer as a child, nothing could equal the thrill of hurling herself into the game.

e Available in the e-Pages: *bedfordstmartins.com/thebedfordreader*

:e: Available in the e-Pages: *bedfordstmartins.com/thebedfordreader*

[e] Available in the e-Pages: *bedfordstmartins.com/thebedfordreader*

:e Available in the e-Pages: *bedfordstmartins.com/thebedfordreader*

THEMATIC
CONTENTS

☷e **Available in the e-Pages:** *bedfordstmartins.com/thebedfordreader*

COMMUNICATION AND LANGUAGE

COMMUNITY

COURAGE

e Available in the e-Pages: bedfordstmartins.com/thebedfordreader

🄴 **Available in the e-Pages:** *bedfordstmartins.com/thebedfordreader*

FOOD

HEALTH AND DISABILITY

HISTORY

HUMOR AND SATIRE

🄴 Available in the e-Pages: *bedfordstmartins.com/thebedfordreader*

MEDIA

MINORITY EXPERIENCE

MYTH AND LEGEND

THE NATURAL WORLD

READING AND WRITING

SCIENCE

SELF-DISCOVERY

e Available in the e-Pages: *bedfordstmartins.com/thebedfordreader*

🄴 Available in the e-Pages: *bedfordstmartins.com/thebedfordreader*

HOW TO USE THIS BOOK

Many prophets have predicted the doom of the word on paper, and they may yet be proved correct. Already, many of us are reading books and magazines mainly on electronic devices and communicating mostly by text messages. But even if we do discard paper and pens, the basic aims and methods of writing will not fundamentally change. Whether on paper or on screen, we will need to explain our thoughts to others plainly and forcefully.

Our aim with *The Brief Bedford Reader* is to provide you with ample and varied resources that will help you develop your skills as a communicator. In this writerly toolbox, you'll find not only interesting models of good writing but also useful advice, reference guides, ideas for writing, and practical strategies that you can apply to your own work.

THE SELECTIONS

Reading and writing are a unity. Deepen your mastery of one, and you deepen your mastery of the other. The experience of carefully reading an excellent writer, noticing not only what the writer has to say but also the quality of its saying, rubs off (if you are patient and perceptive) on your own writing. For any writer, reading is indispensable. It turns up fresh ideas; it

1

stocks the mind with information, understanding, examples, and illustrations; it instills critical awareness of one's surroundings.

In this book, we trust, you'll find at least a few selections you will enjoy and care to remember. *The Brief Bedford Reader* features work by many of the finest nonfiction writers and even a few sterling literary figures. The selections deal with more than just writing and literature and such usual concerns of English courses; they cut broadly across a college curriculum. You'll find essays on science, history, business, popular culture, food, technology, sports, and politics. Some writers recall their childhoods, their problems and challenges. Some writers explore academic concerns such as the uses of language and the physics of free-fall. Some touch on matters likely to spark debate: gay rights, sex roles, race relations, child labor. Some writers are serious; others, funny. In all, these selections mirror the kinds of reading you will meet in other college courses. Such reading is the usual diet of well-informed people with lively minds — who, to be sure, aren't found only on campuses.

We have chosen the essays with one main purpose in mind: to show you how good writers write. Don't feel glum if at first you find an immense gap in quality between E. B. White's writing and yours. Of course there's a gap: White is an immortal with a unique style that he perfected over half a century. You don't have to judge your efforts by comparison. The idea is to gain whatever writing techniques you can. If you're going to learn from other writers, why not go to the best of them?

Student Examples

You can glean many skills by reading the work of seasoned writers, but you can also learn from your peers. Students, too, write essays worth studying, as proved by Brad Manning, Kellie Young, Andrea Roman, and many others. In half of the chapters in Part Two, you'll find an essay written by a student among the professional selections. These essays, you will see, vary in subject and approach, but every one of them shows how much student writers can achieve with a little inspiration and a good deal of effort.

Student writers also provide examples of various GENRES of academic writing, such as a case study or an essay exam. Concluding the introductions to Chapters 4–13, these examples highlight the practical applications of the writing strategies addressed throughout the book.

Visuals

The selections in *The Brief Bedford Reader* go beyond the written word. Much of what we "read" in the world is visual information, such as in paintings and drawings, or visual-with-verbal information, such as in advertisements and infographics. In all, we include fourteen visual works in the printed book. Some of them are subjects of writing, as when a writer analyzes a photograph or a table. Other visual works stand free, offering themselves to be understood, interpreted, and perhaps enjoyed, just as prose and literature do. To help you get the most from these images, we offer advice on reading visuals, with a sample analysis of a photograph, in Chapter 1.

e-Pages

The selections also go beyond the printed page. Take a glance at the table of contents and you'll notice that some of the works listed there are preceded by the symbol **e**. Those selections — audio readings of classic and contemporary essays, short stories, cartoons, videos, infographics, and more — can be accessed online using the code inside the front cover of this book. (If you have a used book, you can purchase a code at *bedfordstmartins.com/ thebedfordreader*.)

We combine multimedia material with printed texts to further a key aim of *The Brief Bedford Reader*: to encourage you to think critically about what you see, hear, and read. Like everyone else, you face a daily barrage of words, sounds, and pictures. Mulling over the views of the writers, artists, and others represented in this book — figuring out their motives and strategies, agreeing or disagreeing with their ideas — will help you learn to manage, digest, and use, in your own writing, what you read, see, and hear.

THE METHODS OF DEVELOPMENT

The selections in *The Brief Bedford Reader* fall into two parts. In Part Two, the heart of the book, each of ten chapters explains a familiar method of developing ideas, such as NARRATION, DESCRIPTION, EXAMPLE, CAUSE AND EFFECT, or DEFINITION. These methods are extraordinarily useful tools for achieving your PURPOSE in writing, whatever that purpose may be. They can help you discover what you know, what you need to know, how to think critically about your subject, and how to shape your ideas.

An introduction to each chapter outlines the method, explains its uses, and shows how you can apply it to your own writing. The reading selections that follow illustrate the method at work. Examining these selections, you'll discover two important facts about the methods of development. First, they are flexible: Two people can use the same method for quite different ends, and just about any method can point a way into just about any subject in any medium. This flexibility is apparent in every chapter of Part Two:

- **A photograph, advertisement, cartoon, or other image** shows how the method can contribute to visual representation of an idea.

- **A passage from a college textbook and a student example of a college assignment** — such as a field observation or an annotated bibliography — demonstrate the method's potential applications in academic writing.

- **A pair of essays** shows authors using the same method to focus on the same general subject but with different purposes and results.

The second fact about the methods of development is this: A writer never sticks to just one method all the way through a piece of writing. Even when one method predominates, you'll see the writer pick up another method, let it shape a paragraph or more, and then move on to yet another method — all to achieve some overriding aim. Part Three offers an anthology of selections by well-known writers that illustrate how, most often, the methods work together.

THE HELP WITH READING AND WRITING

Introductory Chapters

The selections in *The Brief Bedford Reader* are meant to be enjoyed, but also to give you ideas for your own writing. We include three chapters in Part One to help you build your critical reading and writing skills as you work with the readings. You might want to read these chapters straight through as a general guide or turn back to them as necessary for reference, or both.

Chapter 1 explains the goals of CRITICAL READING and provides concrete advice for approaching written and visual works with an open, questioning mind. To demonstrate what academic reading entails, we include a sample essay and accompany it with the notes of one student, Rosie Anaya, and with our own interpretations of the writer's meanings and strategies.

In Chapter 2 we walk you through the stages of the writing process, following the same student as she works from rough idea to final draft. Like the first chapter, this one features bulleted points and boxed checklists to help you find the information you need. It also includes a brief overview of common editing challenges and shows you how to solve them.

In Chapter 3 we address the challenges of ACADEMIC WRITING, whether in responding to individual selections or developing an idea with reference to multiple works. Another essay by Anaya illustrates researched writing using MLA style, and we include her thoughts about using sources. (We present notes on using APA style in the Appendix.)

Journal Prompts, Questions, and Writing Topics

Following every essay in *The Brief Bedford Reader*, you'll find a battery of questions that can help you analyze the selection and respond to it. First, a suggestion for responding in your JOURNAL to what you've just read encourages you to think about the writer's themes and your reactions to them. Next, you'll find questions on meaning, writing strategy, and language that can help you read beneath the surface of the work, teasing out the elements that contribute to the writer's success and even those that don't. (You can see a sample of how these questions work when we analyze Nancy Mairs's "Disability," starting on p. 18.)

After these questions are at least four suggestions for writing, including one that proposes turning your journal entry into an essay, one that links the selection with one or two others in the book, and one that asks you to read the selection and write about it with your critical faculties alert. Additional suggestions for writing appear at the end of each chapter. We intend these prompts not as rigid taskmasters but as helpful guides. Certainly you can respond to them exactly as written, but if they spark other insights for you, by all means pursue your inspiration. Writing is always best when it comes from a real interest in the subject and a desire to write about it.

Glossary

In this introduction and throughout the following chapters, certain terms appear in CAPITAL LETTERS. These are words helpful in discussing both the selections in this book and the reading and writing you do. If you'd like to see such a term defined and illustrated, you can find it in the glossary, Useful Terms, at the back of this book. The glossary offers more than just brief definitions. It is there to provide you with further information and support.

THE WRITERS ON WRITING

A final word. The writers represented in this book did not produce their readable and informative texts on the first try, as if by magic, leaving the rest of us to cope with writer's block, awkward sentences, and all the other difficulties of writing. As proof, we visit their workshops littered with crumpled paper and forgotten coffee cups. Following more than half the selections are statements by their writers, revealing how they write (or wrote), offering their tricks, setting forth things they admire about good writing. (At the very end of the book, an index points you toward the writers' comments on such practical matters as drafting, finding your point, and revising sentences.)

No doubt you'll notice some contradictions in these statements: The writers disagree about when and how to think about readers, about whether outlines have any value, about whether style follows subject or vice versa. The reason for the differences of opinion is, simply, that no two writers follow the same path to finished work. Even the same writer may take the left instead of the customary right fork if the writing situation demands a change. A key aim of providing Anaya's drafts and comments and the other writers' statements on writing is to suggest the sheer variety of routes open to you, the many approaches to writing and strategies for succeeding at it.

Let's get started then.

READING, WRITING, AND RESEARCH

1

CRITICAL READING

Whatever career you enter, much of the reading you will do — for business, not for pleasure — will probably be hasty. You'll glance at words here and there, find essential facts, catch the drift of an argument. By skimming, you'll be able to tear through screens full of e-mail or quickly locate the useful parts of a long report. But other reading that you do for work, most that you do in college, and all that you do in this book call for closer attention. You may be trying to understand a new company policy, seeking the truth in a campaign ad, researching a complicated historical treaty, or (in using this book) looking for pointers to sharpen your reading and writing skills.

Such reading, like writing itself, demands effort. Unlike the casual reading you might do to pass the time or entertain yourself, CRITICAL READING involves looking beneath the surface of a work, whether written or visual, seeking to understand the creator's intentions, the strategies for achieving them, and their worthiness. This book offers dozens of selections that reward critical reading and can teach you how to write better yourself. To learn from a selection, plan to spend an hour or two in its company. Seek out some quiet place — a library, a study cubicle, your room. Switch off the iPod and the phone. The fewer the distractions, the easier your task will be and the more you'll enjoy it.

How do you read critically? Exactly how, that is, do you see beneath the surface of a work, master its complexities, gauge its intentions and techniques, judge its value? To find out, we'll model critical-thinking processes that you can apply to the selections in this book, taking a close look at a sample essay, Nancy Mairs's "Disability" (p. 12), and at a photograph (p. 24).

READING CLOSELY

Previewing

Critical reading starts before you read the first word of a piece of writing. You take stock of what's before you, locating clues to the work's content and the writer's biases. Whenever you approach a written work, make a point of assessing these features:

- **The title.** Often the title will tell you the writer's subject, as with Anna Quindlen's "Homeless" or Dan Ariely's "Why We Lie." Sometimes the title immediately states the THESIS, the main point the writer will make: "I Want a Wife." Some titles spell out the method a writer proposes to follow: "Neat People vs. Sloppy People." The TONE of the title may also reveal the writer's attitude toward the material, as "The Plot against People" or "Live Free and Starve" does.

- **The author.** Whatever you know or can learn about a writer — background, special training, previous works, outlook, or ideology — can often help you predict something about the work before you read a word of it. Is the writer a political conservative or a liberal? a feminist? an athlete? an internationally renowned philosopher? a popular comedian? By knowing something about the background or beliefs of a writer, you may guess beforehand a little of what he or she will say.

- **The genre.** Identifying the type, or GENRE, of a written work can tell you much about the writer's intentions and the content, format, and strategies to expect. Genres vary widely; they include critical analyses, business reports, works of literature, humor pieces, researched essays, arguments, and lab reports — among many others. The conventions of a genre influence a writer's choices and shape readers' expectations. For instance, you can assume that a scholarly article will take a serious, academic tone, lay out its arguments carefully, provide substantial evidence, and cite other published works. If you encountered the same approach in a personal narrative about a life-changing event, however, you'd be surprised.

- **Where the work was published.** Clearly, it matters to a writer's credibility whether an article called "Creatures of the Dark Oceans" appears in

Scientific American, a magazine for scientists and interested nonscientists, or in a popular supermarket tabloid that is full of eye-popping sensationalism. But no less important, examining where a work appears can tell you about the intended AUDIENCE, the readers for whom the writer was writing.

- **When the work was published.** Knowing in what year a work appeared may give you another key to understanding it. A 2014 article on ocean creatures will contain statements of fact more recent and more reliable than an essay printed in 1700 — although the older essay might contain valuable information, too.

To help provide such prereading knowledge, this book supplies biographical information about the writers and tells you something about the sources and original contexts of the selections, in notes just before each essay. (Such a set of notes precedes "Disability" on page 12.)

Writing While Reading

On first reading an essay, you want to focus on what the author has to say. Don't bog down in every troublesome particular: If you meet any words or concepts that you don't know, take them in your stride; you can always circle them and look them up later. The first time you read, get a feel for the gist of the essay; later, you will examine the details and strategies that make it work.

In giving an essay a second or third going-over, many readers find a pencil (or pen or keyboard) indispensable. A pencil in hand concentrates the attention wonderfully, and, as often happens with writing, it can lead you to unexpected questions and connections. (Some readers favor markers that roll pink or yellow ink over a word or line, making the eye jump to that spot, but you can't use a highlighter to note *why* a word or an idea is important.) You can annotate your own printed material in several ways:

- **Underline essential ideas.**
- **Score key passages** with checkmarks or vertical lines.
- **Write questions** in the margins about difficult words or concepts.
- **Note associations** with other works you've read, seen, or heard.
- **Vent your feelings** ("Bull!" "Yes!" "Says who?").

If you can't annotate what you're reading — because it's borrowed or it appears on a screen — make your notes on a separate sheet of paper or in an electronic bookmark or file.

Writing while reading helps you behold the very spine of an essay, so that you, as much as any expert, can judge its curves and connections. You'll develop an opinion about what you read, and you'll want to express it. While reading this way, you're being a writer. Your pencil marks or keystrokes will jog your memory, too, when you review for a test, take part in class discussion, or write about what you've read.

To show what a reader's annotations on an essay might look like, we give you Nancy Mairs's "Disability" with a student's marginal notes, written over the course of several readings. The same student, Rosie Anaya, wrote two essays spurred by the ideas she found in reading Mairs's work; they appear on pages 53 and 84.

NANCY MAIRS

A self-described "radical feminist, pacifist, and cripple," Nancy Mairs aims to "speak the 'unspeakable.'" Her poetry, memoirs, and essays deal with many sensitive subjects, including her struggles with multiple sclerosis. Born in Long Beach, California, in 1943, Mairs grew up in New Hampshire and Massachusetts. She received a BA from Wheaton College in Massachusetts and an MFA in creative writing and a PhD in English literature from the University of Arizona. While working on her advanced degrees, Mairs taught high school and college writing courses. Her second book of poetry, *In All the Rooms of the Yellow House* (1984), received a Western States Arts Foundation book award. Mairs's essays are collected in *Plaintext* (1986), *Remembering the Bone-House* (1988), *Carnal Acts* (1990), *Ordinary Time* (1993), *Waist High in the World: A Life among the Nondisabled* (1996), and *A Troubled Guest* (2001). In 2008 she received the Arizona Literary Treasure Award. In addition to working as a writer, Mairs is a public speaker and a research associate with the Southwest Institute for Research on Women.

Disability

As a writer afflicted with multiple sclerosis, Nancy Mairs is in a unique position to examine how the culture responds to people with disabilities. In this essay from *Carnal Acts*, she examines the media's depiction of disability and argues with her usual unsentimental candor that the media must treat disability as normal. The essay was first published in 1987 in the *New York Times*. To what extent is Mairs's critique of the media still valid today?

For months now I've been consciously searching for repre- 1
sentation of myself in the media, especially television. I know
I'd recognize this self because of certain distinctive, though not
unique, features: I am a forty-three-year-old woman crippled with
multiple sclerosis; although I can still totter short distances with
the aid of a brace and a cane, more and more of the time I ride in
a wheelchair. Because of these appliances and my peculiar gait,
I'm easy to spot even in a crowd. So when I tell you I haven't
noticed any women like me on television, you can believe me.

    Actually, last summer I did see a woman with multiple scle- 2
rosis portrayed on one of those medical dramas that offer an
illness-of-the-week like the daily special at your local diner. In
fact, that was the whole point of the show: that this poor young
woman had MS. She was terribly upset (understandably, I assure
you) by the diagnosis, and her response was to plan a trip to
Kenya while she was still physically capable of making it, against
the advice of the young, fit, handsome doctor who had fallen in
love with her. And she almost did it. At least, she got as far as a
taxi to the airport, hotly pursued by the doctor. But at the last
she succumbed to his blandishments and fled the taxi into his
manly protective embrace. No escape to Kenya for this cripple.

    Capitulation into the arms of a man who uses his medical 3
powers to strip one of even the urge toward independence is
hardly the sort of representation I had in mind. But even if
the situation had been sensitively handled, according to the
woman her right to her own adventures, it wouldn't have been
what I'm looking for. Such a television show, as well as films
like *Duet for One* and *Children of a Lesser God*, in taking disability as its major premise, excludes the complexities that round
out a character and make her whole. It's not about a woman
who happens to be physically disabled; it's about physical disability as the determining factor of a woman's existence.

    Take it from me, physical disability looms pretty large in 4
one's life. But it doesn't devour one wholly. I'm not, for instance,
Ms. MS, a walking, talking embodiment of a chronic incurable degenerative disease. In most ways I'm just like every other
woman of my age, nationality, and socioeconomic background.
I menstruate, so I have to buy tampons. I worry about smoker's
breath, so I buy mouthwash. I smear my wrinkling skin with
lotions. I put bleach in the washer so my family's undies won't

*"myself" = a person
with a disability
living a full life*

!

*Wait, I've seen
characters with
wheelchairs. Lots.*

*A movie shows
disability defining a
woman's life.*

emotions

again!

*Also The Soloist, and
Temple Grandin*

*The complaint: these
shows miss the point*

*Details
have a point*

*she buys things the
advertisers sell.*

be dingy. I drive a car, talk on the telephone, get runs in my pantyhose, eat pizza. In most ways, that is, I'm the advertisers' dream: Ms. Great American Consumer. And yet the advertisers, who determine nowadays who will get represented publicly and who will not, deny the existence of me and my kind absolutely.

Ads don't show disability either—still true?

I once asked a local advertiser why he didn't include dis- 5 abled people in his spots. His response seemed direct enough: "We don't want to give people the idea that our product is just for the handicapped." But tell me truly now: If you saw me pouring out puppy biscuits, would you think these kibbles were only for the puppies of the cripples? If you saw my blind niece ordering a Coke, would you switch to Pepsi lest you be struck sightless? No,

Hah! Snarky. emotions

I think the advertiser's excuse masked a deeper and more anx-ious rationale: To depict disabled people in the ordinary activi-ties of daily life is to admit that there is something ordinary about disability itself, that it may enter anybody's life. If it is

✓ scary thought

effaced completely, or at least isolated as a separate "problem," so that it remains at a safe distance from other human issues, then the viewer won't feel threatened by her or his own physi-cal vulnerability.

effaced? (means erased, or made to disappear)

This kind of effacement or isolation has painful, even dan- 6 gerous consequences, however. For the disabled person, these include self-degradation and a subtle kind of self-alienation not

effects— IMPORTANT

emotions

unlike that experienced by other minorities. Socialized human beings love to conform, to study others and then mold them-selves to the contours of those whose images, for good reasons or bad, they come to love. Imagine a life in which feasible others — others you can hope to be like — don't exist. At the least you might conclude that there is something queer about you, something ugly or foolish or shameful. In the extreme, you

What about individuality?

emotions

might feel as though you don't exist, in any meaningful social sense, at all. Everyone else is "there," sucking breath mints and splashing cologne and swigging wine coolers. You're "not there." And if not there, nowhere.

But this denial of disability imperils even you who are able- 7 bodied, and not just by shrinking your insight into the physi-cally and emotionally complex world you live in. Some disabled people call you TAPs, or Temporarily Abled Persons. The fact is that ours is the only minority you can join involuntarily, without warning, at any time. And if you live long enough, as you're

Problem affects people without disabilities too— interesting point.

✓

increasingly likely to do, you may well join it. The transition will probably be difficult from a physical point of view no matter what. But it will be a good bit easier <u>psychologically</u> if you are accustomed to seeing disability as a normal characteristic, one that complicates but does not ruin human existence. Achieving this integration, for disabled and able-bodied people alike, requires that we insert disability daily into our field of vision: quietly, naturally, in the small and common scenes of our ordinary lives.   *main idea*

DEVELOPING AN UNDERSTANDING

Apart from your specific notes about a text, you'll also need a place to work out your comprehension using the summaries, critical-thinking strategies, and detailed analyses discussed below and on the following pages. For such responses, you may find a JOURNAL handy. It can be a repository of your ideas, a comfortable place to record thoughts about what you read. You may be surprised to find that the more you write in an unstructured way, the more you'll have to say when it's time to write a structured essay. (For more on journals, see p. 30.)

Summarizing

It's usually good practice, especially with more difficult essays, to SUM-MARIZE the content in writing to be sure you understand it or, as often happens, to come to understand it. (We're suggesting that you write summaries for yourself, but the technique is also useful when you discuss other people's works in your writing, as shown on pp. 61–62.) In summarizing a work of writing, you digest, *in your own words*, what the author says: You take the essence of the author's meaning, without the supporting evidence and other details that make that gist convincing or interesting. If the work is short, you may want to make this a two-step procedure: First write a summary sentence for every paragraph or related group of paragraphs; then summarize those sentences in two or three others that capture the heart of the author's meaning.

Here is a two-step summary of "Disability." (The numbers in parentheses refer to paragraph numbers in the essay.) First, the longer version:

(1) Mairs searches the media in vain for depictions of women like herself with disabilities. (2) One TV movie showed a woman recently diagnosed with multiple sclerosis, but she chose dependence over independence.

(3) Such shows oversimplify people with disabilities by making disability central to their lives. (4) People with disabilities live lives and consume goods like everyone else, but the media ignore them. (5) Showing disability as ordinary would remind nondisabled viewers that they are vulnerable. (6) The media's exclusion of others like themselves deprives people with disabilities of role models and makes them feel undesirable or invisible. (7) Nondisabled viewers lose an understanding that could enrich them and would help them adjust to disability of their own.

Now the short summary:

> Mairs believes that the media, by failing to depict disability as ordinary, both marginalize viewers with disabilities and impair the outlook and coping skills of the "Temporarily Abled."

Thinking Critically

Summarizing will start you toward understanding the author's meaning, but it is just a first step. You need tools for discovering the meaning and intentions of an essay or case study or business letter or political message. You need ways to discriminate between the trustworthy and the not so and to apply what's valid in your own work and life.

We're talking here about critical thinking — not "negative," the common conception of *critical*, but "thorough, thoughtful, inquisitive, judgment forming." When you approach something critically, you harness your faculties, your fund of knowledge, and your experiences to understand, appreciate, and evaluate the object. Critical thinking is a process involving several overlapping operations: analysis, inference, synthesis, and evaluation.

- **Analysis.** A way of thinking so essential that it has its own chapter (Chap. 9) in this book, ANALYSIS separates an item into its parts. Say you're listening to a new song by a band you like: Without thinking much about it, you isolate melodies, lyrics, and instrumentals. Critical readers analyze essays more consciously, by looking at the author's main idea, support for that idea, special writing strategies, and other elements. To show you how the beginnings of such an analysis might look, we examine these elements in "Disability" later in this chapter.

- **Inference.** Next you draw conclusions about a work based on your store of information and experience, your knowledge of the creator's background and biases, and your analysis. Say that after listening to the new song, you conclude that it reveals the band's recent preoccupation with Caribbean soca music. Now you are using INFERENCE. When you infer, you add to the work, making explicit what was only implicit. Inference is especially important in discovering a writer's ASSUMPTIONS: opinions or beliefs, often unstated, that direct the writer's ideas, supporting evidence, writing strategies, and language choices. (A writer who favors gun control, for instance, may assume without saying so that an individual's rights may be infringed for the good of the community. A writer who opposes gun control may assume the opposite, that an individual's right is superior to the community's good.)

- **Synthesis.** During SYNTHESIS, you use your special aptitudes, interests, and training to reconstitute a work so that it now contains not just the original elements but also your sense of their underpinnings, relationships, and implications. What is the band trying to accomplish with its new song? Has the musical style changed? Answering such questions leads you to link elements into a whole or to link two or more wholes. Synthesis is the core of much academic writing, as Chapter 3 shows. Sometimes you'll respond directly to a work, or you'll use it as a springboard to another subject. Sometimes you'll show how two or more works resemble each other or how they differ. Sometimes you'll draw on many works to answer a question. In all these cases, you'll put your reading to use to support your own ideas.

- **Evaluation.** When you EVALUATE, you determine the adequacy, significance, or value of a work: Is the band getting better or just standing still? In evaluating an essay you answer a question such as whether you are moved as the author intended, whether the author has proved a case, or whether the argument is even worthwhile. Not all critical thinking involves evaluation, however; often you (and your teachers) will be satisfied with analyzing, inferring, and synthesizing ideas without judging a text's overall merit.

CHECKLIST FOR CRITICAL READING

✔ **Analyze.** Examine the elements of the work, such as thesis, purpose and audience, genre, evidence, structure, and language.

✔ **Infer.** Interpret the underlying meanings of the elements and the ASSUMPTIONS and intentions of the author.

✔ **Synthesize.** Form an idea about how the elements function together to produce a whole and to deliver a message.

✔ **Evaluate.** Judge the quality, significance, or value of the work.

Using this book, you'll learn to think critically about an essay by considering what the author's purpose and main idea are, how clear they are, and how well supported. You'll isolate which writing techniques the author has used to special advantage, what hits you as particularly fresh, clever, or wise — and what *doesn't* work, too. You'll discover exactly what the writer is saying, how he or she says it, and whether, in the end, it was worth saying. In class discussions and in writing, you'll tell others what you think and why.

ANALYZING AN ESSAY

To help you in your critical reading, questions after every selection in this book direct your attention to specific elements of the writer's work. Here we introduce the types of questions — on meaning, writing strategy, and language — and show how they might be applied to Nancy Mairs's "Disability" (p. 12).

Meaning

By *meaning*, we intend what the author's words say literally, of course, but also what they imply and, more generally, what the author's aims are. When reading an essay, look especially for the THESIS and try to determine the author's PURPOSE for writing.

- **Thesis.** Every essay has — or should have — a point, a main idea the writer wants to communicate. Many writers come right out and sum up this idea in a sentence or two, a THESIS STATEMENT. They may provide it in the first or second paragraph, give it somewhere in the middle of the essay, or hold it for the end. Mairs, for instance, develops her thesis over the course of the essay and then states it in paragraph 7:

  Achieving this integration [of seeing disability as normal], for disabled and able-bodied people alike, requires that we insert disability daily into our field of vision: quietly, naturally, in the small and common scenes of our ordinary lives.

  Sometimes a writer will not state his or her thesis outright at all, although it remains in the background controlling the work and can be inferred by a critical reader. If you find yourself confused about a writer's point — "What *is* this about?" — it will be up to you to figure out what the author is trying to say, to clarify what's unclear.

- **Purpose.** By *purpose*, we mean the writer's apparent reason for writing: what he or she was trying to achieve with readers. In making a simple

---

QUESTIONS FOR ANALYZING AN ESSAY

MEANING

✔ **What is the thesis,** or main point? Where is it stated?

✔ **What is the writer's purpose?**

WRITING STRATEGY

✔ **Who is the intended audience?** What assumptions does the writer make about readers' knowledge, perspectives, and interests?

✔ **How are supporting details structured?** What methods does the writer use to organize ideas? How does the writer achieve unity and coherence?

✔ **What evidence does the writer provide** to support the main idea? Is it sufficient and compelling?

LANGUAGE

✔ **What is the overall tone of the essay?** Is it appropriate, given the writer's purpose and audience?

✔ **How effective are the writer's words?** Are their meanings clear? What connotations do they hold?

✔ **Does the writer use any figures of speech,** such as metaphor, simile, hyperbole, personification, or irony? How well do they lend meaning and vibrancy to the writer's thoughts?

---

statement of a writer's purpose, we might say that the writer writes *to entertain* readers, or *to explain* something to them, or *to persuade* them. To state a purpose more fully, we might say that a writer writes not just to persuade but "to motivate readers to write lawmakers and urge more federal spending for the rehabilitation of criminals." In the case of "Disability," it seems that Mairs's purpose is twofold: to explain her view of the media, and to convince readers that lack of representation hurts people without disabilities as much as it does people with disabilities.

Writing Strategy

Almost all writing is a *transaction* between a writer and an audience, maybe one reader, maybe millions. To the extent that writers hold our interest, make us think, and convince us to accept a thesis, it pays to ask, "How do they succeed?" (When writers bore or anger us, we ask why they fail.) Conscious writers make choices intended to get readers on their side so that they can achieve their purpose. These choices are what we mean by STRATEGY in writing.

- **Audience.** We can tell much about a writer's intended audience from the context in which the piece was first published. And when we know something of the audience, we can better analyze the writer's decisions, from the choice of supporting details to the use of a particular tone. Mairs's original audience, for instance, was the readers of the *New York Times*, as the introduction to "Disability" on p. 12 informs us. She could assume educated readers with diverse interests who are not themselves disabled or even familiar with disability. So she fills them in, taking pains to describe her disability (par. 1) and her life (4). For her thoughtful but somewhat blinkered audience, Mairs mixes a blend of plain talk, humor, and insistence to give them the facts they need, win them over with common humanity, and convey the gravity of the problem.

- **Method.** A crucial part of a writer's strategy is how he or she develops ideas to achieve a particular purpose or purposes. As Chapters 4–13 of this book illustrate, a writer may draw on one or more familiar methods of development to make those ideas concrete and convincing. Mairs, for instance, uses COMPARISON AND CONTRAST to show similarities and differences between herself and nondisabled people (pars. 1, 4, 5). She offers EXAMPLES: of dramas she dislikes (2–3), of products she buys (4), and of ads in which people with disabilities might appear (5). With DESCRIPTION she shows the flavor of her life (4) and the feelings she has experienced (6). And with CAUSE AND EFFECT she explains why disability is ignored by the media (5) to show how that affects both people with disabilities (6) and those without (7). Overall, she uses these methods to build an ARGUMENT, asserting and defending an opinion.

- **Evidence.** Typically, each method of development benefits from — and lends itself to — different kinds of support. For this EVIDENCE, the writer may use facts, reasons, expert opinions — whatever best delivers the point. (We have more to say about the uses of evidence in the introductions to Chapters 4–13.) Mairs draws on several types of evidence to develop her claims, including personal experiences and emotions (pars. 1, 4, 5), details to support her generalizations (2, 4, 5), and the opinion of an advertiser (5).

- **Structure.** A writer must mold and arrange ideas to pique, hold, and direct readers' interest. Writing that we find interesting and clear and convincing almost always has UNITY (everything relates to the main idea) and

COHERENCE (the relations between parts are clear). When we find an essay wanting, it may be because the writer got lost in digressions or couldn't make the parts fit together. In "Disability," Mairs first introduces herself and establishes her complaint about the media (pars. 1–5). Then she explains and argues the negative effects of "effacement" on people with disabilities (6) and the positive effects that normalizing disability would have on people who are not presently disabled (7). As often occurs in arguments, Mairs's organization builds to her main idea, her thesis, which readers might find difficult to accept at the outset.

Language

To examine the element of language is often to go even more deeply into an essay and how it was made. A writer's tone, voice, and choice of words in particular not only express meaning but also convey the writer's attitudes and elicit those attitudes from readers.

- **Tone.** The TONE of piece of writing is the equivalent of tone of voice in speaking. Whether it's angry, sarcastic, or sad, joking or serious, tone carries almost as much information about a writer's purpose as the words themselves do. Mairs's tone mixes lightness with gravity, humor with intensity. Sometimes she uses IRONY, saying one thing but meaning another, as in "If you saw my blind niece ordering a Coke, would you switch to Pepsi lest you be struck sightless?" (par. 5). She's blunt, too, revealing intimate details about her life. Honest and wry, Mairs invites us to see the media's exclusion as ridiculous and then leads us to her uncomfortable conclusion.

- **Word choice.** Tone comes in part from DICTION, a writer's choices regarding words and sentence structures — academic, chatty, or otherwise. Mairs is a writer whose diction is rich and varied. Expressions from common speech, such as "what I'm looking for" (par. 3), lend her prose vigor and naturalness. At the same time, Mairs is serious about her argument, so she puts it in serious, firm words, such as "this denial of disability imperils even you who are able-bodied" (7). In everything you read, pay attention also to the CONNOTATIONS of words — their implied meanings and associations. Such subtle nuances can have a profound effect on both the writer's meaning and the readers' understanding of it. In "Disability," the word with the strongest connotations may be "cripple" (2, 5) because it calls up insensitivity: By using this word, Mairs stresses her frankness but also suggests that negative attitudes determine what images the media present.

- **Imagery.** One other use of language is worth noting: those concrete words and phrases that convey concepts by appealing to readers' senses. Such IMAGES might be straightforward, as in Mairs's portrayal of herself as someone who "can still totter short distances with the aid of a brace and a cane" (par. 1). But often writers use FIGURES OF SPEECH, bits of colorful language that capture meaning or attitude better than literal words can. For instance, Mairs says that people "study others and then mold themselves to the contours of those whose images . . . they come to love" (6). That figure of speech is a *metaphor*, stating that one thing (behavioral change) is another (physical change). Elsewhere Mairs uses *simile*, stating that one thing is *like* another ("an illness-of-the-week like the daily special at your local diner," 2), and *understatement* ("physical disability looms pretty large in one's life," 4). More examples of figures of speech appear in Useful Terms, page 568.

Many questions in this book point to figures of speech, to oddities of tone, to particulars of diction, or to troublesome or unfamiliar words. As a writer, you can have no traits more valuable to you than a fondness and respect for words and a yen to experiment with them.

THINKING CRITICALLY ABOUT VISUAL IMAGES

Like everyone else, you are subject to visual representations coming at you continually, unbidden, from all around. Much of the flood of visual information just washes over us. We aren't always thinking that an image, just as much as a sentence, was created by somebody for a reason. No matter what it is — Web advertisement, infographic, painting, music video, photograph, cartoon — a visual image originated with a creator or creators who had a purpose, an intention for how the image should look and how viewers should respond to it.

In their purposefulness, then, visual images are not much different from written texts, and they are no less open to critical thinking that will uncover their meanings and effects. To a great extent, the method for critically "reading" visuals parallels the one for essays outlined on pages 10–12 and 15–18. In short, as the checklist on the facing page indicates, you should start with an overview of the image and then analyze its elements, make inferences, synthesize, and evaluate.

As you do when reading written works, always write while examining a visual image or images. Jotting down responses, questions, and other notes will not only help you remember what you were thinking but also jog further thoughts into being.

QUESTIONS FOR ANALYZING AN IMAGE

THE BIG PICTURE

✔ **What is the source of the work?**

✔ **What does the work show overall?** What appears to be happening?

✔ **Why was the work created** — for instance, to educate, to sell, to shock, to entertain?

ANALYSIS

✔ **Which elements of the image stand out?** What is distinctive about each one?

✔ **What does the composition of the image emphasize?** What is pushed to the background or the sides?

✔ **If words accompany the work, what do they say?** How are they sized and placed in relation to the visual elements?

INFERENCE

✔ **What do the elements of the work say about the creator's intentions and assumptions?** What does the creator seem to think about the subject? What does he or she seem to assume about viewers' backgrounds, needs, interests, and values?

✔ **How do any written or spoken words interact with the visual components?**

SYNTHESIS

✔ **What general appeal does the work make to viewers?** For instance, does it emphasize logical argument, emotion, or the creator's or subject's worthiness?

✔ **What feelings, memories, moods, or ideas does the work summon from viewers' own store of experiences?** Why, given the purpose of the work, would its creator try to establish these associations?

EVALUATION

✔ **Does the work seem to fulfill its creator's intentions?** Does it do what the creator wanted?

✔ **How does the work affect you?** Does it move you? amuse you? bore you? offend you?

✔ **Was the work worth creating?**

To show the critical method in action, we'll look closely at a photograph by Robin Nelson on the next page.

The Big Picture

To examine any visual representation, it helps first to get an overview, a sense of the whole and its context. On such a first glance, consider who created it — for instance, a painter, a teacher, an advertiser — when it was created, and why.

The photograph above was taken by photojournalist Robin Nelson near the Watts Bar nuclear power plant, located on the banks of the Chicamauga reservoir in Spring City, Tennessee. The image was part of a 2011 photo essay in *Mother Jones*, a nonprofit news magazine and Web site known for its progressive outlook. The year before, an earthquake and tsunami had destroyed nuclear reactors in Japan, causing global alarm and renewing concerns about the safety of nuclear power. Nelson's picture shows a solitary older man fishing from a boat with his hands resting on its steering wheel; part of the reservoir and two cooling towers appear in the background. The reactor associated with the tower on the left has operated since 1996. The reactor for the other tower was under construction at the time of the photograph and was slated to begin operation in 2012 (completion has been delayed until 2015 at the earliest).

Analysis

After you've gained an overview of the visual work, begin focusing on the elements that contribute to the whole — not just the people, animals, or objects depicted but also what might be called the artistic elements of lighting, color, shape, and balance. Notice which elements stand out and what seems to be emphasized. If spoken or written words accompany the work, examine their relation to the visual elements as well as what they say.

In Nelson's photograph the dominant elements are the towers and the man, who is presumably content (notice his smile). A fishing rod and line occupy the center of the image, visually connecting the man, the towers, and the water. The pole points at the sun shining brightly in the upper left corner. The sun reflects off the water and puts parts of the man in shadow; the towers are reflected in the water as well. A line of trees runs across the horizontal midline of the photo, highlighting the natural environment. The sky is clear, with a small cloud floating in the upper right. And in the foreground we see what appear to be a container for bait and a cooler, suggesting that the man hopes to get a meal from his catch.

Inference

Identifying the elements of the visual representation leads you to consider what they mean and how the image's creator has selected and arranged them so that viewers will respond in certain ways. As when reading a written text critically, you make explicit what may only be implicit in the work — the creator's own intentions and assumptions.

We can guess Robin Nelson's intentions for the photograph. On the one hand, it seems to support nuclear power as harmless: The bright sun, clear sky, sparkling water, and lush trees show an unspoiled environment; and the casually dressed, smiling man appears unworried about fishing near the plant. Evidently, the water in the reservoir is clean and cool enough to support life. On the other hand, Nelson would know that the readers of *Mother Jones* are generally concerned about the safety of nuclear power — and that the cooling towers alone would raise red flags for many in his audience. The cloud in the otherwise clear sky and the deep shadow enclosing most of the fisherman seem to hint at danger. Nelson may assume more as well: that whatever viewers think about environmental issues, they will empathize with the fisherman. The photographer may see these opposites as reflecting the controversy over nuclear power.

Synthesis

Linking the elements and your inferences about them will move you into a new conception of the visual representation: your own conclusions about its overall message and effect.

As we see it, Nelson's photograph represents Americans' mixed feelings about nuclear power. The looming towers, the cloud, and the shadowing seem ominous, suggesting dangers facing the area around the plant and the United States as a whole. The tranquil beauty of the scenery evokes our appreciation of nature; the implied pleasure of an afternoon fishing evokes our empathy and approval as it also intensifies our concerns for the man's safety and health. The juxtaposition of the towers, the environment, and a single human being seems to represent the intersecting forces of nature and society and the complex implications of nuclear power for both.

Evaluation

Often in criticizing visual works, you'll take one step beyond synthesis to judge the quality, significance, or value of the work.

Robin Nelson's photograph seems to us masterful in delivering a concise and yet big message. As Nelson seems to have intended, he distills strong and even contradictory feelings about nuclear power and environmental protection into a deceptively simple image of a man fishing. Viewers' own biases, whether positive or negative, will affect their responses to Nelson's image and the meanings they derive from it.

Examples of visual works appear elsewhere in this book: For images that support written works, see pages 386 and 394 (tables and graphs). Chapters 4–13 each open with a visual that gives you a chance to try critical viewing yourself. In addition, several visual and multimedia works are included in the e-Pages (*bedfordstmartins.com/thebedfordreader*): multimodal oral histories (Chap. 4), a comedy sketch (Chap. 7), a video advertisement (Chap. 8), maps and charts (Chap. 10), an interactive graphic (Chap. 11), and a cartoon (Chap. 12).

2

THE WRITING PROCESS

The CRITICAL THINKING discussed in the previous chapter will serve you in just about every role you'll play in life — consumer, voter, friend, parent. As a student and a worker, though, you'll find critical thinking especially important as the foundation for writing. Whether to demonstrate your competence or to contribute to discussions and projects, writing will be the main way you communicate with teachers, supervisors, and peers.

Writing is no snap: As this book's Writers on Writing features attest, even professionals do not produce thoughtful, detailed, attention-getting prose in a single draft. Writing well demands, and rewards, a willingness to work recursively — to begin tentatively and then to double back, to welcome change and endure frustration, to recognize and exploit progress.

This recursive writing process is not really a single process at all, not even for an individual writer. Some people work out meticulous plans ahead of time; others prefer to just start writing; still others will work one way for one project and a different way for another. Generally, though, writers do move through five rough stages between assignment or initial idea and finished work: assessment of the writing situation, discovery, drafting, revising, and editing.

In examining these stages, we'll have the help of a student, Rosie Anaya, who wrote an essay for this book responding to Nancy Mairs's essay "Disability." Along with the final draft of her essay (pp. 53–55), Anaya also provided her notes and earlier drafts.

ASSESSING THE WRITING SITUATION

Any writing you do will occur in a specific situation: What are you writing about? Whom are you writing for? Why are you writing about this subject to these people? What will they expect of you? Subject, audience, and purpose are the main components of the writing situation, discussed in detail in this section. We also touch on another component, genre (or type of writing), which relates to audience and purpose.

Subject

Your subject may be specified or at least suggested in a writing assignment you receive. "Discuss one of the works we've read this semester in its historical and social context," reads a literature assignment; "Can you draw up a proposal for holiday staffing?" asks your boss. If you're left to your own devices and nothing occurs to you, try the discovery techniques explained on pages 30–32 to find a subject that interests you.

In this book we've provided ideas for writing that will also give you practice in working with writing assignments. After each selection, a "Journal Writing" prompt encourages you to respond by writing just for yourself. Then, in "Suggestions for Writing," one suggestion proposes turning that journal entry into an essay for others to read. Of the three or four remaining suggestions, one asks you to take a deliberate, critical look at the selection, and another helps you relate the selection to one or two others in the book. More writing topics conclude each chapter. You may not wish to take any of our suggestions as worded; they may merely urge your own thoughts toward what you want to say.

Audience and Purpose

We looked at AUDIENCE and PURPOSE in the previous chapter as concerns of writers that can help you analyze their works. When you are *doing* the writing, considering audience and purpose moves from informative to necessary: Knowing whom you're addressing and why tells you what approach to take, what EVIDENCE to gather, how to arrange ideas, even what words to use.

Audience

You can conceive of your audience generally — for instance, your classmates, subscribers to a particular newspaper, potential blog readers, or members of the city council. Usually, though, you'll want to think about the characteristics of readers that will affect how they respond to you:

- **Who will read your work?** What in the makeup of readers will influence their responses? How old are they? Are they educated? Do they share your values? Are they likely to have some misconceptions about your subject?

- **What do readers need to know?** To get them to understand you or agree with you, how much background should you provide? How thoroughly must you support your ideas? What kinds of evidence will be most effective?

Purpose

While you are considering readers' backgrounds and inclinations, you'll also be refining your purpose. You may know early on whether you want to explain something about your subject or argue something about it — a general purpose. To be most helpful, though, your idea of purpose should include what you want readers to think or do as a result of reading your writing, as in the following examples:

> To explain two treatments for autism in young children so that readers clearly understand the similarities and differences
>
> To defend term limits for state legislators so that readers who are now undecided on the issue will support limits
>
> To analyze Shakespeare's *Macbeth* so that readers see the strengths as well as the flaws of the title character
>
> To propose an online system for scheduling work shifts so that company managers decide to explore the options

We have more to say about audience and purpose in each of the introductions to the rhetorical methods (Chaps. 4–13). The methods, such as DESCRIPTION and CLASSIFICATION, offer useful tools for achieving your purpose in writing. Each one can help you discover what you know, what you need to know, how to think critically about your subject, and how to shape your writing.

Genre

Closely tied to audience and purpose is the type of writing, the GENRE, that you will use to shape your ideas. Your assignment might specify the genre: Have you been asked to write a personal narrative? a critical analysis? an argumentative response? These and other genres have distinctive features — such as organization, kinds of evidence, and even TONE — that readers expect. If you're not already familiar with the expectations for an assigned genre, ask your instructor for guidance and seek out examples.

You will find many examples of different genres in this book. In a sense each method of development (NARRATION, DEFINITION, and so on) is itself a genre, and its conventions and strategies are covered in the chapter devoted to it (Chaps. 4–13). Each introduction also shows the method at work in a specific academic genre, such as a case study or a review. And the book's selections illustrate a range of genres, from personal reflection and memoir to objective reporting and critical evaluation. The best way to learn about genres and readers' expectations is to read widely and attentively.

DISCOVERING IDEAS

During the second phase of the writing process, DISCOVERY, you'll feel your way into an assignment. This is the time when you critically examine any text or image that is part of the assignment and begin to generate ideas for writing. When writing about selections in this book, you'll be reading and rereading and writing, coming to understand the work, figuring out what you think of it, figuring out what you have to *say* about it. From notes during reading to jotted phrases, lists, or half-finished paragraphs after reading, the discovery stage should always be a writing stage. You may even produce a rough draft. The important thing is to let yourself go: Do not, above all, concern yourself with making beautiful sentences or correcting errors. Such self-consciousness at this stage will only jam the flow of thoughts.

Several techniques can help you let go and open up during the discovery stage, among them writing in a journal, freewriting, and using the methods of development.

Journal Writing

A JOURNAL is a record of your thoughts *for yourself*. (Teachers sometimes assign journals and periodically collect them to see how students are doing, but even in such a situation the journal is for you.) You can keep a journal on paper or on a computer or other device. When you write in a journal, you don't have to worry about being understood by a reader or making mistakes: You are free to write however you want in order to get your thoughts down.

Kept faithfully — say, for ten or fifteen minutes a day — a journal can limber up your writing muscles, giving you more confidence and flexibility as a writer. It can also provide a place to work out personal difficulties, explore half-formed ideas, make connections between courses, or respond to reading. Here, for instance, is Rosie Anaya's initial journal entry on Nancy Mairs's "Disability":

I think Mairs is right that disability makes a lot of people uncomfortable. I know that when I see someone in a wheelchair I can feel anxious, but that's usually because I don't know whether I should offer to help or pretend I don't notice. Honestly, I'm more afraid of the woman mumbling to herself on the corner, or the man on the bus rocking back and forth. But why? It's not like they're contagious. I guess I just worry that they might lash out.

Freewriting

Another technique for limbering up is *freewriting*. When freewriting, you write without stopping for ten or fifteen minutes, not halting to reread, criticize, edit, or admire. You can use partial sentences, abbreviations, question marks for uncertain words. If you can't think of anything to write about, jot "can't think" over and over until new words come. (They will.)

You can use this technique to find a subject for writing or to explore ideas on a subject you already have. Of course, when you've finished, you'll need to separate the promising passages from the dead ends, and then use those promising bits as the starting place for more freewriting or perhaps a freely written first draft.

Using the Methods of Development

In Part Two of this book each of the ten chapters explains a familiar method of developing ideas. In the discovery stage, approaching your subject with these methods in mind can reveal its potential:

- **Narration:** Tell a story about the subject, possibly to enlighten or entertain readers or to explain something to them. Answer the journalist's questions: who, what, when, where, why, how?

- **Description:** Explain or evoke the subject by focusing on its look, sound, feel, smell, taste — the evidence of the senses.

- **Example:** Point to instances, or illustrations, of the subject that clarify and support your idea about it.

- **Comparison and contrast:** Set the subject beside something else, noting similarities or differences or both, for the purpose of either explaining or evaluating.

- **Process analysis:** Explain step by step how to do something or how something works — in other words, how a sequence of actions leads to a particular result.

- **Division or analysis:** Slice the subject into its parts or elements in order to show how they relate and to explain your conclusions about the subject.

- **Classification:** Show resemblances and differences among many related subjects, or the many forms of a subject, by sorting them into kinds or groups.

- **Cause and effect:** Explain why or what if, showing reasons for or consequences of the subject.

- **Definition:** Trace a boundary around the subject to pin down its meaning.

- **Argument and persuasion:** Formulate an opinion or make a proposal about the subject.

You can use the methods of development singly or together to find direction, ideas, and supporting details. Say you already have a sense of your purpose for writing: Then you can search the methods for one or more that will help you achieve that purpose by revealing and focusing your ideas. Or say you're still in the dark about your purpose: Then you can apply each method of development systematically to throw light on your subject, helping you see it from many possible angles.

FOCUSING ON A THESIS

Your finished essay will need to center on a THESIS, a core idea to which everything else relates. When you write with a clear-cut thesis in mind, you head toward a goal. Of course, sometimes you just can't know what you are going to say until you wrestle with your subject for a while. In such a situation, your purpose emerges as you write. But the earlier and more exactly you define your goals, the easier you'll find them to fulfill.

Finding a Focus

Every single essay in this book has a thesis because a central, controlling idea is a requirement of good writing. In most cases that main idea is expressed in a sentence or two, called a THESIS STATEMENT, like these from essays in this book:

> That first encounter, and those that followed, signified that a vast, unnerving gulf lay between nighttime pedestrians — particularly women — and me.
> — Brent Staples, "Black Men and Public Space"

Inanimate objects are classified into three major categories — those that don't work, those that break down and those that get lost.

— Russell Baker, "The Plot against People"

A bill [to prohibit import of goods produced with children's labor] is of no use unless it goes hand in hand with programs that will offer a new life to these newly released children.

— Chitra Divakaruni, "Live Free and Starve"

As these diverse examples reveal, an effective thesis shapes an essay. It gives the writer a clearly defined aim, focusing otherwise scattered thoughts on a main idea and providing a center around which the details and supporting points can gather.

You may sometimes start a project with a thesis already in mind. More often, however, your idea will take shape as you proceed through the writing process. Sometimes you may have to write one or more drafts to know exactly what your core idea is. That's okay. Writing about your subject may be the best way for you to find its meaning and significance.

Crafting a Thesis Statement

As you shape your ideas, or even before you start to draft, try to express your main idea in a sentence or two. A thesis statement is a hook on which you can hang the details of your writing. With such a hook, you'll have an easier time drafting an essay. At the same time, readers will have an easier time following you and will more likely appreciate what they read.

An effective thesis statement shares these important qualities with the preceding examples:

- **It asserts an opinion, taking a position on the subject.** A good thesis statement moves beyond facts or vague generalities, as in "That first encounter was troubling" or "This bill is a bad idea."

- **It projects a single, focused idea.** A thesis statement may have parts (such as Baker's three categories of objects), but those parts should all relate to a single, central point.

- **It accurately forecasts the scope of the essay,** neither taking on too much nor leaving out essential parts.

- **It hints at the writer's purpose.** From their thesis statements, we can tell that Staples and Baker mean to explain, whereas Divakaruni intends mainly to persuade.

Don't expect to craft a perfect thesis statement on the first try. Almost always, you will need to revise your statement — and sometimes your thesis itself — as your ideas take form and your purpose for writing becomes clear to you. In each of the following pairs, the first statement is too vague to work as a hook: It conveys the writer's general opinion but not its basis. Each revised statement clarifies the point.

VAGUE   The sculpture is a beautiful piece of work.

REVISED   Although it may not be obvious at first, this smooth bronze sculpture unites urban and natural elements to represent the city dweller's relationship with nature.

VAGUE   The sculpture is a waste of money.

REVISED   The huge bronze sculpture in the middle of McBean Park demonstrates that so-called public art may actually undermine the public interest.

As you will see, writers have great flexibility in presenting a thesis statement — how long it might be, where it appears, even whether it appears. For your own writing, we advise stating your thesis explicitly and putting it near the beginning of your essay — at least until you've gained experience as a writer. The stated thesis will help you check that you have the necessary focus, and the early placement will tell your readers what to expect from your writing. We offer additional suggestions for focusing your thesis and crafting your thesis statement, with examples, in the introductions to the methods of development (Chaps. 4–13).

DRAFTING

Sooner or later, the discovery stage yields to DRAFTING: writing out sentences and paragraphs, linking ideas, focusing them. For most writers, drafting is the occasion for exploring the relations among ideas, filling in the details to support them, beginning to work out the shape and aim of the whole. During drafting, you may clarify or even discover your purpose and your thesis, try out different arrangements of material, or experiment with tone. Sometimes, though, you may find that just spelling out thoughts in complete sentences is challenge enough for a first draft, and you'll leave issues of purpose, thesis, structure, and tone for another round.

A few suggestions for drafting:

- **Give yourself time,** at least a couple of hours.

- **Find a quiet place to work,** somewhere you won't be disturbed.

- **Stay loose** so that you can wander down intriguing avenues or consider changing direction altogether.

- **Keep your eyes on what's ahead,** not on the possible errors, "wrong" words, and bumpy sentences that you can attend to in revision. This is an important message that many inexperienced writers miss: It's okay to make mistakes. You can fix them later.

Expect to draft in fits and starts, working in discrete chunks and fleshing out points as you go. Don't feel compelled to follow a straight path from beginning to end. If the opening paragraph is giving you fits, skip it until later. In fact, most writers find that drafting is easier and more productive if they work on the body of the essay first, leaving the introduction and conclusion until everything else has been worked out.

The Body

The BODY of an essay consists of the subpoints and supporting evidence that develop the main idea. You may have gotten a start at expressing your thoughts in the discovery stage, in which case you can build on what you've already written in your journal or during freewriting sessions. Or you may find yourself staring at a blank screen. In either case, it's usually best to focus first on the points you're most comfortable with, keeping your thesis, your purpose, and your audience in mind.

Supporting a Thesis

In some way, each sentence and PARAGRAPH of the body should serve to support your thesis by making it clear and explicit to readers. You will likely need to experiment and explore your thoughts before they fully take shape, tackling your essay in multiple drafts and filling in (or taking out) details as you go, adjusting your thesis to fit your ideas. Most writers do.

Earlier we saw that the methods of development can help you discover ideas about a subject (see pp. 31–32). They can also help you find, present, and structure evidence as you draft the body of your essay. Suppose, for example, that you set out to explain what makes a certain popular singer unique. You want to discuss her voice, her music, her lyrics, her style. While putting your ideas down, it strikes you that you can best illustrate the singer's distinctions by showing the differences between her and another singer. To achieve your purpose, then, you draw on the method of COMPARISON AND CONTRAST;

and as you proceed, the method prompts you to notice differences you had missed.

Each method typically benefits from — and lends itself to — a particular kind of support. Comparison and contrast may highlight differences, while narration may draw on a sequence of personal experiences and CAUSE AND EFFECT may require objective information such as verifiable facts. Give the methods a try. See how flexible they are, coming into play as you need them to develop parts of your essay. And see how they help you reach your writing goals by giving you more to say, more that you think is worth saying.

Organizing the Evidence

How you organize your support depends on your purpose: What is your aim? What do you want readers to think or feel? What's the best way to achieve that? For instance, anyone writing a proposal to solve a problem wants to cover all the reasonable solutions and make a case for one or more. But one writer might bring readers gradually to her favored solution by first discussing and rejecting the alternatives, while another might grab readers' attention by focusing right away on his own solution, dispensing with alternatives only near the end. In either case, the choices aren't random but depend on the writer's understanding of readers — their assumptions, their biases, and their purposes for reading.

Some methods of development lend themselves to familiar patterns of ORGANIZATION, which we discuss in the introductions to Chapters 4–13. In a narrative essay or a PROCESS ANALYSIS, for instance, you would probably put events in chronological order. Other methods require that you put more thought into how you arrange your points. In an essay developed by EXAMPLE, you might use a climactic organization, starting with the weakest point and ending with the most compelling one (or vice versa). And a descriptive essay might take a spatial order, following details the way an eye might scan a scene: left to right, near to far, and so forth.

Some writers like to plan the order of their points in advance, perhaps with a rough outline or simply a list of points to cover. If concerns about the organization leave you feeling stuck or frustrated, however, focus instead on getting your ideas into sentences and paragraphs; you can always turn to their order in revision.

The Introduction and Conclusion

The opening and closing paragraphs of an essay serve as bookends for the thoughts and information presented in the body. The INTRODUCTION identifies and narrows the subject for readers, capturing their interest and giving them a reason to continue reading. The CONCLUSION creates a sense of completion, bringing readers back to the main idea and satisfying them that you have accomplished what you set out to do as a writer.

Because of the importance of these paragraphs, and because it is difficult to set up and close out material that has not yet been drafted, most writers find that it works best to turn to the introduction and conclusion *after* the rest of the essay has begun to take shape.

The Introduction

The opening paragraph or paragraphs of an essay invite readers in. At a minimum, your introduction will state the subject and lead to your main idea, often presented in a thesis statement. But an effective introduction also grabs readers' attention and inspires them to read on.

Introductions vary in length, depending on their purposes. A research paper may need several paragraphs to set forth its central idea and its plan of organization; a brief, informal essay may need only a sentence or two for an introduction. Whether long or short, a good introduction tells readers no more than they need to know when they begin reading.

Here are a few possible ways to open an essay effectively:

- **Lead up to a statement of your thesis,** or central idea, perhaps showing why you care about it.

- **Present startling facts about your subject.**

- **Tell an ANECDOTE,** a brief story that illustrates your subject.

- **Give background information** so that readers will understand your subject or see why it is important.

- **Begin with an arresting quotation** that sets up your subject or previews your main idea.

- **Ask a challenging question.** (In your essay, you'll go on to answer it.)

Whatever technique you try, strive to make a good first impression and establish a positive, engaging tone, taking care to match the voice in the body of your essay. Don't begin with a hedge such as *It seems important to understand why . . .* ; and don't announce your purpose with mechanical phrasing such as *In this essay, I will explain . . .* or *The purpose of this paper is to show. . . .* Such openings bore readers and give them little incentive to read on.

The Conclusion

A conclusion is purposefully crafted to give a sense of unity to the whole essay. The best conclusions evolve naturally out of what has gone before and convince readers that the essay is indeed at an end, not that the writer has run out of steam.

Conclusions vary in type and length depending on the nature and scope of the essay. A long research paper may require several paragraphs of summary to review and emphasize the main points. A short essay, however, may benefit from a few brief closing sentences.

Although there are no set formulas for closing, the following list presents several options:

- **Restate the thesis of your essay,** and perhaps summarize your main points.

- **Mention the broader implications or significance of your topic.**

- **Give a final example,** pulling all the parts of your discussion together.

- **Offer a prediction for the future.**

- **End with the most important point,** the culmination of your essay's development.

- **Suggest how the reader can apply the information you have provided.**

- **End with a bit of drama or flourish.** Tell an anecdote, offer an appropriate quotation, ask a question, make a final insightful remark, circle back to the introduction. Keep in mind, however, that an ending shouldn't sound false and gimmicky. It truly has to conclude.

In concluding an essay, beware of diminishing the impact of your writing by finishing on a weak note. Don't apologize for what you have or have not written, or cram in a final detail that would have been better placed elsewhere.

REVISING

If it helps you produce writing, you may want to view a draft as a kind of dialog with readers, fulfilling their expectations, answering the questions you imagine they would ask. But some writers save this kind of thinking for the next stage, REVISION. Literally "re-seeing," revision involves stepping outside the intense circle of you-and-the-material to see the work as a reader will, with whatever qualities you imagine that reader to have.

The first task of revising is to step back and view your draft as a whole, looking at the big picture and ignoring pesky details like grammar and spelling. It's always a good idea to let a draft sit for a while before you come back to revise it: at least a few hours, ideally a day or more. When you return with fresh eyes and a refreshed mind, you'll be in a better position to see what works, what doesn't, and what needs your attention. The checklist below and the ensuing discussion can guide you to the big-picture view. Specific revision guidelines for each method of development appear in the introductions to Chapters 4–13.

QUESTIONS FOR REVISION

✔ **Will my purpose be clear to readers?** Have I achieved it?

✔ **What are readers' expectations for this kind of writing?** Have I met them?

✔ **What is my thesis?** Have I supported it for readers?

✔ **Is the essay unified?** Can readers see how all parts relate to the thesis?

✔ **Have I developed my points well?** Have I supplied enough details, examples, and other specifics so that readers can understand me and follow my reasoning?

✔ **Is the essay coherent?** Can readers see how the parts relate?

✔ **Is the organization clear?** Can readers follow it?

Purpose and Genre

Earlier we looked at PURPOSE and GENRE as important considerations in planning an essay. They are even more important in revision. Like many writers, in the discovery and experimentation of drafting you may lose track of your original direction. Did you set out to write a critical analysis of a reading but end up with a summary? Did you rely on personal experience when you were supposed to use evidence from sources? Did you set out to persuade readers but not get beyond explanation? That's okay. You've jumped the first hurdle simply by putting your thoughts into words. Now you can add, delete, and reorganize until your purpose will be clear to readers and you meet their expectations for how it should be fulfilled.

Thesis

As you've developed your ideas and your draft, you've also been developing your THESIS, the main idea that you want to get across to readers. The thesis may be stated up front or hover in the background, but it should be clear to readers and the rest of the essay should in fact support it. You may find that you need to revise your thesis statement to reflect what you ended up writing in your draft, or you may need to rework your supporting ideas so that they develop your thesis. We discussed theses and thesis statements on pages 32–34 and have more to say about them in the introduction to every method chapter in Part Two.

Unity

Drafting freely, as we encourage you to do, can easily take you into some of the byways of your topic. A goal of revision, then, is to deal with digressions so that your essay has UNITY, with every paragraph relating to the thesis and every sentence in a paragraph relating to a single idea, often expressed in a TOPIC SENTENCE. You may choose to cut a digression altogether or to rework it so that it connects to the main idea. Sometimes you may find that a digression is really what you want to write about and then opt to recast your thesis instead. For more help, see "Focus on Paragraph and Essay Unity" on page 408.

Development

While some points in your draft may have to be sacrificed for the sake of unity, others will probably want more attention. Be sure that any general statements you make are backed up with evidence: details, examples, analysis, information from sources, whatever it takes to show readers that your point is valid. The introductions to the methods in Chapters 4–13 offer suggestions for developing specific kinds of essays; take a look, too, at "Focus on Paragraph Development" on page 323.

Coherence

Drafting ideas into sentences can be halting work, and a first draft can seem jumbled as a result. In revision, you want to help readers follow your thoughts by improving COHERENCE: the clear flow and relation of parts. You can achieve coherence through your use of paragraphs, transitions, and organization.

Paragraphs help readers grasp related information in an essay by developing one supporting point at a time: All of the sentences hang together, defining, explaining, illustrating, or supporting one central idea. Check all your paragraphs to be sure that each sentence connects with the one preceding and that readers will see the connection without having to stop and reread. One way to clarify such connections is with TRANSITIONS: linking words and phrases such as *in addition*, *moreover*, and *at the same time*. We have more to say about transitions in "Focus on Paragraph Coherence" on page 287.

No matter what method you use, be sure that each point follows logically from those before it and leads clearly to those that follow. Constructing an outline of what you've written can help you see how well your thoughts hold together. Expect to experiment, moving paragraphs around, deleting some and adding others, before everything clicks into place.

EDITING

You will find that you produce better work when you approach revision as at least a two-step process. First revise, focusing on fundamental, whole-essay matters such as purpose and organization. Only then turn to EDITING, focusing on surface issues such as grammar and word choice to improve the flow of your writing and to fix the mistakes that tend to get in the way of readers' understanding.

The checklist below covers the most common opportunities and problems, which are explained on the pages following. Because some challenges tend to pop up more often when writing with a particular method, we also give additional help in the introductions to Chapters 4–13, in boxes labeled "Focus on . . ." that highlight specific issues and provide tips for solving them.

QUESTIONS FOR EDITING

✔ **Are my language and tone appropriate** for my purpose, audience, and genre?

✔ **Do my words say what I mean,** and are they as vivid as I can make them?

✔ **Are my sentences smooth and concise?** Do they use emphasis, parallelism, variety, and other techniques to clarify meaning and hold readers' interest?

✔ **Are my sentences grammatically correct?** In particular, have I avoided sentence fragments, run-on sentences, comma splices, mismatched subjects and verbs, unclear pronouns, unclear modifiers, and inconsistencies?

✔ **Are any words misspelled?**

Effective Language

Many of us, when we draft, fall back on the familiar language we use when chatting with friends: We might rely on COLLOQUIAL EXPRESSIONS such as *get into* and *freak out* or slip into texting shortcuts such as *u* for "you" and *L8R* for "later." This strategy can let us put our ideas together without getting sidetracked by details. But patterns of casual communication are usually too imprecise for college writing, where word choices can dramatically affect how readers understand your ideas.

As a critical reader, you take note of writers' language and consider how their choices affect the meaning and impact of their work (see pp. 21–22). As a writer, you should devote similar attention to your own choices, adapting your general language and your specific words to reflect your purpose, your meaning, and your audience.

A few guidelines:

- **Adopt a relatively formal voice.** Replace overly casual or emotional language with standard English DICTION and a neutral TONE. (Refer to pp. 565 and 574 of Useful Terms and to "Focus on Tone" on p. 449.)

- **Choose an appropriate point of view.** In most academic writing, you should prefer the more objective third PERSON (*he, she, it, they*) over the first person (*I*) or the second person (*you*). There are exceptions, of course: A personal NARRATIVE written without *I* would ring strange to most ears, and a how-to PROCESS ANALYSIS often addresses readers as *you*.

- **Check that words have the meanings you intend.** The DENOTATION of a word is its dictionary meaning — for example, *affection* means "caring regard." A CONNOTATION, in contrast, is an emotional association that a word produces in readers, as *passion* evokes intensity or *obsession* evokes compulsion. Using a word with the wrong denotation muddies meaning, while using words with strong connotations can shape readers' responses to your ideas — for good or for ill.

- **Use concrete and specific words.** Effective writing balances ABSTRACT and GENERAL words, which provide outlines of ideas and things, with CONCRETE and SPECIFIC words, which limit and sharpen. You need abstract and general words such as *old* and *transportation* for broad statements that set the course for your writing, conveying concepts or referring to entire groups. But you also need concrete and specific words such as *crumbling* and *streetcar line* to make meaning precise and vivid by appealing to readers' senses and experiences. See "Focus on Specific and Concrete Language" on page 134.

- **Be creative.** You can make your writing more lively and forceful with FIGURES OF SPEECH, expressions that imply meanings beyond or different from their literal meanings, such as *curled tight like a rosebud* or *feelings trampled* *to dirt.* Be careful not to resort to CLICHÉS, worn phrases that have lost their power (*hour of need, thin as a rail, goes on forever*), or to combine figures of speech into confusing or absurd images, such as *The players flooded the soccer field like bulls ready for a fight.*

Clear and Engaging Sentences

When you read the selections in this book, you may notice that each writer's sentences have a certain flow, with one idea moving seamlessly into the next. Although the result may seem effortless, we promise you that it was not: Effective sentences are the product of a writer's careful attention to meaning and readability. Editing for emphasis, parallelism, and variety will ensure that readers can follow your ideas without difficulty and stay interested in what you have to say.

Emphasis

While we're drafting, simply getting ideas down in sentence form can be challenge enough. But once the ideas are down, we can see that some are more important than others. Editing offers an opportunity to clarify those relationships for readers. To edit for emphasis, focus on the following changes:

- **Put verbs in the active voice.** A verb in the ACTIVE VOICE expresses action by the subject (*He recorded a new song*), whereas a verb in the PASSIVE VOICE expresses action done *to* the subject (*A new song was recorded*, or, adding who did the action, *A new song was recorded by him*). The active voice is usually more emphatic and therefore easier to follow. See "Focus on Verbs" on page 99.

- **Simplify wordy sentences.** Unnecessary padding puzzles readers and deflates their interest. Weed out any empty phrases or meaningless repetition:

WORDY The nature of social-networking sites is such that they reconnect lost and distant friends but can also for all intents and purposes dredge up old relationships that were better left forgotten.

CONCISE Social-networking sites reconnect lost and distant friends but can also dredge up old relationships that were better left forgotten.

WORDY Many older adults who use the sites have been surprised and shocked to hear from high-school classmates, classmates they had never considered friends in the first place.

CONCISE Many adults who use the sites have been surprised to hear from high-school classmates they had never considered friends.

See also "Focus on Clarity and Conciseness" on page 368.

- **Combine sentences.** You can clarify the importance of ideas by merging sentences to emphasize relationships. Use *coordination* to combine and balance equally important ideas, joining them with *and, but, or, nor, for, so,* or *yet*:

UNEMPHATIC Many restaurant meals are high in fat. Their sodium content is also high. To diners they seem harmless.

EMPHATIC Many restaurant meals are high in fat <u>and</u> sodium, <u>but</u> to diners they seem harmless.

Use *subordination* to de-emphasize less important ideas, placing minor information in modifying words or word groups:

UNEMPHATIC Restaurant menus sometimes label certain options. They use the label "healthy." These options are lower in fat and sodium.

EMPHATIC Restaurant menus sometimes label <u>as "healthy"</u> the options <u>that are lower in fat and sodium.</u>

Parallelism

Another way to clarify the relationship among ideas is to give parallel structure to related words, phrases, and sentences. PARALLELISM is the use of similar grammatical forms for elements of similar importance, either within or among sentences.

PARALLELISM WITHIN A SENTENCE Binge drinking can <u>worsen heart disease</u> and <u>cause liver failure.</u>

PARALLELISM AMONG SENTENCES Binge drinking has less well-known effects, too. <u>It can cause</u> brain damage. <u>It can raise</u> blood sugar to diabetic levels. And <u>it can reduce</u> the body's ability to fight off infections.

Readers tend to stumble over elements that seem equally important but are not in parallel form. As you edit, look for groups of related ideas and make a point of expressing them consistently:

NONPARALLEL Even occasional binges can cause serious problems, from <u>the experience of blackouts</u> to <u>getting arrested</u> to <u>injury.</u>

PARALLEL Even occasional binges can cause serious problems, from <u>blackouts</u> to <u>arrests</u> to <u>injuries.</u>

For more on parallel structure, see "Focus on Parallelism" on page 210.

Sentence Variety

Sentence after sentence with the same length and structure can be stiff and dull. By varying sentences, you can hold readers' interest while also achieving the emphasis you want. The techniques to achieve variety include adjusting the lengths of sentences and varying their beginnings. For examples and specifics, see "Focus on Sentence Variety" on page 174.

Standard Grammar

Writers sometimes think of grammar as a set of rules that exist solely to give nitpickers a chance to point out mistakes. But grammatical errors can undermine an otherwise excellent piece of writing because they are unclear or distracting. The guidelines here can help you catch some of the most common problems.

Sentence Fragments

A *sentence fragment* is a word group that, although punctuated like a sentence, is not a complete sentence. Experienced writers sometimes use fragments deliberately and effectively, but readers usually stumble over fragments and view them as errors. For the sake of clarity, make sure every sentence has a subject and a verb and expresses a complete thought:

FRAGMENT   <u>Snowboarding a relatively young sport.</u>

COMPLETE   Snowboarding <u>is</u> a relatively young sport.

FRAGMENT   Many ski resorts banned snowboards at first. <u>Believing they were dangerous and destructive.</u>

COMPLETE   Many ski resorts banned snowboards at first, <u>believing</u> they were dangerous and destructive.

Run-on Sentences and Comma Splices

Complete sentences need clear separation from each other. When two or more sentences run together with no punctuation between them, they create a *run-on sentence*. When they run together with only a comma between them, they create a *comma splice*. Writers usually correct these errors with a period, with a semicolon, or with a comma along with *and, but, or, nor, for, so,* or *yet:*

RUN-ON Snowboarding has become a mainstream sport riders are now as common as skiers on the slopes.

COMMA SPLICE Snowboarding has become a mainstream sport, riders are now as common as skiers on the slopes.

EDITED Snowboarding has become a mainstream sport. Riders are now as common as skiers on the slopes.

EDITED Snowboarding has become a mainstream sport; riders are now as common as skiers on the slopes.

EDITED Snowboarding has become a mainstream sport, and riders are now as common as skiers on the slopes.

Subject-Verb Agreement

Most writers know to use singular verbs with singular subjects and plural verbs with plural subjects, but matching subjects and verbs can sometimes be tricky. Watch especially for these situations:

- **Don't mistake a noun that follows the subject for the actual subject.** In the examples below, the subject is *appearance*, not *snowboarders* or *Olympics*:

  MISMATCHED The appearance of snowboarders in the Olympics prove their status as true athletes.

  MATCHED The appearance of snowboarders in the Olympics proves their status as true athletes.

- **With subjects joined by *and*, use a plural verb.** Compound word groups are treated as plural even if the word closest to the verb is singular:

  MISMATCHED The cross course and the half-pipe shows the sport's versatility.

  MATCHED The cross course and the half-pipe show the sport's versatility.

Pronouns

We tend to use pronouns without thinking much about them. Problems occur when usage that feels natural in speech causes confusion in writing:

- **Check that each pronoun refers clearly to an appropriate noun.** Rewrite sentences in which the reference is vague or only implied:

  VAGUE Students asked the administration to add more parking spaces, but it had no effect.

  CLEAR Students asked the administration to add more parking spaces, but their pleas had no effect.

IMPLIED Although commuter parking is hard to find, <u>they</u> keep driving to campus.

CLEAR Although <u>commuters know that</u> parking is hard to find, they keep driving to campus.

- **Take care with indefinite pronouns.** We often use singular indefinite pronouns — such as *anybody, anyone, everyone,* and *somebody* — to mean "many" or "all" and then mistakenly refer to them with plural pronouns:

MISMATCHED <u>Everyone</u> should change <u>their</u> passwords frequently.

MATCHED <u>Everyone</u> should change <u>his or her</u> passwords frequently.

MATCHED <u>All computer users</u> should change <u>their</u> passwords frequently.

Misplaced and Dangling Modifiers

A *modifier* describes another word or group of words in a sentence. Make sure that modifiers clearly describe the intended words. Misplaced and dangling modifiers can be awkward or even unintentionally amusing:

MISPLACED I swam away as the jellyfish approached <u>in fear of being stung</u>.

CLEAR <u>In fear of being stung</u>, I swam away as the jellyfish approached.

DANGLING <u>Floating in the ocean</u>, <u>the clouds</u> drifted by.

CLEAR Floating in the ocean, <u>I</u> watched as the clouds drifted by.

Shifts

Be consistent in your use of verb tense (past, present, and so on), person (*I, you, he/she/it, they*), and voice (active or passive). Unnecessary shifts can confuse readers. For details, see "Focus on Verbs" on page 99 and "Focus on Consistency" on page 247.

AN ESSAY-IN-PROGRESS

In the following pages, you have a chance to watch Rosie Anaya as she develops an essay through journal writing and several drafts. She began the writing process early, while reading and annotating Nancy Mairs's "Disability" (p. 13). Inspired by Mairs's argument, Anaya writes about another group that has been "effaced" by the media.

Discovering Ideas and Drafting

Journal Notes on Reading

Haven't the media gotten better about showing people with disabilities since Mairs wrote this essay? Lots of TV shows have characters who just happen to use canes or wheelchairs. But I see why she has a problem: I would be bothered, too, if I didn't see people like me represented. I would feel left out, probably hurt, maybe angry.

Mairs is doing more: Invisibility is a problem for healthy people too—anybody could become disabled and wouldn't know that people with disabilities live full, normal lives.

Interesting that she mentions emotions so many times: the references to feel-ings and psychology raise a question about people with mental disabilities, like depression or schizophrenia. How are *they* represented by the media? Definitely *not* as regular people: Stories in the news about emotionally disturbed people who go over the edge and hurt or even kill people. And *CSI* etc. always using some kind of psychological disorder to explain a crime.

Except the problem with mental illness isn't invisibility—it's negative stereo-typing. What if you're represented as a danger to yourself and others? That's got to be worse.

First Draft

Nancy Mairs is upset with television and movies that don't show physical dis-ability as a feature of normal life. She says the media shows disability consuming a character's life or it doesn't show disability at all, and she wants to see "repre-sentation of myself in the media, especially television." (p. no.).

Mairs makes a convincing argument that the media should portray physi-cal disability as part of everyday life because "effacement" leaves the rest of us unprepared to cope in the case that we should eventually become disabled ourselves. As she explains it, anybody could become disabled, but because we rarely see people with disabilities living full, normal lives on tv, we assume that becoming disabled means life is pretty much over (p. no.). It's been nearly three decades since Mairs wrote her essay, and she seems to have gotten her wish. Plenty of characters on television today who have a disability are not defined by it. But psychological disabilities are disabilities too, and they have never been shown "as a normal characteristic, one that complicates but does not ruin human existence." (p. no.).

Television routinely portrays people with mental illness as threats to them-selves and to others. Think about all those stories on the evening news about a man suffering from schizophrenia who went on a shooting spree before turning his gun on himself, or a mother who drowned her own children in the throes of depression, or a bipolar teenager who commits suicide. Such events are tragic, no doubt, but although the vast majority of people with these illnesses hurt nobody, the news implies that they're all potential killers.

Fictional shows, too, are always using some kind of psychological disorder to explain why someone committed a crime. On *Harry's Law* a domestic abuse victim under treatment for dissociative personality disorder came to believe she was Wonder Woman, turned into a vigilante, and beat several men nearly to death; her sentence after trial was three years in a psychiatric ward. A behavioral analyst on *Criminal Minds* blamed a child abductor's actions on "some kind of psychiatric disorder that drives everything he does." And the entire premise of *Dexter* is that the trauma of witnessing his mother's brutal murder turned the title character into a serial killer. Dexter is an obsessive-compulsive killer who justifies his impulses by killing only other killers. Early in the series, viewers learned that his nemesis, the "Ice Truck Killer," who at one point was engaged to Dexter's adopted sister and then tried to kill her, was actually his long-lost brother. Every season since has featured a different enemy, and each one of them has had some kind of stated or implied mental illness: The "Doomsday Killer" of season six, for example, was a psychotic divinity student who went off his meds and suffered from delusions.

It is my belief that the presentation of psychological disability may do worse than the "effacement" of disability that bothered Mairs. People with mental illness are discouraged from seeking help and are sent deeper into isolation and despair. This negative stereotype hurts us all.

Revising

Anaya's first draft was a good start. She found an idea worth pursuing and explored her thoughts. But as with any first draft, her essay needed work. To improve it, Anaya revised extensively, cutting digressions in some places and adding support in others. Her revised draft, you'll see, responds to "Disability" more directly, spells out Mairs's points and Anaya's own ideas in more detail, and builds more thoroughly on what Mairs had to say.

Revised Draft

Mental Illness on Television

In her essay "Disability" Nancy Mairs ~~is upset with~~ argues that television and movies ~~that don't~~ fail to show physical disability as a feature of normal life. ~~She~~ Instead, Mairs says, the

Uses a less abrupt, more formal tone.

media shows disability consuming a character's life or it doesn't show disability at all~~, and she wants to see "representation of myself in the media, especially television" (p. no.~~13). But Mairs wrote her essay in 1987. Since then the situation has actually improved for physical disability. At the same time, another group—those with mental illness—have come to suffer even worse representation.

~~Mairs makes a convincing argument~~ Mairs's purpose in writing her essay was to persuade her readers that the media should portray physical disability as part of everyday life because ~~"effacement"~~ otherwise it denies or misrepresents disability, and it leaves ~~the rest of us~~ "Temporarily Abled Persons" (those without disability, for now) unprepared to cope in the case that ~~we~~ they should eventually become disabled ~~ourselves~~ themselves (14-15). ~~As she explains it, anybody could become disabled, but because we rarely see people with disabilities living full, normal lives on tv, we assume that becoming disabled means life is pretty much over (p. no.). It's been more than two decades since Mairs wrote her essay, and~~ Nearly three decades later, Mairs ~~she~~ seems to have gotten her wish. Plenty of characters on television today who have a disability are not defined by it. CIA analyst Auggie Anderson on *Covert Affairs* is blind. Daphne Vasquez on *Switched at Birth* (as well as many of her friends and their parents) is deaf. Artie Abrams of *Glee* uses a wheelchair, he sings and dances with a show choir. Joe Swanson of *Family Guy* is also paraplegic. Jimmy on *South Park* uses crutches. The medical examiner on *CSI*, Al Robbins, has prosthetic legs. The media still has a long way to go in representing physical disability, but it has made progress.

However, the media depiction of one type of disability is, if anything, worse than it was three decades ago. Although Mairs doesn't address mental illness in "Disability," mental illness falls squarely into the misrepresentation she criticizes. ~~But p~~Psychological disabilities are disabilities too, ~~and~~ but they have never been shown "as a normal characteristic, one that complicates but does not ruin human existence" (~~p. no.~~ 15). People who cope with a disability such as depression, bipolar disorder, or obsessive-compulsive disorder as parts of their lives do not see

Deletes a quotation to remove a side issue and tighten the introduction.

Adds a thesis statement.

Explains Mairs's idea more clearly.

Provides page numbers in Mairs's essay. (See also p. 70.)

Adds examples to support the assertion about TV today.

Adds a transition to tighten the connection with Mairs's essay.

More fully develops the idea about mental illness as a "normal characteristic."

themselves in the media; those who don't have a psychological disability now but may someday do not see that mental illness is usually a condition they can live with.

The depictions of mental illness actually go beyond Mairs's concerns, as the media actually exploits it. Television routinely portrays people with mental illness as threats to themselves and to others. Think about all those stories on the evening news about a man suffering from schizophrenia who went on a shooting spree before turning his gun on himself, or a mother who drowned her own children in the throes of depression, or a bipolar teenager who commits suicide. ~~Such events are tragic, no doubt, but although the vast majority of people with these illnesses hurt nobody, the news implies that they're all potential killers.~~ Fictional shows, too, are always using some kind of psychological disorder to explain why someone committed a crime. On *Harry's Law* a domestic abuse victim under treatment for dissociative personality disorder ~~came to believe she was Wonder Woman, turned into a vigilante, and~~ beat several men nearly to death~~; her sentence after trial was three years in a psychiatric ward~~. A behavioral analyst on *Criminal Minds* blamed a child abductor's actions on "some kind of psychiatric disorder that drives everything he does." And the entire premise of *Dexter* is that the trauma of witnessing his mother's brutal murder turned the title character into an obsessive-compulsive serial killer. ~~Dexter is an obsessive-compulsive killer who justifies his impulses by killing only other killers. Early in the series, which is now in its seventh season, viewers learned that his nemesis, the "Ice Truck Killer," who at one point was engaged to Dexter's adopted sister and then tried to kill her, is actually his long-lost brother. Every season since has featured a different enemy, and each one of them has had some kind of stated or implied mental illness: The "Doomsday Killer" of season six, for example, was a psychotic divinity student who went off his meds and suffered from delusions.~~

These programs highlight mental illness to get viewers' attention. But the media is also telling us that the proper response to people with mental illness is to be afraid of them. Mairs argues that invisibility in the media can cause people with

Adds a transition to link back to Mairs and the thesis.

Combines related paragraphs ("Fictional shows" used to start a new paragraph).

Removes digressions and simplifies examples to improve unity.

Expands paragraph to link to Mairs's essay and lend authority to Anaya's point.

disabilities to feel unattractive or inappropriate (14). It is my belief that the presentation of psychological disability may do worse. ~~than the "effacement" of disability that bothered Mairs.~~ People with mental illness are discouraged from seeking help and are sent deeper into isolation and despair. Those feelings are often cited as the fuel for violent outbursts, but ironically the media portrays such violence as inevitable with mental illness. ~~This negative stereotype hurts us all.~~

More complex and varied depictions of all kinds of impairments, both physical and mental, will weaken the negative stereotypes that are harmful to all of us. With mental illness especially, we would all be better served if psychological disability was portrayed by the media as a part of everyday life. It's not a crime.

Provides a new conclusion that explains why the topic is important and ends with a flourish.

Works Cited

"Foundation." *Criminal Minds*. 21 Mar. 2012. CBS, 2012. Television.

"Gorilla My Dreams." *Harry's Law*. 11 Jan. 2012. NBC, 2012.
    Television.

Mairs, Nancy. "Disability." *The Bedford Reader*. Ed. X. J. Kennedy
    et al. 12th ed. Boston: Bedford, 2014. 13-15. Print.

"Truth Be Told." *Dexter*. 2006. Showtime, 2007. DVD.

Adds a list of works cited. (See also pp. 73–83.)

Editing

With her thesis clarified, the connections between her argument and Mairs's tightened, and her ideas more fully developed, Anaya was satisfied that her essay was much improved and just about finished. She still had some work to do, though. In editing, she corrected errors, cleaned up awkward sentences, and added explanations. Here we show you her changes to one paragraph.

Edited Paragraph

Mairs's purpose in ~~writing her essay~~ "Disability" ~~was~~ is to persuade ~~her~~ readers that the media should portray physical disability as part of everyday life because otherwise ~~it denies~~ they deny or misrepresent~~s~~ disability~~,~~ and ~~it~~ leaves "Temporarily Abled Persons" (those without disability, for now) unprepared to cope ~~in the case that they should eventually~~ if they become

Reduces wordiness; corrects tense shift.

Corrects pronoun-antecedent and subject-verb agreement (media is plural).

Reduces wordiness.

disabled ~~themselves~~ (14-15). Nearly three decades later, Mairs seems to have gotten her wish~~. Plenty of~~ for characters ~~on television today~~ who have a disability but are not defined by it. CIA analyst Auggie Anderson on *Covert Affairs* is blind. ~~Daphne Vasquez~~ Several characters on *Switched at Birth* ~~(as well as many of her friends and their parents) is~~ are deaf. Artie Abrams of *Glee* uses a wheelchair~~, he~~ and sings and dances with a show choir. Joe Swanson of *Family Guy* is also paraplegic. Jimmy on *South Park* uses crutches. ~~The m~~Medical examiner Al Robbins on *CSI~~, Al Robbins,~~* has prosthetic legs. The media still ~~has~~ have a long way to go in representing physical disability, but ~~it has~~ they have made progress.

Adds coordination for emphasis.

Reduces wordiness.

Fixes comma splice.

Creates parallelism.

Corrects subject-verb and pronoun-antecedent agreement.

Final Draft

Rosie Anaya

Professor De Beer

English 102A

4 February 2013

Mental Illness on Television

In her essay "Disability," Nancy Mairs argues that the media, such as television and movies, fail to show physical disability as a feature of normal life. Instead, Mairs says, they show disability consuming a character's life or they don't show disability at all. Mairs wrote her essay in 1987, and since then the situation has actually improved for depiction of physical disability. At the same time, another group—those with mental illness—has come to suffer even worse representation.

Introduction summarizes Mairs's essay and sets up Anaya's thesis.

Thesis statement establishes Anaya's main idea.

Mairs's purpose in "Disability" is to persuade readers that the media should portray physical disability as part of everyday life because otherwise they deny or misrepresent disability and leave "Temporarily Abled Persons" (those without disability, for now) unprepared to cope if they become disabled (14-15). Nearly three decades later, Mairs seems to have gotten her wish for characters who have a disability but are not defined by it. CIA analyst Auggie Anderson on *Covert Affairs* is blind. Several characters on *Switched at Birth* are deaf. Artie Abrams of *Glee* uses a wheelchair and sings and dances with a show choir. Joe

Page numbers in parentheses refer to "Works Cited" at end of paper. (See also p. 70.)

Examples provide support for Anaya's analysis.

Swanson of *Family Guy* is also paraplegic. Jimmy on *South Park* uses crutches. Medical examiner Al Robbins on *CSI* has prosthetic legs. The media still have a long way to go in representing physical disability, but they have made progress.

However, in depicting one type of disability, the media are, if anything, worse than they were three decades ago. Mairs doesn't address mental illness, but it falls squarely into the misrepresentation she criticizes. It has never been shown, in Mairs's words, "as a normal characteristic, one that complicates but does not ruin human existence" (15). Thus people who cope with a psychological disability such as depression, bipolar disorder, or obsessive-compulsive disorder as part of their lives do not see themselves in the media. And those who don't have a psychological disability now but may someday do not see that mental illness is usually a condition one can live with.

Unfortunately, the depictions of mental illness also go beyond Mairs's concerns, because the media actually exploit it. Television routinely portrays people with mental illness as threats to themselves and to others. TV news features stories about a man suffering from schizophrenia who goes on a shooting spree before turning his gun on himself, a mother with depression who drowns her own children, and a teenager with bipolar disorder who commits suicide. Fictional programs, especially crime dramas, regularly use mental illness to develop their plots. On *Criminal Minds* a child abductor's actions are blamed on "some kind of psychiatric disorder that drives everything he does," and on *Harry's Law* a woman with dissociative personality disorder beats several men nearly to death.

These programs and many others like them highlight mental illness to get viewers' attention, and they strongly imply that the proper response is fear. Mairs argues that the invisibility of physical disability in the media can cause people with disabilities to feel unattractive or inappropriate (14), but the presentation of psychological disability may do worse. It can prevent people with mental illness from seeking help and send them deeper into isolation and despair. Those feelings are often cited as the fuel for violent outbursts, but ironically the media portray such violence as inevitable with mental illness.

Comparison and contrast extend Mairs's idea to Anaya's new subject.

Follow-up comments explain what the quotation contributes to Anaya's thesis. (See also p. 58.)

Topic sentence introduces new idea.

Examples provide evidence for Anaya's point.

Paraphrase explains one of Mairs's points in Anaya's own words. (See also p. 62.)

Cause-and-effect analysis applies Mairs's idea to Anaya's thesis.

Seeing more complex and varied depictions of people living with all kinds of impairments, physical and mental, can weaken the negative stereotypes that are harmful to all of us. With mental illness especially, we would all be better served if the media would make an effort to portray psychological disability as a part of everyday life, not a crime.

Works Cited

"Foundation." *Criminal Minds*. 21 Mar. 2012. CBS, 2012. Television.

"Gorilla My Dreams." *Harry's Law*. 11 Jan. 2012. NBC, 2012. Television.

Mairs, Nancy. "Disability." *The Bedford Reader*. Ed. X. J. Kennedy et al. 12th ed. Boston: Bedford, 2014. 13-15. Print.

Conclusion reasserts the thesis and explains the broader implications of the subject.

"Works Cited" begins on a new page and gives complete publication information for Anaya's sources. (See also pp. 73–83.)

3

ACADEMIC WRITING

In college you will write in many disciplines — history, psychology, chemistry, and so on — each with its own subjects and approaches and GENRES for shaping ideas and information. As varied as your writing projects may be, however, they will share the goals and requirements of ACADEMIC WRITING: They will ask you to build and exchange knowledge by thinking critically (Chap. 1) and writing effectively (Chap. 2) about what you read, see, hear, or do.

For a taste of academic knowledge building, you can take a look at the annotated examples of academic genres that appear in the introductions to Chapters 4–13, such as the case study on pages 101–03, the annotated bibliography on pages 289–90, and the proposal on pages 452–53. You can also examine any of the student essays in this book that use and document sources, such as Rosie Anaya's "The Best Kept Secret on Campus" at the end of this chapter, Marie Javdani's "*Plata o Plomo*: Silver or Lead" (p. 377), and Margaret Lundberg's "Eating Green" (p. 481).

When called on to create academic writing of your own, you will be expected to follow certain conventions:

- **Present a clearly stated** THESIS — a debatable idea about your subject — and attempt to gain readers' agreement with it.

- **Provide EVIDENCE to support the thesis,** drawing on one or more TEXTS, or works that can be examined or interpreted. (A text may be a written document, but it may also be a photograph, an experiment, a conversation, a work of art, a Web site, or any other form of communication.)

- ANALYZE **meaning, infer** ASSUMPTIONS, **and** SYNTHESIZE **texts with your own views.** Academic writers do not merely SUMMARIZE sources; they grapple with them — in short, they read and write critically.

- **Assume an educated audience** — one that can be counted on to read critically in turn. Express your ideas clearly, provide the information readers need to analyze those ideas, and organize points and evidence effectively. Further, approach your subject seriously and discuss evidence and opposing views fairly.

- **Acknowledge the use of** SOURCES, using in-text citations and a bibliography in the format that is appropriate for the discipline you are writing in.

This chapter will show you how to achieve academic writing by responding directly to what you read (below), integrating evidence ethically and effectively (p. 59), orchestrating multiple sources to develop and support your ideas (p. 65), and documenting sources in MLA style (p. 70). (For information on documenting sources in APA style, see the Appendix.) The chapter concludes with a sample research paper (p. 84).

RESPONDING TO A TEXT

The essay by Rosie Anaya in the previous chapter (p. 53) illustrates one genre of academic writing, the critical response: Anaya summarizes Nancy Mairs's essay "Disability" (p. 12), explores its implications, and uses it as a springboard to her own related subject, which she supports with personal observation and experience. Just as Anaya responds to Mairs's essay, so you can respond to any essay in this book or for that matter to any text you read, see, or hear. (A response of this type relies heavily on ANALYSIS, a skill so central to academic writing that we devote an entire chapter to it; see pp. 284–88.)

Using evidence from the text, from your own experiences, and sometimes from additional sources, you can take a variety of approaches:

- **Agree with and extend the author's ideas,** providing additional examples or exploring related ideas, as Anaya does.

- **Agree with the author on some points, but disagree on others.**

- **Disagree with the author on one or more key points.**

- **Explain how the author achieves a particular EFFECT,** such as enlisting your sympathy or sparking your anger.

- **Judge the overall effectiveness of the essay** — for instance, how well the writer supports the thesis, whether the argument is convincing, or whether the author succeeds in his or her stated or unstated purpose.

These suggestions and this discussion assume that you are responding to a single work, but of course you may take on two or even more works at the same time. You might, for instance, use the method of COMPARISON AND CONTRAST to show how two stories are alike or different, or find your own way between competing ARGUMENTS on an issue.

Forming a Response

Some works you analyze will spark an immediate reaction, maybe because you disagree or agree strongly right from the start. Other works may require a more gradual entry into the author's meaning and what you think about it. At the same time, you may have an assignment that narrows the scope of your response — for instance, by asking you to look at TONE or some other element of the work or by asking you to agree or disagree with the author's thesis.

Whatever your initial reaction or your assignment, you can use the tools discussed in Chapter 1 to generate and structure your response: summary, analysis, inference, synthesis, evaluation. (See pp. 15–17 and the questions for analyzing an essay on p. 19.) Your first goal is to understand the work thoroughly, both what it says outright and what it assumes and implies. For this step, you'll certainly need to make notes of some sort: For instance, Rosie Anaya's annotations on Mairs's essay on pages 13–15 and her journal notes on page 48 include questions raised while reading, highlights of key quotations, summaries of Mairs's ideas, interpretations of their meanings, and the beginnings of Anaya's ideas in response. Such notes may grow increasingly focused as you refine your response and return to the work to interpret it further and gather additional passages to discuss.

Synthesizing Your Own and Another's Views

SYNTHESIS, as we note in Chapter 1, is the core of academic writing: Knowledge builds as writers bring their own perspectives to bear on what others have written, making their own contributions to what has come before.

When you write about a text, your perspective on it will be your thesis — the main point you have in response to the text or (if you take off in another direction) as a result of examining the text. As you develop the thesis, always keep your ideas front and center, pulling in material from the text as needed for support. In each paragraph, your idea should come first and, usually, last: State the idea, use evidence from the reading to support it, and then interpret the evidence. (As a way to encourage this final interpretation, some writing teachers ask students not to end paragraphs with source citations.)

You can see a paragraph structured like this in Rosie Anaya's essay "Mental Illness on Television" in Chapter 2:

SYNTHESIS

However, in depicting one type of disability, the media are, if anything, worse than they were three decades ago. Mairs doesn't address mental illness, but it falls squarely into the misrepresentation she criticizes. It has never been shown, in Mairs's words, "as a normal characteristic, one that complicates but does not ruin human existence" (15). Thus people who cope with a psychological disability such as depression, bipolar disorder, or obsessive-compulsive disorder as part of their lives do not see themselves in the media. And those who don't have a psychological disability now but may someday do not see that mental illness is usually a condition one can live with.

[margin notes: Anaya's idea · Evidence from Mairs's text · Anaya's interpretation of Mairs's idea]

Understand that synthesis is more than SUMMARY, which just distills what the text says or shows. Summary has its uses, especially in understanding a writer's ideas (p. 15) and in presenting evidence from source material (p. 61), but it should not substitute for your own ideas. Contrast the preceding paragraph from Anaya's essay with the following draft passage in which Anaya uses summary to present evidence:

SUMMARY

Mairs argues that media misrepresentation of disability hurts not only viewers with disabilities but also those without disabilities (14). The media either ignore disability altogether or present it as the defining characteristic of a person's life (13–14). In doing so, they deny "Temporarily Abled Persons" the opportunity to see disability as something common that may be difficult to adjust to but does not destroy one's life (14–15).

[margin notes: Mairs's idea · Mairs's idea · Mairs's idea]

WORKING WITH EVIDENCE

Much of your synthesis of others' work will come as you decide how to present evidence from your reading (p. 61) and how to integrate that evidence into your own text (p. 64). When making those important decisions, you'll want to avoid plagiarism by tracking and acknowledging others' ideas and information and by using source material honestly.

Avoiding Plagiarism

Academic knowledge building depends on the integrity and trust of its participants. When you write in college, your readers expect you to distinguish your own contributions from those of others. If you do otherwise — if you deliberately or accidentally copy another's idea, data, or even wording without acknowledging your debt — then you steal that person's intellectual property. Called PLAGIARISM, this theft is a serious and often punishable offense.

Caution with Sources

Plagiarism is often a result of careless note taking or drafting. The simplest way to avoid problems is always to acknowledge your sources, clearly marking the boundaries between your original ideas and information and the materials you have gleaned from the work of other writers. Use summary, paraphrase, and quotation carefully, following the suggestions provided in the next section. And cite your sources in an appropriate documentation style, such as MLA for English and some other humanities (explained on pp. 70–83) or APA for the social sciences (explained in the Appendix on pp. 547–60). Whatever system you use, adhere to these guidelines:

- **Identify the sources of all borrowed information and ideas.** Introduce every summary, paraphrase, or quotation and name the author in a SIGNAL PHRASE or a parenthetical citation. See pages 64–65 on integrating source material.

- **Indicate where the material can be found.** Follow any information or idea taken from a source with a parenthetical citation that provides the name of the author (if not mentioned in a signal phrase) and the page number(s), if available. (If you are using APA style, give the year of publication as well.) See pages 70–73 on MLA parenthetical citations and pages 548–51 on APA parenthetical text citations.

- **Mark direct quotations.** Whether sentences, phrases, or distinctive words, another writer's language must be clearly distinguished from your own (see p. 63). Enclose brief quotations in quotation marks. Set off longer quotations with an indention. See page 85 for an example in MLA style and page 559 for an example in APA style.

- **Take care to express all paraphrases and summaries in your own words.** Check your sentences against the original sources, making sure that you haven't picked up any of the writers' phrasings or sentence structures. For examples of acceptable and unacceptable summary and paraphrase, see pages 61–63.

- **Include a list of sources.** On a separate page (or pages) at the end, provide a complete list of the sources cited within your paper, with full publication information for each. See pages 73–83 on an MLA list of works cited and pages 551–58 on APA references.

- **Recognize common knowledge.** Not all information from sources must be cited. Some falls under the category of common knowledge — facts so widely known or agreed upon that they are not attributable to a specific source. You may not know that President Dwight Eisenhower coined the term *military-industrial complex* during his 1961 farewell address, for example, but because anyone can easily find that fact in encyclopedias, in books, and in articles about Eisenhower, it requires no citation (as long as you express it in your own words). In contrast, a scholar's argument that Eisenhower waited too long to criticize the defense industry, or the president's own comments, would need to be credited because each remains the property of its author.

Plagiarism and the Internet

Be especially cautious about plagiarism when you are working online. Whether accidentally or deliberately, you can download source material directly into your own document with a few clicks. And you might be tempted to buy complete papers from term-paper sites. Don't. It is plagiarism to use downloaded material without credit, even accidentally, and it is plagiarism to submit someone else's work as your own, even if you paid for it. Getting caught is more than likely, too, because anything from the Internet is easy to trace.

Summarizing, Paraphrasing, and Quoting

Use the ideas and information in sources to support your own ideas, not to direct or overwhelm them. Depending on the importance and complexity of source material, you may summarize it, paraphrase it, or quote it directly. Remember that *all summaries, paraphrases, and quotations must be acknowledged in source citations.* See the previous section on avoiding plagiarism.

Summary

In a SUMMARY you use your own words to condense a paragraph, an entire article, or even a book into a few lines that convey the source's essential meaning. We discuss summarizing as a reading technique on pages 15–16, and the advice and examples there apply here as well. When responding to a text, you may use a brief summary to catch readers up on the gist of the author's argument or a significant point in the argument. Here, for example, is a summary of Anna Quindlen's "Homeless," which appears on pages 190–92:

> SUMMARY Quindlen argues that reducing homeless people to the abstract issue of homelessness can obscure the fundamental problem of the homeless individual: He or she needs a home (190–92).

Notice that a summary identifies the source author and page numbers and uses words that are *not* the author's. A summary that picks up any of the author's distinctive language or fails to acknowledge that the idea is borrowed from a source counts as plagiarism and must be rewritten. In a draft of "Mental Illness on Television" (p. 53), for instance, Rosie Anaya inadvertently plagiarized this passage from Nancy Mairs's "Disability":

> ORIGINAL QUOTATION "But this [media] denial of disability imperils even you who are able-bodied, and not just by shrinking your insight into the physically and emotionally complex world you live in. Some disabled people call you TAPs, or Temporarily Abled Persons. The fact is that ours is the only minority you can join involuntarily, without warning, at any time. . . . The transition will probably be difficult from a physical point of view no matter what. But it will be a good bit easier psychologically if you are accustomed to seeing disability as a normal characteristic, one that complicates but does not ruin human existence."

> PLAGIARISM Media misrepresentation of disability hurts not only viewers with disabilities but also Temporarily Abled Persons.

In forgetting to name Mairs as the source and in using the phrase "Temporarily Abled Persons" without quotation marks, Anaya stole Mairs's idea. Here is her revision:

> ACCEPTABLE SUMMARY Mairs argues that media misrepresentation of disability hurts not only viewers with disabilities but also "Temporarily Abled Persons," or those without disabilities (14–15).

Paraphrase

When you PARAPHRASE, you restate a specific passage in your own words. Paraphrase adheres more closely than summary to the source author's line of thought, so it's useful for presenting an author's ideas or data in detail. Generally, use paraphrase rather than quotation for this purpose, since paraphrase shows that you're in command of your evidence and lets your own voice come through. Here is a quotation from Quindlen's essay and a paraphrase of it:

ORIGINAL QUOTATION "Homes have stopped being homes. Now they are real estate."

PARAPHRASE Quindlen points out that people's dwellings seem to have lost their emotional hold and to have become just investments (191).

As with a summary, note that a paraphrase cites the original author and page number. And like a summary, a paraphrase must express the original idea in an entirely new way, both in word choice and in sentence structure. The following attempt to paraphrase a line from an essay by David Cole slips into plagiarism through sloppiness:

ORIGINAL QUOTATION "We stand to be collectively judged by our treatment of immigrants, who may appear to be 'other' now but in a generation will be 'us.'"

PLAGIARISM Cole argues that we will be judged as a group by how we treat immigrants, who seem to be different now but eventually will be the same as us (110).

Even though the writer identifies Cole as the source of the information, much of the language and the sentence structure are also Cole's. It's not enough to change a few words — such as "collectively" to "as a group," "they may appear to be 'other'" to "they may seem different," and "in a generation" to "eventually." In contrast, this acceptable paraphrase restates Cole's point in completely new language *and* a new sentence structure:

ACCEPTABLE PARAPHRASE Cole argues that the way the United States deals with immigrants now will come back to haunt it when those immigrants eventually become part of mainstream society (110).

Quotation

Quotations from sources can both support and enliven your own ideas — *if* you choose them well. When analyzing a primary source, such as a work of literature or a historical document, you may need to quote many passages in order to give the flavor of the author's words and evidence for your analysis. With secondary sources, however, too many quotations will clutter an essay and detract from your voice. Select quotations that are relevant to the point you are making, that are concise and pithy, and that use lively, bold, or original language. Sentences that lack distinction — for example, a statement providing statistics on economic growth — should be paraphrased.

Always enclose quotations in quotation marks and cite the source author and page number. For a blatant example of plagiarism, look at the following use of a quotation from Anna Quindlen's "Homeless":

> Original quotation "It has been customary to take people's pain and lessen our own participation in it by turning it into an issue, not a collection of human beings."

> Plagiarism As a society we tend to lessen our participation in other people's pain by turning it into an issue.

By not acknowledging Quindlen at all, the writer takes claim for her idea and for much of her wording. A source citation would help — at least the idea would be credited — but still the expression of the idea would be stolen because there's no indication that it's Quindlen's. Here is a revision with citation and quotation marks:

> Acceptable quotation Quindlen suggests that our tendency "to take people's pain and lessen our own participation in it by turning it into an issue" dehumanizes homeless people (192).

Integrating Source Material

With synthesis, you're always making it clear to readers what your idea is and how the evidence from your reading supports that idea. To achieve this clarity, you want to fit summaries, paraphrases, and quotations into your sentences and show what you make of them.

Signal Phrases

In the passage below, the writer drops a quotation awkwardly into her paragraph and doesn't clarify how the quotation relates to her idea:

> Not introduced The problem of homelessless affects real people. "[W]e work around it, just as we walk around it when it is lying on the sidewalk or sitting in the bus terminal — the problem, that is" (Quindlen 192).

In the following revision, the writer uses "but" and the SIGNAL PHRASE "as Quindlen points out" to link the quotation to the writer's idea and to identify the source author:

> Introduced The problem of homelessness affects real people, but, as Quindlen points out, "we work around it, just as we walk around it when it is lying on the sidewalk or sitting in the bus terminal — the problem, that is" (192).

Signal phrases like "as Quindlen points out" have a number of variations:

> According to one authority . . .

> John Eng maintains that . . .

The author of an important study, Hilda Brown, observes that . . .

Barbara Lazear Ascher, the author of "On Compassion," has a different view, claiming . . .

For variety, such a phrase can also fall elsewhere in the quotation:

"[W]e would be better off," Quindlen says, "if we forgot about the broad strokes and concentrated on the details" (192).

The Ellipsis Mark

When you omit something from a quotation, signal the omission with the three spaced periods of an ellipsis mark as shown:

"This is a difficult problem . . . ," says Quindlen (192).

In Quindlen's view, "the thing that seems most wrong with the world . . . right now is that there are so many people with no homes" (191).

Brackets

If you need to insert words or phrases into a quoted passage to clarify the author's meaning or make the quotation flow with your own language, show that the insertion is yours by enclosing it in brackets:

Quindlen points out that "we work around [the problem], just as we walk around" the homeless people we encounter (192).

WRITING FROM RESEARCH

Responding to a reading — thinking critically about it and synthesizing its ideas into your own — prepares you for the source-based writing that will occupy you for much of your academic career. In researched writing, you test and support your thesis by exploring and orchestrating a range of opinions and evidence found in multiple sources. The writing is source *based* but not source *dominated*: As when responding to a single work, your critical reading and your views set the direction and govern the final presentation.

Using the Library

You have two paths to sources: your school's library and a public search engine such as *Google* or *Bing*. Although it may seem easier to turn to the open Internet first, always start with the library's Web portal: It will lead you to books, scholarly journals, reputable newspapers, and other quality sources that information professionals have deemed worthwhile. Furthermore, some of the most useful source material is not freely available or online at all. Your library can link you to resources that are accessible only to paid subscribers, and it can provide periodical articles and specialized reference works that exist only in print.

The open Internet is also home to many valuable sources, but finding them requires effort and an extra degree of caution. Tapping a few keywords into a commercial search engine will not lead you to the best materials as if by magic. A quick search can give you an overview of your subject and generate ideas, but it can just as easily direct you to the rantings of extremists, advertisements posing as science, and dubious claims in anonymous posts. It will also almost always bring up an overwhelming number of hits, with little indication of which ones are worthy of your attention. Most of the quality material you can find on the Web is indexed on your library's home page; searching from there will save you time and trouble in the long run.

Evaluating Sources

When examining multiple works for possible use in your paper, you of course want each one to be relevant to your subject and to your thesis. But you also want it to be reliable — that is, based on good evidence and carefully reasoned. To evaluate relevance and reliability, you'll depend on your critical-reading skills of analysis, inference, and synthesis (see pp. 16–17). Use the questions for evaluating sources in the box on the facing page and the following discussion of the criteria. Take extra care when evaluating Internet sources you have reached directly, for those materials have not been filtered and are therefore inherently riskier.

Purpose and Audience

The potential sources you find may have been written for a variety of reasons — for instance, to inform the public, to publish new research, to promote a product or service, to influence readers' opinions about a particular issue. The first two of these purposes might lead to a balanced approach to the subject, one that treats all sides fairly. The second two are likely to be biased toward one view, and you'll need to weight what they say accordingly.

A source's intended audience can suggest relevance. Was the work written for general readers? Then it may provide a helpful overview but not much detail. Was the work written for specialists? Then it will probably cover the

QUESTIONS FOR EVALUATING SOURCES

ALL SOURCES

✔ What is the PURPOSE of the source?

✔ Who is the intended AUDIENCE?

✔ Is the material a primary or a secondary source?

✔ Is the author an expert? What are his or her credentials?

✔ Does the author's bias affect the reliability of his or her argument?

✔ Is the argument supported with EVIDENCE that is complete and up to date?

INTERNET SOURCES

✔ What is the origin of the source? Can you identify the author?

✔ Who created the Web site? Does the sponsor have any biases or agendas?

✔ Does the site contain links to sources used as evidence? Is the evidence credible?

✔ How current is the source?

topic in depth, but understanding it may require careful reading or consulting other sources for clarification.

Primary versus Secondary Sources

Primary sources are works by people who conducted or saw events first-hand. They include research reports, eyewitness accounts, diaries, and personal essays as well as novels, poems, and other works of literature. *Secondary sources*, in contrast, present and analyze the information in primary sources and include histories, reviews, and surveys of a field. Both types of source can be useful in research writing. For example, if you were writing about the debate over the assassination of President John F. Kennedy, you might seek an overview in books that discuss the evidence and propose theories about what happened — secondary sources. But you would be remiss if you did not also read eyewitness accounts and law-enforcement documents — the primary sources.

Author's Credentials and Bias

Before you use a source to support your ideas, investigate the author's background to be sure that he or she is trustworthy. Look for biographical information in the introduction or preface of a book or in a note at the beginning or end of an article. Is the author an expert on the topic? Do other writers cite the author of your source in their work?

Often you won't be able to tell easily, or at all, who put a potential source on the Internet and thus whether that author is credible and reliable. Specific background may require digging. On Web sites, look for pages that have information about the author or sponsor or links to such information on other sites. On blogs and social media, ask anonymous writers for information about themselves. If you can't identify an author or a sponsor at all, you probably should not use the source.

Investigating an author's background and credentials will likely also uncover any bias — that is, the author's preference for a particular view of an issue. Bias itself is not a problem: Everyone has a unique outlook created by experience, training, and even research techniques. What does matter is whether the author deals frankly with his or her bias and argues reasonably despite it. (See Chap. 13 for a discussion of reasoning.)

Evidence

Look for strong and convincing evidence to support the ideas in a source: facts, examples, reported experience, expert opinions. A source that doesn't muster convincing evidence, or much evidence at all, is not a reliable source. For very current topics, such as in medicine or technology, the source's ideas and evidence should be as up to date as possible.

The most reliable sources acknowledge borrowed evidence and ideas and tell you where they came from, whether with general mentions in the case of journalism, with formal references in scholarly works, or (sometimes online) with links to the borrowed material. Check out references or links to be sure they represent a range of views. Be suspicious of any work that doesn't acknowledge sources at all.

Currency

If you are writing about a current topic, you want your sources to be up to date. Online sources tend to be more current than print sources. However, online sources also have several potential disadvanges. First, the most current information may not have been tested by others and may not be reliable, so seek to verify recent information in other sources. Second, Web sites change constantly, so information you locate one day could be missing or altered the next. And finally, sites that seem current may actually be dated because their authors or sponsors have not tended them. Always look for a date of copyright, publication, or last revision to gauge currency. If you don't find a date (and you may not), compare the source with others you know to be recent before using its information.

Synthesizing Multiple Sources

In research writing as in response writing, your views should predominate over those of others. You decide which sources to use, how to treat them, and what conclusions to draw from them in order to test and support your thesis. In your writing, this thinking about sources' merits and relevance should be evident to readers. Here, for example, is a paragraph from Rosie Anaya's research paper at the end of this chapter. Notice how Anaya states her idea at the outset, guides us through the presentation of evidence from sources, and finally concludes by tying the evidence back to her idea.

> Despite the prevalence of depression and related disorders on campus, however, most students avoid seeking help when they need it. The American Psychiatric Association maintains that most mental-health issues can be managed or overcome with treatment by therapy and/or medication. But among students with a history of depression, according to the American College Health Association, a mere 10% currently receive any kind of treatment (35). One reason for such low numbers can be found in a study published in *Journal of Mental Health Counseling*: Four in five American students are unwilling to ask for help even when they are certain they need it, because they perceive mental illness as embarrassing or shameful (Aegisdóttir et al. 327–28). Thus students who need help suffer additional pain — and no treatment — because they fear the stigma of mental illness.

(margin annotations) Anaya's idea · Evidence from a Web site · Evidence from a survey · Evidence from a scholarly journal · Anaya's interpretation of the evidence

This paragraph illustrates the techniques of synthesis discussed in the previous section:

- **The writer summarizes and paraphrases data and ideas from sources,** stressing her own voice and her mastery of the source material. (See p. 61.)

- **The writer integrates each summary or paraphrase into her sentence,** using a signal phrase that names the source author and telling readers how the borrowed material relates to her idea. (See p. 64.)

- **The writer clearly indicates what material is borrowed and where it is borrowed from.** Such source citation is crucial to avoid plagiarism. The

MLA citation style that Anaya uses is discussed on the following pages. (APA citation style is discussed in the Appendix.)

SOURCE CITATION USING MLA STYLE

On the following pages we explain the documentation style of the Modern Language Association, as described in the *MLA Handbook for Writers of Research Papers*, 7th edition (2009). This style — used in English, foreign languages, and some other humanities — involves providing a citation in your text that names the author of borrowed material and gives the page number(s) in the source where the material appears. Readers can use the name to locate the full source information in a list of works cited at the end of your text, and they can find the location of the borrowed material in the source itself.

In your text, the author's name may appear in a SIGNAL PHRASE, or it may appear in parentheses. In either case, put any page numbers in parentheses.

TEXT CITATION, AUTHOR NAMED IN SIGNAL PHRASE
As Quindlen suggests, people's dwellings seem to have lost their emotional hold and to have become just investments (191).

TEXT CITATION, AUTHOR NAMED IN PARENTHESES
People's dwellings seem to have lost their emotional hold and to have become just investments (Quindlen 191).

ENTRY IN LIST OF WORKS CITED
Quindlen, Anna. "Homeless." *The Bedford Reader*. Ed. X. J. Kennedy et al.
     12th ed. Boston: Bedford, 2014. 190-92. Print.

MLA Parenthetical Citations

The following examples of MLA text citations show the author named in a signal phrase or named in parentheses.

A work with two or three authors

More than 90% of the hazardous waste produced in the United States comes from seven major industries, all energy-intensive (Romm and Curtis 70).

Educators have been complaining about declining literacy since the late nineteenth century, but such concerns are largely unfounded (Lunsford, Fishman, and Liew 471).

MLA Parenthetical Citations

A work with more than three authors

With more than three authors, name all the authors, or name only the first author followed by et al. (*et alii*, "and others"). Use the same form in your list of works cited.

> Gilman herself created the misconception that doctors tried to ban her story "The Yellow Wallpaper" when it appeared in 1892 (Dock, Allen, Palais, and Tracy 61).

> Gilman herself created the misconception that doctors tried to ban her story "The Yellow Wallpaper" when it appeared in 1892 (Dock et al. 61).

A work with a group author

For a work that lists an organization as author — for instance, a government agency or a corporation — treat the group's name as the author name.

> In a tongue-in-cheek graphic novel, the Centers for Disease Control and Prevention invokes the threat of a zombie apocalypse to encourage Americans to gather materials for an all-purpose emergency kit and keep them readily at hand (5).

An unsigned work

Cite an unsigned work by its title. In a signal phrase, use the full title. In a parenthetical citation, shorten a long title to the first one, two, or three main words.

> In 1995 concern about Taiwan's relationship with China caused investors to transfer capital to the United States ("How the Missiles Help" 45).

Two or more works by the same author(s)

If you cite more than one work by the same author or authors, include a full or shortened version of the the work's title, as explained above. The full title for the first citation below is *Death at an Early Age*.

> In the 1960s Kozol was reprimanded by his principal for teaching the poetry of Langston Hughes (*Death* 83).

> Kozol believes that most people do not understand the effect that tax and revenue policies have on the quality of urban public schools (*Savage Inequalities* 207).

An entire work or a work with no page or other reference numbers

Omit page numbers when you cite an entire work or cite a work that does not number pages, paragraphs, or other parts.

> Lanier argues that the Internet is potentially destructive because of the nature of the medium itself.

A nonprint source

Cite a nonprint source, such as a Web document or a DVD, just as you would a print source: by author's name or, if there is no author, by title. If a source numbers screens or paragraphs instead of pages, give the reference number as in the following model, after par. (one paragraph), pars. (more than one paragraph), screen, or screens. For a source with no reference numbers at all, use the preceding model for an entire work.

> One nurse questions whether doctors are adequately trained in tending patients' feelings (Van Eijk, pars. 6-7).

A work in more than one volume

If you cite two or more volumes of the same work, identify the volume number before the page number. Separate volume number and page number with a colon.

> According to Gibbon, during the reign of Gallienus "every province of the Roman world was afflicted by barbarous invaders and military tyrants" (1: 133).

An indirect source

Use qtd. in ("quoted in") to indicate that you found the source you quote within another source.

Despite his tendency to view human existence as an unfulfilling struggle, Schopenhauer disparaged suicide as "a vain and foolish act" (qtd. in Durant 248).

A literary work

Because novels, poems, and plays may be published in various editions, the page number may not be enough to lead readers to the quoted line or passage. For a novel, specify the chapter number after the page number and a semicolon.

Among South Pacific islanders, the hero of Conrad's *Lord Jim* found "a totally new set of conditions for his imaginative faculty to work upon" (160; ch. 21).

For a verse play or a poem, omit the page number in favor of line numbers.

In "Dulce et Decorum Est," Wilfred Owen undercuts the heroic image of warfare by comparing suffering soldiers to "beggars" and "hags" (lines 1-2) and describing a man dying in a poison-gas attack as "guttering, choking, drowning" (17).

If the work has parts, acts, or scenes, cite those as well (below: act 1, scene 5, lines 16–17).

Lady Macbeth worries about her husband's ambition: "Yet I do fear thy nature; / It is too full o' the milk of human kindness" (1.5.16-17).

More than one work in the same citation

In the post-Watergate era, journalists have often employed aggressive reporting techniques not for the good of the public but simply to advance their careers (Gopnik 92; Fallows 64).

MLA List of Works Cited

Your list of works cited is a complete record of your sources. Follow these guidelines for the list:

- **Title the list** Works Cited.
- **Double-space the entire list.**
- **Arrange the sources alphabetically** by the last name of the first author or by the first main word of the title if the source has no named author.

- **Begin the first line of each entry at the left margin,** and indent subsequent lines one-half inch.

Following are the essentials of a works-cited entry:

- **Reverse the names of the author,** last name first, with a comma between. If there is more than one author, give the other name(s) in normal order.

- **Give the full title of the work,** capitalizing the first, last, and all important words. Italicize the titles of books, periodicals, and Web sites; use quotation marks for the titles of parts of books, articles in periodicals, and pages on Web sites.

- **Give publication information.** For books, this information includes city of publication, publisher, and date of publication. For periodicals, this information includes volume number, issue number, date of publication, and page numbers for the article you cite. For online sources such as Web sites, this information includes the sponsor and date of publication or latest revision of the site and the date you consulted the source. (See pp. 78–81 for more on electronic sources.)

- **Give the medium of publication.** Use a designation such as Print, Web, DVD, Lecture, Performance, Radio, Television, or E-mail.

- **Use periods between parts of each entry.**

You may need to combine the following models for a given source — for instance, combine "Two or three authors" and "An article in a scholarly journal on the Web" for an online journal article with two or three authors.

Authors

One author

Rosen, Kim. "The Healing Power of Poetry." *Utne Reader*. Ogden Pub.,
     Sept./Oct. 2012. Web. 2 Oct. 2012.

Two or three authors

O'Reilly, Bill, and Martin Dugard. *Killing Kennedy: The End of Camelot*. New
     York: Holt, 2012. Print.

Stanton, Wortham, Katherine Mortimer, and Elaine Allard. "Homies in the New
     Latino Diaspora." *Language and Communication* 31.3 (2011): 191-202.
     Print.

MLA List of Works Cited

More than three authors

You may list all authors or only the first author followed by **et al.** (*et alii,*
"and others"). Use the same form in your parenthetical text citation.

Kippax, Susan, R. W. Connel, G. W. Dowsett, and June Crawford. *Gay Communities Respond to Change*. London: Falmer, 2004. Print.

Kippax, Susan, et al. *Gay Communities Respond to Change*. London: Falmer, 2004. Print.

A group author

Reuters. "Top Google Executive in Brazil Faces Arrest over Video." *New York Times*. New York Times, 26 Sept. 2012. Web. 27 Sept. 2012.

An unsigned work

"America's Sleepiest States." *Reader's Digest* June 2012: 48. Print.

More than one work by the same author(s)

Kozol, Jonathan. *Death at an Early Age: The Destruction of the Hearts and Minds of Negro Children in the Boston Public Schools*. New York: Plume, 1967. Print.

---. *Savage Inequalities: Children in America's Schools*. New York: Crown, 1991. Print.

Print Periodicals: Journals, Magazines, and Newspapers

An article in a journal

After the journal title, give the volume and issue numbers separated by a period, the year of publication in parentheses, a colon, the page numbers of the article, a period, and the medium of publication.

Spencer, Renée, and Belle Liang. "'She Gives Me a Break from the World': Formal Youth Mentoring Relationships between Adolescent Girls and Adult Women." *Journal of Primary Prevention* 30.2 (2009): 109-30. Print.

An article in a journal that numbers only issues

If a journal numbers issues but not annual volumes, give just the issue number after the title.

Williams, Jeanne. "Evocations of Enigma in the Work of Ivar Shevtsov." *Review of Poetry* 31 (2006): 21-29. Print.

An article in a monthly or bimonthly magazine

Sirota, David. "The Only Game in Town: An Unlikely Comeback for Dying Newspapers." *Harper's* Sept. 2012: 46-51. Print.

An article in a weekly magazine

Acocella, Joan. "The Lure of the Fairytale." *New Yorker* 23 July 2012: 73-78.
Print.

An article in a newspaper

Neyfakh, Leon. "The Art of Crowdshifting." *Boston Sunday Globe* 23 Sept.
2012, greater Boston ed.: K1+. Print.

The page number K1+ in the example means that the article begins on page 1
of section K and continues on a later page. If the newspaper has an edition,
such as greater Boston ed. in the example, it will be labeled at the top of the
first page.

A review

Iyer, Pico. "Secret Love of the Lost City." Rev. of *The Museum of Innocence*, by
Orhan Pamuk. *New York Review of Books* 19 Nov. 2009: 38-40. Print.

Print Books

A book with an author

Rosin, Hanna. *The End of Men: And the Rise of Women*. New York: Riverhead,
2012. Print.

A book with an editor

Clarke, Jaime, ed. *Don't You Forget about Me: Contemporary Writers on the
Films of John Hughes*. New York: Simon, 2007. Print.

A book with an author and an editor

Emerson, Ralph Waldo. *The Essential Writings of Ralph Waldo Emerson*. Ed.
Brooks Atkinson. New York: Modern, 2000. Print.

A later edition

Bordo, Susan. *Unbearable Weight: Feminism, Western Culture, and the Body*.
2nd ed. Berkeley: U of California P, 2004. Print.

A work in a series

Hall, Donald. *Poetry and Ambition*. Ann Arbor: U of Michigan P, 1998. Print.
Poets on Poetry.

An anthology

Glantz, Michael H., ed. *Societal Responses to Regional Climatic Change*. Lon-
     don: Westview, 2007. Print.

Cite an entire anthology only when you are citing the work of the editor
or you are cross-referencing it, as in the Angelou and Tan models below.

A selection from an anthology

The numbers near the end of the following entry identify the pages on
which the entire cited selection appears.

Kellog, William D. "Human Impact on Climate: The Evolution of an
     Awareness." *Societal Responses to Regional Climatic Change*. Ed.
     Michael H. Glantz. London: Westview, 2007. 283-96. Print.

If you cite more than one selection from the same anthology, you may
give the anthology as a separate entry and cross-reference it by the editor's or
editors' last name(s) in the entries for the selections. Place each entry in its
proper alphabetical place in the list of works cited.

Angelou, Maya. "Champion of the World." Kennedy et al. 104-07.
Kennedy, X. J., et al., eds. *The Bedford Reader*. 12th ed. Boston: Bedford,
     2014. Print.
Tan, Amy. "Fish Cheeks." Kennedy et al. 110-11.

A reference work

Cheney, Ralph Holt. "Coffee." *Collier's Encyclopedia*. 2007 ed. Print.
"Versailles, Treaty of." *World Book Encyclopedia*. 2009 ed. Print.

Online Sources

Online sources vary greatly, and they may be and often are updated. Your
aim in citing such a source should be to tell what version you used and how
readers can find it for themselves. If you don't see a model for the type of
source you used, follow a model that comes close. If you can't find all the
information shown in a model, give what you can find. Substitute an abbreviation for missing information: N.p. for "No publisher" and n.d. for "no date."

Nonperiodical Web publications   Nonperiodical Web publications include most of what you'll find on the open Internet: works that are not pub-

lished on a schedule but just once or irregularly. This definition encompasses online newspapers and magazines as well, because their content is changeable. Thus the Web versions of the *New York Times* and *Wired* magazine are considered nonperiodical publications.

A short work on a Web site

The following example shows the basic elements to include when citing a nonperiodical Web publication: (1) author's name, (2) title of the short work, (3) title of the site, (4) sponsor or publisher of the site, (5) date of the electronic publication or last update, (6) medium of publication, and (7) date you consulted the source.

Speer, Cindy Lynn. "Neil Gaiman's Film Work." *Neil Gaiman*. Harper,
Aug. 2007. Web. 28 Apr. 2013.

An entire Web site

Center for Social Innovation. Stanford Graduate School of Business, 4 Apr.
2013. Web. 17 May 2013.

A newspaper or magazine on the Web

Haspel, Tamar. "Throw Like a Girl? You Can Do Better." *Washington Post*.
Washington Post, 10 Sept. 2012. Web. 4 Oct. 2012.
McWilliams, James. "Vegan Feud." *Slate*. Slate Group, 7 Sept. 2012. Web.
2 Oct. 2012.

A government publication on the Web

United States. Dept. of Educ. "Teaching Literacy in English to K-5 English
Learners." *Doing What Works: Research-Based Education Practices
Online*. US Dept. of Educ., Feb. 2010. Web. 2 Mar. 2013.

A book on the Web

Addington, H. Bruce. *Historic Ghosts and Ghost Hunters*. New York: Moffat,
1908. Internet Archive. Web. 28 Apr. 2013.

A wiki

"Daguerreotype." *Wikipedia*. Wikimedia, 10 Sept. 2012. Web. 24 Sept. 2012.

A television or radio program on the Web

"Radioactive Wolves." *Nature*. Public Broadcasting Service, 19 Oct. 2011. Web.
17 Nov. 2012.

An image on the Web

Doble, Rick. *Spring Rain Abstraction*. 2009. *Digital Art Photography*. Rick
Doble, 2010. Web. 12 Jan. 2013.

If the image originally or simultaneously appeared in another medium,
you may provide the information for the other medium before the Web information:

Matisse, Henri. *La Musique*. 1939. Albright-Knox Gallery, Buffalo. *WebMuseum*.
Web. 3 Mar. 2013.

A video recording on the Web

Jardin, Xeni. *Mardi Gras 1956: Through My Father's Lens*. *YouTube*. YouTube,
2010. Web. 15 Apr. 2013.

If the video originally or simultaneously appeared in another medium, you
may provide the information for the other medium before the Web information:

San Francisco Earthquake and Fire. 18 Apr. 1906. *American Memory*. Lib. of
Congress, n.d. Web. 22 Sept. 2012.

In the preceding example, n.d. means "no date" of publication or posting.

A sound recording or podcast on the Web

Roosevelt, Eleanor. Address at the AFL-CIO Unity Convention. 9 Dec. 1955.
Vincent Voice Lib. Michigan State U, 11 Oct. 2005. Web. 5 Mar. 2013.
Carson, Harry, Stone Phillips, and Bennet Omalu, guests. "The Football
Concussion Crisis, Part 1." *Science Talk*. By Steve Mirsky. *Scientific
American*. Scientific Amer., 15 May, 2012. Web. 13 Sept. 2012.

A posting to a blog

Sullivan, Andrew. "Unfit for Government." *The Dish*. Newsweek/Daily Beast,
12 Sept. 2012. Web. 13 Sept. 2012.

Periodical Web publications

An article in a scholarly journal on the Web

Base an entry for an online journal article on one of the models on page 76 for a print journal article, changing the medium to Web and adding your access date. Use n. pag. if the journal does not number pages.

Sjostrand, Odile. "Law Philosophy in *Mansfield Park*." *Jane Austen Quarterly* 33.1 (1999): n. pag. Web. 12 Oct. 2012.

A periodical article in an online database

For an article that you obtain from a library or other database, provide print publication information using the models for articles in periodicals on pages 76–77. Add the database title, the medium, and your access date.

Conway, Daniel W. "Reading Henry James as a Critic of Modern Moral Life." *Inquiry* 45.3 (2002): 319-30. *Academic Search Elite*. Web. 20 Apr. 2013.

Other online sources

E-mail

Dove, Chris. "Re: Bishop's Poems." Message to the author. 7 May 2013. E-mail.

A posting to a discussion group

Lorenzo, Pamela. "Introduction and Educational Resources." *Adult English Language Learners Literacy Discussion List*. Natl. Inst. for Literacy, 10 Sept. 2012. Web. 3 Feb. 2013.

If the posting has no title, give Online posting instead.

Other Sources

A digital file

For electronic materials stored on mobile devices rather than online — such as e-books, tablet publications, and digital music — follow the documentation guidelines for the basic type of source (book, article in a weekly magazine, sound recording, and so on), and for the medium identify the type of file (MP3, Kindle, PDF, JPEG, XML, and so on, followed by the word "file").

Mitchell, John Cameron. "The Origin of Love." *Hedwig and the Angry Inch: Original Motion Picture Soundtrack*. Hybrid, 2001. MP3 file.

Walker, Jerald. *Street Shadows: A Memoir of Race, Rebellion, and Redemption*. New York: Bantam, 2010. Kindle file.

A photograph, painting, sculpture, or other work of art

For a work of art that you see in the original, follow this format:

van Gogh, Vincent. *The Starry Night*. 1889. Oil on canvas. Museum of Mod. Art, New York.

For a work of art that you see in a reproduction, provide the publication information for the source you used:

Hockney, David. *Nichols Canyon*. 1980. Private collection. *David Hockney: A Retrospective*. Ed. Maurice Tuchman and Stephanie Barron. Los Angeles: Los Angeles County Museum of Art, 1988. 205. Print.

A map or chart

"Annual Rainfall in Las Vegas, 1950-2009." Chart. *The Development of Las Vegas*. By Sarah G. Murphy. Las Vegas: SynthEdge, 2010. 94. Print.

An advertisement

IBM. Advertisement. *New Yorker* 17 Sept. 2012: 13. Print.

A television or radio program

Glass, Ira, host. "The Ghost of Bobby Dunbar." *This American Life*. Natl. Public Radio. KQED, San Francisco, 8 Sept. 2012. Radio.

A sound recording

Mendelssohn, Felix. *A Midsummer Night's Dream*. Cond. Erich Leinsdorf. Boston Symphony Orch. RCA, 1982. LP.

A film, video, or DVD

Achbar, Mark, and Peter Wintonick, dirs. *Manufacturing Consent: Noam Chomsky and the Media*. Zeitgeist, 1992. DVD.

A letter

List a published letter under the author's name, and provide full publication information.

Stetson, James A. Letter to Dolly W. Stetson. 8 Feb. 1845. In *Letters from an American Utopia: The Stetson Family and the Northampton Association, 1843-1847*. Ed. Christopher Clark and Kerry W. Buckley. Amherst: U of Massachusetts P, 2004. 133-34. Print.

For a letter that you receive, list the source under the writer's name, add to the author, provide the date of the correspondence, and end with the medium. Use MS for a manuscript (a letter written by hand) or TS for a typescript (a letter composed on a machine).

Dove, Chris. Letter to the author. 7 May 2013. TS.

An interview

Macedo, Donaldo. Personal interview. 13 May 2013.

Cusack, John. Interview by David Marchese. *Spin*. Spin Media, 27 Apr. 2012. Web. 26 Sept. 2012.

A SAMPLE RESEARCH PAPER IN MLA STYLE

In the previous chapter we saw Rosie Anaya respond to Nancy Mairs's "Disability" with her own essay on television portrayals of psychological disabilities (pp. 53–55). After completing that paper, Anaya began to wonder about some of the disturbing news stories she had seen that linked campus violence with mental illness. For a research assignment, she decided to delve further into the subject and was surprised by what she found. On the following pages, we reprint her research paper for three reasons: It illustrates many techniques of using and documenting sources, which are highlighted in the marginal comments; it shows a writer working with a topic that interests her in a way that arouses the readers' interest as well; and it explores a problem that affects most college students, often profoundly.

Rosie Anaya

Professor De Beer

English 102A

6 May 2013

The Best Kept Secret on Campus

The college experience, as depicted in advertising and the movies, consists of happy scenes: students engrossed in class discussions, partying with friends, walking in small groups across campus. Such images insist that college is a great time of learning and friendship, but some students have a very different experience of emotional and psychological problems, ranging from anxiety to depression to acute bipolar disorder. These students endure social stigma and barriers to treatment that their colleges and universities must do more to help them surmount.

The numbers of college students suffering from psychological problems are staggering. A 2011 survey conducted by the American College Health Association found that 50% of students have experienced overwhelming anxiety, more than 80% have felt emotionally exhausted, 30% have been so depressed that they had trouble functioning, 20% have been formally diagnosed with depression, and 7% have contemplated suicide (31-35, 37). The simple fact, unknown to many, is that a college student is more likely than not to experience a severe psychological problem at least once. In other words, such problems are a common aspect of college life.

Despite the prevalence of depression and related disorders on campus, however, most students avoid seeking help when they need it. The American Psychiatric Association maintains that most mental-health issues can be managed or overcome with treatment by therapy and/or medication. But among students with a history of depression, according to the American College Health Association, a mere 10% currently receive any kind of treatment (35). One reason for such low numbers can be found in a study published in *Journal of Mental Health Counseling:* Four in five American college students are unwilling to ask for help even when they are certain they need it, because they perceive mental illness as embarrassing or shameful (Aegisdóttir et al. 327-28). Thus students who need help suffer additional

---

Side annotations:

Title arouses readers' curiosity.

Images establish contrast between expectations and experiences of college students. No source citation needed for Anaya's generalization.

Thesis statement.

Statistics establish the scope of the problem.

Citation for paraphrase includes only page numbers because author (American College Health Association) is named in the text.

Follow-up comments give Anaya's interpretation of the evidence.

Students' reluctance to seek help for psychological problems.

No parenthetical citation because author (American Psychiatric Association) is named in the text and online source has no page numbers.

Paragraph integrates information from three sources to support Anaya's own idea.

In parenthetical citation, "et al." ("and others") indicates more than three authors.

pain—and no treatment—because they fear the stigma of mental illness.

We've all heard the horror stories about what happens when a college student's mental illness goes untreated. The news media have been reporting such incidents with regularity since a sniper gunned down sixteen classmates at the University of Texas in 1966. In more recent events, a student at Virginia Tech killed thirty-two people before turning his gun on himself, a sophomore at the University of Texas fired an assault rifle in the school library before committing suicide, a suspended Pima Community College student opened fire at a community meeting hosted by an Arizona congresswoman, and a man who had recently dropped out of the University of Colorado killed twelve people and injured fifty-eight others in a movie-theater shooting spree. After repeated exposure to these kinds of stories, fear seems like a natural—and reasonable—response to mental illness on campus.

The news stories are misleading, however. Richard A. Friedman, a psychiatrist and professor at Cornell University, explains that journalists tend to emphasize mental illness in reports of violent crime even though the connection is rare—accounting for less than 5% of all incidents of violence. Friedman warns that this tendency feeds harmful stereotypes:

> Popular media affect not just how the public views people with psychiatric illness but how the public thinks about the disorders themselves. . . . [M]ajor mental disorders are quite treatable and have response rates to psychosocial and biological treatments that are on par with, if not better than, common nonpsychiatric medical illnesses. But the public has little sense from stories in the popular media that mentally ill people can get better with treatment, recover, and go on to lead productive lives.

Although there is little reason to fear people with mental disorders, we are bombarded with the message that they are dangerous and incurable. No wonder, then, that most college students hide their emotional problems from people who could help them,

Perceived consequences of untreated mental illness.

No source citations in this paragraph because it relies on common knowledge: facts available in several sources, not attributable to any one source.

Refutation of common perception of mental illness.

No parenthetical citation for Friedman because author is named in the text and online source has no page numbers.

Quotation of more than four typed lines is set off and indented one inch.

Ellipsis mark indicates deletion of words from original passage. Brackets indicate change in capitalization of original passage.

Long quotation is followed by Anaya's interpretation and explanation of its significance for her thesis.

never guessing that half of their peers are struggling with the same issues.

As unfortunate as it is, social stigma is not the only barrier to treatment faced by students with mental illness. The uncertain availability of on-campus psychological care poses another obstacle. As Richard Kadison and Theresa Foy DiGeronimo explain in a standard work on college mental-health care, creating and running a mental-health system is expensive, and only some schools can afford to offer comprehensive mental-health programming that ranges from outreach to counseling to follow-up treatment. Other schools have minimal resources and can do little more than react to a crisis, while still others offer no counseling or treatment at all (162-66). Struggling students who finally accept that they need help and work up the courage to ask for it may discover that they can't obtain it, at least not easily. It's not hard to imagine that most students—especially those in the grip of depression—would give up.

Even at schools that do offer mental-health services, legal restrictions can make psychiatric intervention difficult or impossible. Benjamin Reiss, a professor at Emory University, points out that the Americans with Disabilities Act protects people with mental illness from discrimination, so schools cannot screen for psychological disorders or force students to obtain treatment unless a court or "threat assessment team" declares them to be dangerous. And because nearly all college students are adults, confidentiality rules prevent schools from notifying parents or teachers of potential problems without the student's consent ("Campus Security" A76). This combination of social stigma and legal obstacle creates an awkward dilemma: Students suffering from mental illness are reluctant to ask for help, yet the very people who can help are prevented from reaching out. The burden of treatment rests squarely on those who are suffering.

So what should concerned colleges and universities do? Perhaps the best solution is for them to take active steps to remove the stigma associated with mental illness. Just being

Mental-health care on college campuses.

Authors' names and parenthetical page numbers clearly indicate the beginning and end of borrowed material.

Anaya's interpretation of the evidence.

Legal issues related to psychiatric care for college students.

Reiss's name above and parenthetical citation below clearly indicate the beginning and end of borrowed material.

Citation includes shortened version of title to distinguish source from another by same author.

Anaya's interpretation of Reiss's article.

Anaya's own suggestions for solving the problem.

open about the extent of depression and related disorders among college students is a start, and it doesn't have to cost a lot of money. For example, a simple poster campaign announcing the basic statistics of mental illness and assuring students that there is no reason to be ashamed of their feelings might reduce reluctance to seek help. Even if a campus has limited mental-health facilities, prominently displaying links to good Web resources on bulletin boards and on the school's Web site is an inexpensive and easy way both to normalize mental illness and to offer help. Two excellent sites are *Active Minds*, which offers, among other things, fact sheets on common psychological disorders and advice on where to go for help, and the American Psychiatric Association's *Healthy Minds*, which offers mental-health information geared to college students, video testimonials, and explanations of available treatments.

No parenthetical citations needed for entire Web sites named in the text.

Students themselves can also take the lead in addressing mental-health issues. At the University of Pennsylvania, junior Alison Malmon responded to her schizophrenic brother's suicide by starting the 350-chapter support group Active Minds, which advocates for students with psychological disorders and stresses that "people with mental illness are no more violent than people without mental illness" (qtd. in Reiss, "Madness" 31). At a smaller college, a freshman who was successfully treated for depression told her story in the school paper and helped dozens of other students to recognize and seek help for their illnesses (Kadison and DiGeronimo 214-17). As these examples show, students everywhere can make an enormous difference simply by sharing their feelings.

Other students' efforts to solve the problem.

Citation of quotation from an indirect source. Citation includes shortened version of title to distinguish source from another by same author.

Anaya's own interpretation.

Students are in a unique position to help each other through mental illness, but they should not be left to do this important work on their own. Colleges and universities need to collaborate with students to erase the stigma associated with mental illness, to encourage students to get help when they need it, and to prevent the kinds of sensational violence that dominate the news.

Conclusion summarizes Anaya's main points and restates her thesis.

Works Cited

Active Minds. Active Minds, 2013. Web. 6 Apr. 2013.

Aegisdóttir, Stefanía, et al. "Enhancing Attitudes and Reducing
    Fears about Mental Health Counseling: An Analogue Study."
    Journal of Mental Health Counseling 33.4 (2011): 327-46.
    Print.

American College Health Association. "National College Health
    Assessment: Fall 2011 Reference Group Data Report." *Publi-
    cations and Reports*. Amer. College Health Assn., 2012. Web.
    4 Apr. 2013.

American Psychiatric Association. "Mental Illness." *Healthy
    Minds*. Amer. Psychiatric Assn., 2011. Web. 8 Apr. 2013.

Friedman, Richard A. "Media and Madness." *American Prospect*.
    The American Prospect, July-Aug. 2008. Web. 20 Mar. 2013.

Kadison, Richard, and Theresa Foy DiGeronimo. *College of the
    Overwhelmed: The Campus Mental Health Crisis and What to
    Do about It*. San Francisco: Jossey, 2004. Print.

Reiss, Benjamin. "Campus Security and the Specter of Mental-
    Health Profiling." *Chronicle of Higher Education* 4 Feb. 2011.
    Academic Search Premier. Web. 26 Mar. 2013.

---. "Madness after Virginia Tech: From Psychiatric Risk to In-
    stitutional Vulnerability." *Social Text* 28.4 (2010): 25-44.
    Academic Search Premier. Web. 4 Apr. 2013.

"Works Cited" begins on a new page.

An entire Web site.

An article in a print journal. "Et al." ("and others") indicates more than three authors.

A research report posted on the Web.

A document from a Web site.

An article in the Web version of a magazine.

A book with two authors.

A newspaper article in an online database.

The second of two works by the same author.

Rosie Anaya on Writing

We asked Rosie Anaya to tell us about her experience writing "The Best Kept Secret on Campus." She focused on the challenges of working with sources and maintaining her own perspective.

Writing "The Best Kept Secret on Campus" started off as a very personal process. I had a tough time adjusting to college and was diagnosed with mild depression about halfway through my first semester. My experience with depression made me more aware of how the media show mental illness, which I wrote about in one of my composition papers. [See pp. 53–55.] When it came time to write a research paper, I was still thinking about the topic and decided to research mental illness among college students.

The research fascinated me. In fact, I got too absorbed. I spent hours on the Internet, reading blogs and magazine articles and psychology sites. I was surprised to learn how common my experience of depression was! It was a huge revelation, especially when I stumbled across the study that said most college students struggle with psychological problems of one sort or another.

I wound up with more material than I could possibly use — and yet not enough, either. I had dozens of stories and examples to work with, but most of it seemed either too personal or too focused on diagnosis. I had to force myself to look for more authoritative sources. I'm glad I did, because the article on stigma helped me pull everything together. Why should anyone feel too embarrassed to get help when mental illness is so common? Once I had that question in mind, it was easier to toss out all of the personal stories and medical details I had collected and focus on the idea that people should never feel ashamed to ask for psychological help if they need it.

Once I started my first draft, I faced another problem: I somehow didn't feel right adding my own thoughts to what the experts had to say. Really, who am I to argue with them? My first draft more or less compiled summaries and quotations from my sources. Here's an example:

> A survey conducted by the National Alliance for the Mentally Ill reports that "one in three students report having experienced prolonged periods of depression; one in four students report having suicidal thoughts or feelings; one in seven students report engaging in abnormally reckless behavior; and one in seven students report difficulty functioning at school due to mental illness" (82). An annual nationwide study noted a rise since 1985 in the number of first-year students struggling with emotional health (Shea), and the American College Health Association announced that more than 80% of college students have felt emotionally exhausted (31). The Web site *Half of Us*, created by and for college students and sponsored by MTV, takes its name from the claim that "nearly half of all college students reported feeling so depressed that they couldn't function during the last school year." One-tenth of college students in the US have seriously considered suicide (Shute).

This patchwork of summaries and quotations didn't work. But then another student in my class pointed out that I didn't have to argue with the experts, I just had to interact with them. I had my own perspectives on this subject after all, and I could use them. I tried describing my personal struggles with depression and using the sources to fill in the blanks:

> I felt alone in my sadness, so I was shocked to find out how many people cope with psychological disabilities. Would you believe that 20% of college

students share my formal diagnosis of depression? According to the American College Health Association, that's only a small part of the problem: More than 80% of us have felt emotionally exhausted, and nearly a third of all college students have been so depressed that we had trouble functioning (31, 37). Given numbers like these, there was no reason for me to be embarrassed about my feelings, and yet I couldn't bring myself to go to the school's counseling office.

But that didn't feel right either. I had to step back and think about what I wanted to accomplish with this paper, and I realized it wasn't all about me. I had a lot of goals, but mainly I wanted to correct stereotypes about students with psychological problems so that readers would view such students fairly and support improved mental-health services at colleges and universities. To get my point across, I went back to a more objective approach, focusing on what I had learned but letting my personal perspective shape it:

> The numbers of college students suffering from psychological problems are staggering. A 2011 survey conducted by the American College Health Association found that 50% of students have experienced feelings of hopelessness, more than 80% have felt emotionally exhausted, 30% have been so depressed that they had trouble functioning, 20% have been formally diagnosed with depression, and 7% have contemplated suicide (31-35, 37). The simple fact, unknown to many, is that a college student is more likely than not to experience a severe psychological problem at least once. In other words, such problems are a common aspect of college life.

In the end, I rewrote the paper three times before I was happy with it. And in case anyone is wondering, I've been going to talk therapy to help manage my depression, and it has helped. Writing this paper was a big step toward healing.

For Discussion

1. In her comments, Anaya reveals a very personal fact about herself. Based on your reading of "The Best Kept Secret on Campus," why do you think she tells us that she struggles with depression?

2. Anaya says of her initial research that it gave her "more material than [she] could possibly use — and yet not enough, either." What does she mean? Have you encountered a similar dilemma in any of your research projects?

3. Why was Anaya dissatisfied with her first two attempts to provide information from her sources? Why didn't they work or "feel right"? How does her final draft resolve those problems?

PART TWO

THE METHODS

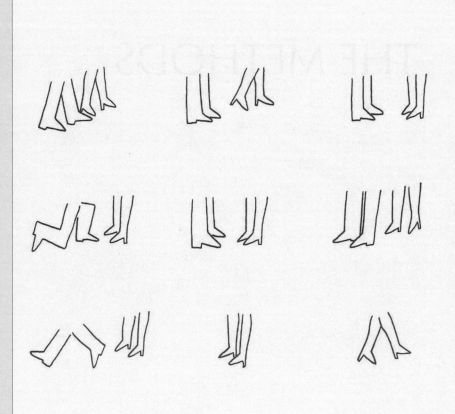

4

NARRATION

Telling a Story

◀ **Narration in a drawing**

Demetri Martin is a popular stand-up comedian known for intelligent wit and for the clever graphs and drawings he incorporates into his act. He has published two books of such artwork: *This Is a Book by Demetri Martin* (2011), which also includes comic essays, and *Point Your Face at This* (2013). "Reality is a concept that depends on where you point your face," he says in the epigraph to the second book — an idea nicely illustrated with this drawing. In Martin's trademark simple style, the sketch focuses on just the lower legs of two people to tell a brief narrative, or story. What experience is depicted here? What do the details in each part of the sequence tell us about the characters, and what do they contribute to the narrative? What effect does Martin achieve by not showing the couple more fully? How does the unusual perspective shape your understanding of what has happened?

THE METHOD

"What happened?" you ask a friend who sports a luminous black eye. Unless he merely grunts "A golf ball," he may answer you with a narrative — a story, true or fictional.

"Okay," he sighs, "you know The Tenth Round? That gym down by the docks that smells of formaldehyde? Last night I heard they were giving away $500 to anybody who could stand up for three minutes against this karate expert, the Masked Samurai. And so . . ."

You lean forward. At least, you lean forward *if* you love a story. Most of us do, particularly if the story tells us of people in action or in conflict, and if it is told briskly, vividly, and with insight into the human heart. NARRATION, or storytelling, is therefore a powerful method by which to engage and hold the attention of listeners — readers as well. A little of its tremendous power flows to the public speaker who starts off with a joke, even a stale joke ("A funny thing happened to me on my way over here . . ."), and to the preacher who at the beginning of a sermon tells of some touching incident.

The term *narrative* takes in abundant territory. A narrative may be short or long, factual or imagined, as artless as a tale told in a locker room or as artful as a novel by Toni Morrison. A narrative may instruct and inform, or simply entertain. It may set forth some point or message, or it may be no more significant than a horror tale that aims to curdle your blood. Because narration can both put across ideas and hold attention, the ability to tell a story — on paper, as well as in conversation — may be one of the most useful skills you can acquire.

THE PROCESS

Purpose and Shape

At least a hundred times a year, you probably resort to narration, not always to tell an entertaining story, but often to report information or to illustrate a point. Every good story has a purpose. A narrative without a purpose is bound to irritate readers, as a young child's rambling can vex an unsympathetic adult.

In academic writing, you will use mainly brief narratives, or ANECDOTES, that recount single incidents as a way of supporting an explanation or an ARGUMENT with the flesh and blood of real life. That is, although a narrative can run from the beginning of an essay to the end, as those later in this chapter do, more often in your writing a narrative will be only a part of what you have to say. It will serve a larger purpose. For instance, say you're writing about therapies for autism and you want readers to see how one particular method works. In a paragraph or so, you can narrate a session you observed between an autistic child and his teacher. Your purpose will determine which of the session's events you relate — not every action and exchange but the ones that, in your eyes, convey the essence of the therapy and make it interesting for readers.

The Thesis

In writing a news story, a reporter often begins by placing the main event in the opening paragraph (called the *lead*) so that readers get the essentials up front. Similarly, in using an anecdote to explain something or to argue a point, you'll want to tell readers directly what the story demonstrates. But in most other kinds of narration, whether fiction or nonfiction, whether to entertain or to make an idea clear, the storyteller refrains from revealing the gist of the story, its point, right at the beginning.

In fact, many narratives do not contain a THESIS STATEMENT, an assertion of the idea behind the story, because such a statement can rob the reader of the very pleasure of narration, the excitement of seeing a story build. That doesn't mean the story lacks a thesis, however — far from it. The writer has every obligation to construct the narrative as if a thesis statement shows the way at the start, even when it doesn't.

By the end of the story, that thesis should become obvious, as the writer builds toward a memorable CONCLUSION. Most storytellers end with a bang if they can, often by surprising the reader with a final moment of IRONY, or an unexpected twist to the tale. In the drawing that opens this chapter, for instance, Demetri Martin shows a marriage proposal that ends in a breakup. The final impact need not be as dramatic as Martin's, either. As Junot Díaz demonstrates in his narrative in this chapter, you can achieve a lot just by leading to your point, stating your thesis at the very end. You can sometimes make your point just by saving the best incident — the most dramatic or the funniest — for last.

The Narrator in the Story

Every story has a NARRATOR, the person telling the tale. The narrator's role in relation to the story determines the POINT OF VIEW, or angle of seeing, that shapes the telling. Generally, writers use different points of view to tell different kinds of stories.

- **Narratives that report personal experience:** Whether you are telling of a real or a fictional event, your narrator will be the one who was there. The telling will probably be SUBJECTIVE: You will use the first PERSON ("I did this; we did that") and choose details and language to express the feelings of the narrator — your own feelings when you are recounting your actual experience or the imagined feelings of a character you have invented. Of course, any experience told in the first person can use some artful telling and some structuring, as the personal narratives in this chapter — by Maya Angelou, Amy Tan, and Annie Dillard — all demonstrate.

- **Narratives that report others' experiences:** When a story isn't your own but someone else's, you proceed differently as narrator. You use the third person, *he, she, it,* or *they*: "The experimenter did this; she did that." Your approach may be subjective, building in the real or imagined feelings of the person experiencing the events — as Junot Díaz does in this chapter, reporting his mother's story. Or your approach may be OBJECTIVE, sticking to the facts as observed by you or by others. In objective narration — typical of writing such as news stories, history books, lab reports, and some fiction — you show what transpired as accurately and dispassionately as possible. In this chapter you can see objective narration in the case study by Emily Thibodeau.

A final element of the narrator's place in the story is verb tense, whether present (*I stare, she stares*) or past (*I stared, she stared*). The present tense is often tempting because it gives events a sense of immediacy. Told as though everything were happening right now, the story of the Masked Samurai might begin: "I duck between the ropes and step into the ring. My heart is thudding fast." But the present tense can seem artificial because we're used to reading stories in the past tense, and it can be difficult to sustain throughout an entire narrative. (See p. 99 on consistency in tenses.) The past tense may be more removed, but it is still powerful: Just look at Maya Angelou's gripping "Champion of the World," beginning on page 104.

What to Emphasize

Discovery of Details

Whether you tell of your own experience or of someone else's, even if it is brief, you need a whole story to tell. If the story is complex, do some searching and discovering in writing. One trusty method to test your memory (or to make sure you have all the necessary elements of a story) is that of a news reporter. Ask yourself:

- **What happened?**
- **Who took part?**
- **When?**
- **Where?**
- **Why did it happen?**
- **How did it happen?**

Journalists call this handy list of questions "the five *W*'s and the *H*." The *H* — *how* — isn't merely another way of asking what happened. It means: In exactly what way or under what circumstances? If the event was a murder, how was it done — with an ax or with a bulldozer?

Scene versus Summary

If you have prepared well — searching your memory or doing some research — you'll have far more information on hand than you can use in your narrative. You'll need to choose carefully, to pick out just those events and details that will accomplish your purpose with your readers.

A key decision is choosing between the two main strategies of narration:

- **Tell a story by SCENE, visualizing each event as vividly and precisely as if you were there.** Think of the scene as if it were in a film, with your reader sitting before the screen. This is the strategy Maya Angelou uses in her account of a tense crowd's behavior as, jammed into a small-town store, they listen to a fight broadcast (in "Champion of the World"). Instead of just mentioning people, you portray them. You recall dialog as best you can, or you invent some that could have been spoken. You include DESCRIPTION (a mode of writing to be dealt with fully in the next chapter). You might prolong one scene for an entire essay, or you could draw a scene in only two or three sentences.

- **Tell a story by SUMMARY, relating events concisely.** Instead of depicting people and their surroundings in great detail, you set down just the essentials of what happened. Such is the strategy Junot Díaz uses, in "The Dreamer" (p. 120), to tell of his mother's childhood determination to get an education. Most of us employ this method in most stories we tell, for it takes less time and fewer words. When chosen well, the economy of a story told in summary may be as effective as the lavish detail of a story told in scenes.

As always, your choice of a strategy depends on your answers to the questions you ask yourself: What is my purpose? Who is my audience? Whether to flesh out a scene fully, how much detail to include — these choices depend on what you seek to do and on how much your audience needs to know to follow you. You may find that you want to use both strategies in telling a single story, passing briskly from one scene to the next, distilling events of lesser importance. Were you to write, let's say, the story of your grandfather's immigration to the United States from Cuba, you might just summarize his decision to leave Cuba and his settlement in Florida. These summaries could frame and emphasize a detailed telling of the events that you consider essential and most interesting — his nighttime escape, his harrowing voyage in a small boat, his surprising welcome by immigration authorities.

Dialog

In this book we are concerned with the kind of writing you do every day in college: nonfiction writing in which you generally explain ideas, organize information you have learned, analyze other people's ideas, or argue a case. In fiction, though, we find an enormously popular and appealing use of narration and certain devices of storytelling from which all storytellers can learn. In the compelling true stories in this chapter, all of the authors strive to make people and events come alive for us. All of them also use a tool that academic writers generally do not: dialog. Reported speech, in quotation marks, is invaluable for revealing characters' feelings.

Organization

In any kind of narration, the simplest approach is to set down events in CHRONOLOGICAL ORDER, following the sequence in which they occurred. To do so is to have your story already organized for you.

Chronological order is an excellent pattern to follow unless you can see some special advantage in violating it. Ask: What am I trying to do? If you are trying to capture your readers' attention right away, you might begin in medias res (Latin, "in the middle of things") and open with a colorful, dramatic event, even though it took place late in the chronology. If trying for dramatic effect, you might save the most exciting or impressive event for last, even though it actually happened early. By this means, you can keep your readers in suspense for as long as possible. (You can return to earlier events in a FLASHBACK, an earlier scene recalled.) Let your purpose be your guide.

No matter what order you choose, either following chronology or departing from it, make sure your audience can follow it. The sequence of events has to be clear. This calls for TRANSITIONS that mark time, whether they are brief phrases that point out exactly when each event happened ("seven years later," "a moment earlier") or whole sentences that announce an event and clearly locate it in time ("Passing by the gym on Friday evening, I noticed the sign: 'Go Three Minutes with the Masked Samurai and Win $500.'"). See *Transitions* in Useful Terms for a list of possibilities.

FOCUS ON VERBS

Narration depends heavily on verbs to clarify and enliven events. Strong verbs sharpen meaning and encourage you to add other informative details:

WEAK   The wind <u>made</u> an awful noise.

STRONG   The wind <u>roared</u> around the house and <u>rattled</u> the trees.

Forms of *make* (as in the example above) and forms of *be* (as in the next example) can sap the life from narration:

WEAK   The noises <u>were</u> alarming to us.

STRONG   The noises <u>alarmed</u> us.

Verbs in the ACTIVE VOICE (the subject does the action) usually pack more power into fewer words than verbs in the PASSIVE VOICE (the subject is acted upon):

WEAK PASSIVE   We <u>were besieged</u> in the basement by the wind, as the water at our feet <u>was swelled</u> by the rain.

STRONG ACTIVE   The wind <u>besieged</u> us in the basement, as the rain <u>swelled</u> the water at our feet.

While strengthening verbs, also ensure that they're consistent in tense. The tense you choose for relating events, present or past, should not shift unnecessarily.

INCONSISTENT TENSES   We <u>held</u> a frantic conference to consider our options. It <u>takes</u> only a minute to decide to stay put.

CONSISTENT TENSE   We <u>held</u> a frantic conference to consider our options. It <u>took</u> only a minute to decide to stay put.

See page 43 for further discussion of passive versus active verbs and page 47 for advice on avoiding shifts in tense.

CHECKLIST FOR REVISING A NARRATIVE

✔ **Thesis.** What is the point of your narrative? Will it be clear to readers by the end? Even if you don't provide a thesis statement, your story should focus on a central idea. If you can't risk readers' misunderstanding — if, for instance, you're using narration to support an argument or explain a concept — then have you stated your thesis outright?

✔ **Point of view.** Is your narrator's position in the story appropriate for your purpose and consistent throughout? Check for awkward or confusing shifts in point of view (subjective or objective; first or third person) and in the tenses of verbs (present to past or vice versa).

✔ **Selection of events.** Have you selected and emphasized events to suit your audience and fulfill your purpose? Tell the important parts of the story in the greatest detail. Summarize the less important, connective events.

✔ **Organization.** If your organization is not strictly chronological (first event to last), do you have a compelling reason for altering it? If you start somewhere other than the beginning of the story or use flashbacks at any point, will your readers benefit from your creativity?

✔ **Transitions.** Have you used transitions to help clarify the order of events and their duration?

✔ **Dialog.** If you have used dialog, quoting participants in the story, is it appropriate for your purpose? Is it concise, telling only the important, revealing lines? Does the language sound like spoken English?

✔ **Verbs.** Do strong, active verbs move your narrative from event to event? Are verb tenses consistent?

NARRATION IN ACADEMIC WRITING

A Geology Textbook

In this paragraph from *The Earth: An Introduction to Physical Geology*, the authors Edward J. Tarbuck and Frederick K. Lutgens use narration to illustrate a powerful geological occurrence. Following a paragraph that explains landslides more generally, this narrative places the reader at a historic event.

The news media periodically relate the terrifying and often grim details of landslides. On May 31, 1970, one such event occurred when a gigantic rock avalanche buried more than 20,000 people in Yungay and Ranrahirca, Peru. There was little warning of the impending disaster; it began and ended in just a matter of a few minutes. The avalanche started 14 kilometers from Yungay, near

Generalization illustrated by narrative

Anecdote helps explain landslides

• *Sudden beginning*

the summit of 6,700-meter-high Nevados Huascaran, the loftiest peak in the Peruvian Andes. Triggered by the ground motion from a strong offshore earthquake, a huge mass of rock and ice broke free from the precipitous north face of the mountain. After plung-ing nearly one kilometer, the material pulverized on impact and immediately began rushing down the mountainside, made fluid by trapped air and melted ice. The initial mass ripped loose additional millions of tons of debris as it roared downhill. The shock waves pro-duced by the event created thunderlike noise and stripped nearby hillsides of vegetation. Although the material followed a previously eroded gorge, a portion of the debris jumped a 200–300-meter-high bedrock ridge that had protected Yungay from past rock avalanches and buried the entire city. After inundating another town in its path, Ranrahirca, the mass of debris finally reached the bottom of the valley where its momentum carried it across the Rio Santa and tens of meters up the opposite bank.

• Fast movement

• Irresistible force

Transitions (under-lined) clarify sequence and pace of events

A Case Study

How did a small, local business solve a marketing problem? What did a company's management do to increase productivity? These questions are typi-cal of those asked by business analysts and students as they read and write case studies. A research method in all the social sciences, the case study examines a particular group, situation, or individual to discover what happened and why.

A business case study often begins with a narrative, telling the story of its subject to establish the background and facts of the case: what happened, who was involved, where and when events took place, and why a problem is relevant. A case study may then proceed to CAUSE AND EFFECT, explaining why this one EXAMPLE happened as it did, and it may draw conclusions about the principles or lessons to be learned from the case.

Emily Thibodeau wrote a case study for an introductory class in business management. Intrigued by the success of Tesla Motors, a manufacturer of luxury electric cars based in California, she wondered how other automobile start-ups had fared in difficult economic climates. Her preliminary research led her to Owen Motors, a builder of luxury cars in the early twentieth cen-tury. In the introduction to her case study, below, Thibodeau narrates Owen's story. Following APA style for in-text citations (see pp. 548–51) she provides page references for direct quotations and paraphrases but not for summaries or facts counted as common knowledge.

History of Owen Motors

The history of Owen Motors is told in *First Cars* by Robert Vigna (1976) and *A History of the Automobile Industry* by Tessa

Smyth and Franco Madrone (1981). The story begins in April of 1909, <u>when</u> Robert and Joseph Owen built a car for themselves in Robert Owen's Detroit, Michigan, garage. The entrepreneurial brothers secured the backing of five investors <u>in January 1910</u> with a design for a luxury automobile <u>and immediately</u> resigned from their jobs at the Packard Motor Car Company. The first automobile manufactured by Owen Motors rolled off the assembly line <u>in 1912</u>. The cars were notable not only for the quality of their interior leather and wood but also for their high-performing multivalve engines and their innovative safety features, including the first padded dashboard (Vigna, 1976, p. 72). <u>By 1917</u> the company was producing almost 4,000 cars annually.

    <u>During America's involvement in World War I (1917–1918)</u>, Owen Motors did not attempt to secure design or manufacturing contracts with the military, as the Ford Motor Company and other car manufacturers did. <u>In the years after the war</u>, Robert Owen came to see this decision as a missed opportunity and wanted the company to diversify its products and expand into new markets; Joseph, in contrast, preferred to keep the company's focus on luxury cars, believing that the market would continue to grow (Smyth & Madrone, 1981, p. 117). <u>Consequently</u>, Joseph bought out Robert's share of the company <u>in 1921</u> and assumed sole leadership. Owen Motors expanded its manufacturing facilities to produce additional models of luxury cars, which continued to be profitable <u>throughout the boom of the 1920s</u> even though the price of an Owen automobile never fell below $3,000. <u>In 1928</u> Owen Motors cleared $2 million in profits.

    <u>In 1929 and 1930, with the onset of the Great Depression</u>, overall car sales in the United States declined rapidly. <u>As the Depression continued</u>, U.S. salaries and wages plummeted and unemployment rose, exceeding 22% in 1933. Larger car companies, such as General Motors and Ford, were able to absorb losses and weather the long economic downturn, but smaller, independent companies like Owen often could not. Consumers <u>now</u> focused almost exclusively on inexpensive cars, which Owen had never made, and its sales had declined almost 50% <u>by 1933</u>. Joseph Owen focused on maintaining quality with just his most popular models and worked with his engineers to make the assembly line

Narrative opens with the company's beginnings

Chronological order

Transitions (<u>underlined</u>) clarify sequence and pace of events

Explanation of the company's changes in response to key historic events:

• World War I

• The economic boom of the 1920s

• The Great Depression

more efficient with technological innovations such as an early welding robot.

The company did survive the Depression, "limping along," as Joseph Owen himself put it (as cited in Vigna, 1976, p. 291). Despite some pressure to sell to a larger company, Owen rejected at least two offers <u>between 1934 and 1938</u>. <u>Then</u> the United States began supplying its allies with arms and supplies <u>in the build-up to World War II</u>, and Owen saw the opportunity that his brother, Robert, had seen with World War I. Trading on the company's reputation for advanced technology and efficient manufacturing, Owen obtained a few small but lucrative contracts to produce trucks. <u>Within two years</u>, the company had abandoned auto manufacturing. <u>In February of 1941</u> Joseph Owen was severely injured in a car accident and he lost control of the company. It was sold to General Motors <u>later that year</u>.

• World War II

Narrative concludes
with the company's sale

Narration

MAYA ANGELOU

Maya Angelou was born Marguerite Johnson in Saint Louis in 1928. After an unpleasantly eventful youth by her account ("from a broken family, raped at eight, unwed mother at sixteen"), she went on to join a dance company, act in the off-Broadway play *The Blacks* and the television series *Roots,* write several books of poetry, produce a TV series on Africa, serve as a coordinator for the Southern Christian Leadership Conference, win the Presidential Medals of Arts and of Freedom, write and deliver the inaugural poem ("On the Pulse of Morning") for President Clinton, and be inducted into the National Women's Hall of Fame. Angelou is the author of thirty best-selling works but is probably best known for the six books of her searching, frank, and joyful autobiography — from *I Know Why the Caged Bird Sings* (1970) through *A Song Flung Up to Heaven* (2002). Her most recent book, *Mom & Me & Mom* (2013), explores her complicated relationship with her mother. Angelou is Reynolds Professor of American Studies at Wake Forest University.

Champion of the World

"Champion of the World" is the nineteenth chapter in *I Know Why the Caged Bird Sings;* the title is a phrase taken from the chapter. Remembering her childhood, the writer tells how she and her older brother, Bailey, grew up in a town in Arkansas. The center of their lives was Grandmother and Uncle Willie's store. On the night of this story, in the late 1930s, the African American community gathers in the store to listen to a boxing match on the radio. Joe Louis, the "Brown Bomber," who was a hero to black people, is defending his heavyweight title against a white contender. (Louis successfully defended his title twenty-five times, a record that stands today.) Angelou's telling of the event both entertains us and explains what it was like to be African American in a certain time and place.

Amy Tan's "Fish Cheeks," following Angelou's essay, also explores the experience of growing up as an outsider in America.

The last inch of space was filled, yet people continued to wedge themselves along the walls of the Store. Uncle Willie had turned the radio up to its last notch so that youngsters on the porch wouldn't miss a word. Women sat on kitchen chairs, dining-room chairs, stools, and upturned wooden boxes.

Small children and babies perched on every lap available and men leaned on the shelves or on each other.

The apprehensive mood was shot through with shafts of gaiety, as a black sky is streaked with lightning.

"I ain't worried 'bout this fight. Joe's gonna whip that cracker like it's open season."

"He gone whip him till that white boy call him Momma."

At last the talking finished and the string-along songs about razor blades were over and the fight began.

"A quick jab to the head." In the Store the crowd grunted. "A left to the head and a right and another left." One of the listeners cackled like a hen and was quieted.

"They're in a clinch, Louis is trying to fight his way out."

Some bitter comedian on the porch said, "That white man don't mind hugging that niggah now, I betcha."

"The referee is moving in to break them up, but Louis finally pushed the contender away and it's an uppercut to the chin. The contender is hanging on, now he's backing away. Louis catches him with a short left to the jaw."

A tide of murmuring assent poured out the door and into the yard.

"Another left and another left. Louis is saving that mighty right . . ." The mutter in the Store had grown into a baby roar and it was pierced by the clang of a bell and the announcer's "That's the bell for round three, ladies and gentlemen."

As I pushed my way into the Store I wondered if the announcer gave any thought to the fact that he was addressing as "ladies and gentlemen" all the Negroes around the world who sat sweating and praying, glued to their "Master's voice."[1]

There were only a few calls for RC Colas, Dr Peppers, and Hires root beer. The real festivities would begin after the fight. Then even the old Christian ladies who taught their children and tried themselves to practice turning the other cheek would buy soft drinks, and if the Brown Bomber's victory was a particularly bloody one they would order peanut patties and Baby Ruths also.

Bailey and I laid the coins on top of the cash register. Uncle Willie didn't allow us to ring up sales during a fight. It was too noisy and might shake up the atmosphere. When the gong rang for the next round we pushed through the near-sacred quiet to the herd of children outside.

---

[1] "His Master's Voice," accompanied by a picture of a little dog listening to a phonograph, was a familiar advertising slogan. (The picture still appears on some RCA recordings.) — Eds.

"He's got Louis against the ropes and now it's a left to the body and a right   15
to the ribs. Another right to the body, it looks like it was low . . . Yes, ladies
and gentlemen, the referee is signaling but the contender keeps raining the
blows on Louis. It's another to the body, and it looks like Louis is going down."

My race groaned. It was our people falling. It was another lynching, yet   16
another Black man hanging on a tree. One more woman ambushed and raped.
A Black boy whipped and maimed. It was hounds on the trail of a man running through slimy swamps. It was a white woman slapping her maid for being
forgetful.

The men in the Store stood away from the walls and at attention. Women   17
greedily clutched the babes on their laps while on the porch the shufflings and
smiles, flirtings and pinching of a few minutes before were gone. This might
be the end of the world. If Joe lost we were back in slavery and beyond help. It
would all be true, the accusations that we were lower types of human beings.
Only a little higher than apes. True that we were stupid and ugly and lazy and
dirty and, unlucky and worst of all, that God Himself hated us and ordained
us to be hewers of wood and drawers of water, forever and ever, world without
end.

We didn't breathe. We didn't hope. We waited.   18

"He's off the ropes, ladies and gentlemen. He's moving towards the center   19
of the ring." There was no time to be relieved. The worst might still happen.

"And now it looks like Joe is mad. He's caught Carnera with a left hook   20
to the head and a right to the head. It's a left jab to the body and another left
to the head. There's a left cross and a right to the head. The contender's right
eye is bleeding and he can't seem to keep his block up. Louis is penetrating
every block. The referee is moving in, but Louis sends a left to the body and
it's an uppercut to the chin and the contender is dropping. He's on the canvas,
ladies and gentlemen."

Babies slid to the floor as women stood up and men leaned toward the   21
radio.

"Here's the referee. He's counting. One, two, three, four, five, six, seven . . .   22
Is the contender trying to get up again?"

All the men in the store shouted, "no."   23

" — eight, nine, ten." There were a few sounds from the audience, but   24
they seemed to be holding themselves in against tremendous pressure.

"The fight is all over, ladies and gentlemen. Let's get the microphone over   25
to the referee . . . Here he is. He's got the Brown Bomber's hand, he's holding
it up . . . Here he is . . ."

Then the voice, husky and familiar, came to wash over us — "The win-   26
nah, and still heavyweight champeen of the world . . . Joe Louis."

Champion of the world. A Black boy. Some Black mother's son. He was   27
the strongest man in the world. People drank Coca-Colas like ambrosia and
ate candy bars like Christmas. Some of the men went behind the Store and
poured white lightning in their soft-drink bottles, and a few of the bigger boys
followed them. Those who were not chased away came back blowing their
breath in front of themselves like proud smokers.

It would take an hour or more before the people would leave the Store   28
and head for home. Those who lived too far had made arrangements to stay in
town. It wouldn't do for a Black man and his family to be caught on a lonely
country road on a night when Joe Louis had proved that we were the strongest
people in the world.

For a reading quiz, visit **bedfordstmartins.com/thebedfordreader**.

Journal Writing

How do you respond to the group identification and solidarity that Angelou writes
about in this essay? What groups do you belong to, and how do you know you're a
member? Consider groups based on race, ethnic background, religion, sports, hobbies,
politics, friendship, kinship, or any other ties. (To take your journal writing further,
see "From Journal to Essay" on the next page.)

Questions on Meaning

1. What do you take to be the author's PURPOSE in telling this story?
2. What connection does Angelou make between the outcome of the fight and the
   pride of African Americans? To what degree do you think the author's view is
   shared by the others in the store listening to the broadcast?
3. To what extent are the statements in paragraphs 16 and 17 to be taken literally?
   What function do they serve in Angelou's narrative?
4. Primo Carnera was probably *not* the Brown Bomber's opponent on the night
   Maya Angelou recalls. Louis fought Carnera only once, on June 25, 1935, and it
   was not a title match. Does the author's apparent error detract from her story?

Questions on Writing Strategy

1. What details in the opening paragraphs indicate that an event of crucial importance is about to take place?

2. How does Angelou build up SUSPENSE in her account of the fight? At what point were you able to predict the winner?
3. Comment on the IRONY in Angelou's final paragraph.
4. What EFFECT does the author's use of direct quotation have on her narrative?
5. **OTHER METHODS** Besides narration, Angelou also relies heavily on the method of DESCRIPTION. Analyze how narration depends on description in paragraph 27 alone.

Questions on Language

1. Explain what the author means by "string-along songs about razor blades" (par. 5).
2. Point to some examples in the essay of Angelou's use of strong verbs.
3. How does Angelou's use of NONSTANDARD ENGLISH contribute to her narrative?
4. Be sure you know the meanings of these words: apprehensive (par. 2); assent (10); ambushed, maimed (16); ordained (17); ambrosia, white lightning (27).

Suggestions for Writing

1. **FROM JOURNAL TO ESSAY** From your journal entry, choose one of the groups you belong to and explore your sense of membership through a narrative that tells of an incident that occurred when that sense was strong. Try to make the incident come alive for your readers with vivid details, dialog, and tight sequencing of events.
2. Write an essay based on some childhood experience of your own, still vivid in your memory.
3. **CRITICAL WRITING** Angelou does not directly describe relations between African Americans and whites, yet her essay implies quite a lot. Write a brief essay about what you can INFER from the exaggeration of paragraphs 16–17 and the oblique-ness of paragraph 28. Focus on Angelou's details and the language she uses to present them.
4. **CONNECTIONS** Angelou's "Champion of the World" and the next essay, Amy Tan's "Fish Cheeks," both tell stories of children who felt like outsiders in pre-dominantly white America. COMPARE AND CONTRAST the two writers' perceptions of what sets them apart from the dominant culture. How does the event each reports affect that sense of difference? Use specific examples from both essays as your EVIDENCE.

Maya Angelou on Writing

Maya Angelou's writings have shown great variety: She has done notable work as an autobiographer, poet, short-story writer, screenwriter, journalist, and song lyricist. Asked by interviewer Sheila Weller, "Do you start each project with a specific idea?" Angelou replied:

It starts with a definite subject, but it might end with something entirely different. When I start a project, the first thing I do is write down, in long-hand, everything I know about the subject, every thought I've ever had on it. This may be twelve or fourteen pages. Then I read it back through, for quite a few days, and find — given that subject — what its rhythm is. 'Cause everything in the universe has a rhythm. So if it's free form, it still has a rhythm. And once I hear the rhythm of the piece, then I try to find out what are the salient points that I must make. And then it begins to take shape.

I try to set myself up in each chapter by saying: "This is what I want to go from — from B to, say, G-sharp. Or from D to L." And then I find the hook. It's like the knitting, where, after you knit a certain amount, there's one thread that begins to pull. You know, you can see it right along the cloth. Well, in writing, I think: "Now where is that one hook, that one little thread?" It may be a sentence. If I can catch that, then I'm home free. It's the one that tells me where I'm going. It may not even turn out to be in the final chapter. I may throw it out later or change it. But if I follow it through, it leads me right out.

For Discussion

1. How would you define the word *rhythm* as Angelou uses it?
2. What response would you give a student who asked, "Doesn't Angelou's approach to writing waste more time and thought than it's worth?"

AMY TAN

Amy Tan is a gifted storyteller whose first novel, *The Joy Luck Club* (1989), met with critical acclaim and huge success. The relationships it details between immigrant Chinese mothers and their Chinese American daughters came from Tan's firsthand experience. She was born in 1952 in Oakland, California, the daughter of immigrants who had fled China's civil war in the late 1940s. She majored in English and linguistics at San Jose State University, where she received a BA in 1973 and an MA in 1974. After two more years of graduate work, Tan became a consultant in language development for disabled children and then started her own company writing reports and speeches for business corporations. Tan began writing fiction to explore her ethnic ambivalence and to find her voice. Since *The Joy Luck Club*, she has published several more novels — most recently *The Valley of Amazement* (2013) — as well as children's books and *The Opposite of Fate* (2003), a collection of autobiographical essays. She sometimes sings with the Rock Bottom Remainders, a "literary garage band" that also includes Dave Barry (p. 220) and Stephen King.

Fish Cheeks

In Tan's novel *The Bonesetter's Daughter* (2001), one of the characters says, "Good manners are not enough. . . . They are not the same as a good heart." Much of Tan's writing explores the tensions between keeping up appearances and having true intentions. In the brief narrative that follows, the author deftly portrays the contradictory feelings and the advantages of a girl with feet in different cultures. The essay first appeared in *Seventeen*, a magazine for teenage girls and young women, in 1987.

For a complementary view of growing up "different," read the preceding essay, Maya Angelou's "Champion of the World."

I fell in love with the minister's son the winter I turned fourteen. He was not Chinese, but as white as Mary in the manger. For Christmas I prayed for this blond-haired boy, Robert, and a slim new American nose.

When I found out that my parents had invited the minister's family over for Christmas Eve dinner, I cried. What would Robert think of our shabby Chinese Christmas? What would he think of our noisy Chinese relatives who lacked proper American manners? What terrible disappointment would he feel upon seeing not a roasted turkey and sweet potatoes but Chinese food?

On Christmas Eve I saw that my mother had outdone herself in creating   3
a strange menu. She was pulling black veins out of the backs of fleshy prawns.
The kitchen was littered with appalling mounds of raw food: A slimy rock cod
with bulging eyes that pleaded not to be thrown into a pan of hot oil. Tofu,
which looked like stacked wedges of rubbery white sponges. A bowl soaking
dried fungus back to life. A plate of squid, their backs crisscrossed with knife
markings so they resembled bicycle tires.

And then they arrived — the minister's family and all my relatives in a   4
clamor of doorbells and rumpled Christmas packages. Robert grunted hello,
and I pretended he was not worthy of existence.

Dinner threw me deeper into despair. My relatives licked the ends of their   5
chopsticks and reached across the table, dipping them into the dozen or so
plates of food. Robert and his family waited patiently for platters to be passed
to them. My relatives murmured with pleasure when my mother brought out
the whole steamed fish. Robert grimaced. Then my father poked his chopsticks just below the fish eye and plucked out the soft meat. "Amy, your favorite," he said, offering me the tender fish cheek. I wanted to disappear.

At the end of the meal my father leaned back and belched loudly, thank-   6
ing my mother for her fine cooking. "It's a polite Chinese custom to show you
are satisfied," explained my father to our astonished guests. Robert was looking down at his plate with a reddened face. The minister managed to muster
up a quiet burp. I was stunned into silence for the rest of the night.

After everyone had gone, my mother said to me, "You want to be the   7
same as American girls on the outside." She handed me an early gift. It was a
miniskirt in beige tweed. "But inside you must always be Chinese. You must be
proud you are different. Your only shame is to have shame."

And even though I didn't agree with her then, I knew that she understood   8
how much I had suffered during the evening's dinner. It wasn't until many
years later — long after I had gotten over my crush on Robert — that I was
able to fully appreciate her lesson and the true purpose behind our particular
menu. For Christmas Eve that year, she had chosen all my favorite foods.

For a reading quiz, visit **bedfordstmartins.com/thebedfordreader**.

Journal Writing

Do you sympathize with the shame Tan feels because of her family's differences from
their non-Chinese guests? Or do you think she should have been more proud to share

her family's customs? Think of an occasion when, for whatever reason, you were acutely aware of being different. How did you react? Did you try to hide your difference in order to fit in, or did you reveal or celebrate your uniqueness? (To take your journal writing further, see "From Journal to Essay" below.)

Questions on Meaning

1. Why does Tan cry when she finds out that the boy she is in love with is coming to dinner?
2. Why does Tan's mother go out of her way to prepare a disturbingly traditional Chinese dinner for her daughter and guests? What one sentence best sums up the lesson Tan was not able to understand until years later?
3. How does the fourteen-year-old Tan feel about her Chinese background? about her mother?
4. What is Tan's PURPOSE in writing this essay? Does she just want to entertain readers, or might she have a weightier goal?

Questions on Writing Strategy

1. How does Tan draw the reader into her story right from the beginning?
2. How does Tan use TRANSITIONS both to drive and to clarify her narrative?
3. What is the IRONY of the last sentence of the essay?
4. **OTHER METHODS** Paragraph 3 is a passage of pure DESCRIPTION. Why does Tan linger over the food? What is the EFFECT of this paragraph?

Questions on Language

1. The simile about Mary in the second sentence of the essay is surprising. Why? Why is it amusing? (See FIGURES OF SPEECH in Useful Terms for a definition of *simile*.)
2. How does the narrator's age affect the TONE of this essay? Give EXAMPLES of language particularly appropriate to a fourteen-year-old.
3. In which paragraph does Tan use strong verbs most effectively?
4. Make sure you know the meanings of the following words: prawns, tofu (par. 3); clamor (4); grimaced (5); muster (6).

Suggestions for Writing

1. **FROM JOURNAL TO ESSAY** Using Tan's essay as a model, write a brief narrative based on your journal sketch about a time when you felt different from others. Try to imitate the way Tan integrates the external events of the dinner with her own feelings about what is going on. Your story may be humorous, like Tan's, or more serious.
2. Take a perspective like that of the minister's son, Robert: Write a narrative essay about a time when you had to adjust to participating in a culture different from your own. It could be a meal, a wedding or other rite of passage, a religious cer-

emony, a trip to another country. What did you learn from your experience, about yourself and others?

3. **CRITICAL WRITING** From this essay one can INFER two very different sets of ASSUMPTIONS about the extent to which immigrants should seek to integrate themselves into the culture of their adopted country. Take either of these positions, in favor of or against assimilation (cultural integration), and make an ARGUMENT for your case.

4. **CONNECTIONS** Both Amy Tan and Maya Angelou, in "Champion of the World" (p. 104), write about difference from white Americans, but their POINTS OF VIEW are not the same: Tan's is a teenager's lament about not fitting in; Angelou's is an oppressed child's excitement about proving the injustice of oppression. In an essay, ANALYZE the two authors' uses of narration to convey their perspectives. What details do they focus on? What internal thoughts do they report? Is one essay more effective than the other? Why, or why not?

ANNIE DILLARD

Annie Dillard is accomplished as a prose writer, poet, and literary critic. Born in 1945, she earned a BA (1967) and an MA (1968) from Hollins College in Virginia. Dillard's first published prose, *Pilgrim at Tinker Creek* (1974), attracted notice for its close, intense, and poetic descriptions of the natural world. It won her a Pulitzer Prize and comparison with Thoreau. Since then, Dillard's entranced and entrancing writing has appeared regularly in *Harper's, The Atlantic Monthly*, and other magazines and in her wide-ranging books, including *Living by Fiction* (1982), literary criticism; *Teaching a Stone to Talk* (1982), nonfiction; *An American Childhood* (1987), autobiography; *The Writing Life* (1989), anecdotes and metaphors about writing; and *The Maytrees* (2007), a novel. In 1999 Dillard was inducted into the American Academy of Arts and Letters. She is professor emeritus at Wesleyan University.

The Chase

Dillard's autobiography, *An American Childhood*, views experience with the sharply perceptive eyes of a child. In this chapter from the book, Dillard leads us running desperately through snow-filled backyards. Like all of her writing, this romp shows unparalleled enthusiasm for life and skill at expressing it.

Some boys taught me to play football. This was fine sport. You thought up   1
a new strategy for every play and whispered it to the others. You went out for
a pass, fooling everyone. Best, you got to throw yourself mightily at someone's
running legs. Either you brought him down or you hit the ground flat on your
chin, with your arms empty before you. It was all or nothing. If you hesitated
in fear, you would miss and get hurt: you would take a hard fall while the kid
got away, or you would get kicked in the face while the kid got away. But if you
flung yourself wholeheartedly at the back of his knees — if you gathered and
joined body and soul and pointed them diving fearlessly — then you likely
wouldn't get hurt, and you'd stop the ball. Your fate, and your team's score,
depended on your concentration and courage. Nothing girls did could compare with it.

Boys welcomed me at baseball, too, for I had, through enthusiastic prac-   2
tice, what was weirdly known as a boy's arm. In winter, in the snow, there was
neither baseball nor football, so the boys and I threw snowballs at passing cars.
I got in trouble throwing snowballs, and have seldom been happier since.

On one weekday morning after Christmas, six inches of new snow had   3
just fallen. We were standing up to our boot tops in snow on a front yard on
trafficked Reynolds Street, waiting for cars. The cars traveled Reynolds Street
slowly and evenly; they were targets all but wrapped in red ribbons, cream
puffs. We couldn't miss.

I was seven; the boys were eight, nine, and ten. The oldest two Fahey   4
boys were there — Mikey and Peter — polite blond boys who lived near me
on Lloyd Street, and who already had four brothers and sisters. My parents
approved Mikey and Peter Fahey. Chickie McBride was there, a tough kid,
and Billy Paul and Mackie Kean too, from across Reynolds, where the boys
grew up dark and furious, grew up skinny, knowing, and skilled. We had all
drifted from our houses that morning looking for action, and had found it here
on Reynolds Street.

It was cloudy but cold. The cars' tires laid behind them on the snowy street   5
a complex trail of beige chunks like crenellated castle walls. I had stepped on
some earlier; they squeaked. We could have wished for more traffic. When a
car came, we all popped it one. In the intervals between cars we reverted to
the natural solitude of children.

I started making an iceball — a perfect iceball, from perfectly white snow,   6
perfectly spherical, and squeezed perfectly translucent so no snow remained
all the way through. (The Fahey boys and I considered it unfair actually to
throw an iceball at somebody, but it had been known to happen.)

I had just embarked on the iceball project when we heard tire chains come   7
clanking from afar. A black Buick was moving toward us down the street. We
all spread out, banged together some regular snowballs, took aim, and, when
the Buick drew nigh, fired.

A soft snowball hit the driver's windshield right before the driver's face. It   8
made a smashed star with a hump in the middle.

Often, of course, we hit our target, but this time, the only time in all of   9
life, the car pulled over and stopped. Its wide black door opened; a man got
out of it, running. He didn't even close the car door.

He ran after us, and we ran away from him, up the snowy Reynolds side-   10
walk. At the corner, I looked back; incredibly, he was still after us. He was in
city clothes: a suit and tie, street shoes. Any normal adult would have quit,
having sprung us into flight and made his point. This man was gaining on
us. He was a thin man, all action. All of a sudden, we were running for our
lives.

Wordless, we split up. We were on our turf; we could lose ourselves in   11
the neighborhood backyards, everyone for himself. I paused and considered.
Everyone had vanished except Mikey Fahey, who was just rounding the

corner of a yellow brick house. Poor Mikey, I trailed him. The driver of the Buick sensibly picked the two of us to follow. The man apparently had all day.

He chased Mikey and me around the yellow house and up a backyard path   12
we knew by heart: under a low tree, up a bank, through a hedge, down some snowy steps, and across the grocery store's delivery driveway. We smashed through a gap in another hedge, entered a scruffy backyard and ran around its back porch and tight between houses to Edgerton Avenue; we ran across Edgerton to an alley and up our own sliding woodpile to the Halls' front yard; he kept coming. We ran up Lloyd Street and wound through mazy backyards toward the steep hilltop at Willard and Lang.

He chased us silently, block after block. He chased us silently over picket   13
fences, through thorny hedges, between houses, around garbage cans, and across streets. Every time I glanced back, choking for breath, I expected he would have quit. He must have been as breathless as we were. His jacket strained over his body. It was an immense discovery, pounding into my hot head with every sliding, joyous step, that this ordinary adult evidently knew what I thought only children who trained at football knew: that you have to fling yourself at what you're doing, you have to point yourself, forget yourself, aim, dive.

Mikey and I had nowhere to go, in our own neighborhood or out of it, but   14
away from this man who was chasing us. He impelled us forward; we compelled him to follow our route. The air was cold; every breath tore my throat. We kept running, block after block; we kept improvising, backyard after backyard, running a frantic course and choosing it simultaneously, failing always to find small places or hard places to slow him down, and discovering always, exhilarated, dismayed, that only bare speed could save us — for he would never give up, this man — and we were losing speed.

He chased us through the backyard labyrinths of ten blocks before he   15
caught us by our jackets. He caught us and we all stopped.

We three stood staggering, half blinded, coughing, in an obscure hilltop   16
backyard: a man in his twenties, a boy, a girl. He had released our jackets, our pursuer, our captor, our hero: He knew we weren't going anywhere. We all played by the rules. Mikey and I unzipped our jackets. I pulled off my sopping mittens. Our tracks multiplied in the backyard's new snow. We had been breaking new snow all morning. We didn't look at each other. I was cherishing my excitement. The man's lower pants legs were wet; his cuffs were full of snow, and there was a prow of snow beneath them on his shoes and socks. Some trees bordered the little flat backyard, some messy winter trees. There was no one around: a clearing in a grove, and we the only players.

It was a long time before he could speak. I had some difficulty at first   17
recalling why we were there. My lips felt swollen; I couldn't see out of the sides of my eyes; I kept coughing.

"You stupid kids," he began perfunctorily.   18

We listened perfunctorily indeed, if we listened at all, for the chewing out   19
was redundant, a mere formality, and beside the point. The point was that he
had chased us passionately without giving up, and so he had caught us. Now
he came down to earth. I wanted the glory to last forever.

But how could the glory have lasted forever? We could have run through   20
every backyard in North America until we got to Panama. But when he
trapped us at the lip of the Panama Canal, what precisely could he have done
to prolong the drama of the chase and cap its glory? I brooded about this for
the next few years. He could only have fried Mikey Fahey and me in boiling
oil, say, or dismembered us piecemeal, or staked us to anthills. None of which
I really wanted, and none of which any adult was likely to do, even in the
spirit of fun. He could only chew us out there in the Panamanian jungle, after
months or years of exalting pursuit. He could only begin, "You stupid kids,"
and continue in his ordinary Pittsburgh accent with his normal righteous
anger and the usual common sense.

If in that snowy backyard the driver of the black Buick had cut off our   21
heads, Mikey's and mine, I would have died happy, for nothing has required
so much of me since as being chased all over Pittsburgh in the middle of
winter — running terrified, exhausted — by this sainted, skinny, furious red-
headed man who wished to have a word with us. I don't know how he found
his way back to his car.

For a reading quiz, visit **bedfordstmartins.com/thebedfordreader***.*

Journal Writing

Why do you suppose Dillard remembers in such vivid detail the rather insignificant
event she describes? What incidents from your childhood seem momentous even
now? List these incidents, along with some notes about their importance. (To take
your journal writing further, see "From Journal to Essay" on the next page.)

Questions on Meaning

1. What is Dillard's PURPOSE in this essay? Obviously, she wants to entertain readers,
   but does she have another purpose as well?
2. Does the persistence of the pursuer seem reasonable to you, given the children's
   prank?

3. What does the pursuer represent for the narrator? How do her feelings about him change after the chase is over, and why?
4. Why does Dillard describe the "chewing out," seemingly the object of the chase, as "redundant, a mere formality, and beside the point" (par. 19)?

Questions on Writing Strategy

1. Why does Dillard open her story with a discussion of football? In what way does the game of football serve as a metaphor in the story? (Hint: Look at par. 13, as well as the sentence "It was all or nothing" in par. 1.) (See FIGURES OF SPEECH in Useful Terms for a definition of *metaphor*.)
2. Identify the two rapid TRANSITIONS in paragraph 2. Do they contribute to or detract from the COHERENCE of the essay?
3. Why does Dillard interrupt the story of the chase with an "immense discovery" (par. 13)? Does this interruption weaken the narrative?
4. Discuss Dillard's POINT OF VIEW. Is her perspective that of a seven-year-old girl or that of an adult writer reflecting on her childhood experience?
5. **OTHER METHODS** Dillard's story implicitly COMPARES AND CONTRASTS a child's and an adult's way of looking at life. What are some of the differences that Dillard implies?

Questions on Language

1. Look up the meaning of any of the following words you don't already know: crenellated (par. 5); translucent (6); nigh (7); impelled, compelled (14); prow (16); perfunctorily (18); redundant (19); piecemeal, exalting, righteous (20).
2. Explain the contradiction in this statement: "I got in trouble throwing snowballs, and have seldom been happier since" (par. 2). Can you find other examples of paradox in what the narrator says? How is this paradox related to the narrator's apparent view of children? (See *Figures of speech* in Useful Terms for a definition of *paradox*.)
3. Why are the strong verbs Dillard uses in paragraph 20 especially appropriate?
4. What is the EFFECT of the last sentence of the essay?

Suggestions for Writing

1. **FROM JOURNAL TO ESSAY** Choose one significant incident from the list of childhood experiences you wrote for your journal, and narrate the incident as vividly as you can. Include the details: Where did the event take place? What did people say? How were they dressed? What was the weather like? Follow Dillard's model in putting CONCRETE IMAGES to work for an idea, in this case an idea about the significance of the incident to you then and now.
2. From what you have seen of children and adults, do you agree with Dillard's characterization of the two groups (see "Writing Strategy" question 5)? Write an essay comparing and contrasting children's and adults' attitudes toward play. (You will have to GENERALIZE, of course, but try to keep your broad statements grounded in a reality your readers will share.)

3. **CRITICAL WRITING** Dillard's narration of the chase is only six paragraphs long (pars. 10–15), but it seems longer, as if almost in real time. What techniques does Dillard use in these paragraphs to hold our attention and re-create the breathlessness of the chase? Look at concrete details, repetition, PARALLELISM, and the near absence of time-marking transitions. In ANALYZING Dillard's techniques, use plenty of quotations from the essay.

4. **CONNECTIONS** Annie Dillard's essay and Brad Manning's "Arm Wrestling with My Father" (p. 138) both deal with childhood values and how they are transformed as one grows older. In an essay, compare and contrast the two writers' treatment of this subject. How does the TONE of each essay contribute to its effect?

Annie Dillard on Writing

Writing for this book, Dillard has testified to her work habits. Rarely satisfied with an essay until it has gone through many drafts, she sometimes goes on correcting and improving it even after it has been published. "I always have to condense or toss openings," she affirms; "I suspect most writers do. When you begin something, you're so grateful to have begun you'll write down anything, just to prolong the sensation. Later, when you've learned what the writing is really about, you go back and throw away the beginning and start over."

Often she replaces a phrase or sentence with a shorter one. In one essay, to tell how a drop of pond water began to evaporate on a microscope slide, she first wrote, "Its contours pulled together." But that sentence seemed to suffer from "tortured abstraction." She made the sentence read instead, "Its edges shrank." Dillard observes, "I like short sentences. They're forceful, and they can get you out of big trouble."

For Discussion

1. Why, according to Dillard, is it usually necessary for writers to revise the opening paragraphs of what they write?

2. Dillard says that short sentences "can get you out of big trouble." What kinds of "big trouble" do you suppose she means?

JUNOT DÍAZ

Junot Díaz is a writer well loved for his unique voice and unflinching fiction, which typically involves young Dominicans struggling with obstacles. Born in 1968 in Santo Domingo, Dominican Republic, he immigrated to New Jersey with his family in 1975. As a poor child who had trouble speaking English and who felt like an outsider, Díaz immersed himself in comic books and science fiction and discovered that writing helped him cope with his difficulties. He earned degrees in literature and history from Rutgers University in 1992 and an MFA in creative writing from Cornell University in 1995. Díaz's critically acclaimed work includes the collections of short stories *Drown* (1996) and *This Is How You Lose Her* (2012) and the novel *The Brief Wondrous Life of Oscar Wao* (2007), which is centered on the brutalities of Dominican history. Díaz won a National Book Critics Circle Award and a Pulitzer Prize for that novel; he has also been recognized with a PEN/Malamud Award, a Dayton Literary Peace Prize, an O. Henry Prize, and a Guggenheim Fellowship. He received a MacArthur "genius" grant in 2012. A frequent contributor to *The New Yorker* and the fiction editor at the *Boston Review*, Díaz teaches writing at the Massachusetts Institute of Technology.

The Dreamer

In this essay Díaz relates a remarkable episode of his mother's life in the Dominican Republic. In expressing his admiration for her determination to learn, Díaz hints at the myriad ways a young girl's daring has influenced his own life and work. "The Dreamer" first appeared in *More*, a women's magazine, in 2011.

I think of my mother, of course. She's one of those ironwill rarely speak 1 figures that haunt. See her in New Jersey, in the house with the squirrels in the back that she feeds sparingly (they shouldn't get fat) and that she chides when she thinks they're acting up. You wouldn't know it looking at her in that kitchen, but she grew up one of those poor Third World–country girls. The brutalized backbone of our world. The kind of Dominican girl who was destined never to get off the mountain or out of the *campo*.[1] Her own mother a straight-haired terror. Expected her to work on the family farm until she died or was married off, but my mother in those small spaces between the work cultivated dreams, that unbreakable habit of the young. When the field hands were hurt or fell ill, she was the one who cared for them. Opened in her a horizon. A dream of being a nurse in the capital, where she heard that every

[1] Spanish, "countryside." — Eds.

block had electricity. But to be a nurse, you needed education, and while there were some girls who attended the one-room school at the base of the hill, my mother was not one of them. Her mother, my grandmother, demanded that she stay on the farm, that she stay a mule. No one more threatened by the thought of an educated girl than my grandmother. Any time my mother was caught near the schoolhouse, my grandmother gave her a beating. And not the beatings of the First World but the beatings of the Third — which you do not so easily shake off.

So the months passed and the horizon started to dim, and that's the way it should have stayed, but then the world, so far away, intervened. For his own complicated reasons the dictator of that time, Trujillo,[2] passed a mandatory-education act stipulating that all Dominican children under the age of fifteen had to be in school and not stuck out in the fields. All children. Any parent keeping a child from school would be imprisoned! Nothing short of the threat of a year inside a Trujillo prison could snap the resistance that rural Dominicans had to the idea of educating their young.

My mother heard about the law, of course. And she brooded on it. The house, like all other houses in the Dominican Republic, had a portrait of Trujillo hanging in it. I guess my mother figured if anyone was going to protect her from my grandmother's wrath, it was going to be him.

She'd only learn later how little our dictator protected her or anyone else.

The news of the school came at a crucial time. My mother's family was preparing for its seasonal move up higher into the hills, in the mist-soaked highlands where the coffee was waiting, but my mother had other plans. Two days before the move, she got down on her knees beside a stagnant puddle of water, put her mouth in it and drank deeply.

She was so sick that the family decided to head into the hills without her. The coffee could not wait. My mother was left with a cousin, and as soon as my grandmother was out of sight, my mother, bent over double from the stomach pains, hobbled down to the schoolhouse and reported my grandmother.

I want to go to school, was what she told the teacher.

What should have happened was that the teacher should have laughed and sent her poor ass back to the hills to pick coffee. But as it turned out, the teacher was an idealistic young woman from the capital — God bless all idealistic educators — and she took my mother's claim seriously. Went to the police, who *always* took Trujillo's laws seriously, and so when my grandmother came back to fetch her daughter, she found my mother attending school.

2 General Rafael Trujillo took over rule of the Dominican Republic in a 1930 military coup. His regime was characterized by violent oppression and lasted until he was assassinated in 1961. — Eds.

And when she tried to drag my mother up to the hills, the police put her   9
in handcuffs, and that was that.

"Your grandmother beat me almost every day," my mother explained, "but   10
I got my education."

She never did become a nurse, my mother. Immigration got in the way   11
of that horizon — once in the United States, my mother never could master
English, no matter how hard she tried, and my God, did she try. But strange
how things work — her son became a reader and a writer, practices she
encouraged as much as possible. I write professionally now, and life is long and
complicated, and who knows how things might have turned out under different circumstances, but I do believe that who I am as an artist, everything that
I've ever written, was possible because a seven-year-old girl up in the hills of
Azua knelt before a puddle, found courage in herself and drank. Every time
I'm in trouble in my art, I try to think of that girl. I think of that thirst, of that
courage. I think of her.

For a reading quiz, visit **bedfordstmartins.com/thebedfordreader**.

Journal Writing

Díaz writes that his mother was severely beaten by her own mother, and distinguishes
"the beatings of the First World [from] the beatings of the Third — which you do not
so easily shake off" (par. 1). How do you react to this distinction? Why would beatings
in developing countries be especially brutal? Do degrees of abuse matter? Why would
any parent beat a child? And why wouldn't families, neighbors, or authority figures
(such as teachers) step in to stop the abuse? Explore your thoughts on any of these
questions in your journal. (To take your journal writing further, see "From Journal to
Essay" on the facing page.)

Questions on Meaning

1. Why does Díaz admire his mother as he does? What does her experience represent to him?
2. Does Díaz have a THESIS? In which sentence or sentences does he state the point
   of his story most directly?
3. What would you say is Díaz's PURPOSE in this essay? Is it simply to inform readers
   about his mother's quest for an education, or does he seem to have another purpose in mind?

4. "She'd only learn later how little our dictator protected her or anybody else," Díaz writes in paragraph 4. What does he mean? Based on this statement and other references to Rafael Trujillo in the essay, what can you INFER about life in the Dominican Republic under his dictatorship?

Questions on Writing Strategy

1. Take note of the first and last sentences in "The Dreamer." How are they related, and what is their effect?
2. In telling his mother's story, does Díaz take mostly an objective or a subjective POINT OF VIEW? How effective do you find his choice?
3. This essay originally appeared in a women's magazine. What evidence in the text reveals that Díaz was writing for an AUDIENCE of female readers?
4. **OTHER METHODS** Explain the CAUSE-AND-EFFECT relationships Díaz outlines in his narrative. What actions — and whose — made it possible for his mother to attend school? What impact did her education have on her life? on his?

Questions on Language

1. Be sure you know how to define the following words: ironwill, chides, cultivated (par. 1); intervened, stipulating (2); brooded (3); stagnant (5).
2. In what sense does Díaz use the word *horizon* (pars. 1, 2, and 11)? What makes this IMAGE particularly appropriate to the story's meaning?
3. The first paragraph of this essay is loaded with sentence fragments, such as "The brutalized backbone of our world." Where else do you find incomplete sentences? What do they contribute to (or take away from) Díaz's VOICE and the effectiveness of his narrative?
4. Díaz quotes his mother twice. Why you do suppose he uses quotation marks around her words in paragraph 10 but not in paragraph 7?

Suggestions for Writing

1. **FROM JOURNAL TO ESSAY** Building on your journal entry (p. 122), compose an essay that examines one of the causes or effects of child abuse, in the United States or elsewhere. If you have had some experience with abuse (as a counselor, a bystander, a victim, or an abuser) and you care to write about it, you might develop your thesis based on your experience and observation; otherwise, draw on information you have gleaned from the media and your reading, being sure to acknowledge any sources you use.
2. Using Díaz's essay as a model, compose an essay in which you contemplate and explain your sense of identity. How do you define yourself? Has any one person had a significant effect on who you are? How so?
3. **CRITICAL WRITING** Write an essay in which you ANALYZE Díaz's use of language in this essay or a portion of it. How would you characterize his DICTION? What are some especially creative uses of language? What overall EFFECT does Díaz create with the language he uses?

4. **CONNECTIONS** In "Superman and Me" (p. 494), Sherman Alexie also writes about learning in desperate circumstances. Write an essay that COMPARES AND CONTRASTS Díaz's and Alexie's attitudes toward formal education. Taken together, what do these two authors seem to believe an education can accomplish for someone struggling in poverty? What do they suggest are a student's responsibilities? How well do public schools, in their view, accomplish their goals? What is each writer saying about the importance of knowledge?

Junot Díaz on Writing

In a 2009 essay for Oprah Winfrey's *O* magazine, Díaz tells the story of how, in his mind, he became a writer. It begins with failure. He had drafted seventy-five pages of his second book, then got stuck. "It wasn't that I couldn't write," he explains. "I wrote every day. I actually worked really hard at writing. At my desk by seven a.m., would work a full eight and more. Scribbled at the dinner table, in bed, on the toilet, on the No. 6 train, at Shea Stadium. I did everything I could. But none of it worked. . . . I wrote and I wrote and I wrote, but nothing I produced was worth a damn."

Díaz goes on to say that he kept trying all the same. "Want to talk about stubborn? I kept at it for five straight years. Five damn years. Every day failing for five years? I'm a pretty stubborn, pretty hard-hearted character, but those five years of fail did a number on my psyche. On me. Five years, sixty months? It just about wiped me out." Frustrated and despondent, he considered pursuing another line of work: "I knew I couldn't go on much more the way I was going. I just couldn't. . . . So I put the manuscript away. All the hundreds of failed pages, boxed and hidden in a closet. I think I cried as I did it."

"I slipped into my new morose half-life," Díaz recalls. "Started preparing for my next stage, back to school in September." And then, on a sleepless night, "sickened that I was giving up, but even more frightened by the thought of having to return to the writing," Díaz pulled the pages out of storage. "I figured if I could find one good thing in the pages I would go back to it," he explains. "Spent the whole night reading everything I had written, and guess what? It was still terrible. In fact with the new distance the lameness was even worse than I'd thought. . . . I didn't have the heart to go on. But I guess I did. . . . I separated the seventy-five pages that were worthy from the mountain of loss, sat at my desk, and despite every part of me shrieking no no no no, I jumped back down the rabbit hole again." And after five more years of struggle and regular bouts "of being utterly, dismayingly lost," he finally completed *The Brief Wondrous Life of Oscar Wao.*

"That," concludes Díaz, is his "tale in a nutshell. Not the tale of how I came to write my novel but rather of how I became a writer. Because, in truth, I didn't become a writer the first time I put pen to paper or when I finished my first book (easy) or my second one (hard). You see, in my view a writer is a writer not because she writes well and easily, because she has amazing talent, because everything she does is golden. In my view a writer is a writer because even when there is no hope, even when nothing you do shows any sign of promise, you keep writing anyway. Wasn't until that night when I was faced with all those lousy pages that I realized, really realized, what it was exactly that I am."

For Discussion

1. Have you ever, like Díaz, tossed out most of a draft? How might "one good thing" justify, or even require, starting over?
2. Discuss a time when you were frustrated with a project, writing or otherwise. What inspired you to persist? (If you quit, how did the failure affect you?)
3. What, to Díaz, does it mean to be a writer?

ADDITIONAL WRITING TOPICS

Narration

1. Write a narrative with one of the following as your subject. It may be (as your instructor may advise) either a first-PERSON memoir or a story written in the third person, observing the experience of someone else. Decide before you begin what your PURPOSE is and whether you are writing (1) an anecdote, (2) an essay consisting mainly of a single narrative, or (3) an essay that includes more than one story.

   A memorable experience from your early life
   A lesson you learned the hard way
   A trip into unfamiliar territory
   An embarrassing moment that taught you something
   A monumental misunderstanding
   An accident
   An unexpected encounter
   A story about a famous person or someone close to you
   A conflict or contest
   A destructive storm
   An assassination attempt
   A historical event of significance

2. Tell a true story of your early or recent school days, either humorous or serious, relating a struggle you experienced (or still experience) in school.

Note: Writing topics combining narration and description appear on page 168.

5

DESCRIPTION

Writing with Your Senses

◀ **Description in a photograph**

Margaret Morton photographs homeless communities in New York City. This photograph, titled *Doug and Mizan's House, East River*, depicts a makeshift dwelling on a Manhattan riverbank. Consider Morton's photograph as a work of description — revealing a thing through the perceptions of the senses. What do you see through her eyes? What is the house made of? What do the overhanging structure on the upper left and the bridge behind the house add to the impression of the house? If you were standing in the picture, in front of the house, what might you hear or smell? If you touched the house, what textures might you feel? What main idea do you think Morton wants this photograph to convey?

THE METHOD

Like narration, DESCRIPTION is a familiar method of expression, already a working part of you. In any talkfest with friends, you probably do your share of describing. You depict in words someone you've met by describing her clothes, the look on her face, the way she walks. You describe somewhere you've been, something you admire, something you just can't abide. In a blog or in a message to a friend, you describe your college (cast concrete buildings, crowded walks, pigeons rattling their wings); or perhaps you describe your brand-new secondhand car, from the glitter of its hubcaps to the odd antiques in its trunk, bequeathed by its previous owner. You can hardly live a day without describing (or hearing described) some person, place, or thing. Small wonder that, in written discourse, description is almost as indispensable as words.

Description reports the testimony of your senses. It invites your readers to imagine that they, too, not only see but perhaps also hear, taste, smell, and touch the subject you describe. Usually, you write a description for either of two PURPOSES:

- **Convey information without bias,** using description that is OBJECTIVE (or *impartial*, *public*, or *functional*). You describe your subject so clearly and exactly that your reader will understand it or recognize it, and you leave your emotions out. The description in academic writing is usually objective: A biology report on a particular species of frog, for instance, might detail the animal's appearance (four-inch-wide body, bright orange skin with light brown spots), its sounds (hoarse clucks), and its feel (smooth, slippery). In writing an objective description your purpose is not to share your feelings. You are trying to make the frog or the subject easily recognized.

- **Convey perceptions with feeling,** using description that is SUBJECTIVE (or *emotional*, *personal*, or *impressionistic*). This is the kind included in a magazine advertisement for a new car. It's what you write in your message to a friend setting forth what your college is like — whether you are pleased or displeased with it. In this kind of description, you may use biases and personal feelings — in fact, they are essential.

For a splendid example of subjective description, read the following passenger's-eye view of a storm at sea, by the nineteenth-century writer Charles Dickens. Notice how Dickens's words convey the terror of the event:

> Imagine the ship herself, with every pulse and artery of her huge body swollen and bursting . . . sworn to go on or die. Imagine the wind howling, the sea roaring, the rain beating; all in furious array against her. Picture the sky both dark and wild, and the clouds in fearful sympathy with the waves, making another ocean in the air. Add to all this the clattering on deck and

down below; the tread of hurried feet; the loud hoarse shouts of seamen; the gurgling in and out of water through the scuppers; with every now and then the striking of a heavy sea upon the planks above, with the deep, dead, heavy sound of thunder heard within a vault; and there is the head wind of that January morning.

Think of what a starkly different description of the very same storm the captain might set down — objectively — in the ship's log: "At 0600 hours, watch reported a wind from due north of 70 knots. Whitecaps were noticed, in height two ells above the bow. Below deck water was reported to have entered the bilge. . . ." But Dickens, not content simply to record information, strives to ensure that his emotions are clear.

Description is usually found in the company of other methods of writing. Often, for instance, it will enliven NARRATION and make the people in the story and the setting unmistakably clear. Writing an ARGUMENT in his essay "Waste Not, Want Not" (p. 468), Bill McKibben begins with a description of a community recycling center. Description will help a writer in examining the EFFECTS of a storm or in COMPARING AND CONTRASTING two paintings. Keep the method of description in mind when you come to try expository and argumentative writing.

THE PROCESS

Purpose and Audience

Understand, first of all, why you are writing about your subject and thus what kind of description is called for. Is it appropriate to perceive and report without emotion or bias — and thus write an objective description? Or is it appropriate to express your personal feelings as well as your perceptions — and thus write a subjective description?

Give some thought to your AUDIENCE. What do your readers need to be told, if they are to share the perceptions you would have them share, if they are clearly to behold what you want them to? If, let's say, you are describing a downtown street on a Saturday night for an audience of fellow students who live in the same city and know it well, then you need not dwell on the street's familiar geography. What must you tell? Only those details that make the place different on a Saturday night. But if you are remembering your home city, and writing for readers who don't know it, you'll need to establish a few central landmarks to sketch (in their minds) an unfamiliar street on a Saturday night.

Before you begin to write a description, go look at your subject. If that is not possible, your next best course is to spend a few minutes imagining the subject until, in your mind's eye, you can see every flyspeck on it. Then, having fixed your subject in mind, ask yourself which of its features you'll need to report to your particular audience, for your particular purpose. Ask, "What am I out to accomplish?"

Dominant Impression and Thesis

When you consider your aim in describing, you'll begin to see what impression you intend your subject to make on readers. Let your description, as a whole, convey this one DOMINANT IMPRESSION. If you are writing a subjective description of an old house, laying weight on its spooky atmosphere for readers you wish to make shiver, then you might mention its squeaking bats and its shadowy halls. If, however, you are describing the house in a classified ad, for an audience of possible buyers, you might focus instead on its eat-in kitchen, working fireplace, and proximity to public transportation. Details have to be carefully selected. Feel no grim duty to include every perceptible detail. To do so would only invite chaos — or perhaps, for the reader, mere tedium. Pick out the features that matter most.

Your dominant impression is like the THESIS of your description — the main idea about your subject that you want readers to take away with them. When you use description to explain or to argue, it's usually a good strategy to state that dominant impression outright, tying it to your essay's thesis or a part of it. In the biology report on a species of frog, for instance, you might preface your description with a statement like this one:

> A number of unique features distinguish this frog from others in the order Anura.

Or in an argument in favor of cleaning a local toxic-waste site, you might begin with a description of the site and then state your point about it:

> This landscape is as poisonous as it looks, for underneath its barren crust are enough toxic chemicals to sicken a small village.

When you use subjective description more for its own sake — to show the reader a place or a person, to evoke feelings — you needn't always state your dominant impression as a THESIS STATEMENT, as long as the impression is there dictating the details.

Organization

To help them arrange the details of a description, many writers rely on their POINT OF VIEW — the physical angle from which they're perceiving and describing. As an observer who stays put and observes steadily, you can make a carefully planned inspection tour of your subject, moving spatially (from left to right, from near to far, from top to bottom, from center to periphery), or perhaps moving from prominent objects to tiny ones, from dull to bright, from commonplace to extraordinary — or vice versa.

The plan for you is the one that best fulfills your purpose, arranging details so that the reader receives the exact impression you mean to convey. If you were to describe, for instance, a chapel in the middle of a desert, you might begin with the details of the lonely terrain. Then, as if approaching the chapel with the aid of a zoom lens, you might detail its exterior before going on inside. That might be a workable method *if* you wanted to create the dominant impression of the chapel as an island of beauty in the midst of desolation. Say, however, that you had a different impression in mind: to emphasize the spirituality of the chapel's interior. You might then begin your description inside the structure, perhaps with its most prominent feature, the stained glass windows. You might mention the surrounding desert later in your description, but only incidentally.

Whatever pattern you follow, stick with it all the way through so that your arrangement causes no difficulty for the reader. In describing the chapel, you wouldn't necessarily proceed in the way you explored the structure, first noting its isolation, then entering and studying its windows, then going outside again to see what the walls were made of, then moving back inside to look at the artwork. Instead, you would lead the reader around and through (or through and around) the structure in an organized manner. Even if a scene is chaotic, the prose should be orderly.

Details

Luckily, to write a memorable description, you don't need a ferocious storm or any other awe-inspiring subject. As Sarah Vowell demonstrates in "Shooting Dad" later in this chapter, you can write about your family as effectively as you write about a hurricane. The secret is in the vividness, the evocativeness of the details. Like most good describers, Vowell uses many IMAGES (language calling up concrete sensory experiences), including FIGURES OF SPEECH (expressions that do not mean literally what they say, often describing one thing in terms of another). For instance, using *metaphor*, Vowell writes that "the respective work spaces governed by my father and me were jealously guarded totalitarian states in which each of us declared ourselves dictator." Using *similes*, Vowell describes shooting a pistol as a six-year-old: "The sound it made was as big as God. It kicked little me back to the ground like a bully, like a foe."

FOCUS ON SPECIFIC AND CONCRETE LANGUAGE

When you write effective description, you'll convey your experience as exactly as possible. You may use figures of speech, as discussed above, and you'll definitely rely on language that is *specific* (tied to actual things) and *concrete* (tied to the senses of sight, hearing, touch, smell, and taste). Specific and concrete language enables readers to behold with the mind's eye — and to feel with the mind's fingertips.

The first sentence below shows a writer's first-draft attempt to describe something she saw. After editing, the second sentence is much more vivid.

VAGUE   Beautiful, scented wildflowers were in the field.

CONCRETE AND SPECIFIC   Backlighted by the sun and smelling faintly sweet, an acre of tiny lavender flowers spread away from me.

When editing your description, keep a sharp eye out for vague words such as *delicious, handsome, loud,* and *short* that force readers to create their own impressions or, worse, leave them with no impression at all. Using details that call on readers' sensory experiences, tell why delicious or why handsome, how loud or how short. When stuck for a word, conjure up your subject and see it, hear it, touch it, smell it, taste it.

Note that *concrete* and *specific* do not mean "fancy": Good description does not demand five-dollar words when nickel equivalents are just as informative. The writer who uses *rubiginous* instead of *rusty red* actually says less because fewer readers will understand the less common word and all readers will sense a writer showing off.

CHECKLIST FOR REVISING A DESCRIPTION

✔ **Subjective or objective.** Given your purpose and audience, is your description appropriately subjective (emphasizing feelings) or objective (unemotional)?

✔ **Dominant impression.** What is the dominant impression of your subject? If you haven't stated it, will your readers be able to express it accurately to themselves?

✔ **Point of view and organization.** Do your point of view and organization work together to make your subject clear in readers' minds? Are they consistent?

✔ **Details.** Have you provided all the details — and just those — needed to convey your dominant impression? What needs expanding? What needs condensing or cutting?

> ✔ **Specific and concrete language.** Have you used words that pin down your meaning exactly and appeal to the senses of sight, hearing, touch, taste, and smell?

DESCRIPTION IN ACADEMIC WRITING

An Art History Textbook

Description interprets a familiar painting in the following paragraphs from *Janson's History of Art* by H. W. Janson et al. The details "translate" the painting, creating a bridge between the reader and the text's reproduction of the work. (You can see the painting on p. 204 of this book.)

The most famous image produced by this group [of Midwest artists] is *American Gothic*, by Grant Wood (1891–1942) of Cedar Rapids, Iowa. The picture was shown at the Art Institute of Chicago in 1930, where it caused a stir and brought Wood to national attention. It was intended as a window into the Midwest world in which the artist grew up and lived. A fictitious father and spinster daughter are presented as the God-fearing descendants of stalwart pioneers who first worked the soil. They are dressed in old-fashioned clothes and stand firmly against the march of progress. The style of their house, from which the title of the painting is taken, is Carpenter Gothic, a nineteenth-century style evoking both the humble modesty and old-fashioned ways of the residents as well as their religious intensity, which parallels the fervor of the medieval period when Gothic cathedrals were built. Wood further emphasizes his characters' faith by developing numerous crosses within the façade, and by putting a church steeple in the distant background.

> Main idea (topic sentence) of the paragraphs, supported by descriptions that follow
>
> Religious ("God-fearing") elements in the painting
>
> Details (underlined) contribute to the dominant impression

In addition to being hard-working and reverent, we also know these farmers are orderly and clean, as suggested by the crisp drawing and severe horizontal and vertical composition. This propriety also stems from the primness of the woman's conservative dress and hair and the suggestion that she carefully tends to the house, as she does to the plants on the front porch. The figures' harsh frontality, the man's firm grasp on his pitchfork, and overalls suggest that they are industrious and strong. There is no hint of modernity, and the simplicity and austerity of the setting suggests they are frugal. Nonetheless, many critics viewed Wood as ridiculing his sitters and their lifestyle, and indeed the painting does contain humor, such as the woman warily looking off to the side as if to make sure nothing untoward is occurring. But regardless of interpretation, no one seemed to deny that the picture captured something fundamentally American, and especially Midwestern.

> Industrious ("stalwart pioneers") elements in the painting
>
> Restatement of the main idea summarizing the effect of the details

A Field Observation

In many of your classes, particularly those in the social sciences, you will be asked to observe people or phenomena in particular settings and to describe what your senses perceive. A systematic observation may produce evidence for an ARGUMENT, as when a writer observes and describes the listlessness of kittens in an animal shelter to encourage support for a citywide spay-and-neuter program. Just as often, however, an observation results in an objective report providing information from which readers draw their own conclusions. Like any description, such a field report emphasizes details and uses concrete language to convey the writer's perceptions. Because the writer's purpose is to inform, the report takes a neutral, third-PERSON (*he, she, they*) point of view, uses unemotional language, and refrains from interpretation or opinion — or withholds such analysis for a separate section near the end.

For an education class in child development, Nick Fiorelli spent a morning in a local private preschool, observing the teachers' techniques and the children's behaviors and taking note of how teachers and children interacted. The paragraphs below, excerpted from his final written report, "Teaching Methodologies at Child's Play Preschool," describe both the classroom itself and some of the activities Fiorelli witnessed while he was there. The full report goes on to outline the educational philosophies and developmental theories that inform the school's approach, with additional examples and descriptions from Fiorelli's visit.

The preschool's Web site explains that it draws on elements of Waldorf, Montessori, Reggio Emillia, and other educational models. This background was evident in the large and colorful classroom, which included separate interest areas for different activities. The room was also open and well lit, with long windows that opened to a playground and an open lawn. The walls of the room were decorated with students' paintings and drawings. Colored rugs, floor tiles, or rubber mats indicated the boundaries of each activity area.

Background information sets the stage

Organization moves from the periphery to the center, then around the room's distinct areas

At first, the general atmosphere appeared noisy and unstructured, but a sense of order emerged within a few minutes of observation. At a large wooden art table, two students used safety scissors to cut shapes from large sheets of red construction paper. Behind them, a child in a red smock stood at a small wooden easel and painted with a large brush. Another strung multicolored beads on a string. Next to the art table, two

Dominant impression: structured creativity

children at a sensory station poured wet sand and rocks through a large funnel into a miniature sandbox, while a third filled a small glass tank with water from a blue enameled pail. A teacher moved between the two tables, encouraging the students and asking questions about their play. In the back of the room, at a literacy area with a thick blue rug and low yellow bookshelves, six students lolled on beanbag chairs, pillows, and a low brown couch, listening to a teacher read a story from an illustrated children's book. She paused on each page to help the children connect the pictures with the story.

Concrete details contribute to the dominant impression

Description

BRAD MANNING

Brad Manning was born in Little Rock, Arkansas, in 1967 and grew up near Charlottesville, Virginia. While a student at Harvard University he played intra-mural sports and wrote articles and reviews for the *Harvard Independent*. He graduated in 1990 with a BA in history and religion. Now living in Charlottes-ville, Manning is a psychiatrist specializing in the treatment of children and adolescents.

Arm Wrestling with My Father

In this essay written for his freshman composition course, Manning explores his physical contact with his father over the years, perceiving gradual changes that are, he realizes, inevitable. For Manning, description provides a way to express his feelings about his father and to comment on relations between sons and fathers. In the essay after Manning's, Sarah Vowell uses description for similar ends, but her subject is the relationship between a daughter and her father.

"Now you say when" is what he always said before an arm-wrestling match. 1
He liked to put the responsibility on me, knowing that he would always con-trol the outcome. "When!" I'd shout, and it would start. And I would tense up, concentrating and straining and trying to push his wrist down to the carpet with all my weight and strength. But Dad would always win; I always had to lose. "Want to try it again?" he would ask, grinning. He would see my downcast eyes, my reddened, sweating face, and sense my intensity. And with squint-ing eyes he would laugh at me, a high laugh, through his perfect white teeth. Too bitter to smile, I would not answer or look at him, but I would just roll over on my back and frown at the ceiling. I never thought it was funny at all.

That was the way I felt for a number of years during my teens, after I 2
had lost my enjoyment of arm wrestling and before I had given up that same intense desire to beat my father. Ours had always been a physical relationship, I suppose, one determined by athleticism and strength. We never communi-cated as well in speech or in writing as in a strong hug, battling to make the other gasp for breath. I could never find him at one of my orchestra concerts. But at my lacrosse games, he would be there in the stands, with an angry look, ready to coach me after the game on how I could do better. He never helped

me write a paper or a poem. Instead, he would take me outside and show me a new move for my game, in the hope that I would score a couple of goals and gain confidence in my ability. Dad knew almost nothing about lacrosse and his movements were all wrong and sad to watch. But at those times I could just feel how hard he was trying to communicate, to help me, to show the love he had for me, the love I could only assume was there.

His words were physical. The truth is, I have never read a card or a letter 3 written in his hand because he never wrote to me. Never. Mom wrote me all the cards and letters when I was away from home. The closest my father ever came, that I recall, was in a newspaper clipping Mom had sent with a letter. He had gone through and underlined all the important words about the dangers of not wearing a bicycle helmet. Our communication was physical, and that is why we did things like arm wrestle. To get down on the floor and grapple, arm against arm, was like having a conversation.

This ritual of father-son competition in fact had started early in my life, 4 back when Dad started the matches with his arm almost horizontal, his wrist an inch from defeat, and still won. I remember in those battles how my tiny shoulders would press over our locked hands, my whole upper body pushing down in hope of winning that single inch from his calm, unmoving forearm. "Say when," he'd repeat, killing my concentration and causing me to squeal, "I did, I did!" And so he'd grin with his eyes fixed on me, not seeming to notice his own arm, which would begin to rise slowly from its starting position. My greatest efforts could not slow it down. As soon as my hopes had disappeared I'd start to cheat and use both hands. But the arm would continue to move steadily along its arc toward the carpet. My brother, if he was watching, would sometimes join in against the arm. He once even wrapped his little legs around our embattled wrists and pulled back with everything he had. But he did not have much and, regardless of the opposition, the man would win. My arm would lie at rest, pressed into the carpet beneath a solid, immovable arm. In that pinned position, I could only giggle, happy to have such a strong father.

My feelings have changed, though. I don't giggle anymore, at least not 5 around my father. And I don't feel pressured to compete with him the way I thought necessary for years. Now my father is not really so strong as he used to be and I am getting stronger. This change in strength comes at a time when I am growing faster mentally than at any time before. I am becoming less my father and more myself. And as a result, there is less of a need to be set apart from him and his command. I am no longer a rebel in the household, wanting to stand up against the master with clenched fists and tensing jaws, trying to impress him with my education or my views on religion. I am no longer a challenger, quick to correct his verbal mistakes, determined to beat him whenever possible in physical competition.

I am not sure when it was that I began to feel less competitive with my father, but it all became clearer to me one day this past January. I was home in Virginia for a week between exams, and Dad had stayed home from work because the house was snowed in deep. It was then that I learned something I never could have guessed.

I don't recall who suggested arm wrestling that day. We hadn't done it for a long time, for months. But there we were, lying flat on the carpet, face to face, extending our right arms. Our arms were different. His still resembled a fat tree branch, one which had leveled my wrist to the ground countless times before. It was hairy and white with some pink moles scattered about. It looked strong, to be sure, though not so strong as it had in past years. I expect that back in his youth it had looked even stronger. In high school he had played halfback and had been voted "best-built body" of the senior class. Between college semesters he had worked on road crews and on Louisiana dredges. I admired him for that. I had begun to row crew in college and that accounted for some small buildup along the muscle lines, but it did not seem to be enough. The arm I extended was lanky and featureless. Even so, he insisted that he would lose the match, that he was certain I'd win. I had to ignore this, however, because it was something he always said, whether or not he believed it himself.

Our warm palms came together, much the same way we had shaken hands the day before at the airport. Fingers twisted and wrapped about once again, testing for a better grip. Elbows slid up and back making their little indentations on the itchy carpet. My eyes pinched closed in concentration as I tried to center as much of my thought as possible on the match. Arm wrestling, I knew, was a competition that depended less on talent and experience than on one's mental control and confidence. I looked up into his eyes and was ready. He looked back, smiled at me, and said softly (did he sound nervous?), "You say when."

It was not a long match. I had expected him to be stronger, faster. I was conditioned to lose and would have accepted defeat easily. However, after some struggle, his arm yielded to my efforts and began to move unsteadily toward the carpet. I worked against his arm with all the strength I could find. He was working hard as well, straining, breathing heavily. It seemed that this time was different, that I was going to win. Then something occurred to me, something unexpected. I discovered that I was feeling sorry for my father. I wanted to win but I did not want to see him lose.

It was like the thrill I had once experienced as a young boy at my grandfather's lake house in Louisiana when I hooked my first big fish. There was that sudden tug that made me leap. The red bobber was sucked down beneath the surface and I pulled back against it, reeling it in excitedly. But when my cousin caught sight of the fish and shouted out, "It's a keeper," I realized that I would be happier for the fish if it were let go rather than grilled for dinner. Arm wrestling my father was now like this, like hooking "Big Joe," the old fish that Lake Quachita holds but you can never catch, and when you finally think you've got him, you want to let him go, cut the line, keep the legend alive.

Perhaps at that point I could have given up, letting my father win. But it was so fast and absorbing. How could I have learned so quickly how it would feel to have overpowered the arm that had protected and provided for me all of my life? His arms have always protected me and the family. Whenever I am near him I am unafraid, knowing his arms are ready to catch me and keep me safe, the way they caught my mother one time when she fainted halfway across the room, the way he carried me, full grown, up and down the stairs when I had mononucleosis, the way he once held my feet as I stood on his shoulders to put up a new basketball net. My mother may have had the words or the touch that sustained our family, but his were the arms that protected us. And his were the arms now that I had pushed to the carpet, first the right arm, then the left. 11

I might have preferred him to be always the stronger, the one who carries me. But this wish is impossible now; our roles have begun to switch. I do not know if I will ever physically carry my father as he has carried me, though I fear that someday I may have that responsibility. More than once this year I have hesitated before answering the phone late at night, fearing my mother's voice calling me back to help carry his wood coffin. When I am home with him and he mentions a sharp pain in his chest, I imagine him collapsing onto the floor. And in that second vision I see me rushing to him, lifting him onto my shoulders, and running. 12

A week after our match, we parted at the airport. The arm-wrestling match was by that time mostly forgotten. My thoughts were on school. I had been awake most of the night studying for my last exam, and by that morning I was already back into my college-student manner of reserve and detachment. To say goodbye, I kissed and hugged my mother and I prepared to shake my father's hand. A handshake had always seemed easier to handle than a hug. His hugs had always been powerful ones, intended I suppose to give me strength. They made me suck in my breath and struggle for control, and the way he would pound his hand on my back made rumbles in my ears. So I offered a handshake; but he offered a hug. I accepted it, bracing myself for the impact. Once our arms were wrapped around each other, however, I sensed a different message. His embrace was softer, longer than before. I remember 13 how it surprised me and how I gave an embarrassed laugh as if to apologize to anyone watching.

I got on the airplane and my father and mother were gone. But as the plane lifted my throat was hurting with sadness. I realized then that Dad must have learned something as well, and what he had said to me in that last hug was that he loved me. Love was a rare expression between us, so I had denied it at first. As the plane turned north, I had a sudden wish to go back to Dad and embrace his arms with all the love I felt for him. I wanted to hold him for a long time and to speak with him silently, telling him how happy I was, telling him all my feelings, in that language we shared.   14

In his hug, Dad had tried to tell me something he himself had discovered. I hope he tries again. Maybe this spring, when he sees his first crew match, he'll advise me on how to improve my stroke. Maybe he has started doing pushups to rebuild his strength and challenge me to another match — if this were true, I know I would feel less challenged than loved. Or maybe, rather than any of this, he'll just send me a card.   15

For a reading quiz, visit **bedfordstmartins.com/thebedfordreader**.

Journal Writing

Manning expresses conflicting feelings about his father. How do you respond to his conflict? When have you felt strongly conflicting emotions about a person or an event, such as a relative, friend, breakup, ceremony, move? Write a paragraph or two exploring your feelings. (To take your journal writing further, see "From Journal to Essay" on the facing page.)

Questions on Meaning

1. In paragraph 3 Manning says that his father's "words were physical." What does this mean?
2. After his most recent trip home, Manning says, "I realized then that Dad must have learned something as well" (par. 14). What is it that father and son have each learned?
3. Manning says in the last paragraph that he "would feel less challenged than loved" if his father challenged him to a rematch. Does this statement suggest that he did not feel loved earlier? Why, or why not?
4. What do you think is Manning's PURPOSE in this essay? Does he want to express love for his father, or is there something more as well?

Questions on Writing Strategy

1. Why does Manning start his essay with a match that leaves him "too bitter to smile" and then move backward to earlier bouts of arm wrestling?
2. In the last paragraph Manning suggests that his father might work harder at competing with him and pushing him to be competitive, or he might just send his son a card. Why does Manning present both of these options? Are we supposed to know which will happen?
3. Explain the fishing ANALOGY Manning uses in paragraph 10.
4. **OTHER METHODS** Manning's essay is as much a NARRATIVE as a description: The author gives brief stories, like video clips, to show the dynamic of his relationship with his father. Look at the story in paragraph 4. How does Manning mix elements of both methods to convey his powerlessness?

Questions on Language

1. Manning uses the word *competition* throughout this essay. Why is this a more accurate word than *conflict* to describe Manning's relationship with his father?
2. What is the EFFECT of "the arm" in this sentence from paragraph 4: "But the arm would continue to move steadily along its arc toward the carpet"?
3. In paragraph 9 Manning writes, "I wanted to win but I did not want to see him lose." What does this apparent contradiction mean?
4. If any of these words is unfamiliar, look it up in a dictionary: embattled (par. 4); dredges, crew (7); conditioned (9); mononucleosis (11).

Suggestions for Writing

1. **FROM JOURNAL TO ESSAY** Expand your journal entry into a descriptive essay that brings to life your mixed feelings about a person or an event. Focus less on the circumstances and happenings than on emotions, both positive and negative.
2. Write an essay that describes your relationship with a parent or another close adult. You may want to focus on just one aspect of your relationship, or one especially vivid moment, in order to give yourself the space and time to build many sensory details into your description.
3. Arm wrestling is a highly competitive sport with a long history. Research the sport in the library or on the Internet. Then write a brief essay that traces its history and explains its current standing.
4. **CRITICAL WRITING** In paragraph 12 Manning writes, "our roles have begun to switch." Does this seem like an inevitable switch, or one that this father and son have been working to achieve? Use EVIDENCE from Manning's essay to support your answer. Also consider whether Manning and his father would respond the same way to this question.
5. **CONNECTIONS** Like "Arm Wrestling with My Father," the next essay, Sarah Vowell's "Shooting Dad," depicts a struggle for communication between child and parent. In an essay, COMPARE AND CONTRAST the two essays on this point. What impedes positive communication between the two authors and their fathers? In what circumstances are they able to communicate?

Brad Manning on Writing

For this book, Brad Manning offered some valuable concrete advice on writing as a student.

You hear this a lot, but writing takes a long time. For me, this is especially true. The only difference between the "Arm Wrestling" essay and all the other essays I wrote in college (and the only reason it's in this book and not thrown away) is that I rewrote it six or seven times over a period of weeks.

If I have something to write, I need to start early. In college, I had a bad habit of putting off papers until 10 p.m. the night before they were due and spending a desperate night typing whatever ideas the coffee inspired. But putting off papers didn't just lower my writing quality; it robbed me of a good time.

I like starting early because I can jot down notes over a stretch of days; then I type them up fast, ignoring typos; I print the notes with narrow margins, cut them up, and divide them into piles that seem to fit together; then it helps to get away for a day and come back all fresh so I can throw away the corny ideas. Finally, I sit on the floor and make an outline with all the cutouts of paper, trying at the same time to work out some clear purpose for the essay.

When the writing starts, I often get hung up most on trying to "sound" like a good writer. If you're like me and came to college from a shy family that never discussed much over dinner, you might think your best shot is to sound like a famous writer like T. S. Eliot and you might try to sneak in words that aren't really your own like *ephemeral* or *the lilacs smelled like springtime*. But the last thing you really want a reader thinking is how good or bad a writer you are.

Also, in the essay on arm wrestling, I got hung up thinking I had to make my conflict with my father somehow "universal." So in an early draft I wrote in a classical allusion — Aeneas lifting his old father up onto his shoulders and carrying him out of the burning city of Troy.[1] I'd read that story in high school and guessed one classical allusion might make the reader think I knew a lot more. But Aeneas didn't help the essay much, and I'm glad my teacher warned me off trying to universalize. He told me to write just what was true for me.

But that was hard, too, and still is — especially in the first draft. I don't know anyone who enjoys the first draft. If you do, I envy you. But in my early drafts, I always get this sensation like I have to impress somebody and I

---

[1] In the *Aeneid*, by the Roman poet Virgil (70–19 BC), the mythic hero Aeneas escapes from the city of Troy when it is sacked by the Greeks and goes on to found Rome. — EDS.

end up overanalyzing the effects of every word I am about to write. This self-consciousness may be unavoidable (I get self-conscious calling L.L. Bean to order a shirt), but, in this respect, writing is great for shy people because you can edit all you want, all day long, until it finally sounds right. I never feel that I am being myself until the third or fourth draft, and it's only then that it gets personal and starts to be fun.

When I said that putting off papers robbed me of a good time, I really meant it. Writing the essay about my father turned out to be a high point in my life. And on top of having a good time with it, I now have a record of what happened. And my ten-month-old son, when he grows up, can read things about his grandfather and father that he'd probably not have learned any other way.

For Discussion

1. What did Manning miss by writing his college papers at the last minute?
2. Why does Manning say that "writing is great for shy people"? Have you ever felt that you could express yourself in writing better than in speech?

SARAH VOWELL

Sarah Vowell is best known for the smart, witty spoken essays she delivers on public radio. Born in Muskogee, Oklahoma, in 1969, Vowell grew up in Oklahoma and Montana. After graduating from Montana State University, she earned an MA in art history and criticism from the School of the Art Institute of Chicago. Radio has played a large part in Vowell's life: She was a DJ for her college station in Montana; published a day-by-day diary of a year spent listening to the radio, *Radio On: A Listener's Diary* (1996); and worked as a contributing editor for *This American Life* on Public Radio International. Many of Vowell's books — such as *Partly Cloudy Patriot* (2002), *The Wordy Shipmates* (2008), and *Unfamiliar Fishes* (2011) — adopt a witty, unexpected perspective on American history. Vowell also works with 826NYC, a nonprofit writing center for children and teenagers, and she was the voice of the young superhero Violet in the animated film *The Incredibles* (2004). She lives in New York City and occasionally writes guest columns for *Salon, Time, San Francisco Weekly*, and the *New York Times*.

Shooting Dad

Vowell read "Shooting Dad," in slightly different form, on *This American Life* and then included it in her essay collection *Take the Cannoli: Stories from the New World* (2000). Like the previous essay, Brad Manning's "Arm Wrestling with My Father," this one explores the relationship between child and father. Engaged in a lifelong opposition to her father, Vowell sees their differences in terms of the Constitution: She cherishes the First Amendment's guarantee of freedom of religion, speech, and assembly, while he holds fast to the Second Amendment's guarantee of the right to bear arms. Then one day, with a jolt, Vowell realizes how much they have in common.

If you were passing by the house where I grew up during my teenage years   1
and it happened to be before Election Day, you wouldn't have needed to come inside to see that it was a house divided. You could have looked at the Democratic campaign poster in the upstairs window and the Republican one in the downstairs window and seen our home for the Civil War battleground it was. I'm not saying who was the Democrat or who was the Republican — my father or I — but I will tell you that I have never subscribed to *Guns & Ammo*, that I did not plaster the family vehicle with National Rifle Association stickers, and that hunter's orange was never my color.

About the only thing my father and I agree on is the Constitution, though ₂ I'm partial to the First Amendment, while he's always favored the Second.

I am a gunsmith's daughter. I like to call my parents' house, located on a ₃ quiet residential street in Bozeman, Montana, the United States of Firearms. Guns were everywhere: the so-called pretty ones like the circa 1850 walnut muzzleloader hanging on the wall, Dad's clients' fixer-uppers leaning into corners, an entire rack right next to the TV. I had to move revolvers out of my way to make room for a bowl of Rice Krispies on the kitchen table.

I was eleven when we moved into that Bozeman house. We had never ₄ lived in town before, and this was a college town at that. We came from Oklahoma — a dusty little Muskogee County nowhere called Braggs. My parents' property there included an orchard, a horse pasture, and a couple of acres of woods. I knew our lives had changed one morning not long after we moved to Montana when, during breakfast, my father heard a noise and jumped out of his chair. Grabbing a BB gun, he rushed out the front door. Standing in the yard, he started shooting at crows. My mother sprinted after him screaming, "Pat, you might ought to check, but I don't think they do that up here!" From the look on his face, she might as well have told him that his American citizenship had been revoked. He shook his head, mumbling, "Why, shooting crows is a national pastime, like baseball and apple pie." Personally, I preferred baseball and apple pie. I looked up at those crows flying away and thought, I'm going to like it here.

Dad and I started bickering in earnest when I was fourteen, after the 1984 ₅ Democratic National Convention. I was so excited when Walter Mondale chose Geraldine Ferraro as his running mate that I taped the front page of the newspaper with her picture on it to the refrigerator door. But there was some sort of mysterious gravity surge in the kitchen. Somehow, that picture ended up in the trash all the way across the room.

Nowadays, I giggle when Dad calls me on Election Day to cheerfully ₆ inform me that he has once again canceled out my vote, but I was not always so mature. There were times when I found the fact that he was a gunsmith horrifying. And just *weird*. All he ever cared about were guns. All I ever cared about was art. There were years and years when he hid out by himself in the garage making rifle barrels and I holed up in my room reading Allen Ginsberg poems, and we were incapable of having a conversation that didn't end in an argument.

Our house was partitioned off into territories. While the kitchen and the ₇ living room were well within the DMZ,¹ the respective work spaces governed by my father and me were jealously guarded totalitarian states in which each of

¹ Abbreviation for *demilitarized zone*, an area off-limits to war making. — EDS.

us declared ourselves dictator. Dad's shop was a messy disaster area, a labyrinth of lathes. Its walls were hung with the mounted antlers of deer he'd bagged, forming a makeshift museum of death. The available flat surfaces were buried under a million scraps of paper on which he sketched his mechanical inventions in blue ballpoint pen. And the floor, carpeted with spiky metal shavings, was a tetanus shot waiting to happen. My domain was the cramped, cold space known as the music room. It was also a messy disaster area, an obstacle course of musical instruments — piano, trumpet, baritone horn, valve trombone, various percussion doodads (bells!), and recorders. A framed portrait of the French composer Claude Debussy was nailed to the wall. The available flat surfaces were buried under piles of staff paper, on which I penciled in the pompous orchestra music given titles like "Prelude to the Green Door" (named after an O. Henry short story by the way, not the watershed porn flick *Behind the Green Door*) I started writing in junior high.

It has been my experience that in order to impress potential suitors, skip the teen Debussy anecdotes and stick with the always attention-getting line "My dad makes guns." Though it won't cause the guy to like me any better, it will make him handle the inevitable breakup with diplomacy — just in case I happen to have any loaded family heirlooms lying around the house. 8

But the fact is, I have only shot a gun once and once was plenty. My twin sister, Amy, and I were six years old — six — when Dad decided that it was high time we learned how to shoot. Amy remembers the day he handed us the gun for the first time differently. She liked it. 9

Amy shared our father's enthusiasm for firearms and the quick-draw cowboy mythology surrounding them. I tended to daydream through Dad's activities — the car trip to Dodge City's Boot Hill, his beloved John Wayne Westerns on TV. My sister, on the other hand, turned into Rooster Cogburn Jr., devouring Duke movies with Dad. In fact, she named her teddy bear Duke, hung a colossal John Wayne portrait next to her bed, and took to wearing one of those John Wayne shirts that button on the side. So when Dad led us out to the backyard when we were six and, to Amy's delight, put the gun in her hand, she says she felt it meant that Daddy trusted us and that he thought of us as "big girls." 10

But I remember holding the pistol only made me feel small. It was so heavy in my hand. I stretched out my arm and pointed it away and winced. It was a very long time before I had the nerve to pull the trigger and I was so scared I had to close my eyes. It felt like it just went off by itself, as if I had no say in the matter, as if the gun just had this *need*. The sound it made was as big as God. It kicked little me back to the ground like a bully, like a foe. It hurt. I don't know if I dropped it or just handed it back over to my dad, but I do know that I never wanted to touch another one again. And, because I 11 believed in the devil, I did what my mother told me to do every time I felt an evil presence. I looked at the smoke and whispered under my breath, "Satan, I rebuke thee."

It's not like I'm saying I was traumatized. It's more like I was decided. 12 Guns: Not For Me. Luckily, both my parents grew up in exasperating households where children were considered puppets and/or slaves. My mom and dad were hell-bent on letting my sister and me make our own choices. So if I decided that I didn't want my father's little death sticks to kick me to the ground again, that was fine with him. He would go hunting with my sister, who started calling herself "the loneliest twin in history" because of my reluctance to engage in family activities.

Of course, the fact that I was allowed to voice my opinions did not mean 13 that my father would silence his own. Some things were said during the Reagan administration that cannot be taken back. Let's just say that I blamed Dad for nuclear proliferation and Contra aid. He believed that if I had my way, all the guns would be confiscated and it would take the commies about fifteen minutes to parachute in and assume control.

We're older now, my dad and I. The older I get, the more I'm interested in 14 becoming a better daughter. First on my list: Figure out the whole gun thing.

Not long ago, my dad finished his most elaborate tool of death yet. A can- 15 non. He built a nineteenth-century cannon. From scratch. It took two years.

My father's cannon is a smaller replica of a cannon called the Big Horn 16 Gun in front of Bozeman's Pioneer Museum. The barrel of the original has been filled with concrete ever since some high school kids in the '50s pointed it at the school across the street and shot out its windows one night as a prank. According to Dad's historical source, a man known to scholars as A Guy at the Museum, the cannon was brought to Bozeman around 1870, and was used by local white merchants to fire at the Sioux and Cheyenne Indians who blocked their trade access to the East in 1874.

"Bozeman was founded on greed," Dad says. The courthouse cannon, 17 he continues, "definitely killed Indians. The merchants filled it full of nuts, bolts, and chopped-up horseshoes. Sitting Bull could have been part of these engagements. They definitely ticked off the Indians, because a couple of years later, Custer wanders into them at Little Bighorn. The Bozeman merchants were out to cause trouble. They left fresh baked bread with cyanide in it on the trail to poison a few Indians."

Because my father's sarcastic American history yarns rarely go on for long 18 before he trots out some nefarious ancestor of ours — I come from a long line of moonshiners, Confederate soldiers, murderers, even Democrats — he cracks that the merchants hired some "community-minded Southern soldiers from North Texas." These soldiers had, like my great-great-grandfather John

Vowell, fought under pro-slavery guerrilla William C. Quantrill. Quantrill is most famous for riding into Lawrence, Kansas, in 1863 flying a black flag and commanding his men pharaohlike to "kill every male and burn down every house."

"John Vowell," Dad says, "had a little rep for killing people." And since   19
he abandoned my great-grandfather Charles, whose mother died giving birth to him in 1870, and wasn't seen again until 1912, Dad doesn't rule out the possibility that John Vowell could have been one of the hired guns on the Bozeman Trail. So the cannon isn't just another gun to my dad. It's a map of all his obsessions — firearms, certainly, but also American history and family history, subjects he's never bothered separating from each other.

After tooling a million guns, after inventing and building a rifle barrel   20
boring machine, after setting up that complicated shop filled with lathes and blueing tanks and outmoded blacksmithing tools, the cannon is his most ambitious project ever. I thought that if I was ever going to understand the ballistic bee in his bonnet, this was my chance. It was the biggest gun he ever made and I could experience it and spend time with it with the added bonus of not having to actually pull a trigger myself.

I called Dad and said that I wanted to come to Montana and watch him   21
shoot off the cannon. He was immediately suspicious. But I had never taken much interest in his work before and he would take what he could get. He loaded the cannon into the back of his truck and we drove up into the Bridger Mountains. I was a little worried that the National Forest Service would object to us lobbing fiery balls of metal onto its property. Dad laughed, assuring me that "you cannot shoot fireworks, but this is considered a fire*arm*."

It is a small cannon, about as long as a baseball bat and as wide as a coffee   22
can. But it's heavy — 110 pounds. We park near the side of the hill. Dad takes his gunpowder and other tools out of this adorable wooden box on which he has stenciled "PAT G. VOWELL CANNONWORKS." Cannonworks: So that's what NRA members call a metal-strewn garage.

Dad plunges his homemade bullets into the barrel, points it at an embank-   23
ment just to be safe, and lights the fuse. When the fuse is lit, it resembles a cartoon. So does the sound, which warrants Ben Day dot[2] words along the lines of *ker-pow!* There's so much Fourth of July smoke everywhere I feel compelled to sing the national anthem.

I've given this a lot of thought — how to convey the giddiness I felt when   24
the cannon shot off. But there isn't a sophisticated way to say this. It's just really, really cool. My dad thought so, too.

---

[2] Ben Day dots are colored dots in various sizes, used in comics to intensify words for actions and loud sounds. — Eds.

Sometimes, I put together stories about the more eccentric corners of the   25
American experience for public radio. So I happen to have my tape recorder
with me, and I've never seen levels like these. Every time the cannon goes off,
the delicate needles which keep track of the sound quality lurch into the bad,
red zone so fast and so hard I'm surprised they don't break.

The cannon was so loud and so painful, I had to touch my head to make   26
sure my skull hadn't cracked open. One thing that my dad and I share is
that we're both a little hard of hearing — me from Aerosmith, him from
gunsmith.

He lights the fuse again. The bullet knocks over the log he was aiming at.   27
I instantly utter a sentence I never in my entire life thought I would say. I tell
him, "Good shot, Dad."

Just as I'm wondering what's coming over me, two hikers walk by. Appar-   28
ently, they have never seen a man set off a homemade cannon in the middle
of the wilderness while his daughter holds a foot-long microphone up into the
air recording its terrorist boom. One hiker gives me a puzzled look and asks,
"So you work for the radio and that's your dad?"

Dad shoots the cannon again so that they can see how it works. The   29
other hiker says, "That's quite the machine you got there." But he isn't talking about the cannon. He's talking about my tape recorder and my microphone — which is called a *shotgun* mike. I stare back at him, then I look over
at my father's cannon, then down at my microphone, and I think, Oh. My.
God. My dad and I are the same person. We're both smart-alecky loners with
goofy projects and weird equipment. And since this whole target practice out-
ing was my idea, I was no longer his adversary. I was his accomplice. What's
worse, I was liking it.

I haven't changed my mind about guns. I can get behind the cannon   30
because it is a completely ceremonial object. It's unwieldy and impractical,
just like everything else I care about. Try to rob a convenience store with
this 110-pound Saturday night special, you'd still be dragging it in the door
Sunday afternoon.

I love noise. As a music fan, I'm always waiting for that moment in a   31
song when something just flies out of it and explodes in the air. My dad is a
one-man garage band, the kind of rock 'n' roller who slaves away at his art for
no reason other than to make his own sound. My dad is an artist — a pretty
driven, idiosyncratic one, too. He's got his last *Gesamtkunstwerk*[3] all planned
out. It's a performance piece. We're all in it — my mom, the loneliest twin in
history, and me.

---

[3] German, "total work of art," specifically a work that seeks to unify all the arts. — Eds.

When my father dies, take a wild guess what he wants done with his ashes.   32
Here's a hint: It requires a cannon.

"You guys are going to love this," he smirks, eyeballing the cannon. "You   33
get to drag this thing up on top of the Gravellies on opening day of hunting
season. And looking off at Sphinx Mountain, you get to put me in little paper
bags. I can take my last hunting trip on opening morning."

I'll do it, too. I will have my father's body burned into ashes. I will pack   34
these ashes into paper bags. I will go to the mountains with my mother, my
sister, and the cannon. I will plunge his remains into the barrel and point it
into a hill so that he doesn't take anyone with him. I will light the fuse. But I
will not cover my ears. Because when I blow what used to be my dad into the
earth, I want it to hurt.

*For a reading quiz, visit **bedfordstmartins.com/thebedfordreader**.*

Journal Writing

How do you respond to Vowell's eccentric, even obsessive, father? Do you basically
come to sympathize with him or not? Who in your life has quirky behavior that you
find charming or annoying or a little of both? Write a paragraph or two about this
person, focusing on his or her particular habits or obsessions. (To take your journal
writing further, see "From Journal to Essay" on the facing page.)

Questions on Meaning

1. In her opening sentence, Vowell describes growing up in "a house divided." What
   does she mean? Where in the essay does she make the divisions in her household
   explicit?
2. Why, given Vowell's father's love of guns, was it "fine" with him that his daughter decided as a young child that she wanted nothing to do with guns (par. 12)?
   What does this attitude suggest about his character?
3. What motivated Vowell to come home to watch her father shoot off his homemade cannon? Why, given her aversion to guns, does she regard this cannon
   positively?
4. What do paragraphs 18–19, about her father's family history, contribute to Vowell's portrait of him?
5. What seems to be Vowell's PURPOSE in writing here? What DOMINANT IMPRESSION
   of her father does she create?

Questions on Writing Strategy

1. Why is the anecdote Vowell relates in paragraph 4 an effective introduction both to her father and to their relationship?
2. Paragraph 8 is sort of an aside in this essay — not entirely on the main topic. What purpose does it serve?
3. What does Vowell's final sentence mean? Do you find it a satisfying conclusion to her essay? Why, or why not?
4. **OTHER METHODS** Throughout her essay, Vowell relies on COMPARISON AND CONTRAST to express her relationship with her father (and with her twin sister in pars. 9–12). Find examples of comparison and contrast. Why is the method important to the essay? How does the method help reinforce Vowell's main point about her relationship with her father?

Questions on Language

1. In paragraph 4 Vowell shows her father "mumbling" that "shooting crows is a national pastime, like baseball and apple pie," while she notes that she herself "preferred baseball and apple pie." How does the language here illustrate IRONY?
2. Pick out five or six concrete and specific words in paragraph 7. What do they accomplish?
3. In paragraph 9 Vowell writes, "My twin sister, Amy, and I were six years old — six — when Dad decided that it was high time we learned how to shoot. Amy remembers the day he handed us the gun for the first time differently. She liked it." What are the EFFECTS of the repetition of the word *six* in the first sentence and of the three-word final sentence?
4. Study the FIGURES OF SPEECH Vowell uses in paragraph 11 to describe shooting a gun. What is their effect?
5. Consult a dictionary if you need help in defining the following: muzzleloader (par. 3); revoked (4); bickering (5); partitioned, respective, totalitarian, labyrinth, lathes, pompous (7); colossal (10); traumatized (12); proliferation, confiscated (13); cyanide (17); nefarious, moonshiners, guerrilla, pharaohlike (18); ballistic (20); giddiness (24); adversary, accomplice (29); unwieldy (30); idiosyncratic (31).

Suggestions for Writing

1. **FROM JOURNAL TO ESSAY** Based on your journal writing, compose an essay that uses description to portray your subject and his or her personal quirks. Be sure to include specific incidents you've witnessed and specific details to create a vivid dominant impression of the person. You may, like Vowell, focus on the evolution of your relationship with this person — whether mainly positive or mainly negative.
2. Conflict between generations is common in many families — whether over music, clothing, hairstyles, friends, or larger issues of politics, values, and religion. Write an essay about generational conflicts you have experienced in your family

or that you have witnessed in other families. Are such conflicts inevitable? How can they be resolved?

3. Gun ownership is a divisive issue in the United States. Research and explain the main ARGUMENTS for and against gun control. Whatever your own position, strive for an objective presentation, neither pro nor con.

4. **CRITICAL WRITING** Vowell's essay divides into several fairly distinct sections: paragraphs 1–4, 5–7, 8, 9–12, 13, 14–31 (which includes an aside in pars. 17–19), and 32–34. In an essay, analyze what happens in each of these sections. How do they fit together to help develop Vowell's dominant impression? How does the relative length of each section contribute to your understanding of her evolving relationship with her father?

5. **CONNECTIONS** Both Sarah Vowell and Brad Manning, in "Arm Wrestling with My Father" (p. 138), describe their fathers. In an essay, examine words Manning and Vowell use to convey their feelings of distance from their fathers and also their feelings of closeness. Use quotations from both essays to support your analysis.

Sarah Vowell on Writing

Writing for both radio and print, Sarah Vowell has discovered differences in listening and reading audiences. On *Transom.org*'s Internet discussion board, she explained how she writes differently for the two media.

[S]ometimes I feel like I'm so much more manipulative on the radio. I know how to use my voice to make you feel a certain way. And that's not writing — that's acting. I get tired of acting sometimes. Which is why it's nice to be able to go back to the cold old page. Also, real time is an unforgiving medium. I still maintain a little academic streak, and any time I read something on the air or out loud, I have to cut back on the abstract, thinky bits. I have to read a story out loud in front of an audience this week and I had to lop it off by half, to prune it of its dull information and, sometimes, its very point. Those things for you, the listener, are bonuses — the listener doesn't get as much filler, the listener gets to feel more. Readers are more patient. . . .

The only real drawback I think from moving between verbal and print media is punctuation. I'm working on another book right now, and there are so many things I want to say that I have to normalize on the page because I do not think in complete, fluid sentences. I seem to think in stopgaps and asides. Which the listener doesn't notice. But the reader, I think, becomes antsy when there are too many dashes and parentheses. So that is a constant battle — (dash!) trying to retain my casual, late twentieth-century (it's where

I'm from), American-girl cadences, but without driving the reader crazy with a bunch of marks all over the place. Also, I love the word *and*. And I start too many sentences with *and*. Again, no one notices out loud because that's normative speech. But do that too much on the page and it's distracting and stupid.

For Discussion

1. What does Vowell mean by having to "normalize [her thoughts] on the page"?
2. What difficulties or rewards have you encountered trying to put ideas into written words for others to read?
3. In your experience as a speaker and a writer, what are the advantages of each form of communication? What are the disadvantages of each?

ELIZABETH GILBERT

Elizabeth Gilbert was born in Waterbury, Connecticut, in 1969 and grew up on her family's Christmas-tree farm. She studied political science at New York University and, after graduating in 1991, took up travel, odd jobs, and constant writing. Many of her experiences on the road found their way into *Pilgrims* (1997), Gilbert's debut collection of short stories. She has written two novels, *Stern Men* (2000) and *The Signature of All Things* (2013); a biography of adventurer Eustace Conway, *The Last American Man* (2002); and a *GQ* article about working in a Manhattan bar that became the basis for the movie *Coyote Ugly*. She is best known, however, for her travel memoir *Eat, Pray, Love: One Woman's Search for Everything across Italy, India, and Indonesia* (2006). The book — which chronicles a year-long quest for indulgence, spirituality, and romance — was translated into thirty languages, earned Gilbert a spot on *Time* magazine's list of the most influential people in the world, and was made into a motion picture. Her next memoir, *Committed: A Skeptic Makes Peace with Marriage* (2010), shows the once-divorced author grappling with the institution of marriage as she prepares to wed again. She and her husband live in Frenchtown, New Jersey, and own an import store called Two Buttons.

The Best Pizza in the World

In this excerpt from *Eat, Pray, Love,* Gilbert depicts an urge to travel that compels her — even while she's already living abroad — to embark on a day trip to Naples, Italy. With her trademark humor and affability, Gilbert describes the "dangerous and cheerful nuthouse" of the city in vivid detail, through a series of impressions, observations, and imagined dialog. As she does throughout her book, Gilbert gives a sense of the disorienting but thrilling experience of stepping outside the familiar.

1   I met a young Australian girl last week who was backpacking through Europe for the first time in her life. I gave her directions to the train station. She was heading up to Slovenia, just to check it out. When I heard her plans, I was stricken with such a dumb spasm of jealousy, thinking, *I want to go to Slovenia! How come I never get to travel anywhere?*

2   Now, to the innocent eye it might appear that I already *am* traveling. And longing to travel while you are already traveling is, I admit, a kind of greedy madness. It's kind of like fantasizing about having sex with your favorite movie star while you're having sex with your *other* favorite movie star. But the fact that this girl asked directions from me (clearly, in her mind, a civilian) suggests that I am not technically traveling in Rome, but living here. However

temporary it may be, I am a civilian. When I ran into the girl, in fact, I was just on my way to pay my electricity bill, which is not something travelers worry about. Traveling-to-a-place energy and living-in-a-place energy are two fundamentally different energies, and something about meeting this Australian girl on her way to Slovenia just gave me such a jones to hit the road.

And that's why I called my friend Sofie and said, "Let's go down to Naples   3
for the day and eat some pizza!"

Immediately, just a few hours later, we are on the train, and then — like   4
magic — we are there. I instantly love Naples. Wild, raucous, noisy, dirty, balls-out Naples. An anthill inside a rabbit warren, with all the exoticism of a Middle Eastern bazaar and a touch of New Orleans voodoo. A tripped-out, dangerous and cheerful nuthouse. My friend Wade came to Naples in the 1970s and was mugged . . . in a *museum*. The city is all decorated with the laundry that hangs from every window and dangles across every street; everybody's fresh-washed undershirts and brassieres flapping in the wind like Tibetan prayer flags. There is not a street in Naples in which some tough little kid in shorts and mismatched socks is not screaming up from the sidewalk to some other tough little kid on a rooftop nearby. Nor is there a building in this town that doesn't have at least one crooked old woman seated at her window, peering suspiciously down at the activity below.

The people here are so insanely psyched to be from Naples, and why   5
shouldn't they be? This is a city that gave the world pizza *and* ice cream. The Neapolitan women in particular are such a gang of tough-voiced, loud-mouthed, generous, nosy dames, all bossy and annoyed and right up in your face and just trying to friggin' *help* you for chrissake, you dope — *why they gotta do everything around here?* The accent in Naples is like a friendly cuff on the ear. It's like walking through a city of short-order cooks, everybody hollering at the same time. They still have their own dialect here, and an ever-changing liquid dictionary of local slang, but somehow I find that the Neapolitans are the easiest people for me to understand in Italy. Why? Because they *want* you to understand, damn it. They talk loud and emphatically, and if you can't understand what they're actually saying out of their mouths, you can usually pick up the inference from the gesture. Like that punk little grammar-school girl on the back of her older cousin's motorbike, who flipped me the finger *and* a charming smile as she drove by, just to make me understand, "Hey, no hard feelings, lady. But I'm only seven, and I can already tell you're a complete moron, but that's cool — I think you're halfway OK despite yourself and I kinda like your dumb-ass face. We both know you would love to be me, but sorry — you can't. Anyhow, here's my middle finger, enjoy your stay in Naples, and *ciao!*"

As in every public space in Italy, there are always boys, teenagers and　6
grown men playing soccer, but here in Naples there's something extra, too. For
instance, today I found kids — I mean, a group of eight-year-old boys — who
had gathered up some old chicken crates to create makeshift chairs and a
table, and they were playing *poker* in the piazza with such intensity I feared
one of them might get shot.

[My friends] Giovanni and Dario . . . are originally from Naples. I cannot　7
picture it. I cannot imagine shy, studious, sympathetic Giovanni as a young
boy amongst this — and I don't use the word lightly — mob. But he is Neapolitan, no question about it, because before I left Rome he gave me the name
of a pizzeria in Naples that I had to try, because, Giovanni informed me, it sold
the best pizza in Naples. I found this a wildly exciting prospect, given that the
best pizza in Italy is from Naples, and the best pizza in the world is from Italy,
which means that this pizzeria must offer . . . I'm almost too superstitious to say
it . . . *the best pizza in the world?* Giovanni passed along the name of the place
with such seriousness and intensity, I almost felt I was being inducted into a
secret society. He pressed the address into the palm of my hand and said, in
gravest confidence, "Please go to this pizzeria. Order the margherita pizza with
double mozzarella. If you do not eat this pizza when you are in Naples, please
lie to me later and tell me that you did."

So Sofie and I have come to Pizzeria da Michele, and these pies we have　8
just ordered — one for each of us — are making us lose our minds. I love my
pizza so much, in fact, that I have come to believe in my delirium that my pizza
might actually love me, in return. I am having a relationship with this pizza,
almost an affair. Meanwhile, Sofie is practically in tears over hers, she's having a metaphysical crisis about it, she's begging me, "Why do they even *bother*
trying to make pizza in Stockholm? Why do we even bother eating food at *all*
in Stockholm?"

Pizzeria da Michele is a small place with only two rooms and one non-　9
stop oven. It's about a fifteen-minute walk from the train station in the rain,
don't even worry about it, just go. You need to get there fairly early in the
day because sometimes they run out of dough, which will break your heart.
By 1:00 p.m., the streets outside the pizzeria have become jammed with Neapolitans trying to get into the place, shoving for access like they're trying
to get space on a lifeboat. There's not a menu. They have only two varieties of pizza here — regular and extra cheese. None of this new age southern
California olives-and-sun-dried-tomato wannabe pizza twaddle. The dough, it
takes me half my meal to figure out, tastes more like Indian *nan* than like any
pizza dough I ever tried. It's soft and chewy and yielding, but incredibly thin.
I always thought we only had two choices in our lives when it came to pizza
crust — thin and crispy, or thick and doughy. How was I to have known there

could be a crust in this world that was thin *and* doughy? Holy of holies! Thin, doughy, strong, gummy, yummy, chewy, salty pizza paradise. On top, there is a sweet tomato sauce that foams up all bubbly and creamy when it melts the fresh buffalo mozzarella, and the one sprig of basil in the middle of the whole deal somehow infuses the entire pizza with herbal radiance, much the same way one shimmering movie star in the middle of a party brings a contact high of glamour to everyone around her. It's technically impossible to eat this thing, of course. You try to take a bite off your slice and the gummy crust folds, and the hot cheese runs away like topsoil in a landslide, makes a mess of you and your surroundings, but just deal with it.

The guys who make this miracle happen are shoveling the pizzas in and out of the wood-burning oven, looking for all the world like the boilermen in the belly of a great ship who shovel coal into the raging furnaces. Their sleeves are rolled up over their sweaty forearms, their faces red with exertion, one eye squinted against the heat of the fire and a cigarette dangling from the lips. Sofie and I each order another pie — another whole pizza each — and Sofie tries to pull herself together, but really, the pizza is so good we can barely cope.

A word about my body. I am gaining weight every day, of course. I am doing rude things to my body here in Italy, taking in such ghastly amounts of cheese and pasta and bread and wine and chocolate and pizza dough. (Elsewhere in Naples, I'd been told, you can actually get something called chocolate pizza. What kind of nonsense is that? I mean, later I did go find some, and it's delicious, but honestly — *chocolate pizza?*) I'm not exercising, I'm not eating enough fiber, I'm not taking any vitamins. In my real life, I have been known to eat organic goat's milk yoghurt sprinkled with wheat germ for breakfast. My real-life days are long gone. Back in America, my friend Susan is telling people I'm on a "No Carb Left Behind" tour. But my body is being such a good sport about all this. My body is turning a blind eye to my misdoings and my overindulgences, as if to say, "OK, kid, live it up, I recognize that this is just temporary. Let me know when your little experiment with pure pleasure is over, and I'll see what I can do about damage control."

Still, when I look at myself in the mirror of the best pizzeria in Naples, I see a bright-eyed, clear-skinned, happy and healthy face. I haven't seen a face like that on me for a long time.

"Thank you," I whisper. Then Sofie and I run out in the rain to look for pastries.

10

11

12

13

*For a reading quiz, visit **bedfordstmartins.com/thebedfordreader**.*

Journal Writing

What food or drink holds a special place in your memory? In your journal, write down as many sensory details about this food or drink as you can. (To take your journal writing further, see "From Journal to Essay" on the facing page.)

Questions on Meaning

1. What DOMINANT IMPRESSION does Gilbert create of Naples and of the pizza she ate there? Does she state this impression in a THESIS STATEMENT, or is it implied?
2. What would you say is Gilbert's PURPOSE in this essay?
3. What distinction does Gilbert make between traveling to a new place and living somewhere temporarily? Into which category does she put herself, and why?
4. In paragraph 8 Gilbert comments that her friend Sofie is "having a metaphysical crisis" over her pizza. What does she mean? How does Sofie's reaction mirror the point of Gilbert's essay?
5. In what ways does pizza serve as a SYMBOL for Gilbert?

Questions on Writing Strategy

1. Most of Gilbert's essay moves in spatial order, from the streets of Naples to a particular pizzeria to the table at which she and her companion ate. Paragraph 7, however, jumps back to another city, as Gilbert explains that a friend gave her the name of the pizzeria and begged her to go there. Why do you think Gilbert placed this paragraph in the middle of her essay, instead of at the beginning?
2. Comment on the IRONY in the last three paragraphs of the essay.
3. As the essay's headnote mentions, Gilbert included this piece in a travel memoir titled *Eat, Pray, Love*. What ASSUMPTIONS does she seem to make about the interests of her readers and their knowledge of Italian culture? Where in the essay do you see EVIDENCE of these assumptions?
4. **OTHER METHODS** Where does Gilbert use CAUSE AND EFFECT to explain something to readers? What does the method contribute to her essay?

Questions on Language

1. Gilbert uses an abundance of FIGURES OF SPEECH in this essay, most notably metaphor and simile, but also hyperbole. Find at least two or three examples of each and comment on their effectiveness.
2. How would you characterize Gilbert's DICTION and TONE? Is her language appropriate? Why, or why not?
3. What is the EFFECT of the imagined dialog in paragraph 5? Why do you suppose Gilbert places quotation marks around the young girl's words but not the women's?
4. Consult a dictionary if you need help defining the following words: jones (par. 2); raucous, warren, exoticism, bazaar (4); Neapolitan, cuff, inference (5); piazza (6); inducted, gravest (7); delirium (8); twaddle, *nan* (9); ghastly (11).

Suggestions for Writing

1. **FROM JOURNAL TO ESSAY** In an essay, describe the food or drink you wrote about in your journal, but also do more: Like Gilbert, focus not just on the food or beverage itself but also on its larger context. Why is it so special? What does it represent to you? Be sure to infuse your writing with vivid IMAGES evoking concrete sensory experiences.

2. In an essay that combines NARRATION and description, write about a memorable experience you have had in your travels. What prompted you to take the trip? Was the place anything like you expected? What about it stands out in your memory, and why? Try to use colorful FIGURES OF SPEECH and specific details to help readers share in your experience.

3. **CRITICAL WRITING** Closely examine how Gilbert appeals to each of the five senses in her descriptions of Naples and its pizza. Choose three to five particularly effective sensory images, and write an essay that explains both their purpose and their effect.

4. **CONNECTIONS** Both Gilbert and Amy Tan, in "Fish Cheeks" (p. 110), write about the emotions they felt while consuming a particular meal. Write an essay in which you COMPARE AND CONTRAST how the two writers describe food and how each writer uses food to make a larger point about desire.

SVEN BIRKERTS

Born in Pontiac, Michigan, in 1951 to immigrants from Latvia, Sven Birkerts grew up near Detroit "wrestling," as he once put it, "with the ghosts of another culture." For much of his childhood he heard only Latvian at home and was regularly regaled with stories of a happier life in northern Europe before World War II. Birkerts was a voracious reader in his youth and studied literature at the University of Michigan, earning a bachelor's degree in 1973. He stumbled on his career as a literary critic in the early 1980s while working as a bookstore clerk. On a whim he wrote a review of a novel for his own enjoyment and submitted it to a journal; to his surprise the amateur effort led to regular assignments. Birkerts's essays have been collected in several volumes, starting with *An Artificial Wilderness: Essays on Twentieth-Century Literature* (1987) and including *The Gutenberg Elegies: The Fate of Reading in an Electronic Age* (1994), *My Sky Blue Trades: Growing Up Counter in a Contrary Time* (2002), and *The Art of Time in Memoir: Then, Again* (2008). He has also taught college writing and is a co-author of two literature textbooks. Often praised for his lack of pretention, Birkerts is known for his skill at distilling complex thoughts into simple prose. He lives in Arlington, Massachusetts, a suburb of Boston.

Ladder

Birkerts's most recent book, *The Other Walk* (2011), mixes critical analysis and personal reflection and was praised by *Publisher's Weekly* for "the humor and insights conveyed in [its] enchanting and well-crafted essays," such as the one we include here. In "Ladder," Birkerts describes with precision and embarrassment what it felt like to discover a crippling phobia at a most inopportune time.

It was already there when I came around the side of the house. I saw it 1 in that sidelong way you register one thing while looking for another. I was trying to find the man I'd spoken to on the phone, who had hired me for the day, and there he was, cross-legged on the grass, wearing a bright white T-shirt, with a full head of silvery hair, camera hair, though he didn't really look like the kind of older man who would go to all the trouble. But maybe he was, because when he heard me coming and turned full-face I saw he was handsome, lady-killer handsome the way some older men are, and these men are always vain. He was cleaning paintbrushes — they were neatly lined up on a sheet of newspaper — and he didn't get up. He had strong-looking arms, maybe even an old-style tattoo. I was looking, staring, at his face, but not so distracted that I didn't take in the other thing. Off to my right, propped up against the side of the house, going up and up in sections, was the tallest ladder

I'd ever seen. I felt a bump in my stomach. I hadn't even really turned yet, or followed the ladder up into the light to see where the ends were propped against the highest gable. I was still making my way across the grass, and the man, I don't remember his name anymore, was squinting up and saluting me, or maybe lifting his arm to block the sun, saying, "Here to do some work?" I nodded and said I was. That was the deal. I'd been living on the edge all winter in our little seaside Maine town, buying dented canned goods at discount and even signing on one day with my girlfriend, Sally, to deliver phone books in nearby Biddeford, the mill town in which every other person was named Pelletier or Thibodeaux — and we were required to check off the right recipient and address. Thibodeaux, Thibodeaux, Thibodeaux . . . We quit after a day. Next I'd put up a sign in our little cracker-box post office offering my odd-job services for a laughably low hourly rate. My logic: who could resist?

And now it was one of the first real spring days and this man had called 2 with a job, and my attention was evenly split between the shock of his seasoned movie-star looks and my growing awareness of that ladder. Did I already know how it was with me and heights? How could I not? I was in my early twenties and had done enough playing in trees and high places as a kid to have an idea. I'd always been a reluctant climber, though maybe I'd later chalked it off as a fear outgrown — as if a decade of not testing the edge would have made it go away. I don't know. I only know that the man — my boss — walked me over to where the ladder stood flat on its grips and showed me my bucket and brushes and handed me a rag that I tucked into my belt. But just before he did that — this comes back with close-up clarity — he reached his thumb and forefinger into the two corners of his mouth and took out his teeth. Out. The whole apparatus. He pulled it from his mouth and held it up like one of those party jokes that you wind with a key. I looked away — I felt embarrassed — and when I glanced back I must have done a double take. Impossible. His face had completely fallen in on itself — the strong jaw was gone, the mouth was crimped like the top of a string bag. I watched as he bent down and set the teeth on another sheet of newspaper in the grass.

When he straightened up, I was face-to-face with an old man with a thick, 3 groomed head of silver hair. I don't know if he had any idea of the effect he had just achieved. He was standing with me by the ladder, telling me to make sure I got enough paint onto the wood, and I was nodding, agreeing, and already registering — I'm sure of it — that first nervous heaviness in my legs, and that tightness in the chest that starts you drawing deep breaths as if a good deep rush of air will make everything better. And then I was on the ladder, starting, a few rungs up, hauling the bucket with my left hand, the shore in sight, the ground still an easy jump. I had that instinct, or instruction, picked up somewhere, to keep my gaze straight ahead, taking in the lapping shingles row by row, the voice that said, "Don't look, just climb." Which I did, so carefully, every bit of my focus on my legs and hands, and on keeping the line of the vertical steady — no twists or turns, just plant the foot on the rung and pull with my one free arm, the right arm, the other gripping the bucket, which I was to hang on a hook next to where I painted — and I was already telling myself the facts of the matter, that people did this all the time, everywhere; that the ladder was strong, well planted at the base; and that little wobbles would naturally be magnified as sensations, that there was no real danger, and that even if I were to fall — *I would not fall* — it would be nothing more than a bad bump and some embarrassment at this point. So I stepped and pulled and steadied and watched myself in slow blurry sections pass by the frame of the first big window, which I knew was about halfway up.

But here the ordinary sequence stops. This upward progress was not happening in units anymore, never mind the rungs lined up ahead of me. Somewhere between one step and another the time stream balked, then stopped and started backing up. Every movement was suddenly breaking into its parts, the one arm aware of itself lifting, wrapping its fingers around the metal of the next rung, the other hand feeling in its joints the cut of the handle, the weight of the bucket, the weathered shingles mere inches away now gathering into the clearest detail: nail heads, streaks and smears and hardened little droplets of ancient paint, the ribbing of the wood grain visible under the color. "Don't look down, just climb." And I could feel it then, on my skin, up the armholes, the April wind, sweetly cool even in the spots of full sun, which I knew without looking was moving in and out behind the clouds. The moment of the shift. It comes now. I hear myself breathing and realize that I've stopped. I don't remember stopping, but all at once I know that I've been staring and staring at the same few warps and scratches. How long? I don't know. The window below me rattles in the breeze, I hear it. Suddenly I can't help myself: I turn my head just slightly to the left and I look down. Mainly to see if the man, my boss, is still there somewhere, but also because I need to know where I am. I feel a kind of thud as the scene clicks in. Ground, grass. He's not anywhere on the left side. Nor — I've moved my head so carefully, as if that little action could make a difference — on the other. The lawn falls away in either direction, empty. I am halfway up the side of the tallest house I've ever seen, and I'm alone. And that little twist of the neck was like breaking the seal. The calm, the focus, whatever story I was telling myself up here, is gone. I take in the great wide lawn, and over there, tiny as a kit for dolls, the newspaper with its row of tiny brushes lined up, and one corner flipping up in the breeze. That repeating movement makes me feel sick, that and the ground all at once so

4

far away, the wind now pulling at the back of my shirt, and I feel the fingers of my right hand tighten their grasp and my chest and stomach push in harder against the rungs. What have I done? I can't unsee the distance down, or lose the sense of the ladder shrinking away to nothing below me and above me. My hand hurts where I hold the metal, and now my knees go soft, just like that. I have the weight of the bucket in my other hand. For the first time I think, *Let it go, just drop it* — drop it and reach up with that hand, as if maybe with both hands gripping I can make it down. But somehow I can't make myself loosen my hold on the bucket, or do anything. Except close my eyes. Close my eyes and start to count, slowly: *One thousand one, one thousand two . . .* I don't know how high I get, but after enough numbers I feel something in me settle, I say to myself, *OK now*, and as I say that I get my fingers to go loose, and then without ever taking them away from the ladder I slide them, along the rung to the right-hand side, and then down the metal slowly, clutching between thumb and forefinger, until I reach the nearer rung, which I grab, and as I do that I let my left leg loose to find the lower support, and this I find, and lower the other leg, foot, shuddering my torso inch by inch down along the rungs, and again repeating the whole sequence, gaining just the first slight ease as the ground lifts slightly toward me, again, again, until I reach the first rung and take the backward step to earth, almost crazy with reaching it, bending to set the bucket down, letting go my other grip and straightening slowly up . . . and only then becoming aware of the man standing right in back of me. He's arrived from somewhere, and I know he's seen the whole of it, and at the same time I can feel that the fingers of my left hand, free from the clutch and the weight, are shaking. But I have no doubt, no question. Standing there, I notice where the shadows — mine, his — break from the grass against the side of the house, and I say to him without turning around, "I can't go up that high. I didn't know it before." I wait for a moment. When I finally turn and meet his eye, he shrugs, saying basically, *What can you do?* He's wearing a painter's cap now, flecked with white paint, and I see that he has put the teeth back in — and he looks good, not quite Paul Newman,[1] but very handsome. Obviously a lady-killer.

For a reading quiz, visit **bedfordstmartins.com/thebedfordreader**.

---

[1] Paul Newman (1925–2008) was a movie actor famous for striking good looks that seemed to improve as he aged. — Eds.

Journal Writing

Using Birkerts's essay as a springboard, consider any irrational fears that you may have. Are you afraid of heights, for instance, or snakes or spiders or tight spaces? Does any one instance involving your phobia stand out in your memory? Write about the experience in your journal. (To take your journal writing further, see "From Journal to Essay" below.)

Questions on Meaning

1. How would you describe the writer's PURPOSE in this essay? What DOMINANT IMPRESSION does Birkerts create?
2. What does Birkerts mean when he says of turning his head while high up during his climb, "that little twist of the neck was like breaking the seal" (par. 4)?
3. Why did the author seek out odd jobs like a day of house painting? How do those circumstances hint at the deeper implications of his fear?
4. Why is Birkerts terrified by the ladder? What does it represent to him?

Questions on Writing Strategy

1. What strategy does Birkerts use to connect with his readers? How well does he succeed, in your estimation?
2. How does Birkerts organize his description?
3. What is the intended effect of the unusually long final paragraph?
4. **OTHER METHODS** Where does Birkerts use COMPARISON AND CONTRAST? What do these passages contribute to the essay?

Questions on Language

1. Consult a dictionary if you are unsure of the meaning of any of the following: sidelong, vain, gable (par. 1); lapping (3); balked (4).
2. In paragraph 1 Birkerts describes his boss as "lady-killer handsome." What does that mean? Where in his essay does Birkerts return to this notion, and what is the EFFECT of the repetition?
3. Point to a few instances in the essay that make particularly effective use of CONCRETE details and sensory IMAGES to convey Birkerts's feelings.

Suggestions for Writing

1. **FROM JOURNAL TO ESSAY** Write an essay on the experience you explored in your journal, using SUBJECTIVE description to convey the effect a phobia had on you.
2. Try to recall an incident in which you struggled with or failed at a job that you expected would be simple. Write a short NARRATIVE about your difficulties. What went wrong? How did the struggle affect you? Did you learn anything about yourself?

3. **CRITICAL WRITING** In an essay, ANALYZE the image that Birkerts presents of himself. Consider specific examples of his language and TONE, along with what he says about himself and his implied attitude toward traditional measures of masculinity.

4. **CONNECTIONS** In "Deadly Mind Traps" (p. 353), Jeff Wise categorizes the kinds of mental errors people make when faced with danger, sometimes with fatal consequences. Read his CLASSIFICATION; then explain what Wise might suggest about how Birkerts should have responded to his fear on the first few steps of the ladder, and why. Which "mind trap" ensnared him?

ADDITIONAL WRITING TOPICS

Description

1. This is an in-class writing experiment. Describe another person in the room so clearly and unmistakably that when you read your description aloud, your subject will be recognized. (Be OBJECTIVE. No insulting descriptions, please!)

2. Write a paragraph describing one subject from *each* of the following categories. It will be up to you to make the general subject refer to a particular person, place, or thing. Write at least one paragraph as an objective description and at least one as a SUBJECTIVE description.

PERSON

A friend or roommate
A typical hip-hop, jazz, or
   country musician
One of your parents
An elderly person you know
A prominent politician
A historical figure

THING

A car
A dentist's drill
A painting or photograph
A foggy day
A season of the year
A musical instrument

PLACE

An office
A classroom
A college campus
A vacation spot
A hospital emergency room
A forest

3. In a brief essay, describe your ideal place — perhaps an apartment, a dorm room, a vacation spot, a restaurant, a gym, a store, a garden, a dance club or other kind of club. With concrete details, try to make the ideal seem actual.

Narration and Description

4. Use a combination of NARRATION and description to develop any one of the following topics:

Your first day on the job
Your first day at college
Returning to an old neighborhood
Getting lost
A brush with a celebrity
Delivering bad (or good) news

LOW-ENERGY DRINKS

LeLIEVRE

6

EXAMPLE

Pointing to Instances

◀ **Examples in a cartoon**

This cartoon by Glen Le Lievre, first published in *The New Yorker*, uses the method of example in a complex way. Most simply, the drawings propose instances of the general category stated in the title — imaginary "low-energy drinks." At the same time, the humor of the examples comes from their contrast with real caffeine-laced high-energy drinks such as Xtreme Shock Fruit Punch, Jolt Cola, Zippfizz Liquid Shot, and AMP High Energy Overdrive. Whom are these drinks marketed to? (Consider visiting a grocery store or a gas station minimart to see some samples up close.) Whom does their marketing ignore? How would you express the general idea of Le Lievre's cartoon?

THE METHOD

"There have been many women runners of distinction," a writer begins, and quickly goes on, "among them Joan Benoit Samuelson, Grete Waitz, Florence Griffith Joyner, and Uta Pippig."

You have just seen examples at work. An EXAMPLE (from the Latin *exemplum*: "one thing selected from among many") is an instance that reveals a whole type. By selecting an example, a writer shows the nature or character of the group from which it is taken. In a written essay, examples will often serve to illustrate a general statement, or GENERALIZATION. Here, for instance, the writer Linda Wolfe makes a point about the food fetishes of Roman emperors (Domitian and Claudius ruled in the first century AD).

> The emperors used their gastronomical concerns to indicate their contempt of the country and the whole task of governing it. Domitian humiliated his cabinet by forcing them to attend him at his villa to help solve a serious problem. When they arrived he kept them waiting for hours. The problem, it finally appeared, was that the emperor had just purchased a giant fish, too large for any dish he owned, and he needed the learned brains of his ministers to decide whether the fish should be minced or whether a larger pot should be sought. The emperor Claudius one day rode hurriedly to the Senate and demanded they deliberate the importance of a life without pork. Another time he sat in his tribunal ostensibly administering justice but actually allowing the litigants to argue and orate while he grew dreamy, interrupting the discussions only to announce, "Meat pies are wonderful. We shall have them for dinner."

Wolfe might have allowed the opening sentence of her paragraph — the TOPIC SENTENCE — to remain a vague generalization. Instead, she supports it with three examples, each a brief story of an emperor's contemptuous behavior. With these examples, Wolfe not only explains and supports her generalization but also animates it.

The method of giving examples — of illustrating what you're saying with a "for instance" — is not merely helpful to all kinds of writing; it is indispensable. Writers who bore us, or lose us completely, often have an ample supply of ideas; their trouble is that they never pull their ideas down out of the clouds. A dull writer, for instance, might declare, "The emperors used food to humiliate their governments," and then, instead of giving examples, go on, "They also manipulated their families," or something — adding still another large, unillustrated idea. Specific examples are *needed* elements in effective prose. Not only do they make ideas understandable, but they also keep readers from falling asleep.

Example   **173**

THE PROCESS
The Generalization and the Thesis

Examples illustrate a generalization, such as Linda Wolfe's opening statement about the Roman emperors. Any example essay is bound to have such a generalization as its THESIS, expressed in a THESIS STATEMENT. Here are two examples from the essays in this chapter:

> Sometimes I think we would be better off [in dealing with social problems] if we forgot about the broad strokes and concentrated on the details.
> — Anna Quindlen, "Homeless"

> That first encounter, and those that followed, signified that a vast, unnerving gulf lay between nighttime pedestrians — particularly women — and me.
> — Brent Staples, "Black Men and Public Space"

The thesis statement establishes the backbone, the central idea, of an essay developed by example. Then the specifics bring the idea down to earth for readers.

The Examples

An essay developed by example will often start with an example or two. That is, you'll see something — a man pilfering a quarter for bus fare from a child's lemonade stand, a friend kissing another friend's fiancé (or fiancée) — and your observation will suggest a generalization (perhaps a statement about how people mishandle ethical dilemmas). But a mere example or two probably won't demonstrate your generalization for readers and thus won't achieve your PURPOSE. For that you'll need a range of instances.

Where do you find more? In anything you know — or care to learn. Start close to home. Seek examples in your own immediate knowledge and experience. Explore your conversations with others, your studies, and the storehouse of information you have gathered from books, newspapers, radio, TV, and the Internet as well as from popular hearsay: proverbs and sayings, popular songs, bits of wisdom you've heard voiced in your family.

Now and again, you may feel an irresistible temptation to make up an example out of thin air. Suppose you have to write about the benefits — any benefits — that recent science has conferred on society. You might imagine one such benefit: the prospect of one day being able to vacation in outer space and drift about like a soap bubble. That imagined benefit would be all right, but it is obviously a conjecture that you dreamed up. An example from fact or experience is likely to carry more weight. Do a little digging on the Internet or in recent books and magazines. Your reader will feel better informed to be told that science — specifically, the NASA space program — has produced useful inventions. You add:

> Among these are the smoke detector, originally developed as Skylab equipment; the inflatable air bag to protect drivers and pilots, designed to cushion astronauts in splashdowns; a walking chair that enables paraplegics to mount stairs and travel over uneven ground, derived from the moonwalkers' surface buggy; the technique of cryosurgery, the removal of cancerous tissue by fast freezing.

By using specific examples like these, you render the idea of "benefits to society" more concrete and more definite. Such examples are not prettifications of your essay; they are necessary if you are to hold your readers' attention and convince them that you are worth listening to.

When giving examples, you'll find other methods useful. Sometimes, as in the paragraph by Linda Wolfe, an example takes the form of a NARRATIVE (Chap. 4): an ANECDOTE or a case history. Sometimes an example embodies a vivid DESCRIPTION of a person, place, or thing (Chap. 5).

Lazy writers think, "Oh well, I can't come up with any example here — I'll just leave it to the reader to find one." The flaw in this ASSUMPTION is that the reader may be as lazy as the writer. As a result, a perfectly good idea may be left suspended in the stratosphere.

FOCUS ON SENTENCE VARIETY

While accumulating and detailing examples during drafting, you may find yourself writing strings of similar sentences:

> UNVARIED   One example of a movie about a disease is *In the Forest*. Another example is *The Beating Heart*. Another is *Tree of Life*. These three movies treat misunderstood or little-known diseases in a way that increases the viewer's sympathy and understanding. *In the Forest* deals with a little boy who suffers from cystic fibrosis. *The Beating Heart* deals with a middle-aged woman who is weakening from multiple sclerosis. *Tree of Life* deals with a father of four who is dying from AIDS. All three movies show complex, struggling human beings caught blamelessly in desperate circumstances.

The writer of this paragraph was clearly pushing to add examples and to expand them — both essential tasks — but the resulting passage needs editing so that the writer's labor isn't so obvious. In the more readable and interesting

Example   **175**

revision, the sentences vary in structure, group similar details, and distinguish the specifics from the generalizations:

> VARIED Three movies dealing with disease are *In the Forest, The Beating Heart,* and *Tree of Life.* In these movies people with little-known or misunderstood diseases become subjects for the viewer's sympathy and understanding. A little boy suffering from cystic fibrosis, a middle-aged woman weakening from multiple sclerosis, a father of four dying from AIDS — these complex, struggling human beings are caught blamelessly in desperate circumstances.

CHECKLIST FOR REVISING AN EXAMPLE ESSAY

✔ **Generalization.** What general statement do your examples illustrate? Will it be clear to readers what ties the examples together?

✔ **Support.** Do you have enough examples to establish your generalization, or will readers be left needing more?

✔ **Specifics.** Are your examples detailed? Does each capture some aspects of the generalization?

✔ **Relevance.** Do all your examples relate to your generalization? Should any be cut because they go off track?

✔ **Sentence variety.** Have you varied sentence structures for clarity and interest?

EXAMPLES IN ACADEMIC WRITING

An Economics Textbook

The following paragraph from *Microeconomics,* by Lewis C. Solmon, appears amid the author's explanation of how markets work. To dispel what might seem like clouds of theory, the author here brings an abstract principle down to earth with a concrete and detailed example.

The primary function of the market is to bring together suppliers and demanders so that they can trade with one another. Buyers and sellers do not necessarily have to be in face-to-face contact; they can signal their desires and intentions through various
$\rfloor$ Generalization to be illustrated

intermediaries. For example, the demand for green beans in California is not expressed directly by the green bean consumers to the green bean growers. People who want green beans buy them at a grocery store; the store orders them from a vegetable wholesaler; the wholesaler buys them from a bean cooperative, whose manager tells local farmers of the size of the current demand for green beans. The demanders of green beans are able to signal their demand schedule to the original suppliers, the farmers who raise the beans, without any personal communication between the two parties.

Single extended example

A Job-Application Letter

To obtain the kinds of jobs a college education prepares you for, you'll submit a résumé that presents your previous work experience, your education, and your qualifications for a specific career field. To capture the prospective employer's interest, you'll introduce yourself and your résumé with a cover letter.

Rather than merely repeat or summarize the contents of a résumé, a job-application letter highlights the connections between your background and the employer's need for someone with particular training and skills. Typically brief and tightly focused on the job in question, an application letter aims to persuade the reader to look at the accompanying résumé and then to follow up with an interview.

When college junior Kharron Reid was applying for a summer internship implementing computer networks for businesses, he put together a résumé tailored for a specific opportunity posted at his school's placement office. (See the résumé on p. 326.) His cover letter, opposite, pulls out examples from the résumé to support the statement (in the second-to-last paragraph) that "my education and my hands-on experience with network development have prepared me for the opening you have."

Example 177

137 Chester St., Apt. E
Allston, MA 02134
February 21, 2014

Ms. Dolores Jackson
Human Resources Director
E-line Systems
75 Arondale Avenue
Boston, MA 02114

Dear Ms. Jackson:

I am applying for the network development internship in your information technology department, advertised in the career services office of Boston University.

Introduction states purpose of letter

I have considerable experience in network development from summer internships at NBS Systems and at Pioneer Networking. At NBS I planned and laid the physical platforms and configured the software for seven WANs on Windows Server 2012. At Pioneer, I laid the physical platforms and configured the software to connect eight workstations into a LAN. Both internships gave me experience in every stage of network development.

Generalization about experience

Two examples of experience

In my three years in Boston University's School of Management, I have concentrated on developing skills in business administration and information systems. I have completed courses in organizational behavior, computer science (including programming), and networking and data communications. At the same time, I have become proficient in Unix, Windows 8/7/Vista, Windows Server 2012/2008, and Red Hat Enterprise Linux.

Generalization about education and skills

Two sets of examples about education and skills

As the enclosed résumé indicates, my education and my hands-on experience with network development have prepared me for the opening you have.

Concluding paragraphs summarize qualifications, refer reader to résumé, and invite a response

I am available for an interview at your convenience. Please call me at (617) 555-4009 or e-mail me at kreid@bu.edu.

Sincerely,

Kharron Reid

Kharron Reid

KELLIE YOUNG

Kellie Young was born and raised in Honolulu, Hawaii, where she attended the Iolani School and volunteered at hospitals over summer breaks. As a Presidential Scholar at the Massachusetts Institute of Technology, she worked as a researcher in the school's biomedical and chemical engineering labs, served as co-president of the Southeast Asian Service Leadership Network, and played on the water polo team. Young graduated in 2011 with a BS in chemical-biological engineering and is currently studying medicine at the University of California at San Francisco. An avid reader, she also loves movies, kites, and ketchup.

The Undercurrent

Young wrote the following essay in her sophomore year in response to a writing assignment that prompted her to reflect on events or emotions that shaped her into the person she is. Focusing on a legacy of incessant and sometimes irrational worries, Young examines her mother's enduring influence on her own thoughts and actions. "The Undercurrent" was selected for the 2010 edition of *Angles*, MIT's annual anthology of exemplary student writing.

In the essay following this one, "XO9," Michael Chabon also shows an interest in family influence on behavior but considers a different kind of mental quirk.

> *The future destiny of a child is always the work of the mother.*
> — Napoleon Bonaparte

The tires crunch heavily over the rocky path, crackling in the still morning air. The truck's headlights flood the darkness in front of us, slicing through the heavy veil to illuminate an unpaved road overshadowed with sweeping branches. When the car has gone as far as it can, we kill the engine and let the silence engulf us. We slip off our seats, tuck our surfboards under our arms, and creep through the trees until the sharp rocks beneath our feet smooth out into fine sand. Only black shadows on the beach, we are utterly and completely alone, blending in with the deepness of the sky and sea.

Quickly, before the sun rises.

Hannah rushes out to meet the black water, her body and board colliding recklessly onto the rough surf. I hesitate before leaping in after her. My stomach flips as the cold Pacific swallows me up, but even more striking is my mother's voice that begins to scream in my mind, freezing me in the water.

You're going to get swept out by the undertow! You're going to get eaten alive by   4
a tiger shark! The coral is poisonous! Get one shard in your toe and you're going to
have to chop it off — the entire thing! What are you thinking? Do you want to die?
Come home!

"I'm going to be fine, this is fine, nothing's wrong, everything's okay," I   5
chant in time to my thrumming heart, as my arms pull me further from home.
I paddle away from my mother, but her voice only becomes muted, a humming
background that does not fade until my arms are outstretched on a perfect
wave, greeting the day.

My mother's voice has been a constant presence throughout my life, from   6
when I was little ("Kellie, get down from that stool! You're going to fall off
and break your leg!") up through high school ("No, you cannot go to that
concert — what if someone starts a mosh pit and you get crushed?"). My life's
roadmap is littered with my mother's interjections and fears about the horrible things that can happen in life. Everything constitutes a risk, and as sentient beings, we should know better than to take those risks that could (and
would!) prematurely cut short our lives. No one better embraces Murphy's
Law[1] than my mother. Her love is thick and binding, and as my mother, she
has always felt responsible for my personal safety; her love constantly drew me
back ("Kellie, did you hear what I said?").

How could I *not* hear?   7

Her cautious attitude toward me was not unfounded. When I was young,   8
I was the maverick. I launched into situations without hesitation, tackling
all obstacles, physical or otherwise, by tucking my chin down and charging
forward. Once in December, when I was twelve, a great and wonderful lightning storm blacked out the bright afternoon sky. Angry, gray clouds blotted
out all semblance of time and the rain fell so thick I could not make out my
neighbor's plumeria tree growing just outside my window. Naturally I ran outside. I slammed the front door behind me, welcoming this phenomenon by
whooping and hollering down the street. I had never seen lightning so close
before; the electric charge in the air felt energizing. It was only after my T-shirt
stuck to my chest and shivers trembled through my body that I discovered the
locked door. My parents found their cold and slightly sick child shivering on
the front steps when they pulled into their driveway later that day.

---

[1] Murphy's Law is a fundamental principle normally associated with pessimists. The law
basically says that if anything can go wrong, it will ("Murphy's Law"). There is a sense of doom
and uncontrollable fate associated with the law and its principles.

My thoughtlessness was a danger to myself, my mother concluded, and ⁹ she determined that if I lacked the capacity to think ahead, she would do it for me. Now whenever I see electric storms, I imagine those poor souls unlucky enough to be struck down by those lightning bolts of doom.

My mother's reach, however, has always extended far beyond natural ¹⁰ disasters and the obvious everyday life-threatening situations. I have often imagined a rapist or mugger waiting in the shadows to attack me as I walked by myself on a sidewalk of a lonely street. Even if I were with a bunch of friends at the mall, my mother's voice would scream at me to stay away from all suspicious-looking adults. If I accidentally looked into strangers' eyes, crazy, irrational thoughts would immediately flood my mind. They were kidnappers, ready to seize me and hold me for an obscenely large ransom, which my parents would have to pay to retrieve their most beloved daughter, forcing the entire family into the utter depths of poverty. Public restrooms were equally dangerous. The toilet seat was swarming with germs so terrible that if I were unfortunate enough to touch the seat with my bare skin, I would contract a disease and die too quickly for doctors to make a saving diagnosis. It would be a tragic death, and at my funeral my mother would cry out in sorrow, "If only she had used a toilet seat cover!" My induced vigilance in public restroom hygiene has called for excessive amounts of the finite paper resources in the stall. For this I am certain that I am on the hit list of countless custodians under the alias: "girl who clogged the toilet with twenty seat covers and yards of toilet paper."

I often feel overwhelmed with the number of decisions that seem to over- ¹¹ run my life, each demanding an extraordinary amount of thought and contemplation. With my mother's voice insisting on caution, I often find myself torn between several paths, trying to project which road will lead me to the best outcome. Once an ingenious, spontaneous idea strikes me, it is abruptly and violently reeled back in. My friends often throw up their hands in despair as I wage war with a restaurant menu. Often I stare between the listed options, calculating the value of each potential meal according to price, nutritional content, and taste, before ordering. "Yes, that is my final answer." After living eighteen years in a house filled with my mother's warnings and cautionary instructions, I unconsciously had begun incorporating her perspective into my own.

Whereas I had been the somewhat unwilling recipient of this seeming ¹² oversensitivity, my mother's situation as a child-adult fostered the growth of these ideals for the survival of her family in a new world. When my grandfather immigrated to paradise with his first wife, he found that life did not simply improve with tropical sunshine and democracy. When his first spouse died, leaving behind four teenagers, he returned to China and brought my grandmother and my mom back home with him to Hawaii. With my grand-mother taking care of the first family, my mother was left to care for herself and her three younger sisters. She was brilliant at juggling work at her father's general store in rainy Manoa and schoolwork, graduating from high school as the top mathematics scholar. Her decisions were all based on taking care of her family, making sure lunches were packed, laces tied, and her sisters equipped with everything her family could afford. In fact, my mom and dad's first date was picking up my aunt from school. My mother's hardships taught her to be cautious and to make wise choices.

Having everything (two parents who do not believe in corporal punish-ment, a financially stable home, abundant opportunities for obtaining a good education), I am buffered from the reality that so educated my mother. Our middle-class status put me at the bottom of this learning curve. Since I could not be poor, my mother made her voice my teacher, hoping I could learn from her what she had learned from life. "Are you listening to me, Kellie?" 13

The home is now empty. All three of my older siblings are in medical school and one is even married. I am the youngest of her followers and am so far from home (a twelve-hour flight with stopovers, six time zones, an ocean, a continent away). In the winter, when I stare out my window at the grey, frozen courtyard covered in brown snow, my mother is staring out of our home win-dow at the brilliant, bright blue sky hanging over the sparkling Pacific Ocean. 14

At the end of summer 2007 when I was at the airport, not at all ready for MIT, my mother checked (four times) the gate and boarding time, even though I had already checked (four times). Separated by towering metal detectors and the mob of people being herded through them, my mom and I shouted our parting farewells. However, our real good-bye was minutes before I turned my phone off for boarding in the form of a text message: "Don't fall asleep at your connection. Someone might steal your laptop. Love you." 15

My mother's voice in my head is something I cannot shake or hide from, but neither is it confining or oppressing. I can sneak out in the morning to surf dawn patrol and meet the eyes of strangers in malls or bars. However, I make these decisions fully aware, consciously, and carefully. Even with so many miles between us now, she is everywhere I go; she is the undercurrent pulling my thoughts, her thoughts, to the forefront of my mind. She slows down my recklessness, throwing caution and wisdom back into the whirlwind of my mind. Although at times her/my fears catch me, freezing me momen-tarily before I leap, she is me, and her voice steers me clear of jumps I realize I cannot make. 16

When my dad is working at the office, my mom sometimes comes home early by herself. All her life, she has always looked after someone, making sure shoelaces are tied and lunches packed. Looking at her spotless house, which 17 in my younger years was fondly nicknamed "pigsty," she likes to call me to talk about her day, my day, and what I should be doing with my life ("Are you studying for the MCATs?"). Occasionally the line phases into static, the airwaves between Boston and Honolulu too filled with distance, and when it's over, my mom will always be frantic on the other end saying, "Kellie? Hello? Can you hear me? Are you still listening?"

"Yup, still listening, go ahead."

18

Work Cited

"Murphy's Law." *WordNet.* Princeton University, June 2010. Web. July 30, 2010.

For a reading quiz, visit **bedfordstmartins.com/thebedfordreader.**

Journal Writing

Young writes about the strong influence her mother has had on her thoughts, on her actions, and on her very sense of who she is. Who has been the strongest influence in your life? It might be a parent, or perhaps another relative, a friend, a religious figure, a celebrity of some sort. Think about what this person has meant to you and how he or she has influenced you, in ways both good and bad. Jot down your musings in your journal. (To take your journal writing further, see "From Journal to Essay" on the facing page.)

Questions on Meaning

1. What do you make of the title of this essay? What is an undercurrent, and what does it have to do with Young's subject? (If necessary, look up *undercurrent* in a dictionary.)
2. What would you say is Young's PURPOSE in this essay? Is it primarily to entertain readers by depicting an obsession, or does she seem to have another purpose in mind?
3. Young explains some of the reasons for her mother's constant worrying in paragraph 12. PARAPHRASE the background information she provides. What circumstances brought Young's mother to Hawaii? Why was she, as a girl, responsible for taking care of three children?
4. What is Young's THESIS? Does she seem to consider her mother's influence on her mostly negative or mostly positive? Explain.

Questions on Writing Strategy

1. Why do you think Young opens her essay as she does? What is the EFFECT of this introduction?
2. What assumptions does the author make about her AUDIENCE?
3. "The Undercurrent" includes quite a few examples. How does Young maintain UNITY and COHERENCE in her essay?
4. **OTHER METHODS**   Where in the essay does Young use NARRATION to relate stories about her experiences? What do these ANECDOTES contribute to her point?

Questions on Language

1. Why does Young quote her mother so extensively? What would the essay lose without this dialog?
2. Point to some instances of hyperbole in the essay. (For a definition of *hyperbole*, see FIGURES OF SPEECH in Useful Terms.) What does Young's language contribute to her TONE?
3. Find definitions of the following words: interjections, sentient (par. 6); maverick, plumeria (8); induced, vigilance, hygiene, finite (10); ingenious (11); corporal, buffered (13).
4. Why do you think Young repeats the parenthetical phrase "(four times)" in paragraph 15?

Suggestions for Writing

1. **FROM JOURNAL TO ESSAY**   Drawing on your journal entry and using your experiences as EVIDENCE, write an essay that explains the influence of a particular person on your identity and behavior. Your essay may be serious or humorous, but it should include plenty of details and focus on CAUSE AND EFFECT.
2. The ability to read other people's and our own thoughts is a key element of emotional intelligence, a relatively new concept that is often evoked in the fields of psychology and education to help people improve their work and life skills. Search your library catalog and databases for books and articles about emotional intelligence; then write a brief DEFINITION of the concept. Consider as well your own emotional intelligence and how you could improve it.
3. **CRITICAL WRITING**   ANALYZE Young's use of humor in this essay. What is it that makes her essay funny? In particular, consider her use of hyperbole, irony, and humorous IMAGES. You might also do some library or Internet research on humor writing to further support your analysis.
4. **CONNECTIONS**   The next essay, Michael Chabon's "XO9," also uses examples to make a point about obsessive thoughts and behaviors. What are some of the similarities and differences in the examples the two writers use? In a brief essay, explore whether and how the examples they choose lead them to different conclusions.

MICHAEL CHABON

Often characterized as a literary rebel, Michael Chabon defies boundaries of genre and style. Born in 1963 in Washington, DC, he grew up in Columbia, Maryland, graduated from the University of Pittsburgh in 1984, and completed his MFA at the University of California at Irvine. A frequent contributor to periodicals ranging in seriousness from *McSweeney's* to the *Paris Review*, Chabon has published two collections of short fiction, two collections of essays, several television and movie screenplays, works of science fiction and fantasy, detective stories, and a serial comic book — all of them consistently praised for their high literary quality. Chabon is probably best known, however, for his bittersweet novels exploring young men's coming of age, especially *The Mysteries of Pittsburgh* (1988), *Wonder Boys* (1995), and *The Amazing Adventures of Kavalier and Clay* (2000), the last of which won the 2001 Pulitzer Prize for fiction. His most recent work, *Telegraph Avenue* (2012), is a comic novel set in a used record store in Chabon's current home of Berkeley, California.

XO9

Whatever genre he tackles, Chabon has a reputation for crafting prose that is inventive and poetic. In this personal essay from *Manhood for Amateurs: The Pleasures and Regrets of a Husband, Father, and Son* (2009), he uses examples to ponder manifestations of obsessive-compulsive disorder among members of his family. Like Kellie Young (p. 178), he discovers that regardless of the frustrations they may bring, obsessions have their uses.

I swear I was twelve years old before my grandmother let me go into a men's room alone. If we were hanging around downtown Washington — and she was a great one for hanging around downtown, a flaneur in White Shoulders[1] and a black sweater set — she used to smuggle me into the ladies' lounge at Garfinckel's department store when I had to go to the bathroom, even if getting there required a twenty-block walk, and when I say *smuggled*, I mean *pushed me like a dollyload of bricks while loudly exhorting me to cut in front of the blind woman with the oxygen tank.* It had to be Garfinckel's, no matter how long a schlep that meant, because only there, amid the caged parakeets and the splendor of the ladies' lounge, did the standard of hygiene come even remotely

[1] A perfume. — EDS.

close to her own. The truth is that even Garfinckel's fell short. Before I was permitted to touch my flesh to the Garfinckel's toilet, she had to enter the stall like a fireman shouldering his way into a burning house, face grim and set, taking minimal sips of air through her nostrils, and wipe down the seat with a paper towel and the Lysol that at all times she kept in a small spray bottle in her handbag. When I was finished with my business, I was expected to summon her so that she could, with a single furious kick of her tiny foot, deploy the flush handle, flush handles being widely known to medical science as festering vectors of disease. Her spray bottle of Lysol came out on buses, too, to render the Naugahyde seats fit for contact, and she whipped it out whenever we went to sit on a bench in Dupont Circle for a session of her favorite pastime in that era: scowling at the "hippies" who gathered there and, in an undertone that was not especially low, mocking them. When she washed the dishes, she would encase each plate and fork in plastic wrap before returning it to the cabinet or drawer. She washed Dixie cups fresh from the package in soap and hot water. She had survived pogrom and transatlantic crossing and Depression and war, and she was not afraid of anything, least of all her son, my father, but she was terrified beyond reason of germs and bacteria.

When I was a kid I found this behavior fascinating, and as I got older, it was good for a laugh, but now I see that the poor woman was suffering from a form of obsessive-compulsive disorder: OCD, or XO9, as my younger son used to believe it was known. He was hearing a lot about XO9 and about my grandmother, because for a while my older son started believing that anything that happened to him on one side of his body — a pinch, a tickle, his mother's taking hold of his hand to cross a busy street — needed to happen right away on the other side of his body, too, or else he would feel "like I'm going to die." This particular form of the disorder, it turned out, meant he had symmetry issues, and there were other ones, including a brief but intense inability to get through five minutes of consciousness without mentioning cows at least once. These things mostly came and went, ramifying wildly, foliating like creepers through the kid's thoughts and, to some degree, the discourse of our family before fading with the help — help that my grandmother never received — of some fairly simple cognitive-therapy techniques and his grateful eagerness to try them. He was so relieved to learn that this thing could be named, could be talked about, that he began to feel better simply through the act of discussing it (which I think is why he consented immediately when I asked his permission to write about it).

This thing runs in families, and I can't help also seeing its signs in my father, an obsessively completist collector of stamps, coins, bubblegum cards, tobacco cards, autographs, Big Little Books, Ovaltine premiums, magazines, books, classical recordings — all kinds of stuff — the collections proliferating, branching off, some running their course, some enduring for decades. He's a man who cannot enter a room without aligning, or suppressing an overwhelming urge to align, the corners of books with the corners of tables they lie upon; a man whose neckties hang in a closet as neatly as the pipes of a church organ and whose desk drawers look like aerial photographs of a secret weapons facility in the Nevada desert.

My grandmother, my father, my son, and me. My few collections are   4
incomplete, I have braved hellish [toilets] without benefit or need of Lysol, and I have never experienced any bodily compulsions beyond those of my animal appetites. But I have this thing where I can't stop trying to fix something that's broken, some lock that won't open even with the right combination, some computer program that won't run or channel that won't TiVo — even if I have to stay up till four o'clock in the morning or miss out on the party in the next room to figure out what's wrong and how to repair it. Even if you resort to physically removing me from the vicinity of the problem, I will not be fully present in conversation or be able to sleep or find any savor in life whatsoever until I have solved it or, at long last, conceded defeat. Over the years certain random words or phrases, such as *Lampedusa, weasels,* and *Ted Kennedy,* have gotten trapped like flies in the casements of my brain and buzzed in fits for months or even years until some unknown hand threw up an invisible sash and they flew out. I must have said the word *monkeys* at least once a day for the past ten years, not counting references to actual simians or my children. And — this is not a boast — I rock. Davening, my wife calls it: steady, rapid, rhythmic rocking, sometimes fitful, sometimes continuous, from foot to foot when I'm standing, and from front to back when I'm sitting down. Rocking like a junkie who needs a fix, a madman on the subway, a devout Jew at prayer, a kid who really needs to pee.

I'm davening as I write these words, and it's always while I'm in the act   5
of writing that the impulse to rock grows strongest, that the rocking feels the best, the most necessary and right. The more easily the words come, the more wildly I rock. When I consider the problem-solving nature of writing fiction — how whatever book I happen to be working on is always broken, stuck, incomplete, a Yale lock that won't open, a subroutine that won't execute, yet day after day I return to it knowing that if I just keep at it, I will pop the thing loose — it begins to seem to me that writing may be in part a disorder: sheer, unfettered XO9. Look at Borges with his knives and his tigers, or Nabokov with his butterflies, or Irving with his bears, or Plath with her camps and her ovens;[2] look at every writer, writing the same damn story, the same poem,

---

[2] Jorge Luis Borges (1899–1986) was an Argentinean novelist, Vladimir Nabokov (1899–1977) was a Russian American novelist, John Irving (born 1942) is an American novelist, and Sylvia Plath (1932–63) was an American poet. — Eds.

returning endlessly to the same themes, the same motifs, the same locales, the same lost summer or girl or father, book after book. *Why do you keep writing about gay men who are friends with straight men?* people want to know. *Why are bad things always happening to dogs in your books? What's with all the sky similes? Why did you use the word* spavined, *like, seventeen times in one novel?* Sometimes I try to come up with sensible answers to these questions, logical explanations for these recurring tropes, motifs, and phrases, but in truth there's only one honest answer that a writer in the grip of XO9 can give:

I can't help it.   6

---

*For a reading quiz, visit **bedfordstmartins.com/thebedfordreader**.*

Journal Writing

Is there anything about your personality that you "can't help"? Do you, for example, worry incessantly, laugh when you're uncomfortable, eavesdrop when you know you shouldn't? Or perhaps you recognize in yourself something like one of the obsessive-compulsive behaviors Chabon writes about. In your journal, brainstorm a list of thoughts and actions you can't control, or keep a list for a few days of habits you notice in yourself. (To take your journal writing further, see "From Journal to Essay" on the next page.)

Questions on Meaning

1. What does "XO9" mean? Where does the term come from?
2. What is Chabon's THESIS? State the main idea of his essay in your own words.
3. Chabon mentions that his obsessive-compulsive son "was so relieved to learn that this thing could be named, could be talked about, that he began to feel better simply through the act of discussing it" (par. 2). What does this statement reveal about Chabon's PURPOSE for writing this essay?

Questions on Writing Strategy

1. Explain how the author organizes his examples. What forms did obsessive-compulsive disorder take in Chabon's grandmother, in his father, in his son, and in himself?
2. How seriously does Chabon expect readers to take his claim that "writing may be in part a disorder" (par. 5)? How can you tell?
3. What ASSUMPTIONS about his readers are evident in Chabon's choice of ALLUSIONS in paragraph 5? Do you need to be familiar with the works of the writers he cites to understand his point?

4. **OTHER METHODS**   What does COMPARISON AND CONTRAST contribute to Chabon's essay?

Questions on Language

1. Be sure you know how to define the following words: flaneur, dollyload, deploy, vectors, Naugahyde, pogrom (par. 1); ramifying, foliating (2); proliferating (3); casements, simians, davening (4); motifs, spavined, tropes (5).
2. Point out some of the FIGURES OF SPEECH Chabon uses in this essay. What metaphors or similes do you find particularly fresh and inventive?
3. Examine the language Chabon uses to describe each of his family member's afflictions, as well as his own. Is it OBJECTIVE? sympathetic? negative?

Suggestions for Writing

1. **FROM JOURNAL TO ESSAY**   Select one of the personality quirks you wrote about in your journal and consider why you behave the way you do. Are your thoughts and actions a matter of habit or of choice? Write an essay about the importance (or unimportance) of self-awareness and conscious decision making, using several concrete examples or a single extended example to support your point. You may refer to some of Chabon's ideas if you wish, but be sure to develop a unique THESIS of your own.
2. Chabon claims that many novelists and poets tend to return to the same themes over and over in their work. Have you noticed this to be true of any one writer you've read, whether for pleasure or for school? Think of a series of novels (or stories or poems) that you have enjoyed. Identify one such recurring motif and, in an essay, ANALYZE its meanings. Why do you suppose the writer keeps returning to it?
3. **CRITICAL WRITING**   Write an essay examining Chabon's TONE. Is it consistent throughout? Are there passages in which he seems self-pitying? mocking? determined? resigned? triumphant? What is the overall tone of the essay? Is it effective? Why?
4. **CONNECTIONS**   Compare and contrast the views of obsessions and their sources and consequences in Michael Chabon's "XO9" and Kellie Young's "The Undercurrent" (p. 178). Use specific passages from each essay to support your comparison.

Michael Chabon on Writing

In "Art of Cake," another essay in *Manhood for Amateurs*, Chabon writes, "cooking entails stubbornness and a tolerance — maybe even a taste — for last-minute collapse. You have to be able to enjoy the repeated and deliberate following of a more or less lengthy, more or less complicated series of steps whose product is very likely — after all that work, with no warning, right at the end — to curdle, sink, scorch, dry up, congeal, burn, or simply taste bad." Carolyn Kellogg, while interviewing him about the book for the *Los Angeles Times*, said of the passage, "I couldn't help wonder if you were also talking a little bit about writing." Chabon's response:

There's definitely a kinship there. . . . I do think writing is a lot like cooking. It might be possible to understand questions that usually get put in terms of things like "influence" and "aesthetic inheritance" and whether you're going to follow the rules or break the rules . . . in terms of recipes and cuisines.

As a cook, I came into this inheritance of different traditions: the American tradition, my Jewish tradition, my mother's family and the family she grew up in. My cooking kind of emerged from . . . a written inheritance, actual recipes written down by my mother and grandmother, and also in the cookbooks that became important to me. [But] I also involve my own approach, my own changes in recipe.

I think in a way, that's sort of what you're engaged in doing as a writer, too. You come into this inheritance of things that have been done and the ways in which they have been done, and people who influence you sort of pass along what they think is important, and what they think you need to know how to do. But over time you begin to make changes, what you think are improvements or alterations, because you like the way it comes out better. In that sense, there's less a question of rejecting or accepting the past, less an anxiety of influence kind of thing, than there is an evolution of your own culinary style as applied to language and storytelling.

You tend to make the things you like to eat. For example, I don't care for fish terribly much, so I don't waste a lot of time trying to figure out how to prepare it. As a writer, I try to write books that I think I would love to read. You cook the foods you'd love to eat; you write the books you'd love to read.

For Discussion

1. What seems to be Chabon's take on the importance of following GENRE conventions while writing? What might be gained — or lost — by breaking "the rules"?
2. Extend Chabon's simile. In what other ways is writing "a lot like cooking"? Or, to take another tack, create and explain a new simile of your own: "Writing is a lot like _____."

ANNA QUINDLEN

Anna Quindlen was born in 1953 and graduated from Barnard College in 1974. She worked as a reporter for the *New York Post* and the *New York Times* before taking over the latter's "About New York" column, serving as the paper's deputy metropolitan editor, and in 1986 creating her own weekly column. In the early 1990s Quindlen wrote a twice-weekly op-ed column for the *Times* on social and political issues, earning a Pulitzer Prize for commentary in 1992. For ten years she wrote a biweekly column for *Newsweek* magazine. Her essays and columns are collected in *Living Out Loud* (1988), *Thinking Out Loud* (1993), and *Loud and Clear* (2004). Much of Quindlen's popular nonfiction — *How Reading Changed My Life* (1998), *A Short Guide to a Happy Life* (2000), and *Being Perfect* (2005) — takes a how-to bent. She has also published two books for children and six successful novels: *Object Lessons* (1991), *One True Thing* (1994), *Black and Blue* (1998), *Blessings* (2002), *Rise and Shine* (2006), and *Every Last One* (2010). Quindlen's memoir *Lots of Candles, Plenty of Cake* appeared in 2012. She lives in New York City.

Homeless

In this essay from *Living Out Loud,* Quindlen mingles a reporter's respect for details with a keen sense of empathy, using examples to explore a persistent social issue. When Quindlen wrote, in 1987, homelessness had become a severe and highly visible problem in New York City and elsewhere in the United States. The problem has not abated since then: Using government data, the National Alliance to End Homelessness estimates that more than 700,000 Americans are homeless on any given day.

Her name was Ann, and we met in the Port Authority Bus Terminal several Januarys ago. I was doing a story on homeless people. She said I was wasting my time talking to her; she was just passing through, although she'd been passing through for more than two weeks. To prove to me that this was true, she rummaged through a tote bag and a manila envelope and finally unfolded a sheet of typing paper and brought out her photographs.

They were not pictures of family, or friends, or even a dog or cat, its eyes brown-red in the flashbulb's light. They were pictures of a house. It was like a thousand houses in a hundred towns, not suburb, not city, but somewhere in between, with aluminum siding and a chain-link fence, a narrow driveway running up to a one-car garage and a patch of backyard. The house was yellow. I looked on the back for a date or a name, but neither was there. There was no need for discussion. I knew what she was trying to tell me, for it was something I had often felt. She was not adrift, alone, anonymous, although her bags and her raincoat with the grime shadowing its creases had made me believe she was. She had a house, or at least once upon a time had had one. Inside were curtains, a couch, a stove, potholders. You are where you live. She was somebody.

I've never been very good at looking at the big picture, taking the global 3 view, and I've always been a person with an overactive sense of place, the legacy of an Irish grandfather. So it is natural that the thing that seems most wrong with the world to me right now is that there are so many people with no homes. I'm not simply talking about shelter from the elements, or three square meals a day or a mailing address to which the welfare people can send the check — although I know that all these are important for survival. I'm talking about a home, about precisely those kinds of feelings that have wound up in cross-stitch and French knots on samplers over the years.

Home is where the heart is. There's no place like it. I love my home with 4 a ferocity totally out of proportion to its appearance or location. I love dumb things about it: the hot-water heater, the plastic rack you drain dishes in, the roof over my head, which occasionally leaks. And yet it is precisely those dumb things that make it what it is — a place of certainty, stability, predictability, privacy, for me and for my family. It is where I live. What more can you say about a place than that? That is everything.

Yet it is something that we have been edging away from gradually during 5 my lifetime and the lifetimes of my parents and grandparents. There was a time when where you lived often was where you worked and where you grew the food you ate and even where you were buried. When that era passed, where you lived at least was where your parents had lived and where you would live with your children when you became enfeebled. Then, suddenly where you lived was where you lived for three years, until you could move on to something else and something else again.

And so we have come to something else again, to children who do not 6 understand what it means to go to their rooms because they have never had a room, to men and women whose fantasy is a wall they can paint a color of their own choosing, to old people reduced to sitting on molded plastic chairs, their skin blue-white in the lights of a bus station, who pull pictures of houses out of their bags. Homes have stopped being homes. Now they are real estate.

People find it curious that those without homes would rather sleep sitting 7 up on benches or huddled in doorways than go to shelters. Certainly some prefer to do so because they are emotionally ill, because they have been locked in before and they are damned if they will be locked in again. Others are afraid of the violence and trouble they may find there. But some seem to want something that is not available in shelters, and they will not compromise, not for a cot, or oatmeal, or a shower with special soap that kills the bugs. "One room," a woman with a baby who was sleeping on her sister's floor, once told me, "painted blue." That was the crux of it; not size or location, but pride of ownership. Painted blue.

This is a difficult problem, and some wise and compassionate people are   8
working hard at it. But in the main I think we work around it, just as we walk around it when it is lying on the sidewalk or sitting in the bus termi‐ nal — the problem, that is. It has been customary to take people's pain and lessen our own participation in it by turning it into an issue, not a collection of human beings. We turn an adjective into a noun: the poor, not poor people; the homeless, not Ann or the man who lives in the box or the woman who sleeps on the subway grate.

Sometimes I think we would be better off if we forgot about the broad   9
strokes and concentrated on the details. Here is a woman without a bureau. There is a man with no mirror, no wall to hang it on. They are not the home‐ less. They are people who have no homes. No drawer that holds the spoons. No window to look out upon the world. My God. That is everything.

---

*For a reading quiz, visit **bedfordstmartins.com/thebedfordreader**.*

Journal Writing

What does the word *home* mean to you? Does it involve material things, privacy, fam‐ ily, a sense of permanence? In your journal, explore your ideas about this word. (To take your journal writing further, see "From Journal to Essay" on the next page.)

Questions on Meaning

1. What is Quindlen's THESIS?
2. What distinction is Quindlen making in her CONCLUSION with the sentences "They are not the homeless. They are people who have no homes"?
3. Why does Quindlen believe that having a home is essential?

Questions on Writing Strategy

1. Why do you think Quindlen begins with the story of Ann? How else might Quindlen have begun her essay?
2. What is the EFFECT of Quindlen's examples about her own home?

3. What key ASSUMPTIONS does the author make about her AUDIENCE? Are the assumptions reasonable? Where does she specifically address an assumption that might undermine her view?
4. How does Quindlen vary the sentences in paragraph 7 that give examples of why homeless people avoid shelters?
5. **OTHER METHODS**   Quindlen uses examples to support an ARGUMENT. What position does she want readers to recognize and accept?

Questions on Language

1. What is the effect of "My God" in the last paragraph?
2. How might Quindlen be said to give new meaning to the old CLICHÉ "Home is where the heart is" (par. 4)?
3. What is meant by "crux" (par. 7)? Where does the word come from?

Suggestions for Writing

1. **FROM JOURNAL TO ESSAY**   Write an essay that gives a detailed DEFINITION of *home* by using your own home(s), hometown(s), or experiences with home(s) as supporting examples. (See Chap. 12 if you need help with definition.)
2. Have you ever moved from one place to another? What sort of experience was it? Write an essay about leaving an old home and moving to a new one. Was there an activity or a piece of furniture that helped ease the transition?
3. Write an essay on the problem of homelessness in your town or city. Use examples to support your view of the problem and a possible solution.
4. **CRITICAL WRITING**   Write a brief essay in which you agree or disagree with Quindlen's assertion that a home is "everything." Can one, for instance, be a fulfilled person without a home? In your answer, take account of the values that might underlie an attachment to home; Quindlen mentions "certainty, stability, predictability, privacy" (par. 4), but there are others, including some (such as fear of change) that are less positive.
5. **CONNECTIONS**   Quindlen makes an emphatic distinction between "the homeless" and "people who have no homes" (par. 9). Read William Lutz's "The World of Doublespeak" (p. 337), which examines how language can be used to distort our perceptions of unpleasant truths. Drawing on what he and Quindlen have to say, write an essay that explores how the way we label a problem like homelessness influences what solutions we may (or may not) be able to find.

Anna Quindlen on Writing

Anna Quindlen started her writing career as a newspaper reporter. "I had wanted to be a writer for most of my life," she recalls in the introduction to her book *Living Out Loud*, "and in the service of the writing I became a reporter. For many years I was able to observe, even to feel, life vividly, but at secondhand. I was able to stand over the chalk outline of a body on a sidewalk dappled with black blood; to stand behind the glass and look down into an operating theater where one man was placing a heart in the yawning chest of another; to sit in the park on the first day of summer and find myself professionally obligated to record all the glories of it. Every day I found answers: who, what, when, where, and why."

Quindlen was a good reporter, but the business of finding answers did not satisfy her personally. "In my own life," she continues, "I had only questions." Then she switched from reporter to columnist at the *New York Times*. It was "exhilarating," she says, that "my work became a reflection of my life. After years of being a professional observer of other people's lives, I was given the opportunity to be a professional observer of my own. I was permitted — and permitted myself — to write a column, not about my answers, but about my questions. Never did I make so much sense of my life as I did then, for it was inevitable that as a writer I would find out most clearly what I thought, and what I only thought I thought, when I saw it written down. . . . After years of feeling secondhand, of feeling the pain of the widow, the joy of the winner, I was able to allow myself to feel those emotions for myself."

For Discussion

1. What were the advantages and disadvantages of news reporting, according to Quindlen?
2. What did Quindlen feel she could accomplish in a column that she could not accomplish in a news report? What evidence of this difference do you see in her essay "Homeless"?

BRENT STAPLES

Brent Staples is a member of the editorial board of the *New York Times*. Born in 1951 in Chester, Pennsylvania, Staples has a BA in behavioral science from Widener University in Chester and a PhD in psychology from the University of Chicago. Before joining the *New York Times* in 1985, he worked for the *Chicago Sun-Times,* the *Chicago Reader, Chicago* magazine, and *Down Beat* magazine. At the *Times,* Staples writes on culture, politics, reading, and special education, advocating for children with learning disabilities. He has also contributed to the *New York Times Magazine, New York Woman, Ms., Harper's,* and other magazines. His memoir, *Parallel Time: Growing Up in Black and White,* appeared in 1994.

Black Men and Public Space

"Black Men and Public Space" first appeared in the December 1986 issue of *Harper's* magazine and was then published, in a slightly different version, in Staples's memoir, *Parallel Time.* To explain a recurring experience of African American men, Staples relates incidents when he has been "an avid night walker" in the urban landscape. Sometimes his only defense against others' stereotypes is to whistle.

My first victim was a woman — white, well dressed, probably in her late 1 twenties. I came upon her late one evening on a deserted street in Hyde Park, a relatively affluent neighborhood in an otherwise mean, impoverished section of Chicago. As I swung onto the avenue behind her, there seemed to be a discreet, uninflammatory distance between us. Not so. She cast back a worried glance. To her, the youngish black man — a broad six feet two inches with a beard and billowing hair, both hands shoved into the pockets of a bulky military jacket — seemed menacingly close. After a few more quick glimpses, she picked up her pace and was soon running in earnest. Within seconds she disappeared into a cross street.

That was more than a decade ago. I was twenty-two years old, a graduate 2 student newly arrived at the University of Chicago. It was in the echo of that terrified woman's footfalls that I first began to know the unwieldy inheritance I'd come into — the ability to alter public space in ugly ways. It was clear that she thought herself the quarry of a mugger, a rapist, or worse. Suffering a bout of insomnia, however, I was stalking sleep, not defenseless wayfarers. As a softy who is scarcely able to take a knife to a raw chicken — let alone hold one to a person's throat — I was surprised, embarrassed, and dismayed all at once. Her flight made me feel like an accomplice in tyranny. It also made it clear that I was indistinguishable from the muggers who occasionally seeped into the area from the surrounding ghetto. That first encounter, and those that followed, signified that a vast, unnerving gulf lay between nighttime pedestrians — particularly women — and me. And I soon gathered that being perceived as dangerous is a hazard in itself. I only needed to turn a corner into a dicey situation, or crowd some frightened, armed person in a foyer somewhere, or make an errant move after being pulled over by a policeman. Where fear and weapons meet — and they often do in urban America — there is always the possibility of death.

In that first year, my first away from my hometown, I was to become thoroughly familiar with the language of fear. At dark, shadowy intersections, I could cross in front of a car stopped at a traffic light and elicit the *thunk, thunk, thunk, thunk* of the driver — black, white, male, or female — hammering down the door locks. On less traveled streets after dark, I grew accustomed to but never comfortable with people crossing to the other side of the street rather than pass me. Then there were the standard unpleasantries with policemen, doormen, bouncers, cabdrivers, and others whose business it is to screen out troublesome individuals *before* there is any nastiness.

I moved to New York nearly two years ago and I have remained an avid night walker. In central Manhattan, the near-constant crowd cover minimizes tense one-on-one street encounters. Elsewhere — in SoHo, for example, where sidewalks are narrow and tightly spaced buildings shut out the sky — things can get very taut indeed.

After dark, on the warrenlike streets of Brooklyn where I live, I often see women who fear the worst from me. They seem to have set their faces on neutral, and with their purse straps strung across their chests bandolier-style, they forge ahead as though bracing themselves against being tackled. I understand, of course, that the danger they perceive is not a hallucination. Women are particularly vulnerable to street violence, and young black males are drastically overrepresented among the perpetrators of that violence. Yet these truths are no solace against the kind of alienation that comes of being ever the suspect, a fearsome entity with whom pedestrians avoid making eye contact.

It is not altogether clear to me how I reached the ripe old age of twenty-two without being conscious of the lethality nighttime pedestrians attributed to me. Perhaps it was because in Chester, Pennsylvania, the small, angry industrial town where I came of age in the 1960s, I was scarcely noticeable against a backdrop of gang warfare, street knifings, and murders. I grew up one of the good boys, had perhaps a half-dozen fistfights. In retrospect, my shyness of combat has clear sources.

As a boy, I saw countless tough guys locked away; I have since buried several, too. They were babies, really — a teenage cousin, a brother of twenty-two, a childhood friend in his mid-twenties — all gone down in episodes of bravado played out in the streets. I came to doubt the virtues of intimidation early on. I chose, perhaps unconsciously, to remain a shadow — timid, but a survivor.

The fearsomeness mistakenly attributed to me in public places often has a   8
perilous flavor. The most frightening of these confusions occurred in the late 1970s and early 1980s, when I worked as a journalist in Chicago. One day, rushing into the office of a magazine I was writing for with a deadline story in hand, I was mistaken for a burglar. The office manager called security and, with an ad hoc posse, pursued me through the labyrinthine halls, nearly to my editor's door. I had no way of proving who I was. I could only move briskly toward the company of someone who knew me.

Another time I was on assignment for a local paper and killing time before   9
an interview. I entered a jewelry store on the city's affluent Near North Side. The proprietor excused herself and returned with an enormous red Doberman pinscher straining at the end of a leash. She stood, the dog extended toward me, silent to my questions, her eyes bulging nearly out of her head. I took a cursory look around, nodded, and bade her good night.

Relatively speaking, however, I never fared as badly as another black male   10
journalist. He went to nearby Waukegan, Illinois, a couple of summers ago to work on a story about a murderer who was born there. Mistaking the reporter for the killer, police officers hauled him from his car at gunpoint and but for his press credentials would probably have tried to book him. Such episodes are not uncommon. Black men trade tales like this all the time.

Over the years, I learned to smother the rage I felt at so often being taken   11
for a criminal. Not to do so would surely have led to madness. I now take pre-cautions to make myself less threatening. I move about with care, particularly late in the evening. I give a wide berth to nervous people on subway platforms during the wee hours, particularly when I have exchanged business clothes for jeans. If I happen to be entering a building behind some people who appear skittish, I may walk by, letting them clear the lobby before I return, so as not to seem to be following them. I have been calm and extremely congenial on those rare occasions when I've been pulled over by the police.

And on late-evening constitutionals I employ what has proved to be an   12
excellent tension-reducing measure: I whistle melodies from Beethoven and Vivaldi and the more popular classical composers. Even steely New Yorkers hunching toward nighttime destinations seem to relax, and occasionally they even join in the tune. Virtually everybody seems to sense that a mugger wouldn't be warbling bright, sunny selections from Vivaldi's *Four Seasons*. It is my equivalent of the cowbell that hikers wear when they know they are in bear country.

*For a reading quiz, visit **bedfordstmartins.com/thebedfordreader**.*

Journal Writing

Staples explains how he perceives himself altering public space. Write in your journal about a time when you felt as if *you* altered public space — in other words, you changed people's attitudes or behavior just by being in a place or entering a situation. If you haven't had this experience, write about a time when you saw someone else alter public space in this way. (To take your journal writing further, see "From Journal to Essay" on the facing page.)

Questions on Meaning

1. What is the PURPOSE of this essay? Do you think Staples believes that he (or other African American men) will cease "to alter public space in ugly ways" (par. 2) in the near future? Does he suggest any long-term solution for "the kind of alienation that comes of being ever the suspect" (5)?
2. In paragraph 5 Staples says he understands that the danger women fear when they see him "is not a hallucination." Do you take this to mean that Staples perceives himself to be dangerous? Explain.
3. Staples says, "I chose, perhaps unconsciously, to remain a shadow — timid, but a survivor" (par. 7). What are the usual CONNOTATIONS of the word *survivor*? Is "timid" one of them? How can you explain this apparent discrepancy?

Questions on Writing Strategy

1. The concept of altering public space is relatively abstract. How does Staples convince you that this phenomenon really takes place?
2. Staples employs a large number of examples in a fairly short essay. How does he avoid having the piece sound like a list? How does he establish COHERENCE among all these examples? (Look, for example, at details and TRANSITIONS.)
3. **OTHER METHODS** Many of Staples's examples are actually ANECDOTES — brief NARRATIVES. The opening paragraph is especially notable. Why is it so effective?

Questions on Language

1. What does the author accomplish by using the word *victim* in the essay's opening line? Is the word used literally? What TONE does it set for the essay?
2. Be sure you know how to define the following words, as used in this essay: affluent, uninflammatory (par. 1); unwieldy, tyranny, pedestrians (2); intimidation (7); congenial (11); constitutionals (12).

3. The word *dicey* (par. 2) comes from British slang. Without looking it up in your dictionary, can you figure out its meaning from the context in which it appears?

Suggestions for Writing

1. **FROM JOURNAL TO ESSAY**   Write an essay narrating your experience of either altering public space yourself or being a witness when someone else did so. What changes did you observe in people's behavior? Was your behavior similarly affected? In retrospect, do you think your reactions were justified?
2. Write an essay using examples to show how a trait of your own or of someone you know well always seems to affect people, whether positively or negatively.
3. The ironic term *DWB* ("driving while black") expresses the common perception that African American drivers are more likely than white drivers to be pulled over by authorities for minor infractions — or no infraction at all. Research and write an essay about the accuracy of this perception in one state or municipality: Is there truth to it? If African Americans have been discriminated against, what if anything has government done to address the problem?
4. **CRITICAL WRITING**   Consider, more broadly than Staples does, what it means to alter public space. Staples would rather not have the power to do so, but it *is* a power, and it could perhaps be positive in some circumstances (wielded by a street performer, for instance, or the architect of a beautiful new building on campus). Write an essay that expands on Staples's idea and examines the pros and cons of altering public space. Use specific examples as your EVIDENCE.
5. **CONNECTIONS**   Like Brent Staples, Gloria Naylor, in "The Meanings of a Word" (p. 412), considers misplaced hostility toward African Americans. In an essay, COMPARE AND CONTRAST the POINTS OF VIEW of these two authors. How does point of view affect each author's selection of details and tone?

Brent Staples on Writing

In comments written especially for this book, Brent Staples talks about the writing of "Black Men and Public Space": "I was only partly aware of how I felt when I began this essay. I knew only that I had this collection of experiences (facts) and that I felt uneasy with them. I sketched out the experiences one by one and strung them together. The bridge to the essay — what I wanted to say, but did not know when I started — sprang into life quite unexpectedly as I sat looking over these experiences. The crucial sentence comes right after the opening anecdote, in which my first 'victim' runs away from me: 'It was in the echo of that terrified woman's footfalls that I first began to know the unwieldy inheritance I'd come into — the ability to alter public space in ugly ways.' 'Aha!' I said. 'This is why I feel bothered and hurt and frustrated when this happens. I don't want people to think I'm stalking them. I want some fresh air. I want to stretch my legs. I want to be as anonymous as any other person out for a walk in the night.'"

A news reporter and editor by training and trade, Staples sees much similarity between the writing of a personal essay like "Black Men and Public Space" and the writing of, say, a murder story for a daily newspaper. "The newspaper murder," he says, "begins with standard newspaper information: the fact that the man was found dead in an alley in such-and-such a section of the city; his name, occupation, and where he lived; that he died of gunshot wounds to such-and-such a part of his body; that arrests were or were not made; that such-and-such a weapon was found at the scene; that the police have established no motive; etc.

"Personal essays take a different tack, but they, too, begin as assemblies of facts. In 'Black Men and Public Space,' I start out with an anecdote that crystallizes the issue I want to discuss — what it is like to be viewed as a criminal all the time. I devise a sentence that serves this purpose and also catches the reader's attention: 'My first victim was a woman — white, well dressed, probably in her late twenties.' The piece gives examples that are meant to illustrate the same point and discusses what those examples mean.

"The newspaper story stacks its details in a specified way, with each piece taking a prescribed place in a prescribed order. The personal essay begins often with a flourish, an anecdote, or the recounting of a crucial experience, then goes off to consider related experiences and their meanings. But both pieces rely on reporting. Both are built of facts. Reporting is the act of finding and analyzing facts.

"A fact can be a state of the world — a date, the color of someone's eyes, the arc of a body that flies through the air after having been struck by a car. A fact can also be a feeling — sorrow, grief, confusion, the sense of being pleased, offended, or frustrated. 'Black Men and Public Space' explores the relationship between two sets of facts: (1) the way people cast worried glances at me and sometimes run away from me on the streets after dark, and (2) the frustration and anger I feel at being made an object of fear as I try to go about my business in the city."

Personal essays and news stories share one other quality as well, Staples thinks: They affect the writer even when the writing is finished. "The discoveries I made in 'Black Men and Public Space' continued long after the essay was published. Writing about the experiences gave me access to a whole range of internal concerns and ideas, much the way a well-reported news story opens the door onto a given neighborhood, situation, or set of issues."

For Discussion

1. In recounting how he developed his essay, what does Staples reveal about his writing process?
2. How, according to Staples, are essay writing and news writing similar? How are they different?
3. What does Staples mean when he says that "writing about the experiences gave me access to a whole range of internal concerns and ideas"?

ADDITIONAL WRITING TOPICS

Example

1. Select one of the following general statements, or set forth a general statement of your own that one of these inspires. Making it your central idea (or THESIS), support it in an essay full of examples. Draw your examples from your reading, your studies, your conversations, or your own experience.

    Compared to voice phone, text messaging has many advantages (or many disadvantages).

    Individual consumers can help slow down global climate change.

    People one comes to admire don't always at first seem likable.

    Good (or bad) habits are necessary to the nation's economy.

    Each family has its distinctive lifestyle.

    Certain song lyrics, closely inspected, promote violence.

    Graphic novels have become a serious form of literary art.

    At some point in life, most people triumph over crushing difficulties.

    Churchgoers aren't perfect.

    TV commercials suggest that buying the advertised product will improve your love life.

    Home cooking can't win over fast food (or vice versa).

    Ordinary lives sometimes give rise to legends.

    Some people I know are born winners (or losers).

    Books can change our lives.

    Certain machines *do* have personalities.

    Some road signs lead drivers astray.

2. In a brief essay, make a GENERALIZATION about the fears, joys, or contradictions that members of minority groups seem to share. To illustrate your generalization, draw examples from personal experience, from outside reading, or from two or three of the essays in this book by the following authors: Nancy Mairs (p. 12), Maya Angelou (p. 104), Amy Tan (p. 110), Junot Díaz (p. 120), Brent Staples (p. 195), Andrea Roman (p. 226), Firoozeh Dumas (p. 252), Gloria Naylor (p. 412), Christine Leong (p. 418), Linda Chavez (p. 454), Sherman Alexie (p. 494), and Martin Luther King, Jr. (p. 507). You might also find useful examples in the multimedia selections at *bedfordstmartins.com/thebedfordreader*, such as those by *National Geographic*, Luis Alberto Urrea, Jamaica Kincaid, and Schroeder Jones.

American Gothic, 1930, painting by Grant Wood, American, 1891–1942. Oil on beaverboard, 30 11/16 × 25 11/16 in. (78 × 65.3 cm) unframed, Friends of American Art Collection, 1930.934, The Art Institute of Chicago. Photography © The Art Institute of Chicago. Art © Figge Art Museum, successors to the Estate of Nan Wood Graham / Licensed by VAGA, New York, NY.

Rural Rehabilitation Client, photograph by Ben Shahn. © Corbis. Reprinted by permission.

7

COMPARISON AND CONTRAST

Setting Things Side by Side

◀ **Comparison and contrast in a painting and a photograph**

Created just five years apart, these works relate in time as well as subject. On the top, the painting *American Gothic,* by the Iowan Grant Wood (1892–1942), depicts farmers in 1930, before the Great Depression was fully under way. On the bottom, the photograph *Rural Rehabilitation Client,* by the Lithuanian-born New Jerseyan Ben Shahn (1899–1969), depicts recipients of a federal aid program in Arkansas in 1935, at the Depression's low point. Closely examine the people in each image (clothes, postures, expressions) and their settings. What striking and not-so-striking similarities do you notice? What is the most obvious difference? What are some more subtle differences? What does the medium of each work (painting versus photography) contribute to the differences? How would you summarize the visions of rural folk conveyed by Wood and Shahn?

THE METHOD

Should we pass laws to regulate pornography or just let pornography run wild? Which team do you place your money on, the Giants or the Patriots? To go to school full-time or part-time: What are the rewards and drawbacks of each way of life? How do the Republican and the Democratic platforms stack up against each other? How are the psychological theories of Carl Jung like or unlike those of Sigmund Freud? These are questions that may be addressed by the dual method of COMPARISON AND CONTRAST. In comparing, you point to similar features of the subjects; in contrasting, to different features. (The features themselves you identify by the method of DIVISION or ANALYSIS; see Chap. 9.)

In practice, comparison and contrast are usually inseparable because two subjects are generally neither entirely alike nor entirely unlike. When student writer Andrea Roman sets out to portray Bolivian and American cultures (p. 226), she considers both their similarities and their differences. Often, as in this case, the similarities make the subjects comparable at all and the differences make comparison worthwhile.

Uses of Comparison and Contrast

Comparison and contrast are especially helpful in academic writing. You can use the method in EXPOSITION to illuminate two or more subjects or in ARGUMENT to show why you prefer one thing to another, one course of action to another, one idea to another.

Because comparison and contrast reveal knowledge about the subjects, you will often be asked to use the method in exams that call for essay answers. Sometimes the examiner will come right out and say, "Compare and contrast nineteenth-century methods of treating drug addiction with those of the present day." Sometimes, however, comparison and contrast won't even be mentioned by name; instead, the examiner may ask, "What resemblances and differences do you find between John Updike's short story 'A & P' and the Grimm fairy tale 'Godfather Death'?" Or, "Explain the relative desirability of holding a franchise as against going into business as an independent proprietor." But those — as you realize when you begin to plan your reply — are just other ways of asking you to compare and contrast.

Purposes

A good essay in comparing and contrasting serves a PURPOSE. Most of the time, the writer of such an essay has one of two purposes in mind:

- **To explain the similarities and differences between two things,** the writer shows each of the subjects distinctly by considering both, side by side. With such a purpose, the writer doesn't necessarily find one of the subjects better than the other. In her essay on growing up Bolivian and American, Andrea Roman does not favor either culture but concludes that each contributes a positive element to her identity.

- **To choose between two things, or** EVALUATE **them,** the writer shows how one of the subjects is better than the other on the basis of some standard: Which of two films more convincingly captures the experience of being a teenager? Which of two chemical processes works better to clean waste water? To answer either question, the writer has to consider the features of both subjects — both the positive and the negative — and then choose the subject whose positive features more clearly predominate.

THE PROCESS

Subjects for Comparison

When you find yourself considering two subjects side by side or preferring one subject over another, you have already embarked on comparison and contrast. Just be sure that your two subjects display a clear basis for comparison. In other words, they should have something significant in common. Comparison usually works best with two of a kind: two means of reading for the visually impaired, two short stories on the same subject, two processes for cleaning waste water, two schools of political thought.

It can sometimes be effective to find similarities between evidently unlike subjects — a city and a country town, say — and a special form of comparison, ANALOGY, always equates two very unlike things, explaining one in terms of the other. In an analogy you might explain how the human eye works by comparing it to a simple camera, or you might explain the forces in a thunderstorm by comparing them to armies in battle. In *Cat-Friend vs. Dog-Friend* (*bedfordstmartins.com/thebedfordreader*), the comedy team of Fatawesome examines animal behaviors by imagining how they'd seem if our human companions acted the same way. In any comparison of unlike things, you must have a valid reason for bringing the two together — that is, the similarities must be significant. In a comparison of a city and a country town, for instance, the likenesses must extend beyond the obvious ones that people live in both places, both have streets and shops, and so on.

Basis for Comparison and Thesis

Beginning to identify the shared and dissimilar features of your subjects will get you started, but the comparison won't be manageable for you or interesting to your readers unless you also limit it. You would be overly ambitious to try to compare and contrast the Russian way of life with the American way of life in five hundred words; you couldn't include all the important similarities and differences. In a brief paper, you would be wise to select a single basis for comparison: to show, for instance, how day-care centers in Russia and the United States are both like and unlike each other.

This basis for comparison will eventually underpin the THESIS of your essay — the claim you have to make about the similarities and dissimilarities of two things or about one thing's superiority over another. Here, from essays in this chapter, are THESIS STATEMENTS that clearly lay out what's being compared and why:

> Neat people are lazier and meaner than sloppy people.
> — Suzanne Britt, "Neat People vs. Sloppy People"

> One would think that language would create the biggest barriers for immigrants but in my mother's case, the biggest obstacles were the small cultural differences.
> — Andrea Roman, "We're Not . . ."

Notice that each author not only identifies her subjects (neat and sloppy people, cultural differences) but also previews the purpose of the comparison, whether to evaluate (Britt) or to explain (Roman).

Organization

Even with a limited basis for comparison, the method of comparison and contrast can be tricky without some planning. We suggest that you make an outline (preferably in writing), using one of two organizations described below: subject by subject or point by point.

Say you're writing an essay on two guitarists, Jed and Jake. Your purpose is to explain the distinctive identities of the two players, and your thesis statement might be the following:

> Jed and Jake are both excellent guitarists whose differences reflect their training.

Here are the two ways you might arrange the body of your comparison:

- **Subject by subject.** Set forth all your facts about Jed, then do the same for Jake. Next, sum up their similarities and differences. In your conclusion, state what you think you have shown.

  1. *Jed*
     Training

Choice of instrument
Technical dexterity
Playing style

2. *Jake*
   Training
   Choice of instrument
   Technical dexterity
   Playing style

This procedure works for a paper of a few paragraphs, but for a longer one, it has a built-in disadvantage: Readers need to remember all the facts about subject 1 while they read about subject 2. If the essay is long and lists many facts, a subject-by-subject arrangement may be difficult to hold in mind.

- **Point by point.** Usually more workable in writing a long paper than the first method, the second scheme is to compare and contrast as you go. You consider one point at a time, taking up your two subjects alternately. In this way, you continually bring the subjects together, perhaps in every paragraph. Notice the differences in the outline:

1. *Training*
   Jed: self-taught
   Jake: classically trained

2. *Choice of instrument*
   Jed: electric
   Jake: acoustic

3. *Technical dexterity*
   Jed: highly skilled
   Jake: highly skilled

4. *Playing style*
   Jed: rapid-fire
   Jake: impressionistic

For either the subject-by-subject or the point-by-point scheme, your conclusion might be: Although similar in skills, the two differ greatly in aims and in personalities. Jed is better suited to a local bar and Jake to a concert hall.

By the way, a subject-by-subject organization works most efficiently for a *pair* of subjects. If you want to write about *three* guitarists, you might first consider Jed and Jake, then Jake and Josh, then Josh and Jed — but it would probably be easier to compare and contrast all three point by point.

Balance and Flexibility

A trick of comparison and contrast is to balance the treatment of both subjects while allowing them to breathe. You do have to give the subjects equivalence: You can't discuss Jed's on-stage manner without discussing Jake's, too. If you have nothing to say about Jake's on-stage manner, then you might as well omit the point. A surefire loser is the paper that proposes to compare and contrast two subjects but then proceeds to discuss quite different elements in each: Jed's playing style and Jake's choice of material, Jed's fondness for Italian food and Jake's hobby of antique-car collecting. The writer of such a paper doesn't compare and contrast the two musicians at all, but provides two quite separate discussions. To be sure you balance the subjects' features, keep an outline like the ones on the previous pages.

At the same time, don't let your outline dictate your every move. The reader of a mechanically written comparison-and-contrast essay comes to feel like a weary tennis spectator whose head has to swivel from side to side: now Jed, now Jake; now Jed again, now back to Jake. You need to mention the same features of both subjects, it is true, but no law decrees *how* you must mention them. You need not follow your outline in lockstep order, or cover similarities and differences at precisely the same length, or spend a hundred words on Jed's fingering skill just because you spend a hundred words on Jake's. As you write, keep casting your thoughts upon a living, particular world — not twisting and squeezing that world into a rigid scheme.

FOCUS ON PARALLELISM

With several points of comparison and alternating subjects, a comparison will be easier for your readers to follow if you emphasize likenesses and differences in your wording. Take advantage of the technique of parallelism discussed on page 44. *Parallelism* — the use of similar grammatical structures for elements of similar importance — balances a comparison and clarifies the relations between elements. At the same time, lack of parallelism can distract or confuse readers.

To make the elements of a comparison parallel, repeat the forms of related words, phrases, and sentences:

NONPARALLEL   Harris expects dieters who follow his plan to limit bread, dairy, and meat, while Marconi's diet forbids few foods.

PARALLEL   Harris's diet limits bread, dairy, and meat, while Marconi's diet forbids few foods.

NONPARALLEL   Harris emphasizes self-denial, but when following Marconi's plan you can eat whatever you want in moderation.

PARALLEL   Harris emphasizes self-denial, but <u>Marconi emphasizes</u> moderation.

NONPARALLEL   <u>If you want to lose weight quickly,</u> choose Harris's diet. <u>You'll have more success keeping the weight off if you</u> follow Marconi's plan.

PARALLEL   If you want to lose weight quickly, choose Harris's diet. <u>If you want to keep the weight off,</u> follow Marconi's plan.

CHECKLIST FOR REVISING A COMPARISON-AND-CONTRAST ESSAY

✔ **Purpose.** What is the aim of your comparison: to explain two subjects or to evaluate them? Will the purpose be clear to readers from the start?

✔ **Subjects.** Are the subjects enough alike, sharing enough features, to make comparison worthwhile?

✔ **Thesis.** Does your thesis establish a limited basis for comparison so that you have room and time to cover all the relevant similarities and differences?

✔ **Organization.** Does your arrangement of material, whether subject by subject or point by point, do justice to your subjects and help readers follow the comparison?

✔ **Balance and flexibility.** Have you covered the same features of both subjects? At the same time, have you avoided a rigid back-and-forth movement that could bore or exhaust a reader?

✔ **Parallelism.** Have you used parallel structure to clarify the subjects and points you are discussing?

COMPARISON AND CONTRAST IN ACADEMIC WRITING

A Communications Textbook

Taken from Steven McCornack's *Reflect and Relate*, the following point-by-point comparison explains a key difference between men and women. The in-text citations, in APA style (see the Appendix), refer readers to a list of sources provided at the end of McCornack's textbook.

<u>Immediately after birth, we begin a lifelong process of gender</u> <u>socialization, learning from others what it means personally, in-</u> <u>terpersonally, and culturally to be "male" or "female."</u> Girls are

> Point-by-point comparison supporting this topic sentence

typically taught feminine behaviors, such as sensitivity to one's own
and others' emotions, nurturance, and compassion (Lippa, 2002).
Boys are usually taught masculine behaviors, learning about asser-
tiveness, competitiveness, and independence from others. As a
result of gender socialization, men and women often end up forming
comparatively different self-concepts (Cross & Madson, 1997). For
example, women are more likely than men to perceive themselves as
connected to others and to assess themselves based on the quality of
these interpersonal connections. Men are more likely than women
to think of themselves as a composite of their individual achieve-
ments, abilities, and beliefs—viewing themselves as separate from
other people. At the same time, the existence of these differences
doesn't mean that all men and all women think of themselves in
identical ways. Many men and women appreciate and embrace both
feminine and masculine characteristics in their self-concepts.

1. First point:
Learned behaviors
Girls
Boys

2. Second point:
Self-concepts
Women
Men

A Review

If you browse the Web or flip through a newspaper, a magazine, or an academic journal, you're bound to spot a review: a writer's assessment of anything
from a restaurant to a scholarly book. Commonly assigned in college courses,
too, reviews rely most heavily on ANALYSIS, identifying and interpreting the
elements of a subject. But because a review EVALUATES quality or value, writers naturally turn to comparison and contrast as well, weighing two or more
products, works, or ideas to determine their relative worth. Such a comparison takes its evidence from the subjects themselves, as in descriptions of the
paintings in an exhibition or quotations from written works.

For a course in popular culture, Charlotte Pak wrote a lengthy review of
singer Beyoncé Knowles's solo career. Pak chose her subject because the enormously successful "Single Ladies (Put a Ring on It)" earned Beyoncé a reputation as a champion of women. Although Pak enjoyed the song, she found
herself bothered by some of the implications in its lyrics, and she decided
to investigate the singer's work for similar themes. In the paragraphs below,
excerpted from her full review, Pak compares "Single Ladies" with a popular
song from the 1960s, with unexpected results.

Critics and fans often view Beyoncé as one of the leaders in
the "strong woman" style that encourages female independence,
equality, and self-worth. These listeners offer Beyoncé's 2009 hit
"Single Ladies (Put a Ring on It)" as a symbol of how far women
have come since the 1950s and 1960s. But this and other songs
by Beyoncé just seem strong when in fact they present women

Basis for comparison:
portrayals of women's
strength

Subject-by-subject
organization supporting
this claim

who are no more independent than the ones portrayed half a
century ago.

  A classic example of the older style is the Dixie Cups' 1964
hit "Chapel of Love." The refrain of the song is familiar even
today: "Goin' to the chapel and we're / Gonna get married / . . .
Goin' to the chapel of love." The song itself seems sentimental
and even naive on the surface. In a sweet, dreamy voice, the
female singer imagines marital bliss, as "Birds all sing as if they
knew / Today's the day we'll say 'I do.' " She sings of marriage
as the fulfillment of her life, implying her dependence on a
man. Yet despite the tone and the sentimentality, the song also
suggests equality between the singer and her husband-to-be
within the bounds of traditional marriage: "I'll be his and he'll
be mine." The possession is mutual. Two independent individuals
will say "I do."

  In contrast, the singer in Beyoncé's "Single Ladies" seems
pleased to be free from an ex-boyfriend. She dances with another
man in a club while her ex jealously watches: "Don't pay him
any attention / 'Cause you had your turn and now you're gonna
learn / What it really feels like to miss me." Her tone is feisty
and no-nonsense, the voice of a sophisticated and independent
woman. Yet she remains preoccupied with her ex-boyfriend and
still sees herself through his eyes. In the song's chorus — "If
you like it then you shoulda put a ring on it" — the "it" suggests that she has a sense of herself as an object to be possessed rather than an independent being. That suggestion is
explicit in the lines "Pull me into your arms, / Say I'm the one
you own." The wimpy "Chapel of Love" at least offers an image
of equality. "Single Ladies" misleads by casting dependency as
strength.

Sidenotes:

1. Representative older song: "Chapel of Love" by the Dixie Cups

Quotations from song

Interpretation

2. Representative Beyoncé song: "Single Ladies (Put a Ring on It)"

Quotations from song

Interpretation

Concluding sentences express judgment

Comparison and Contrast

SUZANNE BRITT

Suzanne Britt was born in Winston-Salem, North Carolina, and studied at Salem College and Washington University, where she earned an MA in English. Britt has written for *Sky Magazine*, the *New York Times*, *Newsweek*, the *Boston Globe*, and many other publications. Her poems have been published in the *Denver Quarterly*, the *Southern Poetry Review*, and similar literary magazines. Britt teaches English at Meredith College in North Carolina and has published a history of the college and two English textbooks. Her other books are collections of her essays: *Skinny People Are Dull and Crunchy like Carrots* (1982) and *Show and Tell* (1983).

Neat People vs. Sloppy People

"Neat People vs. Sloppy People" appears in Britt's collection *Show and Tell*. Mingling humor with seriousness (as she often does), Britt has called the book a report on her journey into "the awful cave of self: You shout your name and voices come back in exultant response, telling you their names." In this essay, Britt uses comparison mainly to entertain by showing us aspects of our own selves, awful or not. For another approach to a similar subject, see the next essay, by Dave Barry.

1   I've finally figured out the difference between neat people and sloppy people. The distinction is, as always, moral. Neat people are lazier and meaner than sloppy people.

2   Sloppy people, you see, are not really sloppy. Their sloppiness is merely the unfortunate consequence of their extreme moral rectitude. Sloppy people carry in their mind's eye a heavenly vision, a precise plan, that is so stupendous, so perfect, it can't be achieved in this world or the next.

3   Sloppy people live in Never-Never Land. Someday is their métier. Someday they are planning to alphabetize all their books and set up home catalogs. Someday they will go through their wardrobes and mark certain items for tentative mending and certain items for passing on to relatives of similar shape and size. Someday sloppy people will make family scrapbooks into which they will put newspaper clippings, postcards, locks of hair, and the dried corsage from their senior prom. Someday they will file everything on the surface of their desks, including the cash receipts from coffee purchases at the snack

shop. Someday they will sit down and read all the back issues of *The New Yorker*.

For all these noble reasons and more, sloppy people never get neat. They 4 aim too high and wide. They save everything, planning someday to file, order, and straighten out the world. But while these ambitious plans take clearer and clearer shape in their heads, the books spill from the shelves onto the floor, the clothes pile up in the hamper and closet, the family mementos accumulate in every drawer, the surface of the desk is buried under mounds of paper, and the unread magazines threaten to reach the ceiling.

Sloppy people can't bear to part with anything. They give loving atten- 5 tion to every detail. When sloppy people say they're going to tackle the sur-face of a desk, they really mean it. Not a paper will go unturned; not a rubber band will go unboxed. Four hours or two weeks into the excavation, the desk looks exactly the same, primarily because the sloppy person is meticulously creating new piles of papers with new headings and scrupulously stopping to read all the old book catalogs before he throws them away. A neat person would just bulldoze the desk.

Neat people are bums and clods at heart. They have cavalier attitudes 6 toward possessions, including family heirlooms. Everything is just another dust-catcher to them. If anything collects dust, it's got to go and that's that. Neat people will toy with the idea of throwing the children out of the house just to cut down on the clutter.

Neat people don't care about process. They like results. What they want 7 to do is get the whole thing over with so they can sit down and watch the rasslin' on TV. Neat people operate on two unvarying principles: Never handle any item twice, and throw everything away.

The only thing messy in a neat person's house is the trash can. The min- 8 ute something comes to a neat person's hand, he will look at it, try to decide if it has immediate use and, finding none, throw it in the trash.

Neat people are especially vicious with mail. They never go through their 9 mail unless they are standing directly over a trash can. If the trash can is beside the mailbox, even better. All ads, catalogs, pleas for charitable contributions, church bulletins, and money-saving coupons go straight into the trash can without being opened. All letters from home, postcards from Europe, bills, and paychecks are opened, immediately responded to, then dropped in the trash can. Neat people keep their receipts only for tax purposes. That's it. No sentimental salvaging of birthday cards or the last letter a dying relative ever wrote. Into the trash it goes.

Neat people place neatness above everything, even economics. They are 10 incredibly wasteful. Neat people throw away several toys every time they walk through the den. I knew a neat person once who threw away a perfectly good dish drainer because it had mold on it. The drainer was too much trouble to wash. And neat people sell their furniture when they move. They will sell a La-Z-Boy recliner while you are reclining in it.

Neat people are no good to borrow from. Neat people buy everything in   11
expensive little single portions. They get their flour and sugar in two-pound bags. They wouldn't consider clipping a coupon, saving a leftover, reusing plastic nondairy whipped cream containers, or rinsing off tin foil and draping it over the unmoldy dish drainer. You can never borrow a neat person's newspaper to see what's playing at the movies. Neat people have the paper all wadded up and in the trash by 7:05 a.m.

Neat people cut a clean swath through the organic as well as the inorganic   12
world. People, animals, and things are all one to them. They are so insensitive. After they've finished with the pantry, the medicine cabinet, and the attic, they will throw out the red geranium (too many leaves), sell the dog (too many fleas), and send the children off to boarding school (too many scuff-marks on the hardwood floors).

*For a reading quiz, visit **bedfordstmartins.com/thebedfordreader**.*

Journal Writing

Britt suggests that grouping people according to oppositions, such as neat versus sloppy, reveals other things about them. Write about the oppositions you use to evaluate people. Smart versus dumb? Fit versus out of shape? Hip versus clueless? Rich versus poor? Outgoing versus shy? Open-minded versus narrow-minded? (To take your journal writing further, see "From Journal to Essay" on the facing page.)

Questions on Meaning

1. "Suzanne Britt believes that neat people are lazy, mean, petty, callous, wasteful, and insensitive." How would you respond to this statement?
2. Is the author's main PURPOSE to make fun of neat people, to assess the habits of neat and sloppy people, to help neat and sloppy people get along better, to defend sloppy people, to amuse and entertain, or to prove that neat people are morally inferior to sloppy people? Discuss.
3. What is meant by "as always" in the sentence "The distinction is, as always, moral" (par. 1)? Does the author seem to be suggesting that any and all distinctions between people are moral?

Questions on Writing Strategy

1. What is the general TONE of this essay? What words and phrases help you determine that tone?
2. Britt mentions no similarities between neat and sloppy people. Does that mean this is not a good comparison-and-contrast essay? Why might a writer deliberately focus on differences and give very little or no time to similarities?
3. Consider the following GENERALIZATIONS: "For all these noble reasons and more, sloppy people never get neat" (par. 4) and "The only thing messy in a neat person's house is the trash can" (8). How can you tell that these statements are generalizations? Look for other generalizations in the essay. What is the EFFECT of using so many?
4. How does Britt use repetition to clarify her comparison?
5. **OTHER METHODS**   Although filled with generalizations, Britt's essay does not lack for EXAMPLES. Study the examples in paragraph 11, and explain how they do and don't work the way they should: to bring the generalizations about people down to earth.

Questions on Language

1. Consult your dictionary for definitions of these words: rectitude (par. 2); métier, tentative (3); accumulate (4); excavation, meticulously, scrupulously (5); salvaging (9).
2. How do you understand the use of the word *noble* in the first sentence of paragraph 4? Is it meant literally? Are there other words in the essay that appear to be written in a similar tone?

Suggestions for Writing

1. **FROM JOURNAL TO ESSAY**   From your journal entry, choose your favorite opposition for evaluating people, and write an essay in which you compare and contrast those who pass your "test" with those who fail it. You may choose to write a tongue-in-cheek essay, as Britt does, or a serious one.
2. Write an essay in which you compare and contrast two apparently dissimilar groups of people: for example, blue-collar workers and white-collar workers, people who send a lot of text messages and people who don't bother with them, runners and football players, readers and TV watchers, or any other variation you choose. Your approach may be either lighthearted or serious, but make sure you come to some conclusion about your subjects. Which group do you favor? Why?
3. ANALYZE the similarities and differences between two characters in your favorite novel, story, film, or TV show. Which aspects of their personalities make them work well together, within the context in which they appear? Which characteristics work against each other, and therefore provide the necessary conflict to hold the reader's or viewer's attention?
4. **CRITICAL WRITING**   Britt's essay is remarkable for its exaggeration of the two types. Write a brief essay analyzing and contrasting the ways Britt characterizes

sloppy people and neat people. Be sure to consider the CONNOTATIONS of the words, such as "moral rectitude" for sloppy people (par. 2) and "cavalier" for neat people (6).

5. **CONNECTIONS**   Neither Suzanne Britt nor the author of the next essay, Dave Barry, seems to have much sympathy for neat people. Write a brief essay in which you explain why neatness matters. Or if you haven't a clue why, then write a brief essay in which you explain the benefits of dirt and disorder.

Suzanne Britt on Writing

Asked to tell how she writes, Suzanne Britt contributed the following comment for this book.

The question "How do you write?" gets a snappy, snappish response from me. The first commandment is "Live!" And the second is like unto it: "Pay attention!" I don't mean that you have to live high or fast or deep or wise or broad. And I certainly don't mean you have to live true and upright. I just mean that you have to suck out all the marrow of whatever you do, whether it's picking the lint off the navy-blue suit you'll be wearing to Cousin Ione's funeral or popping an Aunt Jemimah frozen waffle into the toaster oven or lying between sand dunes, watching the way the sea oats slice the azure sky. The ominous question put to me by students on all occasions of possible accountability is "Will this count?" My answer is rock bottom and hard: "Everything counts," I say, and silence falls like prayers across the room.

The same is true of writing. Everything counts. Despair is good. Numbness can be excellent. Misery is fine. Ecstasy will work — or pain or sorrow or passion. The only thing that won't work is indifference. A writer refuses to be shocked and appalled by anything going or coming, rising or falling, singing or soundless. The only thing that shocks me, truth to tell, is indifference. How dare you not fight for the right to the crispy end piece on the standing-rib roast? How dare you let the fragrance of Joy go by without taking a whiff of it? How dare you not see the old woman in the snap-front housedress and the rolled-down socks, carrying her Polident and Charmin in a canvas tote that says, simply, elegantly, Le Bag?

After you have lived, paid attention, seen connections, felt the harmony, writhed under the dissonance, fixed a Diet Coke, popped a big stick of Juicy Fruit in your mouth, gathered your life around you as a mother hen gathers her brood, as a queen settles the folds in her purple robes, you are ready to write. And what you will write about, even if you have one of those teachers who makes you write about, say, Guatemala, will be something very exclusive and intimate — something just between you and Guatemala. All you have to find out is what that small intimacy might be. It is there. And having found it, you have to make it count.

There is no rest for a writer. But there is no boredom either. A Sunday morning with a bottle of extra-strength aspirin within easy reach and an ice bag on your head can serve you very well in writing. So can a fly buzzing at your ear or a heart-stopping siren in the night or an interminable afternoon in a biology lab in front of a frog's innards.

All you need, really, is the audacity to believe, with your whole being, that if you tell it right, tell it truly, tell it so we can all see it, the "it" will play in Peoria, Poughkeepsie, Pompeii, or Podunk. In the South we call that conviction, that audacity, an act of faith. But you can call it writing.

For Discussion

1. What advice does Britt offer a student assigned to write a paper about, say, Guatemala? If you were that student, how would you go about taking her advice?
2. Where in her comment does the author use colorful and effective FIGURES OF SPEECH?
3. What is the TONE of Britt's remarks? Sum up her attitude toward her subject, writing.

DAVE BARRY

Dave Barry is a humorist whom the *New York Times* has called "the funniest man in America." Barry was born in 1947 in Armonk, New York, and graduated from Haverford College in 1969. He worked as a reporter for five years and lectured businesspeople on writing for eight years while he began to establish himself. As a columnist for the *Miami Herald* for two decades, Barry published humor writing that was syndicated in several hundred newspapers nationwide. He retired from his weekly column in 2005 but still writes occasional essays as well as a blog. He has published more than thirty books, including *Bad Habits: A 100% Fact Free Book* (1985), *The World According to Dave Barry* (1994), *Dave Barry's Money Secrets* (2006), *I'll Mature When I'm Dead* (2010), and *Lunatics* (2012) — the last a comic novel co-authored with fellow humorist Alan Zweibel. In 1988 Barry received the Pulitzer Prize for "distinguished commentary," although, he says, "nothing I've ever written fits the definition." (He thinks he won because his columns stood out from the "earthshakingly important" competition.) He lives in southern Florida.

Batting Clean-Up and Striking Out

This essay from *Dave Barry's Greatest Hits* (1988) illustrates Barry's gift, in the words of critic Alison Teal, "for taking things at face value and rendering them funny on those grounds alone, for rendering every ounce of humor out of a perfectly ordinary experience." Like Suzanne Britt in the previous essay, Barry contrasts two styles of dealing with a mess.

The primary difference between men and women is that women can see 1 extremely small quantities of dirt. Not when they're babies, of course. Babies of both sexes have a very low awareness of dirt, other than to think it tastes better than food.

But somewhere during the growth process, a hormonal secretion takes 2 place in women that enables them to see dirt that men cannot see, dirt at the level of *molecules*, whereas men don't generally notice it until it forms clumps large enough to support agriculture. This can lead to tragedy, as it did in the ill-fated ancient city of Pompeii, where the residents all got killed when the local volcano erupted and covered them with a layer of ash twenty feet deep.[1] Modern people often ask, "How come, when the ashes started falling, the Pompeii people didn't just *leave?*" The answer is that in Pompeii, it was the custom for the men to do the housework. They never even *noticed* the ash until it had for the most part covered the children. "Hey!" the men said (in Latin). "It's mighty quiet around here!" This is one major historical reason why, to this very day, men tend to do extremely little in the way of useful housework.

What often happens in my specific family unit is that my wife will say 3 to me: "Could you clean Robert's bathroom? It's filthy." So I'll gather up the Standard Male Cleaning Implements, namely a spray bottle of Windex and a wad of paper towels, and I'll go into Robert's bathroom, and it *always looks perfectly fine*. I mean, when I hear the word "filthy" used to describe a bathroom, I think about this bar where I used to hang out called Joe's Sportsman's Lounge, where the men's room had bacteria you could enter in a rodeo.

Nevertheless, because I am a sensitive and caring kind of guy, I "clean" 4 the bathroom, spraying Windex all over everything including the six hundred action figures each sold separately that God forbid Robert should ever take a bath without, and then I wipe it back off with the paper towels, and I go back to whatever activity I had been engaged in, such as doing an important project on the Etch-a-Sketch, and a little while later my wife will say: "I hate to rush you, but could you do Robert's bathroom? It's really *filthy.*" She is in there looking at the very walls I *just Windexed*, and she is seeing *dirt! Everywhere!* And if I tell her I already *cleaned* the bathroom, she gives me this look that she has perfected, the same look she used on me the time I selected Robert's outfit for school and part of it turned out to be pajamas.

The opposite side of the dirt coin, of course, is sports. This is an area 5 where men tend to feel very sensitive and women tend to be extremely callous. I have written about this before and I always get irate letters from women who say they are the heavyweight racquetball champion of someplace like Iowa and are sensitive to sports to the point where they could crush my skull like a ripe grape, but I feel these women are the exception.

A more representative woman is my friend Maddy, who once invited 6 some people, including my wife and me, over to her house for an evening of stimulating conversation and jovial companionship, which sounds fine except that this particular evening occurred *during a World Series game*. If you can imagine such a social gaffe.

We sat around the living room and Maddy tried to stimulate a conversa- 7 tion, but we males could not focus our attention on the various suggested

---

[1] Pompeii, in what is now southern Italy, was buried in the eruption of Mount Vesuvius in AD 79. — Eds.

topics because we could actually *feel* the World Series television and radio broadcast rays zinging through the air, penetrating right into our bodies, causing our dental fillings to vibrate, and all the while the women were behaving *as though nothing were wrong*. It was exactly like that story by Edgar Allan Poe where the murderer can hear the victim's heart beating louder and louder even though he (the murder victim) is dead, until finally he (the murderer) can't stand it anymore, and he just *has* to watch the World Series on television.[2] That was how we felt.

Maddy's husband made the first move, coming up with an absolutely brilliant means of escape: *He used their baby*. He picked up Justine, their seven-month-old daughter, who was fussing a little, and announced: "What this child needs is to have her bottle and watch the World Series." And just like that he was off to the family room, moving very quickly for a big man holding a baby. A second male escaped by pretending to clear the dessert plates. Soon all four of us were in there, watching the Annual Fall Classic, while the women prattled away about human relationships or something. It turned out to be an extremely pivotal game.

*For a reading quiz, visit **bedfordstmartins.com/thebedfordreader**.*

Journal Writing

Are you ever baffled by the behavior of members of the opposite sex — or members of your own sex, if you often find yourself behaving differently from most of them? List traits of men or women that you find foreign or bewildering, such as that they do or do not want to talk about their feelings or that they can spend countless hours watching sports on television or shopping. (To take your journal writing further, see "From Journal to Essay" on the facing page.)

Questions on Meaning

1. What is the PURPOSE of Barry's essay? How do you know?
2. How OBJECTIVE is Barry's portrayal of men and women? Does he seem to understand one sex better than the other? Does he seek to justify and excuse male sloppiness and antisocial behavior?

---

[2] Except for the World Series ending, Barry refers to Poe's story "The Tell-Tale Heart" (1843). — EDS.

3. What can you INFER about Barry's attitude toward the differences between the sexes? Does he see a way out?

Questions on Writing Strategy

1. Barry's comparison is organized point by point — differences in sensitivity to dirt, then differences in sensitivity to sports. What is the EFFECT of this organization? Or, from another angle, what would have been the effect of a subject-by-subject organization — just men, then just women (or vice versa)?
2. How does Barry set the TONE of this piece from the very first paragraph?
3. The first sentence looks like a THESIS STATEMENT but turns out not to be complete. Where does Barry finish his statement of the essay's thesis? Does it hurt or help the essay that the thesis is divided? Why?
4. How does the ALLUSION to Poe's "The Tell-Tale Heart" (par. 7) enhance Barry's own story?
5. In paragraph 5, how does Barry indicate that he's changing points of comparison?
6. **OTHER METHODS** How persuasive is the historical EXAMPLE cited in paragraph 2 as EVIDENCE for Barry's claims about men's and women's differing abilities to perceive dirt? Must examples always be persuasive?

Questions on Language

1. Define these words: hormonal (par. 2); implements (3); callous, irate (5); jovial, gaffe (6); prattled, pivotal (8).
2. Paragraph 4 begins with a textbook example of a run-on sentence. Does Barry need a better copy editor, or is he going for an effect here? If so, what is it?
3. What effect does Barry achieve with frequent italics (for example, *"just Windexed,"* par. 4) and capital letters ("Standard Male Cleaning Implements," 3)?
4. Why does Barry use the words *males* and *male* instead of *men* and *man* in paragraphs 7 and 8?

Suggestions for Writing

1. **FROM JOURNAL TO ESSAY** From the list you compiled in your journal, choose the trait of men or women that seems to have the most potential for humor. Write an essay similar to Barry's, exaggerating the difference to the point where it becomes the defining distinction between men and women.
2. How well do you conform to Barry's GENERALIZATIONS about your gender? In what ways are you stereotypically male or female? Do such generalizations amuse or merely annoy you? Why?
3. Considerable research has examined whether the differences between women and men are caused by heredity or by the environment. Explore some of this research, and write an essay ANALYZING what you discover. Based on your reading, do you think gender differences result primarily from biology or from social conditioning?

4. **CRITICAL WRITING**   Barry is obviously not afraid of offending women: He claims to have already done so (par. 5), and yet he persists. Do you take offense at any of this essay's stereotypes of women and men? If so, explain the nature of the offense as coolly as you can. Whether you take offense or not, can you see any virtue in using such stereotypes for humor? For instance, does the humor help undermine the stereotypes or merely strengthen them? Write an essay in which you address these questions, using quotations from Barry as examples and evidence.
5. **CONNECTIONS**   Write an essay about the humor gained from exaggeration, relying on Barry's essay and Suzanne Britt's "Neat People vs. Sloppy People" (p. 214). Why is exaggeration often funny? What qualities does humorous exaggeration have? Quote and PARAPHRASE from Barry's and Britt's essays for your support.

Dave Barry on Writing

For Dave Barry, coming up with ideas for humorous writing is no problem. "Just about anything's a topic for a humor column," he told an interviewer for *Contemporary Authors* in 1990, "any event that occurs in the news, anything that happens in daily life — driving, shopping, reading, eating. You can look at just about anything and see humor in it somewhere."

Writing challenges, for Barry, occur after he has his idea. "Writing has always been hard for me," he says. "The hard part is getting the jokes to come, and it never happens all at once for me. I very rarely have any idea where a column is going to go when it starts. It's a matter of piling a little piece here and a little piece there, fitting them together, going on to the next part, then going back and gradually shaping the whole piece into something. I know what I want in terms of reaction, and I want it to have a certain feel. I know when it does and when it doesn't. But I'm never sure when it's going to get there. That's what writing is. That's why it's so painful and slow. But that's more technique than anything else. You don't rely on inspiration — I don't, anyway, and I don't think most writers do. The creative process is just not an inspirational one for most people. There's a little bit of that and a whole lot of polishing."

A humor writer must be sensitive to readers, trying to make them smile, but Barry warns against catering to an audience. "I think it's a big mistake to write humor for anybody but yourself, to try to adopt any persona other than your own. If I don't at some point think something is funny, then I'm not going to write it." Not that his own sense of humor will always make a piece fly. "Thinking of it in rough form is one thing," Barry confesses, "and shaping and polishing it so that you like the way it reads is so agonizingly slow that

by the time you're done, you don't think anything is funny. You think this is
something you might use to console a widow."

More often, though, the shaping and polishing — the constant revision — do work. "Since I know how to do that," Barry says, "since I do it
every day of the week and have for years and years, I'm confident that if I keep
at it I'll get something."

For Discussion

1. Do you agree with Barry that "[y]ou can look at just about anything and see
   humor in it somewhere"? What topics might be off-limits for humor?
2. What does successful writing depend on, according to Barry? What role does
   inspiration play?
3. How might Barry's views on writing be relevant to your own experiences as a
   writer? What can a humor writer teach a college writer?

ANDREA ROMAN

The daughter of Bolivian immigrants, Andrea Roman was born in 1992 in Washington, DC, and grew up in Rockville, Maryland. She attended Saint Andrews Episcopal School, where she was captain of the varsity girls' soccer team and a volunteer medical translator. As a political science major at Boston College, she volunteers as a Big Sister of Greater Boston, serves on the cabinet for the school's Organization of Latin American Affairs, and remains "extremely devoted" to Caporales, a popular Bolivian folk dance. She expects to graduate in 2014.

"We're Not . . ."

Roman wrote "We're Not . . ." at the end of a first-year writing seminar. She revised it with feedback from her classmates and saw it selected for *Fresh Ink*, Boston College's annual collection of student writing. Assigned to write a personal narrative about a significant event in her life, she chose to focus on a series of disagreements with her mother. The resulting essay compares two important sides of the writer's identity.

"No somos pobres, Andrea. Para qué tienes que prestar ropa?"[1] These were words I heard continually from my mother as I grew up. My parents, being immigrants from Bolivia during the eighties, experienced a complete culture clash when they arrived in America. One would think that language would create the biggest barriers for immigrants but in my mother's case, the biggest obstacles were the small cultural differences. Sooner or later, this became a generic formula for strict rules given by my parents: "We're not _____, Andrea. Why do you have to _____?" Typically, the first blank was filled in by the word "American," while the second invariably changed. My mother could not understand that certain unacceptable actions in our culture were quite acceptable here in the States.

I was eleven years old when I first showed up at my house with an article of clothing that was not mine. I had spilled hot chocolate all over my sweater during lunch that day. Luckily, my best friend Emily had an extra zip-up in her locker. As any good friend would do, she offered me her sweater to wear for the rest of the day since it was the middle of December. Logically, I accepted the sweater with gratitude and went on with my day as if nothing strange had happened. Little did I know, when my mother picked me up from school, I would receive the familiar speech about how embarrassing my act had been.

---

[1] Spanish, "We're not poor, Andrea. Why do you have to borrow clothes?" — Eds.

"*De quien es esa chompa?!*" Those were the very first words that came out   3
of my mother's mouth. Not a breath, not an intake of air, just these words in
a ridiculing tone: "Whose sweater is that?!" I remained clueless and answered
the question, simply, "Emily's." Immediately after my answer, my mother gave
me one of the longest speeches I have ever heard. "We're not poor, Andrea.
Why do you have to borrow clothes? I buy you clothes. You have sweaters. You
wore one this morning!" I could not grasp the magnitude of my mother's anger
or disturbance as I did not see what the big deal was in borrowing a sweater.
Kids in my class did it all the time without any problem. They'd borrow a
sweater one day and give it back the other. It was as simple as that — but not
to my mother. "In Bolivia," my mother said, "we do not borrow clothes from
other people. It is seen as an insult to the family in saying that we cannot
afford to take care of our family. It's a want of an unnecessary thing seeing as
you already have your own." The speech went on and on, usually repeating
the same points, until I finally got a word in: "I stained my sweater. I had nothing to wear and was cold. I just don't see why it's such a big deal." Boy, was that
a mistake. Talking back to my mother was the worst thing I could have done.
The second I got home I got a good deep mouth-washing with dishwasher
soap as punishment.

"We're not American, Andrea. Why do you want a sleepover?" Sleepovers   4
were a big no to my family. In fact, they were unheard of. "You want to sleep
where?" If my girlfriends were having a slumber party over the weekend, I knew
better than to ask for permission. I learned this through multiple attempts
and failed experiences: "*Mami, puedo ir a dormir donde la Caroline este viernes,
porfa?*" "*Para qué?*" Great. Every time I asked to sleep over at a friend's house
my mother's response was always, "Why?"

So I would then respond, "Because all my friends are sleeping over and it's   5
going to be fun and her parents said we could all spend the night."

"Mmm, then no."   6

"*Pero por qué???*"   7

"*Te dije que no.*"[2]   8

And just like that my attempt to go to a sleepover would end.   9

"We're not American, Andrea. We don't do that in Bolivia. Everyone has   10
their own house for a reason. If you want to go over to Caroline's your father
will gladly take you and pick you up later tonight, but don't try to convince
him to stay over because it just won't work."

I suppose my mother letting me go to Caroline's for some time was better   11
than nothing, yet I always longed for that sleepover. Growing up, I quickly

---

[2] Spanish, "I told you no." — Eds.

learned that what my mother said was the rule in the household. After several attempts to attend a sleepover, I gave up — not because I didn't want to sleep over, but because I began to understand why my mother didn't want me to stay over.

Sunday, 1:00 p.m. My family is just getting out of church and deciding   12
where to go for lunch, when all of a sudden I remember that a six-page paper is due in class on Monday. I assume I had a stunned look on my face, because my mother asked what was wrong.

"Oh, nothing. I just remembered that I have an essay due tomorrow, so   13
I'll probably have to start working on that rather soon, if that influences our lunch decision."

"You mean to say that you left all your homework due Monday to do   14
today?"

"Yeah . . ."   15

"Why would you do that? Don't you know Sunday is family day? A day to   16
worship God and be thankful for family?"

"Yes . . ."   17

"Okay then, so you don't have any work due tomorrow right?"   18

"No, Mami, I just said I have an essay due."   19

"Sundays are not the day to leave homework for. That's why you get Fri-   20
day and Saturday. You have two days to complete it; there is no reason why you need Sunday, too."

Geesh. My mother sure did accumulate rules over the years.   21

"Okay, Mami, but I really have to do this essay now."   22

"Well you should have thought of that sooner, no?"   23

Silence overtook the car on our way home and I could feel the disappoint-   24
ment on my mother's face.

When I first arrived at Boston College, I immediately knew that my con-   25
servative cultural position would have to become more open-minded. I knew that not everyone had grown up with strict Bolivian parents, as I had. I would not have to lose my cultural identity, however.

As I lay in my new bed for the very first time in an unfamiliar room filled   26
with familiar things, I started to ask myself the same question that my hall mates confronted me with: "Why do you have such a big American flag?" This question constantly arose when I met someone. Why *did* I have an American flag next to my Bolivian one? My mother instilled Bolivian values in me; Bolivian culture was the only thing I had ever been exposed to, and I loved it. I had just bought this American flag a week before move-in day for my room decorations.

Through my mother's multiple rules, I had become comfortable enough   27
with my identity and culture that showing pride in another country would not
take away from my heritage. I now borrow clothes, have sleepovers, and do
a ton of work on Sundays, but I have not left behind that little Bolivian girl
who received the mouth-washing with dishwasher soap, no matter what flag
hangs on my wall.

For a reading quiz, visit **bedfordstmartins.com/thebedfordreader**.

Journal Writing

Write about a time when you were punished for an act that you didn't think was a
"big deal." What did you do, and what was the punishment? Was it fair? How did the
situation make you feel about your action? about whoever punished you? about yourself? about others involved, such as anyone who may have gotten you into trouble?
(To take your journal writing further, see "From Journal to Essay" on the next page.)

Questions on Meaning

1. What is Roman's THESIS? Where does she state it?
2. What seems to be Roman's PURPOSE in this essay? Does she mean to explain or to
   evaluate? How can you tell?
3. Why was Roman's mother so upset that her daughter borrowed a sweater from a
   classmate? What prompted her to wash Roman's mouth with soap?
4. Why does Roman hang two flags on the wall of her dorm room? What do they
   represent to her?

Questions on Writing Strategy

1. What is the function of the spaces between certain paragraphs in Roman's essay?
   What do they indicate?
2. Roman organizes her essay point by point. What points does she compare? What
   is her basis of comparison?
3. To whom does Roman seem to be writing? Why do you think so?
4. What is notable about Roman's concluding paragraph?
5. **OTHER METHODS**   Roman uses NARRATION to relate three telling episodes involving her mother. What does the dialog contribute to her essay?

Questions on Language

1. How does Roman ensure that English-speaking readers will understand the Spanish phrases she quotes in her essay? Are any statements left unclear to you?

2. Where in the essay does Roman include variations on her mother's complaint "We're not _____, Andrea. Why do you have to _____?" (par. 1)? What is the EFFECT of this repetition?
3. Consult a dictionary if necessary to learn the meanings of the following words: invariably (par. 1), magnitude (3), accumulate (21), instilled (26), heritage (27).

Suggestions for Writing

1. **FROM JOURNAL TO ESSAY** Based on your journal entry, write an essay in which you narrate your experience (or, perhaps, experiences) with being punished while growing up. As you plan and draft your essay, try to draw a larger point about the results of the punishment(s) on your sense of identity. What did you learn about yourself and the world around you?
2. Roman writes of differences with her mother that frustrated her but that also helped form her sense of identity. In a narrative and descriptive essay, relate some aspect of a relationship with a parent or other figure of authority that you found troubling or even maddening at the time but that now seems to have shaped you in positive ways. Did a parent (or someone else) push you to study when you wanted to play sports or hang out with your friends? make you attend religious services when they seemed unimportant to you? refuse to let you participate in certain activities? try to direct you onto a path that you didn't care to take?
3. **CRITICAL WRITING** Roman attributes many of her mother's attitudes to her Bolivian heritage. As an extension of the previous assignment, consider whether Roman's experiences are particular to Bolivian American families or are common in all families, whatever their ethnicity. Are conflicts between children and their parents inevitable, do you think? Why, or why not?
4. **CONNECTIONS** Roman's essay is one of several in this book that explore the experience of growing away from one's parents; other essays include Amy Tan's "Fish Cheeks" (p. 110), Brad Manning's "Arm Wrestling with My Father" (p. 138), Sarah Vowell's "Shooting Dad" (p. 146), Kellie Young's "The Undercurrent" (p. 178), Firoozeh Dumas's "Sweet, Sour, and Resentful" (p. 252), and Jamaica Kincaid's "Girl" (*bedfordstmartins.com/thebedfordreader*). Looking at one or two of these essays along with Roman's, compare and contrast the authors' relationships with their parents. How are the parents themselves and the authors' feelings similar or different? Use quotations or paraphrases from the essays as evidence for your ideas.

Andrea Roman on Writing

Asked how she chose the subject for "We're Not . . . ," Andrea Roman answered, "I had a lot of difficulty in deciding what to write about because truthfully, I didn't think I was all that interesting." Away from her family, she was painfully homesick and seriously contemplated moving back. Being assigned to write about an event in her life prompted Roman to think about why she was having such a hard time adjusting to college. "After a lot of self-reflection," she says, she pinpointed the source of her discomfort: While at home her "school-life was separate from home-life," at college "school *was* home." For the first time, she felt her "two cultures were colliding." The effort to "integrate" her "American and Bolivian lives," she decided, was a struggle worth exploring in writing.

Roman wrote two drafts and then, with "amazing help" from her teacher and her classmates, was able to "refine and refocus the most important aspects" of her experience. "They informed me of the parts they found most interesting," she explains, "so that I could expand on those specific ideas and events." By the time she was finished, she was gratified to discover that writing had "guided" her "in understanding and embracing the difficult time" she was having. Roman encourages other writers to always ask for feedback as well, particularly when writing about their own lives. "You lived through the story," she points out, "but no one else did. An outsider's perspective can highlight ambiguity and confusion" and help you "be as clear as possible."

The best advice Roman ever received? "Don't hold back, be true, and let yourself go." She explains why this mantra has proven so useful: "Our personal experiences and inspirations can never be taken away from us, and we should not shy away from telling our stories. If we do not share our obstacles and adversities, they will be lost and unheard. When you try to write what you think the audience wants, a feeling of forcedness is apparent. Inversely, when you write truthfully, genuineness becomes evident."

For Discussion

1. Have you ever found that writing about a difficult time helped you work through your problems?
2. What are the benefits — and drawbacks — of working with peer reviewers on your writing?
3. What do you think of Roman's advice to draft for yourself, rather than for readers? How can trying to please an audience result in "a feeling of forcedness"?

DAVID SEDARIS

Named Humorist of the Year 2001 by *Time* magazine, David Sedaris was born in 1957 and grew up in North Carolina. After graduating from the School of the Art Institute of Chicago in 1987, Sedaris taught writing there part-time and then moved to New York City, where he took various odd jobs. One of these jobs — a stint as a department-store Christmas elf — provided Sedaris with material for "The Santaland Diaries," the essay that launched his career as a humorist after he read it on National Public Radio's *Morning Edition* in 1993. Since then, Sedaris has contributed numerous commentaries to public radio's *Morning Edition* and *This American Life*, and his work appears frequently in *The New Yorker*, *Esquire*, and other magazines. He has published eight collections of essays and fiction, including *Me Talk Pretty One Day* (2000), *Dress Your Family in Corduroy and Denim* (2004), *When You Are Engulfed in Flames* (2008), and *Let's Explore Diabetes with Owls* (2013). In 2001 Sedaris received the Thurber Prize for American Humor. He lives in England.

Remembering My Childhood on the Continent of Africa

Many of Sedaris's essays locate comedy in exaggerated depictions of his basically normal North Carolina childhood. In this essay from *Me Talk Pretty One Day*, Sedaris highlights that normality by contrasting it with the distinctly unusual childhood of his partner.

When Hugh was in the fifth grade, his class took a field trip to an Ethiopian slaughterhouse. He was living in Addis Ababa at the time, and the slaughterhouse was chosen because, he says, "it was convenient."

This was a school system in which the matter of proximity outweighed such petty concerns as what may or may not be appropriate for a busload of eleven-year-olds. "What?" I asked. "Were there no autopsies scheduled at the local morgue? Was the federal prison just a bit too far out of the way?"

Hugh defends his former school, saying, "Well, isn't that the whole point of a field trip? To see something new?"

"Technically yes, but . . ."

"All right then," he says. "So we saw some new things."

One of his field trips was literally a trip to a field where the class watched a wrinkled man fill his mouth with rotten goat meat and feed it to a pack of waiting hyenas. On another occasion they were taken to examine the bloodied bedroom curtains hanging in the palace of the former dictator. There were tamer trips, to textile factories and sugar refineries, but my favorite is always the slaughterhouse. It wasn't a big company, just a small rural enterprise run by a couple of brothers operating out of a low-ceilinged concrete building. Following a brief lecture on the importance of proper sanitation, a small white piglet was herded into the room, its dainty hooves clicking against the concrete floor. The class gathered in a circle to get a better look at the animal, who seemed delighted with the attention he was getting. He turned from face to face and was looking up at Hugh when one of the brothers drew a pistol from his back pocket, held it against the animal's temple, and shot the piglet, execution-style. Blood spattered, frightened children wept, and the man with the gun offered the teacher and bus driver some meat from a freshly slaughtered goat.

When I'm told such stories, it's all I can do to hold back my feelings of   7
jealousy. An Ethiopian slaughterhouse. Some people have all the luck. When I was in elementary school, the best we ever got was a trip to Old Salem or Colonial Williamsburg, one of those preserved brick villages where time supposedly stands still and someone earns his living as a town crier. There was always a blacksmith, a group of wandering patriots, and a collection of bonneted women hawking corn bread or gingersnaps made "the ol'-fashioned way." Every now and then you might come across a doer of bad deeds serving time in the stocks, but that was generally as exciting as it got.

Certain events are parallel, but compared with Hugh's, my childhood was   8
unspeakably dull. When I was seven years old, my family moved to North Carolina. When he was seven years old, Hugh's family moved to the Congo. We had a collie and a house cat. They had a monkey and two horses named Charlie Brown and Satan. I threw stones at stop signs. Hugh threw stones at crocodiles. The verbs are the same, but he definitely wins the prize when it comes to nouns and objects. An eventful day for my mother might have involved a trip to the dry cleaner or a conversation with the potato-chip deliveryman. Asked one ordinary Congo afternoon what she'd done with her day, Hugh's mother answered that she and a fellow member of the Ladies' Club had visited a leper colony on the outskirts of Kinshasa. No reason was given for the expedition, though chances are she was staking it out for a future field trip.

Due to his upbringing, Hugh sits through inane movies never realizing   9
that they're often based on inane television shows. There were no poker-faced sitcom martians in his part of Africa, no oil-rich hillbillies or aproned brides trying to wean themselves from the practice of witchcraft. From time to time a movie would arrive packed in a dented canister, the film scratched and faded from its slow trip around the world. The theater consisted of a few dozen folding chairs arranged before a bedsheet or the blank wall of a vacant hangar out near the airstrip. Occasionally a man would sell warm soft drinks out of a cardboard box, but that was it in terms of concessions.

When I was young, I went to the theater at the nearby shopping center   10
and watched a movie about a talking Volkswagen. I believe the little car had
a taste for mischief but I can't be certain, as both the movie and the afternoon
proved unremarkable and have faded from my memory. Hugh saw the same
movie a few years after it was released. His family had left the Congo by this
time and were living in Ethiopia. Like me, Hugh saw the movie by himself on
a weekend afternoon. Unlike me, he left the theater two hours later, to find a
dead man hanging from a telephone pole at the far end of the unpaved parking lot. None of the people who'd seen the movie seemed to care about the
dead man. They stared at him for a moment or two and then headed home,
saying they'd never seen anything as crazy as that talking Volkswagen. His
father was late picking him up, so Hugh just stood there for an hour, watching
the dead man dangle and turn in the breeze. The death was not reported in
the newspaper, and when Hugh related the story to his friends, they said, "You
saw the movie about the talking car?"

I could have done without the flies and the primitive theaters, but I   11
wouldn't have minded growing up with a houseful of servants. In North Carolina it wasn't unusual to have a once-a-week maid, but Hugh's family had
houseboys, a word that never fails to charge my imagination. They had cooks
and drivers, and guards who occupied a gatehouse, armed with machetes. Seeing as I had regularly petitioned my parents for an electric fence, the business
with the guards strikes me as the last word in quiet sophistication. Having
protection suggests that you are important. Having that protection paid for
by the government is even better, as it suggests your safety is of interest to
someone other than yourself.

Hugh's father was a career officer with the US State Department, and   12
every morning a black sedan carried him off to the embassy. I'm told it's not
as glamorous as it sounds, but in terms of fun for the entire family, I'm fairly
confident that it beats the sack race at the annual IBM picnic. By the age of
three, Hugh was already carrying a diplomatic passport. The rules that applied
to others did not apply to him. No tickets, no arrests, no luggage search: He
was officially licensed to act like a brat. Being an American, it was expected
of him, and who was he to deny the world an occasional tantrum?

They weren't rich, but what Hugh's family lacked financially they more   13
than made up for with the sort of exoticism that works wonders at cocktail
parties, leading always to the remark "That sounds fascinating." It's a compliment one rarely receives when describing an adolescence spent drinking
Icees at the North Hills Mall. No fifteen-foot python ever wandered onto
my school's basketball court. I begged, I prayed nightly, but it just never happened. Neither did I get to witness a military coup in which forces sympa-

thetic to the colonel arrived late at night to assassinate my next-door neighbor. Hugh had been at the Addis Ababa teen club when the electricity was cut off and soldiers arrived to evacuate the building. He and his friends had to hide in the back of a jeep and cover themselves with blankets during the ride home. It's something that sticks in his mind for one reason or another.

Among my personal highlights is the memory of having my picture taken   14
with Uncle Paul, the legally blind host of a Raleigh children's television show. Among Hugh's is the memory of having his picture taken with Buzz Aldrin on the last leg of the astronaut's world tour. The man who had walked on the moon placed his hand on Hugh's shoulder and offered to sign his autograph book. The man who led Wake County schoolchildren in afternoon song turned at the sound of my voice and asked, "So what's your name, princess?"

When I was fourteen years old, I was sent to spend ten days with my   15
maternal grandmother in western New York State. She was a small and private woman named Billie, and though she never came right out and asked, I had the distinct impression she had no idea who I was. It was the way she looked at me, squinting through her glasses while chewing on her lower lip. That, coupled with the fact that she never once called me by name. "Oh," she'd say, "are you still here?" She was just beginning her long struggle with Alzheimer's disease, and each time I entered the room, I felt the need to reintroduce myself and set her at ease. "Hi, it's me. Sharon's boy, David. I was just in the kitchen admiring your collection of ceramic toads." Aside from a few trips to summer camp, this was the longest I'd ever been away from home and I like to think I was toughened by the experience.

About the same time I was frightening my grandmother, Hugh and his   16
family were packing their belongings for a move to Somalia. There were no English-speaking schools in Mogadishu, so, after a few months spent lying around the family compound with his pet monkey, Hugh was sent back to Ethiopia to live with a beer enthusiast his father had met at a cocktail party. Mr. Hoyt installed security systems in foreign embassies. He and his family gave Hugh a room. They invited him to join them at the table, but that was as far as they extended themselves. No one ever asked him when his birthday was, so when the day came, he kept it to himself. There was no telephone service between Ethiopia and Somalia, and letters to his parents were sent to Washington and then forwarded on to Mogadishu, meaning that his news was more than a month old by the time they got it. I suppose it wasn't much different than living as a foreign-exchange student. Young people do it all the time, but to me it sounds awful. The Hoyts had two sons about Hugh's age who were always saying things like "Hey that's *our* sofa you're sitting on" and "Hands off that ornamental stein. It doesn't belong to you."

He'd been living with these people for a year when he overheard   17
Mr. Hoyt tell a friend that he and his family would soon be moving to Munich,
Germany, the beer capital of the world.

"And that worried me," Hugh said, "because it meant I'd have to find   18
some other place to live."

Where I come from, finding shelter is a problem the average teenager   19
might confidently leave to his parents. It was just something that came with
having a mom and a dad. Worried that he might be sent to live with his
grandparents in Kentucky, Hugh turned to the school's guidance counselor,
who knew of a family whose son had recently left for college. And so he spent
another year living with strangers and not mentioning his birthday. While
I wouldn't have wanted to do it myself, I can't help but envy the sense of
fortitude he gained from the experience. After graduating from college, he
moved to France knowing only the phrase "Do you speak French?" — a question guaranteed to get you nowhere unless you also speak the language.

While living in Africa, Hugh and his family took frequent vacations,   20
often in the company of their monkey. The Nairobi Hilton, some suite of
high-ceilinged rooms in Cairo or Khartoum: These are the places his people
recall when gathered at a common table. "Was that the summer we spent in
Beirut or, no, I'm thinking of the time we sailed from Cyprus and took the
Orient Express to Istanbul."

Theirs was the life I dreamt about during my vacations in eastern North   21
Carolina. Hugh's family was hobnobbing with chiefs and sultans while I ate
hush puppies at the Sanitary Fish Market in Morehead City, a beach towel
wrapped like a hijab[1] around my head. Someone unknown to me was very
likely standing in a muddy ditch and dreaming of an evening spent sitting in
a clean family restaurant, drinking iced tea and working his way through an
extra-large seaman's platter, but that did not concern me, as it meant I should
have been happy with what I had. Rather than surrender to my bitterness,
I have learned to take satisfaction in the life that Hugh has led. His stories
have, over time, become my own. I say this with no trace of a kumbaya.[2]
There is no spiritual symbiosis; I'm just a petty thief who lifts his memories
the same way I'll take a handful of change left on his dresser. When my own
experiences fall short of the mark, I just go out and spend some of his. It is
with pleasure that I sometimes recall the dead man's purpled face or the report
of the handgun ringing in my ears as I studied the blood pooling beneath the

[1] A headscarf worn by Muslim women. — Eds.
[2] From the gospel-folk song with the line "Kumbaya, my Lord, kumbaya," meaning "Come
by here." Probably because of its popularity in folk music, the word now also has negative connotations of passivity or touchy-feely spiritualism. — Eds.

dead white piglet. On the way back from the slaughterhouse, we stopped for Cokes in the village of Mojo, where the gas-station owner had arranged a few tables and chairs beneath a dying canopy of vines. It was late afternoon by the time we returned to school, where a second bus carried me to the foot of Coffeeboard Road. Once there, I walked through a grove of eucalyptus trees and alongside a bald pasture of starving cattle, past the guard napping in his gatehouse, and into the waiting arms of my monkey.

*For a reading quiz, visit **bedfordstmartins.com/thebedfordreader**.*

Journal Writing

When have you envied the life of a friend or relative? Write about what was attractive to you in that person's life. Was it family relationships? educational or employment opportunities? travel experiences? something else? (To take your journal writing further, see "From Journal to Essay" on the next page.)

Questions on Meaning

1. What is the subject of Sedaris's comparison and contrast in this essay?
2. What do you think is the THESIS of this essay? Take into account both Sedaris's obvious envy of Hugh's childhood and Sedaris's awareness that Hugh's life was often lonely and insecure. Is the thesis stated or only implied?
3. There is a certain amount of IRONY in Sedaris's envy of Hugh's childhood. What is this irony? How does Sedaris make this irony explicit in paragraph 21?

Questions on Writing Strategy

1. Does Sedaris develop his comparison and contrast subject by subject or point by point? Briefly outline the essay to explain your answer.
2. Point to some of the TRANSITIONS Sedaris uses in moving between his and Hugh's lives.
3. Sedaris refers to Hugh's monkey in paragraphs 8, 20, and 21. In what sense does he use the monkey as a SYMBOL?
4. The first five paragraphs of the essay include a conversation between Sedaris and Hugh about Hugh's childhood. Why do you think the author opened the essay this way?
5. **OTHER METHODS**   How does Sedaris use NARRATION to develop his comparison and contrast?

Questions on Language

1. How does Sedaris use PARALLEL STRUCTURE in paragraph 8 to highlight the contrast between himself and Hugh? How does he then point up this parallelism?
2. Sedaris offers the image of himself as a "petty thief" in paragraph 21. What is the effect of this IMAGE?
3. Sedaris's language in this essay is notably SPECIFIC and CONCRETE. Point to examples of such language just in paragraph 6.
4. Consult a dictionary if necessary to learn the meanings of the following words: proximity, petty, autopsies, morgue (par. 2); hyenas (6); hawking, stocks (7); leper (8); hangar (9); machetes (11); diplomatic (12); exoticism, coup, evacuate (13); ornamental, stein (16); fortitude (19); hobnobbing, symbiosis, report, canopy, eucalyptus (21).

Suggestions for Writing

1. **FROM JOURNAL TO ESSAY**   Starting from your journal entry, write an essay in which you compare and contrast your own experiences with those of someone whose life you've envied. Have your feelings changed over time? Why, or why not?
2. Hugh's experiences living with strangers gave him a "sense of fortitude" (par. 19), according to Sedaris. When have you ever gone through a difficult experience that left you somehow stronger? Write an essay about such an experience that shows how you were different before and after it.
3. In your library or on the Internet, locate and read reviews of Sedaris's book *Me Talk Pretty One Day*, the source of "Remembering My Childhood," or of another essay collection by Sedaris. Write an essay in which you SYNTHESIZE the reviewers' responses to Sedaris's work.
4. **CRITICAL WRITING**   How seriously does Sedaris want the readers of his essay to take him? Write an essay in which you analyze his TONE, citing specific passages from the text to support your conclusions.
5. **CONNECTIONS**   Gloria Naylor, in "The Meanings of a Word" (p. 412), writes about a childhood very different from either Sedaris's or Hugh's. In an essay, consider how Sedaris and Naylor might view each other's childhoods.

David Sedaris on Writing

Most of us are contented users of word processors, but not David Sedaris. In "Nutcracker.com," an essay in *Me Talk Pretty One Day*, Sedaris explains why he refuses to give up his typewriter.

I hate computers for any number of reasons, but I despise them most for what they've done to my friend the typewriter. In a democratic country you'd think there would be room for both of them, but computers won't rest until I'm making my ribbons from torn shirts and brewing Wite-Out in my bathtub. Their goal is to place the IBM Selectric II beside the feather quill and chisel in the museum of antiquated writing implements. They're power hungry, and someone needs to stop them.

When told I'm like the guy still pining for his eight-track tapes, I say, "You have eight-tracks? Where?" In reality I know nothing about them, yet I feel it's important to express some solidarity with others who have had the rug pulled out from beneath them. I don't care if it can count words or rearrange paragraphs at the push of a button, I don't want a computer. Unlike the faint scurry raised by fingers against a plastic computer keyboard, the smack and clatter of a typewriter suggests that you're actually building something. At the end of a miserable day, instead of grieving my virtual nothing, I can always look at my loaded wastepaper basket and tell myself that if I failed, at least I took a few trees down with me.

For Discussion

1. Why does Sedaris prefer writing with a typewriter instead of with a computer?
2. Defend the word processor from Sedaris's attack. What are some advantages of the newer technology?

ADDITIONAL WRITING TOPICS

Comparison and Contrast

1. In an essay replete with EXAMPLES, compare and contrast the two subjects in any one of the following pairs:

   The main characters of two films, stories, or novels
   Women and men as consumers
   Vampires and zombies
   The styles of two runners
   Liberals and conservatives: their opposing views of the role of government
   How city dwellers and country dwellers spend their leisure time
   The presentation styles of two television news commentators

2. Approach a comparison-and-contrast essay on one of the following general subjects by explaining why you prefer one thing to the other:

   Vehicles: hybrids and conventional engines; sedans and SUVs; American and Asian; Asian and European
   Computers: Macs and PCs
   Two buildings on campus or in town
   Two football teams
   Two horror movies
   Television when you were a child and television today
   City life and small-town or rural life
   Malls and main streets
   Two neighborhoods
   Two sports

3. Write an essay in which you compare a reality (what actually exists) with an ideal (what should exist). Some possible topics:

   The affordable car
   Available living quarters
   A job
   The college curriculum
   Public transportation
   Financial aid for college students

8

PROCESS ANALYSIS

Explaining Step by Step

◀ **Process analysis in a photograph**

In a factory in Shenzhen, China, workers create dolls for export to the United States. This single image catches several steps in the doll-making process. At the very back of the assembly line, flat, unstuffed dolls begin the journey past the ranks of workers who stuff the body parts, using material prepared by other workers on the sides. A supervisor, hands behind his or her back, oversees the process. What do you think the photographer, Wally McNamee, wants viewers to understand about this process? What do you imagine the workers themselves think about it?

THE METHOD

A chemist working for a soft-drink firm is asked to improve on a competitor's product, Hydra Sports Water. First, she chemically tests a sample to figure out what's in the drink. This is the method of DIVISION or ANALYSIS, the separation of something into its parts in order to understand it (see the following chapter). Then the chemist writes a report telling her boss how to make a drink like Hydra Sports Water, but better. This recipe is a special kind of analysis, called PROCESS ANALYSIS: explaining step by step how to do something or how something is done.

Like any type of analysis, process analysis divides a subject into its components: It divides a continuous action into stages. Processes much larger and more involved than the making of a sports drink may also be analyzed. When geologists explain how a formation such as the Grand Canyon developed — a process taking several hundred million years — they describe the successive layers of sediment deposited by oceans, floods, and wind; then the great uplift of the entire region by underground forces; and then the erosion, visible to us today, by the Colorado River and its tributaries, by little streams and flash floods, by crumbling and falling rock, and by wind. Exactly what are the geologists doing in this explanation? They are taking a complicated event (or process) and dividing it into parts. They are telling us what happened first, second, and third, and what is still happening today.

Because it is useful in explaining what is complicated, process analysis is a favorite method of scientists such as geologists. The method, however, may be useful to anybody. Two PURPOSES of process analysis are very familiar to you:

- **A *directive* process analysis explains how to do something or make something.** You meet it when you read a set of instructions for taking an exam or for conducting a chemistry experiment ("From a 5-milliliter burette, add the hydrochloride to a 20-milliliter beaker of water . . .").

- **An *informative* process analysis explains how something is done or how it takes place.** You see it in textbook descriptions of how atoms behave when they split, how lions hunt, and how a fertilized egg develops into a child.

In this chapter, you will find examples of both kinds of process analysis — both the "how to" and the "how." For instance, June Melby offers a directive for making a popular summer treat, while Jessica Mitford spellbindingly explains how corpses are embalmed.

Sometimes process analysis is used very imaginatively. Foreseeing that eventually the sun will burn out and all life on Earth will perish, an astronomer who cannot possibly behold the end of the world nevertheless can write a process analysis of it. An exercise in learned guesswork, such an essay divides a vast and almost inconceivable event into stages that, taken one at a time, become clearer and more readily imaginable.

Whether it is useful or useless (but fun or scary to imagine), an effective process analysis can grip readers and even hold them fascinated. Say you were proposing a change in the procedures for course registration at your school. You could argue your point until you were out of words, but you would get nowhere if you failed to tell your readers exactly how the new process would work: That's what makes your proposal sing. Leaf through a current issue of any magazine, and you will find that process analysis abounds. You may see, for instance, articles telling you how to do a magic trick, make a difficult decision, lose fat, cut hair, arouse a bored mate, and score at stock trading. Less practical, but not necessarily less interesting, are the informative articles: how brain surgeons work, how diamonds are formed, how cities fight crime. Readers, it seems, have an unslakable thirst for process analysis.

THE PROCESS

Here are suggestions for writing an effective process analysis of your own. (In fact, what you are about to read is itself a process analysis.)

1. **Understand clearly the process you are about to analyze.** Think it through. This preliminary survey will make the task of writing far easier for you.

2. **Consider your thesis.** What is the point of your process analysis: Why are you bothering to tell readers about it? The THESIS STATEMENT for a process analysis need do no more than say what the subject is and maybe outline its essential stages, as in this example:

   The main stages in writing a process analysis are listing the steps in the process, drafting to explain the steps, and revising to clarify the steps.

   But your readers will surely appreciate something livelier and more pointed, something that says "You can use this" or "This may surprise you" or "Listen up." Here are two thesis statements from essays in this chapter:

   Granted, the odds of surviving a six-mile plummet [from an airplane] are extraordinarily slim, but at this point you've got nothing to lose by understanding your situation.

   — Dan Koeppel, "Taking a Fall"

[In a mortuary the body] is in short order sprayed, sliced, pierced, pickled, trussed, trimmed, creamed, waxed, painted, rouged, and neatly dressed — transformed from a common corpse into a Beautiful Memory Picture.
— Jessica Mitford, "Behind the Formaldehyde Curtain"

3. **Think about preparatory steps.** If the reader should do something before beginning the process, list these steps. For instance, you might begin, "Assemble the needed equipment: a 20-milliliter beaker, a 5-milliliter burette, safety gloves, and safety goggles."

4. **List the steps or stages in the process.** Try setting them down in chronological order, one at a time — if this is possible. Some processes, however, do not happen in an orderly sequence, but occur all at once. If, for instance, you are writing an account of a typical earthquake, what do you mention first? The shifting of underground rock strata? cracks in the earth? falling houses? bursting water mains? toppling trees? mangled cars? casualties? For this subject the method of CLASSIFICATION (Chap. 10) might come to your aid. You might sort out apparently simultaneous events into categories: injury to people; damage to homes, to land, to public property.

5. **Check the completeness and order of the steps.** Make sure your list includes *all* the steps in the right order. Sometimes a stage of a process may contain a number of smaller stages. Make sure none has been left out. If any seems particularly tricky or complicated, underline it on your list to remind yourself when you write your essay to slow down and detail it with extra care.

6. **Define your terms.** Ask yourself, "Do I need any specialized or technical terms?" If so, be sure to define them. You'll sympathize with your reader if you have ever tried to assemble a bicycle according to a directive that begins, "Position sleeve casing on wheel center in fork with shaft in tongue groove, and gently but forcibly tap in pal-nut head."

7. **Use time-markers or** TRANSITIONS. These words or phrases indicate *when* one stage of a process stops and the next begins, and they greatly aid your reader in following you. Consider, for example, the following paragraph, in which plain medical prose makes good use of helpful time-markers (underlined). (The paragraph is adapted from *Pregnancy and Birth: A Book for Expectant Parents*, by Alan Frank Guttmacher.)

In the human, <u>thirty-six hours after</u> the egg is fertilized, a two-cell egg appears. A twelve-cell development takes place in <u>seventy-two hours</u>. The egg is <u>still</u> round and has increased little in diameter. In this respect it is like a real estate development. <u>At first</u> a road bisects the whole area, then a cross road divides it into quarters, and later other roads divide it into eighths and twelfths. This happens without the taking of any more land, simply by subdivision of the original tract. On the third or fourth day, the egg passes from the Fallopian tube into the uterus. By the fifth day the original single large cell has subdivided into sixty small cells and floats about the slitlike uterine cavity a day or two longer, then adheres to the cavity's inner lining. By the twelfth day the human egg is already firmly implanted. Impregnation is now completed, as yet unbeknown to the woman. At present, she has not even had time to miss her first menstrual period, and other symptoms of pregnancy are still several days distant.

Brief as these time-markers are, they define each stage of the human egg's journey. When using time-markers, vary them so that they won't seem mechanical. If you can, avoid the monotonous repetition of a fixed phrase (*In the fourteenth stage . . . , In the fifteenth stage . . .*). Even boring time-markers, though, are better than none at all. Words and phrases such as *in the beginning, first, second, next, then, after that, three seconds later, at the same time,* and *finally* can help a process move smoothly in the telling and lodge firmly in the reader's mind.

8. **Be specific.** When you write a first draft, state your analysis in generous detail, even at the risk of being wordy. When you revise, it will be easier to delete than to amplify.

9. **Revise.** When your essay is finished, reread it carefully against the checklist on the next page. You might also enlist a friend's help. If your process analysis is directive ("How to Eat an Ice-Cream Cone without Dribbling"), see if the friend can follow your instructions without difficulty. If your process analysis is informative ("How a New Word Enters the Dictionary"), ask the friend whether the process unfolds as clearly in his or her mind as it does in yours.

FOCUS ON CONSISTENCY

While drafting a process analysis, you may start off with subjects or verbs in one form and then shift to another form because the original choice feels awkward. In directive analyses, shifts occur most often with the subjects *a person* and *one*:

> INCONSISTENT To keep the car from rolling while changing the tire, one should first set the car's emergency brake. Then you should block the three other tires with objects like rocks or chunks of wood.

(continued)

Process Analysis

In informative analyses, shifts usually occur from singular to plural as a way to get around *he* when the meaning includes males and females:

> INCONSISTENT   The poll <u>worker</u> first checks each voter against the registration list. Then <u>they</u> ask the voter to sign another list.

To repair inconsistencies, start with a subject that is both comfortable and sustainable:

> CONSISTENT   To keep the car from rolling while changing the tire, <u>you</u> should set the car's emergency brake. Then <u>you</u> should block the three other tires with objects like rocks or chunks of wood.

> CONSISTENT   Poll <u>workers</u> first check each voter against the registration list. Then <u>they</u> ask the voter to sign another list.

Sometimes, writers try to avoid naming or shifting subjects by using PASSIVE verbs that don't require actors:

> INCONSISTENT   To keep the car from rolling while changing the tire, <u>one</u> should first set the car's emergency brake. Then the three other tires <u>should be blocked</u> with objects like rocks or chunks of wood.

> INCONSISTENT   Poll workers first <u>check</u> each voter against the registration list. Then the voter <u>is asked</u> to sign another list.

In directive analyses, avoid passive verbs by using *you*, as shown in the consistent example above, or by using the commanding form of verbs, in which *you* is understood as the subject:

> CONSISTENT   To keep the car from rolling while changing the tire, first <u>set</u> the car's emergency brake. Then <u>block</u> the three other tires with objects like rocks or chunks of wood.

In informative analyses, passive verbs may be necessary if you don't know who the actor is or want to emphasize the action over the actor. But identifying the actor is generally clearer and more concise:

> CONSISTENT   Poll <u>workers</u> first check each voter against the registration list. Then <u>they</u> ask the voter to sign another list.

CHECKLIST FOR REVISING A PROCESS ANALYSIS

✔ **Thesis.** Does your process analysis have a point? Have you made sure readers know what it is?

✔ **Organization.** Have you arranged the steps of your process in a clear chronological order? If steps occur simultaneously, have you grouped them so that readers perceive some order?

> ✔ **Completeness.** Have you included all the necessary steps and explained each one fully? Is it clear how each one contributes to the result?
>
> ✔ **Definitions.** Have you explained the meanings of any terms your readers may not know?
>
> ✔ **Transitions.** Do time-markers distinguish the steps of your process and clarify their sequence?
>
> ✔ **Consistency.** Have you maintained comfortable, consistent, and clear subjects and verb forms?

PROCESS ANALYSIS IN ACADEMIC WRITING

A Psychology Textbook

This passage on our descent into sleep comes from a section in *Psychology*, by Carole Wade and Carol Tavris, on "the most perplexing of all our biological rhythms." Before this paragraph the authors review the history of sleep research; after it they continue to analyze the night-long process that follows this initial descent.

When you first climb into bed, close your eyes, and relax, your brain emits bursts of *alpha waves*. On an EEG recording, alpha waves have a regular, slow rhythm and high amplitude (height). Gradually, these waves slow down even further, and you drift into the Land of Nod, passing through four stages, each deeper than the previous one.

Steps preceding the process

Process to be explained with informative analysis

Stage 1. Your brain waves become small and irregular, and you feel yourself drifting on the edge of consciousness, in a state of light sleep. If awakened, you may recall fantasies or a few visual images.

Step 1

Stage 2. Your brain emits occasional short bursts of rapid, high-peaking waves called *sleep spindles*. Minor noises probably won't disturb you.

Step 2

Stage 3. In addition to the waves that are characteristic of stage 2, your brain occasionally emits *delta waves*, very slow waves with very high peaks. Your breathing and pulse have slowed down, your muscles are relaxed, and you are hard to waken.

Step 3

Stage 4. Delta waves have now largely taken over, and you are in deep sleep. It will take vigorous shaking or a loud noise to awaken you. Oddly, though, if you walk in your sleep, this is when you are likely to do so.

Step 4

Process Analysis

A Lab Report

When scientists conduct experiments to test their hypotheses, or theories, they almost always write reports outlining the processes they followed so that other researchers can attempt to duplicate the outcomes. Laboratory reports are straightforward and objective and are generally organized under standardized headings, such as *Purpose, Materials, Procedure,* and *Results.* They often include tables, figures, and calculations pertaining to the experiment. Most writers of lab reports put the focus on the experiment by keeping themselves in the background: They avoid *I* or *we* and use the PASSIVE VOICE of verbs (*the solution was heated,* as opposed to *we heated the solution*). The passive voice is not universal, however. Most lab assignments you receive in college will include detailed instructions for writing up the experiment and its results, so the best writing strategy is to follow those instructions to the letter.

For a first-year chemistry experiment, Victor Khoury used mostly household materials to extract and isolate deoxyribonucleic acid (DNA) from an onion. Found in all plants and animals, DNA is the molecule that holds the genetic information needed to create and direct living organisms. Khoury's instructor intended the experiment to teach students basic techniques and interactions in chemistry and to help them understand genetics at a molecular level. In the following excerpt from his lab report, Khoury explains the procedure and the main result.

Procedure

A small onion was coarsely chopped and placed in a   Step 1
1000-ml measuring cup along with 100 ml of a solution consisting of 10 ml of liquid dishwashing detergent, 1.5 g of table salt,
and distilled water. The solution was intended to dissolve the   Reason for step
proteins and lipids binding the cell membranes of the onion. The   Step 2
onion pieces were next pressed with the back of a spoon for
30 seconds to break the onion structure down into a mash.   Reason for step

The measuring cup was then placed in a pan of preheated   Step 3
58°C water for 13 minutes to further separate the DNA from the   Reason for step
walls of the onion cells. For the first 7 minutes, the onion was
continuously pressed with a spoon. After 13 minutes of heating,   Step 4
the cup of mixture was then placed in a pan of ice water and
the mixture was pressed and stirred for 5 minutes to cool it and   Reason for step
to slow enzyme activity that would otherwise break down the
DNA. The onion mixture was then placed in a coffee filter over a   Step 5

lab beaker and stored for 1 hour in a 4°C refrigerator in order to   Reason for step
filter and further cool the solution.

    After refrigeration, the filtered solution was stirred for   Steps 6, 7, and 8
30 seconds and 10 ml were poured into a clean vial. A toothpick
dipped in meat tenderizer was placed into the onion solution
so that the enzymes in the tenderizer would further separate   Reason for steps
any remaining proteins from the DNA. Then refrigerated ethyl   Step 9
alcohol was poured into the vial until it formed a 1-cm layer on
top of the onion solution.

Results

    After the solution sat for 2 minutes, the DNA precipitated   Discussion of results
into the alcohol layer. The DNA was long, white, and stringy,
with a gelatinous texture. This experiment demonstrated that
DNA can be extracted and isolated using a process of homogeni-
zation and deproteinization. . . .

FIROOZEH DUMAS

Born in Abadan, Iran, in 1966, Firoozeh Dumas immigrated with her family to Whittier, California, at the age of seven, moved back to Iran two years later, then finally settled for good in the United States two years after that. She earned her bachelor's degree from the University of California at Berkeley in 1988. Dumas, who has said that the worst misconception about Iranians is "that we are completely humorless," took up writing partly to correct such assumptions. Her popular first book, *Funny in Farsi: A Memoir of Growing Up Iranian in America* (2003), portrays the humor in her family's experiences as Middle Eastern immigrants to the United States. Her second book, *Laughing without an Accent: Adventures of an Iranian American, at Home and Abroad* (2008), continues the theme with essays about trying to sell a cross-shaped potato on eBay and taking a cruise with fifty-one family members, among other topics. Dumas contributes to several periodicals — including the *New York Times*, the *Wall Street Journal*, the *Los Angeles Times*, and *Lifetime* — and is an occasional commentator on National Public Radio.

Sweet, Sour, and Resentful

In this 2009 essay from *Gourmet* magazine, Dumas outlines her mother's painstaking process of preparing a traditional Persian meal for the dozens of distant relatives and friends of friends who descended on the family's California condo every weekend. Through her mother's weekly routine — from hunting down ingredients to chopping herbs to refusing praise — Dumas reveals much about family, culture, and humility.

In the next essay, "How to Make a Sno-Cone," June Melby examines another kind of food tradition, from the perspective of a child working in a family business.

My mother's main ingredient in cooking was resentment — not that I can   1
blame her. In 1979, my family was living temporarily in Newport Beach, California. Our real home was in Abadan, a city in the southwest of Iran. Despite its desert location and ubiquitous refineries, Abadan was the quintessential small town. Everybody's father (including my own) worked for the National

Iranian Oil Company, and almost all the moms stayed home. The employees' kids attended the same schools. No one locked their doors. Whenever I hear John Mellencamp's "Small Town," I think of Abadan, although I'm guessing John Mellencamp was thinking of somewhere else when he wrote that song.

By the time of the Iranian revolution,[1] we had adjusted to life in Cali- 2
fornia. We said "Hello" and "Have a nice day" to perfect strangers, wore flip-flops, and grilled cheeseburgers next to our kebabs. We never understood why Americans put ice in tea or bought shampoo that smelled like strawberries, but other than that, America felt like home.

When the revolution happened, thousands left Iran for Southern Califor- 3
nia. Since we were one of the few Iranian families already there, our phone did not stop ringing. Relatives, friends, friends of relatives, friends of friends, and people whose connection we never quite figured out called us with questions about settling into this new land. Displaying the hospitality that Iranians so cherish, my father extended a dinner invitation to everyone who called. As a result, we found ourselves feeding dozens of people every weekend.

The marathon started on Monday, with my mother planning the menu 4
while letting us know that she was already tired. Fortunately, our rice dishes were made to be shared; our dilemma, however, was space. Our condo was small. Our guests squeezed onto the sofa, sat on the floor, or overflowed onto the patio. We eventually had to explain to our American neighbors why there were so many cars parked in front of our place every weekend. My mother, her diplomatic skills in full swing, had me deliver plates of Persian food, decorated with radish roses and mint sprigs, to them. In time, we learned not to share *fesenjan*, pomegranate stew with ground walnuts. "Yes, now that you mention it, it does look like mud, but it's really good," I'd explain, convincing no one.

Because my mother did not drive, my father took her to buy ingredients 5
every Tuesday after work. In Abadan, my mother and I had started most days in the market, going from vendor to vendor looking for herbs, vegetables, and fruits. The fish came from the Karun and Arvand (Shatt al Arab) rivers, the *lavash* and the *sangak* breads were freshly baked, and the chickens were still alive. We were locavores by necessity and foodies without knowing it. In America, I learned that the time my parents spent shopping was in direct correlation to the degree of my mother's bad mood. An extra-long trip meant that my mother could not find everything she needed, a point she would make loud and clear when she got home: "Why don't they let fruit ripen here?" "Why are the chickens so huge and flavorless?" "I couldn't find fresh herbs." "My feet hurt." "How am I supposed to get everything done?"

---

[1] In 1979 fundamentalist rebels led by Ayatollah Ruhollah Khomeini overthrew the Iranian monarchy and established the Islamic Republic of Iran, a theocratic dictatorship. — EDS.

The first step was preparing the herbs. My mother insisted that the pars- 6
ley, cilantro, and chives for *qormeh sabzi*, herb stew, had to be finely chopped
by hand. The food processor, she explained, squished them. As she and my
father sat across the table wielding huge knives, they argued incessantly. My
father did his best to help her. It wasn't enough. As soon as the mountain of
herbs was chopped, my mother started frying them. At any given time, my
mother was also frying onions. Every few days, while my father was watching
the six o'clock news, my mother would hand him a dozen onions, a cutting
board, and a knife. No words were exchanged. Much to my father's relief,
I once volunteered for this task, but apparently my slices were neither thin
enough nor even. It took my father's precision as an engineer to slice correctly.

While all four burners were in use, my mother mixed the ground beef, 7
rice, split peas, scallions, and herbs for stuffed grape leaves. I chopped the
stems of the grape leaves. I had tried stuffing them once, but my rolls, deemed
not tight enough, were promptly unrolled and then rerolled by my mother.

In between cooking, my mother made yogurt — the thick, sour variety 8
that we couldn't find in America. She soaked walnuts and almonds in water to
plump them up; fried eggplants for *kashk-e bademjan*, a popular appetizer with
garlic, turmeric, mint, and whey; made *torshi-e limo*, a sour lemon condiment;
and slivered orange peels. I had been fired from this task also, having left on
far too much pith.

By the time our guests arrived, my mother was exhausted. But the work 9
was not finished. Rice, the foundation of the Persian meal, the litmus test
of the cook's ability, cannot be prepared ahead of time. To wit, one day in
Abadan, the phone rang when my mother was about to drain the rice. During
the time it took her to answer the phone and tell her sister that she would call
her back, the rice overcooked. Almost forty years later, I still remember my
mother's disappointment and her explaining to my father that her sister had
time to talk because my aunt's maid did all the cooking. My aunt did not even
drain her own rice.

We certainly did not have a table big enough to set, so we simply stacked 10
dishes and utensils, buffet-style. As the guest list grew, we added paper plates
and plastic utensils. It was always my job to announce that dinner was ready.
As people entered the dining room, they gasped at the sight of my mother's
table. Her *zereshk polow*, barberry rice, made many emotional. There are no
fresh barberries in America (my mother had brought dried berries from Iran
in her suitcase), and the sight of that dish, with its distinct deep red hue, was
a reminder of the life our guests had left behind.

Our dinners took days to cook and disappeared in twenty minutes. As our 11
guests heaped their plates and looked for a place to sit, they lavished praise
on my mother, who, according to tradition, deflected it all. "It's nothing," she

said. "I wish I could've done more." When they told her how lucky she was to have me to help her, my mother politely nodded, while my father added, "Firoozeh's good at math."

On Sundays, my mother lay on the sofa, her swollen feet elevated, field-   12
ing thank-you phone calls from our guests. She had the same conversation a dozen times; each one ended with, "Of course you can give our name to your cousins." As I watched my mother experience the same draining routine week after week, I decided that tradition is good only if it brings joy to all involved. This includes the hostess. Sometimes, even our most cherished beliefs must evolve. Evolution, thy name is potluck.

For a reading quiz, visit **bedfordstmartins.com/thebedfordreader**.

Journal Writing

Many people have unique rituals, like Dumas's parents' practice of serving elaborate Persian meals to distant acquaintances every weekend. List some rituals that are unique to your family, to another group you belong to, or to you alone — for instance, a holiday celebration, a vacation activity, a way of decompressing after a stressful week. (To take your journal writing further, see "From Journal to Essay" on the next page.)

Questions on Meaning

1. Why were weekend dinners so important to the author's parents and their guests? Consider not just the meals themselves but the larger context that prompted them.
2. In which sentence or sentences does Dumas state her THESIS most directly?
3. What would you say is Dumas's PURPOSE in this essay? Is it primarily to entertain readers by describing her family's weekly routine, or does she seem to have another purpose in mind?
4. What solution to her mother's exhausting role as hostess does Dumas propose in paragraph 12? Do you think her mother would have agreed to it? Why, or why not?

Questions on Writing Strategy

1. Why does Dumas begin her essay with an overview of life in Abadan and an ALLUSION to the Iranian revolution (pars. 1–3)? What purpose does this opening serve?

2. How does Dumas seem to imagine her AUDIENCE? To what extent could she ASSUME that readers would appreciate her mother's situation?
3. What steps does Dumas identify in the process of hosting Iranian guests every weekend? How does she ensure that her analysis has COHERENCE?
4. **OTHER METHODS** What role does COMPARISON AND CONTRAST play in paragraph 5?

Questions on Language

1. Explain how Dumas's TONE contributes to the humor in her essay.
2. Where in this essay does Dumas use Persian words? What is their EFFECT?
3. In paragraph 9, Dumas says that rice is "the litmus test" for Iranian cooks. What does she mean? What is a litmus test, and how does the phrase connect to the focus (and title) of Dumas's essay?
4. Be sure you know the meanings of the following words: ubiquitous, quintessential (par. 1); Persian (4); locavores, correlation (5); pith (8); lavished, deflected (11); potluck (12).

Suggestions for Writing

1. **FROM JOURNAL TO ESSAY**   Write an essay explaining one of the rituals you listed in your journal. Focus on the details and steps of the ritual itself as well as on the significance it holds for you and for any others who participate in it with you.
2. Research the influx of Iranian families into California during the 1970s. What prompted this migration? What quality of life did newcomers face on arrival? What tensions did their arrival create? In an essay, consider these questions and others your research may lead you to. You may prefer to focus on a different migration from the nineteenth or twentieth century — such as that of Irish to the eastern United States, Chinese to the western United States, or African Americans from the southern to the northern United States.
3. **CRITICAL WRITING**   What impression of herself does Dumas create in this essay? What adjectives would you use to describe the writer as she reveals herself on the page? Cite specific language from the essay to support your ANALYSIS.
4. **CONNECTIONS**   "My mother's main ingredient in cooking was resentment," writes Dumas (par. 1). In the next essay, "How to Make a Sno-Cone," June Melby expresses her own feelings of resentment at the necessities of food preparation. Why should making food for others make a person miserable? In an essay, compare and contrast the two writers' perspectives and tones. How do their respective roles in their families' traditions and responsibilities help to shape their attitudes? And how does each writer attempt to lighten the mood with humor?

Firoozeh Dumas on Writing

In a 2004 interview with Khaled Hosseini (author of *The Kite Runner* and *A Thousand Splendid Suns*), Firoozeh Dumas explained how writing awakens her memory. As a girl growing up in Iran and the United States, Dumas says she "was always that quiet kid in a room full of adults" who carefully "listened and observed." When she started writing as an adult, her collected observations "just flooded back." Unlike those who experience writer's block, Dumas was easily inspired: "Every time I finished a story, another popped up in its place. It was like using a vending machine: The candy falls down and is immediately replaced by another."

In order to keep up with her vending machine of ideas — and to accommodate her busy family life — Dumas writes "in spurts," often waking at four in the morning. "Once a story is in my head, I'm possessed, and the only thing I can do is write like mad," she told Hosseini. "This means the house gets very messy and dinner is something frozen. I do not read or go to the movies when I am writing, because I can't concentrate on anything else. I also keep writing in my head when I'm not actually writing, which means that I become a terrible listener."

For Discussion

1. Have you ever found that the act of writing triggers your memory?
2. What does Dumas mean when she says "I . . . keep writing in my head when I'm not actually writing"?
3. For Dumas, what is the relationship between listening and writing?

JUNE MELBY

June Melby is a poet, comedian, and musician who has given prize-winning performances at literary festivals throughout the United States and Europe. She was born in rural Iowa in 1963, studied engineering as an undergraduate, and completed an MFA in nonfiction writing at the University of Iowa. She was also a 2003 resident artist at the Kulturbehörde in Hamburg, Germany, and a 2011 writing fellow at the Virginia Center for the Creative Arts. Melby has given readings on National Public Radio and has published her work in *McSweeney's Internet Tendency*, *Versal*, the *Los Angeles Weekly*, *National Lampoon* magazine, and several German periodicals. She is the author of three poetry collections: *The Chicken Dilemma and Other (Animal) Problems* (1998), *Saltine Crackers Keep Me Alive* (2000), and *Tub Toys* (2012). Melby's forthcoming memoir, *My Family and Other Hazards*, recounts her childhood experiences working with her sisters at her parents' miniature golf course. In addition to writing and performing, she works as a freelance editor and writing coach and teaches at Luther College and at the ArtHaus in Decorah, Iowa.

How to Make a Sno-Cone

Part of a draft chapter for *My Family and Other Hazards*, "How to Make a Sno-Cone" was excerpted in the *Utne Reader* in 2012 from a longer essay published in the *Water-Stone Review*. Like Firoozeh Dumas in the previous essay, Melby considers the challenges and frustrations of preparing food for others, but in her case the effort is for the sake of family income rather than cultural bonding. Using process analysis, she both explains how to shave ice for customers and examines her own resentment at having to do it.

First, don't kill anyone. Don't make them choke on small bits of plastic, which might happen if you push the ice chunks into the grinder with the plastic scoop — something everyone in my family often does. The ice clogs when you dump it in. Also, the chute is metal — ice can stick like a wet tongue on a swing set. You're going to have to shove it in a little, but not so hard that the plastic scoop gets mauled. The shaved ice is white and shiny. By happenstance, the plastic is too. It's hard to know if you've ground up the scoop or not. If you think you might have chewed plastic into the shaved ice, while the customer looks in eagerly through the front window of the Snack Shack, just calmly scoop out the snow from the plexi bin and dump it into the yellow bucket below. Say, "I want to start over; I didn't like that bunch," and put more ice chunks into the machine. The customer will not know of his proximity to death by choking and may be *flattered* that you took the time to chop more ice — better ice — for his sno-cone. One truism about tourists: They like to feel important. A delay, when it's a delay *for* them and not a delay for someone *else* is evidence of your wish to deliver them perfection.

Second, the grape flavor tastes watery. Don't push the grape.   2

Say, "Cherry, blue-raspberry, grape, or a combo?" The cherry flavor is the   3
best single flavor, and you will say so if you're asked, but don't volunteer the information.

Mom says to give one squirt into the ice at the bottom of the cone, then   4
two squirts into the dome on top. Do it slowly so the ice doesn't dent.

The best ice is the cold ice, but customers rarely get that. We grind up   5
ice for sno-cones one at a time because we don't get enough orders to shave up a mountain of ice and leave it to melt there all day. Dad would have a fit. Wasteful, wasteful. For one sno-cone, we only chop one sno-cone's worth. But the best ice comes after five or six sno-cones. The whirling blades get good and cold.

The ice chopped for the seventh or eighth will be so cold and fluffy that it   6
may not even pack into a ball. If that happens, just dig into the mound with your scoop until you're at the bottom, then add some wet (bad) ice to your ball. People like their ice in a ball. It's how they imagine it should be. But we know better. We are sno-cone snobs.

Mom and Dad let us have one free sno-cone a day. But we refuse to eat a   7
sno-cone if it's made from wet ice. Even on the hottest day of July. We wait until the blades are cold from serving up ice for other people, and only then add a few chunks for ourselves.

If the ice is wet, the cone may overflow before you get the third squirt on   8
there. If so, stop. Hand the cone slowly to the customer. Say, "Be careful. This one is pretty full. You'd better take a sip right away." You know — and will never reveal — that if the cone is overflowing it means the ice was not great. It will be gritty and the flavor will be diluted. But the customer always feels privileged that his cone is overflowing.

What the customer wants is what he imagines a sno-cone should look   9
like. This is his vacation, after all. This is his week at the lake, and the family has played mini golf, and the kids have matching Brewers' baseball caps, and the sun is hanging low, and this is the last day before the long drive home. And the little girl looks up at her father and, in her most delicate voice, asks, "Daddy, can we get sno-cones?"

He smiles and says to me, "Do you have rainbow?"   10

"Sure."   11

I drape perfect stripes of brilliant color over the perfect dome of snow. 12
Then they stroll across the parking lot together, sipping cones and leaning
toward each other.

If you see a bug inside the machine when the ice comes out, you can wipe 13
it out with a paper towel even while customers stare through the window at you
from less than two feet away. They won't see that you are removing an insect.

The sno-cone machine rarely breaks down, maybe once every three years. 14
This is something of a miracle. It was purchased when you were young enough
not to question whether your parents understood the idea of food product
safety and potential lawsuits. And nothing bad has ever happened. This, too,
is a miracle. Sometimes, if people come early — it's before 10:00 a.m., but
Mom and Dad let them buy snacks anyway — the sound of grinding ice is the
first thing you hear in the morning. The roar of hungry blades wafts through
the house and wakes you in your bed.

For a reading quiz, visit **bedfordstmartins.com/thebedfordreader**.

Journal Writing

Did you work as a child, whether for a family business or for an unrelated employer?
What was the job? Did you do it because you wanted to, because you needed to, or
because your family required you to? How did you feel about working? Write about the
experience in your journal. (To take your journal writing further, see "From Journal to
Essay" on the facing page.)

Questions on Meaning

1. The "How to" in Melby's title suggests that her essay will be a directive process
   analysis. Does she really intend to teach readers how to make a sno-cone, or does
   she seem to have another PURPOSE in mind?
2. Notice the first sentence of the essay: "First, don't kill anyone." Does Melby mean
   this literally or figuratively? What does the warning tell you about her attitude
   about working in the Snack Shack?
3. Examine Melby's portrayal of her customers. What portrait of them emerges?
4. What would you say is Melby's implied THESIS?

Questions on Writing Strategy

1. What POINT OF VIEW does Melby take? Is she writing from the perspective of a
   child or from that of an adult looking back on her experience? Was her choice
   appropriate, given her subject and purpose?

2. To whom does Melby's NARRATOR seem to be speaking? What makes you think so?
3. How clear are Melby's instructions? What are the steps involved in making a sno-cone, as she presents them?
4. What is the intention of Melby's CONCLUSION? Does the conclusion work well? Why, or why not?
5. **OTHER METHODS** Melby's process analysis relies heavily on DESCRIPTION. To which of the five senses — sight, smell, hearing, touch, taste — does she appeal?

Questions on Language

1. Most, but not all, of Melby's process analysis is written in the second-PERSON *you*, using the commanding form of verbs. Where do you find shifts to first- and third-person? Are these shifts evidence of sloppy writing, or does Melby's use of them have a logic? What is their EFFECT?
2. Identify the places in the essay where Melby gives human qualities to the ice grinder. What is the effect of these uses of PERSONIFICATION?
3. Consult a dictionary if any of the following words are unfamiliar: mauled, happenstance, proximity, truism (par. 1); wafts (14).

Suggestions for Writing

1. **FROM JOURNAL TO ESSAY** Write an essay on the work experience you explored in your journal, using process analysis to explain the mechanics of the job to a new or future employee. Or, if you wish, use NARRATION and description to convey the effect the experience had on you.
2. Melby jokes that her parents might not have "understood the idea of food product safety and potential lawsuits" (par. 14), but the prospect of violating health codes in a restaurant raises a serious issue. Research some lawsuits that have resulted from food poisoning or related threats to public health. Write a report in which you SUMMARIZE several cases and comment on what you think these examples reveal about the food industry and consumer expectations.
3. Write an essay that teaches readers how to do something you're good at, such as baking cupcakes, writing letters of complaint, or unclogging a sink. You might, like Melby, imagine a specific person as your reader, or address your instructions to a more general AUDIENCE.
4. **CRITICAL WRITING** As we mentioned on page 258, "How to Make a Sno-Cone" is from a draft of Melby's memoir. In other words, it is not final. How might her writing be improved? Approach Melby's essay as a peer reviewer and offer suggestions for revision.
5. **CONNECTIONS** Both June Melby and Firoozeh Dumas, in the previous essay, hint at how as children they felt ashamed of their families because of a certain food or drink. Write an essay in which you COMPARE AND CONTRAST the ways the two writers describe food and how each writer uses food to make a larger point about the need to fit in.

DAN KOEPPEL

Journalist and outdoors enthusiast Dan Koeppel is best known for his expertise on extreme sports, such as sky diving and wave running. Born in 1962, he studied at Hampshire College and is a contributing editor at *National Geographic Adventure*. He was inducted into the Mountain Bike Hall of Fame in 2003 and for a time was a commentator on the Public Radio International program *Marketplace*. A productive and eclectic writer, Koeppel has published columns and articles in a wide array of magazines, including *Audubon, Mountain Bike, Outside, Elle, Martha Stewart Living,* and, on a regular basis, *Wired* and *Popular Science*. His books include *Extreme Sports Almanac* (2000), *To See Every Bird on Earth: A Father, a Son, and a Lifelong Obsession* (2005), and *Banana: The Fate of the Fruit that Changed the World* (2008). Koeppel lives in Los Angeles, California, where he is also an occasional film and television screenwriter and a professional roller derby referee.

Taking a Fall

Could you survive a six-mile drop from an airplane? The answer, says Koeppel, is a guarded *yes*. In "Taking a Fall," originally published in *Popular Mechanics* in 2010 and selected for *Best American Science and Nature Writing 2011*, he uses a combination of humor and basic physics to explain the process of long-distance falling and to show how survival is possible, if unlikely.

6:59:00 a.m., 35,000 Feet

You have a late night and an early flight. Not long after takeoff, you drift to sleep. Suddenly you're wide awake. There's cold air rushing everywhere, and sound. Intense, horrible sound. *Where am I?* you think. *Where's the plane?*

You're six miles up. You're alone. You're falling.

Things are bad. But now's the time to focus on the good news. (Yes, it goes beyond surviving the destruction of your aircraft.) Although gravity is against you, another force is working in your favor: time. Believe it or not, you're better off up here than if you'd slipped from the balcony of your high-rise hotel room after one too many drinks last night.

Or at least you will be. Oxygen is scarce at these heights. By now, hypoxia is starting to set in. You'll be unconscious soon, and you'll cannonball at least a mile before waking up again. When that happens, remember what you are about to read. The ground, after all, is your next destination.

Granted, the odds of surviving a six-mile plummet are extraordinarily slim, but at this point you've got nothing to lose by understanding your situation. There are two ways to fall out of a plane. The first is to free-fall, or drop from the sky with absolutely no protection or means of slowing your descent. The second is to become a wreckage rider, a term coined by the Massachusetts-based amateur historian Jim Hamilton, who developed the *Free Fall Research Page* — an online database of nearly every imaginable human plummet. That classification means you have the advantage of being attached to a chunk of the plane. In 1972 a Serbian flight attendant, Vesna Vulovic, was traveling in a DC-9 over Czechoslovakia when it blew up. She fell 33,000 feet, wedged between her seat, a catering trolley, a section of aircraft, and the body of another crew member, landing on — then sliding down — a snowy incline before coming to a stop, severely injured but alive.

Surviving a plunge surrounded by a semiprotective cocoon of debris is   6
more common than surviving a pure free-fall, according to Hamilton's statistics; thirty-one such confirmed or "plausible" incidents have occurred since the 1940s. Free-fallers constitute a much more exclusive club, with just thirteen confirmed or plausible incidents, including perennial *Ripley's Believe It or Not* superstar Alan Magee, blown from his B-17 on a 1943 mission over France. The New Jersey airman, more recently the subject of a *MythBusters* episode, fell 20,000 feet and crashed into a train station; he was subsequently captured by German troops, who were astonished at his survival.

Whether you're attached to crumpled fuselage or just plain falling, the   7
concept you'll be most interested in is *terminal velocity*. As gravity pulls you toward the earth, you go faster. But like any moving object, you create drag — more as your speed increases. When downward force equals upward resistance, acceleration stops. You max out.

Depending on your size and weight, and factors such as air density, your   8
speed at that moment will be about 120 mph — and you'll get there after a surprisingly brief bit of falling: just 1,500 feet, about the same height as Chicago's Sears (now Willis) Tower. Equal speed means you hit the ground with equal force. The difference is the clock. Body meets Windy City sidewalk in twelve seconds. From an airplane's cruising altitude, you'll have almost enough time to read this entire article.

7:00:20 a.m., 22,000 Feet

By now, you've descended into breathable air. You sputter into conscious-   9
ness. At this altitude you've got roughly two minutes until impact. Your plan is simple. You will enter a Zen state and decide to live. You will understand, as Hamilton notes, "that it isn't the fall that kills you — it's the landing."

Keeping your wits about you, you take aim.   10

But at what? Magee's landing on the stone floor of that French train   11
station was softened by the skylight he crashed through a moment earlier.
Glass hurts, but it gives. So does grass. Haystacks and bushes have cushioned
surprised-to-be-alive free-fallers. Trees aren't bad, though they tend to skewer.
Snow? Absolutely. Swamps? With their mucky, plant-covered surface, even
more awesome. Hamilton documents one case of a sky diver who, upon total
parachute failure, was saved by bouncing off high-tension wires. Contrary to
popular belief, water is an awful choice. Like concrete, liquid doesn't com-
press. Hitting the ocean is essentially the same as colliding with a sidewalk,
Hamilton explains, except that pavement (perhaps unfortunately) won't
"open up and swallow your shattered body."

With a target in mind, the next consideration is body position. To slow   12
your descent, emulate a sky diver. Spread your arms and legs, present your
chest to the ground, and arch your back and head upward. This adds friction
and helps you maneuver. But don't relax. This is not your landing pose.

The question of how to achieve ground contact remains, regrettably,   13
given your predicament, a subject of debate. A 1942 study in the journal *War
Medicine* noted "distribution and compensation of pressure play large parts in
the defeat of injury." Recommendation: wide-body impact. But a 1963 report
by the Federal Aviation Agency argued that shifting into the classic sky diver's landing stance — feet together, heels up, flexed knees and hips — best
increases survivability. The same study noted that training in wrestling and
acrobatics would help people survive falls. Martial arts were deemed especially
useful for hard-surface impacts: "A 'black belt' expert can reportedly crack
solid wood with a single blow," the authors wrote, speculating that such skills
might be transferable.

The ultimate learn-by-doing experience might be a lesson from the Japa-   14
nese parachutist Yasuhiro Kubo, who holds the world record in the activity's
banzai category. The sky diver tosses his chute from the plane and then jumps
out after it, waiting as long as possible to retrieve it, put it on, and pull the rip-
cord. In 2000, Kubo — starting from 9,842 feet — fell for fifty seconds before
recovering his gear. A safer way to practice your technique would be at one
of the wind-tunnel simulators found at about a dozen US theme parks and
malls. But neither will help with the toughest part: sticking the landing. For
that you might consider — though it's not exactly advisable — a leap off the
world's highest bridge, France's Millau Viaduct; its platform towers 891 feet
over mostly spongy farmland.

Water landings — if you must — require quick decision-making. Studies   15
of bridge-jump survivors indicate that a feet-first, knifelike entry (aka "the
pencil") best optimizes your odds of resurfacing. The famed cliff divers of

Acapulco, however, tend to assume a head-down position, with the fingers of each hand locked together, arms outstretched, protecting the head. Whichever you choose, first assume the free-fall position for as long as you can. Then, if a feet-first entry is inevitable, the most important piece of advice, for reasons both unmentionable and easily understood, is to *clench your butt.*

No matter the surface, definitely don't land on your head. In a 1977   16
"Study of Impact Tolerance through Free-Fall Investigations," researchers at the Highway Safety Research Institute found that the major cause of death in falls — they examined drops from buildings, bridges, and the occasional elevator shaft (oops!) — was cranial contact. If you have to arrive top-down, sacrifice your good looks and land on your face rather than the back or top of your head. You might also consider flying with a pair of goggles in your pocket, Hamilton says, since you're likely to get watery eyes — impairing accuracy — on the way down.

7:02:19 a.m., 1,000 Feet

Given your starting altitude, you'll be just about ready to hit the ground   17
as you reach this section of instruction (based on the average adult reading speed of 250 words per minute). The basics have been covered, so feel free to concentrate on the task at hand. But if you're so inclined, here's some supplemental information — though be warned that none of it will help you much at this point.

Statistically speaking, it's best to be a flight crew member, a child, or travel-   18
ing in a military aircraft. Over the past four decades, there have been at least a dozen commercial airline crashes with just one survivor. Of those documented, four of the survivors were crew like the flight attendant Vulovic, and seven were passengers under the age of eighteen. That includes Mohammed el-Fateh Osman, a two-year-old wreckage rider who lived through the crash of a Boeing jet in Sudan in 2003, and, more recently, fourteen-year-old Bahia Bakari, the sole survivor of last June's Yemenia Airways plunge off the Comoros Islands.

Crew survival may be related to better restraint systems, but there's no   19
consensus on why children seem to pull through falls more often. The Federal Aviation Agency study notes that kids, especially those under the age of four, have more flexible skeletons, more relaxed muscle tonus, and a higher proportion of subcutaneous fat, which helps protect internal organs. Smaller people — whose heads are lower than the seat backs in front of them — are better shielded from debris in a plane that's coming apart. Lower body weight reduces terminal velocity, and reduced surface area decreases the chance of impalement upon landing.

7:02:25 a.m., 0 Feet

The ground. Like a Shaolin[1] master, you are at peace and prepared. *Impact.*   20
You're alive. What next? If you're lucky, you might find that your injuries are
minor, stand up, and smoke a celebratory cigarette, as the British tail gun-
ner Nicholas Alkemade did in 1944 after landing in snowy bushes following
an 18,000-foot plummet. (If you're a smoker, you're *super extra lucky,* since
you've technically gotten to indulge during the course of an airliner trip.)
More likely, you'll have tough work ahead.

Follow the example of Juliane Koepcke. On Christmas Eve, 1971, the   21
Lockheed Electra she was traveling in exploded over the Amazon. The next
morning the seventeen-year-old German awoke on the jungle floor, strapped
into her seat, surrounded by fallen holiday gifts. Injured and alone, she pushed
the death of her mother, who'd been seated next to her on the plane, out of
her mind. Instead, she remembered advice from her father, a biologist: To find
civilization when lost in the jungle, follow water. Koepcke waded from tiny
streams to larger ones. She passed crocodiles and poked the mud in front of
her with a stick to scare away stingrays. She had lost one shoe in the fall and
was wearing a ripped miniskirt. Her only food was a bag of candy, and she had
nothing but dark, dirty water to drink. She ignored her broken collarbone and
her wounds, infested with maggots.

On the tenth day, she rested on the bank of the Shebonya River. When   22
she stood up again, she saw a canoe tethered to the shoreline. It took her
hours to climb the embankment to a hut, where, the next day, a group of
lumberjacks found her. The incident was seen as a miracle in Peru, and free-
fall statistics seem to support those arguing for divine intervention: According to the Geneva-based Aircraft Crashes Record Office, 118,934 people
died in 15,463 plane crashes between 1940 and 2008. Even when you add
failed-chute sky divers, Hamilton's tally of confirmed or plausible lived-
to-tell-about-it incidents is only 157, with 42 occurring at heights over 10,000
feet.

But Koepcke never saw survival as a matter of fate. She can still recall the   23
first moments of her fall from the plane, as she spun through the air in her
seat. That wasn't under her control, but what happened when she regained
consciousness was. "I had been able to make the correct decision — to leave
the scene of the crash," she says now. And because of experience at her parents' biological research station, she says, "I did not feel fear. I knew how to
move in the forest and the river, in which I had to swim with dangerous animals like caimans and piranhas."

---

[1] A style of Kung Fu associated with the Shaolin Temple, a Buddhist monastery in
China. — EDS.

Or, by now, you're wide awake, and the aircraft's wheels have touched   24
safely down on the tarmac. You understand that the odds of any kind of accident on a commercial flight are slimmer than slim and that you will likely
never have to use this information. But as a courtesy to the next passenger,
consider leaving your copy of this guide in the seat-back pocket.

*For a reading quiz, visit **bedfordstmartins.com/thebedfordreader**.*

Journal Writing

Koeppel writes about the force of gravity from an unusual perspective. In your journal,
write about a powerful natural phenomenon that you have witnessed — for example,
a thunderstorm, a blizzard, an earthquake, a hurricane, a tornado, a fire. What was
your emotional response to the experience? (To take your journal writing further, see
"From Journal to Essay" on the next page.)

Questions on Meaning

1. Is Koeppel's PURPOSE to instruct, to explain, or to entertain? Why, then, do you
   suppose he addresses readers directly, using the second-PERSON *you*? How, if at all,
   does he intend for readers to use the information he provides?
2. What does it mean to be a "wreckage rider" (par. 5)? Why is that preferable to
   free-fall?
3. Explain what Koeppel means by *terminal velocity* (pars. 7, 19). Why does he say
   it's "the concept you'll be most interested in" (7)?
4. How much time elapses between explosion and landing in Koeppel's analysis?
   How does that relate to the time it takes to read his essay? What connection does
   the writer make between these two processes, and why?
5. Does Koeppel have a THESIS? What is the point of his process analysis?

Questions on Writing Strategy

1. Take particular notice of Koeppel's INTRODUCTION and CONCLUSION. What do
   they have in common? What is the EFFECT of this strategy?
2. What function is served by the headings in this essay?
3. "Taking a Fall" originally appeared in *Popular Mechanics*. How can you tell that
   the magazine is intended for general readers, not for a specialized AUDIENCE of
   professional engineers, physicists, or statisticians? What else can you assume
   about the magazine's audience?
4. **OTHER METHODS**   How does Koeppel use EXAMPLES to develop his process analysis? What is the effect of the particular examples he provides?

Questions on Language

1. Be sure you know how to define the following words: hypoxia (par. 4); plausible, constitute, perennial, subsequently (6); fuselage (7); Zen (9); skewer (11); emulate, friction (12); banzai (14); cranial (16); consensus, tonus, subcutaneous, impalement (19); tethered (22); caimans (23); tarmac (24).
2. How would you characterize Koeppel's DICTION in this essay? What does the diction contribute to his TONE? How effective do you find this use of language, given his subject and purpose?
3. What does Koeppel ALLUDE to with the phrase "sticking the landing" (par. 14)?
4. Point to a few sentences in the essay that use vivid IMAGES and FIGURES OF SPEECH to describe the process of surviving a fall from an airplane.

Suggestions for Writing

1. **FROM JOURNAL TO ESSAY**   Write an essay exploring the natural phenomenon that you wrote about in your journal. Like Koeppel, you might begin and end your essay by grounding readers in an imagined experience of it, but focus on analyzing the general process by which it occurs and reflecting on its significance. What makes this force of nature so deadly? What impact does it have on people? How can they improve the odds of survival if they encounter it? Use vivid images that will make the process come to life for your readers.
2. Koeppel writes that Juliane Koepcke "never saw survival as a matter of fate" (par. 23). Write an essay in which you explore this idea from your own experience and your observations of others. Do you believe that people are essentially in charge of their own fates, or do you think fortune is fickle? Develop your ideas using specific examples.
3. Koeppel writes that "the odds of any kind of accident on a commercial flight are slimmer than slim" (par. 24), but fears of terrorism in the wake of the September 11, 2001 attacks have led to increasingly tight airport security measures — to the point that all passengers are subject to physical pat-downs or x-ray scans that reveal blurry outlines of their bodies. To the minds of many, intense screening of airplane passengers is an excessive and ineffective violation of personal liberties, while others argue that such scrutiny is necessary to ensure safety. Do some research to learn more about the ARGUMENTS on both sides of the issue. Then, in an essay, argue your own position on the subject of airport security.
4. **CRITICAL WRITING**   Take a close look at the nature of Koeppel's SOURCES and at his use of SUMMARY, PARAPHRASE, and direct QUOTATION. In an essay, analyze the way he SYNTHESIZES and integrates information and ideas. Why does he quote directly where he does? How effective are his summaries and paraphrases? How does he combine source materials to develop a thesis of his own?
5. **CONNECTIONS**   "Roller Coasters: Feeling Loopy," by Bonnie Berkowitz and Laura Stanton (*bedfordstmartins.com/thebedfordreader*), is another selection about physics written for nonspecialists. In an essay, COMPARE AND CONTRAST Koeppel's essay with Berkowitz and Stanton's interactive graphic. Do the authors present complex concepts in ways that most readers can understand? What strategies do their works have in common? Where do the works diverge? Use quotations and paraphrases from both selections to support your ideas.

JESSICA MITFORD

Born in Batsford Mansion, England, in 1917, the daughter of Lord and Lady Redesdale, Jessica Mitford devoted much of her early life to defying her aristocratic upbringing. In her autobiography *Daughters and Rebels* (1960), she tells how she received a genteel schooling at home, then as a young woman moved to Loyalist Spain during the violent Spanish Civil War. Later she immigrated to the United States, where for a time she worked in Miami as a bartender. She obtained US citizenship in 1944 and became one of her adopted country's most noted reporters: *Time* called her "Queen of the Muckrakers." Exposing with her typewriter what she regarded as corruption, abuse, and absurdity, Mitford wrote *The American Way of Death* (1963, revised as *The American Way of Death Revisited* in 1998), *Kind and Unusual Punishment: The Prison Business* (1973), and *The American Way of Birth* (1992). *Poison Penmanship* (1979) collects articles from *The Atlantic Monthly, Harper's,* and other magazines. *A Fine Old Conflict* (1977) is the second volume of Mitford's autobiography. Her biography of a Victorian lighthouse keeper's daughter, *Grace Had an English Heart* (1989), examines how the media transform ordinary people into celebrities. Mitford died at her home in Oakland, California, in 1996.

Behind the Formaldehyde Curtain

The most famous (or infamous) thing Jessica Mitford wrote is *The American Way of Death,* a critique of the funeral industry. In this selection from the book, Mitford analyzes the twin processes of embalming and restoring a corpse, the practices she finds most objectionable. You may need a stable stomach to enjoy the selection, but you'll find it a clear, painstaking process analysis, written with masterly style and outrageous wit. (For those who want to know, Mitford herself was cremated after her death.)

The drama begins to unfold with the arrival of the corpse at the mortuary. 1

Alas, poor Yorick! How surprised he would be to see how his counterpart 2 of today is whisked off to a funeral parlor and is in short order sprayed, sliced, pierced, pickled, trussed, trimmed, creamed, waxed, painted, rouged, and neatly dressed — transformed from a common corpse into a Beautiful Memory Picture. This process is known in the trade as embalming and restorative art, and is so universally employed in the United States and Canada that the funeral director does it routinely, without consulting corpse or kin. He regards as eccentric those few who are hardy enough to suggest that it might be dispensed with. Yet no law requires embalming, no religious doctrine commends it, nor is it dictated by considerations of health, sanitation, or even of personal daintiness. In no part of the world but in Northern America is it widely used. The purpose of embalming is to make the corpse presentable for viewing in a suitably costly container; and here too the funeral director routinely, without first consulting the family, prepares the body for public display.

Is all this legal? The processes to which a dead body may be subjected are   3
after all to some extent circumscribed by law. In most states, for instance, the signature of next of kin must be obtained before an autopsy may be performed, before the deceased may be cremated, before the body may be turned over to a medical school for research purposes; or such provision must be made in the decedent's will. In the case of embalming, no such permission is required nor is it ever sought.[1] A textbook, *The Principles and Practices of Embalming,* comments on this: "There is some question regarding the legality of much that is done within the preparation room." The author points out that it would be most unusual for a responsible member of a bereaved family to instruct the mortician, in so many words, to "embalm" the body of a deceased relative. The very term *embalming* is so seldom used that the mortician must rely upon custom in the matter. The author concludes that unless the family specifies otherwise, the act of entrusting the body to the care of a funeral establishment carries with it an implied permission to go ahead and embalm.

Embalming is indeed a most extraordinary procedure, and one must won-   4
der at the docility of Americans who each year pay hundreds of millions of dollars for its perpetuation, blissfully ignorant of what it is all about, what is done, how it is done. Not one in ten thousand has any idea of what actually takes place. Books on the subject are extremely hard to come by. They are not to be found in most libraries or bookshops.

In an era when huge television audiences watch surgical operations in   5
the comfort of their living rooms, when, thanks to the animated cartoon, the geography of the digestive system has become familiar territory even to the nursery school set, in a land where the satisfaction of curiosity about almost all matters is a national pastime, the secrecy surrounding embalming can, surely, hardly be attributed to the inherent gruesomeness of the subject. Custom in this regard has within this century suffered a complete reversal. In the early days of American embalming, when it was performed in the home of the deceased, it was almost mandatory for some relative to stay by the embalmer's

---

[1] Partly because of Mitford's attack, the Federal Trade Commission now requires the funeral industry to provide families with itemized price lists, including the price of embalming, to state that embalming is not required, and to obtain the family's consent to embalming before charging for it. Shortly before her death, however, Mitford observed that the FTC had "watered down" the regulations and "routinely ignored" consumer complaints about the funeral industry. — EDS.

side and witness the procedure. Today, family members who might wish to be in attendance would certainly be dissuaded by the funeral director. All others, except apprentices, are excluded by law from the preparation room.

A close look at what does actually take place may explain in large mea-   6
sure the undertaker's intractable reticence concerning a procedure that has become his major *raison d'être*. Is it possible he fears that public information about embalming might lead patrons to wonder if they really want this ser-vice? If the funeral men are loath to discuss the subject outside the trade, the reader may, understandably, be equally loath to go on reading at this point. For those who have the stomach for it, let us part the formaldehyde curtain. . . .

The body is first laid out in the undertaker's morgue — or rather,   7
Mr. Jones is reposing in the preparation room — to be readied to bid the world farewell.

The preparation room in any of the better funeral establishments has the   8
tiled and sterile look of a surgery, and indeed the embalmer–restorative artist who does his chores there is beginning to adopt the term *dermasurgeon* (appro-priately corrupted by some mortician-writers as "demi-surgeon") to describe his calling. His equipment, consisting of scalpels, scissors, augers, forceps, clamps, needles, pumps, tubes, bowls, and basins, is crudely imitative of the surgeon's, as is his technique, acquired in a nine- or twelve-month post-high-school course in an embalming school. He is supplied by an advanced chemi-cal industry with a bewildering array of fluids, sprays, pastes, oils, powders, creams, to fix or soften tissue, shrink or distend it as needed, dry it here, restore the moisture there. There are cosmetics, waxes, and paints to fill and cover features, even plaster of Paris to replace entire limbs. There are ingenious aids to prop and stabilize the cadaver: a Vari-Pose Head Rest, the Edwards Arm and Hand Positioner, the Repose Block (to support the shoulders during the embalming), and the Throop Foot Positioner, which resembles an old-fashioned stocks.

Mr. John H. Eckels, president of the Eckels College of Mortuary Science,   9
thus describes the first part of the embalming procedure: "In the hands of a skilled practitioner, this work may be done in a comparatively short time and without mutilating the body other than by slight incision — so slight that it scarcely would cause serious inconvenience if made upon a living person. It is necessary to remove the blood, and doing this not only helps in the disinfect-ing, but removes the principal cause of disfigurements due to discoloration."

Another textbook discusses the all-important time element: "The ear-   10
lier this is done, the better, for every hour that elapses between death and embalming will add to the problems and complications encountered. . . ." Just how soon should one get going on the embalming? The author tells us, "On the basis of such scanty information made available to this profession through

its rudimentary and haphazard system of technical research, we must conclude that the best results are to be obtained if the subject is embalmed before life is completely extinct — that is, before cellular death has occurred. In the average case, this would mean within an hour after somatic death." For those who feel that there is something a little rudimentary, not to say haphazard, about this advice, a comforting thought is offered by another writer. Speaking of fears entertained in early days of premature burial, he points out, "One of the effects of embalming by chemical injection, however, has been to dispel fears of live burial." How true; once the blood is removed, chances of live burial are indeed remote.

To return to Mr. Jones, the blood is drained out through the veins and   11
replaced by embalming fluid pumped in through the arteries. As noted in *The Principles and Practices of Embalming,* "every operator has a favorite injection and drainage point — a fact which becomes a handicap only if he fails or refuses to forsake his favorites when conditions demand it." Typical favorites are the carotid artery, femoral artery, jugular vein, subclavian vein. There are various choices of embalming fluid. If Flextone is used, it will produce a "mild, flexible rigidity. The skin retains a velvety softness, the tissues are rubbery and pliable. Ideal for women and children." It may be blended with B. and G. Products Company's Lyf-Lyk tint, which is guaranteed to reproduce "nature's own skin texture . . . the velvety appearance of living tissue." Sun-tone comes in three separate tints: Suntan; Special Cosmetic Tint, a pink shade "especially indicated for female subjects"; and Regular Cosmetic Tint, moderately pink.

About three to six gallons of a dyed and perfumed solution of formalde-   12
hyde, glycerin, borax, phenol, alcohol, and water is soon circulating through Mr. Jones, whose mouth has been sewn together with a "needle directed upward between the upper lip and gum and brought out through the left nostril," with the corners raised slightly "for a more pleasant expression." If he should be bucktoothed, his teeth are cleaned with Bon Ami and coated with colorless nail polish. His eyes, meanwhile, are closed with flesh-tinted eye caps and eye cement.

The next step is to have at Mr. Jones with a thing called a trocar. This is a   13
long, hollow needle attached to a tube. It is jabbed into the abdomen, poked around the entrails and chest cavity, the contents of which are pumped out and replaced with "cavity fluid." This done, and the hole in the abdomen sewn up, Mr. Jones's face is heavily creamed (to protect the skin from burns which may be caused by leakage of the chemicals), and he is covered with a sheet and left unmolested for a while. But not for long — there is more, much more, in store for him. He has been embalmed, but not yet restored, and the

best time to start the restorative work is eight to ten hours after embalming, when the tissues have become firm and dry.

The object of all this attention to the corpse, it must be remembered, is to make it presentable for viewing in an attitude of healthy repose. "Our customs require the presentation of our dead in the semblance of normality . . . unmarred by the ravages of illness, disease, or mutilation," says Mr. J. Sheridan Mayer in his *Restorative Art*. This is rather a large order since few people die in the full bloom of health, unravaged by illness and unmarked by some disfigurement. The funeral industry is equal to the challenge: "In some cases the gruesome appearance of a mutilated or disease-ridden subject may be quite discouraging. The task of restoration may seem impossible and shake the confidence of the embalmer. This is the time for intestinal fortitude and determination. Once the formative work is begun and affected tissues are cleaned or removed, all doubts of success vanish. It is surprising and gratifying to discover the results which may be obtained." 14

The embalmer, having allowed an appropriate interval to elapse, returns to the attack, but now he brings into play the skill and equipment of sculptor and cosmetician. Is a hand missing? Casting one in plaster of Paris is a simple matter. "For replacement purposes, only a cast of the back of the hand is necessary; this is within the ability of the average operator and is quite adequate." If a lip or two, a nose, or an ear should be missing, the embalmer has at hand a variety of restorative waxes with which to model replacements. Pores and skin texture are simulated by stippling with a little brush, and over this cosmetics are laid on. Head off? Decapitation cases are rather routinely handled. Ragged edges are trimmed, and head joined to torso with a series of splints, wires, and sutures. It is a good idea to have a little something at the neck — a scarf or a high collar — when time for viewing comes. Swollen mouth? Cut out tissue as needed from inside the lips. If too much is removed, the surface contour can easily be restored by padding with cotton. Swollen necks and cheeks are reduced by removing tissue through vertical incisions made down each side of the neck. "When the deceased is casketed, the pillow will hide the suture incisions . . . as an extra precaution against leakage, the suture may be painted with liquid sealer." 15

The opposite condition is more likely to present itself — that of emaciation. His hypodermic syringe now loaded with massage cream, the embalmer seeks out and fills the hollowed and sunken areas by injection. In this procedure the backs of the hands and fingers and the under-chin area should not be neglected. 16

Positioning the lips is a problem that recurrently challenges the ingenuity of the embalmer. Closed too tightly, they tend to give a stern, even 17 disapproving expression. Ideally, embalmers feel, the lips should give the impression of being ever so slightly parted, the upper lip protruding slightly for a more youthful appearance. This takes some engineering, however, as the lips tend to drift apart. Lip drift can sometimes be remedied by pushing one or two straight pins through the inner margin of the lower lip and then inserting them between the two front upper teeth. If Mr. Jones happens to have no teeth, the pins can just as easily be anchored in his Armstrong Face Former and Denture Replacer. Another method to maintain lip closure is to dislocate the lower jaw, which is then held in its new position by a wire run through holes which have been drilled through the upper and lower jaws at the midline. As the French are fond of saying, *il faut souffrir pour être belle*.[2]

If Mr. Jones has died of jaundice, the embalming fluid will very likely turn   18
him green. Does this deter the embalmer? Not if he has intestinal fortitude. Masking pastes and cosmetics are heavily laid on, burial garments and casket interiors are color-correlated with particular care, and Jones is displayed beneath rose-colored lights. Friends will say "How *well* he looks." Death by carbon monoxide, on the other hand, can be rather a good thing from the embalmer's viewpoint: "One advantage is the fact that this type of discoloration is an exaggerated form of a natural pink coloration." This is nice because the healthy glow is already present and needs but little attention.

The patching and filling completed, Mr. Jones is now shaved, washed,   19
and dressed. Cream-based cosmetic, available in pink, flesh, suntan, brunette, and blond, is applied to his hands and face, his hair is shampooed and combed (and, in the case of Mrs. Jones, set), his hands manicured. For the horny-handed son of toil special care must be taken; cream should be applied to remove ingrained grime, and the nails cleaned. "If he were not in the habit of having them manicured in life, trimming and shaping is advised for better appearance — never questioned by kin."

Jones is now ready for casketing (this is the present participle of the verb   20
"to casket"). In this operation his right shoulder should be depressed slightly "to turn the body a bit to the right and soften the appearance of lying flat on the back." Positioning the hands is a matter of importance, and special rubber positioning blocks may be used. The hands should be cupped slightly for a more lifelike, relaxed appearance. Proper placement of the body requires a delicate sense of balance. It should lie as high as possible in the casket, yet not so high that the lid, when lowered, will hit the nose. On the other hand, we are cautioned, placing the body too low "creates the impression that the body is in a box."

[2] You have to suffer to be beautiful. — Eds.

Jones is next wheeled into the appointed slumber room where a few last   21
touches may be added — his favorite pipe placed in his hand or, if he was a
great reader, a book propped into position. (In the case of little Master Jones
a Teddy bear may be clutched.) Here he will hold open house for a few days,
visiting hours 10 a.m. to 9 p.m.

All now being in readiness, the funeral director calls a staff conference   22
to make sure that each assistant knows his precise duties. Mr. Wilber Kriege
writes: "This makes your staff feel that they are a part of the team, with a
definite assignment that must be properly carried out if the whole plan is to
succeed. You never heard of a football coach who failed to talk to his entire
team before they go on the field. They have drilled on the plays they are to
execute for hours and days, and yet the successful coach knows the importance of making even the benchwarming third-string substitute feel that he
is important if the game is to be won." The winning of *this* game is predicated
upon glass-smooth handling of the logistics. The funeral director has notified
the pallbearers whose names were furnished by the family, has arranged for the
presence of clergyman, organist, and soloist, has provided transportation for
everybody, has organized and listed the flowers sent by friends. In *Psychology
of Funeral Service* Mr. Edward A. Martin points out, "He may not always do as
much as the family thinks he is doing, but it is his helpful guidance that they
appreciate in knowing they are proceeding as they should. . . . The important
thing is how well his services can be used to make the family believe they are
giving unlimited expression to their own sentiment."

The religious service may be held in a church or in the chapel of the   23
funeral home; the funeral director vastly prefers the latter arrangement, for
not only is it more convenient for him but it affords him the opportunity to
show off his beautiful facilities to the gathered mourners. After the clergyman
has had his say, the mourners queue up to file past the casket for a last look
at the deceased. The family is *never* asked whether they want an open-casket
ceremony; in the absence of their instruction to the contrary, this is taken for
granted. Consequently well over 90 percent of all American funerals feature
the open casket — a custom unknown in other parts of the world. Foreigners
are astonished by it. An English woman living in San Francisco described her
reaction in a letter to the writer:

> I myself have attended only one funeral here — that of an elderly fellow
> worker of mine. After the service I could not understand why everyone was
> walking towards the coffin (sorry, I mean casket), but thought I had better
> follow the crowd. It shook me rigid to get there and find the casket open and
> poor old Oscar lying there in his brown tweed suit, wearing a sun-tan makeup
> and just the wrong shade of lipstick. If I had not been extremely fond of the

old boy, I have a horrible feeling that I might have giggled. Then and there I decided that I could never face another American funeral — even dead.

The casket (which has been resting throughout the service on a Classic 24 Beauty Ultra Metal Casket Bier) is now transferred by a hydraulically operated device called Porto-Lift to a balloon-tired, Glide Easy casket carriage which will wheel it to yet another conveyance, the Cadillac Funeral Coach. This may be lavender, cream, light green — anything but black. Interiors, of course, are color-correlated, "for the man who cannot stop short of perfection."

At graveside, the casket is lowered into the earth. This office, once 25 the prerogative of friends of the deceased, is now performed by a patented mechanical lowering device. A "Lifetime Green" artificial grass mat is at the ready to conceal the sere earth, and overhead, to conceal the sky, is a portable Steril Chapel Tent ("resists the intense heat and humidity of summer and the terrific storms of winter . . . available in Silver Gray, Rose, or Evergreen"). Now is the time for the ritual scattering of earth over the coffin, as the solemn words "earth to earth, ashes to ashes, dust to dust" are pronounced by the officiating cleric. This can today be accomplished "with a mere flick of the wrist with the Gordon Leak-Proof Earth Dispenser. No grasping of a handful of dirt, no soiled fingers. Simple, dignified, beautiful, reverent! The modern way!" The Gordon Earth Dispenser (at $5) is of nickel-plated brass construction. It is not only "attractive to the eye and long wearing"; it is also "one of the 'tools' for building better public relations" if presented as "an appropriate noncommercial gift" to the clergyman. It is shaped something like a saltshaker.

Untouched by human hand, the coffin and the earth are now united. 26

It is in the function of directing the participants through this maze of 27 gadgetry that the funeral director has assigned to himself his relatively new role of "grief therapist." He has relieved the family of every detail, he has revamped the corpse to look like a living doll, he has arranged for it to nap for a few days in a slumber room, he has put on a well-oiled performance in which the concept of *death* has played no part whatsoever — unless it was inconsiderately mentioned by the clergyman who conducted the religious service. He has done everything in his power to make the funeral a real pleasure for everybody concerned. He and his team have given their all to score an upset victory over death.

*For a reading quiz, visit **bedfordstmartins.com/thebedfordreader**.*

Journal Writing

Presumably, morticians embalm and restore corpses, and survivors support the work, because the practices are thought to ease the shock of death. Now that you know what goes on behind the scenes, how do you feel about a loved one's undergoing these procedures? (To take your journal writing further, see "From Journal to Essay" on the next page.)

Questions on Meaning

1. What was your emotional response to this essay? Can you analyze your feelings?
2. To what does Mitford attribute the secrecy surrounding the embalming process?
3. What, according to Mitford, is the mortician's intent? What common obstacles to fulfilling it must be surmounted?
4. What do you understand from Mitford's remark in paragraph 10, on dispelling fears of live burial: "How true; once the blood is removed, chances of live burial are indeed remote"?
5. Do you find any implied PURPOSE in this essay? Does Mitford seem primarily out to rake muck, or does she offer any positive suggestions to Americans?

Questions on Writing Strategy

1. What is Mitford's TONE? In her opening two paragraphs, exactly what shows her attitude toward her subject?
2. Why do you think Mitford goes into so much grisly detail in analyzing the processes of embalming and restoration? How does the detail serve her purpose?
3. What is the EFFECT of calling the body Mr. Jones?
4. Paragraph by paragraph, what TRANSITIONS does the author employ?
5. To whom does Mitford address her process analysis? How do you know she isn't writing for an AUDIENCE of professional morticians?
6. Choose one of the quotations from the journals and textbooks of professionals and explain how it serves the author's general purpose.
7. Why do you think Mitford often uses the PASSIVE VOICE to describe the actions of embalmers — for instance, "the blood is drained," "If Flextone is used," and "It may be blended" in paragraph 11? Are the verbs in passive voice effective or ineffective? Why?
8. **OTHER METHODS** In paragraph 8, Mitford uses CLASSIFICATION in listing the embalmer's equipment and supplies. What groups does she identify, and why does she bother sorting the items at all?

Questions on Language

1. Explain the ALLUSION to Yorick in paragraph 2.
2. What IRONY do you find in this statement in paragraph 7: "The body is first laid out in the undertaker's morgue — or rather, Mr. Jones is reposing in the

preparation room"? Pick out any other words or phrases in the essay that seem ironic. Comment especially on those you find in the essay's last two sentences.
3. Why is it useful to Mitford's purpose that she cites the brand names of morticians' equipment and supplies (the Edwards Arm and Hand Positioner, Lyf-Lyk tint)? List all the brand names in the essay that are memorable.
4. Define the following words or terms: counterpart (par. 2); circumscribed, autopsy, cremated, decedent, bereaved (3); docility, perpetuation (4); inherent, mandatory (5); intractable, reticence, *raison d'être*, formaldehyde (6); "derma-" (in *dermasurgeon*), augers, forceps, distend, stocks (8); somatic (10); carotid artery, femoral artery, jugular vein, subclavian vein, pliable (11); glycerin, borax, phenol, bucktoothed (12); trocar, entrails (13); stippling, sutures (15); emaciation (16); jaundice (18); predicated (22); queue (23); hydraulically (24); sere, cleric (25); therapist (27).

Suggestions for Writing

1. **FROM JOURNAL TO ESSAY**   Drawing on your personal response to Mitford's essay in your journal, write a brief essay that ARGUES either for or against embalming and restoration. Consider the purposes served by these practices, both for the mortician and for the dead person's relatives and friends, as well as their costs and effects.
2. Search the Web or consult a periodical index for sources of information about the phenomenon of quick-freezing the dead. Set forth this process, including its hoped-for result of being able to revive the corpses in the far future.
3. ANALYZE some other process whose operations may not be familiar to everyone. (Have you ever held a job, or helped out in a family business, that has taken you behind the scenes? How is fast food prepared? How are cars serviced? How is a baby sat? How is a house constructed?) Detail it step by step, including transitions to clarify the steps.
4. **CRITICAL WRITING**   In attacking the funeral industry, Mitford also, implicitly, attacks the people who pay for and comply with the industry's attitudes and practices. What ASSUMPTIONS does Mitford seem to make about how we ought to deal with death and the dead? (Consider, for instance, her statements about the "docility of Americans . . . , blissfully ignorant" [par. 4] and the funeral director's making "the funeral a real pleasure for everybody concerned" [27].) Write an essay in which you interpret Mitford's assumptions and agree or disagree with them, based on your own reading and experience. If you like, defend the ritual of the funeral, or the mortician's profession, against Mitford's attack.
5. **CONNECTIONS**   In "Vampires Never Die" (p. 291), Guillermo del Toro and Chuck Hogan also comment on fears of death, noting that "we have no true jurisdiction over our bodies." Taken together, what do Mitford's and del Toro and Hogan's essays say about the importance of the body in Western culture? Write an essay either defending or criticizing the desire for physical immortality, whether real or imagined.

Jessica Mitford on Writing

"Choice of subject is of cardinal importance," declared Jessica Mitford in *Poison Penmanship*. "One does by far one's best work when besotted by and absorbed in the matter at hand." After *The American Way of Death* was published, Mitford received hundreds of letters suggesting alleged rackets that ought to be exposed, and to her surprise, an overwhelming majority of these letters complained about defective and overpriced hearing aids. But Mitford never wrote a book blasting the hearing aid industry. "Somehow, although there may well be need for such an exposé, I could not warm up to hearing aids as a subject for the kind of thorough, intensive, long-range research that would be needed to do an effective job." She once taught a course at Yale on muckraking, with each student choosing a subject to investigate. "Those who tackled hot issues on campus, such as violations of academic freedom or failure to implement affirmative-action hiring policies, turned in some excellent work; but the lad who decided to investigate 'waste in the Yale dining halls' was predictably unable to make much of this trivial topic." (The editors interject: We aren't sure that the topic is necessarily trivial, but obviously not everyone would burn to write about it!)

The hardest problem Mitford faced in writing *The American Way of Death*, she recalled, was doing her factual, step-by-step account of the embalming process. She felt "determined to describe it in all its revolting details, but how to make this subject palatable to the reader?" Her solution was to cast the whole process analysis in the official JARGON of the mortuary industry, drawing on lists of taboo words and their EUPHEMISMS (or acceptable synonyms), as published in the trade journal *Casket & Sunnyside:* "Mr., Mrs., Miss Blank, not corpse or body; preparation room, not morgue; reposing room, not laying-out room. . . ." The story of Mr. Jones thus took shape, and Mitford's use of jargon, she found, added macabre humor to the proceedings.

For Discussion

1. What seem to be Mitford's criteria for an effective essay or book?
2. What is muckraking? Why do you suppose anyone would want to do it?

ADDITIONAL WRITING TOPICS

Process Analysis

1. Write a *directive* process analysis (a "how-to" essay) in which, drawing on your own knowledge, you instruct someone in doing or making something. Divide the process into steps, and be sure to detail each step thoroughly. Here are some possible subjects (any of which may be modified or narrowed):

How to create a Web site or a blog
How to post a video on *YouTube*
How to enlist people's confidence
How to bake bread
How to meditate
How to teach a child to swim
How to select a science fiction novel
How to drive a car in snow or rain
How to prepare yourself to take an intelligence test
How to compose a photograph
How to judge cattle
How to buy a used motorcycle
How to enjoy an opera
How to organize your own rock group
How to eat an artichoke
How to groom a horse
How to belly dance
How to build (or fly) a kite
How to start weight training
How to aid a person who is choking
How to behave on a first date
How to get your own way
How to kick a habit
How to lose weight
How to win at poker
How to make an effective protest or complaint

Or, if you don't like any of those topics, what else do you know that others might care to learn from you?

2. Step by step, working in chronological order, write a careful *informative* analysis of any one of the following processes. (This is not to be a "how-to" essay, but an essay that explains how something works or happens.) Make use of DESCRIPTION wherever necessary, and be sure to include frequent TRANSITIONS. If one of these topics gives you a better idea for a paper, go with your own subject.

How a student is processed during orientation or registration
How the student newspaper gets published
How a particular Web search engine works
How a stereo amplifier or an MP3 player works

How a professional umpire (or an acupuncturist, or some other professional) does his or her job

How an air conditioner (or other household appliance) works

How birds teach their young (or some other process in the natural world: how sharks feed, how a snake swallows an egg, how the human liver works)

How police control crowds

How people usually make up their minds when shopping for new cars (or new clothes)

3. Write a directive process analysis in which you use a light TONE. Although you need not take your subject in deadly earnest, your humor will probably be effective only if you take the method of process analysis seriously. Make clear each stage of the process and explain it in sufficient detail. Here are a few possible topics:

How to get through the month of November (or March)

How to flunk out of college swiftly and efficiently

How to outwit a computer game

How to choose a mate

How to go broke

How to sell something that nobody wants

9

DIVISION OR ANALYSIS

Slicing into Parts

◀ **Division or analysis in a cartoon**

The cartoonist Roz Chast is well known for witty and perceptive comments on the everyday, made through words and simple, almost childlike drawings. Dividing or analyzing, this cartoon identifies the elements of a boy's sandwich to discover what they can tell about the values and politics of the parent who made the sandwich. The title, "Deconstructing Lunch," refers to a type of analysis that focuses on the multiple meanings of a subject and especially its internal contradictions. Summarize what the sandwich reveals about the boy's parent. What contradictions do you spot in his or her values or politics? What might Chast be saying more generally about food choices?

THE METHOD

A chemist working for a soft-drink company is asked to improve on a competitor's product, Hydra Sports Water. (In the previous chapter the same chemist was working on a different part of the same problem.) To do the job, the chemist first has to figure out what's in the drink. She smells the stuff and tastes it. Then she tests a sample chemically to discover the actual ingredients: water, corn syrup, sodium citrate, potassium chloride, coloring. Methodically, the chemist has performed DIVISION or ANALYSIS: She has separated the beverage into its components. Hydra Sports Water stands revealed, understood, ready to be bettered.

Division or analysis (the terms are interchangeable) is a key skill in learning and in life. It is an instrument allowing you to slice a large and complicated subject into smaller parts that you can grasp and relate to one another. In fact, it is so fundamental that it underlies every other method of development discussed in this book — for instance, it helps you identify features for DESCRIPTION or spot similarities for COMPARISON AND CONTRAST. With analysis you comprehend — and communicate — the structure of things. And when it works, you find in the parts an idea or conclusion about the subject that makes it clearer, truer, more comprehensive, or more vivid than it was before you started.

Kinds of Division or Analysis

Although division or analysis always works the same way — separating a whole, singular subject into its elements, slicing it into parts — the method can be more or less difficult depending on how unfamiliar, complex, and abstract the subject is. Obviously, it's going to be much easier to analyze a chicken (wings, legs, thighs, . . .) than a poem by Rita Dove (this image, that allusion, . . .), easier to analyze the structure of a small business than that of a multinational conglomerate.

There are always multiple ways to divide or analyze a subject. One literary critic, for instance, might divide a poem by looking at its rhymes, meter, imagery, and so forth — following its internal components — while another might examine the poem as an artifact of the author's time and place — connecting its elements to its context. In other words, the outcome of an analysis depends on the rule or principle used to conduct it. This fact accounts for some of the differences among academic disciplines: A psychologist, say, may look at the individual person primarily as a bundle of drives and needs, whereas a sociologist may emphasize the individual's roles in society. Even within disciplines, different factions analyze differently, using different principles of division or analysis. Some psychologists are interested mainly in perception, others mainly in behavior; some focus mainly on emotional development, others mainly on brain chemistry.

Analysis and Critical Thinking

Analysis plays a fundamental role in CRITICAL THINKING, READING, AND WRITING, topics discussed in Chapters 1 and 3. In fact, *analysis* and *criticism* are deeply related: The first comes from a Greek word meaning "to undo"; the second from a Greek word meaning "to separate."

Critical thinking, reading, and writing go beneath the surface of the object, word, image, or whatever the subject is. When you work critically, you divide the subject into its elements, INFER the buried meanings and ASSUMPTIONS that define its essence, and SYNTHESIZE the parts into a new whole that is now informed by your perspective. Say a campaign brochure quotes a candidate as favoring "reasonable government expenditures on reasonable highway projects." The candidate will support new roads, right? Wrong. As a critical reader of the brochure, you quickly sense something fishy in the use (twice) of *reasonable*. As an informed reader, you know (or find out) that the candidate has consistently opposed new roads, so the chances of her finding a highway project "reasonable" are slim. At the same time, her stand has been unpopular, so of course she wants to seem "reasonable" on the issue. Read critically, then, a campaign statement that seems to offer mild support for highways is actually a slippery evasion of any such commitment.

Analysis (a convenient term for the overlapping operations of analysis, inference, and synthesis) is very useful for exposing such evasiveness, but that isn't its only function. If you've read this far in this book, you've already done quite a bit of analytical/critical thinking as you read and analyzed the selections. The method will also help you understand a sculpture, perceive the importance of a case study in sociology, or form a response to an environmental impact report. And the method can be invaluable for straight thinking about popular culture, from TV to toys.

THE PROCESS

Subject and Purpose

Keep an eye out for writing assignments requiring division or analysis — in college and work, they won't be few or hard to find. They will probably include the word *analyze* or a word implying analysis, such as *evaluate, examine, explore, interpret, discuss,* or *criticize.* Any time you spot such a term, you know your job is to separate the subject into its elements, to infer their meanings, to explore the relations among them, and to draw a conclusion about the subject.

Almost any coherent entity — object, person, place, concept — is a fit subject for analysis *if* the analysis will add to the subject's meaning or significance. Little is deadlier than the rote analytical exercise that leaves the parts neatly dissected and the subject comatose on the page. As a writer, you have to animate the subject, and that means finding your interest. What about your subject seems curious? What's appealing? or mysterious? or awful? And what will be your PURPOSE in writing about the subject: Do you simply want to explain it, or do you want to argue for or against it?

Such questions can help you find the principle or framework you will use to divide the subject into parts. Say you've got an assignment to write about a sculpture in a nearby park. Why do you like the sculpture, or why don't you? What elements of its creation and physical form make it art? What is the point of such public art? What does this sculpture do for this park, or vice versa? Any of these questions could suggest a slant on the subject, a framework for analysis, and a purpose for writing, getting your analysis moving.

Principle of Analysis and Thesis

Finding your principle of analysis will lead you to your essay's THESIS as well — the main point you want to make about your subject. Expressed in a THESIS STATEMENT, this idea will help keep you focused and help your readers see your subject as a whole rather than as a bundle of parts. Here are the thesis statements in two of this chapter's selections:

> Monsters, like angels, are invoked by our individual and collective needs. Today, much as during that gloomy summer in 1816 [when Dracula was conceived], we feel the need to seek their cold embrace.
> — Guillermo del Toro and Chuck Hogan, "Vampires Never Die"

> Boys — and more and more girls — who accept Jock Culture values often go on to flourish in a competitive sports environment that requires submission to authority, winning by any means necessary, and group cohesion.
> — Robert Lipsyte, "Jock Culture"

Readers will have an easier time following your analysis — and will more likely appreciate it — if they have a hook on which to hang the details. Your thesis statement can be that hook if you use it to establish your framework, your principle of analysis. A well-focused thesis statement can help you as well, because it gives you a yardstick to judge how complete, consistent, and supportive your analysis is. Don't be discouraged, though, if your thesis statement doesn't come to you until *after* you've written a first draft and had a chance to discover your interest. Writing about your subject may be the best way for you to find its meaning and significance.

Evidence

Making a valid analysis is chiefly a matter of giving your subject thought, but for the result to seem useful and convincing to your readers, it will have to refer to the concrete world. The method, then, also requires open eyes and a willingness to provide EVIDENCE. The nature of the evidence will depend entirely on what you are analyzing — physical details for a sculpture, quotations for a poem, financial data for a business review, statistics for a psychology case study, and so forth. The idea is to supply enough evidence to justify and support your particular slant on the subject.

In developing an essay by analysis, having an outline at your elbow can be a help. You don't want to overlook any parts or elements that should be included in your framework. (You needn't mention every feature in your final essay or give them all equal treatment, but any omissions or variations should be conscious.) And you want to use your framework consistently, not switching carelessly (and confusingly) from, say, the form of the sculpture to the cost of public art.

A final caution: It's possible to get carried away with one's own analysis, to become so enamored of the details that the subject itself becomes dim or distorted. You can avoid this danger by keeping the subject literally in front of you as you work (or at least imagining it vividly). It often helps to reassemble your subject at the end of the essay, placing it in a larger context, speculating on its influence, or affirming its significance. By the end of the essay, your subject must be a coherent whole truly represented by your analysis, not twisted, inflated, or obliterated. The reader should be intrigued by your subject, yes, but also able to recognize it on the street.

FOCUS ON PARAGRAPH COHERENCE

Because several elements contribute to the whole of a subject, your analysis will be easier for readers to follow if you frequently clarify what element you are discussing and how it fits with your principle of analysis. Two techniques, especially, can help you guide readers through your analysis: transitions and repetition or restatement.

- **Use TRANSITIONS as signposts to tell readers where you, and they, are headed.** Among other uses, transitions may specify the relations between your points and your principle of analysis (*first, second, another feature*) or

(continued)

may clarify the relations among the points themselves (*even more important, similarly*). Consider how transitions keep readers focused in the following paragraph:

Many television comedies, even some that boast live audiences, rely on laugh tracks to fill too-quiet moments. To create a laugh track, an editor uses four overlapping elements of a laugh. The first is style, from titter to belly laugh. The second is intensity, the volume, ranging from mild to medium to earsplitting. The third ingredient is duration, the length of the laugh, whether quick, medium, or extended. And finally, there's the number of laughers, from a lone giggler to a roaring throng. When creating a canned laugh, the editor draws from a bank of hundreds of prerecorded laugh files and blends the four ingredients as a maestro weaves a symphony out of brass, woodwinds, percussion, and strings.

- **Use repetition and restatement to link sentences and tie them to your principle of analysis.** In the preceding paragraph, two threads run through the sentences to maintain the focus: *laugh tracks, laugh track, laugh, laughers,* and *canned laugh*; and *editor, editor,* and *maestro*.

CHECKLIST FOR REVISING A DIVISION OR ANALYSIS ESSAY

✔ **Principle of analysis and thesis.** What is your particular slant on your subject, the rule or principle you have used to divide your subject into its elements? Do you specify it in your thesis statement?

✔ **Completeness.** Have you considered all the subject's elements required by your principle of analysis?

✔ **Consistency.** Have you applied your principle of analysis consistently, viewing your subject from a definite slant?

✔ **Evidence.** Is your division or analysis well supported with concrete details, quotations, data, or statistics, as appropriate?

✔ **Significance.** Why should readers care about your analysis? Have you told them something about your subject that wasn't obvious on its surface?

✔ **Truth to subject.** Is your analysis faithful to the subject, not distorted, exaggerated, or deflated?

DIVISION OR ANALYSIS IN ACADEMIC WRITING

A Political Science Textbook

In this paragraph adapted from *Government by the People*, an introductory political science textbook focused on American government, authors David

B. Magleby, Paul C. Light, and Christine L. Nemacheck divide the US Constitution into its essential elements. The careful analysis supports their admiration for the document's simplicity and flexibility.

Despite its brevity, the Constitution firmly established the Framers' experiment in free-government-in-the-making that each generation reinterprets and renews. That is why after more than 225 years we have not had another written Constitution — let alone two, three, or more, like other countries around the world. Part of the reason is the public's widespread acceptance of the Constitution. But the Constitution has also endured because it is a brilliant structure for limited government and one that the Framers designed to be adaptable and flexible. Article I establishes a bicameral Congress, with a House of Representatives and a Senate, and empowers it to enact legislation — for example, governing foreign and interstate commerce. Article II vests the executive power in the president, and Article III vests the judicial power in the Supreme Court and other federal courts that Congress may establish. Article IV guarantees the privileges and immunities of citizens and specifies the conditions for admitting new states. Article V provides for the methods of amending the Constitution, and Article VI specifies that the Constitution and all laws made under it are the supreme law of the land. Finally, Article VII provides that the Constitution had to be ratified by nine of the original thirteen states to go into effect. In 1791, the first ten amendments, the Bill of Rights, were added, and another seventeen amendments have been added since.

> Principle of analysis: "brilliant" structure of the Constitution
> 1. Legislative branch
>
> 2. Executive branch
> 3. Judicial branch
> 4. Protections for citizens
> 5. Procedures for amendment
> 6. Authority
> 7. Ratification
>
> 8. Bill of Rights and later amendments

An Annotated Bibliography

As a college student, you are likely to write research papers in many of your courses. Whether for your own use or as part of the research-writing assignment, preparing an annotated bibliography during research can help you keep track of your sources and use them effectively.

A common form of annotated bibliography contains a two-part entry for every potential source: (1) full publication information for the source, so that you can find it again and cite it accurately in your paper; and (2) your own comments on the source, including a brief summary and a brief analysis that addresses its value in its field, its usefulness to you, and other matters. If you include an annotation along with the publication information in your final paper, the two together can help readers locate and assess the source for themselves.

For a course in American literature, sophomore Lauren Soto researched and wrote a literary analysis about revenge in the works of Edgar Allan Poe, focusing on the parallels in Poe's life and fiction. Soto read and reread several of Poe's short stories and then searched her school's library and the Internet

for critical analyses of the author's work. At her instructor's request, she compiled an annotated bibliography that listed and commented on the sources she
thought would be most helpful in writing her paper, using MLA style (p. 70)
to format the publication information. Here are two of Soto's entries:

Allen, Brooke. "The Tell-Tale Artist: Edgar Allan Poe Turns 200."   Source: magazine
    Weekly Standard 28 Sept. 2009: 28-31. Print.   article

A literary critic's view of Poe's place in literary history and   Elements of article
popular culture on the 200th anniversary of his birth. Allen
claims that Poe essentially invented horror fiction, science   1. Poe's influence
fiction, and the detective story. She also sees parallels between 2. Parallels between
Poe himself and the characters in his fiction. Allen's focus on   Poe's life and work
Poe's mental instability and its effects on his creativity is   Potential use of source
helpful in understanding some themes in his work, particularly
revenge. Poe's sensitivity to insults, for example, connects to
Montressor in "The Cask of Amontillado," who kills to avenge an
unnamed slight.

Edgar Allan Poe Society of Baltimore. Edgar Allan Poe Society   Source: Web site
    of Baltimore, 2013. Web. 26 Feb. 2013.

A comprehensive online collection of all of Poe's works, in-   Elements of Web site
cluding letters and other documents, as well as links to critical 1. Collection of Poe's
articles from the journal *Poe Studies/Dark Romanticism*. The   works
site's most useful features are essays by scholars that address   2. Scholarly criticism
common misconceptions about Poe, particularly that his poems
and stories about anger, loss, fear, and vengeance mirror events
and relationships in his own life. This perspective is valuable to 3. Balancing
balance Allen and other writers who make a great deal of the   perspectives
connections between Poe's life and work. At the same time, the   Potential use of source
site seems somewhat defensive about Poe and protective of him,
so information about Poe and his life needs to be verified in
other sources.

GUILLERMO DEL TORO AND CHUCK HOGAN

Guillermo del Toro and Chuck Hogan are coauthors of *The Strain* (2009), *The Fall* (2010), and *The Night Eternal* (2011) — a trilogy of vampire novels. Although they share an interest in telling a new kind of story about vampires, the authors arrived at their collaboration from very different backgrounds. Born in Guadalajara, Mexico, del Toro began his career as a cinematic makeup artist. He debuted as a director with *Cronos* (1993) and has directed six other movies, including both *Hellboy* films (2004, 2008), *Pan's Labyrinth* (2006), which won three Academy Awards, and *Pacific Rim* (2013). Hogan, by contrast, is a Boston-based novelist who was working as a video-store manager when he made his breakthrough with *The Standoff* (1995), a thriller about a tense hostage negotiation. Hogan has since published *The Blood Artists* (1998), *Prince of Thieves* (2004), *The Killing Moon* (2007), and *Devils in Exile* (2010). *Prince of Thieves* won the 2005 Hammett Award for literary crime writing and was the basis for the 2010 motion picture *The Town*.

Vampires Never Die

Filmmaker del Toro and novelist Hogan bonded over their fascination with how ancient myths about vampires have been adapted and readapted in popular culture. In this 2009 essay, first published in the *New York Times*, they trace the perpetual craving for vampire stories back to its historical, literary, and scientific roots.

In the essay following this one, "Our Zombies, Ourselves," James Parker extends del Toro and Hogan's fascination with monster legends by examining a related pop culture phenomenon.

Tonight, you or someone you love will likely be visited by a vampire — on cable television or the big screen, or in the bookstore. Our own novel describes a modern-day epidemic that spreads across New York City.

It all started nearly two hundred years ago. It was the "Year without a Summer" of 1816, when ash from volcanic eruptions lowered temperatures around the globe, giving rise to widespread famine. A few friends gathered at the Villa Diodati on Lake Geneva and decided to engage in a small competition to see who could come up with the most terrifying tale — and the two great monsters of the modern age were born.

One was created by Mary Godwin, soon to become Mary Shelley, whose   3
Dr. Frankenstein gave life to a desolate creature. The other monster was less created than fused. John William Polidori stitched together folklore, personal resentment and erotic anxieties into "The Vampyre," a story that is the basis for vampires as they are understood today.

With "The Vampyre," Polidori gave birth to the two main branches of   4
vampiric fiction: the vampire as romantic hero, and the vampire as undead monster. This ambivalence may reflect Polidori's own, as it is widely accepted that Lord Ruthven, the titular creature, was based upon Lord Byron — literary superstar of the era and another resident of the lakeside villa that fateful summer. Polidori tended to Byron day and night, both as his doctor and most devoted groupie. But Polidori resented him as well: Byron was dashing and brilliant, while the poor doctor had a rather drab talent and unremarkable physique.

But this was just a new twist to a very old idea. The myth, established   5
well before the invention of the word "vampire," seems to cross every culture, language and era. The Indian Baital, the Ch'ing Shih in China, and the Romanian Strigoi are but a few of its names. The creature seems to be as old as Babylonia and Sumer.[1] Or even older.

The vampire may originate from a repressed memory we had as primates.   6
Perhaps at some point we were — out of necessity — cannibalistic. As soon as we became sedentary, agricultural tribes with social boundaries, one seminal myth might have featured our ancestors as primitive beasts who slept in the cold loam of the earth and fed off the salty blood of the living.

Monsters, like angels, are invoked by our individual and collective needs.   7
Today, much as during that gloomy summer in 1816, we feel the need to seek their cold embrace.

Herein lies an important clue: In contrast to timeless creatures like the   8
dragon, the vampire does not seek to obliterate us, but instead offers a peculiar brand of blood alchemy. For as his contagion bestows its nocturnal gift, the vampire transforms our vile, mortal selves into the gold of eternal youth and instills in us something that every social construct seeks to quash: primal lust. If youth is desire married with unending possibility, then vampire lust creates within us a delicious void, one we long to fulfill.

---

[1] Countries of ancient Mesopotamia (in the vicinity of modern-day Iraq), dating back to approximately 4000 BC and 2000 BC, respectively. They are generally considered the origins of Western civilization. — Eds.

In other words, whereas other monsters emphasize what is mortal in us,   9
the vampire emphasizes the eternal in us. Through the panacea of its blood it
turns the lead of our toxic flesh into golden matter.

In a society that moves as fast as ours, where every week a new "block-   10
buster" must be enthroned at the box office, or where idols are fabricated
by consensus every new television season, the promise of something everlasting, something truly eternal, holds a special allure. As a seductive figure,
the vampire is as flexible and polyvalent as ever. Witness its slow muta-
tion from the pansexual, decadent Anne Rice[2] creatures to the current
permutations — promising anything from chaste eternal love to wild nocturnal escapades — and there you will find the true essence of immortality:
adaptability.

Vampires find their niche and mutate at an accelerated rate now — in the   11
past one would see, for decades, the same variety of fiend, repeated in multiple
storylines. Now, vampires simultaneously occur in all forms and tap into our
every need: soap opera storylines, sexual liberation, noir detective fiction, etc.
The myth seems to be twittering promiscuously to serve all avenues of life,
from cereal boxes to romantic fiction. The fast pace of technology accelerates
its viral dispersion in our culture.

But if Polidori remains the roots in the genealogy of our creature, the most   12
widely known vampire was birthed by Bram Stoker in 1897.

Part of the reason for the great success of his "Dracula" is generally   13
acknowledged to be its appearance at a time of great technological revolution.
The narrative is full of new gadgets (telegraphs, typing machines), various
forms of communication (diaries, ship logs), and cutting-edge science (blood
transfusions) — a mash-up of ancient myth in conflict with the world of the
present.

Today as well, we stand at the rich uncertain dawn of a new level of sci-   14
entific innovation. The wireless technology we carry in our pockets today
was the stuff of the science fiction in our youth. Our technological arrogance
mirrors more and more the Wellsian[3] dystopia of dissatisfaction, while allowing us to feel safe and connected at all times. We can call, see or hear almost
anything and anyone no matter where we are. For most people then, the only
remote place remains within. "Know thyself" we do not.

---

[2] Anne Rice (born 1941) is an American novelist best known for *Interview with the Vampire* (1976), *The Vampire Lestat* (1985), and *The Queen of the Damned* (1988). — Eds.
[3] H. G. Wells (1866–1946) was an influential English science fiction writer whose
works include *The Time Machine* (1895), *The Island of Doctor Moreau* (1896), and *War of the
Worlds* (1898). — Eds.

Despite our obsessive harnessing of information, we are still ultimately   15
vulnerable to our fates and our nightmares. We enthrone the deadly virus
in the very same way that "Dracula" allowed the British public to believe in
monsters: through science. Science becomes the modern man's superstition.
It allows him to experience fear and awe again, and to believe in the things
he cannot see.

And through awe, we once again regain spiritual humility. The current   16
vampire pandemic serves to remind us that we have no true jurisdiction over
our bodies, our climate or our very souls. Monsters will always provide the
possibility of mystery in our mundane "reality show" lives, hinting at a larger
spiritual world; for if there are demons in our midst, there surely must be
angels lurking nearby as well. In the vampire we find Eros and Thanatos[4] fused
together in archetypal embrace, spiraling through the ages, undying.

Forever.   17

For a reading quiz, visit **bedfordstmartins.com/thebedfordreader***.*

Journal Writing

Do you enjoy vampire stories, whether in books, in movies, or on television? Of the
vampire characters in popular culture (past or present), who is your favorite? Why do
you think this character appeals to you? In your journal, explore what vampires mean
to you. If you don't care for vampire fiction, consider why it leaves you cold. (To take
your journal writing further, see "From Journal to Essay" on the facing page.)

Questions on Meaning

1. Why do you suppose del Toro and Hogan wrote this essay? Are they merely pro-
   moting their novels, or do they have a more serious PURPOSE as well?
2. What is the THESIS of "Vampires Never Die"? Where, if at all, is it stated
   succinctly?
3. How do del Toro and Hogan explain the appeal of vampires in contemporary culture? In what ways has that appeal changed across time and geography? In what
   ways has it remained consistent?
4. What is a "social construct" (par. 8)? How is the concept central to the authors'
   interpretation of vampires?

---

[4] Greek gods of love (Eros) and death (Thanatos). — EDS.

5. In paragraph 15, del Toro and Hogan say, "Science becomes the modern man's superstition." What do they mean? How do you explain the PARADOX in that statement?

Questions on Writing Strategy

1. "Vampires Never Die" uses advanced academic vocabulary and contains several literary, historical, scientific, and psychological references. How, then, do the authors imagine their AUDIENCE? Are their ASSUMPTIONS reasonable in your case?
2. What principle of analysis do del Toro and Hogan use in examining vampire stories? What enduring elements do they perceive in the characters?
3. Why do del Toro and Hogan speculate in their introduction about the "resentment and erotic anxieties" (par. 3) felt by John William Polidori, the author of the first modern vampire story? What do his personal conflicts have to do with how we think about vampires today?
4. What is the EFFECT of the essay's final paragraph?
5. **OTHER METHODS**   Del Toro and Hogan COMPARE AND CONTRAST new technologies from the late nineteenth and early twenty-first centuries. What similarities do they find?

Questions on Language

1. Make sure you know the meanings of the following words: desolate (par. 3); ambivalence, titular, dashing (4); repressed, sedentary, seminal, loam (6); invoked (7); obliterate, primal (8); panacea (9); consensus, polyvalent, pansexual, permutations, chaste (10); noir, promiscuously, dispersion (11); mash-up (13); dystopia (14); pandemic, mundane, archetypal (16).
2. Explain the double meaning of "twittering" in paragraph 11. Why do you think del Toro and Hogan chose this particular word?
3. What do the authors mean by "a peculiar brand of blood alchemy" (par. 8)? Where else do they use this metaphor? Why is it particularly appropriate for their subject? (For a definition of *metaphor*, see FIGURES OF SPEECH in Useful Terms.)

Suggestions for Writing

1. **FROM JOURNAL TO ESSAY**   Expanding on your journal entry, write an essay that analyzes one vampire character from popular culture — such as Bram Stoker's Dracula, Edward from the *Twilight* series, Yvette from Anne Rice's novels, Bill Compton from *True Blood*, or The Master from del Toro and Hogan's trilogy. Break the character down into his (or her) elements, considering backstory as well as personality, and reassemble the parts into a new whole of your understanding.
2. Write an essay that analyzes several examples of another type of writing by examining their shared characteristics and hidden meanings. You may choose any narrowly defined GENRE that's familiar to you: food blog, parenting-advice column, amateur film review, gay romance, alternative-history science fiction, and so on. Be sure to make your principle of analysis clear to your readers.

3. Some cultural analysts have said that the resurgence of vampire stories in the last quarter century can be attributed to the AIDS epidemic that emerged in the 1980s. In your library's database of scholarly journal articles, conduct a keyword search with "vampires and AIDS," and read one or two of the arguments in favor of this theory. (If you prefer, you may search for other academic analyses of vampire lore.) How do you respond to the articles? Do alternate interpretations undermine del Toro and Hogan's analysis, or do they simply complicate it?

4. **CRITICAL WRITING**   Del Toro and Hogan explore CAUSES AND EFFECTS to explain the prevalence of vampires in popular culture. How persuasive is their analysis? Do you agree with them that vampire legends fill psychological and spiritual voids that have been created by advances in science and technology? Why, or why not?

5. **CONNECTIONS**   James Parker, in "Our Zombies, Ourselves" (the next essay), also writes about monsters. In an essay, compare and contrast Parker's and del Toro and Hogan's assumptions about the sources and functions of monster mythologies. Consider, as well, your own thoughts about the value of such interpretations: Are vampires and zombies in popular culture worthy of serious inquiry?

Guillermo del Toro and Chuck Hogan on Writing

"Vampires Never Die" was by no means Guillermo del Toro and Chuck Hogan's first experience working together as writers. In 2006 they began collaborating on a trilogy of horror novels about vampires. The project started when Hogan's literary agent sent him a twelve-page outline of del Toro's story idea, originally conceived for the small screen, and told him the director was thinking about trying a novel. "I got a page and a half in before calling [my agent] back and essentially telling him that I would do anything to be involved," Hogan gushed in a 2009 interview with blogger Sarah Weinman. In lieu of a publishing deal or any kind of contract, the authors made a pact on a handshake — "actually more of a bro-hug," according to Hogan — and agreed to join forces. They finished the first installment of the trilogy, *The Strain*, after three years.

Hogan admits to being apprehensive about writing with del Toro, whom he calls "a god of the genre," especially since the storyline was the director's. However, he says that del Toro "completely opened up his story," giving Hogan the freedom to expand and change the narrative in the drafting stage. In a separate interview with Rick Kleffel on KUSP Central Coast Public Radio, del Toro praised Hogan's contributions to the shape of the story: "The

book is full of intimate moments of terror that come from personal experience, and others that Chuck created. . . . Some of the best, most disturbing
moments in the book come from his imagination, curiously enough."

Both authors note that, though their drafting processes were loose, revising the book was "rigorous." Exchanging drafts by e-mail, they commented
extensively on each other's chapters, a practice that del Toro calls "riffing."
As he explains, "I was merciless with his chapters; he was merciless with my
chapters." Revisions involved moving or cutting large portions of text. Del
Toro often rearranged chapters, and Hogan sometimes scrapped entire sections. Speaking of Hogan's editing style, del Toro jokes that some changes
were made "subverticiously" (a word of his own invention): "All of a sudden
I would get the manuscript and it was missing one chapter I wrote or half a
chapter I wrote." However, it was this kind of harsh revision that in the end
made for the "seamless blending" of two writers' talents.

For Discussion

1. Why do you think del Toro and Hogan write freely but revise rigorously?
2. Have you ever worked collaboratively on a writing project? What were some of
   the advantages or frustrations of working that way?

JAMES PARKER

A prolific journalist fascinated with popular culture in general and horror stories in particular, James Parker writes regularly for *Slate*, the *Boston Globe*, the *New York Times*, *In These Times*, and *Barnes & Noble Review*, among other publications. He is a contributing editor for *The Atlantic Monthly* and the author of *Turned On* (1998), a biography of punk musician Henry Rollins. He also edits the *Pilgrim*, a literary magazine written and produced by homeless people in the Boston area. Parker was born in 1968 in London, England, and lives in Brookline, Massachusetts, with his wife and son.

Our Zombies, Ourselves

Parker wrote "Our Zombies, Ourselves" in 2011 for his entertainment column in *The Atlantic Monthly*. Like Guillermo del Toro and Chuck Hogan in the previous selection, Parker analyzes the role of fictional monsters in the popular imagination, seeking to understand the current resurgence of the undead among the living.

The most surprising thing about the modern zombie — indeed, the *only* surprising thing about the modern zombie — is that he took so long to arrive. His slowness is a proverb, of course: his museumgoer's shuffle, his hospital plod. Plus he's a wobbler: The shortest path between two points is seldom the one he takes. Nonetheless, given all that had been going on, we might reasonably have expected the first modern zombies to start showing up around 1919.[1] Twentieth-century man was already moaning and scratching his head; shambling along with bits falling off him; desensitized, industrialized, hollowed out, metaphysically evacuated — *A crowd flowed over London Bridge, so many*[2]. . . . Had some trash visionary produced a novel or play about the brain-eating hordes, or a *vers libre*[3] epic of viral undeadness, it would have gone down rather well, at this point. And yet not until 1968, at the dawning of the Age of Aquarius, did the zombie as we know him really make the scene.

---

[1] World War I ended in November 1918. — EDS.

[2] Parker quotes a line from T. S. Eliot's epic poem *The Waste Land* (1922), which draws on mythology to ponder themes of postwar destruction, disillusionment, and despair. — EDS.

[3] French, "free verse." A free-verse poem is loosely structured and does not have a rhyming scheme. — EDS.

Look: There he is, out of focus and deep in the shot, in the fifth minute 2
of George A. Romero's *Night of the Living Dead*. He's wandering through a
cemetery, wearing a shabby blazer, with the air of a distracted groundskeeper.
In the foreground are two soberly dressed young people, Barbara and Johnny.
They are visiting their father's grave. Barbara kneels and bows her head, but
Johnny's a scoffer. "Hey, c'mon, Barb — church was this morning, huh? Hey, I
mean praying's for church, huh?" Sniffs Barbara: "I haven't seen *you* in church
lately." A breeze rises. Dark, frondy tree limbs wave above them like seaweed
in the black-and-white afternoon, and the zombie draws near. He has begun
to reel and lurch. He grabs Barbara. There's death in his skin tone, but his face
is alive with a kind of stricken fixity. He bashes Johnny against a tombstone.
Barbara flees in a car, but wrecks it. And now we *really* see him, framed disas-
trously in the skewed rear windshield, advancing toward us at an off-kilter
zombie trot. No mistaking the message: The world is out of whack, the car is
off the road, here comes the zombie.

And he's never stopped coming. After fertile decades bumbling in the 3
gore/horror subbasement, he veered toward the mainstream in the early 2000s
and currently enjoys a cultural profile unmatched even by his fancy-pants
cousin, the vampire. Sure, we've all enjoyed *Twilight*, *True Blood*, vampire
love, the pallor and the pangs, etc. — but it's the zombie, Old Reliable, who's
really bringing home the bacon. He's the one who rides the best-seller lists
and consumes the pop unconscious, whose titles spatter the humor section of
your local bookstore: *Zombie Haiku*, *The Zen of Zombie*, *It's Beginning to Look a
Lot Like Zombies: A Book of Zombie Christmas Carols*. People, sometimes hundreds of people, go on processional "zombie walks." Video gamers are mowing down fresh multitudes of zombies with a fervor undimmed by habit. And
AMC's zombie series, *The Walking Dead* — the DVD of which is released this
month — was the surprise cable smash of last year. Are we approaching, have
we already reached, a zombie saturation point, or "burnout," as Max Brooks,
author of the (very good) 2006 zombie novel *World War Z*, has put it? I say
no. The zombie keeps on: It's what he does.

His origins, we learn — we who dabble in the recklessly expanding field 4
of zombie studies — are in Caribbean folk nightmare. For the people of Haiti,
the *zombi* was one who had died and been buried, only to be malignantly
revived and enslaved by a sorcerer, or *bokor*. Look: There's the zombie in
1929, the year William Seabrook published his sensational account of Haitian voodoo lore, *The Magic Island*. He's working in the cane fields, his eyes
like "the eyes of a dead man" but his hands "callused, solid, human." And
there he is in 1932, in the Halperin brothers' *White Zombie* — his cinematic
debut — trudging with alienated obedience behind his dark master (played
by Béla Lugosi). At night he works with other zombies in the sugar mill. The

blades of the great thresher groan magnificently, zombifigently, as they turn. A zombie falls in. Oh well.

So Romero did not invent the zombie. But he cut him loose: The grave-   5
yard zombie in *Night of the Living Dead* may be punishing Johnny, in the finest horror-flick tradition, for being cheeky on hallowed ground, but he himself is no longer a supernatural figure. No demon or magus possesses him, no enchantment holds him. The zombifier seems to be technology: radioactive contamination from an exploded space probe. Zombiedom runs amok, mov- ing virally through the population. The zombie wants live human flesh, and those still in possession of it are advised, via TV and radio, to barricade them- selves indoors. Romero was laying down the new canons of zombiehood: the wobbliness of the zombie, the terrible mobility of the virus, the pockets of survival, the squall of information as the grid collapses.

Severed thus from his heritage, sent freewheeling into postmodernity   6
with nothing to say on his own behalf (because he can't talk, because he's a *zombie*), our hero would seem to be in a position of great semiotic vulnerabil- ity. And so it has proved: All manner of meanings have been and continue to be plastered onto the zombie. Much can be made of him, because he makes so little of himself. He is the consumer, the mob, the Other, the proletariat, the weight of life, the dead soul. He is too many e-mails in your inbox, a kind of cosmic spam. He is everything rejected and inexpugnable. He comes back, he comes back, feebly but unstoppably, and as he drags you down, a fatal lethargy overtakes you. What is it, this victim's inanition? We all feel it. One of the great statements of the zombie plague was uttered in 1989 by the Canadian punk band NoMeansNo, with its song "It's Catching Up." "Have you heard the news?" it begins, sardonically, over a ticking mesh of guitar and hi-hat.[4] "The dead walk." The last verse rises to a scream:

> There are some things that never die
> Things that never really were alive
> I've shut them out!
> I've slammed the door!
> But I can't keep them back
> Anymore!

None of this is to ignore the plentiful variations that have been worked   7
upon Romero's zombie theme since 1968. Recent years, for example, have given us both the Sprinting or Galloping Zombie of Danny Boyle's *28 Days Later* and Zack Snyder's *Dawn of the Dead* remake, and the Comic-Existential Zombie of Edgar Wright's *Shaun of the Dead*. In the Boyle/Snyder model, the

---

[4] A type of cymbal. — Eds.

zombie is wild-eyed and very fast. The virus, too, has been ferally accelerated: Now, scant seconds after having your throat ripped out, you stand up snarling and race off in search of prey. *Shaun of the Dead* is gentler and more profound: Here zombiedom seems to germinate through a fog of hangovers, Monday mornings, lapses in conversation. Shaun refuses to *become*; his job (selling televisions) demeans him; his nice girlfriend wants him to give up smoking and stop spending so much time down the pub. He will not, he cannot, and the dead throng the streets. As the future peters out, the present blooms with zombies.

But sometimes a zombie is just a zombie. Strike that: A zombie is *always* just a zombie. The blow-'em-all-away success of *The Walking Dead* is no mystery: The show, and the comic-book series by Robert Kirkman on which it's based, mark a triumphant return to zombie orthodoxy, to the non-galloping zombie and his icons. Once again, and with great gladness, we see shotguns, frantically tuned radios, smoke pillars of apocalypse on the horizon — the full zombie opera. The zombie himself has never looked better, dripping with wounds, full of conviction. With his dangling stethoscope, or his policeman's uniform, or his skateboard, he exhibits the pathos of his ex-personhood. He flaps and sighs. He crookedly advances. He's taking his time. But he'll get there.

8

For a reading quiz, visit **bedfordstmartins.com/thebedfordreader**.

Journal Writing

Every region of the world has folklore and urban legends similar to the Haitian accounts of zombie slaves sensationalized in William Seabrook's *The Magic Island*: hitchhiking ghosts, flickering orbs, gas-station carjackings, haunted cemeteries, buried treasures, and so forth. Think of one such story you have heard. Do you believe it? Why, or why not? Why do you think people tell such tales? (To take your journal writing further, see "From Journal to Essay" on page 303.)

Questions on Meaning

1. What seems to have prompted Parker to compose this essay? Where does he reveal his PURPOSE for writing?
2. When, according to Parker, did zombies fully emerge in popular fiction? Why did they not attract much attention when they first appeared in published literature?

3. What seems to have initially turned people into zombies in George A. Romero's *Night of the Living Dead*? Why is this "zombifier" (par. 5) significant to Parker's analysis?
4. Parker suggests that critics tend to see zombies as SYMBOLS: "All manner of meanings have been and continue to be plastered onto the zombie," he says (par. 6). What are some of those meanings? What, to Parker, do zombies signify?
5. Parker states his THESIS near the end of his essay. What is it? Why doesn't he include it in his introduction?

Questions on Writing Strategy

1. What does Parker seem to ASSUME about his AUDIENCE? To what extent do you fit his assumptions?
2. "A zombie is *always* just a zombie," writes Parker (par. 8). What does he mean? What are the elements of "zombiehood" (5), as he presents them?
3. What EVIDENCE does Parker offer to support his analysis? How seriously does he seem to take his subject?
4. Parker's essay feels impressionistic, almost entranced. What strategies does he use to give his musings UNITY and COHERENCE?
5. **OTHER METHODS**   Parker COMPARES AND CONTRASTS three recent zombie movies in paragraph 7. Why? What does the comparison contribute to his point?

Questions on Language

1. The line from *The Waste Land* cited in paragraph 1 is part of the last stanza in the poem's first part:

    > Unreal City,
    > Under the brown fog of a winter dawn,
    > A crowd flowed over London Bridge, so many,
    > I had not thought death had undone so many.
    > Sighs, short and infrequent, were exhaled,
    > And each man fixed his eyes before his feet.
    > Flowed up the hill and down King William Street,
    > To where Saint Mary Woolnoth kept the hours
    > With a dead sound on the final stroke of nine.

    How does this ALLUSION serve Parker? Do you recognize any other references to literary and cultural history in the essay? What do you take to be their intended effect?
2. Parker uses a number of words that may be unfamiliar to you. Consult a dictionary if you need help defining any of the following: proverb, desensitized, metaphysically (par. 1); foreground, frondy, reel, fixity (2); fertile, pallor, processional, fervor (3); recklessly, malignantly, alienated (4); magus, canons (5); postmodernity, semiotic, proletariat, inexpugnable, inanition, sardonically (6); existential, ferally, germinate (7); orthodoxy, pathos. From what field of academic study does much of his vocabulary derive?

3. How would you characterize Parker's DICTION and TONE in this essay? Are they appropriate for a formal analysis? Why, or why not?

Suggestions for Writing

1. **FROM JOURNAL TO ESSAY** Building on your journal entry and using Parker's analysis of zombies and your own experiences as evidence, write an essay that explores the function of folk tales and urban legends. Where do they come from? What purpose do they serve in contemporary American culture? How do they compare to other forms of mythology?

2. Parker's essay is essentially a review of a popular television show. Pick a program you especially like or dislike and use division or analysis to EVALUATE it in an essay. What elements contribute to the show's appeal for viewers? What is your take on its effectiveness or enjoyability? Why do you feel as you do?

3. **CRITICAL WRITING** Watch an episode of *The Walking Dead* or one of the zombie movies Parker cites: *Night of the Living Dead*, *White Zombie*, *28 Days Later*, *Dawn of the Dead*, or *Shaun of the Dead*. How accurate and fair is Parker's portrayal of the work? Do you agree with his interpretations, or do you attach different meanings to zombies in popular culture? What meanings do you see? Answer these questions in an essay.

4. **CONNECTIONS** Parker asserts that at the moment, the zombie is more popular than even "his fancy-pants cousin, the vampire" (par. 3). Why should this be? And how do you think Guillermo del Toro and Chuck Hogan would respond to Parker's claim? Using "Our Zombies, Ourselves" and "Vampires Never Die" (p. 291) as a starting point, write an essay that compares and contrasts the portrayals of zombies and vampires in popular culture. What do the two types of fictional monster have in common? How are they different? Which, in your view, is the superior character? Why?

James Parker on Writing

Most writing teachers and guides caution students to avoid CLICHÉS, or common FIGURES OF SPEECH that have grown tired from overuse (see our advice, p. 43). But in a 2009 column for the *Boston Globe*, Parker takes a different view of such time-worn expressions.

He begins with a challenge: "Who will say a good word for the cliché? Its sins are so numerous." Because critics deride clichés as "[e]xhausted tropes, numb descriptors, zombie proverbs, hackneyed sentiments, rhetorical rip-offs, metaphorical flat tires, ideas purged of thought and symbols drained of power," he says, people who trade in words "have always been extra-spooked" by fears of slipping on overused phrases. But maybe they shouldn't be. "Durable, easily handled, yet retaining somehow the flavor of its coinage," Parker claims, "the classic cliché . . . sticks and it stays, and not by accident."

As proof, Parker turns to etymology: "Let's consider the origin of the word. For nineteenth-century typesetters, a cliché was a piece of language encountered so often in the course of their work that it had earned its own printing plate — no need to reset the individual letters, just stamp that thing on the page and keep going. So the cliché was an object, and a useful one: a concrete unit of communication that minimized labor and sped things up. I imagine that a nice hardy cliché like 'on its last legs' or 'tempest in a teapot' does more or less the same thing inside our heads: one bash of the stamp, one neat little payload of meaning, and on we go."

Sure, says Parker, evasive political shorthand and quickly dated media catchphrases are probably best shunned. "But what of the timeless cliché, the cliché you can steer your course by, the cliché that carries a small freight not just of meaning, but of wisdom?" That kind of cliché, Parker insists, has value. "I sometimes think," he writes, "that my entire psychological and ethical structure, such as it is, falls somewhere between 'There's no such thing as a free lunch,' and 'It takes two to tango.' Observations like these have been road-tested, times beyond number, and discovered to be sound. They are laden with experience, and yet somehow jaunty. Some witty individual must have coined them, somewhere, but they glow with the accumulated knowledge of the [human] race. They are clichés, and they belong to you: As a speaker of English, they are your birthright. Use them proudly. And when life hands you a lemon, remember that it's better than a poke in the eye with a sharp stick."

For Discussion

1. Why does Parker believe that clichés can be useful to writers? Do you agree with him?
2. Take another look at "Our Zombies, Ourselves" (p. 298). To what extent does Parker follow his own advice? Does his use of clichés strengthen or weaken his essay?

ROBERT LIPSYTE

Robert Lipsyte is a sportswriter and broadcast journalist who is equally well known for his young-adult novels. Born in 1938 in the Bronx, he grew up feeling bullied and outcast in the Queens borough of New York City, earned a BA in English from Columbia University at the age of nineteen, and received an MA from the Columbia School of Journalism in 1959. As a reporter and writer for the *New York Times*, Lipsyte published more than five hundred columns; he is also the author of nearly thirty books, including *The Masculine Mystique* (1966), *Free to Be Muhammad Ali* (1978), *An Accidental Sportswriter: A Memoir* (2011), and novels such as *The Contender* (1967) and *The Twinning Project* (2012). Lipsyte was a sports commentator for National Public Radio from 1976 to 1982, an on-air essayist for CBS and NBC from 1982 to 1988, and the host of the public television show *The Eleventh Hour* in the late 1980s, for which he won an Emmy for on-camera achievement in 1990. He continues to write both fiction and nonfiction.

Jock Culture

As Lipsyte tells it, he came into his career by happenstance: Fresh out of college, he needed a job and the *Times* gave him one. That his entry-level position morphed into a career immersed in sports continues to surprise him. Long a sportswriter but never a particular fan, Lipsyte is in a unique position to examine what he sees as a damaging obsession with athleticism and competition in American life. "Jock Culture" first appeared in a special 2011 sports issue of *The Nation*, a newsmagazine usually focused on politics.

In the spring of that hard year, 1968, the Columbia University crew coach, Bill Stowe, explained to me that there were only two kinds of men on campus, perhaps in the world — Jocks and Pukes. He explained that Jocks, such as his rowers, were brave, manly, ambitious, focused, patriotic, and goal-driven, while Pukes were woolly, distractible, girlish, and handicapped by their lack of certainty that nothing mattered as much as winning. Pukes could be found among "the cruddy weirdo slobs" such as hippies, pot smokers, protesters, and, yes, former English majors like me.

I dutifully wrote all this down, although doing so seemed kind of Puke-ish. But Stowe was such an affable ur-Jock,[1] twenty-eight years old, funny and articulate, that I found his condescension merely good copy. He'd won

[1] The German prefix *ur-* means "thorough" or "perfect." — EDS.

an Olympic gold medal, but how could I take him seriously, this former Navy officer who had spent his Vietnam deployment rowing the Saigon River and running an officers' club? Not surprisingly, he didn't last long at Columbia after helping lead police officers through the underground tunnels to roust the Pukes who had occupied buildings during the antiwar and antiracism demonstrations.

As a thirty-year-old *New York Times* sports columnist then, I was not 3 handicapped by as much lack of certainty about all things as I am now. It was clear to me then that Bill Stowe was a "dumb jock," which does not mean stupid; it means ignorant, narrow, misguided by the values of Jock Culture, an important and often overlooked strand of American life.

These days, I'm not so sure he wasn't right; the world may well be divided 4 into Jocks and Pukes. Understanding the differences and the commonalities between the two might be one of the keys to understanding, first, the myths of masculinity and power that pervade sports, and then why those myths are inescapable in everyday life. Boys — and more and more girls — who accept Jock Culture values often go on to flourish in a competitive sports environment that requires submission to authority, winning by any means necessary, and group cohesion. They tend to grow up to become our political, military, and financial leaders. The Pukes — those "others" typically shouldered aside by Jocks in high school hallways and, I imagine, a large percentage of those who are warily reading this special issue of *The Nation* — were often turned off or away from competitive sports (or settled for cross-country). They were also more likely to go on to question authority and seek ways of individual expression.

This mental conditioning of the Jocks was possible because of the intrin- 5 sic joy of sports. Sports is good. It is the best way to pleasure your body in public. Sports is entertaining, healthful, filled with honest, sustaining sentiment for warm times and the beloved people you shared them with. At its simplest, think of playing catch at the lake with friends.

Jock Culture is a distortion of sports. It can be physically and mentally 6 unhealthy, driving people apart instead of together. It is fueled by greed and desperate competition. At its most grotesque, think killer dodgeball for prize money, the Super Bowl. (The clash between sports and the Jock Culture version is almost ideological, at least metaphorical. Obviously, I am for de-emphasizing early competition and redistributing athletic resources so that everyone, throughout their lives, has access to sports. But then, I am also for world peace.)

Kids are initiated into Jock Culture when youth sports are channeled into 7 the pressurized arenas of elite athletes on travel teams driven by ambitious parents and coaches. A once safe place to learn about bravery, cooperation, and respect becomes a cockpit of bullying, violence, and the commitment to a win-at-all-costs attitude that can kill a soul. Or a brain. It is in Pee Wee football, for example, that kids learn to "put a hat on him" — to make tackles head first rather than the older, gentler way of wrapping your arms around a ball carrier's legs and dragging him down. Helmet-to-helmet hits start the trauma cycle early. No wonder the current concussion discussion was launched by the discovery of dementia and morbidity among former pro players.

There is no escape from Jock Culture. You may be willing to describe yourself as a Puke, "cut" from the team early to find your true nature as a billionaire geek, Grammy-winning band fag, wonkish pundit, but you've always had to deal with Jock Culture attitudes and codes, and you have probably competed by them. In big business, medicine, the law, people will be labeled winners and losers, and treated like stars or slugs by coachlike authority figures who use shame and intimidation to achieve short-term results. Don't think symphony orchestras, university philosophy departments, and liberal magazines don't often use such tactics.

Jock Culture applies the rules of competitive sports to everything. Boys, in particular, are taught to be tough, stoical and aggressive, to play hurt, to hit hard, to take risks to win in every aspect of their lives. To dominate. After 9/11, I wondered why what seemed like a disproportionate number of athletic women and men were killed. From reading their brief *New York Times* memorials, it seemed as though most were former high school and college players, avid weekend recreationists, or at least passionate sports fans. When I called executives from companies that had offices in the World Trade Center, I discovered it was no coincidence; stock-trading companies in particular recruited athletes because they came to work even if they were sick, worked well in groups, rebounded quickly from a setback, pushed the envelope to reach the goal, and never quit until the job was done. They didn't have to be star jocks, but they did have to have been trained in the codes of Jock Culture — most important, the willingness to subordinate themselves to authority.

The drive to feel that sense of belonging that comes with being part of a winning team — as athlete, coach, parent, cheerleader, booster, fan — is a reflection of Jock Culture's grip on the male psyche and on more and more women. Men have traditionally been taught to pursue their jock dreams no matter the physical, emotional, or financial cost. Those who realized those dreams have been made rich and famous; at the least, they were waved right through many of the tollbooths of ordinary life. Being treated like a celebrity at twelve, freed from normal boundaries, excused from taking out the garbage and from treating siblings, friends, girls responsibly, is no preparation for a fully realized life. No wonder there are so many abusive athletes, emotionally stunted ex-athletes, and resentful onlookers.

At a critical time when masculinity is being redefined, or at least re-   11
examined seriously, this sports system has become more economically, culturally, and emotionally important than ever. More at service to the empire.
More dangerous to the common good.

Games have become our main form of mass entertainment (including   12
made-for-TV contests using sports models). Winners of those games become
our examples of permissible behavior, even when that includes cheating, sexual crimes, or dog torturing. And how does that lead us to the cheating, the
lying, the amorality in our lives outside the white lines? It's not hard to connect the moral dots from the field house to the White House.

The recent emergence of girls as competitors of boys has also raised the   13
ante. Boys have traditionally been manipulated by coaches, drill sergeants,
and sales managers by the fear of being labeled a girl ("sissy" and "faggot"
have less to do with homophobia than misogyny). Despite the many ways
males can identify themselves as "real men" in our culture — size, sexuality,
power, money, fame — nothing seems as indelible as the mark made in childhood when the good bodies are separated from the bad bodies, the team from
the spectators. The designated athletes are rewarded with love, attention,
and perks. The leftovers struggle with their resentments and their search for
identity.

Of course, the final score is not always a sure thing. There are sensitive   14
linebackers and CEOs, domineering shrinks and violinists. Who won in the
contest between the *Facebook* Puke Mark Zuckerberg and his fiercest competitors, the Olympic rowing Jocks Tyler and Cameron Winklevoss?[2]

"I don't follow that stuff these days," says Bill Stowe, now living in Lake   15
Placid, New York, after retiring as crew coach and fundraiser for the Coast
Guard Academy, a far more comfortable fit than Columbia. "And I have to
tell you, I don't remember separating the world into Jocks and Pukes, although
it sounds good. I liked good brains in my boats, as long as they were willing to
concentrate and pay the price."

Stowe, at seventy-one, is still a conservative Republican. But he doesn't   16
like to talk politics. "It's time to give up the torch," he says. "People are still
living in ignorance, but I'm not running it up the flagpole anymore. Life's
too short to fight." He surprises me when we talk sports. "The big-league
thing, that's a circus. I don't understand how anyone could look up to those
guys. But the real issue is with the kids. Did you read where they're building a
$60 million football stadium for a high school in Texas? Just for the Jocks.

[2] Mark Zuckerberg (born 1984) is the founder and CEO of *Facebook*. Tyler and Cameron
Winkelvoss (born 1981) are twins who accused Zuckerberg, once a fellow Harvard student, of
stealing their idea and computer codes to create his social network. After a protracted legal
battle, the brothers settled for a deal valued at $65 million. — Eds.

Have you got any idea how much good you could do, even just in athletics, for all the other kids with that much money?"

I dutifully write all this down, which doesn't at all seem Puke-ish now.   17
We're on the same page, the coach and I. There's hope.

For a reading quiz, visit **bedfordstmartins.com/thebedfordreader**.

Journal Writing

Are you a "Jock" or a "Puke"? Do you play on any athletic teams, or are you content to stay on the sidelines? Did you ever experience or witness any of the aspects of youth sports that Lipsyte describes, whether positive or negative? How did you respond? In your journal, reflect on one such memory. (To take your journal writing further, see "From Journal to Essay" on the next page.)

Questions on Meaning

1. Reread the first three paragraphs of this essay. What do you make of Lipsyte's INTRODUCTION? What event is he reporting, and why is it relevant to his subject?
2. What does Lipsyte mean by "Jock Culture"? How is it distinct from sports in general?
3. In your own words, what is Lipsyte's THESIS? For whom is Jock Culture harmful, and why?
4. How would you describe the apparent PURPOSE of this essay? What is Lipsyte trying to accomplish?

Questions on Writing Strategy

1. What, according to Lipsyte, are the "codes" (par. 8), or elements, of Jock Culture — both positive and negative? What principle of analysis does he apply to his subject?
2. To whom does Lipsyte seem to be writing? Athletes, coaches, students, business leaders, someone else? What ASSUMPTIONS does he make about his readers?
3. Lipsyte brings up the terrorist attacks of September 11, 2001 in paragraph 9, commenting that "a disproportionate number of athletic women and men were killed" at the World Trade Center. Why? What does this detail contribute to his analysis?
4. Why does Lipsyte quote crew coach and former Olympian Bill Stowe in his opening and closing paragraphs? What is the EFFECT of using Stowe's words to frame the essay?

5. **OTHER METHODS**   How does Bill Stowe use CLASSIFICATION to categorize people? How does Lipsyte? What characteristics do "Jocks" have that "Pukes" lack?

Questions on Language

1. What are the CONNOTATIONS of the words *Jock* and *Puke*? Why do you suppose the author chose to repeat these labels coined by Bill Stowe?
2. How would you characterize Lipsyte's TONE? Is it appropriate, given his purpose and AUDIENCE?
3. Point to a few of the metaphors Lipsyte uses to enliven his prose. (See FIGURES OF SPEECH in Useful Terms for a definition of *metaphor*.) What do they have in common? What is their effect?
4. Consult a dictionary if any of the following words are unfamiliar: affable, deployment, roust (par. 2); submission, cohesion (4); sustaining (5); distortion, grotesque, ideological, metaphorical (6); dementia, morbidity (7); wonkish, pundit (8); stoical, subordinate (9); psyche (10); amorality (12); ante, misogyny (13).

Suggestions for Writing

1. **FROM JOURNAL TO ESSAY**   Respond to Lipsyte's concerns about the effects of Jock Culture. Do you agree that pressures to compete and a "win-at-all-costs attitude" (par. 7) are destructive forces in society, or do you believe that the values taught by team sports bring positive effects? Why? Start your response with the experience you recounted in your journal, adding additional examples from your observations of others.
2. Think about the virtues Bill Stowe cites in paragraph 1: "brave, manly, ambitious, focused, patriotic, and goal-driven." Choose one of these words, or another of the values Lipsyte mentions in the essay, and write a DEFINITION essay that explains its meanings for you. Use examples from your own experience, observations, and reading to make the definition complete.
3. The concussion crisis that Lipsyte ALLUDES to in paragraph 7 has led some to call for an end to football altogether, or at least for new regulations intended to protect players from brain damage. Research the main arguments for and against such regulations. Then write an essay in which you SUMMARIZE your findings. If your research — or your own experience — leads you to form an opinion favoring one side of the issue, present and support that as well.
4. **CRITICAL WRITING**   Based on this essay, analyze Lipsyte's apparent attitude toward masculinity and the feminist movement. How does he characterize attempts to shift cultural assumptions about men's and women's competitive abilities? Does he believe that gender equity is possible or even desirable? What does he suggest have been (or will be) the effects of feminism? Support your ideas with EVIDENCE from the essay.
5. **CONNECTIONS**   In "Why Women Still Can't Have It All" (*bedfordstmartins.com/thebedfordreader*), Anne-Marie Slaughter explains how the intense pressure to put work above family prompted her to quit a high-profile government job. In an essay, consider how Slaughter's experience supports or contradicts Lipsyte's analysis of the implications of Jock Culture for individuals and society.

FRANCINE PROSE

Francine Prose is the author of more than twelve novels as well as several children's books, short-story collections, and works of nonfiction, such as *Gluttony* (2003) and *Anne Frank: The Book, the Life, the Afterlife* (2009). She was born in Brooklyn, New York, in 1947 and graduated from Radcliffe College in 1968. She has received Guggenheim and Fulbright fellowships and has served as a judge for literary prizes. Prose's novel *Blue Angel* (2000), a satire set on a college campus, was nominated for the National Book Award. *A Changed Man* (2005), her novel about a reformed neo-Nazi, won the Dayton Literary Peace Prize for fiction. From 2007 to 2009 Prose served as president of PEN American Center, the US branch of an international literary organization; she was elected to the American Academy of Arts and Letters in 2009. Prose lives in New York and teaches writing at Bard College.

What Words Can Tell

"What Words Can Tell" (editors' title) comes from Prose's book *Reading like a Writer: A Guide for People Who Love Books and for Those Who Want to Write Them* (2006). In this excerpt, Prose gives a detailed reading of the opening paragraph of "A Good Man Is Hard to Find," a short story by the southern American writer Flannery O'Connor (1925–64). In the story a family on vacation intersects the path of an escaped convict, known only as "The Misfit." Prose's analysis of O'Connor's words is a model of close attention illuminating a written work.

Part of a reader's job is to find out why certain writers endure. This may 1 require some rewiring, unhooking the connection that makes you think you have to have an *opinion* about the book and reconnecting that wire to whatever terminal lets you see reading as something that might move or delight you. . . .

With so much reading ahead of you, the temptation might be to speed up. 2 But in fact it's essential to slow down and read every word. Because one important thing that can be learned by reading slowly is the seemingly obvious but oddly underappreciated fact that language is the medium we use in much the same way a composer uses notes, the way a painter uses paint. I realize it may seem obvious, but it's surprising how easily we lose sight of the fact that words are the raw material out of which literature is crafted.

Every page was once a blank page, just as every word that appears on it 3 now was not always there, but instead reflects the final result of countless large and small deliberations. All the elements of good writing depend on the writer's skill in choosing one word instead of another. And what grabs and keeps our interest has everything to do with those choices.

One way to compel yourself to slow down and stop at every word is to ask yourself what sort of information each word — each word choice — is conveying. Reading with that question in mind, let's consider the wealth of information provided by the first paragraph of Flannery O'Connor's "A Good Man Is Hard to Find":   4

> The grandmother didn't want to go to Florida. She wanted to visit some of her connections in east Tennessee and she was seizing at every chance to change Bailey's mind. Bailey was the son she lived with, her only boy. He was sitting on the edge of his chair at the table, bent over the orange sports section of the *Journal*. "Now look here, Bailey," she said, "see here, read this," and she stood with one hand on her thin hip and the other rattling the newspaper at his bald head. "Here this fellow that calls himself The Misfit is aloose from the Federal Pen and headed toward Florida and you read here what it says he did to these people. Just you read it. I wouldn't take my children in any direction with a criminal like that aloose in it. I couldn't answer to my conscience if I did."

The first simple declarative sentence could hardly be more plain: subject, verb, infinitive, preposition. There is not one adjective or adverb to distract us from the central fact. But how much is contained in these eight little words!   5

Here, as in the openings of many stories and novels, we are confronted by one important choice that a writer of fiction needs to make: the question of what to call her characters. Joe, Joe Smith, Mr. Smith? Not, in this case, Grandma or Grandma Smith (no one in this story has a last name) or, let's say, Ethel or Ethel Smith or Mrs. Smith, or any of the myriad terms of address that might have established different degrees of psychic distance and sympathy between the reader and the old woman.   6

Calling her "the grandmother" at once reduces her to her role in the family, as does the fact that her daughter-in-law is never called anything but "the children's mother." At the same time, the title gives her (like The Misfit) an archetypal, mythic role that elevates her and keeps us from getting too chummy with this woman whose name we never learn, even as the writer is preparing our hearts to break at the critical moment to which the grandmother's whole life and the events of the story have led her.   7

The grandmother didn't want to go to Florida. The first sentence is a refusal, which, in its very simplicity, emphasizes the force with which the old woman is digging in her heels. It's a concentrated act of negative will, which we will come to understand in all its tragic folly — that is, the foolishness of attempting to exert one's will when fate or destiny (or as O'Connor would argue,   8

God) has other plans for us. And finally, the no-nonsense austerity of the sentence's construction gives it a kind of authority that — like *Moby-Dick's*[1] first sentence, "Call me Ishmael" — makes us feel that the author is in control, an authority that draws us farther into the story.

The first part of the second sentence — "She wanted to visit some of   9
her connections in east Tennessee" — locates us in geography, that is, in the South. And that one word, *connections* (as opposed to *relatives* or *family* or *people*), reveals the grandmother's sense of her own faded gentility, of having come down in the world, a semi-deluded self-image that, like the illusions of many other O'Connor characters, will contribute to the character's downfall.

The sentence's second half — "she was seizing at every chance to change   10
Bailey's mind" — seizes our own attention more strongly than it would have had O'Connor written, say, "*taking* every chance." The verb quietly but succinctly telegraphs both the grandmother's fierceness and the passivity of Bailey, "the son she lived with, her only boy," two phrases that convey their domestic situation as well as the infantilizing dominance and the simultaneous tenderness that the grandmother feels toward her son. That word *boy* will take on tragic resonance later. "Bailey Boy!" the old woman will cry after her son is killed by The Misfit, who is already about to make his appearance in the newspaper that the grandmother is "rattling" at her boy's bald head. Meanwhile, the paradox of a bald, presumably middle-aged boy leads us to make certain accurate conclusions about the family constellation.

The Misfit is "aloose" — here we find one of those words by which   11
O'Connor conveys the rhythm and flavor of a local dialect without subjecting us to the annoying apostrophes, dropped *g*'s, the shootin' and talkin' and cussin', and the bad grammar with which other authors attempt to transcribe regional speech. The final sentences of the paragraph — "I wouldn't take my children in any direction with a criminal like that aloose in it. I couldn't answer to my conscience if I did" — encapsulate the hilarious and maddening quality of the grandmother's manipulativeness. She'll use *anything*, even an imagined encounter with an escaped criminal, to divert the family vacation from Florida to east Tennessee. And her apparently unlikely fantasy of encountering The Misfit may cause us to reflect on the peculiar egocentrism and narcissism of those people who are constantly convinced that, however minuscule the odds, the stray bullet will somehow find *them*. Meanwhile, again because of word choice, the final sentence is already alluding to those questions of conscience, morality, the spirit and soul that will reveal themselves as being at the heart of O'Connor's story.

---

[1] A novel by the American writer Herman Melville (1819–91). — EDS.

Given the size of the country, we think, they can't *possibly* run into the criminal about whom the grandmother has warned them. And yet we may   12 recall Chekhov's[2] remark that the gun we see onstage in an early scene should probably go off by the play's end. So what *is* going to happen? This short passage has already ushered us into a world that is realistic but at the same time beyond the reach of ordinary logic, and into a narrative that we will follow from this introduction as inexorably as the grandmother is destined to meet a fate that (we *do* suspect) will involve The Misfit. Pared and edited down, highly concentrated, a model of compression from which it would be hard to excise one word, this single passage achieves all this, or more, since there will be additional subtleties and complexities obvious only to each individual reader.

Skimming just won't suffice if we hope to extract one fraction, such as the fraction above, of what a writer's words can teach us about how to use the   13 language.

---

*For a reading quiz, visit **bedfordstmartins.com/thebedfordreader**.*

Journal Writing

Prose's book *Reading like a Writer* holds that careful reading like she demonstrates in this excerpt can teach the skills of effective writing. How convinced are you of this connection between reading and writing? Is it reasonable to expect student writers to follow the example set by professionals? In your journal, consider what you've learned about writing from your reading. How, if at all, have you tried to adopt another writer's techniques, and how successful was the effort? (To take your journal writing further, see "From Journal to Essay" on the facing page.)

Questions on Meaning

1. To what end does Prose examine the first paragraph of Flannery O'Connor's short story? What is her PURPOSE?
2. What is Prose's THESIS?
3. Why is Prose so impressed by the introductory paragraph of "A Good Man Is Hard to Find"?

---

[2] Anton Chekhov (1860–1904), Russian writer of plays and stories. — EDS.

Questions on Writing Strategy

1. For whom is Prose writing? What clues in the text reveal how she imagines her AUDIENCE?
2. To what extent does Prose ASSUME that her readers are familiar with Flannery O'Connor's "A Good Man Is Hard to Find"? How does she ensure that readers can follow her analysis even if they haven't read the story?
3. Prose uses analysis to illuminate O'Connor's writing. How does she reassemble the parts to reach a conclusion about a broader subject?
4. **OTHER METHODS**   How does Prose use a single extended EXAMPLE to make a point about reading and writing?

Questions on Language

1. Identify two FIGURES OF SPEECH in Prose's first three paragraphs and explain what they contribute to her essay.
2. Why do you suppose the author switches from the second person (*you*) in her introduction to the first-person plural (*we*) in her examination of O'Connor's paragraph? What is the EFFECT of this shift?
3. What are the implications of Prose's ALLUSIONS to Herman Melville's *Moby-Dick* (par. 8) and Anton Chekhov's axiom about guns appearing onstage (12)?
4. Check a dictionary if any of the following words are unfamiliar to you: deliberations (par. 3); conveying (4); declarative (5); myriad, psychic (6); archetypal (7); austerity (8); gentility (9); succinctly, telegraphs, infantilizing, resonance, constellation (10); transcribe, encapsulate, egocentrism, narcissism, minuscule (11); inexorably, excise (12).

Suggestions for Writing

1. **FROM JOURNAL TO ESSAY**   Building on the comments you made in your journal, write an essay for an audience of novice writers that explains what, if anything, they can learn about writing from reading.
2. At *bedfordstmartins.com/thebedfordreader*, listen to Jamaica Kincaid's short story "Girl," Joan Didion's "The Santa Ana," or Luis Alberto Urrea's "Life on the Mississippi." Alternatively, read one of the works of creative nonfiction in this book, such as Maya Angelou's "Champion of the World" (p. 104), George Orwell's "Shooting an Elephant" (p. 527), or E. B. White's "Once More to the Lake" (p. 538). Following Prose's analysis as a model, do a close reading of a short passage from the story or essay. (You may choose the first paragraph, as Prose does, or any brief passage that conveys a lot of meaning, but be sure to select an excerpt that has enough substance to support an analysis.) Explain your interpretation in a brief essay.
3. **CRITICAL WRITING**   Locate a copy of Flannery O'Connor's short story "A Good Man Is Hard to Find," and read it for yourself. Then write an essay that responds to Prose's analysis of the first paragraph. Do you agree with her analysis, or do you read the paragraph differently? Why?

4. **CONNECTIONS**   In her essay "But What Do You Mean?" (p. 327), Deborah Tannen looks at some of the ways in which men and women communicate. In a brief essay, consider how Tannen's discussion of gender differences might add another layer of meaning to the grandmother's words in the passage from "A Good Man Is Hard to Find."

Francine Prose on Writing

On the Web site *Barnes & Noble Book Clubs* ("Where Readers and Writers Meet"), Francine Prose was asked by a reader about an apparent contradiction in her book *Reading like a Writer:* She stresses the importance of correct grammar in writing, and yet she admiringly quotes an ungrammatical passage by the noted American fiction writer Philip Roth. "The problem with so many grammatical mistakes," Prose responds, "is that they call attention to themselves. You know that something is wrong with the sentence even if you don't know precisely what it is. And it's distracting. The whole point of grammar is clarity — to help us to write, and to understand, as clearly and comprehensively as possible." As for Philip Roth's errors, Prose explains, "Never — not for a moment — are we confused about what Roth means, nor do we feel he's making a mistake or that he's not in control of the language."

For Discussion

1. Why does Prose accept Roth's grammatical errors but disapprove of those made by others?
2. In what way does grammar "help us to write, and to understand, as clearly and comprehensively as possible"? Have you had the experience of reading someone else's writing and not being able to understand it at first — finding it "distracting" — because of grammatical errors? Or has your own writing been misunderstood because of such errors?

ADDITIONAL WRITING TOPICS

Division or Analysis

Using the method of division or analysis, write an essay on one of the following sub-jects (or choose your own subject). In your essay, make sure your purpose and your principle of division or analysis are clear to your readers. Explain the parts of your sub-ject so that readers know how each relates to the others and contributes to the whole.

1. The slang or technical terminology of a group such as stand-up comedians or computer hackers
2. An especially bad movie, television show, or book
3. A doll, game, or other toy from childhood
4. A typical TV commercial for a product such as laundry soap, deodorant, beer, a luxury car, or an economy car
5. An appliance or a machine, such as a stereo speaker, a motorcycle, a microwave oven, or a camera
6. An organization or association, such as a social club, a sports league, or a support group
7. The characteristic appearance of a rock singer or a classical violinist
8. A year in the life of a student
9. Your favorite poem
10. A short story, an essay, or another work that made you think
11. The government of your community
12. The most popular restaurant (or other place of business) in town
13. The Bible
14. A band or an orchestra
15. A painting or a statue

How the Poor, the Middle Class, and the Rich Spend Their Money

Type of Spending	Household Income		
	$15,000–$19,999	**$50,000–$69,999**	**Above $150,000**
Food at Home	10.2%	7.7%	5.4%
Food at Restaurants, etc.	4.7%	5.4%	5.4%
Housing	29.2%	26.7%	27.5%
Utilities	11.1%	8.2%	4.8%
Clothes & Shoes	3.6%	3.2%	3.7%
Transportation & Gasoline	20.4%	21.3%	15.5%
Health Care & Health Insurance	8.2%	7.1%	4.5%
Entertainment	4.8%	5.1%	5.7%
Education	1.5%	1.3%	4.4%
Saving for Retirement	2.6%	9.6%	15.9%

10

CLASSIFICATION

Sorting into Kinds

◀ **Classification in a table**

How do you spend your money? Does most of it go for rent and utilities, for instance, or is the bulk of your budget earmarked for tuition, fees, and books? How do your income and expenses compare to those of your peers? In this infographic, National Public Radio's *Planet Money* translates data from the Bureau of Labor Statistics to show how household budgets in the United States typically sort out. NPR's table classifies spending patterns for three economic groups: "the Poor, the Middle Class, and the Rich." Notice, first, how NPR defines each class. Then examine the data. The column on the left identifies ten types of spending; the three other columns compare the percentages of household income devoted to each category by the groups. What similarities and differences among the categories strike you? Are you surprised by any of the numbers? Why, or why not?

THE METHOD

To CLASSIFY is to make sense of some aspect of the world by arranging many units — trucks, chemical elements, wasps, students — into more manageable groups. Zoologists classify animals, botanists classify plants — and their classifications help us understand a vast and complex subject: life on earth. To help us find books in a library, librarians classify books into categories: fiction, biography, history, psychology, and so forth. For the convenience of readers, newspapers run classified advertising, grouping many small ads into categories such as "Help Wanted" and "Cars for Sale."

Subjects and Reasons for Classification

The subject of a classification is always a number of things, such as peaches or political systems. (In contrast, DIVISION or ANALYSIS, the topic of the preceding chapter, usually deals with a solitary subject, a coherent whole, such as *a* peach or *a* political system.) The job of classification is to sort the things into groups or classes based on their similarities and differences. Say, for instance, you're going to write an essay about how people write. After interviewing a lot of writers, you determine that writers' processes differ widely, mainly in the amount of planning and rewriting they entail. On the basis of your findings, you create groups for planners, one-drafters, and rewriters. Once your groups are defined (and assuming they are valid), your subjects (the writers) almost sort themselves out.

Just as you can ANALYZE a subject in many ways, you can classify a subject according to many principles. One travel guide, for instance, might group places to stay by style of accommodation: resorts, hotels, motels, bed-and-breakfasts, boarding houses, and hostels. A different guidebook might classify options according to price: grand luxury, luxury, moderate, low-priced, flea-bag, and flophouse.

The principle used in classifying things depends on the writer's PURPOSE. A guidebook classifies accommodations by price to match visitors with hotels that fit their pocketbooks. A linguist might explain the languages of the world by classifying them according to their origins (Romance languages, Germanic languages, Coptic languages . . .), but a student battling with a college language requirement might try to entertain fellow students by classifying languages into three groups: hard to learn, harder to learn, and unlearnable.

Kinds of Classification

Classification schemes vary in complexity, depending on the groups being sorted and the basis for sorting them. In classifying methods of classification, we find two types: binary and complex.

- **Binary classification.** The simplest classification is binary (or two-part), in which you sort things out into (1) those with a certain distinguishing feature and (2) those without it. You might classify a number of persons, let's say, into smokers and nonsmokers, runners and nonrunners, believers and nonbelievers. Binary classification is most useful when your subject is easily divisible into positive and negative categories.

- **Complex classification.** More often, a classification sorts things into multiple categories, sometimes putting members into subcategories. Such is the case with a linguist who categorizes languages by origin. Writing about the varieties of one Germanic language, such as English, the writer could identify the subclasses of British English, North American English, Australian English, and so on.

As readers, we like to meet classifications that strike us as true and familiar. This pleasure may account for the appeal of magazine articles that classify things ("The Seven Common Varieties of Moocher," "Five Embarrassing Types of Social Blunder"). Usefulness as well as pleasure may explain the popularity of classifications that EVALUATE things. The magazine *Consumer Reports* sorts products as varied as computer monitors and frozen dinners into groups based on quality (excellent, good, fair, poor, and not acceptable), and then, using DESCRIPTION, discusses each product (of a frozen pot pie: "Bottom crust gummy, meat spongy when chewed, with nondescript old-poultry and stale-flour flavor").

THE PROCESS

Purposes and Theses

Classification will usually come into play when you want to impose order on a complex subject that includes many items. In one essay in this chapter, for instance, Deborah Tannen tackles the seemingly endless opportunities for men and women to miscommunicate with each other. Sometimes you may use classification humorously, as Russell Baker does in another essay in this chapter, to give a charge to familiar experiences.

Whatever use you make of classification, do it for a reason. Classifications can reveal truth or amuse us, but they can also reveal nothing and bore us. To sort ten US cities according to their relative freedom from air pollution or their cost of living or the range of services offered to residents might prove highly informative and useful to someone looking for a new place to live. But to sort the cities according to a superficial feature such as the relative size of their cat and dog populations wouldn't interest anyone, probably, except a veterinarian looking for a job.

Your purpose, your THESIS, and your principle of classification will all over-lap at the point where you find your interest in your subject. Say you're curi-ous about how other students write. Is your interest primarily in the materials they use (keyboard, pencil, voice recorder), in where and when they write, or in how much planning and rewriting they do? Any of these could lead to a principle for sorting the students into groups. And that principle should be revealed in your THESIS STATEMENT, letting readers know why you are classify-ing. Here, from the essays in this chapter, are two examples of classification thesis statements:

> Inanimate objects are classified into three major categories — those that don't work, those that break down and those that get lost.
> — Russell Baker, "The Plot against People"

> Research shows [that] self-defeating behavior is usually far from random. We tend to make mistakes in ways that cluster under a few categories of screwup.
> — Jeff Wise, "Deadly Mind Traps"

Categories

For a workable classification, make sure that the categories you choose don't overlap. If you were writing a survey of popular magazines for adults and you were sorting your subject into categories that included women's magazines and sports magazines, you might soon run into trouble. Into which category would you place *Women's Sports*? The trouble is that both categories take in the same item. To avoid this problem, you'll need to reorganize your classifica-tion on a different principle. You might sort out the magazines by their audi-ences: magazines mainly for women, magazines mainly for men, magazines for both women and men. Or you might group them according to subject matter: sports magazines, literary magazines, fashion magazines, celebrity magazines, and so on. *Women's Sports* would fit into either of those classification schemes, but into only *one* category in each scheme.

When you draw up a scheme of classification, be sure also that you include all essential categories. Omitting an important category can weaken the effect of your essay, no matter how well written it is. It would be a major over-sight, for example, if you were to classify the residents of a dormitory accord-ing to their religious affiliations and not include a category for the numerous nonaffiliated.

Some form of outline can be helpful to keep the classes and their mem-bers straight as you develop and draft ideas. You might experiment with a diagram in which you jot down headings for the groups, with plenty of space around them, and then let each heading accumulate members as you think of them. This kind of diagram offers more flexibility than a vertical list or an outline, and it may be a better aid for keeping categories from overlapping or disappearing.

FOCUS ON PARAGRAPH DEVELOPMENT

A crucial aim of classification is to make sure each group is clear: what's counted in, what's counted out, and why. You'll provide the examples and other details that make the groups clear as you develop the paragraph(s) devoted to each group.

The following paragraph barely outlines one group in a four-part classification of ex-smokers into zealots, evangelists, the elect, and the serene:

> The second group, evangelists, does not condemn smokers but encourages them to quit. Evangelists think quitting is easy, and they preach this message, often earning the resentment of potential converts.

Contrast this bare-bones adaptation with the actual paragraphs written by Franklin E. Zimring in his essay "Confessions of a Former Smoker":

> By contrast, the antismoking evangelist does not condemn smokers. Unlike the zealot, he regards smoking as an easily curable condition, as a social disease, and not a sin. The evangelist spends an enormous amount of time seeking and preaching to the unconverted. He argues that kicking the habit is not *that* difficult. After all, *he* did it; moreover, as he describes it, the benefits of quitting are beyond measure and the disadvantages are nil.
>
> The hallmark of the evangelist is his insistence that he never misses tobacco. Though he is less hostile to smokers than the zealot, he is resented more. Friends and loved ones who have been the targets of his preachments frequently greet the resumption of smoking by the evangelist as an occasion for unmitigated glee.

In the second sentence of each paragraph, Zimring explicitly contrasts evangelists with zealots, the group he previously defined. And he does more as well: He provides specific examples of the evangelist's message (first paragraph) and of others' reactions to him (second paragraph). These details pin down the group, making it distinct from other groups and clear in itself.

CHECKLIST FOR REVISING A CLASSIFICATION

✔ **Purpose.** Have you classified for a reason? Will readers see why you bothered?

✔ **Principle of classification.** Will readers also see what rule or principle you have used for sorting individuals into groups? Is this principle apparent in your thesis sentence?

> ✔ **Consistency.** Does each representative of your subject fall into one category only, so that categories don't overlap?
>
> ✔ **Completeness.** Have you mentioned all the essential categories suggested by your principle of classification?
>
> ✔ **Paragraph development.** Have you provided enough examples and other details so that readers can easily distinguish each category from the others?

CLASSIFICATION IN ACADEMIC WRITING

An Anthropology Textbook

This paragraph comes from *Humankind Emerging,* a textbook on human physical and cultural evolution by Bernard Campbell. The author offers a standard classification of hand grips in order to explain one of several important differences between human beings and their nearest relatives, apes and monkeys.

There are two distinct ways of holding and using tools: the *power grip* and the *precision grip,* as John Napier termed them. Human infants and children begin with the power grip and progress to the precision grip. Think of how a child holds a spoon: first in the power grip, in its fist or between its fingers and palm, and later between the tips of the thumb and first two fingers, in the precision grip. Many primates have the power grip also. It is the way they get firm hold of a tree branch. But neither a monkey nor an ape has a thumb long enough or flexible enough to be completely *opposable* through rotation at the wrist, able to reach comfortably to the tips of all the other fingers, as is required for our delicate yet strong precision grip. It is the opposability of our thumb and the independent control of our fingers that make possible nearly all the movements necessary to handle tools, to make clothing, to write with a pencil, to play a flute.

Topic sentence names the principle of classification

Two categories explained side by side

Second category explained in greater detail

A Résumé

Sooner or later, every college student needs a résumé: a one-page overview of skills and experiences that will appeal to a potential employer. Part of the challenge in drafting a résumé is to bring order to what seems a complex and unwieldy subject, a life. The main solution is to classify activities and interests into clearly defined groups: typically work experience, education, and special skills.

The group that poses the biggest challenge is usually work experience: Some résumés list jobs with the most recent first, detailing the specifics of each one; others sort experience into skills (such as computer skills, administrative skills, and communication skills) and then list job specifics under each subcategory. The first arrangement tends to be more straightforward and potentially less confusing to readers. However, college students and recent graduates with few previous jobs often find the second arrangement preferable because it downplays experience and showcases abilities.

The résumé on the next page was prepared by Kharron Reid, who was seeking an internship in the field of information systems for the summer between his junior and senior years of college. After experimenting with organizational strategies, he decided to put the category of work experience first because it related directly to the internships he sought. And he chose to organize his work experience by jobs rather than skills because the companies he had worked for were similar to the companies he was applying to.

For the cover letter Reid wrote to go with the résumé, see page 177.

Kharron Reid
137 Chester Street, Apt. E
Allston, MA 02134
(617) 555-4009
kreid@bu.edu

OBJECTIVE

An internship that offers experience in information systems

EXPERIENCE

Pioneer Networking, Damani, MI, May to September 2013

As an intern, worked as a LAN specialist using a Unix-based server

- Connected eight workstations onto a LAN by laying physical platform and configuring software
- Assisted network engineer in monitoring operations of LAN

NBS Systems Corp., Denniston, MI, June to September 2012

As an intern, helped install seven WANs using Windows Server 2012

- Planned layout for WANs
- Installed physical platform and configured servers

SPECIAL SKILLS

Computer proficiency:

Windows 8/7/Vista	QuarkXPress	HTML
Unix	Adobe Photoshop	XML
Red Hat Enterprise Linux	Adobe InDesign	JavaScript

Internet research

EDUCATION

Boston University, School of Management, 2011 to present

Double major: business administration and information systems

Courses: organizational behavior, computer science, advanced programming, networking and data communications

Lahser High School, Bloomfield Hills, MI, 2007 to 2011

Similar to a thesis statement, an objective expresses the applicant's purpose

First major category: work experience

A subcategory for each job includes summaries and specific details

Second major category: special skills

Specific skills

Third major category: education

Specific information relevant to job objective

DEBORAH TANNEN

Deborah Tannen is a linguist who is best known for her popular studies of communication between men and women. Born and raised in New York City, Tannen earned a BA from Harpur College (now part of Binghamton University), MAs from Wayne State University and the University of California at Berkeley, and a PhD in linguistics from Berkeley. She is University Professor at Georgetown University, has published many scholarly articles and books, and has lectured on linguistics all over the world. But her renown is more than academic: With television talk-show appearances, speeches to businesspeople and senators, and best-selling books, Tannen has become, in the words of one reviewer, "America's conversational therapist." The books include *You Just Don't Understand* (1990), *The Argument Culture* (1998), *I Only Say This Because I Love You* (2001), and *You Were Always Mom's Favorite!* (2009), the last about communication between sisters. Tannen sits on the board of directors at the PEN/ Faulkner Foundation, a nonprofit organization devoted to building audiences for literature.

But What Do You Mean?

Why do men and women so often communicate badly, if at all? This question has motivated much of Tannen's research and writing, including the essay reprinted here. Excerpted in *Redbook* magazine from Tannen's book *Talking from 9 to 5* (1994), "But What Do You Mean?" classifies the conversational areas where men and women have the most difficulty communicating in the workplace.

William Lutz's "The World of Doublespeak," the essay following Tannen's, also uses classification to examine communication problems, in the form of misleading verbal substitutions that make "the bad seem good, the negative appear positive."

Conversation is a ritual. We say things that seem obviously the thing to 1
say, without thinking of the literal meaning of our words, any more than we
expect the question "How are you?" to call forth a detailed account of aches
and pains.

Unfortunately, women and men often have different ideas about what's 2
appropriate, different ways of speaking. Many of the conversational rituals
common among women are designed to take the other person's feelings into
account, while many of the conversational rituals common among men are

designed to maintain the one-up position, or at least avoid appearing one-down. As a result, when men and women interact — especially at work — it's often women who are at the disadvantage. Because women are not trying to avoid the one-down position, that is unfortunately where they may end up.

Here, the biggest areas of miscommunication. 3

1. Apologies

Women are often told they apologize too much. The reason they're told 4 to stop doing it is that, to many men, apologizing seems synonymous with putting oneself down. But there are many times when "I'm sorry" isn't self-deprecating, or even an apology; it's an automatic way of keeping both speakers on an equal footing. For example, a well-known columnist once interviewed me and gave me her phone number in case I needed to call her back. I mis-placed the number and had to go through the newspaper's main switchboard. When our conversation was winding down and we'd both made ending-type remarks, I added, "Oh, I almost forgot — I lost your direct number, can I get it again?" "Oh, I'm sorry," she came back instantly, even though she had done nothing wrong and *I* was the one who'd lost the number. But I understood she wasn't really apologizing; she was just automatically reassuring me she had no intention of denying me her number.

Even when "I'm sorry" *is* an apology, women often assume it will be the 5 first step in a two-step ritual: I say "I'm sorry" and take half the blame, then you take the other half. At work, it might go something like this:

A: When you typed this letter, you missed this phrase I inserted.

B: Oh, I'm sorry. I'll fix it.

A: Well, I wrote it so small it was easy to miss.

When both parties share blame, it's a mutual face-saving device. But if one 6 person, usually the woman, utters frequent apologies and the other doesn't, she ends up looking as if she's taking the blame for mishaps that aren't her fault. When she's only partially to blame, she looks entirely in the wrong.

I recently sat in on a meeting at an insurance company where the sole 7 woman, Helen, said "I'm sorry" or "I apologize" repeatedly. At one point she said, "I'm thinking out loud. I apologize." Yet the meeting was intended to be an informal brainstorming session, and *everyone* was thinking out loud.

The reason Helen's apologies stood out was that she was the only person 8 in the room making so many. And the reason I was concerned was that Helen felt the annual bonus she had received was unfair. When I interviewed her colleagues, they said that Helen was one of the best and most productive workers — yet she got one of the smallest bonuses. Although the problem might have been outright sexism, I suspect her speech style, which differs from that of her male colleagues, masks her competence.

Unfortunately, not apologizing can have its price too. Since so many women use ritual apologies, those who don't may be seen as hard-edged. What's important is to be aware of how often you say you're sorry (and why), and to monitor your speech based on the reaction you get.

2. Criticism

A woman who cowrote a report with a male colleague was hurt when she read a rough draft to him and he leapt into a critical response — "Oh, that's too dry! You have to make it snappier!" She herself would have been more likely to say, "That's a really good start. Of course, you'll want to make it a little snappier when you revise."

Whether criticism is given straight or softened is often a matter of convention. In general, women use more softeners. I noticed this difference when talking to an editor about an essay I'd written. While going over changes she wanted to make, she said, "There's one more thing. I know you may not agree with me. The reason I noticed the problem is that your other points are so lucid and elegant." She went on hedging for several more sentences until I put her out of her misery: "Do you want to cut that part?" I asked — and of course she did. But I appreciated her tentativeness. In contrast, another editor (a man) I once called summarily rejected my idea for an article by barking, "Call me when you have something new to say."

Those who are used to ways of talking that soften the impact of criticism may find it hard to deal with the right-between-the-eyes style. It has its own logic, however, and neither style is intrinsically better. People who prefer criticism given straight are operating on an assumption that feelings aren't involved: "Here's the dope. I know you're good; you can take it."

3. Thank-Yous

A woman manager I know starts meetings by thanking everyone for coming, even though it's clearly their job to do so. Her "thank-you" is simply a ritual.

A novelist received a fax from an assistant in her publisher's office; it contained suggested catalog copy for her book. She immediately faxed him her suggested changes and said, "Thanks for running this by me," even though her contract gave her the right to approve all copy. When she thanked the assistant, she fully expected him to reciprocate: "Thanks for giving me such a quick response." Instead, he said, "You're welcome." Suddenly, rather than an equal exchange of pleasantries, she found herself positioned as the recipient of a favor. This made her feel like responding, "Thanks for nothing!"

Many women use "thanks" as an automatic conversation starter and   15
closer; there's nothing literally to say thank you for. Like many rituals typical of women's conversation, it depends on the goodwill of the other to restore the balance. When the other speaker doesn't reciprocate, a woman may feel like someone on a seesaw whose partner abandoned his end. Instead of balancing in the air, she has plopped to the ground, wondering how she got there.

4. Fighting

Many men expect the discussion of ideas to be a ritual fight — explored   16
through verbal opposition. They state their ideas in the strongest possible terms, thinking that if there are weaknesses someone will point them out, and by trying to argue against those objections, they will see how well their ideas hold up.

Those who expect their own ideas to be challenged will respond to anoth-   17
er's ideas by trying to poke holes and find weak links — as a way of *helping*. The logic is that when you are challenged you will rise to the occasion: Adrenaline makes your mind sharper; you get ideas and insights you would not have thought of without the spur of battle.

But many women take this approach as a personal attack. Worse, they   18
find it impossible to do their best work in such a contentious environment. If you're not used to ritual fighting, you begin to hear criticism of your ideas as soon as they are formed. Rather than making you think more clearly, it makes you doubt what you know. When you state your ideas, you hedge in order to fend off potential attacks. Ironically, this is more likely to *invite* attack because it makes you look weak.

Although you may never enjoy verbal sparring, some women find it help-   19
ful to learn how to do it. An engineer who was the only woman among four men in a small company found that as soon as she learned to argue she was accepted and taken seriously. A doctor attending a hospital staff meeting made a similar discovery. She was becoming more and more angry with a male colleague who'd loudly disagreed with a point she'd made. Her better judgment told her to hold her tongue, to avoid making an enemy of this powerful senior colleague. But finally she couldn't hold it in any longer, and she rose to her feet and delivered an impassioned attack on his position. She sat down in a panic, certain she had permanently damaged her relationship with him.

To her amazement, he came up to her afterward and said, "That was a great rebuttal. I'm really impressed. Let's go out for a beer after work and hash out our approaches to this problem."

5. Praise

A manager I'll call Lester had been on his new job six months when he [20] heard that the women reporting to him were deeply dissatisfied. When he talked to them about it, their feelings erupted; two said they were on the verge of quitting because he didn't appreciate their work, and they didn't want to wait to be fired. Lester was dumbfounded: He believed they were doing a fine job. Surely, he thought, he had said nothing to give them the impression he didn't like their work. And indeed he hadn't. That was the problem. He had said *nothing* — and the women assumed he was following the adage "If you can't say something nice, don't say anything." He thought he was showing confidence in them by leaving them alone.

Men and women have different habits in regard to giving praise. For ex- [21] ample, Deirdre and her colleague William both gave presentations at a conference. Afterward, Deirdre told William, "That was a great talk!" He thanked her. Then she asked, "What did you think of mine?" and he gave her a lengthy and detailed critique. She found it uncomfortable to listen to his comments. But she assured herself that he meant well, and that his honesty was a signal that she, too, should be honest when he asked for a critique of his performance. As a matter of fact, she had noticed quite a few ways in which he could have improved his presentation. But she never got a chance to tell him because he never asked — and she felt put down. The worst part was that it seemed she had only herself to blame, since she *had* asked what he thought of her talk.

But had she really asked for his critique? The truth is, when she asked [22] for his opinion, she was expecting a compliment, which she felt was more or less required following anyone's talk. When he responded with criticism, she figured, "Oh, he's playing 'Let's critique each other'" — not a game she'd initiated, but one which she was willing to play. Had she realized he was going to criticize her and not ask her to reciprocate, she would never have asked in the first place.

It would be easy to assume that Deirdre was insecure, whether she was [23] fishing for a compliment or soliciting a critique. But she was simply talking automatically, performing one of the many conversational rituals that allow us to get through the day. William may have sincerely misunderstood Deirdre's intention — or may have been unable to pass up a chance to one-up her when given the opportunity.

6. Complaints

"Troubles talk" can be a way to establish rapport with a colleague. You 24
complain about a problem (which shows that you are just folks) and the other
person responds with a similar problem (which puts you on equal footing).
But while such commiserating is common among women, men are likely to
hear it as a request to *solve* the problem.

One woman told me she would frequently initiate what she thought would 25
be pleasant complaint-airing sessions at work. She'd talk about situations that
bothered her just to talk about them, maybe to understand them better. But
her male office mate would quickly tell her how she could improve the situation. This left her feeling condescended to and frustrated. She was delighted
to see this very impasse in a section in my book *You Just Don't Understand*,
and showed it to him. "Oh," he said, "I see the problem. How can we solve
it?" Then they both laughed, because it had happened again: He short-
circuited the detailed discussion she'd hoped for and cut to the chase of finding
a solution.

Sometimes the consequences of complaining are more serious: A man 26
might take a woman's lighthearted griping literally, and she can get a reputation as a chronic malcontent. Furthermore, she may be seen as not up to solving the problems that arise on the job.

7. Jokes

I heard a man call in to a talk show and say, "I've worked for two women 27
and neither one had a sense of humor. You know, when you work with men,
there's a lot of joking and teasing." The show's host and the guest (both
women) took his comment at face value and assumed the women this man
worked for were humorless. The guest said, "Isn't it sad that women don't
feel comfortable enough with authority to see the humor?" The host said,
"Maybe when more women are in authority roles, they'll be more comfortable
with power." But although the women this man worked for *may* have taken
themselves too seriously, it's just as likely that they each had a terrific sense
of humor, but maybe the humor wasn't the type he was used to. They may
have been like the woman who wrote to me: "When I'm with men, my wit or
cleverness seems inappropriate (or lost!) so I don't bother. When I'm with my
women friends, however, there's no hold on puns or cracks and my humor is
fully appreciated."

The types of humor women and men tend to prefer differ. Research has 28
shown that the most common form of humor among men is razzing, teasing, and mock-hostile attacks, while among women it's self-mocking. Women

often mistake men's teasing as genuinely hostile. Men often mistake women's mock self-deprecation as truly putting themselves down.

Women have told me they were taken more seriously when they learned   29
to joke the way the guys did. For example, a teacher who went to a national conference with seven other teachers (mostly women) and a group of admin-istrators (mostly men) was annoyed that the administrators always found rea-sons to leave boring seminars, while the teachers felt they had to stay and take notes. One evening, when the group met at a bar in the hotel, the principal asked her how one such seminar had turned out. She retorted, "As soon as you left, it got much better." He laughed out loud at her response. The playful insult appealed to the men — but there was a trade-off. The women seemed to back off from her after this. (Perhaps they were put off by her using joking to align herself with the bosses.)

There is no "right" way to talk. When problems arise, the culprit may be   30
style differences — and *all* styles will at times fail with others who don't share or understand them, just as English won't do you much good if you try to speak to someone who knows only French. If you want to get your message across, it's not a question of being "right"; it's a question of using language that's shared — or at least understood.

For a reading quiz, visit **bedfordstmartins.com/thebedfordreader**.

Journal Writing

Tannen's ANECDOTE about the newspaper columnist (par. 4) illustrates that much of what we say is purely automatic. Do you excuse yourself when you bump into inani-mate objects? When someone says, "Have a good trip," do you answer, "You, too," even if the other person isn't going anywhere? Do you find yourself overusing certain words or phrases such as "like" or "you know"? Pay close attention to these kinds of verbal tics in your own and others' speech. Over the course of a few days, note as many of them as you can in your journal. (To take your journal writing further, see "From Journal to Essay" on the following page.)

Questions on Meaning

1. What is Tannen's PURPOSE in writing this essay? What does she hope it will accomplish?

2. What does Tannen mean when she writes, "Conversation is a ritual" (par. 1)?
3. What does Tannen see as the fundamental difference between men's and women's conversational strategies?
4. Why is "You're welcome" not always an appropriate response to "Thank you"?

Questions on Writing Strategy

1. This essay has a large cast of characters: twenty-three to be exact. What function do these characters serve? How does Tannen introduce them to the reader? Does she describe them in sufficient detail?
2. Whom does Tannen see as her primary AUDIENCE? ANALYZE her use of the pronoun *you* in paragraphs 9 and 19. Whom does she seem to be addressing here? Why?
3. Analyze how Tannen develops the category of apologies in paragraphs 4–9. Where does she use EXAMPLE, DEFINITION, and COMPARISON AND CONTRAST?
4. How does Tannen's DESCRIPTION of a columnist as "well-known" (par. 4) contribute to the effectiveness of her example?
5. **OTHER METHODS**   For each of her seven areas of miscommunication, Tannen compares and contrasts male and female communication styles and strategies. SUMMARIZE the main source of misunderstanding in each area.

Questions on Language

1. What is the EFFECT of "I put her out of her misery" (par. 11)? What does this phrase usually mean?
2. What does Tannen mean by a "right-between-the-eyes style" (par. 12)? What is the FIGURE OF SPEECH involved here?
3. What is the effect of Tannen's use of figurative verbs, such as "barking" (par. 11) and "erupted" (20)? Find at least one other example of the use of a verb in a nonliteral sense.
4. Look up any of the following words whose meanings you are unsure of: synonymous, self-deprecating (par. 4); lucid, tentativeness (11); intrinsically (12); reciprocate (14); adrenaline, spur (17); contentious, hedge (18); sparring, rebuttal (19); adage (20); soliciting (23); commiserating (24); initiate, condescended, impasse (25); chronic, malcontent (26); razzing (28); retorted (29).

Suggestions for Writing

1. **FROM JOURNAL TO ESSAY**   Write an essay classifying the examples from your journal entry into categories of your own devising. You might sort out the examples by context ("phone blunders," "faulty farewells"), by purpose ("nervous tics," "space fillers"), or by some other principle of classification. Given your subject matter, you might want to adopt a humorous TONE.
2. How well does your style of communication conform to that of your gender as described by Tannen? Write a short essay about a specific communication prob-

lem or misunderstanding you have had with someone of the opposite sex (sibling, friend, parent, significant other). How well does Tannen's differentiation of male and female communication styles account for your particular problem?

3. How true do you find Tannen's assessment of miscommunication between the sexes? Consider the conflicts you have observed between your parents, among fellow students or coworkers, in fictional portrayals in books and movies. You could also go beyond your personal experiences and observations by researching the opinions of other experts (linguists, psychologists, sociologists, and so on). Write an essay confirming or questioning Tannen's GENERALIZATIONS, backing up your (and perhaps others') views with your own examples.

4. **CRITICAL WRITING**   Tannen insists that "neither [communication] style is intrinsically better" (par. 12), that "There is no 'right' way to talk" (30). What do you make of this refusal to take sides in the battle of the sexes? Is Tannen always successful? Is absolute neutrality possible, or even desirable, when it comes to such divisive issues?

5. **CONNECTIONS**   Tannen offers some of her own experiences as examples of communication blunders, and she often uses the first-person *I* or *we* in explaining her categories. In contrast, the author of the next essay, William Lutz, takes a more distant approach in classifying types of misleading language called *doublespeak*. Which of these approaches, personal or more distant, do you find more effective, and why? When, in your view, is it appropriate to inject yourself into your writing, and when is it not?

Deborah Tannen on Writing

Though Deborah Tannen's "But What Do You Mean?" is written for a general audience, Tannen is a linguistics scholar who does considerable academic writing. One debate among scholarly writers is whether it is appropriate to incorporate one's experiences and biases into academic writing, especially given the goal of objectivity in conducting and reporting research. The October 1996 *PMLA* *(Publications of the Modern Language Association)* printed a discussion of the academic uses of the personal, with contributions from more than two dozen scholars. Tannen's comments, excerpted here, focused on the first-person *I*.

When I write academic prose, I use the first person, and I instruct my students to do the same. The principle that researchers should acknowledge their participation in their work is an outgrowth of a humanistic approach to linguistic analysis. . . . Understanding discourse is not a passive act of decoding but a creative act of imagining a scene (composed of people engaged in culturally recognizable activities) within which the ideas being talked about have meaning. The listener's active participation in sense making both results from and creates interpersonal involvement. For researchers to deny their involvement in their interpreting of discourse would be a logical and ethical violation of this framework. . . .

[O]bjectivity in the analysis of interactions is impossible anyway. Whether they took part in the interaction or not, researchers identify with one or another speaker, are put off or charmed by the styles of participants. This one reminds you of a cousin you adore; that one sounds like a neighbor you despise. Researchers are human beings, not atomic particles or chemical elements. . . .

Another danger of claiming objectivity rather than acknowledging and correcting for subjectivity is that scholars who don't reveal their participation in interactions they analyze risk the appearance of hiding it. "Following is an exchange that occurred between a professor and a student," I have read in articles in my field. The speakers are identified as "A" and "B." The reader is not told that the professor, A (of course the professor is A and the student B), is the author. Yet that knowledge is crucial to contextualizing the author's interpretation. Furthermore, the impersonal designations A and B are another means of constructing a false objectivity. They obscure the fact that human interaction is being analyzed, and they interfere with the reader's understanding. The letters replace what in the author's mind are names and voices and personas that are the basis for understanding the discourse. Readers, given only initials, are left to scramble for understanding by imagining people in place of letters.

Avoiding self-reference by using the third person also results in the depersonalization of knowledge. Knowledge and understanding do not occur in abstract isolation. They always and only occur among people. . . . Denying that scholarship is a personal endeavor entails a failure to understand and correct for the inevitable bias that human beings bring to all their enterprises.

For Discussion

1. In arguing for the use of the first-person *I* in academic prose, Tannen is speaking primarily about its use in her own field, linguistics. From your experience with academic writing, is Tannen's argument applicable to other disciplines as well, such as history, biology, psychology, or government? Why, or why not? What have your teachers in various courses advised you about writing in the first person?

2. Try this experiment on the effects of the first person and third person (*he, she, they*): Write a passage of academic prose in one person or the other. (Tannen's example of professor A and student B can perhaps suggest a direction for your passage, or you may have one already written in a paper you've submitted.) Rewrite the passage in the other person, and ANALYZE the two versions. Does one sound more academic than the other? What are the advantages and disadvantages of each one?

WILLIAM LUTZ

William Lutz was born in 1940 in Racine, Wisconsin. He received a BA from Dominican College, an MA from Marquette University, a PhD from the University of Nevada at Reno, and a JD from Rutgers School of Law. For much of his career, Lutz's interest in words and composition has made him an active campaigner against misleading and irresponsible language. For fourteen years he edited the *Quarterly Review of Doublespeak,* and he has written three popular books on such language, the last being *Doublespeak Defined: Cut through the Bull**** and Get to the Point!* (1999). He has also written for many periodicals, including the *Los Angeles Times,* the *London Times,* and *USA Today.* In 1996 Lutz received the George Orwell Award for Distinguished Contribution to Honesty and Clarity in Public Language. He is professor emeritus at Rutgers University in Camden, New Jersey.

The World of Doublespeak

In the previous essay, Deborah Tannen examines the ways gender differences in speaking can cause innocent misunderstandings. But what if misunderstandings are the result of speech crafted to obscure meaning? Such intentional fudging, or *doublespeak,* is the sort of language Lutz specializes in, and here he uses classification to expose its many guises. "The World of Doublespeak" abridges the first chapter in Lutz's book *Doublespeak: From Revenue Enhancement to Terminal Living* (1989); the essay's title is the chapter's subtitle.

There are no potholes in the streets of Tucson, Arizona, just "pavement deficiencies." The Reagan Administration didn't propose any new taxes, just "revenue enhancement" through new "user's fees." Those aren't bums on the street, just "non–goal oriented members of society." There are no more poor people, just "fiscal underachievers." There was no robbery of an automatic teller machine, just an "unauthorized withdrawal." The patient didn't die because of medical malpractice, it was just a "diagnostic misadventure of a high magnitude." The US Army doesn't kill the enemy anymore, it just "services the target." And the doublespeak goes on.

Doublespeak is language that pretends to communicate but really doesn't. It is language that makes the bad seem good, the negative appear positive, the unpleasant appear attractive or at least tolerable. Doublespeak is language that avoids or shifts responsibility, language that is at variance with its real or purported meaning. It is language that conceals or prevents thought; rather than extending thought, doublespeak limits it.

Doublespeak is not a matter of subjects and verbs agreeing; it is a matter of words and facts agreeing. Basic to doublespeak is incongruity, the incongruity between what is said or left unsaid, and what really is. It is the incongruity between the word and the referent, between seem and be, between the essential function of language — communication — and what doublespeak does — mislead, distort, deceive, inflate, circumvent, obfuscate.

How to Spot Doublespeak

How can you spot doublespeak? Most of the time you will recognize doublespeak when you see or hear it. But, if you have any doubts, you can identify doublespeak just by answering these questions: Who is saying what to whom, under what conditions and circumstances, with what intent, and with what results? Answering these questions will usually help you identify as doublespeak language that appears to be legitimate or that at first glance doesn't even appear to be doublespeak.

First Kind of Doublespeak

There are at least four kinds of doublespeak. The first is the euphemism, an inoffensive or positive word or phrase used to avoid a harsh, unpleasant, or distasteful reality. But a euphemism can also be a tactful word or phrase which avoids directly mentioning a painful reality, or it can be an expression used out of concern for the feelings of someone else, or to avoid directly discussing a topic subject to a social or cultural taboo.

When you use a euphemism because of your sensitivity for someone's feelings or out of concern for a recognized social or cultural taboo, it is not doublespeak. For example, you express your condolences that someone has "passed away" because you do not want to say to a grieving person, "I'm sorry your father is dead." When you use the euphemism "passed away," no one is misled. Moreover, the euphemism functions here not just to protect the feelings of another person, but to communicate also your concern for that person's feelings during a period of mourning. When you excuse yourself to go to the "restroom," or you mention that someone is "sleeping with" or "involved with" someone else, you do not mislead anyone about your meaning, but you do respect the social taboos about discussing bodily functions and sex in direct terms. You also indicate your sensitivity to the feelings of your audience, which is usually considered a mark of courtesy and good manners.

However, when a euphemism is used to mislead or deceive, it becomes   7
doublespeak. For example, in 1984 the US State Department announced that
it would no longer use the word "killing" in its annual report on the status of
human rights in countries around the world. Instead, it would use the phrase
"unlawful or arbitrary deprivation of life," which the department claimed
was more accurate. Its real purpose for using this phrase was simply to avoid
discussing the embarrassing situation of government-sanctioned killings in
countries that are supported by the United States and have been certified by
the United States as respecting the human rights of their citizens. This use of
a euphemism constitutes doublespeak, since it is designed to mislead, to cover
up the unpleasant. Its real intent is at variance with its apparent intent. It is
language designed to alter our perception of reality.

The Pentagon, too, avoids discussing unpleasant realities when it refers   8
to bombs and artillery shells that fall on civilian targets as "incontinent ord-
nance." And in 1977 the Pentagon tried to slip funding for the neutron bomb
unnoticed into an appropriations bill by calling it a "radiation enhancement
device."

Second Kind of Doublespeak

A second kind of doublespeak is jargon, the specialized language of a   9
trade, profession, or similar group, such as that used by doctors, lawyers, engineers, educators, or car mechanics. Jargon can serve an important and useful
function. Within a group, jargon functions as a kind of verbal shorthand that
allows members of the group to communicate with each other clearly, efficiently, and quickly. Indeed, it is a mark of membership in the group to be able
to use and understand the group's jargon.

But jargon, like the euphemism, can also be doublespeak. It can be — and   10
often is — pretentious, obscure, and esoteric terminology used to give an air
of profundity, authority, and prestige to speakers and their subject matter.
Jargon as doublespeak often makes the simple appear complex, the ordinary
profound, the obvious insightful. In this sense it is used not to express but
impress. With such doublespeak, the act of smelling something becomes
"organoleptic analysis," glass becomes "fused silicate," a crack in a metal support beam becomes a "discontinuity," conservative economic policies become
"distributionally conservative notions."

Lawyers, for example, speak of an "involuntary conversion" of property   11
when discussing the loss or destruction of property through theft, accident,
or condemnation. If your house burns down or if your car is stolen, you have
suffered an involuntary conversion of your property. When used by lawyers in
a legal situation, such jargon is a legitimate use of language, since lawyers can
be expected to understand the term.

However, when a member of a specialized group uses its jargon to communicate with a person outside the group, and uses it knowing that the nonmember does not understand such language, then there is doublespeak. For example, on May 9, 1978, a National Airlines 727 airplane crashed while attempting to land at the Pensacola, Florida, airport. Three of the fifty-two passengers aboard the airplane were killed. As a result of the crash, National made an after-tax insurance benefit of $1.7 million, or an extra 18¢ a share dividend for its stockholders. Now National Airlines had two problems: It did not want to talk about one of its airplanes crashing, and it had to account for the $1.7 million when it issued its annual report to its stockholders. National solved the problem by inserting a footnote in its annual report which explained that the $1.7 million income was due to "the involuntary conversion of a 727." National thus acknowledged the crash of its airplane and the subsequent profit it made from the crash, without once mentioning the accident or the deaths. However, because airline officials knew that most stockholders in the company, and indeed most of the general public, were not familiar with legal jargon, the use of such jargon constituted doublespeak.

Third Kind of Doublespeak

A third kind of doublespeak is gobbledygook or bureaucratese. Basically, such doublespeak is simply a matter of piling on words, of overwhelming the audience with words, the bigger the words and the longer the sentences the better. Alan Greenspan, then chair of President Nixon's Council of Economic Advisors, was quoted in *The Philadelphia Inquirer* in 1974 as having testified before a Senate committee that "It is a tricky problem to find the particular calibration in timing that would be appropriate to stem the acceleration in risk premiums created by falling incomes without prematurely aborting the decline in the inflation-generated risk premiums."

Nor has Mr. Greenspan's language changed since then. Speaking to the meeting of the Economic Club of New York in 1988, Mr. Greenspan, now Federal Reserve chair, said, "I guess I should warn you, if I turn out to be particularly clear, you've probably misunderstood what I've said." Mr. Greenspan's doublespeak doesn't seem to have held back his career.[1]

Sometimes gobbledygook may sound impressive, but when the quote is later examined in print it doesn't even make sense. During the 1988 presidential campaign, vice-presidential candidate Senator Dan Quayle explained the need for a strategic-defense initiative by saying, "Why wouldn't an enhanced

---

[1] Greenspan retired from the Federal Reserve in 2006. He is now a private consultant. — EDS.

deterrent, a more stable peace, a better prospect to denying the ones who enter conflict in the first place to have a reduction of offensive systems and an introduction to defense capability? I believe this is the route the country will eventually go."

The investigation into the *Challenger* disaster in 1986 revealed the doublespeak of gobbledygook and bureaucratese used by too many involved in the shuttle program. When Jesse Moore, NASA's associate administrator, was asked if the performance of the shuttle program had improved with each launch or if it had remained the same, he answered, "I think our performance in terms of the liftoff performance and in terms of the orbital performance, we knew more about the envelope we were operating under, and we have been pretty accurately staying in that. And so I would say the performance has not by design drastically improved. I think we have been able to characterize the performance more as a function of our launch experience as opposed to it improving as a function of time." While this language may appear to be jargon, a close look will reveal that it is really just gobbledygook laced with jargon. But you really have to wonder if Mr. Moore had any idea what he was saying.   16

Fourth Kind of Doublespeak

The fourth kind of doublespeak is inflated language that is designed to make the ordinary seem extraordinary; to make everyday things seem impressive; to give an air of importance to people, situations, or things that would not normally be considered important; to make the simple seem complex. Often this kind of doublespeak isn't hard to spot, and it is usually pretty funny. While car mechanics may be called "automotive internists," elevator operators members of the "vertical transportation corps," used cars "pre-owned" or "experienced cars," and black-and-white television sets described as having "non-multicolor capability," you really aren't misled all that much by such language.   17

However, you may have trouble figuring out that, when Chrysler "initiates a career alternative enhancement program," it is really laying off five thousand workers; or that "negative patient-care outcome" means the patient died; or that "rapid oxidation" means a fire in a nuclear power plant.   18

The doublespeak of inflated language can have serious consequences. In Pentagon doublespeak, "pre-emptive counterattack" means that American forces attacked first; "engaged the enemy on all sides" means American troops were ambushed; "backloading of augmentation personnel" means a retreat by American troops. In the doublespeak of the military, the 1983 invasion of Grenada was conducted not by the US Army, Navy, Air Force, and Marines,   19 but by the "Caribbean Peace Keeping Forces." But then, according to the Pentagon, it wasn't an invasion, it was a "predawn vertical insertion." . . .

The Dangers of Doublespeak

Doublespeak is not the product of carelessness or sloppy thinking. Indeed,   20
most doublespeak is the product of clear thinking and is carefully designed and
constructed to appear to communicate when in fact it doesn't. It is language
designed not to lead but mislead. It is language designed to distort reality and
corrupt thought. . . . In the world created by doublespeak, if it's not a tax
increase, but rather "revenue enhancement" or "tax base broadening," how
can you complain about higher taxes? If it's not acid rain, but rather "poorly
buffered precipitation," how can you worry about all those dead trees? If that
isn't the Mafia in Atlantic City, but just "members of a career-offender cartel," why worry about the influence of organized crime in the city? If Supreme
Court Justice William Rehnquist wasn't addicted to the pain-killing drug his
doctor prescribed, but instead it was just that the drug had "established an
interrelationship with the body, such that if the drug is removed precipitously,
there is a reaction," you needn't question that his decisions might have been
influenced by his drug addiction. If it's not a Titan II nuclear-armed intercontinental ballistic missile with a warhead 630 times more powerful than the
atomic bomb dropped on Hiroshima, but instead, according to air force colonel Frank Horton, it's just a "very large, potentially disruptive reentry system,"
why be concerned about the threat of nuclear destruction? Why worry about
the neutron bomb escalating the arms race if it's just a "radiation enhancement weapon"? If it's not an invasion, but a "rescue mission" or a "predawn
vertical insertion," you won't need to think about any violations of US or
international law.

Doublespeak has become so common in everyday living that many people   21
fail to notice it. Even worse, when they do notice doublespeak being used on
them, they don't react, they don't protest. Do you protest when you are asked
to check your packages at the desk "for your convenience," when it's not for
your convenience at all but for someone else's? You see advertisements for
"genuine imitation leather," "virgin vinyl," or "real counterfeit diamonds,"
but do you question the language or the supposed quality of the product? Do
you question politicians who don't speak of slums or ghettos but of the "inner
city" or "substandard housing" where the "disadvantaged" live and thus avoid
talking about the poor who have to live in filthy, poorly heated, ramshackle
apartments or houses? Aren't you amazed that patients don't die in the hospital anymore, it's just "negative patient-care outcome"?

Doublespeak such as that noted earlier that defines cab drivers as "urban   22
transportation specialists," elevator operators as members of the "vertical
transportation corps," and automobile mechanics as "automotive internists"
can be considered humorous and relatively harmless. However, when a fire in
a nuclear reactor building is called "rapid oxidation," an explosion in a nuclear
power plant is called an "energetic disassembly," the illegal overthrow of a
legitimate government is termed "destabilizing a government," and lies are
seen as "inoperative statements," we are hearing doublespeak that attempts to
avoid responsibility and make the bad seem good, the negative appear positive, something unpleasant appear attractive; and which seems to communicate but doesn't. It is language designed to alter our perception of reality and
corrupt our thinking. Such language does not provide us with the tools we
need to develop, advance, and preserve our culture and our civilization. Such
language breeds suspicion, cynicism, distrust, and, ultimately, hostility.

Doublespeak is insidious because it can infect and eventually destroy the   23
function of language, which is communication between people and social
groups. This corruption of the function of language can have serious and far-
reaching consequences. We live in a country that depends upon an informed
electorate to make decisions in selecting candidates for office and deciding
issues of public policy. The use of doublespeak can become so pervasive that it
becomes the coin of the political realm, with speakers and listeners convinced
that they really understand such language. After a while we may really believe
that politicians don't lie but only "misspeak," that illegal acts are merely
"inappropriate actions," that fraud and criminal conspiracy are just "miscerti-
fication." President Jimmy Carter in April of 1980 could call the aborted raid
to free the American hostages in Teheran an "incomplete success" and really
believe that he had made a statement that clearly communicated with the
American public. So, too, could President Ronald Reagan say in 1985 that
"ultimately our security and our hopes for success at the arms reduction talks
hinge on the determination that we show here to continue our program to rebuild and refortify our defenses" and really believe that greatly increasing the
amount of money spent building new weapons would lead to a reduction in the
number of weapons in the world. If we really believe that we understand such
language and that such language communicates and promotes clear thought,
then the world of 1984,[2] with its control of reality through language, is upon us.

---

[2] In a section omitted from this abridgement of his chapter, Lutz discusses *Nineteen Eighty-
Four*, the 1949 novel by George Orwell in which a frightening totalitarian state devises a language, called *newspeak*, to shape and control thought in politically acceptable forms. (For an
example of Orwell's writing, see p. 527.) — Eds.

*For a reading quiz, visit **bedfordstmartins.com/thebedfordreader***.

Journal Writing

Now that you know the name for it, when have you read or heard examples of double-speak? Over the next few days, jot down examples of doublespeak that you recall or that you read and hear — from politicians or news commentators; in the lease for your dwelling or your car; in advertising and catalogs; from bosses, teachers, or other figures of authority; in overheard conversations. (To take your journal writing further, see "From Journal to Essay" on the facing page.)

Questions on Meaning

1. What is Lutz's THESIS? Where does he state it?
2. According to Lutz, four questions can help us identify doublespeak. What are they? How can they help us distinguish between truthful language and double-speak?
3. What, according to Lutz, are "the dangers of doublespeak"?
4. What ASSUMPTIONS does the author make about his readers' educational back-grounds and familiarity with his subject?

Questions on Writing Strategy

1. What principle does Lutz use for creating his four kinds of doublespeak — that is, what mainly distinguishes the groups?
2. How does Lutz develop the discussion of euphemism in paragraphs 5–8?
3. Lutz quotes Alan Greenspan twice in paragraphs 13–14. What is surprising about the comment in paragraph 14? Why does Lutz include this second quotation?
4. Lutz uses many quotations that were quite current when he first published this piece in 1989 but that now may seem dated — for instance, references to Presi-dents Carter and Reagan or to the nuclear arms race. Do these EXAMPLES under-mine Lutz's essay in any way? Is his discussion of doublespeak still valid today? Explain your answers.
5. **OTHER METHODS**   Lutz's essay is not only a classification but also a DEFINITION of *doublespeak* and an examination of CAUSE AND EFFECT. Where are these other methods used most prominently? What do they contribute to the essay?

Questions on Language

1. How does Lutz's own language compare with the language he quotes as double-speak? Do you find his language clear and easy to understand?

2. ANALYZE Lutz's language in paragraphs 22 and 23. How do the CONNOTATIONS of words such as "corrupt," "hostility," "insidious," and "control" strengthen the author's message?
3. The following list of possibly unfamiliar words includes only those found in Lutz's own sentences, not those in the doublespeak he quotes. Be sure you can define variance (par. 2); incongruity, referent (3); taboo (5); esoteric, profundity (10); condemnation (11); ramshackle (21); cynicism (22); insidious (23).

Suggestions for Writing

1. **FROM JOURNAL TO ESSAY**   Choose at least one of the examples of doublespeak noted in your journal, and write an essay explaining why it qualifies as doublespeak. Which of Lutz's categories does it fit under? How did you recognize it? Can you understand what it means?
2. Just about all of us have resorted to doublespeak at one time or another — when making an excuse, when trying to wing it on an exam, when trying to impress a potential employer. Write a NARRATIVE about a time you used deliberately unclear language, perhaps language that you yourself didn't understand. What were the circumstances? Did you consciously decide to use unclear language, or did it just leak out? How did others react to your use of this language?
3. Although the *Quarterly Review of Doublespeak,* which Lutz once edited, is now defunct, your library may carry back issues of the journal or offer access through a database. Read a few related articles from the journal, and based on them write an essay in which you challenge, expand, or add more examples to Lutz's categories.
4. **CRITICAL WRITING**   Can you determine from his essay who Lutz believes is responsible for the proliferation of doublespeak? Whose responsibility is it to curtail the use of doublespeak: just those who use it? the schools? the government? the media? we who hear it? Write an essay that considers these questions, citing specific passages from the essay and incorporating your own ideas.
5. **CONNECTIONS**   While Lutz looks at language "carefully designed and constructed to appear to communicate when in fact it doesn't," Deborah Tannen, in the previous essay, takes the position that "conversation is a ritual" — that we don't often think about what we're saying and miscommunicate as a result. How do you resolve the apparent contradictions in these two writers' underlying assumptions about language? Is most of our speech deliberate, or is it automatic? Why do you think so? In an essay that draws on examples and EVIDENCE from each of these two essays as well as from your own experience, explain what you see as the major causes of miscommunication.

William Lutz on Writing

In 1989 C-SPAN aired an interview between Brian Lamb and William Lutz. Lamb asked Lutz about his writing process. "I have a rule about writing,"

Lutz answered, "which I discovered when I wrote my dissertation: You never write a book, you write three pages, or you write five pages. I put off writing my dissertation for a year, because I could not think of writing this whole thing. . . . I had put off doing this book [*Doublespeak*] for quite a while, and my wife said, 'You've got to do the book.' And I said, 'Yes, I am going to, just as soon as I . . . ,' and, of course, I did every other thing I could possibly think of before that, and then I realized one day that she was right, I had to start writing. . . . So one day, I sit down and say, 'I am going to write five pages — that's all — and when I am done with five pages, I'll reward myself.' So I do the five pages, or the next time I will do ten pages or whatever number of pages, but I set a number of pages."

Perhaps wondering just how high Lutz's daily page count might go, Lamb asked Lutz how much he wrote at one time. "It depends," Lutz admitted. "I always begin a writing session by sitting down and rewriting what I wrote the previous day — and that is the first thing, and it does two things. First of all, it makes your writing a little bit better, because rewriting is the essential part of writing. And the second thing is to get you flowing again, get back into the mainstream. Truman Capote[3] once gave the best piece of advice for writers ever given. He said, 'Never pump the well dry; always leave a bucket there.' So, I never stop writing when I run out of ideas. I always stop when I have something more to write about, and write a note to myself, 'This is what I am going to do next,' and then I stop. The worst feeling in the world is to have written yourself dry and have to come back the next day, knowing that you are dry and not knowing where you are going to pick up at this point."

For Discussion

1. Though his work is devoted to words and writing, William Lutz once spent a great deal of time avoiding writing. What finally got him to stop procrastinating? When you are avoiding a writing assignment, is it the length of the project or something else that prevents you from getting to work?
2. Lutz always rewrites before he starts writing about the idea that he didn't develop on the previous day. How come? Do you think Lutz's strategy is a good one?

---

[3] Truman Capote (1924–84) was an American journalist and fiction writer. — EDS.

Notes and Resources for Teaching

with
INTEGRATED
MEDIA

The Brief Bedford Reader

X. J. Kennedy • Dorothy M. Kennedy

Jane E. Aaron • Ellen Kuhl Repetto

Manufactured in the United States of America.

8   7   6   5   4   3
f   e   d   c   b   a

For information, write: Bedford/St. Martin's, 75 Arlington Street, Boston, MA 02116   (617-399-4000)

ISBN 978-1-4576-4893-9

PREFACE

In finding your way to this preface, you may already have discovered the innovations in the twelfth edition of *The Brief Bedford Reader*. (If not, they are summed up in the text's own preface.) Here we describe the various resources for teachers provided in this manual.

"Teaching with Journals and Collaboration" (p. 1). *The Brief Bedford Reader* includes quite a bit on journal writing and many opportunities for small-group collaboration, and here we support the text with background on these popular techniques — benefits, pitfalls, suggestions.

"Teaching Visual and Multimodal Literacy" (p. 4). We suggest ways to use an exciting feature of *The Brief Bedford Reader*: the introductory material on critical reading of visuals and the many images and multimedia selections appearing throughout the book and in the integrated e-Pages.

"Reading, Writing, and Research" (p. 7). This section gives an overview of the text's crucial chapters on critical reading, the writing process, and academic writing in Part One, as well as the Appendix on documenting sources in APA style.

Chapter introductions. For each rhetorical chapter we preview the method, predicting difficulties that students may have with it and suggesting various uses for the selections that illustrate the method.

Selection introductions. For each selection we highlight what students may like (or dislike) about the piece, suggest topics for discussion and collaboration, and mark connections to other selections.

Answers to questions. For each selection we also give answers to the questions on meaning, writing strategy, and language that follow the selection in the text.

Comments on the "Writers on Writing." For each comment by a selection author on his or her process, we suggest how the author's reported experience may be instructive for students. Note that the index at the end of the text lists each of these comments under the topic it addresses, such as choosing a subject or outlining or revising.

As always, these resources are intended not as a pedagogic *CliffsNotes* but as the notes of colleagues with whom you might care to hold a dialog. The answers to questions, especially, are necessarily brief, and undoubtedly you and your students will find much to disagree with. We hope you will also find views to test and enlarge your own questions to prompt better answers.

CONTENTS

TEACHING WITH JOURNALS AND COLLABORATION

Our users report that they often employ journal writing and small-group collaboration in their writing classes. *The Brief Bedford Reader* and this instructor's manual support these techniques in several ways.

JOURNALS

The Brief Bedford Reader includes a discussion of journal writing in Chapter 2 (see p. 30) and a journal-writing assignment just after every selection in the printed book (for example, pp. 107 and 111).

More and more instructors use the journal as a teaching tool because it offers students a place to experiment with their ideas without the pressure of producing a crafted, polished essay. This opportunity for creative thinking can also lead to more provocative classroom discussions and formal essays.

One advantage of journals from the teacher's perspective is that they encourage students to share the responsibility of preparing for discussion. You can require a journal entry as part of every assignment, as the first step of writing a paper, or as an integrated part of class discussion. You can allow students to keep their entries on loose pages for easy submission or ask them to keep a paper or electronic notebook so they (and you) have all their entries in one place. You can use the structured journal prompts at the end of each selection, or you can allow students to write anything at all, in any direction, as long as they write something. Most instructors find that journal writing, like any other teaching technique, requires trial and error in the classroom. One teacher's pleasure is another's pain, after all; and some classes will sit slack-jawed before the same assignment that fires others into animated participation. Following are some general guidelines for those who do or want to use journals.

However often or seldom you require journal entries, try to present them in the context of other writing and discussion in the course; the danger of using journals in an unstructured way is that they can become busywork. Explain to students that it's in their best interest to use their journals as idea books: safe places to record notes and impressions, grapple with difficult issues, respond to the essays in *The Brief Bedford Reader*, and generate ideas for more formal writing assignments. They'll find that papers, discussions, and tests are easier because of the time they spend responding to what they read. Your promise not to grade the entries will guarantee more experimentation. However, you may need scheduled or surprise checks to ensure that

1

writing is actually being committed to paper, and of course some students will be disappointed if you don't personally respond to their personal entries. One productive system is to schedule one or two submissions — emphasizing that they're just for a check in the gradebook toward a discussion grade — while encouraging unscheduled submissions for your comments on a particular entry whenever a student wants them. A student who is worried about a paper can get your early feedback, or a student who prefers writing to speaking can have a conversation with you.

Many students will be unfamiliar, even uncomfortable, with required writing that is informal and ungraded, so you may want to coax and guide them into writing. For those who are anxious about your expectations, emphasize that a journal provides a free space where there are no right answers and where organization and sentence structure may simply reflect the student's train of thought. For everyone, make use of the open-ended journal assignment after every selection in the printed book: It asks students for personal recollections or gut responses to the selection, in an effort to help them recognize their own connection to it. Farther on, a "From Journal to Essay" writing topic asks students to hone their personal responses into structured essays, sometimes personal, often critical. You can use the journal prompt by itself to get students writing and talking. Even if you don't build journals into your course, you might find some of the prompts useful as in-class freewriting prompts or as remedies for dull discussions. Try assigning a journal entry for a particular selection and then asking volunteers to read theirs aloud and lead a discussion for five minutes or so. Try asking pairs of students to trade journals, read each other's entries on a given topic, and write responses. Try giving the journal assignments as starting points for small-group discussions.

Some students will have strong responses to the essays in *The Brief Bedford Reader* and will not need any prompting to come up with "something to write about." Definitely encourage students to stray from our suggested avenues of response if they have another idea to explore. The main purpose of journals, after all, is to challenge students to articulate their own ideas more fully.

COLLABORATION

Working in small groups creates unique opportunities for students to examine the concepts of a course and the process of writing. Like journals, small groups are a useful testing ground for ideas and a means for exploring the nuances of issues. Often less intimidating than a whole-class discussion, a small group can provide students with a more collaborative forum for voicing their opinions. In fact, many teachers find that a major benefit of small groups is that they require all students to participate actively both as talkers and as listeners.

Small groups can augment learning in a variety of ways. Discussions might center on an opinion presented in a selection on writing style or rhetorical strategy or on solving a problem raised by an author. (This manual's introductions to the selections often suggest possible directions.) The result could be a collaborative written response that you collect or a series of brief presentations in which groups explain their responses to the rest of the class. Or, keeping it more informal, you may choose simply to roam and eavesdrop throughout the group sessions to see that groups stay focused and to discover what kinds of conclusions they are reaching.

Groups can also enhance whole-class discussions. Try having small groups spend the first fifteen minutes of class brainstorming answers to difficult questions as a precursor to a whole-class discussion. Have groups do outside research related to upcoming essays and report their findings to the class as a whole. Toward the end of the semester, you may feel confident enough in your groups to allow them to take turns planning and running class discussions.

Small groups can also be invaluable as writing workshops, to help students learn to become better readers and revisers of their own essays. Once students get to know members of their group well, they will begin to trust the feedback they receive. From brainstorming on an essay topic to providing suggestions on drafts, peer readers are often uniquely able to point out what works in an essay, what is confusing, what needs expanding, and so on.

You may have to teach students how to give this kind of feedback. Toward that end, Chapter 2 sets the stage with ideas about what problems to look for in a draft and suggestions for revising effectively. With the general checklists for revision and editing in hand (see pp. 39 and 41), try modeling a workshop process for the class, beginning with a conversation about what *constructive criticism* means. Ask a volunteer to bring copies of a draft paper to class, or copy a paper from a previous term, or even copy something of your own. Distribute copies to the class. Have the author read the paper aloud, as would occur in the small group. (If the author isn't present, ask a volunteer to read.) Ask the author to explain his or her main concerns about the essay (introduction doesn't seem to fit rest of paper, organization feels choppy, transitions awkward, and so on) — or if there is no author, take this role yourself. Then lead the whole class in a discussion of the essay, starting with what works particularly well and moving to what doesn't work. (Often students will shy away from criticizing a peer, and you may need to get the discussion going.) Give the author (you, if you're role-playing) plenty of opportunities to respond to people's comments. During the discussion, point out what works in workshopping and what doesn't. The most useful feedback will reflect the reader's understanding of the essay ("I got confused when you . . ." or "I wish you would give more details so I could see this place better" or "I don't follow your logic in paragraph 3"). *Discussion* of how to solve such problems will be more fruitful than blunt suggestions like "This passage should be cut" or "You should just rewrite this sentence like this."

Of course, negotiating personality conflicts and overcoming shyness and other qualities that can silence a small group can sometimes be tricky. To minimize these problems, have students compose a "personals" ad on an index card at the beginning of the term, explaining that they're searching for their workshop soul mates. Write a few questions on the board, such as what their strengths and weaknesses are as writers, readers, and talkers or how they respond to constructive criticism. Such self-portraits may not be entirely accurate, but they can help you group students according to complementary abilities and attitudes: You can group some who like to do research with others who like to talk in front of a large group; some who struggle to organize essays with others who feel that organizing is their biggest strength; some who are experienced in collaboration with others who aren't.

Small groups give students a chance to practice the ideas and strategies gleaned from lectures and reading. And such collaborative learning eases some of the burden on you, too: Students will not only gain a great sense of authority over their learning but also share the hot seat at the front of the room.

TEACHING VISUAL
AND MULTIMODAL LITERACY

Throughout *The Brief Bedford Reader* we provide many opportunities to incorporate visuals and multimedia into writing classes: A section in Chapter 1 extends critical thinking from texts to illustrations; every rhetorical chapter opens with an image or related images, along with a caption that prompts students' critical responses; a few of the written selections center on illustrations that we also reprint; and in the integrated e-Pages (*bedfordstmartins .com/thebedfordreader*), at least one multimedia selection — video, audio, visual, or textual — enhances the possibilities for engaging students with each rhetorical method.

THINKING CRITICALLY ABOUT VISUAL IMAGES

In Chapter 1 on reading we offer a detailed approach to thinking critically about visuals (pp. 22–26). Paralleling the method for evaluating written texts, the approach involves five steps: getting the big picture, analyzing, inferring, synthesizing, and evaluating. A photograph provides a rich opportunity to apply the method.

Students generally like looking at images, and they often form immediate, almost visceral responses to what they see. The challenge, then, may be to guide their responses along critical pathways. For instance, they may need coaching to perceive the value of information about artists or advertisers or historical and cultural contexts — and they may need help gathering such information. In analyzing an image, they often benefit from small-group discussions in which they hear several points of view. Similarly, in the inference phase they can listen to the meanings attributed by others with different backgrounds and outlooks. Finally, as they evaluate images, they may need encouragement to step back from their natural emotional responses and judge the worthiness of the image's purpose and its success in fulfilling that purpose.

CHAPTER-OPENING IMAGES

Each rhetorical chapter in Part Two opens with a visual representation of the chapter's method at work, accompanied by background information and questions about the image(s).

- A drawing tells a story of romantic disappointment (narration, Chap. 4)
- A photograph depicts a riverside shanty (description, Chap. 5)

4

- A cartoon proposes "low-energy drinks" that could counteract today's trendy jolters (example, Chap. 6)
- A well-known painting and a contemporaneous photograph play off each other (comparison and contrast, Chap. 7)
- A photograph makes a telling comment on a doll-making factory (process analysis, Chap. 8)
- A cartoon deconstructs a kid's bologna sandwich (division or analysis, Chap. 9)
- A table categorizes typical household budgets by income status (classification, Chap. 10)
- A cartoon examines the effects of texting while driving (cause and effect, Chap. 11)
- A US Army advertisement probes the meaning of *strong* (definition, Chap. 12)
- An alternative version of the Stars and Stripes makes a strong argument about the United States (argument and persuasion, Chap. 13)

We anticipate that these images will inspire you and your students in several possible ways:

- Because each chapter opener shows a rhetorical method at work, it provides an additional way to introduce the method. The images may especially help students who resist or struggle with reading.
- The caption accompanying each chapter opener provides background on the image so that students have essential information for a critical response. The questions in each caption encourage reflection and discourage a snap judgment such as "I like it" or "I don't like it" or "I don't get it," and they can serve as journal or discussion prompts. Using the caption questions or your own assignments, you can devise various class or small-group projects centered on the chapter openers. For instance, the Grant Wood painting and the Ben Shahn photograph in Chapter 7 open up worlds to investigate — the backgrounds and interests of the artists, the effects of the Great Depression on farmers, the effect of medium on perception (note that the sample textbook passage in Chapter 5 offers an art historian's take on the painting; see p. 135). For another example, the cartoon in Chapter 11 practically begs for a more detailed and substantiated examination of the problem of distracted driving and presents an opportunity to discuss the advantages of simplifying causes and effects.

ILLUSTRATIONS ACCOMPANYING TEXT SELECTIONS

Two of *The Brief Bedford Reader*'s text selections include illustrations. In each case, the juxtaposition deepens the meaning of both the written text and the illustration.

- "Why We Lie" (p. 384) reproduces a sample math puzzle to help explain Dan Ariely's unusual research project and includes an infographic that visually summarizes his cause-and-effect analysis.
- Christopher Beam's "Blood Loss" (p. 393), about changing trends in murder and mayhem, includes a bar graph interpreted by the author.

MULTIMEDIA SELECTIONS

The Brief Bedford Reader now has integrated e-Pages — videos, audio selections, comics, graphics, and essays accessible online (*bedfordstmartins .com/thebedfordreader*). Chosen for their value as models of the rhetorical methods in everyday life, each of these selections demonstrates the richness and complexity that be achieved when words are combined with visuals or sounds. Each is also accompanied by a streamlined set of editorial apparatus: full introductions to the creator and the piece, three or four questions on meaning and strategy, and two suggestions for writing, one of them pointing out connections between the e-Pages selection and a traditional essay in the printed book.

In most cases you might wish to share these pieces in class, viewing or listening with your students as a group; or you could assign them just as you would the traditional essays in the book. They are all the work of quality writers or artists and will reward close examination; each of them is not only entertaining but also thought-provoking.

- Native Americans on a South Dakota reservation use an online tool that combines photography, audio, and text to share stories about their lives (narration, Chap. 4).
- "The Santa Ana," a classic by beloved essayist Joan Didion, is read by a popular actress for a recently released audiobook (description, Chap. 5).
- A prizewinning Mexican American writer with a growing fan base reads his own essay about the transformative powers of fiction (example, Chap. 6).
- A video sketch by a popular comedy team examines behaviors of our pets that we might not endure from our friends (comparison and contrast, Chap. 7).
- A viral marketing video criticizes manipulative advertising tactics (process analysis, Chap. 8).
- Caribbean novelist Jamaica Kincaid performs her always enjoyable and always provocative short story "Girl" (division or analysis, Chap. 9).
- The US Census Bureau charts historical immigration trends in a series of interrelated graphics (classification, Chap. 10).
- A reporter and a graphic artist use interactive Web technology to explain the physics of roller coasters (cause-and-effect analysis, Chap. 11).
- A digital cartoon explains a misunderstood personality type and offers suggestions to help people get along with each other (definition, Chap. 12).
- A lengthy (and controversial) magazine article, accompanied by several snippets of readers' online reactions and one self-contained response, presents an opportunity to examine both a complex argument and critical reading in action (argument, Chap. 13).

READING, WRITING, AND RESEARCH

The first three chapters of *The Brief Bedford Reader* provide a substantial and well-illustrated discussion of critical reading, the writing process, and academic writing (including research and documentation in MLA style), and an Appendix offers guidelines for citing sources using APA style. The outline of this material (below) is followed by a description of the contents.

Chapter 1 gives step-by-step instructions on attentive, critical reading, including examples of annotating a text, summarizing, and using analysis, interpretation, synthesis, and evaluation. A sample essay by Nancy Mairs and a student's marginal notes along with our commentary illustrate the steps. Then a section shows students, again by example, how to apply their faculties for critical thinking to visual images. (For more on this topic, see p. 4 of this manual.)

Chapter 2 then details the stages of the writing process, including aids to discovery (journals, freewriting, and the rhetorical methods themselves); a stress on the thesis and thesis statement; suggestions for drafting the introduction, body, and conclusion of an essay; and detailed advice on and examples of revising and editing. This section also includes the stages of a student's response to Mairs's essay, from first journal entry through annotated final draft. This paper also serves the next chapter as an example of response writing.

Chapter 3, "Academic Writing," aims to help students surmount one of their biggest hurdles: learning to write critically about what they have read. The chapter focuses on response writing and research writing, emphasizing synthesis in both cases. The writing and research help includes extensive sections on synthesizing ideas; avoiding plagiarism while integrating summaries, paraphrases, and quotations; evaluating both print and online sources; and documenting sources in MLA style. Concluding the chapter is an annotated research paper by the same student who wrote the response paper in Chapter 2. She writes on a similar subject, modeling the way reading can expand and refine ideas, and reflects on the process in a writers-on-writing commentary.

We provide the Appendix, "APA Documentation," as a resource for students who are writing in the social sciences or who might be asked to use the American Psychological Association's documentation system for any of their papers. Designed as a reference tool, this section includes an overview of APA style, models of parenthetical citations, and guidelines and sample entries for a list of references. The Appendix concludes with excerpts from the research paper in Chapter 3 adapted to APA style, showing how the documentation system works in practice.

You can use Part One and the Appendix in various ways, depending on your students' needs and, of course, your own inclinations. Many instructors teach directly from this material, especially when students are unfamiliar with the processes of critical reading and writing, have little experience with academic writing or with research, or have no other text to rely on. Other instructors ask their students to read the material on their own — it does not assume previous knowledge and so can be self-teaching. Still others select for classwork the parts they wish to stress (summary, say, or the thesis statement) and ask students to cover the remaining sections on their own.

PART TWO

THE METHODS

4
NARRATION
Telling a Story

To write a short account of a personal experience is, for many students, a first assignment that looks reassuring and possible to fulfill. Instructors who wish to begin in this way may assign for reading one or more of this chapter's essays by Angelou, Tan, and Dillard: These writers give students a sense of what a good writer can do with material perhaps much like their own: recollections and observations of ordinary experience from childhood and high school days. Díaz takes a different approach and shares a story told to him by his mother, expressing with awe what another person experienced in another time.

The e-Pages for narration present intriguing multimodal oral histories, a collection of first-person accounts of life on an Indian reservation along with a "true" ghost story.

Not all freshmen feel comfortable writing in the first person. Some may writhe under a burden of self-consciousness. Some may feel guilty about not following the doctrine of a high-school teacher who once urged them to avoid *I*. A few members of the composition staff at Chapel Hill reported encountering this problem, and because of it, some preferred to begin their courses with *The Brief Bedford Reader*'s chapter on description. Writing in the third person seems to give some students greater assurance about constructing that crucial first paper in which they're trying hard to please.

MAYA ANGELOU
Champion of the World

A story within a story, Maya Angelou's suspenseful narrative invites attention to both its method and its matter. Inside the story of what happens in the general store (told in the first person, as Angelou looks back to her childhood), we follow the story of the Louis-Carnera fight. Suspense builds from the beginning, in the introductory glimpse of the people crowding in eagerly, in the "apprehensive mood" compared to a sky "streaked with lightning" (par. 2), and in the scraps of conversation. Larger events of the history of civil rights form a background to this narrative—for example, the fact that African Americans were not safe at night, although we learn this only at the end of the story.

You might begin by asking students what they know of the career of Joe Louis. (In some classes no one may know of him.) You could break the class into groups of three or four and have them research what it meant in the 1930s for an African American to become a prominent and universally admired athlete. Come up with a few contextual categories: Louis's career overall; other firsthand reminiscences of boxing in the 1930s; African American life in the 1930s. Each group could then present its findings for five to ten minutes, ending with a whole-class discussion of Angelou's memoir. (Note: If this sort of background research is something you'd like to have students do fairly regularly, you might consider rotating the responsibility so that just one group works and reports on any given essay.)

Audio aids: Angelou reads excerpts from *I Know Why the Caged Bird Sings* on a set of CDs with the same title, produced by Random House Audiobooks. The recordings may be ordered or downloaded from *Amazon.com*.

Angelou's essay is paired with Amy Tan's narrative "Fish Cheeks" (p. 110) for discussion and writing. Both writers recall experiences as "outsider" children in a predominantly white culture.

QUESTIONS ON MEANING

1. Like the rest of the autobiography from which this selection is taken, "Champion of the World" seems written for a dual purpose: to recall vivid and significant moments of the author's life and to reveal the ironic situation of African Americans in the United States in the 1930s—able to become world champions but not able to walk a country road at night. This irony is given great weight by being placed at the end of the story.
2–3. As Angelou indicates in much of her story, and especially in paragraphs 16 and 17, the pride of the race depends on the fight. Not only pride but a whole future rides on the outcome: "If Joe lost we were back in slavery. . . ." Everyone in the store believes this, but the author's view is not so simple. Obviously she doesn't share the notion that if Joe Louis lost it would be clear that "God Himself hated us"; she is exaggerating the assumptions of the people in the store to emphasize the ideological importance of the fight.

4. The error makes untrue a small corner of the story (and might distract people who recognize it), but the fact that Angelou mixed up Louis's fights does not discredit what she reports experiencing.

QUESTIONS ON WRITING STRATEGY

1. Every sentence in the first paragraph contributes to our sense of the importance of the coming events. Note that, with space inside the store at such a premium, children (except infants and toddlers who could fit on a lap) are banished to the porch outside.
2. From paragraph 1 we feel anticipation and a tension that mounts to a crisis in paragraph 15, when the contender rains blows on Louis and staggers him. Short, punchy sentences add speed and force to Angelou's account: "We didn't breathe. We didn't hope. We waited" (par. 18—and, incidentally, a good example of parallelism). The whole device of telling the story of the fight through a radio announcer's spiel is particularly effective because, as Angelou makes clear, the listeners in the store hang on the announcer's every word. Using radio as a medium in story-telling can increase suspense by leaving much to the imagination.
    Anyone familiar with the history of boxing will predict the winner as soon as the name of Joe Louis emerges; others may not be sure until Louis rallies in paragraph 20.
3. Students who sense the irony will probably express it in any of several ways. Some will say that despite all the hopes and dreams bound up in the fight, Louis's victory hasn't delivered his people. Maybe Louis is the strongest man in the ring, but African Americans in rural Arkansas are still vulnerable. Angelou's irony in the final line is so strong that it is practically sarcasm. Isn't there a suggestion, too, that on this particular night some whites, resenting the Louis victory, will be out to punish any African Americans they can find alone or in small numbers?
4. Here, as everywhere, direct quotation lends immediacy to any scene an author creates.
5. The descriptive details in paragraph 27—drinking Coke "like ambrosia," eating candy "like Christmas," boys "blowing their breath in front of themselves like proud smokers"—move the story ahead and recreate the special joy and pride of the occasion.

QUESTIONS ON LANGUAGE

1. Singing commercials for razor blades; sales pitches designed to "string" the listener along. It is possible that Angelou finds irony in the sponsor's product, too, since a racist, stereotypical view of poor African Americans might have them fighting with razors or razor blades.
2. Examples of strong verbs include "perched" (par. 1); "grunted" (6); "poured" (10); "pushed" (12); "groaned," "ambushed," "raped," "whipped," "maimed," "slapping" (16); "clutched" (17); "slid" (21); and "shouted" (23).
3. Nonstandard English here makes the people gathered in the store come alive for us. (This story offers a great opportunity to point out the occasional high value of nonstandard English. The comments in pars. 4 and 8 are so well put that they're hard to forget.)
4. The definition of *white lightning* is hard to find in standard dictionaries. *The Dictionary of American Slang* defines it as "cheap, inferior, homemade, or bootleg whisky, usually uncolored corn whisky."

MAYA ANGELOU ON WRITING

Here are some responses to the questions for discussion.

1. What Angelou means by rhythm won't be easily defined, but for her, finding the rhythm of a subject is that early stage all writers go through when first preparing to write. It means (we'd guess) getting a sense of the size and shape of a subject—or perhaps working up some feeling for it.
2. Writing twelve or fourteen pages of longhand notes, setting down all she knows about the subject, may seem to some students an excessive amount of toil. But Angelou invites the observation that the more work you do before you write, the easier it is to write.

AMY TAN

Fish Cheeks

Amy Tan remains one of the best-known Chinese American writers on the current scene. This brief, amusing piece about a shock between two cultures is a good example of how much can be accomplished in very little space. Every detail contributes to the contrast between the two families and their cultures.

We have paired "Fish Cheeks" with Maya Angelou's "Champion of the World." Both essays illuminate the experience of being an outsider in America and the ways family can ameliorate or exacerbate a child's grappling with social identity. Tan, by the way, discussed the influences of such childhood experiences on her work as a writer with Roger Rosenblatt as part of the 2008 Chautauqua Institution morning lecture series; a video of their conversation, "Finding Meaning through Writing," is available on *YouTube*.

Some students may take offense at Tan's use of stereotypes for humor, while others may see her Asian Americanness as exempting her from criticism on those grounds. If this issue is controversial in your class, consider setting up small-group debates on the "political correctness" of the essay. Students who enjoy Tan's story should be encouraged to look further into Tan's works—such as *The Joy Luck Club* (1989), *The Kitchen God's Wife* (1991), *The Hundred Secret Senses* (1995), *The Bonesetter's Daughter* (2001), *The Opposite of Fate* (2003), and *The Valley of Amazement* (2013).

QUESTIONS ON MEANING

1. Tan believes that her family will embarrass her.
2. Tan's mother wants to teach her not to be ashamed of her Chineseness, not to become completely Americanized. "Your only shame is to have shame" (par. 7).
3. Tan is ashamed of her background, referring to her family's "shabby Chinese Christmas" and "noisy Chinese relatives who lacked proper

American manners" (par. 2). She resents her mother at the time, but eventually learns to appreciate the lesson she has taught her.

4. Tan's purpose is to amuse and entertain, yes, but possibly also to thank her mother and to impart her lesson to the reader.

QUESTIONS ON WRITING STRATEGY

1. Tan sets us up for a story right away. We know immediately that we're going to hear an anecdote about the minister's cute son—and an ethnic conflict.
2. The narrative progression is straightforward; each paragraph starts with a transition that places us in time: "the winter I turned fourteen" (par. 1); "When I found out" (2); "On Christmas Eve" (3); "And then" (4); "Dinner" (5); "At the end of the meal" (6); "After everyone had gone" (7); "And even though I didn't agree with her then" (8). This gives a sense of constant forward momentum to the story.
3. The irony lies in the narrator's inability to acknowledge or realize that the dishes she has described with such disgust in paragraph 3 are in fact her favorites. The Chinese Tan and the American Tan conflict with each other.
4. The descriptive paragraph is meant to be humorous and entertaining, and it will probably have the desired effect on non-Chinese readers: to make clear the culture shock the narrator thinks the minister's family will experience. (Some readers, though, may relish the description.)

QUESTIONS ON LANGUAGE

1. The comparison is amusing because the minister's son is compared to a chaste female figure even though it's a first crush and the narrator is "in love"; it also underscores both the cultural and nonsexual nature of her love.
2. Tan's language is typical of a young adolescent girl: "my mother had outdone herself" (par. 3); "Robert grunted hello, and I pretended he was not worthy of existence" (4); "Dinner threw me deeper into despair," "I wanted to disappear" (5).
3. Students' opinions may differ, but Tan's use of verbs in paragraph 5 is especially strong.
4. Tofu (a curd of soybean milk) comes from the Chinese *dòu*, "bean," and *fu*, "curdled." Once exotic in the United States, tofu is now a staple of many American diets.

ANNIE DILLARD

The Chase

This portrait of childhood beautifully captures the energy and idealism of youth. It originally appeared as a chapter in *An American Childhood* (1987), which one reviewer described as being "less about a coming-to-age than about a coming-to-consciousness, a consciousness so heightened by what appears to be an overactive autonomic nervous system that one sometimes fears her nerves will burst through her skin."

The narration of the chase itself (pars. 10–15) is an excellent model for students' own narrative writing. Point out the rhetorical devices Dillard uses to vary the narration and to make the chase seem endless (such as asyndeton, repetition, use of the plural in par. 13).

The story is also a good example of how narration can be used in the service of a larger theme, with implications that go beyond the events recounted. Dillard does more than simply tell a story; she makes an interesting observation about the death of enthusiasm.

Students might want to share in small groups their reactions to Dillard's contrast between a child's and an adult's point of view. Some may find Dillard's description of adulthood overly cynical and her portrait of childhood romanticized. Others may recall a time when they themselves expected more from life, when their own senses of joy were greater. (Or they may have experienced moments when they suddenly caught themselves thinking or speaking like their parents.) Encourage students to discuss their reactions to this theme and to come up with other examples of it from literature and movies.

QUESTIONS ON MEANING

1. Dillard wants to show how a harmless chase can take on epic proportions in the mind of a child. She wants to point out valuable qualities of childhood lost in adulthood: energy and wholeheartedness.
2. No. This driver is exceptional, the only one who has ever left his car (par. 9).
3. The pursuer is the only adult the narrator has encountered who "knew what I thought only children who trained at football knew: that you have to fling yourself at what you're doing, you have to point yourself, forget yourself, aim, dive" (par. 13). At the end of the chase he comes "down to earth" (19), addressing the children in the banal, perfunctory tones of an ordinary adult. Dillard is disillusioned because of the gap between her ideals and reality.
4. Nothing can live up to the glorious moment that was the chase. The pursuer has resumed the role of just another adult, parroting the words all adults are required to say at such moments.

QUESTIONS ON WRITING STRATEGY

1. Football serves as a metaphor for life in the story: Everything you do, you have to tackle, giving 100% of yourself.
2. From football to baseball, from baseball to snowball throwing: These transitions contribute to the essay's coherence. Baseball is a logical link between football (another boys' sport) and snowball throwing, in which the throwing arm is all-important. The lesson Dillard has learned from playing sports is carried over to a more general lesson about life.
3. Far from weakening the narrative, this is the story's epiphany, where Dillard explains the larger meaning the chase was to take on.

4. Dillard's narration seamlessly combines the articulateness and sophistication of an adult interpreter with a child's view of the events taking place.

5. Adults are lazy and take shortcuts. ("Any normal adult would have quit, having sprung us into flight and made his point," par. 10.) Unlike children playing football, adults are unwilling to fling themselves "wholeheartedly" (1) into things. With their "normal righteous anger" and "usual common sense" (20), they are victims of habit and routine. Children are willing to go all out; they know that life is "all or nothing" (1). (See also the second writing suggestion.)

QUESTIONS ON LANGUAGE

1. Dillard uses language with religious connotations to describe her pursuer. Besides "exalting" and "righteous," she also uses "glory" (par. 19) and "sainted" (21).

2. The children, though playing together, exhibit a "natural solitude" (par. 5). While being chased they are at once "exhilarated" and "dismayed" (14). The man chasing them is referred to as "our pursuer, our captor" and "our hero" (16). Dillard portrays childhood as a time of confusion and contradiction.

3. Dillard is imagining what the pursuer might have done if he had "trapped" her and her companion in crime: "fried" them in boiling oil, "dismembered" them, "staked" them to anthills; but his only option, disappointingly to her, is to "chew [them] out."

4. The sentence indicates how long and complicated the chase was and helps to bring the pursuer back down to earth. It is also anticlimactic after the imaginative digression about the Panama Canal and the lyrical tribute to the pursuer that precede it. It is a typically banal, "adult" question.

ANNIE DILLARD ON WRITING

Any student who has ever become tangled in a long, complicated sentence and gone around in circles, losing track of an idea, will find sense in Dillard's remark that short sentences "can get you out of big trouble." If we teach sentence combining, we sometimes risk creating monsters; some students—often the best ones—may try to make a sentence carry too much weight. But Dillard's advice shouldn't be construed as urging us to write in nothing but short, simple sentences, sounding like a first-grade reader as a result. A good point to suggest: Mix up your sentences; vary them in length. And don't worry at all about your sentences while you write a draft; deal with them when you edit.

JUNOT DÍAZ
The Dreamer

In this brief, personal story, the author captures the desperation of a young girl in a developing country while expressing the influence she had on him as a writer. For students accustomed to taking their own education for granted, the lengths to which Díaz's mother went to secure her schooling is likely to come as a shock.

Some discussion should certainly focus on Díaz's unique voice as a writer (see the questions on language and the critical-writing prompt). He is known for his loose, conversational style and a predilection for sentence fragments; this is the only work of his we have encountered that isn't also riddled with profanity. Although his style is unusual, it has won Díaz legions of admirers, not to mention a MacArthur grant and multiple literary prizes.

Students can be expected to know little or nothing about Dominican history, and so they may tend to gloss over the essay's hints at the brutalities inflicted by Trujillo. You may want to encourage them to do some research on the subject, but at least have them focus on those details in the story that suggest what it was like to live in the Dominican Republic under a harsh dictatorship (see the last question on meaning). Díaz tells readers just enough for them to understand why a girl would court sickness and abuse for a dream of a better life.

QUESTIONS ON MEANING

1. It seems that Díaz admires his mother for her defiance and determination in the face of impossible odds. That she would, as a young child, make herself physically ill and risk violence for an education is impressive. And as he explains in his conclusion, she represents desire and "courage" (par. 11)—a source of inspiration for his work and life. (We see evidence of his own determination and stubbornness in his comments on writing, p. 124.)
2. Díaz states his main idea in his conclusion: "I do believe that who I am as an artist, everything that I've ever written, was possible because a seven-year-old girl up in the hills of Azua knelt before a puddle, found courage in herself and drank" (par. 11).
3. Díaz writes to inspire his readers and to encourage them to take risks. He also wants to explain his sense of who he is as a writer.
4. The line suggests that Trujillo and his government inflicted great harm on the people of the Dominican Republic. Much can be inferred from the writer's casual remarks. We can tell, for instance, that rural Dominicans were desperately poor and generally uneducated (to the point of resisting education for their children). We know that they were "brutalized" (par. 1)—not only by the demands of field labor, but also by the police (2)—and that they feared Trujillo (3). We can guess that political dissenters were jailed and also that prison conditions were extremely bad. We see that some "idealistic educators" did what they could and that even the police were afraid of Trujillo (8). All told, Díaz paints a portrait

of a nation suffering extreme oppression and violence at the hands of a cruel dictator.

QUESTIONS ON WRITING STRATEGY

1. By opening his essay with "I think of my mother" (par. 1) and closing it with "I think of her" (11), he frames his narrative in a dreamlike state of admiration. The device of introducing and closing the essay with variations on the same sentence creates a satisfying coherence.
2. Although he is telling someone else's story and relates the bulk of it in the third person, Díaz writes from a very subjective point of view: He imagines his mother's feelings as well as those of his grandmother, and he allows his own feelings to infuse most every line of the story. Given that the point of the story is the effect it had on him (par. 11), the choice seems highly appropriate.
3. He focuses almost exclusively on female characters and stresses the difficulties faced by girls in the Dominican Republic. Although male readers can certainly appreciate the story, Díaz's obvious admiration for women in general and the resilience of a young girl in particular seems intended to appeal to a female readership.
4. A convergence of circumstances opened the possibility of education for the author's mother: Trujillo decreed mandatory education for children her age, a teacher accepted her into the school when she "should have laughed and sent her poor ass back to the hills" (par. 8), and the police intervened when her mother tried to pull her out of school—but it was his mother's own action, Díaz stresses, that saved her. Astonishingly, she deliberately ingested dirty water to make herself so sick that her family would have to leave her behind, and then she walked to the school and demanded an education. Although the education didn't help her much and she did not realize her dream of becoming a nurse, she passed her values on to her son, who did benefit from her daring by becoming a successful writer.

QUESTIONS ON LANGUAGE

1. Our dictionary doesn't define the idiomatic *ironwill*, but students should appreciate the implications of Díaz's adjective: It creates an image of his mother as a strong, stubborn woman.
2. *Horizon* can refer to the apparent convergence of earth and sky in the distance; it can also mean a person's goals and interests. Díaz uses the word in the second sense, but for most readers it will conjure an image of open space in the distance. By stressing the word, Díaz effectively creates a metaphor equating his mother's dreams with distant realities that are, eventually, illusions.
3. Fragments can be found throughout the essay. Díaz knows what he's doing: His heavy use of deliberately incomplete sentences—especially in paragraph 1—creates a brooding tone and rhythm; it also creates emphasis and, in some cases, a sense of indignation.
4. The second quotation is from a direct conversation Díaz had with his mother. The first is something he might have been told or have imagined she said, but since he didn't witness the conversation he reports it as dialog the way fiction writers often do, without quotation marks.

JUNOT DÍAZ ON WRITING

It seems to us that Díaz inherited a good streak of his mother's determination and willingness to make personal sacrifices—as indeed he suggests in "The Dreamer" (p. 120). We like his comments both for the reassurance they offer struggling writers and for their raw honesty. Although few students can imagine discarding hundreds of pages of manuscript, most should be able to empathize with the frustrations of failed writing and the agony of starting over. Incidentally, Díaz's comments bear comparison with Michael Chabon's "XO9" (p. 184). Both portray the writing process as something of a painful compulsion that nonetheless has healing qualities.

NATIONAL GEOGRAPHIC

from The Pine Ridge Community Storytelling Project

In an extraordinarily ambitious undertaking, Aaron Huey, *National Geographic,* and the makers of Cowbird have collaborated with the residents of the Pine Ridge Reservation in South Dakota to create an extensive archive of multimodal oral histories documenting the lives, frustrations, and hopes of one group of Oglala Lakota Sioux. We had a difficult time picking out just a handful of the more than two hundred submissions made to date, and so we tried to select representative stories that hit on what seem to be the most common themes found among the collection—such as pride, politics, tradition, and community—without presenting a grouping that would paint the reservation as either romantic or tragic.

We settled on five narratives by four contributors. In "Unci Maka or Grandmother Earth," Marisa Snider recalls an important life lesson her grandmother taught her while planting flowers. Tom Swift Bird, in "First Racist I Ever Encountered," relates a painful childhood experience with a sense of befuddled humor. Monique M. Apple, in "Becoming a Lakota Woman," describes a traditional ceremony that had been long forbidden by the federal government. Leon Matthews tells a ghost story in "I See Spirits." And the final piece, "Faces I Do Not Worship," another entry by Marisa Snider, neatly encapsulates the community's longstanding issues with the American government.

A risk in offering only five stories is that the limited sample undermines one of the major goals of the storytelling project: to let the residents of Pine Ridge speak for themselves and express the full complexities of their experiences in ways that no reporters or editors could ever hope to accomplish. We would, then, encourage students to visit the project's home page at *ngm .nationalgeographic.com/2012/08/pine-ridge/community-project* and take in as many more stories as time and interest allow. We have no doubt that they will be fascinated and fully engaged by what's there.

QUESTIONS ON MEANING AND STRATEGY

1. The general tone might best be described as ambivalent. Although the storytellers express pride, hope, determination, and humor, there is also an underlying sense of resentment and struggle. Forcefully countering stereotypes of reservation Indians as desperate addicts, these stories portray the Pine Ridge Lakota as complex human beings who are deeply connected: to the earth and spirituality yes, but also to tradition, family, and community. They also reveal that the speakers are politically involved, very intelligent, and devoted to changing their circumstances in whatever ways they can.

2. Issues touched upon include education ("Unci Maka or Grandmother Earth," "First Racist I Ever Encountered"); racism and oppression ("First Racist I Ever Encountered," "Faces I Do Not Worship"); religion ("First Racist I Ever Encountered," "I See Spirits," "Faces I Do Not Worship"); hardship ("Becoming a Lakota Woman"); outlawed ceremonies ("Becoming a Lakota Woman"); land ownership ("Faces I Do Not Worship"); and broken treaties ("Faces I Do Not Worship"). The underlying theme, it seems to us, is a desire for sovereignty and respect. Students' interpretations may vary.

3. The Lakota have a long tradition of storytelling. Not surprisingly, then, the narratives abound in creative metaphors and analogies especially. There is, of course, the daffodil in Marisa Snider's "Unci Maka or Grandmother Earth," a tale of overcoming weakness; the ghosts of the past in Leon Matthews's "I See Spirits"; the understatement of Tom Swift Bird's "First Racist I Ever Encountered"; and the political and religious similes in Marisa Snider's "Faces I Do Not Worship." Students may well latch onto others as their favorites.

4. The integrated multimedia components bring depth and additional meaning to the texts; in some cases they *are* the texts. The speakers' voices, when offered, help listeners connect with the narrators as real people; we can hear their laughter and their pride. The singing and drumming in some instances juxtapose assumptions about native culture with the spoken words, often creating an intentionally jarring dissonance. And in most cases the photographs illustrate key points of the stories while allowing viewers to visualize both the beauty and the poverty on the reservation. None of the stories would have been as effective and powerful if they were limited to written words.

5
DESCRIPTION
Writing with Your Senses

Because most instructors make much of descriptive writing, this chapter offers an ample choice of illustrations. Students tend to think of descriptive writing as a kind of still-life painting in words: An apple or a banana sits on a table and you write about it. In this chapter we strive to demonstrate that, on the contrary, description can involve the testimony of all the senses. All the writers employ description in fresh and engaging ways.

For our pairing in this chapter, we have chosen Brad Manning's "Arm Wrestling with My Father" (Manning wrote the essay as a college freshman) and Sarah Vowell's "Shooting Dad." Both authors look at their fathers, but otherwise their views (and their descriptions) are quite different. Note that each essay is followed by a "Connections" writing suggestion involving the other.

BRAD MANNING

Arm Wrestling with My Father

Manning's essay specifically addresses the male experience by exploring how masculine ideals (such as strong, silent, athletic) can affect father-son relations. Most students will have something to say about the general difficulties of parent-child communication, and you may want to extend discussion to how Manning's personal experience represents larger issues. That men communicate nonverbally and women verbally is a commonly held belief. Ask students whether they agree with this gender generalization. Is it easier, more common, or more acceptable for mothers to talk openly with their daughters than for fathers to do so with their sons? What about for mothers and sons, for fathers and daughters? (For a take on the latter relationship, see Sarah Vowell's "Shooting Dad," the essay following this one.) Students may need encouragement to complicate their answers to these questions with specific reasons for their generalizations.

To enhance class discussion, small groups could initially be asked to spend ten to fifteen minutes brainstorming stereotypes about a particular gendered parent-child relationship: one group working with fathers and sons, one with mothers and daughters, and so on (you could even throw stepparents into the mix). When the class reassembles, groups should both respond to each other's ideas and connect their claims to the relationship and standard of communication that Manning describes with his father.

QUESTIONS ON MEANING

1. Manning's father communicates through gestures rather than words.
2. They have learned primarily that they don't have to compete to express affection and that there are many different kinds of communication.
3. Clearly Manning has always felt loved, but he recognizes that these challenges *show* that his father loves him.
4. His purpose is definitely to express love for his father. In a larger context he also wants to suggest the strength of a nonverbal relationship between fathers and sons.

QUESTIONS ON WRITING STRATEGY

1. Manning begins with his bitterness to set us up for the emotional progress of the essay, which moves from frustration and anger to acceptance (all responses to various arm-wrestling competitions).
2. These options suggest that he believes they have both learned something about new avenues of communication. We aren't supposed to predict anything; just knowing options exist shows progress is being made.
3. Manning compares the thrill of hooking his first big fish (par. 10) to the sense of accomplishment he initially felt when he realized that he was going to win his first arm-wrestling match with his father. Although both events are exciting firsts that suggest the approach toward manhood, Manning is a little sorry in both cases to know that he can defeat (kill?) a worthy and longtime foe: "I wanted to win but I did not want to see him lose" (9); "when you finally think you've got him, you want to let him go, cut the line, keep the legend alive" (10). Still, these poetic and self-sacrificing impulses stand in contrast to the end of this wrestling match, which Manning, despite his regrets, won't lose on purpose (11).
4. The narrative progresses through events that demonstrate Manning's boyish powerlessness: his "whole upper body pushing down in hope of winning," his father would "grin with his eyes fixed on me," Manning would "start to cheat and use both hands," his brother once even tried to help, and yet "the man would win." The description emphasizes the contrast between the boy and the man in terms of size ("tiny shoulders" are no match for the man's "calm, unmoving forearm"); effort (the father "not seeming to notice his own arm" while the boy's "greatest efforts" were useless); and power (the father's arm moves "steadily . . . regardless of the opposition").

QUESTIONS ON LANGUAGE

1. *Competition* suggests sportsmanship, organized rivalry with a goal, rather than the discordant clash of wills that *conflict* suggests.

2. This reduces the father to just the arm, giving the reader a greater sense of how large a role the father's arms play in characterizing the man as a whole. The image of him as "the arm" suggests both his competitiveness and his protectiveness (par. 4).

3. Manning still feels competitive with his father but is loath to sacrifice his sense of being protected by a father who is stronger than he is.

4. *Mononucleosis* is a disease involving a high white-blood-cell count, causing fever, weakness, swollen lymph nodes, and a sore throat.

BRAD MANNING ON WRITING

Manning has some good advice for college writers, especially about taking the time to plan and revise and working for one's own voice. Students who struggle to write may dispute Manning's implication that writing can be a better means of self-expression than speaking. You might reinforce Manning's message that writing, unlike speaking, provides a chance to build and shape thought.

SARAH VOWELL

Shooting Dad

To begin discussion of this essay, consider the particular cleverness of Vowell's title: Her father is literally a "shooting dad" (a dad whose pastime is shooting firearms), and, in her conclusion, Vowell says that after his death the family will fulfill his request to bag his ashes and shoot them from his cannon (thus, the family will be literally "shooting Dad").

If you pair this with the previous essay, Brad Manning's "Arm Wrestling with My Father," consider asking students to compare and contrast the father-child relationships these two writers present. One interesting difference is that Manning focuses much more overtly on the love he feels for his father and his father's love for him than Vowell does in describing her relationship with her father. Why might this be less of an issue for Vowell? How would students characterize Vowell's feelings for her father and his feelings for her? Her portrait is for the most part quite affectionate, but she also treats her father with considerable humor, poking fun at his various foibles. Despite their differences, as Vowell has grown older, she and her father seem to have developed an easygoing relationship, with little if any of the unspoken baggage Manning describes between himself and his father. Do students think this a reflection more of gender, age, or basic family dynamics? (Note that Vowell's family seems far less "shy" than the family Manning describes.)

Another focus of discussion might be Vowell's highly polished comic tone, her delightful way of casually tossing in a verbal joke—having "to move revolvers out of my way to make room for a bowl of Rice Krispies" (par. 3), for example, or referring to the floor of her father's shop as "a tetanus shot waiting to happen" (7). You could divide students into groups, have each group analyze Vowell's essay for further examples, and then report on their findings and how the examples contribute to the persona Vowell presents in this essay. What relationship does she establish with her readers?

QUESTIONS ON MEANING

1. Throughout their lives, Vowell and her father have been at odds over political issues and divided in their interests—she the liberal, he the conservative; she antigun, he progun; she artistic, he mechanical. The division is made explicit in paragraphs 1–2, 5, 7–8, and 13.
2. Vowell writes that both her parents grew up in controlling households "where children were considered puppets and/or slaves" (par. 12). In reaction to the rigidity of his own parents, her father wanted his children to have the freedom to make their own choices. We see him, then, as fundamentally open-minded.
3. Vowell had reached a point in adulthood where she wanted to connect more closely with her father and decided that sharing in this major project of his was a good place to start—particularly since it represents "a map of all his obsessions" (par. 19). She isn't bothered by her father's cannon as she is by other guns because "it is a completely ceremonial object" (30), not a weapon that could readily be used to harm others. Also, she enjoys the noise it makes and the way its smoke fills the air.
4. Vowell's father is proud to be the descendant of reactionaries and renegades and enjoys recalling tales of his "nefarious" ancestors (par. 18). His slyly ornery streak helps explain his outspoken individualism.
5. Vowell's purpose seems to be to trace her evolving view of her father, from seeing him as her polar opposite to realizing that they have more in common—in terms of being "smart-alecky loners with goofy projects and weird equipment" (par. 29)—than she ever expected. She creates the impression of a man who is exasperating, obsessive in his beliefs and habits, but somehow endearing, finally, because of his idiosyncratic devotion to "his art" (31).

QUESTIONS ON WRITING STRATEGY

1. The anecdote demonstrates in a nutshell her father's penchant for guns and his tendency to behave as he sees fit. It also shows that, even at eleven, Vowell saw things completely differently and welcomed the restrictions that town life would place on her father's behavior.
2. The paragraph provides a bit of humor with its suggestion that boyfriends feared Vowell just might shoot them if they betrayed her. It also acts as a transition into the following paragraph, where Vowell admits that she has shot a gun only once in her life. While this aside doesn't contribute directly to the portrait of Vowell's father, it does bring in outsiders' views of her father's guns.
3. The final sentence suggests the depth of Vowell's feelings for her father: When he dies, she will and wants to feel pain. The double meaning of "hurt"—the pain of the cannon noise and the pain of loss—ties together the threads of guns and father and sharply etches Vowell's love for her father.
4. Comparison and contrast is found in paragraphs 1–2, 6–7, 13, and 29. The method is important to show how different Vowell believed herself and her father to be until she came to share one of his pleasures and realized that they were surprisingly alike.

QUESTIONS ON LANGUAGE

1. Shooting crows is clearly not "a national pastime, like baseball and apple pie." Vowell points up the irony of her father's statement by stating her own preference.
2. Our favorite concrete and specific words: *labyrinth*, *bagged*, *blue ballpoint pen*, *spiky*, *cramped*, the list of musical instruments, *penciled*, *pompous*. The words create two vividly real spaces, down to the writing on paper.
3. Repeating the word *six* asks the reader to focus on the young age of the twins when they were first allowed to shoot a gun. The short final sentence neatly summarizes, by contrast, Vowell's own bad experience with shooting.
4. In personification and similes, Vowell says the gun "kicked little me back to the ground like a bully, like a foe." It's not just big and heavy and dangerous to others but malevolent to her, "an evil presence."
5. *Pharaohlike* (par. 18) will not show up in students' dictionaries, though of course *pharaoh* will ("a king of ancient Egypt; a tyrant"). Vowell alludes to the biblical story of Moses, in which the ruler of Egypt ordered all Hebrew boy babies killed.

SARAH VOWELL ON WRITING

Most students won't share Vowell's experience of writing for radio and print, but they will know some frustrations of getting thoughts into writing and they may, like Vowell, have experienced distinct advantages and disadvantages in speaking and in writing. For instance, in speaking, as Vowell says, you can leave some things unsaid and can be a bit slapdash. But in writing you don't have to face your audience and can take time to work out your ideas.

ELIZABETH GILBERT

The Best Pizza in the World

An excerpt from one of the most widely read memoirs in recent memory, "The Best Pizza in the World" is great fun to read. Most of us have, at one point or another, experienced gastronomic delight of the kind Gilbert describes, but few could express it as forcefully or with as much originality as she does. Students should enjoy both Gilbert's infectious enthusiasm for her subject and her strikingly fresh figures of speech, many of which are irresistible.

You may want to spend some time considering Gilbert's overwhelmingly colloquial language (see question 2 on language). Such casual, everyday usage is normally frowned upon in formal writing, but in Gilbert's case it works quite well, creating a strong writer's voice, infusing a sense of intimacy with her readers, and forging an unmistakably clear emotional image of her joy at being in Naples.

Students interested in Elizabeth Gilbert's thoughts on the writing process can find several video interviews with the author at *bigthink.com/users/elizabethgilbert*.

QUESTIONS ON MEANING

1. The essay does not include an explicit thesis statement, but the dominant impression is of a breathless joy, even ecstasy, in the experience of chaos and sensory overload.

2. Gilbert means to entertain her readers, no doubt, but also, it seems, to persuade them to seek out pleasure for themselves. She appeals to readers directly in paragraph 9, enjoining them to not "even worry about it, just go," to "get there fairly early," and when "[y]ou try to take a bite off your slice and the gummy crust folds, and the hot cheese runs away like topsoil in a landslide . . . just deal with it." The suggestion is that readers should undertake the same journey Gilbert describes.

3. As Gilbert sees it, "[t]raveling-to-a-place energy and living-in-a-place energy are two fundamentally different energies" (par. 2). Travelers seek out new places "just to check [them] out" (1) and focus on novel experiences; temporary residents necessarily get caught up in the mundane aspects of real life, such as paying utility bills. Gilbert places herself in both categories: She's temporarily living in Rome but travels to Naples to reignite a traveler's sense of newness and wonder.

4. *Metaphysics* is the philosophical study of reality and being. The pizza is so good, and so beyond the realm of anything she's ever experienced, that it causes Sofie to question everything she ever knew—about pizza, about eating, about her place in the world, and perhaps even the meaning of life. The same is true for Gilbert.

5. The pizza represents everything that is good and special about Naples and serves as the embodiment of the "pure pleasure" (par. 11) Gilbert sought as a visitor to Italy.

QUESTIONS ON WRITING STRATEGY

1. Gilbert didn't go to Naples for the pizza, but it turned out to be the defining moment of her trip. The jump back to Rome serves as a transition between the two halves of Gilbert's essay: her description of Naples and her description of the pizza.

2. The irony is that, although Gilbert thinks she is abusing her body, she feels better than she has in a very long time. She seems to conclude that sometimes the healthiest thing a person can do is abandon all concerns about health and focus, instead, on pleasure.

3. Readers of a book titled *Eat, Pray, Love* would presumably expect and appreciate ecstatic descriptions of food that holds a special significance for the writer. Gilbert assumes that her readers are interested in traveling to new places and that, if they haven't done so themselves, they've at least read about exotic destinations (notice, for instance, her casual reference to "Tibetan prayer flags" in par. 4). She also assumes that they have some general idea of what Italy is like, yet she is careful to describe the specific experience of Naples with vivid and unforgettable images, such as a "crooked old woman seated at her window, peering suspiciously down at the activity below" (4) and pizza makers whose "sleeves are rolled up over their sweaty forearms, their faces red with

exertion, one eye squinted against the heat of the fire and a cigarette dangling from the lips" (10).

4. The first two paragraphs explain that Gilbert met somebody who was traveling for pleasure, and the encounter made her jealous, sparking a desire for adventure. The introduction establishes Gilbert's reasons for traveling to Naples and puts her experience in a broader context.

QUESTIONS ON LANGUAGE

1. *Similes*: "undershirts and brassieres flapping in the wind like Tibetan prayer flags" (par. 4); "The accent in Naples is like a friendly cuff on the ear," "It's like walking through a city of short-order cooks . . ." (5); "shoving for access like they're trying to get space on a lifeboat," "much the same way one shimmering movie star . . . ," "hot cheese runs away like topsoil in a landslide" (9); "looking for all the world like the boilermen in the belly of a great ship . . ." (10). *Metaphors*: "longing to travel while you are already traveling is . . . a kind of greedy madness," "a jones to hit the road" (2); "An anthill inside a rabbit warren . . . ," "A tripped-out, dangerous and cheerful nuthouse" (4); "I almost felt I was being inducted into a secret society" (7); "contact high of glamour" (9). *Hyperbole*: "There is not a street in Naples in which some tough little kid in shorts and mismatched socks is not screaming up from the sidewalk . . . ," "Nor is there a building in this town that doesn't have at least one crooked old woman seated at her window . . ." (4); "I feared one of them might get shot" (6). We also particularly enjoy the writer's *personification* of her pizza in paragraph 8, where she imagines that it loves her back. Every one of Gilbert's figures of speech is fresh, imaginative, and highly evocative.

2. Gilbert's diction is profoundly colloquial. Just a few examples include "gave me such a jones to hit the road" (par. 2); "tripped-out" (4); "so insanely psyched," "right up in your face," "flipped me the finger" (5); "don't even worry about it," "wannabe pizza twaddle," "deal with it" (9); "can barely cope" (10). Piled one on top of the next, her colloquialisms build a tone that is breathless and exuberant. She is utterly thrilled by Naples and can't contain her excitement, which she wants to share with her readers. Her choice of language therefore strikes us as not only appropriate but also effective.

3. The effect is one of intensity and immediacy. Students may have trouble finding a reason for the inconsistent use of quotation marks, but it seems that the girl's thoughts are directed at Gilbert, whereas the women's (in italics) are more general, meant for everyone, and possibly muttered to themselves.

4. Students may have difficulty finding *nan* (sometimes spelled *naan*) in a general dictionary, but recipes abound online. The slightly sweet and aromatic leavened flat bread, similar to pita bread but fluffier and more flavorful, is common in south Asian cuisine.

SVEN BIRKERTS

Ladder

Anybody who suffers from a fear of heights, and of ladders in particular, will nod knowingly as they read Birkerts's amusing account of the physical and emotional panic he experienced as a hired painter. But his description is so precise and vivid that even readers who have no issues with wobbling up high on a narrow contraption can imagine his terrors for themselves.

The symbolism of the ladder as career trajectory and the deeper points of the essay will likely escape students on a first (or even second or third) reading. Encourage them to think carefully about and discuss the writer's meaning, focusing on the third and fourth questions on meaning and the third writing suggestion, labeled "Critical Writing."

QUESTIONS ON MEANING

1. The writer means to entertain, but also to mull over a defining moment in his life. The dominant impression he creates is a mixed sense of deep fear and shame as a young man.
2. He means that by abandoning his determination not to look down he suddenly lost his focus and became aware of the precariousness of his position. In other words, he panicked. (Some readers may recognize the somewhat vulgar slang usage of "breaking the seal," referring to the first trip to a bathroom in a night of drinking, which supposedly causes a person to need to urinate more frequently afterward. There's a slight implication that Birkerts may have wet himself in fear.)
3. As Birkerts explains in paragraph 1, he was young and unemployed. He sought out short-term menial tasks because he was broke but also, he suggests, because he didn't want or hadn't settled on a permanent job. The background details establish an aimlessness that sets up the ladder's function as a symbol (see the next question).
4. As we see it, the ladder symbolizes an adult career path (the proverbial "ladder to success"). Birkerts is afraid of responsibility. He is also afraid of getting old (like his employer) and dying.

QUESTIONS ON WRITING STRATEGY

1. Birkerts makes repeated self-deprecating remarks to establish humor and to make readers sympathize with and even like him. We think he succeeds quite well.
2. The essay is only four paragraphs long, with no formal introduction or conclusion. Birkerts takes a point of view that is simultaneously spatial and moving, and he arranges his description chronologically (with the exception of the end of paragraph 1, where he flashes back to provide the background to the story).
3. The unfocused structure of the last paragraph—and especially of the nearly 200-word sentence within it—conveys the author's feelings of panic, creating for readers the same sense of disembodiment and breathlessness that Birkerts experienced.

4. Birkerts compares the old man's appearance with and without teeth at the beginning of paragraph 1 and the end of paragraph 2. The striking difference creates humor; it also suggests that appearances can be deceiving and implies a not-so-flattering comparison between the employer (a successful man at the end of his career) and the author (an unsuccessful man at the beginning of his adult life).

QUESTIONS ON LANGUAGE

1. Notice the connotations of *lapping* in paragraph 3. Rather than describing the shingles with the more commonly used *overlapping*, Birkerts deftly chooses a word that also hints at competitive racing, wagging tongues, and the waves of the nearby ocean.
2. *Lady-killer* is a colloquial term for a man so attractive that women swoon over him. In using the term in both his introduction and conclusion, however, Birkerts seems to suggest that his employer's attractiveness and competence, especially compared to his own, left him feeling emasculated.
3. Students should have no difficulty finding examples: Birkerts masterfully employs vivid details and fresh figures of speech to render his sensations unmistakably clear. Some of our favorites include "a bump in my stomach" (par. 1); the "mouth . . . crimped like the top of a string bag" (2), "that first nervous heaviness in my legs" (3); "the time stream balked, then stopped and started backing up" (4); "the other hand feeling in its joints the cut of the handle, the weight of the bucket, the weathered shingles mere inches away" (4); and "shuddering my torso inch by inch down along the rungs" (4).

JOAN DIDION

The Santa Ana

If there were any doubt about the lasting relevance of Joan Didion's *Slouching Towards Bethlehem*, Diane Keaton's 2012 reading for Audible should remove it. In a review of the audiobook for *Salon*, Kyle Minor exclaims that Keaton's performance reminds us that the value of Didion's writing "has only deepened with time." Didion remains, he says, "the most consistently interesting and quotable essayist in the English language." We tend to agree.

Like all of Didion's work, "The Santa Ana" offers an excellent example of descriptive writing. Her colorful yet unsettling images appeal to the senses — sight, sound, taste, and touch. Didion's precision permits the listener to share her sensual impressions of and experiences with the "persistent [and] malevolent" Santa Ana wind. Perhaps the most interesting question to begin discussion with your students is whether Didion admires the destructive force she writes about. Because it may remind students of some phenomenon that drives them crazy where they live, Didion's essay could start a discussion about such phenomena, leading into the first suggestion for writing.

QUESTIONS ON MEANING AND STRATEGY

1. The essay uses the Santa Ana to make a larger point about the craziness of life in Los Angeles. Didion seems to be responding to the problem she identifies: "It is hard for people who have not lived in Los Angeles to realize how radically the Santa Ana figures in the local imagination." The essay also has a self-expressive element: Such a potent force begs to be written about and affords Didion the opportunity to explore its dramatic effects on herself and her surroundings.

2. The wind leaves the city dry, hot, and still. It makes people a little crazy, "drying the hills and the nerves to the flash point." "The baby frets. The maid sulks." It makes Didion testy and argumentative, causing her to "rekindle a waning argument with the telephone company." Natives used to throw themselves into the sea when the Santa Ana came. Didion's neighbor holes up inside, and the neighbor's husband runs around with a machete. People go to their doctors complaining of "headaches and nausea and allergies, about 'nervousness,' about 'depression.'" School-children become unmanageable. People have even committed murder.

3. A mechanistic view holds that human behavior is entirely controlled by outside forces (in this case, a force of nature). The opposite view would be that humans act of their own accord, that they have free will.

4. Didion's description relies on concrete examples because her subject, the wind itself, is nearly intangible. She is therefore limited to describing its physical and psychological effects: on nature (the Pacific, peacocks, the sky), on property (fires and property damage), and on people (see the second question on meaning and strategy). By describing these effects so vividly and thoroughly, she brings to life a phenomenon that people who have not lived in Los Angeles would otherwise have trouble understanding. Her examples are colorful and memorable and paint a vivid portrait for the outsider of what it's like to deal with such a malign phenomenon.

6
EXAMPLE
Pointing to Instances

Some essays in this chapter use only a few examples; others use many. They all show the ways examples can pin down and give meaning to generalizations.

Kellie Young's and Michael Chabon's essays are connected by theme as well as by method: Both treat obsessions—where they come from and how to deal with them. Anna Quindlen explores with a moving case the problem of homelessness. Brent Staples's personal memoir, "Black Men and Public Space," provides instances when the author aroused suspicion simply because of his skin color—anecdotes that generally arouse keen interest and lively discussion. And Luis Alberto Urrea's "Life on the Mississippi," an audio reading in the e-Pages, considers the ways "ritual nightly reading" of an American classic shaped one boy's view of the world.

Some students find difficulty in seeing the difference between giving an example and giving evidence to support a general statement. The latter is a larger concern, in which example is only one strategy. It may help to explain that, usually, an example backs up a general statement ("There have been many fine woman runners: Grete Waitz . . ."), but not everything supporting a general statement is an example. Statistics and other data, factual statements, expert opinions, and quotations also serve as evidence. The distinction may not be worth losing sleep over, but if a class has trouble seeing it, ask them to take a more painstaking look at "The Method" at the beginning of this chapter.

KELLIE YOUNG

The Undercurrent

Young's student essay on coping with dangers both real and imagined forms a pair with the next essay, Michael Chabon's "XO9." Both concern the effects that families have on mental health, as well as the ways we all tend to obsess over small things.

Students should enjoy Young's entertaining reflections on her anxious mother's incessant worries and their effects on her. For a generation raised by "helicopter parents," many will undoubtedly have similar tales to tell of overprotectiveness and nagging reminders. A good way to begin classroom discussion might be to ask students how Young's experience compares with their own. Why do parents worry so much about their children, especially after they leave home? Are they right to be concerned?

For students interested in learning more about emotional intelligence for the second writing suggestion (or simply for their own edification), the tenth anniversary edition of Daniel Goleman's *Emotional Intelligence: Why It Can Matter More than IQ* (2006) is an obvious starting point.

QUESTIONS ON MEANING

1. An *undercurrent* is a marine phenomenon in which a strong stream of water under the surface pulls back from the shore, often catching swimmers off guard and pulling them under and out to sea. (Warning signs on beaches usually advise bathers not to fight the current but to swim with it until it subsides.) According to Merriam-Webster's online dictionary, the word also refers to "a hidden opinion, feeling, or tendency often contrary to the one publicly shown." Young, a surfer, uses the concept as a metaphor for the nagging warnings from her mother that she hears in her head and struggles to overcome. As a swimmer must, she finds that the best approach is to follow the flow.

2. We outline Young's purpose in the essay headnote: Her essay is a response to a college composition assignment that specified she should reflect on events or emotions that shaped her into the person she is.

3. Her grandparents' relationship was not unusual for immigrant families in the mid-twentieth century. Young's widowed grandfather went to China to find a new wife to take care of his four teenage children; the wife brought a daughter from a previous relationship with her. Young doesn't make it terribly clear, but it seems that the couple had three children together after marriage. Because Young's grandmother was occupied with caring for her husband and his older children (the "first family," par. 12), it fell to her daughter to care for their younger children. Young's point is that her mother was laden with adult responsibilities from a young age and through hardships learned early the dangers of living.

4. Young seems to consider the influence somewhat mixed, as she states in paragraph 16: "My mother's voice in my head is something I cannot shake or hide from, but neither is it confining or oppressing. . . . Although at times her/my fears catch me, freezing me momentarily before I leap, she is me, and her voice steers me clear of jumps I realize I cannot make."

QUESTIONS ON WRITING STRATEGY

1. Young's description of surfing in the dark (pars. 1–3) and of the warnings in her head (4) is entertaining, surprising, and thoroughly engaging—a hook practically guaranteed to grab readers' interest in a personal topic that might otherwise seem irrelevant or abstract. At the same time, the story's focus, fears of injury or death while participating in an obviously risky endeavor, sets an ironic tone and establishes Young's overarching

point that while her mother's worries may sometimes seem overblown, the writer has learned that it's best to heed them.

2. The writer assumes an audience of peers: college students familiar with the struggles and ambivalent feelings that accompany growing up and away from a parent as they try to become independent.

3. Young covers a lot of ground in "The Undercurrent"; she maintains unity by ensuring that each paragraph includes a clear topic sentence that makes a generalization related to the thesis. Young is also careful to mark transitions among her paragraphs and to repeat key words such as *mother, hear, life,* and *danger.*

4. Young provides three anecdotes: the morning of pre-dawn surfing (pars. 1–5), the afternoon locked out in the rain (8), and the departure to Boston at the airport (15). The stories are meant both to amuse readers and to illustrate Young's point that her mother has good reason to worry about her.

QUESTIONS ON LANGUAGE

1. The quotations—both real and imagined—are essential examples of the voice and the warnings that have become engrained in Young's mind. Without them, the essay would contain only vague generalizations and would lose its effectiveness entirely.

2. "The Undercurrent" is loaded with examples of hyperbole, whether from Young's and her mother's overstatements of the dangers facing her—*"Get one shard in your toe and you're going to have to chop it off—the entire thing!"* (par. 4); "what if someone starts a mosh pit and you get crushed? (6); "if I were unfortunate enough to touch the seat with my bare skin, I would contract a disease and die too quickly for doctors to make a saving diagnosis" (10)—or from Young's predilection for exaggerated phrases, such as "risks that could (and would!) prematurely cut short our lives (6), "lightning bolts of doom" (9), "utter depths of poverty" (10), and " 'twenty seat covers and yards of toilet paper' " (10). The abundance of hyperbole is amusing, of course, but it also establishes a wry, self-mocking tone that lets readers know Young doesn't take herself or her worries too seriously.

3. *The American Heritage Dictionary* tells us that *maverick* can mean not only a stubbornly independent person but also an "unbranded range animal, especially a calf that has become separated from its mother." We don't know if Young intended the second meaning, but it seems especially fitting for her subject.

4. The repetition points out the parallels between her mother's behavior and Young's own.

MICHAEL CHABON

XO9

Chabon makes his living by undermining genre expectations while sticking to form. This ostensibly personal essay is no exception. Dwelling through most of it on the obsessive-compulsive disorders that have plagued many members of his family including himself, Chabon switches gear in his conclusion and transforms his musings into sly literary criticism aimed both at his own work and that of "every writer" (par. 5).

The essay also gives an opportunity to talk to students about control: Which parts of their lives do they have direct control over? What lies beyond their control? What can they gain from the latter? Does Chabon gain the upper hand in his concession to the "grip of XO9" (par. 5), or has OCD defeated him?

Kellie Young's "The Undercurrent" complements Chabon's essay. A "Connections" writing suggestion after each essay helps students compare them. In class, you might want to emphasize the differences in the writer's tones. Both write openly and honestly about their own psychological quirks, but while Young emphasizes humor, Chabon starts with mockery and quickly turns to compassion. Why do students think that is?

QUESTIONS ON MEANING

1. We have no idea where or how Chabon's son came up with the odd label (he doesn't tell us), nor can we guess what it might refer to (although we have tried, obsessively), but XO9 is the writer's family's name for obsessive-compulsive disorder.
2. Chabon's thesis, stated in paragraph 5, is that writing fiction is a kind of obsessive-compulsive disorder, comparable to his desperate need to fix anything that's broken. He does it because he feels compelled to.
3. Writing the essay is a kind of cognitive therapy for Chabon. His purpose, it seems, is to "feel better" (par. 2) about his own OCD by talking about it openly.

QUESTIONS ON WRITING STRATEGY

1. Each member of his family suffers from a different kind of obsession, or compulsion, and Chabon groups his examples around those types. For his grandmother, it's germophobia. His son has symmetry issues and a habit of repeating words (Chabon shares that tic). His father is compulsively organized. Chabon needs to fix things; he also needs to "rock" (par. 4).
2. Chabon takes his thesis very seriously and develops it thoroughly. Students should note that he leads to it carefully, laying out several examples of OCD that affect members of his family before turning the lens on himself and the ways the disorder manifests in his behaviors. He then makes a point of showing how his impulses as writer compare to his other impulses. To further verify his claim, he cites examples of

other writers whose "recurring tropes, motifs, and phrases" (par. 5) suggest that they, too, suffer from similar compulsions.

3. Clearly, Chabon assumes an educated audience of sophisticated fiction readers, especially fans of his own novels and stories. Although it would help to have a familiarity with the writers he mentions and their novels, he offers just enough information about each—an example or two of a recurring aspect of their work—to support his claim that many writers tend to return to the same ideas in their fiction.

4. Chabon compares the forms of OCD experienced by his family members and himself to show why his obsessions are real and to acknowledge that they cause him the same kinds of frustration and discomfort (albeit at a less extreme level). As he writes in paragraph 4, "My few collections are incomplete, I have braved hellish [toilets] without benefit or need of Lysol, and I have never experienced any bodily compulsions beyond those of my animal appetites. But I have this thing where I can't stop trying to fix something that's broken. . . ."

QUESTIONS ON LANGUAGE

1. *Daven* comes from the Yiddish *davnen* and refers to the ritualized recital of Jewish liturgy. For Chabon then, the act of rocking back and forth, especially while writing, is a form of prayer.

2. The most obvious metaphor, of course, is writing as obsession; notice also how neatly Chabon ties the lock metaphor of paragraph 5 back to his expressed need to fix things that are broken. As Chabon acknowledges in his conclusion, he is a writer particularly prone to simile. Some examples: "*pushed me like a dollyload of bricks*," "she had to enter the stall like a fireman shouldering his way into a burning house (par. 1); "foliating like creepers though the kid's thoughts" (2); "as neatly as the pipes of a church organ" (3); "trapped like flies in the casements of my brain," "like a junkie who needs a fix, a madman on the subway, a devout Jew at prayer, a kid who really needs to pee" (4). Students' favorites will vary.

3. Chabon is openly mocking of his grandmother's germophobia in his introduction because he's writing from his perspective as a child. As an adult, he explains, he came to understand that she suffered from a disorder. His descriptions of his son's and his father's compulsions, accordingly, are highly empathetic, not least so because he has experienced them himself.

MICHAEL CHABON ON WRITING

Delivered off the cuff, this comparison of writing and cooking is both clever and illuminating. Students should have fun elaborating on the similarities between the processes: Some, for instance, might comment that reading, like eating, can provide sustenance (or indigestion); others might invoke vocabulary as ingredients, or grammar as recipes. Encourage them to be creative. You might discuss with students how to follow Chabon's example and "write the kinds of" essays they'd want to read.

ANNA QUINDLEN

Homeless

In this direct, personal essay, Quindlen uses detailed examples to explore what it is to be without a home. The third question on meaning provides a likely occasion for class discussion of the importance of a home and what a home is.

If you think your students may need more background on the issue of homelessness, the third writing suggestion gives them a chance to do research into and write about the rights of the homeless—to supplement the evidence of their own experience with facts, expert opinions, and so on. Students could research collaboratively, with small groups focusing on each of the following questions to cover more ground: How widespread is homelessness in your area? What are local attitudes toward homeless people? What provisions are made for the homeless? Is homelessness thought of differently on the national level? Each group could report its findings back to the class. (If this sort of research is something you'd like to have students do fairly regularly, you might consider rotating the responsibility so that just one group works and reports on any given essay.)

If students already have enough background on the issue, you might use Quindlen's essay as a springboard for discussing practical measures to help solve the problem. Working in groups of three or four, students could discuss the practicalities of Quindlen's claim that nothing but a home will solve the problems of the homeless: With this as a premise, what can be done to achieve this goal? Fifteen minutes of collaborative brainstorming on this question should give students enough time to prepare for a whole-class discussion of the issues Quindlen raises.

QUESTIONS ON MEANING

1. Quindlen's thesis (in pars. 8–9) is that abstraction from particular human beings to "issues" may distance us from problems and impede their solution—in this case, solving homelessness with homes.
2. The key is in paragraph 8: Use of the term "the homeless" distances us from the problem suffered by particular people with particular needs.
3. Having a place to live makes you "somebody" (par. 2); it provides "certainty, stability, predictability, privacy" (4), and "pride of ownership" (7). Students' opinions about the importance of a home will vary. This question and the fourth writing suggestion provide good opportunities to discuss just what a home is, anyway: a house or an apartment? a room in a dorm? a heating grate?

QUESTIONS ON WRITING STRATEGY

1. Quindlen might have begun with a statement of her opinion (among other options), but the story of Ann draws the reader in and illustrates Quindlen's point. It also, perhaps even more important, reinforces

Quindlen's argument that we should focus more on particular people with particular problems.

2. The examples bring Quindlen to earth and magnify the loss suffered by the homeless.
3. The author assumes that the reader has a home and feels strongly about it. Some students may not feel as strongly about having a home as Quindlen does. In paragraph 7 she addresses readers' likely assumption that shelters are better than the streets.
4. The second through fourth sentences enumerate examples and could be parallel simple sentences, but Quindlen varies their structures and complexity (notice the distribution of subordinate clauses), building to the brief, poignant fragment spoken by the mother.
5. She wants readers to agree that nothing short of homes will solve the problems of homeless people.

QUESTIONS ON LANGUAGE

1. It invests her opinion with passion and urgency.
2. Not only do our hearts reside in and take nourishment from our homes, but we can show heart by providing homes for those who lack them.
3. *Crux* is a Latin word meaning "cross." In English it is a critical point or essential feature.

ANNA QUINDLEN ON WRITING

Analyzing the differences between Quindlen's essay and a conventional news report (the second question for discussion) may engage students. To us, the myriad differences come down to "My God" (par. 9): Such a fervently personal exclamation would never appear in straight news, not even in feature writing. Other examples include statements of belief, such as "You are where you live" (par. 2) and "That [a home] is everything" (4), or personal details, such as the Irish grandfather (3) and the beloved hot-water heater (4).

BRENT STAPLES

Black Men and Public Space

As Brent Staples demonstrates, the most gripping and convincing examples are often brief anecdotes. In this essay examples of Staples's discovery—of the "alienation that comes of being ever the suspect"—take up most of the room. In addition, Staples gives examples of "tough guys" who died in street violence (par. 7) and precautions he takes to appear less threatening (11–12). His vivid opening paragraph, with its first sentence pretending that he is a killer, deserves special scrutiny.

For collaborative work on this essay, we suggest focusing on just what public space is and what happens to us when we enter it. Students might try to define *public space* by coming up with examples and discovering what the examples have in common. How do they feel different in private and in public space? Once they have their examples and definitions, the groups could reassemble as a class to arrive at a generally accepted definition.

As an alternative, you could encourage students to explore their own feelings about public space. Are there places they feel more or less welcome, safe, at home? The "Journal Writing" prompt after the essay gives students an opportunity to explore such questions. They might also find it helpful to generate a list of generalizations in small groups. What does it mean to be a student, a woman, a man, a member of a particular religious or ethnic group, and so on, in American public spaces? Working in small groups, students will probably feel freer to discuss their experiences; you might even consider dividing the groups along gender lines for those women and men who might be reluctant to speak up otherwise.

QUESTIONS ON MEANING

1. Students will state the author's purpose variously. Staples writes to communicate his experience as a black man of whom others are needlessly frightened. He writes to explain his discovery that, when mistaken for a criminal, it is wiser not to react with rage but to take precautions to appear less threatening. However the writer's purpose is put, this is personal experience and observation; we do not see Staples trying to predict the future or proposing any long-term solutions.
2. If we keep on reading, we find Staples acknowledging that women are often the victims of street violence, some of it perpetrated by young African American males. He believes, though, that reports have been exaggerated. He takes pains to make clear that he isn't dangerous. He considers himself not a tough guy but a "softy" who hates to cut up a raw chicken (par. 2); he has shrunk from street fights (6); his own brother and others have been killed in "episodes of bravado" (7).
3. By using it in this context, Staples gives the word *survivor* fresh connotations. Usually it suggests rugged strength, ability to endure, and so on, but here Staples helps us to understand that, in an area of gang warfare, knifings, and murders, timidity is a form of self-preservation.

QUESTIONS ON WRITING STRATEGY

1. Staples convinces by giving examples: anecdotes from his own experience (pars. 1, 5, 8, 9) and that of another African American male (10).
2. The examples are set forth in detail too rich to seem a mere bare-bones list. The similar nature of all the examples lends the essay coherence, and to give it even more Staples uses transitions skillfully. In nearly every paragraph, the opening sentence is transitional, and transitional phrases indicate time: "One day," "Another time," "a couple of summers ago."
3. Beginning with the scene of a near-empty street at night and a frightened woman fleeing him, Staples dramatizes his thesis and immediately sets forth a typical, recurrent situation.

QUESTIONS ON LANGUAGE

1. As we have seen, Staples's essay uses a narrative hook at the start, and to make the hook grab hard, the writer deliberately misleads us. The word *victim* leads us to take him for a self-confessed criminal. By the end of the paragraph, we doubt our impression, and in his second paragraph, Staples explains that he is harmless; he can hardly take a knife to a chicken. If we look back on the opening paragraph, we see the discrepancy between the word *victim* and reality. In truth, the fleeing woman is mistaken and fearful, a person on whom the innocent narrator has no designs. This discrepancy makes clear the writer's ironic attitude. As the essay proceeds, he expresses a mingling of anger, humor, and resignation.
2. We admire Staples's use of that fine old formal word *constitutionals*, "walks taken for health." Like the expression "robust constitution," though, it seems a throwback to another era.
3. Students will have fun defining *dicey* ("risky, unpredictable"), recalling that shooting dice is, of course, a game of chance.

BRENT STAPLES ON WRITING

Staples provides a clear and enlightening illustration of how writing generates ideas, instead of simply recording them, as most inexperienced writers seem to believe. His comparison of essay- and news-writing is related: The work begins in the details, in the data, the observations, the feelings—in the facts, as Staples says. The big picture depends on the details.

LUIS ALBERTO URREA

Life on the Mississippi

Luis Alberto Urrea is known for his disarming ability to portray bleak circumstances with an uplifting tone, a skill he applies in full force to this lyrical essay on the strategies he used to cope with living in a rough neighborhood as a child. Literature, he suggests, is a saving force. We strongly encourage you and your students to listen to Urrea's audio performance of the piece; his cheerful, unassuming voice brings the work to life—just as his imagination brought to life the stories he read in his youth.

Sherman Alexie, in "Superman and Me" (p. 494), also writes about the life-saving power of reading; we point out the link between the two selections in the writing suggestion labeled "Connections" following Alexie's essay. Students may be interested to know that Urrea and Alexie are friends.

QUESTIONS ON MEANING AND STRATEGY

1. Everything to do with the Mississippi River is, of course, the product of Urrea's childhood imagination as fueled by reading *The Adventures of Tom Sawyer*. A dirt alley becomes a river, rickety porches transform into docks, and disabled cars turn into boats. (The same happens in Urrea's conclusion, where the front stoop morphs into the wilds of Rudyard Kipling's *The Jungle Book*.) The real world of his urban neighborhood is bleak and rife with crime; the imaginary world is Urrea's salvation.

2. Urrea's purpose goes beyond offering examples of childhood adventures. His essay is a hymn to the transformative power of literature—reading, he implies, let him escape the deprivations and all too real dangers of his neighborhood and very likely saved his life.

3. No doubt Urrea assumes intimate familiarity with Twain's *The Adventures of Tom Sawyer* and Kipling's *The Jungle Book* (1894), both classic works of literature for children. He alludes to Sawyer's famous fence-painting ruse, to Becky Thatcher, and to several of the friends' adventures and scrapes in Twain's novel. Clearly, too, Urrea assumes that readers know that Mowgli is a boy raised by wolves and that Rikki-Tikki-Tavi is a mongoose adopted to protect a family from poisonous snakes. Even if readers aren't familiar with these works, however, Urrea offers enough detail to get across his point that the stories (and presumably many others) colored his imagination and shaped his view of the world around him.

4. Students may not catch at first that Urrea describes a neighborhood plagued by gangs—or, in his mind, the "river urchins and cut-pockets" that swarm the back alleys. He implicitly compares the black and red ants in constant, futile battle with the neighborhood's competing gangs; the analogy supports Urrea's understated claim that "[m]ost of the strife in that little dirt alley world was racial."

7
COMPARISON AND CONTRAST
Setting Things Side by Side

Many students dread the method of comparison and contrast, perhaps because of meeting it on essay examinations. We do our best to reassure them (in "The Method") that it is manageable with a little planning. The chapter offers extra help with outlining; we try to take some of the mystique out of it, and we urge the student not to feel a slave to a mere charting of letters and numerals. For a short paper, the formal outline—of the Roman numeral *I*, capital *A* variety—is surely more trouble than it's worth. But in writing any paper that compares and contrasts, a plan to follow, at least a rough plan, is especially useful.

Suzanne Britt's "Neat People vs. Sloppy People" is easy reading, but it makes sharp comments on human behavior. We've paired it with another humorous piece on human behavior, Dave Barry's "Batting Clean-Up and Striking Out." Both essays contrast neatniks and others, but they explain the differences differently.

Keeping up the humor, David Sedaris amusingly contrasts his dull life in an American suburb with his partner's garishly textured life as the child of a nomadic diplomat, and Fatawesome uses analogy to compare pets and friends. The remaining selection in this chapter is more serious, though not somber. In "We're Not . . . ," student writer Andrea Roman contrasts her Bolivian heritage with her American upbringing.

For introducing the method of comparison and contrast, here's a light-weight illustration possibly worth reading to your class. At least it suggests that in comparing and contrasting, a writer has to consider a whole series of points. Craig Hosmer, a Republican and, at the time, representative from California's thirty-second district, introduced the following advice into the *Congressional Record* for October 1, 1974. (We found this item in *American Humor: An Interdisciplinary Newsletter*, Fall 1983, and offer it in a slightly abbreviated version, the better to illustrate comparison and contrast.)

How to Tell Republicans from Democrats

Republicans employ exterminators.
Democrats step on bugs.

Democrats name their children after popular sports figures, politicians, and entertainers.
Republican children are named after their parents or grandparents, according to where the money is.

Republicans tend to keep their shades drawn, although there is seldom any reason why they should.
Democrats ought to, but don't.

Republicans study the financial pages of the newspaper.
Democrats put them in the bottom of the bird cage.

Democrats buy most books that have been banned somewhere.
Republicans form censorship committees and read them as a group.

Democrats give their worn-out clothes to those less fortunate.
Republicans wear theirs.

Democrats raise Airedales, kids, and taxes.
Republicans raise dahlias, Dalmatians, and eyebrows.

Democrats eat the fish they catch.
Republicans hang them on the wall.

Republicans sleep in twin beds—some even in separate rooms.
That is why there are more Democrats.

SUZANNE BRITT

Neat People vs. Sloppy People

Whatever Suzanne Britt believes, she believes wholeheartedly. Then she merrily sets out to convince her readers that she's right. A danger in teaching this essay, perhaps, is that students without Britt's skill may be inspired to emulate her slapdash unreasonableness without quite achieving the desired effect. Some students, though, just might surprise you with the delightful writing they can produce with this essay as their inspiration.

Small groups can be useful for helping students through the brainstorming part of writing an essay. Students might appreciate having time to talk about the points of comparison they have come up with in preparing to write an essay for either of our first two writing suggestions. Group members can help each other expand their lists of comparative points and find the details that will bring these points to life.

QUESTIONS ON MEANING

1. Whoever said it failed to perceive Britt's humor.
2. Britt is hardly impartial. It's easy to see that her sympathies lie with sloppy people and that she considers herself one of them. Mostly, she writes to amuse and entertain.
3. "As always" means what it says. Yes, Britt is saying—with tongue only partially in cheek—the distinctions among people are moral.

QUESTIONS ON WRITING STRATEGY

1. Britt's tone is blunt, assured, and, of course, hyperbolic. The tone is es-tablished from the start: "Neat people are lazier and meaner than sloppy people." Words and phrases that illustrate the tone abound throughout the essay.
2. Britt finds no similarities at all between the two. Had she mentioned any, her essay would be less exaggerated and would therefore lose some of its force. Writers who aren't exaggerating might give short shrift to similarities, too, if they are obvious or irrelevant.
3. These broad statements are generalizations because they make con-clusive assertions on the basis of some evidence—although, of course, Britt is deliberately exaggerating whatever evidence she has. By using so many generalizations, Britt compounds the outrageous nature of her essay. Her humor derives from her being unfair to neat people and find-ing no fault at all with their opposites.
4. Britt constantly clarifies her subjects by repeating *sloppy people* and *neat people*.
5. The examples do specify the kinds of behavior Britt has in mind, but they are themselves generalizations about the two kinds of people. They illustrate behavior but not particular persons.

QUESTIONS ON LANGUAGE

1. *The American Heritage Dictionary* tells us that *métier* is a word that began as the Latin *ministerium* ("occupation") and then became the Vulgar Latin *misterium* and the Old French *mestier* before assuming its present spelling and meaning ("specialty") in modern French and English.
2. The word is not to be understood literally, but humorously, as are *rec-titude, stupendous* (par. 2), *excavation* (5), and *vicious* (9). Students may argue for one or two others that they perceive are not to be taken literally.

SUZANNE BRITT ON WRITING

Here are some responses to the questions for discussion.

1. Britt doesn't offer much specific advice for the student assigned to write about Guatemala. But the method she urges, it seems, is to study the subject long enough to discover some personal connection or interest in it.
2. Britt's first paragraph yields at least two metaphors ("you have to suck out all the marrow of whatever you do" and "My answer is rock bottom and hard") and a simile ("silence falls like prayers across the room"). More colorful still are the similes two paragraphs later, in which the student is advised to gather "your life around you as a mother hen gath-ers her brood, as a queen settles the folds in her purple robes." There's hyperbole, too, in the next paragraph: "an interminable afternoon in a biology lab."
3. What is the tone of Britt's remarks? Though she regards writing with humor and zest, and doesn't take it in grim earnest, clearly she deeply cares about it. In the end, she equates it with an act of faith.

DAVE BARRY

Batting Clean-Up and Striking Out

Dave Barry is one of America's best-known and most prolific humorists, and his essay makes a perfect companion piece to Suzanne Britt's. Both writers rely on exaggeration and generalization to make readers laugh.

Students respond differently to humor based on stereotypes. While some will see this kind of humor as cathartic, others will be annoyed or even angered by it. The second through fourth writing suggestions all ask students to respond to Barry's use of stereotypes for their humorous potential. In addition, you might want to give students a chance to express their reactions in class. Encourage those who were offended by the essay to voice and clarify their objections; encourage those who enjoyed the essay to defend it.

QUESTIONS ON MEANING

1. Barry's purpose is to entertain and amuse. His humor is characterized by broad generalizations (such as the first sentence); tall tales (the "hormonal secretion" and the Pompeii example, par. 2); exaggeration ("clumps large enough to support agriculture," 2; "bacteria you could enter in a rodeo," 3); self-effacement ("an important project on the Etch-a-Sketch" and the pajamas anecdote, 4); and a tongue-in-cheek tone ("my specific family unit" and "Standard Male Cleaning Implements," 3; "a sensitive and caring kind of guy," 4; "human relationships or something," 8).
2. Barry is anything but objective. He is clearly writing from a male point of view, and he understands male behavior. However, his tone is far too facetious for the essay to be taken as a justification of boorish behavior. He makes as much fun of himself as of anyone else.
3. Barry seems to take the differences between the sexes as a given. He is less interested in reconciliation than in exploiting gender misunderstandings for their humorous potential.

QUESTIONS ON WRITING STRATEGY

1. A subject-by-subject organization would have undermined Barry's examples, which depend on the interaction of women and men to make their point.
2. From the first ironic sentence we know to take everything Barry says with a grain of salt.
3. The second half of Barry's thesis sentence is in paragraph 5: "The opposite side of the dirt coin, of course, is sports. This is an area where men tend to feel very sensitive and women tend to be extremely callous." Students (and teachers) may disagree over whether the divided thesis sentence helps or hurts. A single, early sentence might have tied the parts together, but it also would have stolen an element of surprise from the essay.

4. Barry effectively appropriates the force of Poe's story, giving his own anecdote an added dimension. The incongruity of Poe's horror story and Barry's domestic scene produces a comic effect.
5. He uses the phrase "the opposite side of the . . . coin."
6. This example is obviously invented. Its purpose is not to persuade but, like everything else in the essay, to amuse.

QUESTIONS ON LANGUAGE

1. Students sensitive to its connotation may object to Barry's use of *prattled* to describe the women's talk, even though he clearly intends it humorously. The word means "to talk idly or meaninglessly" and comes from a Dutch word, *praten*, with the same meaning.
2. The breathless, digressive nature of the sentence adds to the humor of the anecdote. It has the oral quality of someone gossiping on the telephone.
3. Again, the orality of the text is increased. We can hear the emphasis in Barry's voice, the near hysteria of "*during a World Series Game*" (par. 6), the sports-announcer tone of "Annual Fall Classic" (8).
4. By using *males* and *male*, Barry creates an anthropological distance between himself and his subject.

DAVE BARRY ON WRITING

Writing is a serious job for this humor writer, and students may be surprised at how difficult it can be for a funny man to wring a laugh from a reader. We appreciate Barry's observation that writing is, to quote Edison on genius, "one percent inspiration and ninety-nine percent perspiration." We also appreciate Barry's insistence that experience helps, a lesson that students may learn themselves as they gain more practice writing.

ANDREA ROMAN

"We're Not ..."

This engaging and well-written student essay is sure to resonate with many students who have shared Roman's frustrations with a parent's oppositions to their quest for independence, as well as those who have struggled to shape their own identities. For students who are children of immigrants, the essay may be especially affecting because cultural differences often exacerbate the normal parent-child conflicts, as Roman demonstrates.

Two possible approaches to discussing this essay: Focus on how your students define *American* and the degree to which their families contribute to that definition, directly or indirectly; or focus on how differences between parents and children nourish or thwart the children. For either approach, students will be drawing on their own experiences, so small groups may encourage freer discussion than a whole-class setting. Hearing their classmates' experiences and ideas will broaden students' own perspectives and prepare them for work on the second, third, and fourth writing suggestions.

QUESTIONS ON MEANING

1. Roman states her thesis in paragraph 1: "One would think that language would create the biggest barriers for immigrants but in my mother's case, the biggest obstacles were the small cultural differences." The last sentence of the paragraph reiterates that idea.
2. Roman's purpose is to explain the differences between her mother's Bolivian cultural assumptions and her own American assumptions. She makes it clear in her conclusion that she considers neither cultural heritage superior to the other: "Through my mother's multiple rules, I had become comfortable enough with my identity and culture that showing pride in another country would not take away from my heritage" (par. 27).
3. To her mother's Bolivian eye, borrowing clothing indicated to others that the Roman family was too poor to provide for their children. It was, in other words, a source of shame. She punished Roman not for the borrowing but for having the audacity to question her mother's rules, for "talking back."
4. Each flag—one Bolivian, one American—represents an important part of the author's identity.

QUESTIONS ON WRITING STRATEGY

1. Although we have included Roman's essay as a model of comparison and contrast, it is also an episodic narrative (see question 5, below), an assignment we have noticed is becoming increasingly popular in college writing courses. The blank spaces separate the three major episodes Roman recounts, breaking the essay into its parts and lending a reflective quality to her story.
2. Roman's basis of comparison, identified in her introduction, is "that certain unacceptable acts in [Bolivian] culture were quite acceptable here in the States" (par. 1). Her points of comparison focus on three of those acts: borrowing clothing (2–3), attending sleepover parties (4–11), and working on Sundays (12–24).
3. Roman is writing for her peers—other students at Boston College, specifically her hall mates who asked why she displayed a large American flag in her dorm room. The essay answers their question, which had become her own. To some extent, then, Roman is also writing for herself.
4. In her concluding paragraph Roman not only explains the significance of her thesis but circles back neatly to each of the major points in her essay without resorting to dull summary: "I now borrow clothes, have sleepovers, and do a ton of work on Sundays, but I have not left behind that little Bolivian girl who received the mouth-washing with dishwasher soap, no matter what flag hangs on my wall."
5. Dialog lends immediacy and vibrancy to each episode and expresses each participant's lack of understanding better than summary or explanation could. In Roman's case it also reveals the linguistic and cultural differences she asserts in her introduction. The conversations mingle English and Spanish for both mother and daughter.

QUESTIONS ON LANGUAGE

1. In almost every instance Roman restates the Spanish phrase in English, usually within the space of a sentence or two. There are two exceptions. The opening quotation from her mother is translated in paragraph 3 (we provide it in a gloss note as well because students may not recognize the relationship). She doesn't translate "*Te dije qué no*," but most readers can figure out its meaning by context.
2. "We're not poor, Andrea. Why do you have to borrow clothes?" (par. 3); "We're not American, Andrea. Why do you want a sleepover?" (4); "We're not American, Andrea. We don't do that in Bolivia" (10). The repetition gives the essay coherence, but it also does more: In repeating her mother's continued assertion that she's not American, Roman emphasizes the cultural conflict she felt and is able to conclude with some defiance that she is, indeed, American.
3. Notice the paradox in Roman's statement that the specifics of her mother's objections "invariably changed" (par. 1): *invariable* means unchanging, constant.

ANDREA ROMAN ON WRITING

Although Andrea Roman may not have thought she's "all that interesting," we have to disagree. Her comments offer useful points about the personal benefits to be derived from writing—and from seeking and accepting feedback. Her advice to draft from the heart should prove especially useful to other students struggling with the pressures of writing for an audience. Being "true" to themselves and then letting others help refine their work can help them work through their own difficulties, as Roman illustrates.

DAVID SEDARIS

Remembering My Childhood on the Continent of Africa

This essay is humorist David Sedaris's account of the exotic childhood and adolescent experiences of his partner Hugh—who grew up in various African outposts as the son of a US diplomat—as contrasted with Sedaris's far more mundane youth in suburban North Carolina. Students may initially have some trouble with Sedaris's subtle irony. You could begin discussion by asking class members whether they think Sedaris truly wishes he could have traded places with Hugh, whose youth, while "fascinating" in retrospect (par. 13), was in fact marked by some pretty gruesome and dangerous events. Sedaris admits that he can't acknowledge this fact because it means "I should have been happy with what I had" (21). Instead he retreats into fantasy, safely appropriating the stories he has heard from Hugh as memories of his own.

To pursue this question further, you could divide the class into small groups and have each group analyze the essay for evidence of Sedaris's clear awareness that Hugh's childhood was "not as glamorous as it sounds" (12). In reporting back their findings to the class, each group could consider what Sedaris seems to be suggesting about his own personality.

Sedaris's reading of *Me Talk Pretty One Day*, from which this essay comes, is available on CD and for download. Students may enjoy his distinctive delivery, familiar to anyone who has heard him on National Public Radio.

QUESTIONS ON MEANING

1. Sedaris contrasts his own "unspeakably dull" middle-class American childhood (par. 8) with the much more exotic and eventful childhood of his partner Hugh, who, as the son of a diplomat, grew up in various countries in Africa.
2. The thesis might seem to be that Sedaris's life was dull compared to Hugh's (par. 8) or that Sedaris makes up for his dull life by appropriating Hugh's (21). But hovering over all, just hinted, is the larger idea that Hugh's childhood, while much more exciting than Sedaris's and food for resentment and imagination, had terrible costs that Sedaris would not have wanted to pay.
3. Sedaris's envy is essentially ironic because many of Hugh's childhood experiences seem pretty lonely and harrowing, beginning with the field trip to the slaughterhouse. This is true even when Sedaris writes of something that one might indeed be envious of: For example, Hugh's family had servants, but they included guards with machetes (par. 11), suggesting that the family was always in danger. In paragraph 21 Sedaris notes that while he was longing for more exotic adventures as a child, Hugh ("[s]omeone unknown to me" at the time) was probably longing for something more normal.

QUESTIONS ON WRITING STRATEGY

1. Sedaris's point-by-point organization can be outlined as follows: comparison of field trips (pars. 1–7); of daily life (8); of access to popular culture, specifically movies and the circumstances of viewing them (9–10); of servants and security (11); of dangerous experiences (12–13); of meeting a celebrity (14); of Sedaris's ten-day visit with his senile grandmother and Hugh's two years living with strangers (15–19); and of vacations (20–21).
2. Transitions include "[w]hen I was in elementary school" (par. 7), "[w]hen I was seven years old" and "[w]hen he was seven years old" (8), "[u]nlike me" (10), "but" (11), and "[a]bout the same time" (16).
3. A monkey is a particularly exotic pet that many children might long to own. Hugh's monkey comes to represent for Sedaris everything that he envies about Hugh's childhood.
4. The opening conversation establishes the relationship between Sedaris and Hugh and particularly the fact that Hugh seems unfazed by his odd experiences. This opening also makes clear that Sedaris has had many such conversations with Hugh, on which he bases his knowledge of Hugh's experiences.

5. Sedaris narrates stories from his own life and from Hugh's to point up how different their experiences have been.

QUESTIONS ON LANGUAGE

1. The second and third, fourth and fifth, and sixth and seventh sentences in the paragraph are parallel in structure, which highlights the contrast that concludes each sentence. As Sedaris wittily puts it, "The verbs are the same, but [Hugh] definitely wins the prize when it comes to nouns and objects."
2. The term "petty thief" emphasizes the self-deprecating portrait that Sedaris has presented throughout. His use of Hugh's memories represents no "spiritual symbiosis" but is merely a way for Sedaris to live vicariously through the other man's experiences.
3. Almost any paragraph will provide examples of specific, concrete language. In paragraph 6 examples include "low-ceilinged concrete building," "small white piglet," "its dainty hooves clicking against the concrete floor," "class gathered in a circle," "turned from face to face," "drew a pistol from his back pocket, held it against the animal's temple, and shot the piglet, execution-style," "Blood-spattered, frightened children wept."
4. *Symbiosis*, from the Greek word for "living together," implies the intimate union of two dissimilar types.

DAVID SEDARIS ON WRITING

You might take a poll of the students in your class: How many have ever used a typewriter? Sedaris's animus against the computer and love of the typewriter probably grows quainter by the day, but we like what he says about the feel of writing, the sense "that you're actually building something."

FATAWESOME

Cat-Friend vs. Dog-Friend

With more than 13 million views on *YouTube* as well as national media attention for the piece, there's a good chance that many of your students have seen "Cat-Friend vs. Dog-Friend" before. But they probably haven't thought of this highly entertaining video as the excellent model of comparison and contrast it is. Clearly ordered point by point, the video is especially effective in that it makes two distinct comparisons — of dogs and cats, and of pets and friends. You might wish to spend some time in class having students tease out the implied meaning of Fatawesome's central analogy, a mental exercise we encourage with the third question on meaning and strategy. You could also extend that analogy by asking your students what other sorts of animal characteristics can be ascribed to humans. What characteristics would they like to see more—or less—of in their friends, their family, and others?

Students who enjoy "Cat-Friend vs. Dog-Friend" might be pointed to *fatawesome.com* for additional works. The comedy team regularly posts new videos, comics, and sketches and also gives on-campus performances by appointment.

QUESTIONS ON MEANING AND STRATEGY

1. "Cat-Friend vs. Dog-Friend" is clearly meant to entertain, but notice *how* it entertains. The actors portray human characters with animal qualities, implying a secondary focus on how human friends interact. Students might express the thesis as some variation of "dogs make better pets than cats do" or "friends who act like dogs are better than friends who act like cats," but Fatawesome offers a more nuanced thesis in the *YouTube* tagline for the video: "If your friends acted like your pets, you might not keep them around" (see the first suggestion for writing). Students might paraphrase the thesis as "people who are overly needy or overly independent do not make desirable friends" or, from another perspective, "we wouldn't accept our pets' quirks and behaviors if they were human."

2. The cat-and-dog comparison is structured point by point, and the points of comparison focus on behavior. For example, dog-friend greets his human friend enthusiastically, while cat-friend runs away; dog-friend cuddles on the couch, but cat-friend nonchalantly walks all over; dog-friend regrets spilling the milk, but cat-friend spills it deliberately; and so on. Dog-friend comes off as the better companion, although certainly not without flaws. (The portrayals of sniffing a person's rear, sulking over spilled milk, and volunteering to eat vomit are clearly negatives, although such behaviors are encouraged with "That's a good boy!" at the end.) At the same time, cat enthusiasts might argue that cat-friend's indifferent independence is preferable to dog-friend's overeager enthusiasm.

3. Viewers who have any familiarity with cats or dogs will not need the captions to grasp which actor plays which role, but the graphic cues help clarify the comparison from the start. The analogy, too, is simple enough: In comparing two unlike things (pets and people), the video makes concrete the abstract notion that behaviors acceptable or even endearing in animal companions would be irritating (or worse) coming from human friends.

4. Students' choices will, of course, vary, but each example illustrates an easily understood (if unstated) generalization. The coming-home scene, for instance, illustrates the idea that dogs are loyal and enthusiastic while cats are independent and rebellious; the spilled-milk scene could be said to exemplify the point that dogs are more attuned to disapproval than cats are; and the vomit scene suggests that both animals eat things they shouldn't. Such generalizations are somewhat stereotypical, of course, but that's where the humor lies.

8
PROCESS ANALYSIS
Explaining Step by Step

This chapter provides a good sampling of process analyses, ranging from the directions in June Melby's "How to Make a Sno-Cone" (albeit directions that are not to be followed) to the informative analyses in Dan Koeppel's "Taking a Fall," Jessica Mitford's "Behind the Formaldehyde Curtain," and Dove's "Evolution." Mixing both types is Firoozeh Dumas's personal reflection in "Sweet, Sour, and Resentful," which opens the chapter and is paired with Melby. Both essays treat processes of food preparation—for houseguests in Dumas's case, customers in Melby's.

Incidentally, the opening of this chapter explains the *analysis* part of process analysis. We continue to introduce process analysis *before* analysis (Chap. 9) because we expect that many students find the former easier to understand. Process analysis thus becomes a way into analysis. But if you'd rather cover analysis itself first, nothing in the text discussion or essays will impede you.

FIROOZEH DUMAS
Sweet, Sour, and Resentful

Popular humorist Firoozeh Dumas has made it her mission to humanize Iranian people in the American consciousness, a mission that seems especially important in the context of political unrest and wars in the Middle East, nuclear proliferation, and terrorism.

Younger readers may not be familiar with the Iranian revolution to which Dumas refers or with the ensuing exodus of Iranian families to America and Americans' distrust of them in the 1970s and 1980s. We encourage students to research this background in the second writing suggestion, but you may also want to flesh out the basic outline provided in the gloss note on page 253: In the late 1970s fundamentalist Muslims fostered political and religious unrest in the country, culminating in a coup and the exile of American-backed Shah Reza Pahlavi. In his place revolutionaries installed Ayatollah Ruhollah Khomeini, who was determined to jettison Western influence and

restructure Iranian culture and politics around strict interpretation of Islamic religious rule. In 1979, Khomeini supporters captured fifty-three
Americans at the US embassy in Tehran, precipitating a hostage crisis that
lasted 444 days and ended in a botched rescue attempt and embarrassment
for the Carter administration; the hostages were released upon Ronald Reagan's inauguration in 1981. (During the same period Iran was attacked by
Iraq, leading to a brutal war that lasted until 1988.) Backlash against Iranians in the United States—the vast majority of whom had fled the violence
and repression in their country—was severe and included general hostility,
physical attacks, and demands for universal deportation.

We have paired "Sweet, Sour, and Resentful" with June Melby's "How to
Make a Sno-Cone" because both writers examine the frustrations that seem
often to accompany the task of feeding others. But if you assign Amy Tan's
"Fish Cheeks" (p. 110), another short piece about a family tradition surrounding food, you might prefer to have students compare and contrast
Dumas's essay with Tan's. Both writers, whose families immigrated to the
United States in the wake of political unrest, explore the difficulty of keeping
a tradition alive in their new country. Whereas Tan's difficulty stems from a
desire to fit in with her American peers, Dumas's mother's difficulty is purely
logistic. Nevertheless, the two essays make a similar point about the importance of maintaining family tradition and cultural ties. And although both
writers focus on the difficulty of adjusting to American life, Dumas states her
thesis explicitly while Tan leaves it up to readers to work out the significance
of her story.

QUESTIONS ON MEANING

1. The dinners provided an opportunity to orient recent Iranian immi-
    grants to life in California; they also allowed the hosts to share "the
    hospitality that Iranians so cherish" (par. 3) as well as stay connected
    to their roots. For both the hosts and the guests, the elaborate and
    traditional Persian meals helped to maintain a sense of community;
    they also served as a bittersweet "reminder of the life [they] had left
    behind" (10).
2. "As I watched my mother experience the same draining routine week
    after week, I decided that tradition is good only if it brings joy to all
    involved. . . . Sometimes, even our most cherished beliefs must evolve"
    (par. 12).
3. Dumas wants to share a belief that she developed as a witness to her
    mother's exhaustion and resentment—the importance of adapting tra-
    dition and beliefs when circumstances demand it. To some extent, she
    is also relating the impetus behind her own assimilation into American
    culture.
4. Dumas suggests potluck, or requiring guests to contribute to the meals
    by bringing food with them. Based on the way Dumas characterizes
    her (traditional, diplomatic, judgmental of inadequate or lazy cooks,
    perfectionist, and controlling), we doubt her mother would have relin-
    quished the role of hostess, no matter how much it strained her. How-
    ever, Dumas does relate the process in the past tense, so it's possible
    that her mother did, indeed, scale back her efforts—or that the number
    of guests dwindled after the first wave of Iranian immigration in the late
    1970s and early 1980s.

QUESTIONS ON WRITING STRATEGY

1. The introductory paragraphs establish the context behind the elaborate weekly meals: The guests who came to the author's parents' condo
every weekend were reluctant immigrants, possibly even refugees, displaced from their "real home" (par. 1) by war. At the same time, the
introduction indicates the parallels between Iranian culture and American culture to help make Iranians seem less "foreign" to readers—one
of Dumas's overriding goals as a writer.

2. "Sweet, Sour, and Resentful" was, as the introduction to the essay indicates, first published in the now-defunct *Gourmet*, an upscale magazine
for "foodies" (par. 5) that often featured complicated recipes and travel
essays. Dumas could reasonably assume, then, that her readers held a
strong interest in food and culture. Most readers of the magazine would
have had some experience preparing elaborate dishes, hunting down
elusive ingredients, and hosting large gatherings, so it's likely they
could empathize with the difficulties and stresses the author's mother
endured—if not, perhaps, her resentment.

3. Although Dumas identifies the "first step" as "preparing the herbs"
(par. 6), the process actually began with her father taking phone calls
and extending invitations to near strangers. Next came menu planning
(on Mondays) and softening the neighbors with gifts of food (par. 4), followed by Tuesday shopping trips that usually ended in frustration. With
all ingredients corralled, by midweek the author's parents began the simultaneous tasks of chopping by hand and frying herbs and onions (6);
mixing, cooking, and rolling the contents of stuffed grape leaves (7); and
preparing homemade yogurt and other side dishes (8). The guests would
arrive on the weekends, at which time Dumas's mother cooked and
drained the rice. The meals would then be served "buffet-style" (10) and
consumed in a matter of minutes (11). The final step was "fielding
thank-you phone calls from . . . guests" (12) and extending more invitations. With several overlapping stages occurring over the course of a
week, Dumas ensures coherence by providing clear time-markers and
transitions throughout her analysis, then circling back to the first stage
in her conclusion, implying that the process never ended.

4. By comparing bucolic local market days in Abadan with frustrating car-
dependent shopping trips in California, Dumas harkens back to her introduction and underscores her point that adjusting to life in the United
States was challenging and unpleasant for Iranian immigrants. At the
same time, she emphasizes how much additional trouble her mother
went to in order to give her guests a taste of home.

QUESTIONS ON LANGUAGE

1. Characteristically, Dumas's ironic tone in this essay borders on sarcasm but is nonetheless good-natured and appreciative. She tempers
the implied criticism of her parents' and guests' behavior with several self-deprecating remarks, which is where most of her humor lies.
You might ask students how the writer's attitude toward her parents
would have come across without the mocking comments about her own
abilities.

2. Dumas provides the Persian names for most of the dishes her mother
prepared and served to guests every week. In doing so, she emphasizes

the sense of home those meals provided for both her family and their guests. She ensures that American readers will understand the meaning by renaming each dish in an appositive phrase, such as "*fesenjan*, pomegranate stew with ground walnuts" (par. 4) or "*qormeh sabzi*, herb stew" (6).

3. In its literal sense a "litmus test" is a chemical process that measures the pH level of a substance to determine where it falls within a range from base to acid; colloquially, the phrase refers to a basis for making a judgment. Dumas uses the term in its colloquial meaning, but we like the echo of "sweet" (base) and "sour" (acidic) with the title and the concept's effectiveness in evoking her mother's bitterness about performing her tasks.

4. *Locavore*—a combination of *local* and the Latin *vorare*, "to eat"—is a recent coinage and does not appear in all dictionaries. The word refers to a politically and environmentally motivated movement advocating a preference for organic, local foods, rather than those that have been processed or shipped long distances. Students may be interested to know that Barbara Kingsolver (p. 430) is a strong proponent of local eating.

FIROOZEH DUMAS ON WRITING

Many students may identify with Dumas's childhood memory of soaking up observations in a room full of adults. Fewer will relate to her experience of feeling almost intoxicated with the inspiration to write them down. One way to simulate the experience is to have students write for ten minutes from observation or from a prompt. Try having them write about their favorite Halloween costume or the first time they can remember feeling guilty. The only rule is to keep the pencil moving (or the fingers typing) until you call time.

JUNE MELBY

How to Make a Sno-Cone

In this excerpt from a forthcoming comic memoir about her family's failed mini-golf course, June Melby combines tongue-in-cheek process analysis with personal reflection to contemplate a childhood living on and working in a lowbrow tourist attraction. We pair this essay with the work of another humorist, Firoozeh Dumas, because both "How to Make a Sno-Cone" and "Sweet, Sour, and Resentful" touch on food, family, and resentment in telling and insightful ways.

As we point out in the headnote and in the fourth writing topic, Melby's essay is a work in progress. An earlier draft is available on the author's Web site: *junemelby.com/artwork/2472512_Take_a_Break_for_a_Delicious_Sno _cone.html*. It might be instructive to spend some classroom time examining her revisions and discussing Melby's writing process in general. What has she changed, and why? What further revisions might she make?

QUESTIONS ON MEANING

1. Readers could certainly follow Melby's instructions (assuming they had access to an industrial ice grinder and flavoring syrups), but this essay comes from her memoir-in-progress. The writer's purpose is to reflect on her experiences as a child.
2. The statement is meant both literally and figuratively. Although there is a real risk of injuring customers with plastic shards mixed in with ice, the warning and Melby's follow-up statement, "Don't make them choke . . ." (par. 1), reveal her feelings of hostility toward those customers.
3. The portrait is not a flattering one. Melby portrays her customers as clueless tourists who are easily fooled (pars. 1, 13), who "like to feel important" and exude a sense of privilege (pars. 1, 8, 9), who don't know a good Sno-cone from a bad one (6, 8), and who could be litigious (14). At the same time, however, she reveals feelings of jealousy in her tender description, in paragraphs 9–12, of a vacationing father's loving relationship with his daughter.
4. Melby's thesis, it would seem, is that she hated working in her parents' Snack Shack and would have preferred a more typical childhood.

QUESTIONS ON WRITING STRATEGY

1. The essay mingles both points of view. The present tense and the references to "Mom" and "Dad" indicate a child's perspective, but the vocabulary of the first paragraph and the detachment of the last, along with the insights into customers' needs and emotions, suggest an adult reflecting on the past. The choice seems appropriate, although some readers may find the mixture confusing: It shows that Melby is still coming to understand her experience and has not yet finished maturing.
2. In the instructive passages (pars. 1–8, 13) she is giving instructions to a new employee—specifically, one of her sisters (students may need to be reminded to read the headnotes before the essay to grasp this information). The more reflective paragraphs (9–12, 14) seem to be addressed to herself.
3. The instructions are clear enough, if presented in a deliberately muddled order. To make a Sno-cone, a person should grind enough ice for one serving (par. 5) while being careful not to damage the plastic scoop (1), pack the ice into a ball if necessary (6, 8), ask the customer what flavor he or she wants (2–3), apply three squirts of flavoring slowly and in stages (4), hand the finished product to the customer slowly (8), and wipe the machine clean as necessary (13).
4. Melby's intention is to step back and reflect on the implications of her experience, implying a judgment that her parents probably shouldn't have had their children making Sno-cones. Some readers will likely find the conclusion unsatisfying. As an excerpt from a longer work, the last paragraph does feel somewhat lingering, yet we think it creates a nice, dreamlike closing impression.
5. Melby's descriptions appeal to every sense but smell.

QUESTIONS ON LANGUAGE

1. Paragraphs 1–4, part of 6, 8, and 13–14 are written in the second person; paragraphs 5–7 are in the first-person plural, 9 is in the third person, and 10–12 are in the first-person singular. The shifts are problematic

and some readers will find them jarring (we encourage students to try resolving them in the fourth writing prompt, labeled "Critical Writing"). Melby does seem to have a logic to the shifts, however: The instructions themselves are written in the imperative, mixing in *we* when Melby refers to her family; the first-person singular passage reverts to a specific memory. Overall the effect is conversational and creates a sense of daydreaming, which we imagine the author did a good bit of while working the stand.

2. Melby gives the machine human qualities in her introduction and her conclusion: "ice can stick like a wet tongue on a swing set" (par. 1), "The roar of hungry blades" (14). As personification tends to do, these figures of speech make the machine seem alive—and in Melby's case, threatening.

3. Melby uses *wafts* to describe the transmission of sound (an appropriate usage), but most readers will associate the verb with smells. It could be argued, then, that her descriptions in this essay (see question 5 on writing strategy) appeal to all five of the senses.

DAN KOEPPEL

Taking a Fall

Students should enjoy Koeppel's highly entertaining romp into survival strategies for those unlucky enough to fall from an airplane unexpectedly. In just a few pages the author traces the physical and biological processes of free-fall, at the same time providing details from physics and aviation history and showing what research has taught us about statistical probabilities. It sounds unreadable, but Koeppel pulls it off wonderfully. In his hands what could be dry, impenetrable science turns amusing and informative, even life saving.

At the same time, Koeppel offers glorious proof that researched writing need not be dull or mechanical (we encourage students to analyze his use of sources in the fourth writing topic). Drawing on sources both popular (*Mythbusters*, even!) and scholarly, his essay is a model of synthesis. Koeppel paraphrases and summarizes materials in such a way that anybody can follow their ideas, and quotes only the most delectable language. At no point does he lose his delightfully insouciant voice.

In case some of your students resist science writing, even comical science writing, you might start off by dividing the class into small groups to work on the first and third questions on meaning. When they see clearly *why* Koeppel goes the trouble of explaining the intricacies of terminal velocity, students will be able to relax and enjoy the ride.

QUESTIONS ON MEANING

1. Koeppel writes to explain and to entertain. His use of the second person for an informative process analysis is unusual, but by addressing readers directly he engages them in a process that might otherwise come

across as theoretical and dry. He doesn't expect that readers will actually need to use the information, as he makes clear in his thesis and in the middle of the essay: "Granted, the odds of surviving a six-mile plummet are extraordinarily slim, but at this point you've got nothing to lose by understanding your situation" (par. 5); "here's some supplemental information, though be warned that none of it will help you at this point" (17).

2. A "wreckage rider" is somebody whose fall is cushioned and slowed by virtue of "being attached to a chunk of the plane" (par. 5). Such crash victims have a higher chance of survival.

3. As Koeppel explains it, *terminal velocity* is the point at which a faller reaches the highest speed of descent. (The word *terminal*, in this case, refers to a limit, rather than an end.) If a person hits that limit while still falling, the possibility of slowing ("drag") and reducing the intensity of impact comes into play. This is why, Koeppel says, a person is more likely to survive a fall from an airplane than a fall from, say, a tall building.

4. Judging by the time-markers in the essay's headings, the fall Koeppel analyzes takes three minutes and twenty-five seconds—almost as much time he estimates it should take a person to read the essay (pars. 8, 17). (Note that a few minutes might be enough for a first quick read, but we would argue that students should take significantly more time to fully digest his work.) The connection helps make it clear just how long three and a half minutes actually is, while also stressing to readers that Koeppel is unfolding events in (almost) real time.

5. Koeppel's straightforward thesis appears in paragraph 5: "Granted, the odds of surviving a six-mile plummet are extraordinarily slim, but at this point you've got nothing to lose by understanding your situation." One might say that his point is to have fun with some useless information.

QUESTIONS ON WRITING STRATEGY

1. Koeppel opens and closes his essay by having readers imagine themselves sleeping on an airplane. By putting them in the situation he means to explore, he makes a potentially abstract concept concrete and understandable. At the same time, the framing device reassures readers that the rare horrors he examines were nothing but a dream.

2. The headings break the process into its stages, both in terms of time and height.

3. Koeppel's analysis of what a person endures in a six-mile fall shows that he assumes a general audience. He explains the process carefully and with no small amount of cheek, using simple language and humor to convey complicated scientific concepts. He defines certain physics terms, such as *terminal velocity* (par. 7), and he draws comparisons to sports, such as martial arts (13) and cliff diving (15) to help clarify his points. He does assume, however, that his audience is well educated and somewhat knowledgeable about science, using terms such as *hypoxia* (4), *friction* (12), *cranial* (16), *tonus* (19), and *subcutaneous* (19) without defining them.

4. Koeppel cites eight examples of people who have survived falls from airplanes: Vesna Vulovic (pars. 5, 18), Alan Magee (6, 11), an unnamed sky diver (11), Yasuhiro Kubo (14), Mohammed el-Fateh Osman (18), Bahia Bakari (18), Nicholas Alkemade (20), and Juliane Koepcke (21–23). Ranging in detail from quick mention to extended consideration, the

examples prove his claim that survival is possible and help him to illustrate each of his recommended moves; they're also quite gripping and morbidly entertaining.

QUESTIONS ON LANGUAGE

1. The connotations of *banzai* for most readers will bring up images of reckless attack, as Koeppel intends. Students may enjoy learning that according to *The American Heritage Dictionary*, the Japanese battle cry translates into "(may you live) ten thousand years!"—a nice touch of irony, we think.
2. Koeppel deftly overshadows formal, scientific language and technical terms with giddily colloquial expressions, conversational sentence structures, and black humor. Taken together, the writer's language choices clearly communicate the details of a complicated scientific process while making that process surprisingly entertaining and easily understandable, even for general readers with no background in science.
3. The allusion is to acrobatics, which Koeppel first brings up as good training for fall survival in paragraph 13. In gymnastics (and also in figure skating) "sticking the landing" means completing a jump gracefully, without wobbling or falling down.
4. Although Koeppel uses a few figures of speech, such as the metaphor "a semiprotective cocoon of debris" (par. 6) and the simile "[h]itting the ocean is essentially the same as colliding with a sidewalk" (11), he relies much more heavily on literal images which are no less vivid (although admittedly gruesome) for being real. Some of our favorites include Vesna Vulovic "wedged between her seat, a catering trolley, a section of aircraft, and the body of another crew member, landing on—then sliding down—a snowy incline" (5); "Magee's landing on the stone floor of that French train station . . . softened by the skylight he crashed through" (11); the "mucky, plant-covered surface" of swamps (11); the clear description of the classic sky diver pose (12); and Juliane Koepcke waking "on the jungle floor, strapped into her seat, surrounded by fallen holiday gifts" (21).

JESSICA MITFORD

Behind the Formaldehyde Curtain

For that soporific class that sits and looks at you, here is a likely rouser. If Mitford can't get any response out of them, they're in a league with her Mr. Jones, and you might as well devote the rest of the course to silent study periods. Sometimes, it is true, a class confronted with this essay will just sit there like people in whose midst a large firecracker has been hurled, watching it sputter. Give them time to respond with five or ten minutes to freewrite about whatever Mitford's essay first inspires them to say. Then have them trade papers in groups of three or four, read the papers, and discuss their responses with each other. You can turn these smaller group discussions into a whole-class conversation whenever it seems appropriate.

Teaching Mitford's essay invites one possible danger: that someone in the class, having recently experienced the death of a loved one, will find Mitford's macabre humor cruel and offensive. We once received a painful letter from a student in Wenatchee, Washington, who complained bitterly about this "hideous" essay. "My husband was crushed in a logging accident," she wrote. "If Mitford also learned a little about grief, she would know that those people who view a body have an easier time with grief than those who don't. She wouldn't hate funeral directors. I guess Mitford would have had me view my husband's mangled body, but I'm glad the funeral director prepared his body for viewing."

How can you answer such a protest? Before assigning this essay for reading, you might ask the class whether anyone present has suffered a death in the family. At least warn students what to expect. Anyone recently bereaved might be given the option of skipping both Mitford's essay and the class discussion. If a student in mourning reads Mitford's essay anyway and protests its seeming callousness, you might see whether that student feels impelled to write a personal response to Mitford and her essay—as our correspondent did so effectively. The first and fourth writing suggestions may be helpful.

The painstaking legwork that Mitford did before she wrote *The American Way of Death* is documented in *Poison Penmanship: The Gentle Art of Muckraking* (1979). Much of her information came from professional journals, such as *Casket & Sunnyside, Mortuary Management*, and *Concept: The Journal of Creative Ideas for Cemeteries*. While laying stress on the value of such research, Mitford adds that a muckraker profits from sheer luck. A friend happened to recall a conversation with an undertaker when she was arranging for her brother-in-law's funeral. She had insisted on the cheapest redwood coffin available, but the undertaker objected. The deceased was too tall to fit into it; a costly coffin was required. When she continued to insist, the undertaker said, "Oh, all right, we'll use the redwood, but we'll have to cut off his feet." This grim example of high-pressure sales tactics supplied Mitford's book with one of its "more shining jewels."

When Mitford first showed her analysis of the embalming process (as a manuscript chapter for *The American Way of Death*) to her British and her American publishers, "it was met with instantaneous and thunderous disapproval from the editors on both sides of the Atlantic; this chapter is too revolting—it must go, they said." She insisted on keeping it, and lost the publishers. A year after Simon & Schuster brought out the book, she recalls, "those self-same embalming passages were chosen for inclusion in a college textbook on writing. Well! Of course I felt vindicated. The obvious moral is that although *some* editors can *sometimes* perform wonders in improving your work, in the last analysis your own judgment must prevail" (from *Poison Penmanship*, pp. 22–23).

QUESTIONS ON MEANING

1. In case anyone finds this essay repulsive and resents your assigning it, we suggest you begin by inviting reactions of all kinds. Let students kick the essay about, and, if they hate it, encourage them to say why. Almost certainly some will find it hilarious and will defend it as humor. Others will probably say that they didn't like it, that it's unpleasant, but that it tells truths we ought to know. You'll usually get more reactions if you are slow to advance your own. If the sense of the meeting should

be vehemently against this essay, you may care to stick up for it (or you may want to skip on to the next selection in a hurry). But if, as is likely, most students are intrigued by it, they'll indicate this by their reactions, and your ensuing class discussion can ride on this momentum.

2. She speculates that perhaps undertakers keep it secret for fear that patrons, knowing what it is, wouldn't want it done (par. 6).

3. "To make the corpse presentable for viewing in a suitably costly container" (par. 2). Most of the usual obstacles to presentability are itemized in paragraphs 14–18: the effects of mutilation, emaciation, and disease.

4. If the subject was not dead, the undertaker will have killed him.

5. Her purpose is to attack the custom of embalming (and to chide the society that permits it). Mitford finds Americans "docile" and "ignorant" in tolerating such a procedure (par. 4). From her concluding paragraphs (23–27), we infer that she would urge Americans not to embalm, to admit the fact of death, and to bury the dead in closed coffins, as is done in much of the rest of the Western world.

QUESTIONS ON WRITING STRATEGY

1. Mitford's tone is cheerful scorn. Her verbs for the treatments inflicted on the corpse—"sprayed," "sliced," "pierced," "pickled," and so on—clearly show that she regards the process as ridiculous. The ironic phrase "suitably costly container" strongly hints that she regards morticians as racketeers.

2. She is determined to show that if we knew what embalming and restoration entailed—its every detail—we wouldn't stand for it.

3. The body becomes a character in her drama—whether it is that of an adult or a child.

4. Mitford's opening sentence indicates the start of a time sequence, and students should easily be able to find the ensuing time-markers. Her favorites are the small words "next" and "now," and most of the paragraphs about Mr. Jones contain one or the other.

5. Her audience is American general readers, whom she distinguishes from "funeral men" in paragraph 6.

6. The quotation in paragraph 3 suggests that embalming (and all it entails) may be illegal; the one in paragraph 10 suggests that dolling up the corpse is more important to the mortician than possibly saving a life. Mr. Kriege (quoted in par. 22) makes the undertaker sound like a funeral football coach, in whose hands the corpse is a helpless ball. In offering these quotations, Mitford hangs the ethics and professional behavior of morticians by their own words and once more questions the desirability of embalming.

7. Mitford's passive verbs are to us very effective. They keep the focus on the grisly process, and they undermine her target actors, funeral directors.

8. The groups are "surgery" tools, tissue chemicals, restorative cosmetics and plasters, and props and stabilizers. The groups make the catalog of equipment and supplies more intelligible and reinforce Mitford's point about the pretentions and absurdities of the process.

QUESTIONS ON LANGUAGE

1. By alluding to the Prince of Denmark's speech with skull in hand (*Hamlet* 5.1), Mitford suggests that perhaps Yorick's "counterpart of today" is

another luckless jester or clown. This theatrical allusion also enforces her metaphor of the drama that begins and the curtain that must be lifted.

2. Mitford delights in citing undertakers' euphemisms. The morticians, she implies, dislike plain words—in paragraph 20 she quotes one who warns against creating the impression "that the body is in a box" (which, of course, is fact). There seems an ironic discrepancy between the attitudes expressed in the last two sentences and Mitford's own view. A funeral, she implies, shouldn't be a "real pleasure" but an occasion for grief. Death isn't an opposing football team.

3. To the general reader, these brand names carry unpleasant connotations, and a lively class discussion may be devoted to unraveling what these are. Lyf-Lyk tint seems cutesy in its spelling, like some drugstore cosmetic item. Other brand names seem practical and unfeeling: Throop Foot Positioner, Armstrong Face Former and Denture Replacer. Porto-Lift and the Glide Easy casket carriage stress slickness and efficiency. Classic Beauty Ultra Metal Casket Bier seems absurdly grand. Mitford's purpose is to attack our sympathy and tolerance for the undertaker's art, and certainly these names rub us the wrong way.

4. "Dermasurgeon" (par. 8) is a euphemism Mitford especially relishes. Although it tries to dignify the mortician, Mitford points out how (unlike the surgeon he imitates) the embalmer acquired his training in a quick post–high-school course.

JESSICA MITFORD ON WRITING

Surprisingly often, authors are in total agreement when they discuss the art of writing. Mitford takes the common view that to write well, you have to care deeply about your subject. (We love that British phrase "besotted by.") Like so many writers, both amateur and professional, she knows that writing is hard work. Like George Orwell, muckraker Mitford sees writing as a valuable tool for righting the world's wrongs.

From what Mitford says about her research for *The American Way of Death*, students can learn how important it is to get the facts straight when doing an exposé. The author makes clear as well that in writing, as in most other activities, a sense of humor is a valuable asset.

DOVE

Evolution

In this clever bit of viral marketing, Dove reveals the extent to which images of women are manipulated by the media, arguing that (other) advertisers have created false standards of beauty. Although most of us are aware that photographs are routinely tweaked for publication, the degrees of alteration in "Evolution" will surprise—and possibly even outrage—many viewers. Others, accustomed to digital manipulations by the media, might not be troubled by the practice at all.

For the most part Dove's "Campaign for Real Beauty" has been met with praise for showcasing "real" women in its advertising and for attempting to redefine beauty with more realistic criteria. (The campaign worked, too: In just the first year after its launch Dove's sales increased by some 5%.) Yet some of your students may raise the criticism that many viewers have: Dove's parent company, Unilever, has been known to use blatantly sexist images in ads for other products, such as Axe body spray. You might use this point to spark discussion of the contradictions inherent in the campaign: Although Dove questions contemporary standards of beauty promoted by advertisers, the company itself makes and advertises beauty products. What do your students make of the paradox? How, if at all, can it be resolved?

QUESTIONS ON MEANING AND STRATEGY

1. The video's purpose is to expose and criticize the manipulations, both physical and digital, that advertisers use when creating images to promote beauty and fashion products. The "perception of beauty" that results, claims Dove, is "distorted"—not only entirely false but also unattainable. (Judging from comments attached to the video on *YouTube*, a surprising number of viewers miss the point entirely, mistaking this for an actual advertisement for the fictional "Fasel" makeup named in the billboard at the end. We expect your students are more savvy than that.)

2. Seconds 0:19 to 0:39 show how a team of makeup artists and hair stylists transform a woman's physical appearance; the next ten seconds show how a photograph of the resulting look is further transformed with computer software (such as *Photoshop*). Most viewers will be startled by the digital alterations that take an already attractive image and render it completely divorced from reality—particularly the lengthening of the model's neck, the enlargement of her eyes, and the slimming of her shoulders.

3. The word *evolution* alludes to Darwin's theory of the gradual process, over several generations, of a species' biological improvement. The irony in the title is that the supposed perfection achieved for the model is quick and illusory; the video suggests that our standards of beauty are actually degrading to humans.

4. The video contrasts three versions of the model's face: a natural look, a glamorized look, and a digitally enhanced look. The final, billboard image bears no resemblance to the woman's actual appearance (and not much resemblance to the original photograph). The comparisons support Dove's thesis, stated in the frames from 1:00 to 1:05, that "our perception of beauty is distorted."

9
DIVISION OR ANALYSIS
Slicing into Parts

Division and classification have long been combined and confused in composition textbooks, so it is no wonder that some authors, some teachers, and many students cannot tell them apart. The true loser has seemed to be division. Indeed, some texts dispose of division as the mere servant of classification, the operation required to sort (divide) things into classes.

At the same time, first-year writing classes are absorbed in critical thinking, reading, and writing. Scholarly journals, textbooks, and teachers are inventing and experimenting with ways to teach these crucial skills. Yet all along we have had the means to introduce the skills through the Cinderella of the division and classification pair. Though generally treated, when treated at all, as a simple cutting operation, division is of course *analysis*. And what is analysis but the basis of criticism?

We have tried to rescue division/analysis and give it useful work in the composition course. We have, most noticeably, given the method its own chapter (and classification its own), in which we stress analytic thinking and discuss critical thinking. We have also made much more explicit the analytical underpinnings of the other methods of development, including (but not only) classification. (Two of these related methods—comparison/contrast and process analysis—continue to be covered before this chapter on the theory that they may be more familiar and accessible to students, even without explicit discussion of analysis. Of course, you may change the order of chapters if you see it differently.)

The magic of e-Pages allows us to bring back Jamaica Kincaid's provocative short story "Girl"—as read by the author herself. We now pair "Vampires Never Die" by Guillermo del Toro and Chuck Hogan with "Our Zombies, Ourselves" by James Parker, for what students should find an irresistibly fascinating look at monster legends in the media. Robert Lipsyte's "Jock Culture" forms a bridge from simple division to critical analysis, illustrated by Francine Prose's "What Words Can Tell."

GUILLERMO DEL TORO AND CHUCK HOGAN
Vampires Never Die

Students may be surprised to discover that the creators of such pulp fiction as *Hell Boy*, *Blade II*, and *Prince of Thieves* are also capable of writing a poetic, sophisticated, and seriously academic literary analysis of a trend in popular culture. In just a few pages, del Toro and Hogan survey the complete history of vampire lore and offer a fresh take on what it reveals about the human condition, especially within contemporary culture. Some of their literary and philosophical allusions, as well as their unstated reliance on the psychological theories of Carl Jung, may wash over students, yet the analysis as a whole remains compelling and understandable. (We've glossed those allusions that seem most important to following the authors' ideas; others we leave to students to investigate if they're so inclined.) Fans of current vampire stories will surely be interested to learn of the legacy behind them and be intrigued by the idea that those stories could mean anything more than just good entertainment.

"Vampires Never Die" forms a pair with James Parker's "Our Zombies, Ourselves," an examination of similar monster mythologies on television and in the movies. You may wish to begin class discussion with the question likely to be on many students' minds: Does popular culture, especially something as seemingly trivial as vampire fiction and zombie lore, merit academic study? Why, or why not? What can we learn from analyses such as these? Or, as an alternative, you might consider encouraging students to find and share criticism of del Toro's and Hogan's own literary and filmic productions. To what extent has their creative work been the subject of similar kinds of interpretation? And does "Vampires Never Die" make readers more—or less—inclined to read the authors' collaborative vampire novels for pleasure?

QUESTIONS ON MEANING

1. There's no question that "Vampires Never Die" serves as clever and well-conceived publicity for the authors' vampire trilogy. However, the authors also examine the larger cultural meanings of vampire stories in general, over time and across cultures. The essay is a sophisticated psychological analysis of one particular literary genre.
2. "Monsters, like angels, are invoked by our individual and collective needs. Today, much as during that gloomy summer in 1816, we feel the need to seek their cold embrace" (par. 7).
3. The authors posit that the concept of vampiric immortality fills a universal psychological and spiritual void. By tapping into deep-seated fears and desires, vampire stories both reassure us and "provide the possibility of mystery in our mundane . . . lives" (par. 16). The particulars of those fears and desires might change over time and across cultures, but the basic truths of death and sexuality do not. Vampires, say del Toro and Hogan, represent a powerful mixture of the two most profound aspects of human existence.

4. Students should be able to infer from the context that a *social construct* is any custom, taboo, philosophy, or law designed to govern human conduct by repressing base urges. (The idea also refers to any cultural infusion of meaning onto abstractions, but the authors aren't using it that way.) The concept is important to del Toro and Hogan's analysis because they see the vampire character as one released from the pressures of civilization, who allows human beings to reconnect vicariously with their primal instincts.

5. Although science appears to be rational and objective, new technologies can seem mysterious, even ominous to laypersons. Even those with a scientific mindset tend to embrace innovation and understanding as a faith in itself and, in so doing, to "experience fear and awe again, and to believe in the things [they] cannot see" (par. 15).

QUESTIONS ON WRITING STRATEGY

1. Writing for the *New York Times*, del Toro and Hogan assume an audience of well-educated readers with wide-ranging interests. At the same time, they assume a familiarity with popular culture, from classic novels to *American Idol*, and an immersion in communication technologies. Some students may object that several of the authors' allusions go above readers' heads, but other students will surely appreciate the apparent respect for their intelligence.

2. Their principle of analysis is the question of what makes vampires appeal across time and culture. The two basic elements identified by del Toro and Hogan are lust and death, introduced as "romantic hero" and "undead monster" (par. 4) and reiterated in the conclusion as "Eros and Thanatos fused together in archetypal embrace" (16). Subsets of those elements include primal fear (6), immortality (8), adaptability (10), uncertainty (13–14), superstition (15), and spirituality (16).

3. Their point is that the folklore taps into something deeply personal—yet primal and universal. That the first written story might have stemmed from deep-seated emotional, psychological, and sexual tensions is therefore highly significant (even if students don't recognize Jung's theory of the collective unconscious lurking behind the authors' assumptions).

4. The single word *forever* evokes immortality, both of vampires as individual characters and as a universal cultural need. Coming on the heels of a paragraph about faith and spirituality, it also echoes the concluding sentiment of Christian prayers: *Amen.*

5. The authors compare two eras "of great technical revolution" in paragraphs 13–15. Both in the early nineteenth century and now, people were confronted with "new gadgets . . . , various forms of communication . . . , and cutting-edge science" (par. 13). Del Toro and Hogan name those new technologies in the case of the nineteenth century but leave it to readers to fill in the details for the twenty-first. In either case, such innovations were both liberating and disorienting, leaving us "still ultimately vulnerable to our fates and our nightmares" (15).

QUESTIONS ON LANGUAGE

1. For a definition of *mash-up*, students may need to turn to the Internet or to a recent dictionary of slang. The term, similar in meaning to *remix*,

applies to the creative process that combines elements of multiple existing productions (songs, film clips, video clips, and the like) to create something new, a technique often used by avant-garde musicians and filmmakers. We find it interesting that del Toro and Hogan manage to apply a cutting-edge (and controversial) creative trend to "ancient myth" and folklore.

2. Traditionally, *twitter* means to chirp or speak excitedly, but the word also refers to the recent and fast-growing social networking application. The verb is especially effective, given that del Toro and Hogan are writing about the psychological effects of fast-paced technology and overwhelming torrents of communication.

3. *Alchemy* refers to medieval beliefs that an as-yet-undiscovered chemical process could transform base metals, lead in particular, into gold; the hope was that such transformations would form the foundation for an elixir for everlasting youth. The metaphor fits the vampire subject very well, both in the idea that commingling of blood would transform both biter and victim into something better and that the transformation would enable immortality; it also reinforced the suggestion that science is superstition (see par. 15). The authors return to the metaphor in the next paragraph (9).

GUILLERMO DEL TORO AND CHUCK HOGAN ON WRITING

Del Toro and Hogan provide valuable insight into their collaborative writing process. Their committal "bro-hug" and their banter during the interview indicate a rapport between the two men. Is a friendly relationship a prerequisite for the deep (and sometimes ruthless) revision del Toro and Hogan do? Students may want to discuss best practices for giving feedback and ways to approach suggested revisions with an open mind, especially if peer revision is part of your course.

JAMES PARKER

Our Zombies, Ourselves

With its abundance of allusions and jargon drawn from literary criticism, Parker's whimsical essay may prove difficult to students. And yet they should have fun with "Our Zombies, Ourselves," even if much of Parker's meaning eludes them. Who doesn't enjoy a good look at zombies these days?

We pair this selection with "Vampires Never Die," by Guillermo del Toro and Chuck Hogan, for what should be obvious reasons. Vampires and zombies pervade popular culture at the moment (even the normally staid Centers for Disease Control and Prevention circulated a tongue-in-cheek guide to surviving a zombie apocalypse). We expect that college students will find both essays interesting and relevant, maybe even entertaining. It may surprise students that such characters can support academic study, but the authors of these two pieces do an exemplary job of lending intellectual rigor to a potentially frivolous topic.

A good place to begin discussion is to focus on the journal prompt. Zombies, in some cultures, are taken to be very real. Why would anyone believe they exist? What kinds of folk tales or urban legends have students heard in their hometowns or at school? How do they compare to zombie stories? Campus folklore can be especially evocative: If a popular legend or rumor circulates at your school, encourage students to investigate it, perhaps visiting the site involved or searching the campus newspaper's archives for details, and then report on what they learn.

QUESTIONS ON MEANING

1. Parker reveals his purpose in paragraph 3: He was prompted to write about zombies by the DVD release of the first season of *The Walking Dead*, "the surprise cable smash" of 2010 (and still one of the most popular programs on television). His essay is an oblique review of the show, which readers can see he admires and enjoys.
2. Although the first appearance he cites seems to be the shuffling masses in T. S. Eliot's poem *The Waste Land* (1922), and although he acknowledges that zombies figured in the book *The Magic Island* (1929) and the movie *White Zombie* (1932), Parker claims that the "modern zombie" of popular culture was born in George A. Romero's cult favorite film *Night of the Living Dead* (1968) and really took off at the start of the twenty-first century. He seems to think that the character should have been able to gain traction with the postwar industrialization of the early twentieth century, but suggests that the subject required a "trash visionary" (par. 1)—a less serious artist than someone like Eliot—to grasp the interest of a broad audience.
3. In Romero's film, zombies are the result of "radioactive contamination from an exploded space probe" (par. 5). Parker's point is that modern technology is the impetus behind and the propagator of today's cultural sense of not living fully, of a general zombified malaise, much as Guillermo del Toro and Chuck Hogan argue (p. 291) that new technologies explain the popularity of vampires in the late nineteenth century.
4. Zombies, Parker says, have been seen as metaphors for "the consumer, the mob, the Other, the proletariat, the weight of life, the dead soul" (par. 6), but he argues that they have no meaning: "A zombie is *always* just a zombie" (8). At most, he suggests, zombies represent the current national mood—a generalized sense of exhaustion and purposelessness in life.
5. Parker's thesis appears in paragraph 8: "The blow-'em-all-away success of *The Walking Dead* is no mystery: The show, and the comic-book series by Robert Kirkman on which it's based, mark a triumphant return to zombie orthodoxy, to the non-galloping zombie and his icons." He withholds it because he spends his time in the essay building to this idea, broadening his focus beyond *The Walking Dead* to establish what he means by "zombie orthodoxy" and to explain its appeal.

QUESTIONS ON WRITING STRATEGY

1. As we mention in the headnote to this essay, Parker was writing for his entertainment column in *The Atlantic Monthly*, a fairly intellectual

magazine focused on culture and politics. Accordingly, he assumes a well-educated audience grounded in literary theory and basic history, but who also happen to enjoy "trash" (par. 1) media productions, possibly as guilty pleasure. Students will probably fit the latter part of his assumptions, if not the former.

2. Students may not recognize the allusion to the (supposedly) Freudian disclaimer that "sometimes a cigar is just a cigar" (see the first question on language), but Parker is saying that zombies carry no deep symbolic meaning; they just are. He outlines the basic elements of zombiedom in paragraph 5: "the wobbliness of the zombie, the terrible mobility of the virus, the pockets of survival, the squall of information as the grid collapses." Each of these elements is elaborated on in more detail in the rest of the essay. Zombies, as Parker portrays them, walk unsteadily (pars. 1–2), cannot be stopped easily (3), lack free will (4–5), crave "human flesh" (5), cannot speak (6), and multiply their number by taking victims (7).

3. For evidence Parker cites multiple media productions centered on zombie lore: George A. Romero's *Night of the Living Dead* (pars. 2, 5), a spate of parodies and video games (3), the novel *World War Z*, the Béla Lugosi movie *White Zombie* (4), a punk song from the 1980s (6), and the movies *28 Days Later, Dawn of the Dead,* and *Shaun of the Dead.* We know he takes his subject seriously because he also draws on literary and quasi-scholarly works (T. S. Eliot's *The Waste Land,* 1, and William Seabrook's *The Magic Island,* 4), claims that "zombie studies" is an emerging academic field (4), and uses terminology from literary theory (see the second question on language). But as serious as he is, readers can tell that Parker is also having fun.

4. Parker uses topic sentences as transitions that preview clearly the focus of each paragraph; repeats key words such as *zombie* (and our favorite invented variation, *zombificently,* in par. 4), *shuffle/wobble/plod /bumble/lurch, slow,* and *dead;* and deftly circles back to his introduction with his concluding sentences: "He crookedly advances. He's taking his time. But he'll get there" (8).

5. Parker compares the movies, examples of two distinct variations on the classic zombie popularized by *Night of the Living Dead,* to lead to his point that the show *The Walking Dead* and the comic-book series it's based on "mark a triumphant return to zombie orthodoxy" (par. 8).

QUESTIONS ON LANGUAGE

1. The allusion to *The Waste Land* is obscure; we include the full stanza with the question because students undoubtedly won't catch it (it blew past us on the first few readings, and then we had to look it up). Parker seems to expect that the one line will evoke for readers an image of the walking dead and his implication that Eliot somehow presaged the emergence of zombies in fiction; we think that's unlikely. The same may or may not be the case for his several other allusions. These include his title, a reference to the 1970s self-help book *Our Bodies, Ourselves;* his oblique reference to World War I in the introduction (which we have glossed for students); "the Age of Aquarius" (1); the Jungian theory of the collective unconscious (3); the "horror-flick tradition" in which immorality and irreverence are punished (5); the concept of "the Other" (6); the sly reference to Freud with "sometimes a zombie is just a zombie" (8); and of course the zombie films and books Parker brings

up. Students may catch some of these allusions, and will probably miss most of the non-zombie ones, but they certainly reveal the depth of Parker's analysis and show that he knows his theory.

2. Notice how many of Parker's words hail from literary criticism: *proverb, metaphysically, alienated* (from the Marxist school), *canons, postmodernity, semiotic, proletariat* (Marxism, again), *existential, pathos.* Parker's allusions to Carl Jung (par. 3) and Sigmund Freud (8) add the psychological school of theory to the mix.

3. Parker mixes academic vocabulary and colloquial expressions with a dose of cliché (see James Parker on Writing, p. 303); his tone strikes us as simultaneously lyrical and fun. Neither the diction nor the tone are appropriate for a formal analysis, but Parker doesn't mean to be formal. He's having a good time and means for his readers to enjoy themselves, as well.

JAMES PARKER ON WRITING

Parker makes an interesting, if debatable, point that some clichés convey depths of meaning more effectively and more efficiently than fresh language is capable of. A risk of exposing students to his argument, of course, is that they may fail to make distinctions between those phrases that are "laden with experience" and those that are merely trite. You might ask them to dispute his claims, arguing among themselves for the benefits of fresher, creative language.

ROBERT LIPSYTE
Jock Culture

While sports are an integral part of American culture, Robert Lipsyte argues in this compelling essay, the values instilled by competition are harmful and counterproductive, both for those who embrace them and those who don't.

The sports fans in your class will likely have a strong reaction against the writer's negative assessment of "Jock Culture," while the indifferent will probably be relieved to find a sympathetic friend—especially if your school has a vibrant athletic program. It may be worth reminding both camps that although Lipsyte self-identifies as a "Puke," he has made his career writing about sports.

"Jock Culture" is one of several pieces in *The Brief Bedford Reader* that touch on sports (albeit the only one that's overtly critical). To appease students hostile to Lipsyte's criticisms, you may wish to assign his essay in conjunction with one or more of the following: Maya Angelou, "Champion of the World" (p. 104); Annie Dillard, "The Chase" (p. 114); Brad Manning, "Arm Wrestling with My Father" (p. 138); Dave Barry, "Batting Clean-Up and Striking Out" (p. 220). How well does Lipsyte's analysis hold up when compared with the positive feelings others have derived from watching or participating in athletics?

QUESTIONS ON MEANING

1. Lipsyte describes an interview he held with Columbia University's crew coach in the midst of student occupations of the school's buildings in protest of the Vietnam War. It would seem that Stowe was involved in breaking up the demonstrations. The student occupations are relevant to Lipsyte's subject for several reasons. First, his interview with Stowe introduced him to the concept of Jocks and Pukes: Stowe, of course, is an example of the former; and Lipsyte (and the protesting students) of the latter. By placing his analysis in the context of the Vietnam War, Lipsyte also highlights the conflicts between athleticism and intellectualism and previews his claim that Jock Culture can be blamed, at least in part, for violence and warfare.

2. Jock Culture is the set of values instilled by devotion to overly competitive team sports: "submission to authority, winning by any means necessary, and group cohesion" (par. 4). Sports themselves, Lipsyte acknowledges, are beneficial (5), but Jock Culture debases them through "greed and desperate competition" (6) that turn people against each other in other aspects of life, particularly business, school, and government. It pits aggression against cooperation and results in "the cheating, the lying, the amorality" (12) that seems to mark contemporary society.

3. Lipsyte introduces his thesis in paragraph 4: "Boys—and more and more girls—who accept Jock Culture values often go on to flourish in a competitive sports environment that requires submission to authority, winning by any means necessary, and group cohesion." Implied in this statement and developed in the rest of the essay is Lipsyte's claim that those values are damaging to society as a whole. In a culture focused on winning, everybody—Jocks, Pukes, men, women, business leaders, workers, professionals, artists, intellectuals, and children especially—loses.

4. "Jock Culture" is an argument against aggressive, competitive values in American business and leisure. Lipsyte aims to persuade his readers to question those values and, perhaps, to support "de-emphasizing early competition and redistributing athletic resources" (par. 6), especially in schools (16).

QUESTIONS ON WRITING STRATEGY

1. Using the "myths of masculinity and power" (par. 4) instilled by competitive team sports as his principle of analysis, Lipsyte identifies several elements of Jock Culture, among them "greed and desperate competition" (6); "bullying, violence, and the commitment to a win-at-all-costs attitude that can kill a soul" (7); division into "winners and losers" (8); "coachlike authority figures who use shame and intimidation to achieve short-term results (8); expectations for people "to be tough, stoical, and aggressive, to play hurt, to hit hard, to take risks to win in every aspect of their lives" (9); desires to "pursue . . . jock dreams no matter the physical, emotional, or financial cost" (10); and "misogyny" (13). The positive aspects of sports—"entertaining, healthful, filled with honest, sustaining sentiments for warm times and the beloved people you shared them with" (5); "a once safe place to learn about bravery, cooperation, and respect" (7); learning teamwork and developing the ability

to reach a goal despite setbacks (9)—are completely overshadowed by the damaging effects of Jock Culture.

2. As he indicates, Lipsyte is writing to other Pukes like himself—educated, politically aware readers of *The Nation* who "were often turned off or away from competitive sports" (par. 4). He assumes his audience consists of liberals who "question authority and seek ways of individual expression" (4), and anticipates that many of them identify as artsy misfits, whether they work in "business, medicine, the law," or in "symphony orchestras, university philosophy departments, and liberal magazines" like *The Nation* (8). He seems to want them to understand that even if they think they live apart from Jock Culture, it permeates every aspect of their lives and affects them more than they may realize.

3. Although the 9/11 example may seem gratuitous to some readers, it neatly encapsulates the entirety of Lipsyte's analysis. It shows, first of all, that Jocks—both male and female—have an advantage in business yet also are harmed by that advantage. It reinforces his implication, in paragraphs 1–4, that competitive values lead to military action and outright war. It hints at why "submission to authority" (4) is a dangerous trait. And it lets Lipsyte show empathy for those who embrace the values he disdains.

4. By quoting the "affable *ur*-Jock" (par. 2) in his introduction, Lipsyte establishes the position that he intends to counter while simultaneously distancing himself from terms that some readers will find offensive. Returning to Stowe four decades later in his conclusion, Lipsyte circles back to his introduction (creating unity) and reveals that even a devoted athlete has changed his mind about the value of sports and come around to the author's way of thinking.

5. Lipsyte starts off with Bill Stowe's binary classification, which ascribes positive characteristics to Jocks: They are, he claims, "brave, manly, ambitious, focused, patriotic, and goal-driven" (par. 1). Pukes are exactly the opposite: "wooly, distractible, girlish, and handicapped by their lack of certainty that nothing mattered as much as winning" (1). In Lipsyte's own reckoning, however, the characteristics are different. As he presents them, Pukes "question authority and seek ways of individual expression," while Jocks are conformists who do whatever is asked of them (4).

QUESTIONS ON LANGUAGE

1. Although Stowe uses the word *Jock* approvingly, both words have derogatory connotations, especially *Puke*, which brings up images of sickliness and weakness. If nothing else, the labels capture readers' attention and stress the different personalities more colorfully than *athlete* and *intellectual* would.

2. No doubt Lipsyte himself would describe his tone as "Puke-ish" (par. 2)—in a good way. His words are calm, reasoned, intellectual, and infused with empathy.

3. Lipsyte's invective against sport mentality is riddled with sport metaphors. Some examples: "mental conditioning" (par. 4); "arenas of elite athletes," "cockpit of bullying" (7); "'cut' from the team early" (8); "pushed the envelope" (9); "our lives outside the white lines" (12). Taken together with Bill Stowe's mixed metaphors/clichés in paragraph 16 ("It's time to give up the torch. . . . I'm not running it up the flagpole

anymore"), they show that while the author might reject Jock Culture, he understands it fully—and probably better than Jocks do.

4. *Wonkish* is a relatively new coinage and could be counted as slang. The word refers to a student or analyst (a *wonk*) who focuses excessively on a particular subject.

FRANCINE PROSE

What Words Can Tell

Francine Prose's book *Reading like a Writer* holds that thoughtful reading is the key to good writing. This excerpt from Prose's best-selling writing guide both reinforces our own assumptions about the benefits of close reading and serves beautifully as a model of such reading. We hope students will be inspired by Prose's example to attempt similar analyses of both the fiction and the nonfiction included in *The Brief Bedford Reader*. As Prose demonstrates, even a few sentences of a quality work reveal much meaning and have much to teach about the value of words.

Students who want to read "A Good Man Is Hard to Find" can locate it in many venues. Flannery O'Connor's marvelous collection "*A Good Man Is Hard to Find" and Other Stories* is available in almost any library, and it can also be found online via the University of Central Florida at *pegasus.cc.ucf .edu/~surette/Goodman.html*. The critical writing topic following Prose's analysis invites students to read the story and then respond to Prose's interpretation of its opening paragraph. This topic could also spark class discussion as students share their responses to Prose and to the story itself.

QUESTIONS ON MEANING

1. Prose examines the paragraph to demonstrate just how informative and rewarding it can be to "slow down and read every word" (par. 2) of an enduring writer's work.
2. The author's thesis is stated in paragraph 3: "All the elements of good writing depend on the writer's skill in choosing one word instead of another. And what grabs and keeps our interest has everything to do with those choices."
3. Prose admires the passage for O'Connor's skill in establishing every character's personality, setting the tone, and foreshadowing the plot in a "highly concentrated . . . model of compression from which it would be hard to excise one word" (par. 12).

QUESTIONS ON WRITING STRATEGY

1. Prose's intended audience is made clear in the title of her book: *Reading like a Writer: A Guide for People Who Love Books and for Those Who Want to Write Them*. Her use of the language of literary criticism further suggests that she imagines her readers to be well educated, or at least somewhat experienced in reading literature.

2. Given that Prose has no qualms about including spoilers, she does seem to assume that most members of her audience have read O'Connor's short story. Yet she is careful to reprint the full passage under analysis and to alert readers to its connections with later plot developments. Even those who have never read "A Good Man Is Hard to Find" learn enough about it from Prose's essay to follow her examination of its introduction. (And we hope that those who have not yet had the pleasure of reading O'Connor's masterful story will be inspired by Prose's analysis to track it down for their own enjoyment.)

3. Prose ties her analysis together in paragraph 13: "Skimming just won't suffice" to "teach us about how to use the language."

4. By giving a close reading of one short passage from a famous story, Prose proves her point that writers can learn a lot by reading the masters.

QUESTIONS ON LANGUAGE

1. Figures of speech in the lead-in to Prose's analysis include her analogy of wiring to explain how readers need to relearn their approach to fiction (par. 1) and her similes comparing a writer's words to a composer's notes and an artist's paints (2). Each of these turns of phrase demonstrates the author's appreciation for colorful, meaningful writing and encourages her readers to think in creative terms.

2. The switch in address reflects Prose's switch in emphasis and purpose. The introductory paragraphs are meant as instruction for the readers who are the subject of Prose's lesson, so the second person is appropriate. In the analysis itself, however, Prose is more interested in the intricacies of reading and thinks of her audience (and herself) as the objects of O'Connor's efforts, hence the third-person *we*.

3. The allusions stress that Flannery O'Connor is part of a community of revered literary masters whose work continues to influence contemporary writers.

4. Notice that many of Prose's word choices—*psychic, archetypal, infantilizing, egocentrism, narcissism*—reveal her interest in the psychological school of literary criticism.

FRANCINE PROSE ON WRITING

Prose's statement about grammatical errors may puzzle those students who have been taught that errors are always wrong. Her point, we think, is that Philip Roth can get away with what might be considered a textbook error because he knows what he's doing—the error is deliberate—and because his meaning is clear. What distinguishes his error from that of a less experienced writer is his control and clarity.

JAMAICA KINCAID

Girl

The writer Stephanie Vaughn has said that Kincaid's story "spills out in a single breath. . . . Its exhilarating motion gives . . . the sense of a writer carried over the precipice by the energy of her own vision." Even so, students may need a little guidance on how to follow and understand this evocative piece of fiction. They may complain that as a story, it unfolds much less clearly and logically than, say, the narrative essays in Chapter 4. For those who resist the unorthodox style, you might ask students to compare Kincaid's spoken version with the written transcript. The story's form, especially when read out loud, helps emphasize the mother and daughter's relationship.

Students will certainly notice that this story is not set in the United States. Encourage them in small groups to locate the details that make this fact obvious. How does the foreignness of the location help or hinder understanding of the story? Are there things in "Girl" that suggest the universal experience of growing up? How would they rewrite this story to capture the lessons their parents repeat?

QUESTIONS ON MEANING AND STRATEGY

1. These are any boys who hang around without enough to do—boys without motivation. She should avoid them because, presumably, they would be interested in "ruining" her.
2. A life full of risk, danger, and vigilance—risks including miscooked food and bad sex, dangers including becoming pregnant and becoming a "slut," vigilance with household chores, social obligations, health, and personal morality.
3. This advice lightens with a little laugh the heavy sense of obligation conveyed by all the other advice. If it were the last line, it might detract from the seriousness of the rest of the piece.
4. The categories include how to wash, cook, sew, iron, sing, grow food, sweep, smile, set the table, interact with men, and make medicine. The categories show that the roles of women are methodical, not random, and should be appreciated for their subtlety, efficiency, and complexity.

10
CLASSIFICATION
Sorting into Kinds

In our general comments on Chapter 9, we explain our reasons for divorcing the hoary pair of division and classification. Our reasons have mainly to do with salvaging division/analysis, but benefits accrue to classification, too. For one thing, it doesn't have to compete for attention (ours, yours, students'), so it's much clearer. For another, we can provide more illustrations.

The selections in this chapter range from humorous to serious, reflecting the classifications we find in the publications we read. Deborah Tannen and William Lutz look at miscommunications inadvertent and deliberate, respectively. Russell Baker contributes a well-known humorous piece of curmudgeonly confusion over our material possessions. Adventure writer Jeff Wise uses psychology to group mistakes that can lead to death, or at the very least embarrassment. And in the e-Pages, a compelling infographic from the US Census Bureau shows the changing face of American immigration.

Troubleshooting: All our efforts to keep division/analysis and classification separate and equal are hampered by the inescapable fact that *divide* is sometimes taken to mean *classify*, as in "Divide the students into groups." You might want to point out this issue directly to students if you think the terminology will confuse them. We maintain that division/analysis treats a singular, whole, coherent subject (a camera, a theory, a poem), whereas classification treats a plural, numerous subject (cameras, theories, poems).

The confusion between division and classification may account for the tendency of some students to "classify" by taking a single item (say, the television show *Survivor*) and placing it in a category (say, reality shows). We'd explain that they haven't classified anything; they have just filed an item in a pigeonhole. If they'll remember that classification begins not with one thing but with several things, they may avoid much perplexity.

DEBORAH TANNEN
But What Do You Mean?

The linguist Deborah Tannen came to national prominence with *You Just Don't Understand*, a book about misunderstandings between men and women in conversation. Since then, she has continued to disseminate much of her research through the mass media, trying to help people solve the communication problems of daily life. Oliver Sacks, another intellectual who often addresses a general audience, wrote of *You Just Don't Understand*: "Deborah Tannen combines a novelist's ear for the way people speak with a rare power of original analysis. It is this that makes her an extraordinary sociolinguist, and it is this that makes her book such a fascinating look at that crucial social cement, conversation."

This is one essay that students should be able to apply easily to their own lives, although the men in your class may be more resistant than the women. The essay will certainly evoke a wide range of student response, which should lead to lively class discussion. Here is an in-class exercise to test Tannen's theories: Ask students to bring in dialogs that illustrate conflict from novels, plays, or movie scripts, deleting characters' names and direct references to gender. Have students read the dialogs out loud and try to guess characters' genders, justifying their choices. Encourage students to look for instances of Tannen's seven categories of miscommunication in the dialogs. (A variation is to cross-cast the dialogs, with women reading men's lines, and vice versa, and see if they are still believable.)

While Tannen examines innocent misunderstandings, William Lutz, in the next essay, takes on language that misleads on purpose. The "Connections" questions following both essays will help students consider what both kinds of miscommunication have in common, as well as how such confusions might be avoided.

QUESTIONS ON MEANING

1. Tannen is pointing out the areas of communication in which misunderstandings between the sexes are most frequent. She seems to hope that a better understanding of how men's and women's communication styles differ will help eliminate such misunderstandings. A secondary purpose is to show women how their problems in the workplace may be linked to their style of communication.
2. Much of what we say is based on pure protocol, which serves as a kind of social cement. We're not so much communicating facts as establishing a rapport with the other person. This speech is often so automatic and predictable that we aren't even aware of what we're saying. (See also the journal prompt and the first writing suggestion.)
3. "Many of the conversational rituals common among women are designed to take the other person's feelings into account, while many of the conversational rituals common among men are designed to maintain the one-up position, or at least avoid appearing one-down" (par. 2).
4. "Thank you" is not always used as an expression of gratitude, but is simply a ritual, "an automatic conversation starter and closer" (par. 15).

An answer of "You're welcome" results in an imbalance between the speakers.

QUESTIONS ON WRITING STRATEGY

1. Tannen uses these characters as examples of the points she is making. She adds variety to the essay by referring to people alternately by their first names (real or fictitious) and by their functions ("a well-known columnist," par. 4; "[a] woman manager I know," 13). These characters are ciphers, empty vessels in the service of Tannen's argument, and as such do not need to be described in detail. Tannen reveals only what is relevant to her point. (See also question 4.)

2. Because the essay appeared in *Redbook,* a women's magazine, Tannen uses *you* to address women readers: "What's important is to be aware of how often you say you're sorry (and why), and to monitor your speech based on the reaction you get" (par. 9); "Although you may never enjoy verbal sparring, some women find it helpful to learn how to do it" (19). (Tannen takes a broader approach for a male *and* female audience in *Talking from 9 to 5,* the book from which this essay was excerpted.)

3. Tannen begins by redefining women's apologizing not as self-deprecation but as a "way of keeping both speakers on an equal footing." She then offers an extended example of this redefinition and expands on it further through a brief dialog that reveals apologizing as "a mutual face-saving device." In paragraphs 6 and 7, she gives an example of a woman whose constant apologies may have limited others' perceptions of her competence. Finally, she poses a contrast: the negative response women may get if they don't use "ritual apologies."

4. That the columnist is well known makes her apology all the more unexpected, less likely to be chalked up to insecurity.

5. (1) *Apologies*: Women apologize more than men do. They see apology as a way of keeping both speakers on an equal footing, of sharing responsibility. Men take apologies at face value, seeing them as self-deprecating. (2) *Criticism*: Women tend to soften criticism more than men do. Men prefer "straight answers." (3) *Thank-yous*: Women say "thank you" more often, as a ritual. Men take "thank you," like "I'm sorry," more literally. (4) *Fighting*: Men see conversation as a battleground, stating their ideas and criticizing those of others in the strongest possible terms. Women often perceive this approach as a personal attack. (5) *Praise*: Women often assume that the absence of praise is the equivalent of criticism. For men, in contrast, praise is often implied when no criticism is given. Women who ask for criticism may really be asking for praise, but men will give them what they ask for. (6) *Complaints*: Women complain as a way of bonding with others. Men see these complaints as a call for a solution. (7) *Jokes*: "[T]he most common form of humor among men is razzing, teasing, and mock-hostile attacks, while among women it's self-mocking. Women often mistake men's teasing as genuinely hostile. Men often mistake women's mock self-deprecation as truly putting themselves down."

QUESTIONS ON LANGUAGE

1. The humor here relies on exaggeration. It usually refers to finishing off a suffering animal.
2. Tannen uses the metaphor of a gun: criticism as shooting.

3. These verbs liven up the essay and inspire a strong visual or auditory impression. Other examples are "*leapt* into a critical response" (par. 10) and "*poke* holes" (17).

4. Note Tannen's vocabulary of physical and verbal conflict: "contentious," "hedge," "sparring," "rebuttal," "retorted," as well as "disadvantage" (par. 2), "attack" (18), and "enemy" (19). You might discuss whether Tannen loads her case with such words, perhaps exaggerating the conflicts between genders.

DEBORAH TANNEN ON WRITING

Students may not be aware of the debate about the personal in scholarly writing, but many have probably been told at some time not to use *I* in their academic papers. Tannen suggests why and also argues in favor of the first person on scholarly grounds. Students in the natural and applied sciences may be more likely than others in the class to resist Tannen's argument, contending that they don't write about personal interactions. Uncovering resistance and getting a discussion going are of course the aims of the first follow-up question. For the second one, collaboration in small groups is ideal: Working together, students will find it easier to draft the third-person or first-person passage and then revise it, seeing firsthand what the differences are.

WILLIAM LUTZ

The World of Doublespeak

William Lutz is a leading figure in the campaign against the dishonest language that he (and others) call doublespeak. This essay, extracted from the first chapter of his book-length treatment of the subject, both defines the term and classifies its varieties. The many, many examples will leave students in no doubt about the meaning of doublespeak and should make it relatively easy for them to spot it.

One problem with doublespeak is that it often relies on multisyllabic words and complicated syntax. As a result, the most example-heavy parts of Lutz's essay may be difficult reading for some students. Lutz himself practices what he preaches, writing clearly and concisely, but you may want to warn students that some passages in the essay require patience.

Probably the best way to make this essay immediate and significant for students is to have them locate doublespeak in what they read and hear. Indeed, you may want to ask them to try the journal-writing assignment as soon as they've read the essay and to bring their examples to class. Even if each student contributes only one or two examples, you'll have a good collection. Working as a whole class or in small groups to sort their examples into Lutz's categories, students will be writing a continuation of the essay.

We pair Lutz's essay with the previous one, Deborah Tannen's "But What Do You Mean?" While Tannen deals with gender communications and Lutz with a subtle form of deception, both authors look at how our uses of language can hinder understanding. The fifth writing suggestion following each essay can be used as an assignment or to spark discussion.

QUESTIONS ON MEANING

1. Lutz's thesis might be stated briefly as follows: The four kinds of doublespeak all include language "that avoids or shifts responsibility, language that is at variance with its real or purported meaning" (par. 2). The thesis accumulates over paragraphs 2–3, with the addition of the intention to classify in paragraph 5.
2. Paragraph 4 offers the following questions: "Who is saying what to whom, under what conditions and circumstances, with what intent, and with what results?" These questions locate the motivation for dishonesty that would indicate doublespeak.
3. The greatest danger is that, as in Orwell's *Nineteen Eighty-Four*, doublespeak will lead to the "control of reality through language" (par. 23). Doublespeak "alter[s] our perception of reality and corrupt[s] our thinking. . . . [It] breeds suspicion, cynicism, distrust, and, ultimately, hostility" (22). It can "infect and eventually destroy the function of language" (23).
4. Lutz clearly assumes an educated reader, someone able to perceive the fundamental dishonesty in his examples. At the same time, his careful classification, scores of examples, and extensive discussion of the dangers indicate that he believes his reader probably is not sensitive to doublespeak and needs help to recognize it.

QUESTIONS ON WRITING STRATEGY

1. Lutz's principle of classification is the intention of doublespeakers. Those who use euphemisms are trying to "mislead or deceive" (par. 7) with inoffensive words. Those who use jargon seek to give their words "an air of profundity, authority, and prestige" (10). Those who use gobbledygook or bureaucratese are bent on "overwhelming the audience with words" (13). And those who use inflated language seek "to make the ordinary seem extraordinary; . . . to make the simple seem complex" (17).
2. Lutz begins by offering a definition of the category. Then he offers examples of euphemisms used to spare others' feelings or to avoid language regarded as taboo—euphemisms he finds acceptable. Finally, he contrasts these kinds of euphemism with three examples of euphemism used by government agencies to "mislead or deceive"—in which case it becomes doublespeak.
3. Greenspan's second comment is surprising because he acknowledges that he is deliberately unclear. With the quotation Lutz shows that doublespeak is intentional.
4. Many of Lutz's examples are dated, and some students may at first think that doublespeak is an old, not a current, problem. The first writing suggestion, asking students to find current examples of their own, should help them see that doublespeak is no less a problem now than it was more than two decades ago.
5. Definition appears mainly in paragraphs 2 and 3 and in the explanations of each kind of doublespeak (pars. 5, 7, 9–10, 13, 17). Cause and effect also figures in the explanation of categories, as Lutz gives the

intentions of doublespeakers, but mainly it develops the last section of the essay (20–23). The definition, of course, clarifies Lutz's subject and his categories. The cause-and-effect analysis shows what is at stake with this dishonest language.

QUESTIONS ON LANGUAGE

1. Lutz's language provides a good foil to the quotations of doublespeak: He uses plain language and relatively simple syntax.
2. The words listed all have negative connotations, suggesting undesirable or even dangerous effects of doublespeak. More neutral language would not make Lutz's point as sharply. For just a few examples, see paragraph 1.
3. *Taboo* now refers to a prohibition against the use or practice of something. The word comes from the Tongan word *tabu*, an adjective meaning "set apart, consecrated to a special use or purpose." Captain Cook traveled to Tonga in 1777; his widely read narrative of his experiences, including an explanation of *tabu*, brought the term into common use in England.

WILLIAM LUTZ ON WRITING

Students may be encouraged to see recognizable behaviors, particularly procrastination, in a successful writer. Students aren't writing whole books for their classes, of course, but Lutz's advice, scaled down, should remind them that they needn't try to write an essay all at once, only a few paragraphs. The longer students wait to write a paper, the greater the chance they will have to do it in one sitting and will be daunted by the task.

The writer and humorist Fran Lebowitz once joked that being a writer was a bit like being a perpetual student . . . except you can't write a book the night before it is due. "I know," Lebowitz deadpanned, "because I tried twice."

RUSSELL BAKER

The Plot against People

In this essay, the well-known humorist Russell Baker makes a common use of classification—for humor. Baker takes a wry look at the universal human feeling that the material world is conspiring against us. Ask the class to come up with more examples of things that "have it in" for people.

Writing humor is difficult, as students who have tried can attest. Give students an opportunity to try their hands at a collaborative essay modeled on Baker's. What conspiracy theories can the class generate? (These might include the school's conspiracy to keep students from registering for any of the classes they most need, the local market's conspiracy to run out of Diet Coke when you most need one, and so on.) Make a list of ideas on the board, and have small groups of students write a short essay describing this conspiracy in detail. You might ask the groups to read their finished products.

Students who enjoy Baker's approach can be encouraged to look into some of his collections, such as *Poor Russell's Almanac* (1972) and *So This Is Depravity* (1980).

QUESTIONS ON MEANING

1. Baker's thesis is stated in paragraph 1. His larger meaning is that inanimate objects conspire to frustrate humans.
2. The reason may be that objects are doing humans a favor (par. 11) or that they are "incredibly stupid" (12).
3. He may also want to point out how ridiculous we are when we become infuriated with inanimate things.
4. By not working, thus "conditioning him never to expect anything of them" (par. 16).

QUESTIONS ON WRITING STRATEGY

1. Baker classifies objects by the ways they thwart human wishes. He might have included things that work for a while and then break, or even things that work fine; but his use of extreme cases adds to the essay's humor.
2. Baker begins by contrasting the category with the previous category. Next he provides two examples (pliers and keys) and then an additional example (women's purses). Finally, he again contrasts things that break down with things that get lost, using the examples of a furnace and a woman's purse.
3. "[A]ny object capable of breaking down at the moment when it is most needed will do so" (par. 2); "A furnace . . . will invariably break down . . ." (10); "Thereafter, they never work again" (13). (Students will, of course, find others.) Hyperbole establishes Baker's comic tone of exasperation.
4. His pseudoscientific classification, with its dogmatic assertion of the three categories of objects, is a parody of intellectual authority. The pseudophilosophical discussion of spiritual "peace" in the conclusion reinforces the essay's mock-serious tone.
5. Baker's little stories (the cunning automobile of paragraph 3, or paragraph 8's climbing pliers) capture the reader's attention. Shared experiences provide a sense of recognition and help make the essay funny.

QUESTIONS ON LANGUAGE

1. The vocabulary words highlighted here all contribute to the essay's mock-serious tone. In general, the essay's diction is quite simple.
2. Clever, malicious, plotting. Its effect is to personify the automobile.
3. The general terms make the shared experiences more universal. Had Baker used *I*, he might have seemed more of a crank, less persuasive.

RUSSELL BAKER ON WRITING

What do lead pencils, Shakespeare, eternal quests, cave writing, dreaming, Luddites, and cornpone politicians have to do with computers? In Russell Baker's fertile mind, everything and nothing. In addition to enjoying the fun of the piece, students may be interested in noting how he cleverly shows a mind in the act of composition. Stream-of-consciousness writing has been used more often in confessions, but with some behind-the-scenes crafting, Baker demonstrates its humorous potential.

———————

JEFF WISE

Deadly Mind Traps

Mixing academic psychology with a morbid sense of humor in this blog post turned essay, journalist Jeff Wise effectively offers practical tips for overcoming common cognitive errors while keeping his readers thoroughly entertained.

"Deadly Mind Traps" is one of several selections in this book that use humor, sometimes dark humor, to impart scientific information to a general audience. We point to one, Dan Koeppel's "Taking a Fall," in the writing suggestion labeled "Connections." Others include Jessica Mitford's "Behind the Formaldehyde Curtain" (p. 269), Dan Ariely's "Why We Lie" (p. 384), and Bonnie Berkowitz and Laura Stanton's "Roller Coasters: Feeling Loopy" (in the e-Pages, at *bedfordstmartins.com/thebedfordreader*). You might want to ask students what it is about hard science that leads some writers to look to irreverence as a way to hook readers in. And why do people writing about death (Wise, Koeppel, Mitford) so often turn to gallows humor? Are such attempts to amuse ever appropriate? Why do students think so?

QUESTIONS ON MEANING

1. Wise gives two reasons in paragraph 7: Altruism is a "deep-seated emotion" that is difficult to control to begin with, and in an emergency situation panic kicks in and causes irrational thinking. Essentially, instinct overpowers reason.
2. He cites our "irrational assessment of risks and rewards" (par. 12). Most people, Wise explains, would rather risk a large loss when there's a potential for gain than take a certain small loss. But they fail to consider the real possibility of losing when there's any chance for gain.
3. Situational blindness is "the failure to remain aware of one's environment" (par. 16), or not paying attention; confirmation bias, or "bending the map" (19), is the failure to recognize an incorrect theory or assumption in the face of new evidence. The terms come from psychology.
4. Wise is referring to the foreclosure crisis: the housing market collapse and credit meltdown caused by a rash of risky mortgage lending and securities bundling in the late 1990s and early 2000s. His point is that

confirmation bias can affect enormous groups of people at once and cause widespread disaster.

5. If the limits were set for safety reasons, you could die. In less serious situations "redlining" (par. 28) simply causes people to lose their way and miss whatever goal the limits were meant to define.

6. Wise's thesis, stated in paragraph 3, is that potentially deadly cognitive errors generally fall into one of a few simple categories. His purpose is to inform readers of what those categories are and to show how an awareness of them can be applied to less harrowing aspects of daily life; he also means to entertain.

QUESTIONS ON WRITING STRATEGY

1. Absolutely. Even if readers won't ever find themselves in one of the life-or-death situations he recounts, Wise explains that the general concepts he delineates can be applied to everyday life and offers examples of such applications in the sections labeled "Avoid the trap."

2. Each category starts off with a brief, real-life narrative that illustrates the consequences of the error for one person or group of people, moves to an explanation of the psychological concept at hand, and ends with suggested real-life applications for the knowledge. We think the strategy is very effective: The stories are engaging, the explanations are clear and to the point, and the applications are practical and useful. Also, the predictable pattern pulls readers along and gives the essay unity and coherence.

3. It may interest students to know that in his first draft of this essay, published in his blog for *Psychology Today*, Wise used a different order and concluded with "Bending the Map." In this revised version he seems to order his categories of errors from those least to most likely to apply to readers' own lives. In essence, he starts with the most compelling point and ends with the most relevant one. Many readers will wish, however, that the essay didn't end quite as abruptly as it does.

4. Wise, a journalist, quotes experts in psychology to lend authority to his explanations and to give them a bit of extra color.

5. We'd say that "Deadly Mind Traps" is as much a cause-and-effect analysis as it is a classification. In each category of his essay, Wise identifies a specific type of cognitive error and examines both why it happens and what might result. Without the cause-and-effect analysis, his classification would seem a rather hollow exercise.

QUESTIONS ON LANGUAGE

1. Examples of colloquial language include the phrases "suck three buddies to their doom" (par. 1), "keeled over" (5), "no big deal" (11), and "in a hole" (13); the comments "take a breath" (4), "you'll be completely clueless about what to do next" (17), and "We look at clouds and see sheep" (19); and the casual vocabulary, such as "boneheaded" (2), "screwup" (3), and "bushwhacked" (21). Some students may like the playful tone for its humor and accessibility; others may find that it detracts from the seriousness of Wise's subject or inappropriately makes light of real human tragedies.

2. *Hydrogen sulfide*, a poisonous gas emitted by rotting organic matter and typically smelling of rotten eggs, is something of a euphemism for

"sewer gas" in the context of Showalter's demise. It is heavier than air and thus tends to float just above its source.

3. Some metaphors: "autopilot" (par. 3), "mental traps from which there is no escape" (3), "blind faith" (16), "the human maze" (18), "Our minds are wired to find order in randomness" (19), and "windows of good weather can shut abruptly" (25). Some understatements: "mistakes best described as boneheaded" (2); "each one died in turn" (5); "another goes in after him, then another" (5); "a jump would cause serious injury at best" (11); "the gamble that he might be able to ride the gondola safely back to the ground seems preferable to a guaranteed pair of broken legs" (12); "In this particular case, the water had to be flowing uphill" (20); "it was too late" (26); and "Today his body remains where he sat" (27). The metaphors, of course, bring freshness and vibrancy to Wise's prose. And as they often do, the understatements lend a sense of (dark) humor to his subject.

US CENSUS BUREAU

America's Foreign Born in the Last 50 Years

Immigration continues to be a contentious topic in American politics and culture, and this multilayered infographic from the US Census Bureau might help to explain, in part, why that is. Students may be surprised to learn that in their grandparents' time, most immigrants to the United States came from Europe, Canada, and the Soviet Union. Today, in contrast, foreign-born residents *look* foreign. They're also more likely to live next door.

To engage your students in the topic before they get into the data, you might begin discussion by focusing on their assumptions about recent immigrants. What, if anything, do they know about them, and what have they heard? Are they immigrants or children (or grandchildren) of immigrants themselves? Would they ever consider moving to another country? Why, or why not?

QUESTIONS ON MEANING AND STRATEGY

1. The first bar graph puts the immigrant population at 40 million. Some students may add up the numbers for the top ten countries of origin (23.8 million), but that graphic doesn't account for the total number of immigrants. The percentage has increased since 1960, from 5.4% to 12.9%. Interestingly, however, the percentage today is lower than it was at the beginning of the twentieth century (and for the second half of the nineteenth).

2. In this particular infographic the Census Bureau classifies immigrants by country of birth. The vast majority of foreign-born residents are from Latin America (Mexico, El Salvador, and Guatemala, as well as Cuba and the Dominican Republic), followed by Asia (China, India, the Philip-

pines, Vietnam, and Korea). In contrast to the past, Europe accounts for a relatively small portion of immigrants today.

3. The West and the South have the most foreign-born residents today, with pockets in Florida and the Northeast (New York and New Jersey, especially). California, the Census Bureau reports, has the highest concentration of immigrants in the country, at 27% of the state's population.

4. The immigrant population today is far more diverse than it was half a century ago. Although most foreign-born residents in 1960 were white Europeans who shared a common cultural heritage with the native-born majority, now they tend to be Latino or Asian. They are younger (in their early forties, compared to late fifties), and they've settled across a broader swath of the United States.

11
CAUSE AND EFFECT
Asking Why

As you know, the matter of cause and effect can plunge a class into many complexities, and it can sometimes lead to fruitless wrangles. Still, many instructors find that this chapter leads to unusually satisfying results.

We start off with two complementary essays, Chitra Divakaruni's "Live Free and Starve" and student Marie Javdani's "*Plata o Plomo*: Silver or Lead" (Javdani's essay is documented), both examining effects of globalization. Then Dan Ariely's "Why We Lie" explains how small-scale cheating wreaks wide-scale damage, and Christopher Beam's "Blood Loss" considers interrelated trends in crime and journalism. And in the e-Pages, Bonnie Berkowitz and Laura Stanton make clever use of Web technology to immerse readers in the physics of a roller-coaster ride.

We have endeavored to clarify the difference between process analysis and cause-and-effect analysis, a frequent source of confusion for students. Process asks *how*; cause and effect asks *why*. Further, process deals with events that are repeated or repeatable or even just theoretically repeatable (like the creation of the Grand Canyon); cause and effect deals with singular events, one-time happenings.

Studying cause and effect can lead to a discussion of common errors in reasoning, as we indicate in this chapter when we touch on the fallacy of *post hoc*. If you wish to bring up logical fallacies, a few are listed, defined, and illustrated in Chapter 13, on argument and persuasion (pp. 445–47). Perhaps it is enough at this point merely to call students' attention to them. Cause and effect may be complicated enough without trying to tackle logical fallacies at the same time.

CHITRA DIVAKARUNI
Live Free and Starve

Both Chitra Divakaruni's "Live Free and Starve" and the essay we pair it with, Marie Javdani's "*Plata o Plomo*," tackle globalization—specifically, the effects that policies or actions in the United States can have on those in the developing world.

Divakaruni focuses on the drastically limited choices of child laborers: If they don't work, even under terrible conditions, they starve. Divakaruni argues that Americans should not try to stop child labor abroad without also taking responsibility for the terrible deprivation that sends children into labor in the first place. That "without also" is crucial for students to understand: Divakaruni may show the unintended consequences of a bill banning goods produced with child labor, but she certainly does not argue *for* child labor. For readers inclined to favor US action on unjust labor practices and similar issues of human rights around the world, Divakaruni's paragraph 5 presents a warning not to evaluate others' situations from a strictly American perspective. In the end, the author suggests the kinds of measures Americans would need to take if they really want to help child laborers.

We have previously included Divakaruni's essay in the argument chapter, and it could still be taught as an argument. It provides an excellent chance to discuss emotional appeals. Ask students to mark places in the essay where Divakaruni works to touch the emotions of readers, and then in class spend some time at the board noting the relevant passages. Small groups of students could each analyze one of the passages: What beliefs and values does Divakaruni appeal to? How accurate is she in gauging her readers' sympathies? Do the appeals work to strengthen her argument? (If you would like students to write on Divakaruni's emotional appeals, see the fourth writing suggestion.)

QUESTIONS ON MEANING

1. Divakaruni wants to make her readers think with greater complexity about the solutions available—or not available—for the problem of child labor in developing countries. The title alerts the readers that the author's perspective is perhaps unusual. The brief paragraph 2 makes it clear that she disagrees with the House's solution. Then in paragraph 4 she begins to explain why.
2. Divakaruni's thesis is stated in paragraph 8: "A bill like the one we've just passed is of no use unless it goes hand in hand with programs that will offer a new life to these newly released children."
3. Third World countries are the developing nations of Asia, Africa, and Latin America. The term comes from the Cold War: The First and Second Worlds were the non-Communist and Communist industrialized nations.
4. Divakaruni means that most Americans have already met their survival needs (for "bread," as she puts it) and thus can afford the relative luxury of seeking freedom and other needs at the top of the pyramid.

5. The children lack "food and clothing and medication," there are no
    schools for them, their governments can't provide these things, and
    ultimately no one takes responsibility for them.

QUESTIONS ON WRITING STRATEGY

1. The rhetorical questions expand on the opening (thesis) sentence.
    They push readers to think hard about the negative effects the legisla-
    tion could have on child laborers and to consider their willingness to
    "shoulder the responsibility" for the children when they are jobless.
2. Divakaruni explains in this paragraph how child labor affects children.
    The first words ("It is true that child labor is a terrible thing") establish
    the idea of the paragraph, and the remainder concisely itemizes the
    effects.
3. In telling the detailed story of one child, Divakaruni grounds her es-
    say in a specific case. She establishes her authority as an observer of
    child labor abroad, and an open-eyed and sympathetic observer at that.
    Though Nimai had a life that was "hardly a desirable existence for a
    child," he still was better off, Divakaruni contends, than the nonwork-
    ing children in his village.

QUESTIONS ON LANGUAGE

1. The survival of the families is so borderline that caring for their own
    children could ruin them.
2. The words show compassion—"ribs sticking out," "hunger was too
    much to bear," "ate whatever they could find," "knew they'd be beaten
    for it."
3. *Blithe* has roots in Old Saxon, Middle Dutch, Old High German, and Old
    Norse. It earlier referred to the outward expression of a kindly feeling
    but has come to mean "heedless or careless, unaware of the full impli-
    cations of an act."

CHITRA DIVAKARUNI ON WRITING

For Divakaruni, social activism broadens and sensitizes her and is thus
a boon to her writing. Our questions prompt students to consider just what
a writer gains from having her or his "preconceptions" challenged and from
understanding the lives of others. The questions could open up a discussion
of critical thinking, not just about others' ideas but about one's own as well.

MARIE JAVDANI

Plata o Plomo: Silver or Lead

Paired with the previous essay—Chitra Divakaruni's look at child labor
in developing countries—this essay focuses on another problem that affects
children in the Third World: drug production and trafficking. In a good ex-

ample of student research writing, Marie Javdani explores the plight of Colombian peasants caught between rebels who finance their cause through drug trafficking and government-condoned forces who battle the rebels. Extensive financial aid to the Colombian government from the United States has done little to stem the production and flow of drugs from the country, largely because of government corruption. Javdani argues that US money would be better spent drastically reducing US demand for drugs, which would, in turn, significantly decrease the profitability of the drug trade and thus improve the situation in places like Colombia.

Students may be surprised by the connection Javdani makes between young Americans' use of illegal drugs and the death of a young Colombian. Class discussion might focus on this connection, which brings the abstractions of globalization down to concrete cases. Do students accept the connection? Do they accept Javdani's conclusion that Americans have a responsibility to change their own behavior in order to help improve conditions in developing countries?

QUESTIONS ON MEANING

1. Javdani states her thesis at the end of paragraph 3, forecasting the organization of the essay. In paragraphs 4–7 she describes "what's happening in drug-source countries," in paragraphs 8–9 she covers "how the United States can and cannot help there," and in paragraphs 10–11 she makes a case for "what, instead, can be done at home."
2. Many peasants fear the government more than the rebels, in part because the rebels can provide protection from the government, whereas the government provides little protection from the rebels. Also, the peasants evidently receive money from the rebel drug lords to farm coca.
3. As Javdani writes in paragraph 8, money used to eradicate coca fields has "alienated peasants" and "escalated violence," and money intended to "help peasants establish alternative crops" and further legitimate police efforts has wound up helping arm paramilitary forces or simply disappearing. Javdani argues that greater efforts must be made to reduce the US market for drugs.

QUESTIONS ON WRITING STRATEGY

1. Students may have different thoughts about Javdani's intended audience, but in her final paragraph she clearly appeals to people her own age to recognize the extent to which their use of and tolerance for drug use in this country has harmful effects elsewhere. Javdani wrote the essay in a freshman writing class, so she may have had in mind an audience of her classmates.
2. Javdani's sympathies seem to lie with the Colombian peasants. For evidence, students might point to her opening description of Miguel and her discussion throughout of the Colombians' plight and the atrocities they face.
3. Javdani's extensive use of sources backs up her claims and gives her writing authority. The source citations are particularly effective in the detailed descriptions of the situation in Colombia.
4. The contrast Javdani sets up in her opening paragraphs is between a suburban teenager scoring drugs in the United States and a peasant boy facing execution because of his family's resistance to drug trafficking in

Colombia. She creates a connection between the two that she returns to in her conclusion: It is the demand for drugs in the United States, typified by Eric, that endangers peasants in Colombia, typified by Miguel.

QUESTIONS ON LANGUAGE

1. The phrase "between a rock and a hard place" means being stuck between two equally bad choices with no alternative. The peasants can either work with the government and face torture and execution by the rebel drug lords or work with the drug lords and face the same fate from government-condoned paramilitary forces.
2. Javdani writes that Eric lives in a "suburban paradise" and yet still faces the "stress of homework and ex-girlfriends"; obviously, she intends readers to see his life as not terribly stressful at all and certainly not an excuse to use drugs. Students should see immediately that Javdani has no sympathy for Eric.
3. The peasants are "traitors" to one side or the other no matter what their choice, so they are not literally traitors, and the "cooperation" the peasants are accused of is not voluntary but forced, so it is not literally cooperation.
4. *Guerilla* comes from the Spanish word for war, *guerra*, with the diminutive ending *-illa*; it might be translated literally as "small war." The word was coined in the early nineteenth century to describe the Spanish resistance movement against the French regime established by Napoleon Bonaparte. The Spanish word for "guerilla fighter" is *guerillero*, but in English *guerilla* has long referred to those who participate in guerilla warfare, as well as to the warfare itself.

MARIE JAVDANI ON WRITING

Javdani offers much useful advice for other student writers. We emphasize her counsel to care about one's topic because inexperienced writers, especially reluctant ones, often don't make the effort to find their own angle on a subject. We also like Javdani's warning that interest doesn't justify the speechifying of a soapbox orator: Moderation is the key.

DAN ARIELY

Why We Lie

In this accessible and compelling overview of his own scholarly research, renowned behavioral economist Dan Ariely challenges accepted models of human decision making and proposes a new understanding of both why people lie and how they might be persuaded to be more honest. A glance through the comments on the *Wall Street Journal's* Web site reveals that readers can easily misinterpret Ariely's ideas if they don't read carefully. Students, too, might be surprised by Ariely's apparent acceptance that most people lie, if only "just by a little." You might wish, then, to begin discussion with the

question of Ariely's purpose (the first question on meaning). Far from justifying or condoning such behavior, as some might think, Ariely seeks to put
a stop to it.

When assigning Ariely's essay, you could also conduct an exercise to
make his point concrete for students. Set a timer, and ask them to solve the
puzzle on page 386. How long does it take them? Do they think they could
solve four such puzzles in five minutes? Can they understand why most test
participants cheated?

Some longer works on Ariely's topic are *Lying: Moral Choice in Public
and Private Life,* by Sissela Bok (1978); the title essay in *On Lies, Secrets,
and Silence,* by Adrienne Rich (1979); and of course Ariely's *The (Honest)
Truth about Dishonesty: How We Lie to Everyone—Especially Ourselves*
(2012), from which this piece is adapted. Students who enjoy Ariely's voice
and would like to hear his suggestions for overcoming procrastination when
facing a writing assignment or similar task could be directed to his video
comments on the subject at *bigthink.com/users/danariely.*

QUESTIONS ON MEANING

1. Ariely is writing mainly to examine the implications of his research and
   to use them to propose a better way to prevent dishonesty.
2. As Ariely explains in paragraphs 4–5, cost-benefit analysis is the mental
   practice of weighing potential benefits of an action against the potential
   risks. Although it is "the traditional, rational model of human behavior"
   (5) that most people assume drives decision making, Ariely stresses
   that his research has shown the model is wrong. Efforts to prevent
   cheating by raising the potential costs (fines, punishments, shame, and
   so forth) are therefore doomed to fail.
3. By testing multiple variables with the "matrix task" (par. 5), Ariely and
   his colleagues discovered several factors that increase the likelihood of
   dishonesty: "making the prospect of a monetary payoff more 'distant,'
   in psychological terms" (11), witnessing another person cheating (12),
   a weak sense of ethics (13), mental depletion (13), and a belief that the
   dishonesty will benefit others (13). The infographic on p. 389 lists additional factors: "ability to rationalize, conflicts of interest, creativity, previous immoral acts, being depleted, others benefiting from our dishonesty, watching others behave dishonestly, culture that gives examples of
   dishonesty." A reduced "probability of getting caught" (9), surprisingly,
   is not a factor.
4. Ariely suggests that reminding people of morality before they may be
   tempted to lie is the best way to prevent dishonesty, and he is guard-
   edly optimistic that "[s]uch tricks" (par. 22) could have wide-ranging
   effects. Although he acknowledges that his suggested tactic won't prevent "flagrant misbehaviors" (25), he insists that it would, indeed, prevent most people from cheating "just by a little" (22) when the opportunity arises.
5. Ariely hints at his thesis early in the essay, with "it is this kind of
   small-scale mass cheating, not the high-profile cases, that is most corrosive to society" (par. 4). He previews his solution in the middle, when
   he first says "simply being reminded of moral codes has a significant
   effect on how we view our own behavior" (17). He then continues building to his thesis, which he states in his conclusion: "All of this means
   that, although it is obviously important to pay attention to flagrant

misbehaviors, it is probably even more important to discourage the small and more ubiquitous forms of dishonesty—the misbehavior that affects all of us, as both perpetrators and victims" (25).

QUESTIONS ON WRITING STRATEGY

1. Ariely's mix of academic and colloquial diction, along with his examples from business, sports, culture, and politics, reveal that he is writing for a general audience of educated readers who are interested in the psychology of human behavior. Presumably he counts researchers, insurance administrators, bankers, the IRS, and his study participants among the "perpetrators and victims" of "the misbehavior that affects all of us" (par. 25).

2. Paragraphs 4–9 report the results of Ariely's matrix experiments to establish that most people cheat on a small scale, 10–14 examine the causes of that cheating, and 15–21 explore an idea for making people more honest. Ariely gives the essay unity by ensuring that each section is clearly introduced with a transitional topic sentence (or question) that establishes its relation to his thesis. And the repetition of certain key words and phrases (see question 3 on language)—such as *dishonesty, cheat, lie,* and, most notably, *just by a little*—adds to the essay's coherence.

3. The joke previews the moral of Ariely's story, so to speak, and offers a nice transition to his proposed solution. As he explains, the joke "suggests . . . that simply being reminded of moral codes has a significant effect on how we view our own behavior" (par. 17). Repeating it also lets the author inject some humor into his essay.

4. The matrix presents an example of the puzzle Ariely challenged his research subjects to solve and helps readers visualize what might otherwise be an abstract concept. The infographic summarizes in clear visual form both the causes of dishonesty and the proposed solution that Ariely outlines in his essay.

5 The anecdote encapsulates Ariely's main point, or, as he puts it, "captures rather nicely our society's misguided efforts to deal with dishonesty" (par. 1). The idea that we lock our doors to keep honest people honest offers a nice metaphor for Ariely's moral-reminder solution, and so he circles back to it in his conclusion.

QUESTIONS ON LANGUAGE

1. Examples of colloquial language include "just by a little" and "just by a bit" (pars. 4, 7, 9, 10, 23, 24), "a simple little experiment" (5), "something funny happens" (7), "putting more money on the line" (8), "mini-Madoff" (12), and "the 'What the hell' effect" (13). Among Ariely's figures of speech are the understatement "Unable to get the IRS to give our theory a go in the real world" (20) and the metaphors (verging on clichés) "a few bad apples spoil the bunch" (3), "in a nutshell" (4), "waltz away with a wad of cash" (12), "balancing act" (13), "game the system" (24), and "grease the psychological skids" (25). Such language lends authenticity to Ariely's voice and makes his ideas more accessible, although some readers may find it inconsistent with an academic subject and purpose.

2. *Integrity,* from the Latin *integer,* "whole" or "complete," can refer to a state of being complete or undivided (as in the integrity of a geometric form) or to a condition that is sound or unimpaired (as in the integrity

of a mechanical system). Ariely uses it in its more common sense of "adherence to a code of moral or ethical values."

3. *Cheat* and *lie* are harsh synonyms for *dishonesty*; they connote judgment. *Just by a little,* on the other hand, implies self-delusive rationalization. Repeating the terms as much as he does lets Ariely underscore his main idea: that the accumulation of minor transgressions among the bulk of the population poses a greater problem than the major frauds that usually capture people's attention.

CHRISTOPHER BEAM

Blood Loss

Prompted to write by the lackluster media response to a serial killer's conviction and sentencing, Christopher Beam comes up with an interesting theory to explain a decline in serial killings over the past few decades. Drawing on examples of sensational crimes throughout the twentieth century (and the early twenty-first), he concludes that we are most caught up with those misdoings that tap into generalized anxieties. Ignored by the media because more pressing concerns have moved to the forefront of the national consciousness, serial killers have less incentive to do what they do. And in their place, it seems, we have an epidemic of mass murders.

Students may have a hard time accepting Beam's suggestion that media coverage contributes to the incidence of some types of crime. The author is, after all, a crime reporter. You may want to begin discussion by asking the class to recall examples of recent "media frenzies" over sensational crimes. What elements do the big stories have in common? Did the perpetrators, in fact, seem to want the notoriety their actions brought them? Could they have been motivated by a desire for fame? If so, what responsibility do the media bear for their actions?

QUESTIONS ON MEANING

1. As the structure of the essay suggests, Beam has a dual purpose: to report that serial killings have declined significantly since their peak in the 1980s, and to propose a theory explaining why. In the first four paragraphs he establishes the fact of the trend, showing that the number of serial murders has dropped dramatically, and with it the public's fascination with serial killers. The next two paragraphs examine possible explanations for the drop but dismiss them, and the remainder of the essay develops the idea, introduced in paragraph 7, that media coverage of serial killers "tapped into the obsessions and fears of the time."

2. Beam assumes an audience of true-crime buffs, it seems. At the very least, he expects that readers will have a passing knowledge of the events and cases he cites, whether recent or historic. Even if they don't, however, Beam's interest is not in the individual crimes but in their accumulation and their cultural symbolisms. The details are not necessary to get his point across.

3. Yes, he does. Beam suggests a correlation between sensational crimes and media coverage, claiming that the "short path to celebrity" offered by the "media's growing obsession with serial killers in the 1970s and '80s" (par. 5) helped to fuel such killings. He adds, in paragraph 7, that one serial killer (David Berkowitz) went as far as to contact the news media directly. His point seems to be that by sensationalizing certain kinds of crimes, the media give criminals an added incentive to commit them.

4. Beam's thesis is that the crimes that attract the most media attention are those that resonate with or somehow symbolize prevailing cultural fears — such as kidnappings and "societal decay during the Depression" (par. 9), serial murders by "sex-addled psychopaths" (7) in the 1970s and 1980s, and terrorism today. Serial killings don't capture our attention anymore because we're worried about "instant mass annihilation" (11). He comes closest to stating his general idea in paragraph 9: "Infamous crimes almost always needle the anxieties of their periods."

QUESTIONS ON WRITING STRATEGY

1. The gruesome details in Beam's story about an archetypal serial killer grab readers' interest. That the "crossbow cannibal" was more or less ignored by the media starts the essay on an ironic note and sets up Beam's claim that serial killers murder partly for the media attention.

2. Beam uses the word *structural* in its sense of "related to or concerned with systematic structure in a particular field of study" (*The American Heritage Dictionary*). His point in paragraph 5 is that serial killings didn't necessarily increase in the 1970s and 1980s: It's possible, he acknowledges, that they were simply better documented. But as he goes on to say in paragraph 6, that questionable cause-and-effect relationship is not relevant to his inquiry. Regardless of whether or not there was an actual rise in serial killings four decades ago, the number has declined since then.

3. In paragraph 6 Beam considers the possibility that police work and longer jail terms for captured killers might have contributed to the decline in serial killings. But he has a different explanation: He suggests that serial killings have dropped off the radar because the public isn't as fascinated by them as it once was, giving "psychopaths" (par. 7) less reason to kill.

4. The statistics support Beam's claim that "serial murders peaked in the 1980s and have been declining ever since" (par. 4). Readers may reasonably question their reliability: The data were gathered by a single scholar and represent cases reported in popular sources. But there is little other data available, according to Beam.

5. Beam cites James Alan Fox's definition in paragraph 4: "a string of four or more homicides committed by one or a few perpetrators that spans a period of days, weeks, months, or even years." He also identifies the first recorded instance of "serial murderer" (as cited in *The Oxford English Dictionary*) and the source of the synonym "serial killer" (it was coined by an FBI agent in 1981) in paragraph 8.

QUESTIONS ON LANGUAGE

1. Beam uses complex, formal words and phrases — such as *incarceration* and *caveat* (par. 6), *conversely* (10), "structural explanations for

the rise of reported serial murders" (5), and "As the raw numbers have declined" (7)—alongside colloquial expressions, including "just aren't the sensation they used to be" (1), "hard to come by" (4), and "returned the favor" (8). The informal language helps him connect with readers and build a casual tone; the formal language emphasizes that he has studied his subject thoroughly and takes his argument seriously.

2. "Golden boy" carries with it a sense of resentment for somebody who appears to be perfect; it also implies that such a person is an insincere sycophant. Applied to Ted Bundy, a wealthy political supporter, the term also hints at Americans' distrust of the greedy and powerful in the 1980s.

3. Beam uses *needle* as a transitive verb ("needle the anxieties of their periods"), whereas students may know it only as a noun (a sewing implement). The informal use creates a compelling image, implying both a prick of conscience and the lethal injection of a death sentence.

BONNIE BERKOWITZ AND **LAURA STANTON**

Roller Coasters: Feeling Loopy

As print journalism struggles to survive in the early twenty-first century, online editions of newspapers have become almost mandatory. Bonnie Berkowitz and Laura Stanton worked together to create "Roller Coasters: Feeling Loopy" for the Web version of the *Washington Post*, one of the most respected and enduring newspapers in the United States (perhaps tellingly, it was purchased by *Amazon* founder and CEO Jeff Bezos in 2013). The benefits of online technology are evident in their interactive graphic, which relies on the viewer to click the play button in the center of a roller coaster to virtually travel through the ride and get information about popular features and their effects along the way.

Berkowitz and Stanton are not, of course, physicists, doctors, or roller-coaster experts: They rely on data and information from others. You might want to spend some time in class evaluating the credibility of the sources they list below the graphic. Given the emphasis that roller coasters are safer than they seem, what kinds of expertise seem most reliable? Do students detect any potential bias from the authors' sources? Does such bias detract from the effectiveness of the graphic's central point? Why, or why not?

QUESTIONS ON MEANING AND STRATEGY

1. The graphic's primary purpose is informative, with an objective focus on the most popular features built into modern roller coasters and the physical effects they have on riders. (The section below the coaster provides additional information for readers interested in coaster innovations.) Students might note that the authors use simple language and graphics to make the information presented easy to understand. "Roller Coasters: Feeling Loopy" also makes a subtle argument that roller

coasters are safe despite what riders may experience or what readers may assume; the persuasive element is reinforced by the use of expert sources for evidence (particularly the early quotation from coaster designer Rob Decker) as well as the playful, even childlike, tone used to impart the information.

2. Individual causes and effects are explained in each of the seven stages depicted in the interactive graphic: (1) rapid acceleration ("linear G-force") pushes riders' cheeks and bodies backward; (2) steep drops intensify the effects of gravity ("positive G-force"), pushing blood toward riders' feet and creating a sense of heaviness; (3) the effect of circling through loops ("centripetal force") keeps riders in their seats even though they're upside-down; (4) the initial descent after a hill counteracts gravity ("negative G-force"), temporarily causing internal organs to shift position and blood to rush upward; (5) deceptive visual cues induce "fear and adrenaline," increasing riders' heart rates; (6) sharp turns ("lateral G-force") push riders to the outside of a car and may cause injury if not tempered by banking of the track; and (7) the cumulative effect of multiple unfamiliar motions sometimes causes a stomach valve to release, making a rider nauseous.

3. Berkowitz and Stanton use a combination of division or analysis and process analysis to organize the causes and effects of the imagined coaster ride, with their principle of analysis being the physics behind common design features and what they do to the human body. While there is a clear beginning, middle, and end to their interactive graphic, the parts in the middle are not chronological because the design features appear in varying order on actual roller coasters: Drops, banks, loops, crests, and so forth do not necessarily occur in the order described by the graphic.

4. Terms such as *positive G-force*, *lateral G-force*, *negative G-force*, and *centripetal force* may be unfamiliar to a general audience, but Berkowitz and Stanton use simple language and clever illustration to ensure that the scientific terms are adequately defined for their purposes (see the answer to question 2, above). Interested readers should have no trouble grasping the basic concepts and how they apply to the experience of a typical roller-coaster ride. Notice in particular the authors' animated definition for stage 3, in which the path of a bird in flight clearly shows the difference between a circular loop and a clothoid loop. If any students complain that the concepts are unclear, you might ask them to examine the stages in question more closely or to consider what might have been lost if the graphic didn't include the technical language.

12
DEFINITION
Tracing Boundaries

"When they come to definition," said the late Richard Beal, an author of textbooks, a director of composition, and our sage adviser, "most authors of rhetorically organized readers seem not to know what it is nor what to do about it."

Definition, he suggested, is not in itself a distinct and separate expository method, but a catchall name for a kind of explaining that involves whatever method or methods it can use. It would break with tradition, Beal said, to place definition last among methods of exposition. Then the instructor might use it to review all the rest.

We hope that this ordering of the book's contents proves useful to you. You will also find the book carefully distinguishing a short definition (the kind found in a dictionary), a stipulative definition (the kind that pins down an essential term in a paragraph or two), and an extended definition (the kind found in whole essays).

All the essays in this chapter trace the shape of a definite territory and attempt to set forth its nature. In the paired selections, Gloria Naylor and Christine Leong demonstrate how words change meanings in different contexts: Each explores the alterations in a derogatory word for her race depending on who uses it. (As a bonus, Leong, a student, responds directly to Naylor—thus modeling a common writing assignment.) Meghan Daum takes issue with popular usage of *narcissist*, insisting on the value of the psychological term's clinical meaning. Barbara Kingsolver defines what *rural* means to people like her, who live far from urban centers. And in the e-Pages, graphic artist Schroeder Jones offers a useful explanation of a misunderstood minority.

GLORIA NAYLOR

The Meanings of a Word

Focusing on the highly charged word *nigger*, Naylor maintains that context determines interpretation. Many students will disagree with this assertion, arguing that language carries its own meaning, so it might be useful to open up this issue right away. Students will certainly agree that saying something like "It was all my fault" carries a completely different meaning depending on whether it is uttered with sincerity or with sarcasm. Can students think of other instances when they have relied on inflection to convey meaning? Have they manipulated language—through exaggerations or half-truths, for example—for their own benefit? William Lutz's "The World of Doublespeak" (p. 337) provides another perspective on how we can (and often do) twist language to suit ourselves.

Part of Naylor's point, too, is that speech can be more precise (or more nuanced) than writing. How do writers overcome (or try to overcome) the limitations of written language? Students can explore the connections among tone, context, and meaning. Give groups fifteen or twenty minutes to look over essays they have already read this semester, in search of sentences, ideas, or passages that might be easily misinterpreted if read out of context. (It will be helpful if you read aloud a few examples as models. Promising examples appear in Anna Quindlen's "Homeless," Chap. 6, and Jessica Mitford's "Behind the Formaldehyde Curtain," Chap. 8.) Have students identify different interpretations for an isolated excerpt as well as interpretations for the excerpt when considered in the context of the entire selection. After each group explains its examples, the class will be better prepared for a discussion of writing strategies and/or Naylor's sense of the multiple meanings of language.

QUESTIONS ON MEANING

1. Written language, with less inflection and immediacy, doesn't offer the variety and richness of spoken language.
2. This was the first time it sounded offensive, so it was the first time she was shocked enough to really notice—"hear"—it.
3. They took a derogatory term and redefined it, gaining power from using it as a form both of praise and of informed condemnation rather than simply as a term of prejudice.
4. She wants to show how the meanings of a word change with the context in which it is used. (See the next question.)

QUESTIONS ON WRITING STRATEGY

1. Naylor holds that spoken language is richer and more powerful than written language and that the power of words derives from their context. The rest of the essay presents examples of these assertions in uses of *nigger*. To us, the opening is a bit flat and perhaps unnecessary: The assertions are well made through the examples. But some students may appreciate the initial overview.

2. Paragraphs 3, 14, and 15 discuss racist uses of the term: They sandwich nonracist uses, as the African American experience is sandwiched by racism. At the same time, the discussion of nonracist uses is longer, emphasizing the positive. The two definitions come together in paragraphs 14–15, in which Naylor sums up the nonracist uses and distinguishes them from the racist uses.
3. These last sentences make clear that despite the empowering use of the word within her family and community, her mother knows Naylor will face more uses of the word in a racist context. It also suggests a protective bond between Naylor and her mother.
4. They suggest how the word might be used in a sentence, so that the audience can get a sense of different inflections. Through them Naylor tries to add a spoken component to written language.

QUESTIONS ON LANGUAGE

1. The old question is "Which came first, the chicken or the egg?" This debate helps Naylor show the circular ways that language and reality influence one another.
2. They identify, respectively, a sex-crazed woman and a person sexually interested in corpses. Both connote perversion, twistedness. Naylor uses the words to emphasize the unfamiliarity of *nigger*, but she implies with them just how venomous was the little boy's insult.
3. The religious connotations of *mecca* suggest a sense of reverence for a place that offers a retreat from daily strife. The word can be understood both in a religious sense (a spiritual center in Islam) and in a secular sense (a center for people who share a common interest). Describing the grandmother's house as a *mecca* identifies it as a safe and spiritual gathering place.

GLORIA NAYLOR ON WRITING

Naylor's remarks could fuel a discussion about the literary canon—what's included, what's excluded, who decides. Naylor turned a perceived disadvantage, a dearth of "approved" African American literature, into an advantage by deciding to help right the wrong herself. When she says she attempts to "articulate experiences that want articulating," she evokes many silenced forebears.

CHRISTINE LEONG

Being a Chink

Leong's essay is clearly modeled on Gloria Naylor's "The Meanings of a Word." Like Naylor, Leong explores the power to be gained from refusing to allow words, especially those originally intended as demeaning or offensive, to have fixed meanings. For students who resist the idea that language is flexible and that context often determines meaning, you might wish to consider some of the suggestions and questions we pose in the introduction to Naylor's essay.

Deborah Tannen's "But What Do You Mean?" (p. 327) is another interesting counterpart to this essay; both discuss ways that communication relies on mutual assumptions about the meanings of words. In clusters of three or four, students could brainstorm a list of groups that have "private" language. (Students may need to be reminded that groups may be defined not just by race, ethnicity, or gender, but also by age, occupation, marital status, education, hobby, and so on.) How does knowing the private language create a position of power for a speaker or a listener?

QUESTIONS ON MEANING

1. Leong explains *chink* in paragraph 10: a label that describes specific external characteristics but not internal ones.
2. For this group of friends the word has become a way to comfort each other by acknowledging the way they have all had to deal with racism (par. 11).
3. Her purpose is the last one listed: Although her essay does both of the other things to some degree, Leong wants to show the reader how the flexible nature of language allows for power through redefining racist terms. You know this from the conjunction of her first and last paragraphs.

QUESTIONS ON WRITING STRATEGY

1. Both essays have an introduction on language and meaning, a story that starts "I remember the first time . . . ," and a conclusion that explains the power in co-opting racist terms. Leong places her experiences in the context of racist issues generally and of Naylor's reading of them specifically.
2. Leong builds suspense as she sifts through the trash. Ending with the envelope accomplishes several things: The envelope is both grouped with other forgotten rubbish and set apart by its racist inscription.
3. This example sets up the parallel between Naylor's family's redefinition of *nigger* and Leong's redefinition of *chink*, enhancing Leong's explanation of the way she and her friends dealt with the label and their reasons for doing so.
4. To make clear that they are consciously subverting the original meaning of *chink* and not misunderstanding it.
5. She assumes the slur is directed at her father, and she is outraged on his behalf.

QUESTIONS ON LANGUAGE

1. Words like "imposed," "small," "weak," "insignificant," "paralyze," and "belittle" all suggest that racist language is debilitating.
2. This characterization of their use of *chink* suggests affection, gentleness, and mutual understanding, almost like a nickname—all of which are in contrast to racist uses.
3. Students should notice how careful Leong is with the language of labels: In terms of both race and gender, she is very politic, using "Cau-

casian" instead of "white," and "human" or "person" instead of "man."
You might ask students how this care contributes to her essay's
message.

CHRISTINE LEONG ON WRITING

Leong's insistence on the writer's personal involvement in writing is
refreshing, especially coming from a student. Your students may be surprised by Leong's assertion that inspiration counts more than grammar and
sense in reaching readers. With "Being a Chink" and her comments on writing—both not only correct but sensible—Leong makes a strong case for
clarity informed by passion.

MEGHAN DAUM

Narcissist—Give It a Rest

In Greek mythology Narcissus was a handsome Greek youth who, as
punishment for ignoring the advances of the nymph Echo, was made to fall
in love with his own image. He then pined away, changing into the flower
that bears his name. *Narcissism* has come to mean excessive self-love, and
Daum has a problem with that. In this column abridged from the *Los Angeles
Times*, she examines popular usage of the word, explains why such usage is
inappropriate, and begs people to stop.

Students may not catch the significance of this essay's timing and
context, although Daum hints at it in paragraph 5. She published "Narcissist—Give It a Rest" about a month after the American Psychiatric Association announced the controversial decision to drop narcissistic personality
disorder from the latest edition of the *Diagnostic and Statistical Manual of
Mental Disorders*, or DSM-V, psychologists' official catalog of mental illness.
We point that out in the writing suggestion labeled "Critical Writing" and
encourage students to learn why the decision sparked debate.

QUESTIONS ON MEANING

1. Daum asserts that the misuse of the word began in the 1970s and by the
1990s became so overused as to become meaningless, apparently dropping out of popular use in the first decade of the twenty-first century. As
she sees it, however, people have just recently begun flinging it around
again as an insult, giving "the impression that they just discovered it"
(par. 3) when in fact it's been around for decades.
2. Daum's essay goes beyond defining *narcissist*. She is writing to explain
how others use the word inappropriately, to complain vocally about the
misuse, and to implore people to stop.
3. Daum divides her thesis between paragraphs 5 and 7: "The term has
been misused and overused so flagrantly that it's now all but meaningless when it comes to labeling truly destructive tendencies. . . . So

perhaps it's time to declare a moratorium on the indiscriminate use of this particular n-word."

QUESTIONS ON WRITING STRATEGY

1. The "[p]rofessional pundits . . . , bloggers, politicians, religious leaders, celebrity shrinks, cultural critics, Internet commenters and blowhards at parties" (par. 3) whom Daum criticizes would likely take umbrage at her accusations and her tone. Actual narcissists probably would not care what she thinks, one way or the other.
2. While popular usage of *narcissist* treats the word as a synonym for "any behavior you don't like" (par. 4), Daum argues for the American Psychiatric Association's clinical definition as it appeared in the *Diagnostic and Statistical Manual of Mental Disorders* for more than four decades—a serious disorder that causes "self-destructive" (pars. 1, 5) behavior.
3. Daum opens with her complaint that "a whole lot of people" (par. 1) are using the word *narcissist* as a general insult. In paragraph 2 she establishes the history of the popular usage. Paragraphs 3 and 4 rattle off examples of people who use the word and people to whom it's applied. In paragraph 5 Daum explains her objection to the usage. Her conclusion (6–7) offers her alternate characterization of Americans' behavior. Each paragraph relates directly to Daum's thesis, includes a topic sentence, and is developed with details.
4. Daum gives examples of "narcissistic" people in paragraph 4: "Democrats, Republicans, red state folks, blue state folks, baby boomers, Gen Xers, millenials . . . , [p]arents, nonparents, vegans, meat eaters, city dwellers, rural dwellers, people who travel a lot, people who refuse to travel, writers who use the first person. . . ." By setting up most of her examples as diametrically opposed pairs (implicitly comparing and contrasting the two groups) in a breathless string, she emphasizes her point that *everybody* can be accused of narcissism, usually by someone whose tendencies are different.

QUESTIONS ON LANGUAGE

1. The writer is clearly annoyed.
2. A *vector*, from the Latin *vehere*, "to carry," is an organism that transmits disease. Given that Daum is arguing to preserve the clinical meaning of *narcissist*, readers should appreciate her implication that people casually refer to the disorder as though it's contagious, even though it's not.
3. Both phrases connote shame and taboo (especially the latter); Daum is taking her own advice and refusing to use the word.

MEGHAN DAUM ON WRITING

Daum's comments on a reader's responsibilities reinforce our own advice about reading actively and critically, as well as about writing being a transaction between writer and reader. The questions for discussion encourage students to explore in more detail what a reader brings to that transaction.

BARBARA KINGSOLVER
Rural Delivery

With Michael Pollan's *The Omnivore's Dilemma* (2006), Barbara King-solver's *Animal, Vegetable, Miracle* has been credited with galvanizing the local-food movement, exposing the dangers of commercial agriculture, and inspiring thousands to pay more attention to what they eat and where it comes from. Our food, both writers have argued, has physical, cultural, eco-nomic, and political consequences. In this excerpt from her book, Kingsolver draws attention to a few of the political implications by asking readers to reconsider what the word *rural* (and by extension, *farmer*) means to them.

You may want to point out that Kingsolver defines largely by negation, explaining what rural people are not—"hick, redneck, hayseed, bumpkin" (par. 3) and so forth—to show them instead as she sees them. For King-solver, rural communities are not only sophisticated, cultured, and diverse but also essential to everybody else's survival, so we'd all better start show-ing more respect, both culturally and politically.

The vast majority (83%) of people in the United States live in urban or suburban areas, and many more relocate to densely populated areas every day. To engage your class in the topic before getting into the essay itself, you might begin discussion by focusing on students' own assumptions about rural living. What, if anything, do they know about it, and what have they heard? Would they ever willingly live "*so far from everything*" (par. 6)? Why, or why not?

QUESTIONS ON MEANING

1. Here is a possible summary: Rural communities are sparsely populated areas where farming dominates the landscape and the economy. They are characterized by a proud insularity, unacknowledged sophistica-tion, a strong sense of community, cultural and political diversity, and a history of being exploited by urban dwellers—who would starve without them.

2. Yes and no. Kingsolver was not raised on a farm, but because her family did not live in town, others classified them as "farm" people (par. 1). As an adult, however, Kingsolver strongly identifies with farmers and does seem to count herself among them, even if she does not make a living from working the land. (She currently cultivates a small plot to feed her family, something we mention in the introduction to the essay, but which Kingsolver does not discuss in it.)

3. Paragraphs 9–11 expand Kingsolver's definition to the landscape and politics of the nation as a whole, highlighting the significance of her subject for readers in rural and urban areas alike.

4. Kingsolver's purpose goes well beyond defining *rural*. The essay is a tribute to the lives and cultures of rural Americans, farmers in particu-lar. Kingsolver wants to share her vision with readers from all back-grounds and counter negative assumptions about rural life and politics. Most important, she wants readers to understand that the nation liter-ally cannot survive without the contributions of its rural communities.

QUESTIONS ON WRITING STRATEGY

1. Opening with a depiction of a nonsensical "caste" system imposed by classmates draws readers in and shares an experience to which most can relate. Kingsolver's point is that distinctions between rural and urban are as arbitrary—and as relative—as were the distinctions between "farm" and "town" where she grew up.
2. Kingsolver covers quite a bit of ground in "Rural Delivery"; she maintains unity by ensuring that each paragraph includes a clear topic sentence related to the thesis. Kingsolver is also careful to mark transitions among her paragraphs and to repeat key words such as *farm*, *rural*, and *urban*.
3. Stipulative definitions in the essay include those of "farmer" (par. 1), "everything" (6), "Interior" (6), "Conservative" (7), and "insider" and "outsider" (8). With each definition Kingsolver emphasizes that common assumptions about rural America are wrong.
4. During the 2000 presidential campaign political commentators and newscasters began categorizing states as either Democratic (blue) or Republican (red), based on predicted election results. The labels have stuck in the popular consciousness and are still used to characterize whole regions by their supposed political leanings—even though, as Kingsolver asserts, such labels are grossly oversimplified and misleading. She considers the political divide at length because it has come to signify a country polarized by difference and because it parallels the urban/rural "antipathy" that so concerns her. Ultimately, she hopes to bridge the gulf by questioning its existence.

QUESTIONS ON LANGUAGE

1. Berry is a well-known and respected writer who also happens to be a practicing farmer, so he lends authority to Kingsolver's arguments on two levels. The first quotation helps her to establish the importance of recognizing the politics of food; the second, which closes the essay, raises a dire warning of what will happen if the politics of food is not recognized and dealt with.
2. Kingsolver uses complex, formal words—such as *numinous* (par. 1), *bourgeoisie* (2), *symptomatic* (6), and *extractive* (9)—alongside colloquial expressions, including "Maybe you see where I'm going with this" (3) and "Okay, I'm exaggerating a little" (6). The informal language helps her connect with readers and build an earnest tone; the formal language expressly counters assumptions that rural people like Kingsolver are uneducated or unsophisticated.
3. Some readers will detect Marxist connotations in *bourgeoisie*, French for "middle class." By using that word in the same introductory paragraphs with *castes* (a reference to India) and *apartheid* (a reference to South Africa), Kingsolver strongly hints that her essay will emphasize political and class issues.

SCHROEDER JONES

Dr. Carmella's Guide to Understanding the Introverted

Although he has illustrated two books and self-published dozens of cartoons on *DeviantART*, Schroeder Jones is largely unknown as an artist. If the immediate popularity of "Dr. Carmella's Guide to Understanding the Introverted" is any indication, we suspect obscurity will soon be behind him. Already, Jones has translated the cartoon into multiple languages (German, Chinese, Polish, and Czech) and created a pamphlet version to satisfy demand; he's also expanding the viral hit into book form. In a short space and an accessible format, he has managed to define a complex psychological concept in a way that both introverts and extroverts can appreciate and apply to their own interactions with others.

Students interested in reading more about introversion might be referred to Jonathan Rauch's enduringly popular essay "Caring for Your Introvert" (*theatlantic.com/magazine/archive/2003/03/caring-for-your-introvert/302696*). For a longer, more recent consideration on the subject, see Susan Cain's *Quiet: The Power of Introverts in a World That Can't Stop Talking* (2012). Students may enjoy taking Cain's introvert/extrovert quiz, offered at the Web site for her book (*thepowerofintroverts.com*). Some may be surprised (even relieved) to discover where their own social preferences land them on the spectrum.

QUESTIONS ON MEANING AND STRATEGY

1. Here is a possible summary: An introvert is a person who is drained by socializing with other people, *not* somebody who is withdrawn, lonely, or unfriendly.
2. Jones's definition is clarified with an analogy, an extended metaphor that uses something immediate and familiar (a hamster ball) to provide insight into something that is difficult to envision (personal space). This visual device, which encourages readers to apply their knowledge of the concrete subject to the artist's definition of the abstract, allows Jones to explain something complex with a minimum of words.
3. Upon close inspection of the cartoon, students may notice missing periods, comma splices, run-on sentences, sentence fragments, vague and implied pronoun references, and an unnecessary exclamation point in addition to the pronoun-antecedent mismatches. Although sticklers may well be distracted by these apparent errors and deem Jones's cartoon weakened by them, others might respond that the standards of written grammar and punctuation are looser for visual works—much as they are for spoken conversation.
4. Jones's purpose is to help extroverts understand introverts and thus get along with them better (implied throughout the cartoon is the assumption that extroverts find introverts withdrawn or hostile, when really what they are is quiet sometimes). The process analysis is essential to show nonintroverts how to use the artist's definition in their own lives.

13
ARGUMENT AND PERSUASION
Stating Opinions and Proposals

Argument and persuasion are often difficult for students to master, so the introduction to this chapter is more detailed than the others. We spell out the elements of argument, integrating the Rogerian and Toulmin methods and the more traditional inductive and deductive reasoning. Then we cover the most common fallacies and (in the section headed "The Process") discuss possible structures for arguments. We also give emphasis to anticipating likely objections when conceiving and writing an argument.

This chapter's selections start with one piece that flies solo: Linda Chavez's "Supporting Family Values," a liberal argument by a conservative writer. Then we present three casebooks:

- Katha Pollitt and Charles Colson on gay marriage
- Bill McKibben, Derrick Jensen, and Margaret Lundberg (a student), on the effects of individual actions on the environment
- Anne-Marie Slaughter's controversial and widely read article from *The Atlantic Monthly* on the challenges of balancing work and family life is accompanied in the e-Pages by a sampling of responses collected by the editors of *Reader's Digest* and one blogger's reflections on the debate Slaughter revived.

LINDA CHAVEZ

Supporting Family Values

Chavez, a politically conservative writer who hails from a Spanish-speaking background, insists in this essay that Hispanic immigrants are both willing and able to adapt to American life and culture. Even more, Chavez suggests, that same group of immigrants so often vilified as lazy, uneducated, or criminal are in fact exemplars of virtue and should be honored, even rewarded, for their moral contributions to American society.

This essay is notable for using conservative ideals (family values) to argue for liberal policy (amnesty for illegal immigrants). Students may have some difficulty reconciling two points of view that would seem almost mu-

106

tually exclusive, but we find it quite clever of Chavez to intertwine them in such a way that neither position can be easily refuted: As Chavez presents her argument, readers on either side of the conservative-liberal divide have little choice but to accept at least part of their opponents' way of thinking.

QUESTIONS ON MEANING

1. Chavez opens her essay by noting it was prompted by a "new report out this week from the Pew Hispanic Center" (par. 1), but perceptive readers will notice from her remarks in the final two paragraphs that her argument was inspired as well by the ongoing conflict between efforts to aggressively identify and deport illegal immigrants and proposals to offer amnesty to illegal immigrants who meet certain criteria.

2. Although she mentions slight differences in family structure, education level, and income among illegal and legal immigrants, the only real distinction Chavez makes between the two groups is their legal status. Especially because so many immigrant families consist of both illegal and legal residents, Chavez suggests, the distinctions are practically meaningless.

3. Chavez's comparison of attitudes toward current Mexican and "other Latin American" immigrants with attitudes toward European immigrants of a century ago is a commonly used argument in favor of relaxed immigration controls. Her point is that a century of experience has shown that immigrants do assimilate into the larger culture over time and that fears of unfamiliar ethnic groups are unfounded. At the same time, because most of her readers are presumably of European heritage, Chavez subtly chides them for perpetuating the same hostilities that were once directed at their own ancestors—and reassures them that Spanish-speaking immigrants will, indeed, become an integral part of American culture if given the opportunity.

4. Chavez's purpose is revealed in the last two paragraphs: She is writing to argue in favor of "granting amnesty" to a qualified category of illegal immigrants. Her thesis might best be expressed in the penultimate sentence: "A better approach [to deportation] would allow those who have made their lives here, established families, bought homes, worked continuously and paid taxes to remain after paying fines, demonstrating English fluency, and proving they have no criminal record." By withholding her thesis and purpose until the end, Chavez acknowledges that her position will be difficult for readers to accept; she therefore fully makes her case before letting them in on what she wants them to believe.

QUESTIONS ON WRITING STRATEGY

1. Chavez characterizes opponents as unreasonable to the point of hysteria, referring to "hard-line immigration restrictionists," "alarm" (par. 2); "fear" (5); "worries [that] are no more rational today—or born out of actual evidence—than they were a hundred years ago" (6); and "popular but uninformed opinion" (8). In doing so, Chavez suggests that some readers may hold these views, yet she forces them to reexamine their beliefs by portraying them as irrational. She seems to trust that most of her readers—"the rest of us" (2)—are reasonable people who can be persuaded to change their minds if presented with sufficient information.

2. Chavez states her main assumption in paragraph 2: "One of the chief so-cial problems afflicting this country is the breakdown in the traditional family." Many readers, especially those of a conservative medium like *townhall.com*, will presumably share the writer's concern about family values; others will reject it outright. In either case readers are likely to find Chavez's approach creative at the very least.

3. Chavez appeals to both reason and emotion. She is careful to base her argument on statistical evidence from a published report in para-graphs 1, 3, 6, 7, and 8, using the numbers to draw inferences about the character, values, and potential for success of undocumented Spanish-speaking immigrants, especially as they compare to legal immigrants and native-born families. But she appeals to emotion throughout, citing both family values and fears of cultural disintegration as she makes her case.

4. Chavez names three categories of American "households" in para-graph 3: native, legal, and illegal. As she explains, native families are the least likely to be "made up of two parents living with their own children," while a third of legal immigrant households and nearly half of all illegal immigrant households consist of traditional nuclear families. The point is central to her argument that immigrant families represent a positive influence on the rest of the country and should therefore be supported and encouraged, not broken apart by deportation or harassment.

QUESTIONS ON LANGUAGE

1. *Amnesty* is a political term for a government's pardon of illegal activi-ties; in Chavez's essay, it refers explicitly to ongoing proposals to grant legal status to illegal residents who have nonetheless established them-selves successfully. The word comes from the same Latin and Greek roots as *amnesia*, or forgetting.

2. By "native" Chavez means those born in the United States and thus automatically granted citizenship. There are at least two layers of irony in her use of the term: First is the subtle reference to Native Americans, the peoples who were displaced with the first wave of European settle-ment in the fifteenth century; but Chavez also points out that nearly three-quarters of the children of illegal immigrants are "American-born" (par. 1) and thus citizens—a fact that complicates the issue of deporta-tion, especially for readers with a strong interest in family values.

3. Most students will likely find Chavez's tone reasonable and levelheaded, even appealing. The diction is for the most part plain; Chavez avoids sarcasm and hectoring, and in her conclusion she becomes somewhat informal, saying her evidence "should give pause to those who'd like to see all illegal immigrants rounded up and deported or their lives made so miserable they leave on their own" (par. 9).

LINDA CHAVEZ ON WRITING

Chavez's nostalgia for the old days of sentence diagramming might prompt students to reflect on their own grammatical education. How were they taught the rules? You might point out that understanding the rules is different from following them. Plenty of writers occasionally write "incorrect" sentences, but they do so on purpose and for a particular effect. Readers can tell the difference between intentional rule breaking and error.

KATHA POLLITT

What's Wrong with Gay Marriage?

Pollitt's essay is the first of a pair on marriage between homosexuals. She takes the "pro" position. Charles Colson, in the next essay, takes the "con." Though not directly, Pollitt in essence addresses Colson's main objections to same-sex marriage. In paragraphs 1, 2, 3, and 6 she presents opposing arguments and then refutes them. Even students who do not agree with her position should be able to learn a great deal from her model.

Students may have difficulty grasping Pollitt's conclusion about the separation of church and state. For all its religious trappings, she argues, marriage is ultimately a civil union—conferred by the government—and thus a civil right. If any man and woman can be married in the eyes of the government—no matter how ill suited—then, she asks, why should this status be denied to same-sex couples? Religious objections are irrelevant to Pollitt because religion does not figure in the civil relationship between marrying couples and the government.

One way to begin discussion might be to ask students to consider Pollitt's point in paragraph 6 that "people can live with civil unions but draw the line at marriage." What is it that makes marriage such a hot-button issue?

QUESTIONS ON MEANING

1. Pollitt first presents the argument that the fundamental purpose of marriage is procreation; this she attempts to refute by noting the fact that heterosexuals with no intention of having children are allowed to marry. Then she deals with George Gilder's claim that marriage must be a union of a man and a woman because marriage is "the way women domesticate men." She questions Gilder's premise but then says that allowing same-sex marriage would in no way change the relationship between men and women in a heterosexual union. Finally, she presents the "argument from history"—"marriage has been around forever"—which she claims is false because marriage as currently defined does not have a particularly long history. Pollitt's implicit point here is that the concept of marriage has evolved and there is no reason it should not continue to do so.
2. Pollitt says that marriage "as we understand it" is "voluntary, monogamous, legally egalitarian, based on love, involving adults only" (par. 3); it is "love, commitment, stability" (4). Pollitt herself is not a proponent of marriage, believing that it reinforces unfairness in society and in relations between men and women.
3. Pollitt argues that the basic objection to same-sex marriage is really "religious prejudice" (par. 6)—that those who believe homosexuality to be a sin believe that same-sex marriage rewards sinful behavior.
4. Pollitt's thesis is stated at the end of paragraph 6: "People may think *marriage* is a word wholly owned by religion, but actually it's wholly owned by the state. . . . [T]wo men or two women should be able to marry, even if religions oppose it and it makes some heterosexuals, raised in those religions, uncomfortable."

QUESTIONS ON WRITING STRATEGY

1. The opening question brings to the essay a very human, somewhat grumbling voice, and it immediately establishes Pollitt's topic and viewpoint. The questions in paragraphs 2 and 5 ask readers to see that there is no affirmative answer—or that to answer affirmatively is to answer unreasonably.
2. The concessions make Pollitt sound reasonable. Still, once she makes each concession, she goes on to argue that the point conceded is not really significant.
3. The transitions make it clear where Pollitt is in her argument: Each one refers in some way to the preceding paragraph or paragraphs. (The one in paragraph 3 does so by asking a question that echoes paragraph 2's "How about: Marriage is the way women domesticate men.")
4. Some students may think that Pollitt includes the paragraph because it personalizes the essay or because it reduces the importance of marriage. Others may think that it weakens the argument because it shows that Pollitt doesn't value marriage anyway, so she wouldn't care about undermining it.
5. Pollitt identifies what she sees as the elements of the opposition to gay marriage—the subarguments to the main argument that it threatens traditional marriage.

QUESTIONS ON LANGUAGE

1. Examples of humorous language in paragraph 2 include the "husbandly failings" in various domestic crimes, "barbarian-adoption program," women "haven't been too successful at it anyway," "male-improvement project," and "heterosexual pothead with plans for murder and suicide." The language suggests that Pollitt doesn't take Gilder's argument seriously and underscores her rejection of it.
2. With the phrase "live in sin" Pollitt is adopting the language of social conservatives for rhetorical purposes. She obviously would not agree with the characterization.
3. Putting "sacred" and "gay lifestyle" in quotation marks distances Pollitt from them: These are terms conservatives would use, but she would not.
4. The parallelism and repetition stress the contrast between the view of marriage as a solely religious institution and the reality of marriage as a government institution.
5. *Monogamous* comes from the Greek for "one" and "marriage." It originally meant being married to one person for life, but it now means being married to only one person at a time.

CHARLES COLSON

Gay "Marriage": Societal Suicide

Colson's essay and the preceding one by Katha Pollitt form a pair on the issue of marriage between homosexuals. The arguments in the two essays cover opposing sides of similar points, so you'll probably want students to read and discuss the essays together.

In dealing with Colson's essay, students may have difficulty considering the effectiveness of the argument, particularly those who are opposed to same-sex marriage. Colson stresses his moral grounds for opposing gay marriage only in paragraph 8. For the most part he makes a sociological argument, linking gay marriage to an increasing "decoupling of marriage and procreation" that "would pull them completely apart, leading to an explosive increase in family collapse, out-of-wedlock births—and crime" (par. 4). His reasoning is deductive, and he offers statistics and expert opinion to back it up. In evaluating the argument, students will have to judge first whether the deduction holds up (see the first question on writing strategy). Do they agree that legalizing homosexual marriage would lead more heterosexuals to view marriage as no longer a requirement for having children and thus would increase single-parent households and societal problems?

QUESTIONS ON MEANING

1. Colson states his thesis in the final sentence of paragraph 4 and rephrases it in his concluding sentence.
2. Colson uses the example of Norway—where a rise in rates of out-of-wedlock births followed the legalization of same-sex marriage—to support the first assertion (par. 6). He offers his own experience in prison ministry and the results of "[d]ozens of studies" to support the second (par. 5). We find the evidence for the first assertion shaky: It could illustrate the *post hoc* fallacy as much as a cause-and-effect relationship, and Norway is of course quite different from the United States. In paragraph 5 Colson might have bolstered his statistics by referring to their sources, but perhaps he did not see the need because, as he says at the start of paragraph 6, "Critics agree with this."
3. In paragraph 8 Colson makes a moral argument based on "[h]istory and tradition" that "[t]he family, led by a married mother and father, is the best available structure for both child rearing and cultural health." He also asserts in the final paragraph that marriage is "not a private institution designed solely for the individual gratification of its participants," though he doesn't really make a case for this point. You might ask students to consider the extent to which they can support this assertion.

QUESTIONS ON WRITING STRATEGY

1. Colson's claim is that gay marriage will cause family breakdown and societal problems. His assumption is that any form of marriage besides the traditional one will undermine the traditional one. His syllogism runs something like this: Any form of marriage besides the traditional one will lead to family breakdown and societal problems; gay marriage is not traditional; therefore, gay marriage will lead to family breakdown and societal problems.
2. With the quotation marks Colson shows that he does not accept the word *marriage* when it is applied to same-sex couples.
3. The question provides an arresting opening, suggesting the worst-case scenario should same-sex unions become legal.

4. Paragraph 7 concedes an argument made by proponents of same-sex marriage: that heterosexuals themselves—including Christian heterosexuals—have weakened marriage. The concession supports Colson's reasonableness: He sees validity in the opponents' side. He then goes on to argue that the issue is not people's behavior but the institution of marriage.
5. The argument is based on cause and effect: Same-sex marriage will lead to a rise in single-parent households, which, in turn, will lead to an increasing number of children who pose a threat to themselves and society.

QUESTIONS ON LANGUAGE

1. "Lawlessness," "gleefully mocking," "egged them on," and "chaos" all have very negative connotations.
2. The words imply that same-sex marriage was forced on the people of Norway against their will. It is not clear if indeed it was.
3. Although *unorthodox* has come to be a fairly neutral word for action or belief that is not commonly accepted but not necessarily wrong, etymologically its meaning is more like "not right or proper" (from the Greek *ortho*, "correct, right," and *doxa*, "opinion").

BILL McKIBBEN

Waste Not, Want Not

"Waste Not, Want Not" is the first of three essays focused on issues related to climate change. Like Derrick Jensen and Margaret Lundberg following him, Bill McKibben considers the effects of individual lifestyle choices on the environment.

McKibben uses an arsenal of persuasive strategies in this essay, including ethical appeals, emotional appeals, and rational appeals (such as statistics and examples), and a clear problem-solution organization. The first two questions on writing strategy will help students see that McKibben takes great care to bond with his audience, perhaps because his proposal may not be easy for even the most environmentally conscious readers to act on.

To introduce the essay, you might have the class as a whole compile a list of objections to reducing personal consumption for environmental reasons. After reading the essay, students can discuss whether—and how effectively—McKibben counters each objection. Then, when they've read Derrick Jensen's rebuttal of McKibben's proposal, they can compare the two essays for their strategies and effectiveness. You could apply the same strategy when introducing Margaret Lundberg's argument for a vegetarian lifestyle. See the discussions of Jensen's and Lundberg's essays on pp. 115 and 117 of this manual.

QUESTIONS ON MEANING

1. Paragraphs 4–5 and 9–10 center on environment, paragraphs 7 and 11–13 center on economy, and paragraphs 6, 8, and 14–15 touch on both at the same time. According to McKibben, adopting a simpler lifestyle would improve the world in two ways: by protecting the planet from the devastation caused by waste, and by allowing people more time and money to pursue relationships, cultural enlightenment, and the common good.

2. McKibben blames the consumer economy, especially the actions of manufacturers and advertisers, but also individuals' desire for money and things. Among the examples of waste he cites are disposable water bottles (par. 3), manufacturing that favors cost-savings over efficiencies (4–5, 8), junk mail (6), automotive torque (7), personal trash (9–10), education (11), military spending (13), soil (14), talent (14), executive excess (15), and large houses (17).

3. McKibben's proposed solution is to reduce personal consumption: "The economic mess now transfixing us will mean some kind of change. We can try to hang onto the status quo—living a Wal-Mart life so we can buy cheaply enough to keep the stream of stuff coming. Or we can say uncle" (par. 18). He asks readers to embrace a lifestyle of thrift, returning to a time of "Yankee frugality" when "we couldn't imagine wasting money on ourselves, made do or did without" (16).

QUESTIONS ON WRITING STRATEGY

1. McKibben seems to expect that many if not most readers will agree with his assessment of the problem but not necessarily his solution—a reasonable expectation, given that he's writing for *Mother Jones*, with its mostly liberal and environmentally aware audience. In opening with a personal tale of the satisfaction of recycling, McKibben presents himself as someone who holds the same values his readers do, but then attempts to jar them into deeper consciousness by stressing the quantity of "unnecessary" waste (3). Throughout his examples of shameful behavior in the rest of the essay, he addresses the perpetrators as *you* and *we*—implicating his readers in the wastefulness and unacceptable behavior he describes. By the time he reaches his proposal, the resulting sense of shared responsibility for the problem should, he seems to hope, soften readers' resistance to change and sacrifice.

2. Examples of *emotional appeals*: the mention of trees and time wasted by junk mail (par. 6); the suggestion that fast acceleration "makes you look like an idiot, or a teenager" (7); the concern for workers and children (12); the examples of profligate CEOs (15). Examples of *ethical appeals*: McKibben's presentation of his community recycling experience (1–3); his admiration for learning (11); his use of *we* (throughout). Examples of *rational appeals*: statistical evidence (e.g., 7, 9); the structure of the argument; dealing with opponents' arguments (see question 4, below). Students' judgments of these appeals will of course vary widely depending on their knowledge and beliefs.

3. The syllogism:

   Major premise: All waste hurts the economy and the environment.
   Minor premise: Personal consumption produces waste.
   Conclusion: Personal consumption hurts the economy and the environment.

Some students might point out, like Derrick Jensen does in "Forget Shorter Showers" (p. 475), that not all consumption is personal; others might reject the premise that waste is harmful: Either complication could render the conclusion invalid.

4. McKibben addresses opposing viewpoints somewhat obliquely, usually making an attempt at common ground then following it with his own assertion. He acknowledges the effectiveness of the Clean Air and Clean Water Acts in paragraph 4, for instance, and accepts that clean-burning engines reduce carbon emissions before asserting that such emissions still contribute to global warming (5). He accepts that some efforts are "maybe perhaps vaguely useful" before suggesting that other efforts could be "actually useful instead" (8). The closest he seems to come to a direct counterargument is in paragraph 9, where he establishes the volumes of waste produced by a large population before refuting the idea that "population is at the root of our troubles." Some students might feel that the author's attempts at counterargument are unfair or at the very least grudging; others may not be able to identify them at all; still others might report that they enjoyed them.

5. McKibben identifies nine categories of waste in paragraphs 4–14: "old-fashioned waste, the dangerous, sooty kind" (4); "waste that comes from everything operating as it should, only too much so" (5); waste that comes from doing something that manifestly doesn't need doing" (6–7); "waste that comes with doing something maybe perhaps vaguely useful when you could be doing something actually useful instead" (8); solid waste (9–10); wasted education (11); waste of human capital (12); government waste (13); and waste of natural resources (14). In each case he offers examples of the kinds of waste he means and establishes their effects. The distinctions establish the scope of the problem and suggest that personal waste is not only significant but the only kind that readers have the power to reduce: "Our wasteful habits wouldn't matter much if there were just a few of us," McKibben says (9).

QUESTIONS ON LANGUAGE

1. McKibben counts himself among the people overwhelmed by waste. By peppering the essay with colloquialisms and attempts at humor, he lightens the mood and establishes a bond with readers. The tone also allows him to express frustration at the situation.

2. "Stuffporn" is jargon for advertising; "throughput" is jargon for production or output. Other examples of language borrowed from business and economics include "multiply it by proximity" (par. 9), "inefficiencies" (12), "margin" (14), "open sourcing" (18), "stimulus" (19), and "hyperconsumerism" (19). McKibben uses most of these words ironically, highlighting the absurdity of business philosophies and practices.

3. Literally a decorative cord braided by a child as busywork and typically worn with a uniform (such as those for the Boy Scouts), a *boondoggle* is also a colloquial word for a wasteful or unnecessary task.

DERRICK JENSEN
Forget Shorter Showers

Both Derrick Jensen and Bill McKibben are regular contributors to *Orion* magazine. Although McKibben's essay (p. 468) was published in *Mother Jones*, Jensen's essay, published a month later in *Orion*, seems a direct response to his colleague. Read together, these essays should help students recognize that ideas need not be dual opposites or rigid pro/con debates to merit argument. Jensen's strong reaction to McKibben's proposal (and others like it) also shows students how an intelligent and knowledgeable reader like Jensen can counter what may have seemed airtight arguments. Following Jensen's example, students may in turn question some of his arguments, evidence, or assumptions (the first writing suggestion offers a specific approach).

The essay following Jensen's, "Eating Green" by Margaret Lundberg, adds another perspective on personal choices and their potential for effecting environmental change.

QUESTIONS ON MEANING

1. Jensen's thesis, stated in the first and last sentences of paragraph 8, is that simple living "is ineffective at causing the sorts of changes necessary to stop this culture from killing the planet." What Jensen wants, instead, is to "destroy the industrial economy that is destroying the real, physical world"—a revolution. His purpose is to refute claims that cutting back on personal consumption will help the environment.
2. Jensen agrees with McKibben on many points: Both believe the environment is in trouble, both place a great deal of the blame on consumer economy and inadequate government, and both see a desperate need for change. They disagree, however, on one key point: whether consuming less as individuals will do any good. McKibben sees personal choice as the primary driver of consumer economy; therefore, reducing consumption will reduce the damage caused by industry. Jensen, on the other hand, sees industrial culture as the driver; therefore that culture must be rejected and replaced with a different system of values.
3. A *double bind* is an either-or situation in which both choices lead to bad results. Jensen believes that we've become trapped into seeing only two options: continue consuming and harming the planet at our current pace, or reduce consumption and harm the planet more slowly. Both have the end result of "killing the planet" (par. 7). Jensen proposes a third option: dismantling the consumer economy altogether. (Although note that he doesn't specify what system he proposes in its stead.)
4. By stating that he is a practitioner of simple living himself, Jensen attempts to build common ground with his opponents. He applauds the practice but wants readers to accept that they need to do more.

QUESTIONS ON WRITING STRATEGY

1. *Rational appeals*: Jensen uses statistics and other evidence to support his argument (e.g., pars 2, 3, 5), and he walks readers through his deductive reasoning (e.g., 7–11). *Ethical appeals*: as an environmental activist, Jensen portrays himself as someone who cares deeply about the environment; he also concedes that he practices simple living (6). *Emotional appeals*: questioning the sanity of simple living proponents (1), depictions of death and dying (3, 7–8, 11), multiple repetitions of the phrase "killing the planet" (7–8), the suggestion that humans can help the earth as well as harm it (8, 10, 12), absolving readers from blame (9), the assertion that simple living is an act of "suicide" (11).

2. The examples are shocking and grab readers' attention from the start. But Jensen has a stronger reason for invoking them: He sees the environmental crisis as being on a par with the political crises he uses to frame the essay. Much as activists refused to work within the systems of Nazi Germany, antebellum America, Tsarist Russia, and gender and racial oppression—and instead revolted against them—Jensen believes that environmental activists today must reject the status quo and take decisive political action for radical change.

3. Jensen seems to address environmental activists (*Orion* magazine states that its mission is "to inform, inspire, and engage individuals and grassroots organizations in becoming a significant cultural force for healing nature and community"). He apparently hopes to jolt readers out of what he views as dangerous complacency and persuade them to take, or at least support, strong political action. Students' responses will depend on their openness to his arguments.

4. Jensen suggests from the beginning that simple-living advocates ignore the question and fail to see the real issue at hand. He accuses them of oversimplification in paragraphs 2–5 especially, portrays them as falling victim to either-or thinking in paragraph 7, and questions their deductions by claiming that simple living is "predicated on the flawed notion that humans inevitably harm the planet" (8) and asserting that "the logic behind simple living as a political act is suicide" (11).

    Some students might see an element of ad hominem attack in Jensen's portrayal of simple living advocates "dancing naked around a fire" (1). Those unconvinced of global warming or climate change might accuse Jensen of begging the question: Because the planet is dying, we must do something radical to save it. Those who do worry about the environment, on the other hand, might consider Jensen's conclusion—the planet is in trouble, so we must abolish capitalism—a non sequitur, although he takes great pains to explain the connection.

5. The main point—that the current global economic system is destroying the planet—has more punch because Jensen enumerates specific effects of consumer culture.

QUESTIONS ON LANGUAGE

1. *Agribusiness* was coined in the mid-1950s in response to economic and cultural shifts: family-run farms to large corporate interests, individual labor to mass production, local consumption to national distribution.

2. Of the given adjectives, *frustrated* and *militant* seem to be the most appropriate to describe Jensen's tone. At times the author sounds exasperated and condescending, as in "well, no" (paragraph 3) and "Uh, I've

got some bad news" (5). At other times he seems cautiously optimistic, especially when he reminds readers that there are positive actions they can take to help the planet (8, 10, 12). Overall, he takes a strong militant tone urging readers to revolution.

3. "Or lets talk water. . . . Or let's talk energy. . . . Or let's talk waste." Each of these deliberate sentence fragments follows the same grammatical pattern. The fragments and the parallelism together build a sense of urgency.

4. Jensen knows his proposal is radical and will come off as extreme. By quoting a respected environmental writer, he attempts to persuade readers that his ideas are both reasonable and shared by others.

DERRICK JENSEN ON WRITING

We find ourselves hard-pressed to disagree with Jensen's rules for writing. Keeping readers in mind at all times is the key to communicating with them. And communication, of course, is the reason for writing in the first place. Jensen does have other rules that he shares with his students—cited elsewhere in his book, they include provide the right details, be very clear, and aim for realistic dialog—but as far as we can see his rules are all variations of the first: "don't bore the reader."

MARGARET LUNDBERG

Eating Green

In the last of three essays that examine how personal choices affect the environment, returning student writer Margaret Lundberg makes an unusual case in favor of vegetarianism. If everybody stopped eating meat or at least ate substantially less of it, she claims, global climate change and overpopulation might cease to be problems.

Lundberg's argument is heartfelt, thoroughly researched, and compelling, although other students may take issue with a few of her sources or the organization of her points; we encourage readers to tackle these complexities in the third writing suggestion and the second question on meaning. We think they'll find that despite some minor flaws, their peer has done an admirable job of researching a challenging subject, synthesizing information, and putting her ideas into writing.

As a small-group activity, you could have students investigate the eating habits of students on your campus. Each group should devise a plan for observing places to eat both on and near campus, with members reporting back their individual findings and then the group as a whole drafting a brief report. These group reports could then be compared in class.

QUESTIONS ON MEANING

1. Lundberg sets up her thesis with a question in paragraph 2: "If all of us adopting a vegetarian diet could slow or stop all of these [environmental] ills, shouldn't we consider it?" She then develops her argument through the body of the essay and answers her question with a thesis statement in the concluding paragraph: "A vegetarian diet would enable us to healthfully feed many more people, and make much better use of the resources we have."

2. Focusing on the environmental damage caused by large-scale, industrialized beef production, Lundberg presents several points to support her claim. First, she says, the diets fed to cows raised for commercial slaughter make them ill, causing them to release large amounts of methane and nitrous oxide into the atmosphere, contributing to global warming (pars. 5–6). "Raising and packaging livestock animals" (6) uses far more energy, water, and chemicals than growing plants, depleting natural resources and increasing pollution (7). At the same time, more land is used to grow animal feed than food for human consumption, to the point that rainforests are being cleared to create more farmable land, contributing more greenhouse gases to the atmosphere; and with less land available for tending vegetables and grains to feed a growing human population, food shortages become a real possibility, especially for people in developing countries (7–8, 11).

3. Increasing levels of greenhouse gases are largely responsible for the recent rise in global temperatures. Lundberg's point is that the gases released by cows' bodily functions—especially on a mass scale—are more damaging to the environment than the carbon-dioxide emissions that are usually blamed for climate change.

4. Lundberg assumes that her readers have children or plan to have children, and that they're concerned for their own health, for their family's health, and for the health of the environment. She also assumes that most are not vegetarians but are willing to consider the idea.

5. Not necessarily. Although Lundberg clearly wishes that everybody on the planet could be persuaded to adopt a vegetarian diet if not a vegan one, at the very least she hopes to convince her readers to cut back significantly on their meat consumption. She makes this concession in the middle of her essay: Although "giving up meat seems like an unreasonable thing to ask" (par. 9), Lundberg admits, she stresses that the sheer quantities of meat in the typical American diet are unhealthful and unnecessary. It seems she'd settle for a few billion converts (8).

QUESTIONS ON WRITING STRATEGY

1. The personal details set the context for Lundberg's proposal and help to establish her ethical appeal as a reasonable, caring person rather than a militant proselytizer. She has taken up vegetarianism and veganism only recently, she says, and has seen her own health improve; that experience made her wonder how her diet choices could improve the planet's health. In admitting to liking meat herself, she anticipates objections and establishes common ground with nonvegetarian readers.

2. In paragraph 9 Lundberg concedes that meat is nutritious, and in paragraphs 10 and 11 she concedes that corporations are trying to find ways to reduce the environmental impacts of factory farming. She quickly dismisses each claim. Some readers may wish she addressed the coun-

terarguments in more detail; others may have different objections that she failed to address.

3. Lundberg intends these rhetorical questions, all of which suggest the long-term implications of dietary choices, to get her readers to think seriously about the problem she has been describing. The final question, in particular, lets Lundberg end with a flourish.

4. Answers will vary. We think Lundberg does an adequate job of examining the environmental effects of industrialized beef, given her focus and purpose. Some readers may think she overlooks the animal-rights arguments for vegetarianism, but those don't seem important to her. Other readers may question the validity of some of her statistics, especially those from potentially biased sources like the Vegan Society or from questionable authorities like the author of a cookbook. (We encourage them to examine her sources more carefully in the third writing suggestion.)

QUESTIONS ON LANGUAGE

1. Lundberg uses quotation marks around "went vegan" (par. 2), "just what the doctor ordered" (2), "Where's the beef?" (3), "do their part" (10), "cow pies" (11), and "Corn Belt" (12). The quotation marks acknowledge that Lundberg is aware she's slipping into colloquialisms. Some readers may feel that she could have edited them out, but the casual language helps to humanize the author.

2. Wendy's and McDonald's are both huge corporate entities that rely on industrial beef production while feeding the demand for large-scale factory farming. In focusing on fast-food franchises who advertise heavily and whose food few would consider healthy, Lundberg implies that much of the meat we eat is junk food or at best a guilty pleasure that could be given up without great sacrifice.

3. We enjoy the word play in Lundberg's title. *Green* refers both to the color of many vegetables and to environmentally conscious practices. By eating greens, she suggests, we're eating green.

4. Students may not be aware that *vegetarian* and *vegan* have slightly different meanings. A vegetarian does not eat meat but will consume animal products that don't require slaughter, such as eggs and dairy products; a vegan eschews consumption of *any* product derived from animals, often extending the ban to nonedibles such as leather and wool.

MARGARET LUNDBERG ON WRITING

Margaret Lundberg's thoughts on writing could help students who think they have nothing to write about or who have trouble starting to write. If they work from their own experiences and feelings, they'll have an easier time finding a subject.

ANNE-MARIE SLAUGHTER
Why Women Still Can't Have It All

As we mention in the headnote to "Why Women Still Can't Have It All," Anne-Marie Slaughter's new feminist manifesto created an enormous stir when it was published in June 2012. We accompany her article in the e-Pages with two samplings of reader responses: quotations collected by *Reader's Digest* in "The Essay That *Rocked* the Internet," and one man's befuddled perspective on the hubbub in Andrew Cohen's blog entry, "'Having It All'? How about 'Doing the Best I Can'?"

Your students may or may not be parents yet, but as Slaughter suggests at several points in her article, the issue of work-life balance affects everybody—especially college students aspiring for professional careers and future families. Although she pointedly acknowledges that her essay is addressed to a very narrow and very privileged segment of the population, her argument for family-friendly working conditions struck a chord with readers of all socioeconomic backgrounds. Some embraced her ideas wholeheartedly; others objected vociferously. We have no doubt that students' own reactions will be equally mixed, and just as strong; classroom debate is sure to be lively. If you have a mix of younger and older students, you might ask if their experiences bear out the contention of the sources quoted by Slaughter that college women today dismiss the possibility of "having it all" or deny that women (or men) of the author's generation ever achieved it.

Note, too, that Slaughter's article is very long: At more than twelve thousand words, it would have taken up approximately twenty pages in the print version of *The Brief Bedford Reader.* Be sure to tell your students to allow themselves plenty of time to read it—at least an hour or two—and then even more time to reread it closely.

QUESTIONS ON MEANING AND STRATEGY

1. "Having it all," in the feminist sense, might be described as pursuing a rewarding career while raising a happy family. Or as Slaughter puts it, "to rise up the ladder as fast as men and also have a family and an active home life (and be thin and beautiful to boot)." Slaughter argues that the juggling involved in having both work and children is impossible for women because of the social assumptions underlying the way most professional jobs are structured, *not* because working mothers are insufficiently motivated or committed. Citing limited opportunities for women to obtain leadership positions, impossibly long hours and travel requirements, work schedules that conflict with school schedules and family activities, deeply felt motherly instincts, and pressure to prioritize career growth, Slaughter insists that women who value their children are left with no choice but to opt out. Men are better able to combine work and family, Slaughter asserts, but only because they have been socialized to sacrifice family; she would like to see that change.

2. Slaughter introduces her thesis in the paragraph that closes her introduction: "The best hope for improving the lot of all women, and for closing . . . a 'new gender gap'—measured by well-being rather than wages—is to close the leadership gap: to elect a woman president and fifty women senators; to ensure that women are equally represented in the ranks of corporate executives and judicial leaders. Only when women wield power in sufficient numbers will we create a society that genuinely works for all women. That will be a society that works for everyone." Short of achieving an all-female legislature, Slaughter's solutions are outlined in the sections titled "Changing the Culture of Face Time," "Revaluing Family Values," "Redefining the Arc of a Successful Career," and "Rediscovering the Pursuit of Happiness." In practical terms her proposals might be summarized thus: encourage flexible working hours and telecommuting; create workplace "defaults" that align business and family schedules; establish corporate policies that prioritize family; teach leaders and coworkers to respect the discipline and time management required of caregivers; shift hiring and promotion assumptions to allow for occasional steps down or away (what Slaughter calls "investment intervals"); and normalize family commitments by openly acknowledging them and the happiness they bring. Businesses that take these steps, she argues in the section labeled "Innovation Nation," can expect to see higher productivity and creativity from all of their employees as a result. In sum, as she stresses in the final section, "Enlisting Men," Slaughter's thesis is that women in the workplace should stop trying to adhere to traditional masculine values and work instead to persuade men to adopt traditional feminine values.

3. Slaughter is clearly targeting readers like herself—"elite" middle-aged professional women who have children and jobs that allow them some control over their schedules, and who publicly lament that younger women seem to have given up the idea of combining career and family. As she states toward the end of her introductory section, "I am writing for my demographic—highly educated, well-off women who are privileged enough to have choices in the first place." Slaughter addresses these peers directly, informing them that "members of the younger generation have stopped listening" to feminist claims and insisting that "it's time to talk." She acknowledges that for the majority of women, the concept of "having it all" is beyond the realm of possibility, and explains that younger readers don't even see it as an option, but the urgency of her essay and the care with which she outlines causes and effects make it clear that she is also targeting the other readers of the *The Atlantic Monthly*—male and female alike.

4. Slaughter is writing to call into question the assumptions propagated by her generation of feminists and to persuade women in leadership positions to push for change. In the section titled "The Half-Truths We Hold Dear," she enumerates "the stories we tell ourselves, the clichés that [we] typically fall back on when younger women ask us how we have managed to 'have it all.'" Those assumptions are (1) that younger women aren't determined enough to strike a balance between work and family, (2) that women are comfortable relinquishing parenting responsibilities to their partners, and (3) that women can time having children in such a way that they can build careers in their late thirties and early forties. None of them, Slaughter argues, is true. She is pushing for a new wave of feminism that prioritizes family over career.

READER'S DIGEST

The Essay That *Rocked* the Internet

We include "The Essay That *Rocked* the Internet" as a follow-up to Anne-Marie Slaughter's essay for a simple reason. In curating responses to "Why Women Still Can't Have It All" from around the Web, *Reader's Digest* offers a concise and complex overview of real-world critical reading in action. Students will likely see some of their own opinions reflected in the quotations, but they just as likely will be surprised by how differently other readers interpreted aspects of Slaughter's argument—not to mention how many thousands of people voluntarily wrote about something they read outside of school.

We follow this compilation of excerpts with one full and nuanced reader response from Andrew Cohen, " 'Having It All'? How about 'Doing the Best I Can'?" That blog entry, too, offers students a model of carefully considered reflective writing in response to reading.

QUESTIONS ON MEANING AND STRATEGY

1. Characterizing "Why Women Still Can't Have It All" as a provocative essay that is "[p]art confessional, part sociological analysis, and part call to arms," the *Reader's Digest* editors focus on the parenting and gender aspects of Slaughter's article (the "confessional" and "sociological analysis") and overlook much of her argument (the "call to arms")—especially her proposals for solving the problem of work-life balance for both women and men. The oversimplification is almost unavoidable, given that the editors attempt to condense a 12,000-word essay to one paragraph and five key points—at the same time, the magazine tends to lean conservative in its political outlook. In general, we'd say it offers a serviceable summary that hits at most of the major issues Slaughter addresses, especially those points that sparked the most debate.

2. As a glance at the magazine's audience demographics shows, the average *Reader's Digest* reader is a middle-aged adult with some college education, a household income of around $60,000, and one or more children living at home; fewer than half are homeowners. More women than men read the magazine (60% of the audience is female), and fewer than a quarter of the readers hold professional or managerial positions (17% are unemployed or retired). They are not, in other words, the "elite" women in leadership roles that Slaughter identifies as her target audience, but average working parents. Accordingly, *Reader's Digest* focuses on those points and responses that would resonate most with its readers, emphasizing middle- and working-class struggles to balance jobs, families, and traditional gender roles.

3. The examples bear out *Reader's Digest*'s assertion that "[w]omen of every age and background (and plenty of men) let Slaughter know what they thought of her and her ideas about women, work, and family." Offering quotations both critical and supportive of Slaughter's points from women and men of varying socioeconomic statuses—single mothers, stay-at-home fathers, professional writers, "pink collar" workers, older

and younger readers, conservatives, feminists, and so forth—the magazine attempts to convey that what readers "thought" of her argument was complex, varied, and deeply felt.

ANDREW COHEN

"Having It All"? How about "Doing the Best I Can"?

Andrew Cohen's impassioned blog entry, the last of three contributions to a debate on work-life balance, offers a man's perspective on what the author believes is at heart a women's issue. As a "single father and a work-at-home dad," Cohen is in a strong position to counter Anne-Marie Slaughter's assumption that men are somehow naturally more inclined to let their partners take care of the children while they climb a career ladder. He is also, like Slaughter, in the enviable position of being able to wield some control over his work schedule; but unlike Slaughter, he doesn't believe that the flexibility gives him any particular advantage as a working parent.

Students may note that although Cohen claims that "earnest public conversation on this topic between and among men is impossible to imagine," several men are among those quoted in the selection sandwiched between his and Slaughter's, "The Essay That *Rocked* the Internet" from *Reader's Digest*. A good starting point for discussion could be to expand on the first question on meaning and strategy: Is "having it all" really a women's-only issue, as Cohen insists? If men really have given up any hope of achieving that state, doesn't that make the issue even more relevant? Why, or why not?

QUESTIONS ON MEANING AND STRATEGY

1. Cohen offers his tentative definition of the phrase: an occasional, temporary feeling of "pride and peace" in having successfully contributed to both work and family. Men can't be part of the debate, he claims, because "having it all," at least as conceived as a "pursuit of a lifestyle that is rich, rewarding and successful in all of its many facets," is solely a women's issue. Most men, he claims, have never believed they could commit equally to their careers and their children, and they understand that they must make sacrifices on both fronts. Although he admires women who aspire to reach the pinnacles in both areas of their lives, Cohen believes that the goal is an impossible one.

2. Cohen is writing to analyze and contribute to the debate spurred by Slaughter's article, but also to defend himself—and other fathers like him—against her claim that men are more comfortable than women sacrificing family life for career aspirations. Most emphatically, he insists that they are not.

3. Cohen gives multiple examples drawn from personal experience and cites the experiences and attitudes of other men in his life to demonstrate his understanding of the issue and to prove his claim that most

fathers (and mothers) are deeply committed parents who "live nanny-less lives of quiet desperation, just hoping that the choices we make, for ourselves and our families, end up being sound ones." At the same time, he stresses throughout his blog entry that he respects women and applauds their efforts to do better; he also goes out of his way to "give Slaughter credit" for those aspects of her argument that he either agrees with or finds illuminating. Some readers may feel that he's a little too earnest in his self-deprecations or may doubt the sincerity of his praises of women, but he certainly makes the effort.

4. Throughout his piece Cohen compares men and women, each time concluding that women are stronger, smarter, braver, and so forth. The comparisons help him to establish common ground with readers—especially women—who may not agree with his position.

MIXING THE METHODS

In this part of the book we provide an anthology, arranged alphabetically by author, of five works by very well-known writers. The collection has a dual purpose. First, we want to widen the tight focus of the previous ten chapters so that students see the methods as a kit of tools to be used *in combination* as the need arises. All five selections demonstrate just this flexibility in approach, narrating here, comparing there, analyzing a process for a couple of paragraphs, defining a term when helpful. The headnote to each selection lists the methods the author most relies on, pointing to specific paragraphs. And the introduction to Part Three gives students a list of questions—a kind of crib sheet of the methods—that they can use to explore or focus any subject.

The second goal of this anthology is to give you more leeway in your assignments. You can teach this part as a "mixing the methods" unit, of course, but you can also pluck out individual selections for any number of uses. If you want to show how a particular method works with other methods, you can point to, say, the classification in Judy Brady's "I Want a Wife" or the description in E. B. White's "Once More to the Lake." If you're just seeking another example of a particular method, you can turn to, say, Martin Luther King's "I Have a Dream" for argument and persuasion or George Orwell's "Shooting an Elephant" for narration. If you think students will respond to the thematic pairing of White's "Once More to the Lake" with Brad Manning's "Arm Wrestling with My Father" (in Chap. 5), you can assign them together.

We have highlighted the possible links in several ways. As we mentioned above, the headnote to each essay in this part itemizes the main methods used by the author. Among the writing suggestions for each selection in this part is at least one "Connections" topic that pulls in an essay from Part Two. For more general thematic links among selections, we provide a "Thematic Table of Contents" just after the book's main contents.

SHERMAN ALEXIE
Superman and Me

In this touching essay, Sherman Alexie charts both the plight of American Indians living on reservations and his own escape from that plight through a devotion to reading and sheer willpower. You might begin discussion by asking the class to enumerate the problems that Alexie suggests American Indians face: poverty, malnutrition, addiction, prejudice, an overriding sense of helplessness and failure. Students might then consider the personal qualities they see in the writer that helped him overcome such adverse circumstances. Make sure that students recognize Alexie's deep sense of ambivalence as he tries to cast himself as a saving hero.

Some discussion should certainly focus on Alexie's unorthodox writing style. Students should consider the effect of the very short sentences and relentless repetition. The accumulation of these devices gives the essay much of its power and suggests Alexie's overriding theme of childlike stubbornness and determination to be heard. This aspect of the piece could be the subject of small-group discussion.

Students interested in exploring more of Alexie's prose (he is also a poet) can be referred to his short-story collections *The Lone Ranger and Tonto Fistfight in Heaven* (1993), *The Toughest Indian in the World* (2000), *War Dances* (2009), and *Blasphemy* (2012). In addition, Alexie wrote the screenplays for the independent films *Smoke Signals* and *The Business of Fancydancing*, which are available for download and on DVD; you might consider screening portions of either film to shed light on reservation life. (The oral histories from a Lakota Sioux reservation collected by *National Geographic,* available in the e-Pages, could accomplish the same goal.) Alexie also has a Web site at *fallsapart.com.*

QUESTIONS ON MEANING

1. On its surface a literacy narrative, "Superman and Me" is also a plea for better education for American Indians and a statement of why the author writes. Or as Alexie expresses the purpose of all his work so poignantly in his concluding sentence, "I am trying to save our lives."
2. Alexie's childhood on the reservation was painful, except when he was reading—although even then he read "with equal parts joy and desperation" (par. 7). Speaking and writing about himself in the third person in paragraph 5 allows him to distance himself from the past while downplaying his success, especially for "Indians and non-Indians" who distrust intelligent Native Americans (6). Students should note that paragraph 5 is the only place in the essay Alexie uses the third person to speak about himself. The statement is ironic.
3. A "smart Indian," as Alexie suggests, threatens the status quo and is "widely feared and ridiculed by Indians and non-Indians alike" (par. 6) because he (or she) challenges assumptions, battles complacency, aims for improvement, and seeks change for the community. Notice that Alexie explicitly states that he is smart in paragraphs 7 and 8, asserting that he himself is dangerous.

4. Both Superman and Alexie are in the process of "breaking down the door" (par. 4). In each case the door serves as a metaphor for illiteracy and resistance, for the author as a child and for the students he attempts to reach as an adult. By casting Superman as his role model, Alexie implies that he sees himself as something of a reluctant hero. He managed to extract himself from the difficulties of reservation life through education, and he wants the same for others.

QUESTIONS ON WRITING STRATEGY

1. Alexie seems to be writing for a wider audience. He takes pains to describe the conditions of reservation life and the weaknesses of reservation schooling; he also refers to other Indians in the third person, as *they* and *them* (pars. 6, 8).
2. Alexie repeats himself relentlessly throughout the essay. Some examples: "Superman is breaking down the door" / "I am breaking down the door" (par. 4); "I pretend to read the words" (4); "an Indian boy living on the reservation" (4); "I was smart. I was arrogant. I was lucky" (7, 8); "I was trying to save my life" (7) / "They are trying to save their lives" (8) / "I am trying to save our lives" (8); "novels, short stories, and poems" (8); and "'Books,' I say" (8). In paragraph 7 the fourteen instances of "I read" stress that the process of learning to read required persistence and ingenuity. Here and elsewhere, the repetitions create a forceful staccato rhythm that is almost hypnotic; they also reinforce the sense of a stubborn child who is determined to learn—and to be heard. And, of course, they give the essay an irresistible coherence.
3. We can infer that Alexie writes serious but accessible fiction and poetry about the struggles of American Indian life, especially on reservations, and that he uses his writing to subvert stereotypes and empower Indian readers.
4. Alexie's sentences in this paragraph (and elsewhere) are a model of parallel structure, both within sentences and among them. Each sentence of comparison shows students performing poorly in school but using the same skills quite well on their own. His point is that these children are much more intelligent than their teachers give them credit for, and that low expectations encourage students to fail.
5. Alexie paints a picture of determination under desperate circumstances. As he portrays it, reservation life is characterized by unemployment and poverty (par. 1), illness and premature death (2), emotional pain (5), illiteracy (6), and fighting (6)—but also celebrations, storytelling, and laughter (6), and perhaps most of all, hope (8).

QUESTIONS ON LANGUAGE

1. The short sentences and simple structure mimic the writing level one would expect of a child in grade school. Alexie writes from the perspective of his childhood self learning to read and write.
2. Paragraphs, Alexie explains, group like things together and help them work "for a common purpose" (par. 4)—in other words, they facilitate unity and coherence. Just as written paragraphs hold together thoughts on a page, Alexie's conceptual paragraphs—communities, families, individual family members—help people stick together and work toward a goal.
3. From the Latin *prōdigium*, or "portent," the word *prodigy* originally referred to an omen of danger; now it is used to describe a person, usually

a child, with exceptional abilities. We enjoy the hints of its obsolete usage in Alexie's emphasis on the dangers of intelligence.

SHERMAN ALEXIE ON WRITING

Alexie speaks and writes freely about his role as an "American Indian writer." The quotations we've selected emphasize the mix of humor and pain evident in "Superman and Me" and his other writing. Most students will be familiar with "the Earth Mother and Shaman Man thing" that colors much writing by and about Native Americans. Indeed, it may color students' own impressions of Indian life, so that Alexie's depiction comes as a surprise.

JUDY BRADY

I Want a Wife

In the late 1980s newspapers and magazines quoted an instantly famous remark attributed to the actress Joan Collins after her divorce from musician Peter Holm. Declaring that her bitter public divorce battle had soured her on remarrying, Collins is also said to have quipped, "I don't need a husband, I need a wife." But we suspect that the credit for originating this epigram belongs to Judy Brady.

Instructors who have taught this essay in earlier editions report that it's a trusty class-rouser, evoking lively comments and a few intense disputes. Does Brady overstate her case in "I Want a Wife"? Some students, reading her essay in the new millennium, may think so. Perhaps their skepticism indicates real advances in the status of women since Brady first wrote in 1972. Do wives today play roles as humble and exacting as the one Brady details here? Are men as well as women freer today to depart from prescribed patterns of behavior? Are women still as angry as Brady was? Note that similar questions are addressed in the third writing suggestion. The trio of arguments about balancing work and family that appear in the e-Pages implicitly and explicitly counter some of Brady's attitudes toward men and feminism, so the four selections together create an even stronger basis for discussion and writing.

Give students some time to consider the above questions by having them collaboratively update Brady's essay: What are the requirements of a wife these days? Students can replace "wife" with "husband," "girlfriend," or "boyfriend" if they prefer. You might ask a few groups to read their responses aloud to the class as a way to open discussion of Brady's essay.

QUESTIONS ON MEANING

1. The essay lists them all. In general, the duties of a wife seem to entail making life easy and comfortable for everyone in the family—except the wife herself.

2. What it all boils down to, in Brady's view, is that husbands shoulder whatever responsibilities they want to assume. All others they assign to their wives.
3. The thesis is implied: Wives are not persons but conveniences whose subservient roles have been fashioned by husbands.
4. Answers will vary. Are all men as demanding and insensitive as the composite male chauvinist Brady draws? Are there fewer who resemble him nowadays than there were in 1972, when the essay was first published? The class might like to consider the extent to which traditional roles have changed in the past decade.

QUESTIONS ON WRITING STRATEGY

1. Because the author's name clearly indicates that she is a woman, the title is a surefire attention-getter.
2. The first two paragraphs establish Brady's credentials, position her essay in the real world, and show from the outset that wishing for a wife is not uncommon—among men.
3. Brady's tone is sardonic.
4. Avoiding the pronoun, though a bit awkward here and there, contributes greatly to the irony of "I Want a Wife." It dehumanizes a wife; she is not a woman but a thing to be used.
5. Readers of *Ms.* have feminist leanings. To us, the essay's observations of husbands and wives remain fresh: "Supermom" is, after all, a recent coinage. However, not everyone will agree.
6. The principle of analysis is determined by the thesis: The role of a wife can be divided into jobs that serve others, especially the husband. Other principles of analysis might be the jobs a wife does that require brainpower or the satisfactions of the role of wife—but these, of course, would produce entirely different essays.
7. The groups of duties are nurse-governess (par. 3), maid (4), confidante (5), social planner (6), and sex object (7). Today, "bread winner" might get more play than Brady gives it (par. 3).

QUESTIONS ON LANGUAGE

1. It emphasizes the selfishness and the demanding tone of the words. The words themselves reduce a wife to the level of a possession.
2. You might be able to elicit a definition of *monogamy* by asking your class to list other words they know that contain *mono-* and to list what all the definitions have in common.
3. The essay's diction is appropriate, the words easy for any intelligent reader to understand. The repetition of "I want a wife" and the author's use of short sentences give the essay a staccato beat that underscores the anger behind it.

JUDY BRADY ON WRITING

Brady's essay is a perfect example of writing derived from the rhetorical situation. She went from "complaining" at a meeting of frustrated women to reading her essay in front of a crowd to, later, publishing it. Students should be made aware of their own opportunities to turn their private gripes into coherent and audience-appropriate public arguments, perhaps in the form of an opinion piece for the campus newspaper.

MARTIN LUTHER KING, JR.
I Have a Dream

Although King's speech was meant to be heard aloud, it remains impressive on the page, and it supplies a splendid illustration of a proposal that appeals to emotion. You will probably wish to point out, however, that some of its strategies are directed primarily toward listeners: the strong use of repetition, parallelism, and direct references to the audience.

Your students will better appreciate the power of this speech if they see or at least hear it as delivered by King in 1963. (One source for video of the speech: *youtube.com/watch?v=iEMXaTkUFA*.) Have students in small groups discuss the differences between reading and hearing this speech. Alternately, have a group of students listen to the speech and make a presentation to the rest of the class, playing certain brief selections and commenting on the differences in hearing versus reading.

If you do have students listen to the speech, you might encourage them to consider the textual differences in the spoken and printed versions. King revised the original text of his speech, no doubt after he had received many requests for a printable version. (Speakers often make such changes, either because a transcription from spoken delivery might contain elements that would transfer awkwardly to the page or because they want to make improvements.) The printed version of King's speech adds a few passages that were not part of his original delivery, including from "*Now* is the time" through "1963 is not an end, but a beginning" in paragraphs 4 and 5, and paragraphs 8 and 9 in their entirety. In our view, the new passages are wonderful: "to lift our nation from the quicksands of racial injustice to the solid rock of brotherhood" (4) and "You have been the veterans of creative suffering" (8) in particular. We don't believe that in making changes Dr. King lost the power of his spoken discourse; if anything, he strengthened it. Some students, however, may disagree.

QUESTIONS ON MEANING

1. The purpose is to inspire its hearers, despite their setbacks and disappointments, to go on working for civil rights.
2. African American people have yet to receive the freedom and the justice that the nation's founders guaranteed.
3. While King praises the rise of black activism, he believes it can advance its cause by nonviolent means, as he makes clear in this paragraph.
4. King recalls both early American history and the present occasion in his opening paragraph and in paragraphs 3 and 5.

QUESTIONS ON WRITING STRATEGY

1. Besides directly addressing his followers (in pars. 6–8), King employs parallelism in phrases such as "from the dark and desolate valley of segregation to the sunlit path of racial justice" (4). Still more impressively, he builds parallel structures by repeating phrases and clauses,

lending them tremendous emphasis. This strategy informs much of the essay. In paragraph 2 there is a refrain ("One hundred years later"), and in paragraph 4 another ("*Now* is the time"). Most powerful of all are "I have a dream" (11–18) and "Let freedom ring" (20–27)—repeated again and again, at the start of each paragraph.

2. Paragraph 6.
3. Though he begins by recalling the past and its disappointments, he devotes by far the largest part of his speech to the future, in his extended description of his dream (pars. 10–27).
4. King's reasonableness is especially evident in his condemnation of bitterness and violence (par. 6). His personal authority—having been discriminated against and failing, having led demonstrations and achieving victories—combines with his rhetoric to give the speech its power.
5. In paragraph 2 the metaphors strengthen King's connection with the African Americans in his audience by showing his understanding of his race's hobbled, outcast state. In paragraph 4 the extended metaphor of the promissory note gives an argument by analogy, linking African American history to something concrete. The remaining metaphors in this paragraph intensify King's urgent appeal by contrasting what is with what could (and should) be.

QUESTIONS ON LANGUAGE

1. King uses concrete words in much of his imagery: the metaphors of "manacles" and "chains" (par. 2), that of the "check" (4), the visualization of the "governor's lips" (16). But for most of the speech his diction is largely abstract, as seems necessary to encompass two centuries of the past and the whole of the future.
2. King employs many figures, some biblical in connotation. Besides those noted in question 5 on writing strategy and in the preceding question, they include "summer of . . . discontent" (5), an echo from Shakespeare ("Now is the winter of our discontent / Made glorious summer by this sun of York"—the opening lines of *Richard III*); "the palace of justice," "the cup of bitterness" (6); "justice rolls down like waters" and "righteousness like a mighty stream" (7); "storms of persecution" and "winds of police brutality" (8); "valley of despair" (9); the "heat of injustice and oppression" and the "oasis of freedom and justice" (13); the topographical references in paragraph 18; the "mountain of despair" and the "stone of hope" (19); and the "symphony of brotherhood" (19).
3. There seems freshness in King's application of *curvaceous* to California mountain peaks, instead of to (as in the usual cliché) Hollywood film goddesses.

MAXINE HONG KINGSTON

No Name Woman

Students are usually moved by Kingston's evocation of a haunting childhood story. Ask them to describe their own reactions to the tale of Kingston's aunt. Does it seem completely alien, from a world far away, or more immediate? Does it hold students' imaginations?

Kingston's books *The Woman Warrior* and *China Men* are sources of further mystery and understanding about Chinese and American culture. In addition, a number of films have depicted Chinese village life: *Ju Dou, Raise the Red Lantern*, and *To Live* are just a few available on DVD. Students who are interested in the films might consider writing a comparative paper on the role of women, for example, in Kingston's essay and in one of the films. How important is the medium to the message? What do the two media say in common? Another use of the films, given their complicated imagery, is to assign a collaborative paper. Interested students could watch one film together, discuss it, and prepare a comparison between it and Kingston's essay, addressing the questions above.

QUESTIONS ON MEANING

1. Kingston and her mother share the purpose of telling a riveting story. Kingston's purpose is also self-examination and an inquiry into Chinese cultural attitudes; her mother's is also to instill these cultural attitudes in her.
2. Her aunt's husband could not have been the child's father (par. 3). Kingston posits two possible fathers: a man who "commanded [the aunt] to be with him" (15), and a man she herself was drawn to (21).
3. It is meant to warn her against adultery and, by extension, sexuality.
4. Kingston is haunted by her Chinese heritage; she seeks "ancestral help" (par. 22). Her aunt is a powerful representative of that heritage, an example of its grip on women and their emotions. Her life and death are a profound "family secret" that transcends Kingston's own immediate family.

QUESTIONS ON WRITING STRATEGY

1. Kingston's family and other older Chinese would be unlikely to read the essay: Kingston does address Chinese Americans directly (par. 12), and her detailed descriptions of Chinese and Chinese American cultures indicate that she is trying to explain them to other Americans. Older Chinese, and particularly her family, would be shocked that she is breaking the silence about her aunt. Chinese Americans would see themselves and their own "haunting" in her story. Other Americans might be enlightened about the complexity and power the Chinese heritage holds.
2. The story of the aunt is supposed to be kept secret by the mother. The mother's tale is supposed to be kept secret by Kingston but is instead examined minutely in this essay. Kingston's telling the secret of her aunt's story is an act of rebellion equivalent to her aunt's. Thus, the opening line presages all the themes of the essay (and creates suspense as well).
3. The effect is to intensify the confusion of reality and truth and to show the subjective nature of memory and family history. Kingston creates this effect in passages such as "I want her fear to have lasted just as long as rape lasted" (par. 18), "I hope that the man my aunt loved appreciated a smooth brow" (25), and "She may have gone to the pigsty as a

last act of responsibility" (44). You might want to draw students' attention to places where Kingston's different sources are intertwined—for
example, "My mother spoke about the raid as if she had seen it, when
she and my aunt, a daughter-in-law to a different household, should not
have been living together at all" (19).

4. The details in paragraphs 15–18 tell a much bleaker story: "She obeyed
    him" (par. 16), "No one talked sex, ever" (18). The details in para-
    graphs 21–28 are those of a more romantic tale: "she often worked at
    herself in the mirror" (23), "my aunt combed individuality into her bob"
    (25), "she dreamed of a lover for the fifteen days of New Year's" (28).
    Kingston seems more caught up in the romantic version of the story, in
    her aunt's desire and need to rebel.

5. Her aunt might have been "commanded . . . to lie with" the father of her
    child (par. 15), or she might have "let dreams grow" and "offered us up
    for a charm that vanished" (21). The raid might have been organized
    by her rapist (16) or by villagers who were "speeding up the circling of
    events" (39). She might have killed her child because it was "a foreign
    growth that sickened her every day" (43) or because "Mothers who love
    their children take them along" (46). In the end Kingston concludes that
    her aunt's suicide was caused by her feelings of imprisonment within
    the conventions of village life.

QUESTIONS ON LANGUAGE

1. Kingston's poetic language shows how deeply she responds to her Chi-
    nese heritage and its tales. Some striking phrases include "a protrud-
    ing melon of a stomach" (par. 3), "the heavy, deep-rooted women were
    to maintain the past against the flood" (20), "women looked like great
    sea snails" (27), "violence could open up a black hole, a maelstrom that
    pulled in the sky" (37).

2. You might want to explain the "commensal" tradition (par. 19), in which
    food is shared by the generations of an extended family. The idea of food
    and its allocation is central to societies, like China's, where resources
    are stretched to their utmost. Kingston underscores this in paragraph 15,
    when she describes her ancestors as "people who hatch their own chicks
    and eat the embryos and the heads for delicacies and boil the feet in
    vinegar for party food, leaving only the gravel, eating even the gizzard
    lining."

3. Kingston blurs the distinction between history and her interpretation
    of it.

MAXINE HONG KINGSTON ON WRITING

In this interview Kingston discloses a profound belief in the power of
writing to generate writing, even to bring order and meaning to one's life.
Some students may have had this experience of writing, and perhaps they
can confirm Kingston's words for students who haven't. (Students often
don't realize that the turmoil of writing can actually be productive.) Kingston
also slips in a small warning: It's fine to let yourself go in drafting, but eventually the "intellectual" (Kingston seems to mean "critical") side must kick
in for revision.

GEORGE ORWELL

Shooting an Elephant

Orwell's gripping narrative, told with vivid detail and an appealing self-effacement, tends to stick in the memory of anyone who studies it. Orwell's elegant prose may at first put some students off, but even they will soon enough be caught up in the narrator's tale.

Indelible as it is, the essay may strike students as remote from their concerns because it takes place in a country and a time far from their own. If you find this response, point out that the essay tells of doing what seems necessary, even what's wrong, to save face. Governments and their representatives everywhere, including our own, commit dubious actions for just this reason. The second writing suggestion can help students discover the relation between Orwell's experience and their own: Ask students to scour newspapers, TV news programs, or news blogs for examples of contemporary face-saving among public officials. In small groups each student could present one such example for discussion of the perpetrator's likely motives as well as the effects of such behavior.

QUESTIONS ON MEANING

1. Orwell explains that he took his .44 Winchester with him because "the noise might be useful *in terrorem*" (par. 3). His borrowing the elephant rifle later (4) seems a wise precaution because the elephant had killed a man. As he explains in paragraph 5, the rifle was for self-defense only.
2. The answer is twofold. He had to save face—that was the more important reason. But, as he mentions in paragraph 9, his being a bad shot also influenced his behavior by injecting an element of fear.
3. He expresses the epiphany most clearly and vehemently in paragraph 7: "I perceived in this moment that when the white man turns tyrant it is his own freedom that he destroys." And so on to the end of the paragraph.
4. The coolie's death put the young Orwell "legally in the right." By the time he wrote "Shooting an Elephant," though, Orwell was no longer motivated by any need to save face. He had the courage to tell his story truthfully and unsparingly, awful as it was. It seems clear that the mature Orwell did not share his younger self's view of the coolie's death.
5. Orwell's purpose is clearly to show, through his experience of shooting the elephant, how the need to save face motivates—indeed, compels—the actions of himself and every other imperialist.

QUESTIONS ON WRITING STRATEGY

1. These paragraphs, because they reveal so much about the author's feelings toward his job and toward the Burmese who made it difficult, shed light on the complex motives that resulted in the unnecessary shooting. They also, perhaps, somewhat justify the author's behavior—to himself and to us.

2. He explains the circumstances best in his opening paragraphs. He had come to hate imperialism and all that it stood for. Still, because it was his job, he had to do "the dirty work of Empire." Adding to his misery was the abuse he and his English compatriots had to endure from the Burmese.

3. With hindsight, Orwell has a broader and deeper perspective on the events. At the time, he was bitter, embarrassed, and a little afraid. In retrospect, he can see his foolishness and the tyranny he helped to further.

4. The paragraphs seem to unfold almost in real time, and the details of the wounded elephant are excruciating. We understand, almost too plainly, Orwell's horror at his act.

5. The Burmese are portrayed as both detestable (spitting on European women, yelling "with hideous laughter," "sneering") and pitiable ("wretched prisoners huddling in the stinking cages," "gray, cowed faces," "scarred buttocks"). The contradiction makes Orwell's position "perplexing and upsetting."

QUESTIONS ON LANGUAGE

1. The term refers to the annual period during which a male elephant is most sexually aroused and is often violent.

2. Some examples: "chucked up my job" (par. 2), "had taken the wrong direction" (3), "rubbish van" (3), "had come suddenly upon him round the corner of the hut" (4), "I ought not to shoot him" (6), and various uses of *got*, such as "I had got to do it" (7), "I had got to shoot" (7), and "I had got to act quickly" (8).

3. *Sahib* is a title of respect from the Urdu use of the Arabic *cahib*, meaning "friend."

GEORGE ORWELL ON WRITING

This is a grim account of the writing process! "Writing a book is a horrible, exhausting struggle, like a long bout of some painful illness." But students who have suffered when writing even a brief paper may take heart from Orwell's account of his agonies.

Orwell's remark about the need to efface one's own personality (cited in the second discussion question) echoes similar advice given by T. S. Eliot in his familiar essay "Tradition and the Individual Talent" (1919). Blasting the Romantic poets' notion of writing as self-expression, Eliot finds the poet obligated to do something more interesting than vent personal emotions. He adds: "But, of course, only those who have personality and emotions to express know what it means to want to escape from these things."

Orwell here stresses the importance of writing both to achieve something readable and beautiful and—more important, because it affects the artistry of the finished work—writing to improve society.

E. B. WHITE

Once More to the Lake

Among White's essays, this is one of the most often reprinted. In July 1941 White made a pilgrimage back to the Belgrade Lakes, northwest of Augusta, Maine, together with his young son, Joel. "This place is as American as a drink of Coca Cola," he wrote to his wife, Katharine. "The white collar family having its annual liberty. I must say it seems sort of good" (*Letters of E. B. White,* 1976). After his return to civilization, White produced "Once More to the Lake" for a column he was then contributing to *Harper*'s magazine. Too marvelous to be a reasonable model for most student writers, the essay can encourage them to believe that their own memories are worth recording and can interest others. "Once More to the Lake" exhibits a whole array of rhetorical methods, too: description, narration, exemplification, comparison and contrast, even process analysis.

Of course, it is White's description—of place, people, feelings—that is most inimitable, but students can try their hand in a small way at first. Give them a one-paragraph writing assignment—even with a word limit, if you desire—to describe a place that is highly familiar to them. Working in small groups, students can read aloud their paragraphs and get feedback on how they might revise them to make the images more vivid, the phrasing more precise, the details more developed. (This will work best if students bring copies of their paragraphs for the other members of their group.) Fine-tuning their own writing on this small scale should give students the confidence to undertake larger writing projects (like those in the writing suggestions).

QUESTIONS ON MEANING

1. White senses that nothing essential at the lake has changed; besides, he sustains the illusion that his son is himself as a boy and that he has become his own father (par. 4 and later passages).
2. Once, inboard motors had made a sleepy sound; today, the outboards seem "petulant, irritable." A central detail: "this was the note that jarred, the one thing that would sometimes break the illusion and set the years moving."
3. White's son is engaged by the same attractions: the joy of getting up early and going off by himself in a boat (par. 4), the fun of learning tricks with a motor (10). But the essay sets forth an insight that is White's alone, and the boy is not portrayed in any clear detail until the final paragraph.
4. White's purpose, made explicit in the final paragraph, is to set forth a theme: that although time at the lake seems to have stood still, time for the writer has been passing. He has aged and he will die like his father before him.

QUESTIONS ON WRITING STRATEGY

1. The repetitions help set forth the central theme of the essay. (In the answer to question 4 above we suggest one way of stating it.)

2. Beautifully arranged, this essay doesn't completely unfold its purpose until its final line. By a multitude of details, we have been lulled into accepting the illusion that time stands still. Suddenly, in one unforgettable image, White invokes reality. The feeling of donning an ice-cold bathing suit is a familiar sensation from childhood, but the cold of the suit also suggests the cold of the grave.

3. Young readers, we trust, will understand and appreciate it, too. Ask them. Students might not be greatly excited by White's slowly unfolding account at first, but most do warm to it.

4. The author's tone, sometimes gently humorous, in general is nostalgic, even dreamlike—as if he were viewing the lake and his early adventures there through a gentle haze.

5. White's images appeal to all five senses. They capture the smells of the bedroom and wet woods (par. 2); the sight of a dragonfly, the boat, and its contents (5); the sounds of motors (10); the taste of donuts dipped in sugar (11); and the tactile sense of damp moss in the bait can (5), of the "soggy, icy" bathing trunks (13).

6. The comparison, notably between White's childhood experiences and his son's, contains the essay's theme of time and mortality.

QUESTIONS ON LANGUAGE

1. For the word *cultist* (par. 6), it might be worth pointing out that White apparently means an enthusiast for cleanliness.

2. The diction might sound exaggerated, but "unique" and "holy" describe the way the lake appears to White in memory.

3. White's description of a thunderstorm is only one of the essay's rich array of figurative language. The lake in early morning preserves "the stillness of the cathedral" (par. 2). Waves keep "chucking the rowboat under the chin" (5). In paragraph 10 a one-cylinder engine was like a wild animal "eating out of your hand," and a boat could approach a dock like a charging bull. In paragraph 11 a steamboat used to look like a Ubangi, and a drink of soda pop would backfire like an engine. In paragraph 12 the storm becomes a wild concert, and the generations are linked "in a strong indestructible chain." The essay ends in a splendid metaphor.

E. B. WHITE ON WRITING

For aspiring writers—probably every class has at least one or two—E. B. White's advice must be among the most encouraging in existence. To the discouraged seventeen-year-old who wrote to him, White simply said, "Write." What eager aspirants might fail to notice at first glance is White's confession that he wrote "half a million words" before trying to get any of them into print. This statement comes as a cool, refreshing breeze in a world where too many people try to get published before they are ready.

E. B. White isn't big on market tips, either. His whole point is that if you really care about what you write, if you really work at it until it's as good as it can be, someone will want to read it. Clearly, not every aspiring writer was born with a gift equal to White's. Still, we hope you agree that one of the most helpful things you can impress upon students is that their writing will be better if they care about what they're saying.

RUSSELL BAKER

Russell Baker is one of America's notable humorists and political satirists. Born in 1925 in Virginia, Baker was raised in New Jersey and Maryland by his widowed mother. After serving in the navy during World War II, he earned a BA from Johns Hopkins University in 1947. He became a reporter for the *Baltimore Sun* that year and then joined the *New York Times* in 1954, covering the State Department, the White House, and Congress. From 1962 until he left the *Times* in 1998, he wrote a popular syndicated column that ranged over the merely bothersome (unreadable menus) and the serious (the Cold War). Many of Baker's columns and essays have been collected in books, such as *There's a Country in My Cellar* (1990). Baker has twice received the Pulitzer Prize, once for distinguished commentary and again for the first volume of his autobiography, *Growing Up* (1982). He has also written fiction and children's books, edited *Russell Baker's Book of American Humor* (1993), and served as host of *Masterpiece Theatre* on public television. Now retired, Baker lives in Leesburg, Virginia.

The Plot against People

The critic R. Z. Sheppard has commented that Baker can "best be appreciated for doing what a good humorist has always done: writing to preserve his sanity for at least one more day." In this piece from the *New York Times* in 1968, Baker uses classification for that purpose, taking aim, as he has often done, at inanimate objects. In the decades since this piece was written, the proliferation of electronic gadgets has, if anything, intensified the plot Baker imagines.

Inanimate objects are classified into three major categories — those that 1
don't work, those that break down and those that get lost.

The goal of all inanimate objects is to resist man and ultimately to defeat 2
him, and the three major classifications are based on the method each object uses to achieve its purpose. As a general rule, any object capable of breaking down at the moment when it is most needed will do so. The automobile is typical of the category.

With the cunning typical of its breed, the automobile never breaks down 3
while entering a filling station with a large staff of idle mechanics. It waits until it reaches a downtown intersection in the middle of the rush hour, or until it is fully loaded with family and luggage on the Ohio Turnpike.

Thus it creates maximum misery, inconvenience, frustration and irritability among its human cargo, thereby reducing its owner's life span.   4

Washing machines, garbage disposals, lawn mowers, light bulbs, automatic laundry dryers, water pipes, furnaces, electrical fuses, television tubes, hose nozzles, tape recorders, slide projectors — all are in league with the automobile to take their turn at breaking down whenever life threatens to flow smoothly for their human enemies.   5

Many inanimate objects, of course, find it extremely difficult to break down. Pliers, for example, and gloves and keys are almost totally incapable of breaking down. Therefore, they have had to evolve a different technique for resisting man.   6

They get lost. Science has still not solved the mystery of how they do it, and no man has ever caught one of them in the act of getting lost. The most plausible theory is that they have developed a secret method of locomotion which they are able to conceal the instant a human eye falls upon them.   7

It is not uncommon for a pair of pliers to climb all the way from the cellar to the attic in its single-minded determination to raise its owner's blood pressure. Keys have been known to burrow three feet under mattresses. Women's purses, despite their great weight, frequently travel through six or seven rooms to find hiding space under a couch.   8

Scientists have been struck by the fact that things that break down virtually never get lost, while things that get lost hardly ever break down.   9

A furnace, for example, will invariably break down at the depth of the first winter cold wave, but it will never get lost. A woman's purse, which after all does have some inherent capacity for breaking down, hardly ever does; it almost invariably chooses to get lost.   10

Some persons believe this constitutes evidence that inanimate objects are not entirely hostile to man, and that a negotiated peace is possible. After all, they point out, a furnace could infuriate a man even more thoroughly by getting lost than by breaking down, just as a glove could upset him far more by breaking down than by getting lost.   11

Not everyone agrees, however, that this indicates a conciliatory attitude among inanimate objects. Many say it merely proves that furnaces, gloves and pliers are incredibly stupid.   12

The third class of objects — those that don't work — is the most curious of all. These include such objects as barometers, car clocks, cigarette lighters, flashlights and toy-train locomotives. It is inaccurate, of course, to say that they never work. They work once, usually for the first few hours after being brought home, and then quit. Thereafter, they never work again.   13

In fact, it is widely assumed that they are built for the purpose of not working. Some people have reached advanced ages without ever seeing some of these objects — barometers, for example — in working order.   14

Science is utterly baffled by the entire category. There are many theories   15
about it. The most interesting holds that the things that don't work have
attained the highest state possible for an inanimate object, the state to which
things that break down and things that get lost can still only aspire.

They have truly defeated man by conditioning him never to expect any-   16
thing of them, and in return they have given man the only peace he receives
from inanimate society. He does not expect his barometer to work, his electric
locomotive to run, his cigarette lighter to light or his flashlight to illuminate,
and when they don't it does not raise his blood pressure.

He cannot attain that peace with furnaces and keys and cars and women's   17
purses as long as he demands that they work for their keep.

For a reading quiz, visit **bedfordstmartins.com/thebedfordreader**.

Journal Writing

What other ways can you think of to classify inanimate objects? In your journal, try
expanding on Baker's categories, or create new categories of your own based on a
different principle — for example, objects no student can live without or objects no
student would want to be caught dead with. (To take your journal writing further, see
"From Journal to Essay" on the next page.)

Questions on Meaning

1. What is Baker's THESIS?
2. Why don't things that break down get lost, and vice versa?
3. Does Baker have any PURPOSE other than to make his readers smile?
4. How have inanimate objects "defeated man" (par. 16)?

Questions on Writing Strategy

1. What is the EFFECT of Baker's principle of classification? What categories are
   omitted here, and why?
2. In paragraphs 6–10, how does Baker develop the category of things that get lost?
   Itemize the strategies he uses to make the category clear.
3. Find three places where Baker uses hyperbole. (See FIGURES OF SPEECH in Useful
   Terms if you need a definition.) What is the effect of the hyperbole?
4. How does the essay's INTRODUCTION help set its TONE? How does the CONCLUSION
   reinforce the tone?
5. **OTHER METHODS**   How does Baker use NARRATION to portray inanimate objects
   in the act of "resisting" people? Discuss how these mini-narratives make his classification more persuasive.

Questions on Language

1. Look up any of these words that are unfamiliar: plausible, locomotion (par. 7); invariably, inherent (10); conciliatory (12).
2. What are the CONNOTATIONS of the word "cunning" (par. 3)? What is its effect in this context?
3. Why does Baker use such expressions as "man," "some people," and "their human enemies" rather than *I* to describe those who come into conflict with inanimate objects? How might the essay have been different if Baker had relied on *I?*

Suggestions for Writing

1. **FROM JOURNAL TO ESSAY**   Write a brief, humorous essay based on one classification system from your journal entry. It may be helpful to use narration or DESCRIPTION in your classification. Figures of speech, especially hyperbole and understatement, can help you establish a comic tone.
2. Think of a topic that would not generally be considered appropriate for a serious classification (some examples: game-show winners, body odors, stupid pet tricks, knock-knock jokes). Select a principle of classification, and write a brief essay sorting the subject into categories. You may want to use a humorous tone; then again, you may want to approach the topic "seriously," counting on the contrast between subject and treatment to make your IRONY clear.
3. **CRITICAL WRITING**   In a short essay, discuss the likely AUDIENCE for Baker's essay. (Recall that it first appeared in the *New York Times*.) What can you INFER from his EXAMPLES about Baker's own age and economic status? Does he ASSUME his audience is similar? How do the connections between author and audience help establish the essay's humor? Does this humor exclude some readers?
4. **CONNECTIONS**   Baker's essay bears comparison with "Remembering My Childhood on the Continent of Africa" by another humorist, David Sedaris (p. 232). Each man writes about himself with a self-deprecating, mock-serious tone. Read both works closely, and write an essay in which you COMPARE AND CONTRAST the words the authors use to present themselves and their situations.

Russell Baker on Writing

In "Computer Fallout," an essay from the October 11, 1987, *New York Times Magazine,* Baker sets out to prove that computers make a writer's life easier, but he ends up somewhere else entirely. Although Baker wrote this piece when word processors were still fairly new on the writing scene, those who share his affliction will recognize the experience even today.

The wonderful thing about writing with a computer instead of a typewriter or a lead pencil is that it's so easy to rewrite that you can make each sentence almost perfect before moving on to the next sentence.

An impressive aspect of using a computer to write with

One of the plusses about a computer on which to write

Happily, the computer is a marked improvement over both the typewriter and the lead pencil for purposes of literary composition, due to the ease with which rewriting can be effectuated, thus enabling

What a marked improvement the computer is for the writer over the typewriter and lead pencil

The typewriter and lead pencil were good enough in their day, but if Shakespeare had been able to access a computer with a good writing program

If writing friends scoff when you sit down at the computer and say, "The lead pencil was good enough for Shakespeare

One of the drawbacks of having a computer on which to write is the ease and rapidity with which the writing can be done, thus leading to the inclusion of many superfluous terms like "lead pencil," when the single word "pencil" would be completely, entirely and utterly adequate.

The ease with which one can rewrite on a computer gives it an advantage over such writing instruments as the pencil and typewriter by enabling the writer to turn an awkward and graceless sentence into one that is practically perfect, although it

The writer's eternal quest for the practically perfect sentence may be ending at last, thanks to the computer's gift of editing ease and swiftness to those confronting awkward, formless, nasty, illiterate sentences such as

Man's quest is eternal, but what specifically is it that he quests, and why does he

Mankind's quest is

Man's and woman's quest

Mankind's and womankind's quest

Humanity's quest for the perfect writing device

Eternal has been humanity's quest

Eternal have been many of humanity's quests

From the earliest cave writing, eternal has been the quest for a device that will forever prevent writers from using the word "quest," particularly when modified by such adjectives as "eternal," "endless," "tireless" and

Many people are amazed at the ease

Many persons are amazed by the ease

Lots of people are astounded when they see the nearly perfect sentences I write since upgrading my writing instrumentation from pencil and typewriter to

Listen, folks, there's nothing to writing almost perfect sentences with ease and rapidity provided you've given up the old horse-and-buggy writing mentality that says Shakespeare couldn't have written those great plays if he had enjoyed the convenience of electronic compositional instrumentation.

Folks, have you ever realized that there's nothing to writing almost

Have you ever stopped to think, folks, that maybe Shakespeare could have written even better if

To be or not to be, that is the central focus of the inquiry.

In the intrapersonal relationships played out within the mind as to the relative merits of continuing to exist as opposed to not continuing to exist

Live or die, a choice as ancient as humanities' eternal quest, is a tough choice which has confounded mankind as well as womankind ever since the option of dreaming was first perceived as a potentially negating effect of the quiescence assumed to be obtainable through the latter course of action.

I'm sick and tired of Luddites saying pencils and typewriters are just as good as computers for writing nearly perfect sentences when they — the Luddites, that is — have never experienced the swiftness and ease of computer writing which makes it possible to compose almost perfect sentences in practically no time at

Folks, are you sick and tired of

Are you, dear reader

Good reader, are you

A lot of you nice folks out there are probably just as sick and tired as I am of hearing people say they are sick and tired of this and that and

Listen, people, I'm just as sick and tired as you are of having writers and TV commercial performers who oil me in cornpone politician prose addressed to "you nice folks out

A curious feature of computers, as opposed to pencils and typewriters, is that when you ought to be writing something more interesting than a nearly perfect sentence

Since it is easier to revise and edit with a computer than with a typewriter or pencil, this amazing machine makes it very hard to stop editing and revising long enough to write a readable sentence, much less an entire newspaper column.

For Discussion

1. What is Baker's unstated THESIS? Does he convince you?
2. Do you find yourself ever having the problem Baker finally admits to in the last paragraph?

JEFF WISE

Jeff Wise is a journalist who writes about science, psychology, technology, and adventure. He earned a BS in evolutionary biology from Harvard University in 1988 and freelanced with Time Inc. for ten years. Currently a contributing editor for *Popular Mechanics* and *Travel + Leisure,* Wise blogs regularly for the *Huffington Post* and *Psychology Today* and has published articles in many periodicals, including *Men's Health, Outside, National Geographic Adventure, Esquire, Popular Science, Details,* and the *New York Times.* He is also the author of *Extreme Fear: The Science of Your Mind in Danger* (2009). An adventure seeker who is willing to "try anything," Wise pilots gliders and small airplanes as a hobby. He lives in New York City.

Deadly Mind Traps

Wise is known for his witty but carefully researched explanations of scientific concepts. In "Deadly Mind Traps," he explains how common mental errors can lead to doom and offers practical suggestions for outwitting our tendencies toward self-destruction. Wise first wrote the essay as a 2012 blog post for *Psychology Today* and thoroughly revised it for inclusion in *Reader's Digest* six months later.

1   The hiker who leaves a well-marked trail and wanders off, cross-country. The pilot who flies his perfectly maintained airplane into the ground. The kayaker who dives into a hydraulic whitewater "grinder" even though he's just seen it suck three buddies to their doom. "Gee," you think when you hear such tales, "*I'd* never do something like that."

2   But would you? We like to think of ourselves as pretty rational, but that's hardly how we seem from the perspective of accident investigators and search-and-rescue crews, who can tell you all too well that otherwise normal, healthy individuals are exceptionally predisposed to making mistakes best described as boneheaded in life-or-death situations.

3   Research shows this kind of self-defeating behavior is usually far from random. We tend to make mistakes in ways that cluster under a few categories of screwup. Most of the time, we're on autopilot, relying on habit and time-saving rules of thumb known as heuristics. For the most part, these rules work just fine. But when the stakes are higher, they can lead us into mental traps from which there is no escape. One slipup leads to another and to another, in an ever-worsening spiral. The pressure ratchets up, and our ability to make sound decisions withers.

4   These cognitive errors are most dangerous in a potentially lethal environment like the wilderness or the cockpit of an aircraft, but versions of them

can crop up in everyday life, too, such as when making decisions about what to eat or how to invest. The best defense? Just knowing they exist. When you recognize yourself starting to glide into one of these mind traps, stop, take a breath, and turn on your rational brain.

1. The Domino Effect

The problem began with a minor malfunction. Scott Showalter, a 34-year-old Virginia dairy farmer, was trying to transfer manure from one holding pit to another when the pipe between them became clogged. As he'd done before, he climbed down to free the obstruction. But what he neither saw nor sensed was the invisible layer of hydrogen sulfide gas that filled the bottom of the pit. He keeled over within seconds. When an employee, Amous Stoltzfus, climbed down to Showalter's aid, he too succumbed, but not before his shouts drew the attention of Showalter's wife and two of their daughters, aged 9 and 11. One by one, each climbed down to rescue the others, and each one died in turn.

Similar tragedies play out time and again when people try to rescue companions. A teen jumps from a dangerous waterfall and disappears; his buddies follow, one after the other, until they all drown. A firefighter goes into a burning building to rescue a comrade; another goes in after him, then another.

In each case, the domino effect results from a deep-seated emotion: the need to help others. The fear response shuts down areas of the brain that handle complex thoughts and planning, but it doesn't affect simple emotions or well-learned habits like altruism. So we're driven to think about helping others instead of rationally identifying potential hazards, like invisible poison gas or an underwater hydraulic. "People lose the ability to think about the long-term consequences of their actions," says Sian Beilock, PhD, a professor of psychiatry at the University of Chicago.

Avoid the trap: If you ever find yourself in an unfolding tragedy like the Showalters', Beilock recommends pausing for a moment to take a deep breath and think about what's going on. "Even taking one step back sometimes allows you to see it in a different light, to maybe think, My efforts would be better spent running to get help," she says. Of course, it's extremely difficult to separate rational thought from emotion during an unfamiliar crisis. Planning for potential dangers can help; for instance, every family should practice a fire drill routine in their home.

2. Double or Nothing

In February 2003, a group of foreign tourists visiting Northern California prepared to watch a hot-air balloon take off at the Domaine Chandon vineyard near Yountville. Shortly before 8 a.m., the ground crew was repositioning the inflated balloon when one of the tourists, a 33-year-old Scot named Brian Stevenson, grabbed hold of the basket, perhaps in an attempt to help.

But when the balloon began to rise, Stevenson held on, despite a chorus   10
of shouts from the ground urging him to let go. The balloon rose quickly: 10 feet, 20, 40, 100. The empty air below Stevenson's dangling feet stretched to a horrifying distance; pretty soon, he could hold on no longer. His fellow tourists watched as their companion plummeted fatally to the earth.

If a balloon unexpectedly begins to rise, a person hanging on can follow   11
a deadly logic: When he's only been lifted a foot or two into the air, he may think, Oh, that's no big deal, I can just step down if I need to. Then suddenly he's at six feet and thinks, I could twist an ankle, I'd better hang on and wait until it gets lower. Before he knows it, he's at 25 feet, realizing that a jump would cause serious injury at best.

The runaway-balloon problem is a manifestation of our irrational assess-   12
ment of risks and rewards. We tend to avoid risk when contemplating poten-tial gains but seek risk to avoid losses. For instance, if you offer people a choice between a certain loss of $1,000 and a fifty-fifty chance of losing $2,500, the majority will opt for the riskier option, to avoid a definite financial hit. From the perspective of someone dangling 20 feet in the air, the gamble that he might be able to ride the gondola safely back to the ground seems preferable to a guaranteed pair of broken legs. But in the moment, he can't factor in the price he'll pay if he loses.

Avoid the trap: Casinos make a good profit from our flawed ability to   13
calculate true risk. Gamblers wind up in a hole, then instinctively take bigger and bigger risks in an attempt to recoup the losses. To a veteran in the field of applied psychology, it's a foregone conclusion. "I always tell my students, if you're tempted to go to Vegas, just write me a check instead," says Art Markman, PhD, a professor of psychology at the University of Texas at Austin.

3. Situational Blindness

In December 2009, John Rhoads and his wife, Starry Bush-Rhoads, headed   14
back to their home in Nevada after a visit to Portland, Oregon. Following the directions of their GPS, they drove south on US Highway 97 through Bend, then turned left on Oregon Highway 31, passing through a dramatically beau-tiful high desert landscape before they connected with the highway to Reno near the California border.

Near the town of Silver Lake, Oregon, their GPS told them to turn off   15
the highway onto a little-used forest road. If they'd continued straight, they'd

have been home in under six hours. But their GPS was programmed to take the "shortest route," not the "fastest." The narrow road took them into ever-deepening snow. After driving more than 30 miles, they got stuck, managed to dig themselves out, drove further, and then got stuck again. They tried calling 911 but couldn't get cell phone reception. For three days, the couple huddled for warmth until they finally managed to get a cell phone signal and call for help. A sheriff's deputy came to winch out their car.

As GPS units and satellite navigation smart-phone apps have flourished recently, there's been a spate of similar cases in which travelers follow their devices blindly and wind up getting badly lost. The underlying mistake is not merely technological but perceptual: the failure to remain aware of one's environment, what aviation psychologists call situational awareness, or SA. People have always had difficulties maintaining SA, psychologists say, but the proliferation of electronics, and our blind faith that these devices will keep us safe, has led to an epidemic of absentmindedness.

Avoid the trap: Full situational awareness requires incorporating outside information into a model of your environment and using that model to predict how the situation might change. If all you're doing is following the lines of the GPS, and it turns out to be wrong, you'll be completely clueless about what to do next.

In daily life, we rely on what Beth Blickensderfer, PhD, a professor of applied psychology at Embry-Riddle Aeronautical University, calls social SA to navigate our way through the human maze. It's especially relevant when you're traveling in another country, for example. If you're not paying attention, you might not realize that it's considered unacceptable for a man to talk to a woman in some cultures or to refuse to eat a delicacy, and you wind up committing a serious faux pas that could ruin the occasion.

4. Bending the Map

Our minds are wired to find order in randomness. We look at clouds and see sheep. This can be useful for making decisions, since we're helpless without a theory that makes sense of our quandary. But once we form a theory, we tend to see everything through it. A consequence is that when people get lost in the backcountry, they can convince themselves that they know exactly where they are, a problem sometimes called bending the map.

A few years ago, three twenty-something skiers went out-of-bounds at the Jackson Hole Mountain Resort at Teton Village in Wyoming. Looking for fresh powder in Rock Springs Bowl, they took a wrong turn, headed north instead of south, and wound up at the bottom of Granite Canyon. If they'd been where they thought they were, the stream should have been flowing right to left, and heading left would have taken them back to the ski area. Instead, they found the stream flowing left to right. They knew they needed to go left to get home, but based on the topography of where they thought they were, they also had to go downhill. Eventually, they decided on a solution: In this particular case, the water had to be flowing uphill.

The group marched upstream, away from the ski area, and wound up hav-   21
ing to spend the night in the snow without any survival gear. The next morning, they reconsidered their earlier logic and decided that, yes, the stream must indeed be flowing uphill. They had bushwhacked another quarter mile in the wrong direction before a rescue helicopter found them and flew them to safety.

Such errors of overconfidence are due to a phenomenon psychologists   22
call confirmation bias. "When trying to solve a problem or troubleshoot a problem, we get fixated on a specific option or hypothesis," explains Jason Kring, president of the Society for Human Preference in Extreme Environments, "and ignore contradictory evidence and other information that could help us make a better decision."

A vast collective error of confirmation bias unfolded in the past decade   23
as investors, analysts, and financial advisers all convinced themselves that legions of financial derivatives based on subprime mortgages were all fundamentally sound. There was plenty of evidence to the contrary, but the money was so good that too many found it easier to believe. They kept convincing themselves right up until the roof caved in.

Avoid the trap: To outsmart confirmation bias, make a habit of skepti-   24
cism, including skepticism toward your own gut feelings and assumptions. If you're part of a group that seems prone to agreement, play devil's advocate to encourage others to share different points of view. "Don't use your intuition to convince yourself that things are going right; use it to alert you to potential problems," says Jeff Haack, a former search-and-rescue specialist for Emergency Management British Columbia. "Listen to those niggling doubts."

5. Redlining

Mountain climbing at high altitudes is a race against time. Our endur-   25
ance is severely limited in the face of extreme cold and limited oxygen, and windows of good weather can shut abruptly. Lingering too long is an invitation to disaster, so when mountaineers prepare to summit, they need to set a turnaround time and strictly abide by it.

The consequence of failing to heed this sacred rule was made gruesomely 26 manifest on May 10, 1996. On that date, an unprecedented number of climbers were preparing to make the final stage of their ascent of Mount Everest, including some who had paid as much as $65,000 each. For expedition leader Rob Hall, getting his clients safely to the top and back meant a turnaround time of 2 p.m. But the turnaround time came and went. Finally, at 4 p.m., the last straggler arrived at the summit, and Hall headed down. But it was too late.

Already a deadly storm had begun, lashing the mountain with hurricane- 27 force winds and whiteout snow. Stuck on Everest's exposed face, eight climbers died, one by one. Hall was one of the last to succumb. Trapped a few hundred feet below the summit, paralyzed by the cold and a lack of oxygen, he radioed base camp and was patched through via satellite to his wife back home in New Zealand. "Sleep well, my sweetheart," he told her. "Please don't worry too much." Today his body remains where he sat.

Hall fell victim to a simple but insidious cognitive error that I call redlin- 28 ing. Anytime we plan a mission that requires setting a safety parameter, there's a risk that in the heat of the moment we'll be tempted to overstep it. Divers see an interesting wreck just beyond the limit of their dive tables. Pilots descend through clouds to their minimum safe altitude, fail to see the runway, and decide to go just a little bit lower.

It's easy to think, I'll just go over the redline a little bit. What's the big 29 deal? The problem is that once we do, there are no more cues reminding us that we're heading in the wrong direction. A little bit becomes a little bit more, and at some point, it becomes too much. Nothing's calling you back to the safe side.

A similar phenomenon has been dubbed the what-the-hell effect, such as 30 when dieters control impulses with strict limits on their eating, a nutritional redline. One day, they slip up, eat a sundae, and boom — they're over the line. "Now they're in no-man's-land," says Markman, "so they just blow the diet completely. They binge."

Avoid the trap: As in mountain climbing, the best response to passing a 31 redline is to recognize what you've done, stop, and calmly steer yourself back toward the right side. When it's not life-or-death stakes, know that redlining is a reality, and try to check it as much as possible.

For a reading quiz, visit **bedfordstmartins.com/thebedfordreader**.

Journal Writing

Have you ever fallen into one of the "mental traps" (par. 3) Wise discusses? In your journal, write about some preventable mistakes you have made. When is the last time you remember slipping up? What was the most significant mistake you ever made? Could it have killed you, or were the potential consequences less serious? What actually happened? (To take your journal writing further, see "From Journal to Essay" on the next page.)

Questions on Meaning

1. Why, according to Wise, do people try to help others even when doing so might put their own lives at risk?
2. How does Wise explain the flawed logic behind gambling?
3. What is situational blindness? confirmation bias? From what field(s) of study does Wise borrow these terms?
4. To what set of recent events does Wise refer in paragraph 23? How does this ALLUSION serve him?
5. Why is it important to set limits and stick to them? What could happen if you push past pre-established boundaries?
6. Does Wise have a THESIS? What is his PURPOSE for classifying mental errors?

Questions on Writing Strategy

1. Does Wise expect that readers will actually be able to use the information he provides? How can you tell?
2. Wise develops every one of his categories the same way. What pattern does he follow, and how effective do you find this strategy?
3. Do you detect any organizing principle in the way Wise orders his five categories of mental errors? Why do you suppose he starts and ends his classification the way he does?
4. Wise quotes several psychologists in the course of his essay. What do these SOURCES contribute to his explanations?
5. **OTHER METHODS**   What role does CAUSE AND EFFECT play in Wise's classification?

Questions on Language

1. Locate several examples of COLLOQUIAL language in this selection, and explain how such language sets Wise's TONE. How appropriate do you find this tone, given Wise's subject and purpose?
2. Find definitions of the following words: hydraulic (par. 1); predisposed (2); heuristics (3); hydrogen sulfide (5); comrade (6); altruism (7); manifestation (12); recoup, foregone (13); spate, proliferation (16); faux pas (18); quandary (19); topography (20); legions, derivatives (23); ascent (26); insidious, parameter (28).

3. Identify some FIGURES OF SPEECH in Wise's essay, especially metaphors and understatements, and explain their EFFECT. Why do some of the stories of tragedy, in particular, come off as slightly funny?

Suggestions for Writing

1. **FROM JOURNAL TO ESSAY**   Develop one or more of the mistakes you recalled in your journal into an essay. You may choose to elaborate on your mistakes by classifying according to some principle or by NARRATING the story of a particular mistake and its outcome. Give your reader a sense of your mental state that led to the mistake in the first place.

2. Wise suggests that, for a variety of reasons, human beings have a surprising tendency to get themselves killed through acts of thoughtlessness. How common do you think such incidents really are? In a library or local bookstore, find a copy of Wendy Northcutt's *The Darwin Awards*, an annual collection of news stories about people who die or seriously injure themselves in "an astonishingly stupid way that is verifiably true." (You might also visit her blog at *darwinawards.com*.) Is it fair of Northcutt to mock these victims? Select a dozen or so of your favorite examples in the book or on the blog, and write an essay explaining how those people's actions illustrate any of Wise's categories of "Deadly Mind Traps."

3. **CRITICAL WRITING**   EVALUATE Wise's success in making complicated psychological concepts clear and engaging for a nonspecialist audience. Consider, in particular, his use of colloquial language, ANECDOTES, and quotations from experts. What do these techniques contribute to the essay?

4. **CONNECTIONS**   "Taking a Fall," by Dan Koeppel (p. 262), is another essay that SYNTHESIZES scientific research for a nonspecialist audience. In an essay, COMPARE AND CONTRAST Wise's essay with Koeppel's. What strategies do the two writers use to make complex concepts easy to understand? Do both writers succeed equally well at engaging and informing their readers? Use quotations and PARAPHRASES from both essays to support your ideas.

ADDITIONAL WRITING TOPICS

Classification

Write an essay by the method of classification, in which you sort one of the following subjects into categories of your own. Make clear your PURPOSE in classifying and the basis of your classification. Explain each class with DEFINITIONS and EXAMPLES (you may find it helpful to make up a name for each group). Check your classes to be sure they neither gap nor overlap.

1. Commuters, or people who use public transportation
2. Environmental problems or environmental solutions
3. Social media users
4. Vegetarians
5. Talk shows
6. The ills or benefits of city life
7. Your playlists
8. Families
9. Stand-up comedians
10. Styles of marriage
11. Vacations
12. College students
13. Movies for teenagers or men or women
14. Waiters you'd never tip
15. Comic strips
16. Movie monsters
17. Sports announcers
18. Inconsiderate people
19. Radio stations
20. Shoppers

11

CAUSE AND EFFECT

Asking Why

◀ **Cause and effect in a cartoon**

With simple drawings and perhaps a few words, editorial cartoonists often make striking comments on events and trends. This cartoon by Mike Luckovich, published in the *Atlanta Journal Constitution*, proposes a disturbing effect of a common cause. What is the cause? What, according to Luckovich, is the effect? How does the content of both text messages in the cartoon reinforce Luckovich's position? What other effects might result from the cause depicted here? Do you agree or disagree with Luckovich's view? Why?

THE METHOD

Press the button of a doorbell and, inside the house or apartment, chimes sound. Why? Because the touch of your finger on the button closed an electrical circuit. But why did you ring the doorbell? Because you were sent by your dispatcher: You are a bill collector calling on a customer whose payments are three months overdue.

The touch of your finger on the button is the *immediate cause* of the chimes: the event that precipitates another. That you were ordered by your dispatcher to go ring the doorbell is a *remote cause:* an underlying, more basic reason for the event, not apparent to an observer. Probably, ringing the doorbell will lead to some results: The door will open, and you may be given a check — or have the door slammed in your face.

To figure out reasons and results is to use the method of CAUSE AND EFFECT. Either to explain events or to argue for one version of them, you try to answer the question "Why did something happen?" or "What were the consequences?" or "What might be the consequences?" Seeking causes, you can ask, for example, "Why do birds migrate?" "What led to America's involvement in the war in Vietnam?" Looking for effects, you can ask, "How has the birth-control pill changed the typical American family?" "What impact have handheld computers had on the nursing profession?" You can look to a possible future and ask, "Of what use might a course in psychology be to me if I become an office manager?" "Suppose an asteroid the size of a sofa were to strike Philadelphia — what would be the probable consequences?"

Don't confuse cause and effect with the method of PROCESS ANALYSIS (Chap. 8). Some process analysis essays, too, deal with happenings; but they focus more on repeatable events (rather than unique ones) and they explain *how* (rather than why) something happened. If you were explaining the process by which the doorbell rings, you might break the happening into stages — (1) the finger presses the button; (2) the circuit closes; (3) the current travels the wire; (4) the chimes make music — and you'd set forth the process in detail. But why did the finger press the button? What happened because the doorbell rang? To answer those questions, you need cause and effect.

In trying to explain why things happen, you can expect to find a whole array of causes — interconnected, perhaps, like the strands of a spiderweb. To produce a successful essay, you'll want to do an honest job of unraveling, and this may take time. Before you start to write, you may want to devote extra thought to seeing which facts are the causes and which matter most. To answer the questions "Why?" and "What followed as a result?" may sometimes be hard, but it can be satisfying — even illuminating. Indeed, to seek causes and effects is one way for the mind to discover order in a reality that otherwise might seem random and pointless.

THE PROCESS

Subject and Purpose

The method of cause and effect tends to suggest itself: If you have a subject and soon start thinking "Why?" or "What results?" or "What if?" then you are on the way to analyzing causation. Your subject may be impersonal — like a change in voting patterns or the failure or success of a business — or it may be quite personal. Indeed, an excellent cause-and-effect paper may be written on a subject very near to you. You can ask yourself why you behaved in a certain way at a certain moment. You can examine the reasons for your current beliefs and attitudes. Writing such a paper, you might happen upon a truth you hadn't realized before.

Whether your subject is personal or impersonal, make sure it is manageable: You should be able to get to the bottom of it, given the time and information available. For a 500-word essay due Thursday, the causes of teenage rebellion would be a less feasible topic than why a certain thirteen-year-old you know ran away from home.

Before rushing to list causes or effects, stop a moment to consider what your PURPOSE might be in writing. Much of the time you'll seek simply to explain what did or might occur, discovering and laying out the connections as clearly and accurately as you can. But when reasonable people could disagree over causes or effects, you'll want to go further, arguing for one interpretation over others. You'll still need to be clear and accurate in presenting your interpretation, but you'll also need to treat the others fairly. (See Chap. 13 on argument and persuasion.)

Thesis

When you have a grip on your subject and your purpose, you can draft a tentative THESIS STATEMENT to express the main point of your analysis. The essays in this chapter provide good examples of thesis statements that put across, concisely, the author's central finding about causes and effects. Here are two examples:

> A bill like the one we've just passed [to ban imports from factories that use child labor] is of no use unless it goes hand in hand with programs that will offer a new life to these newly released children.
> — Chitra Divakaruni, "Live Free and Starve"

> To begin to solve the problem [of the illegal drug trade], we need to understand what's happening in drug-source countries, how the United States can and can't help there, and what, instead, can be done at home.
> — Marie Javdani, "*Plata o Plomo:* Silver or Lead"

Your own thesis statement may be hypothetical at the discovery stage, before you have gathered EVIDENCE and sorted out the complexity of causes and effects. Still, a statement framed early can help direct your later thinking and research.

Causal Relations

Your toughest job in writing a cause-and-effect essay may be figuring out what caused what. Sometimes one event will appear to trigger another, and it in turn will trigger yet another, and another still, in an order we call a *causal chain*. Investigators at the scene of a ten-car pileup, for instance, might determine that a deer ran across the highway, causing a driver to slam on the brakes suddenly, causing another driver to hit the first car, causing the next driver to swerve and hit the embankment, and so on.

In reality, causes are seldom so easy to find as that stray deer: They tend to be many and complicated. Even a simple accident may happen for more than one reason. Perhaps the deer was flushed out of the woods by a hunter. Perhaps the first driver was distracted by a crying child in the back seat. Perhaps winter had set in and the road was icy. Perhaps the low glare of the setting sun made it difficult for any of the drivers to see clearly. Still, one event precedes another in time, and in discerning causes you don't ignore chronological order; you pay attention to it.

When you can see a number of apparent causes, weigh them and assign each a relative importance. Which do you find matter most? Often, you will see that causes are more important or less so: major or minor. If you seek to explain why your small town has fallen on hard times, you might note that two businesses shut down: a factory employing three hundred and a drugstore employing six. The factory's closing is a *major cause*, leading to significant unemployment in the town, while the drugstore's closing is perhaps a *minor cause* — or not a cause at all but an effect. In writing about the causes, you would emphasize the factory and mention the drugstore only briefly if at all.

When seeking remote causes, look only as far back as necessary. Explaining your town's misfortunes, you might see the factory's closing as the immediate cause. You could show what caused the shutdown: a dispute between union and management. You might even go back to the cause of the dispute (announced layoffs) and the cause of the layoffs (loss of sales to a competitor). A paper showing effects might work in the other direction, moving from the factory closing to its impact on the town: unemployment, the closing of stores (including the drugstore), people packing up and moving away.

Two cautions about causal relations are in order here. One is to beware of confusing coincidence with cause. In the logical FALLACY called *post hoc* (short for the Latin *post hoc, ergo propter hoc*, "after this, therefore because of this"), one assumes, erroneously, that because A happened before B, A must have caused B. This is the error of the superstitious man who decides that he lost his job because a black cat walked in front of him. Another fallacy is to oversimplify causes by failing to recognize their full number and complexity — claiming, say, that violent crime is simply a result of "all those first-person shooter games." Avoid such wrong turns in reasoning by patiently looking for evidence before you write, and by giving it careful thought. (For a fuller list of logical fallacies, or errors in reasoning, see pp. 445–47.)

Discovery of Causes

To help find causes of actions and events, you can ask yourself a few searching questions. These have been suggested by the work of the literary critic Kenneth Burke:

1. **What act am I trying to explain?**
2. **What is the character, personality, or mental state of whoever acted?**
3. **In what scene or location did the act take place, and in what circumstances?**
4. **What instruments or means did the person use?**
5. **For what purpose did the person act?**

Burke calls these elements a *pentad* (or set of five): the *act*, the *actor*, the *scene*, the *agency*, and the *purpose*. If you were a detective trying to explain why a liquor store burned down, you might ask these questions:

1. **Act:** Was the fire deliberately set by someone, or was there an accident?
2. **Actors:** If the fire was arson, who set it: the store's worried, debt-ridden owner? a mentally disturbed anti-alcohol crusader? a drunk who had been denied a purchase?
3. **Scene:** Was the store near a church? a mental hospital? a fireworks factory?
4. **Agency, or means of the act:** Was the fire caused by faulty electrical wiring? a carelessly tossed cigarette? a flaming torch? rags soaked in kerosene?
5. **Purpose:** If the fire wasn't accidental, was it set to collect insurance? to punish drinkers? to get revenge?

You can further deepen your inquiry by seeing relationships between the terms of the pentad. Ask, for instance, what does the actor have to do with this

Cause and Effect

scene? (Is he or she the neighbor across the street, who has been staring at the liquor shop resentfully for years?)

Don't worry if not all the questions apply or if not all the answers are immediately forthcoming. Burke's pentad isn't meant to be a grim rigmarole; it is a means of discovery, to generate a lot of possible material for you — insights, observations, hunches to pursue. It won't solve each and every human mystery, but sometimes it will helpfully deepen your thought.

Educated Guesses

In stating what you believe to be causes and effects, don't be afraid to voice a well-considered hunch. Your instructor doesn't expect you to write, in a short time, a definitive account of the causes of an event or a belief or a phenomenon — only to write a coherent and reasonable one. To discern all causes — including remote ones — and all effects is beyond the power of any one human mind. Still, admirable and well-informed writers on matters such as politics, economics, and world and national affairs are often canny guessers and brave drawers of inferences. At times, even the most cautious and responsible writer has to leap boldly over a void to strike firm ground on the far side. Consider your evidence. Focus your thinking. Look well before leaping. Then take off.

FOCUS ON CLARITY AND CONCISENESS

While drafting a cause-and-effect analysis, you may need to grope a bit to discover just what you think about the sequence and relative importance of reasons and consequences. Your sentences may grope a bit, too, reflecting your initial confusion or your need to circle around your ideas in order to find them. The following draft passage reveals such difficulties:

> WORDY AND UNCLEAR   Employees often worry about suggestive comments from others. The employee may not only worry but feel the need to discuss the situation with coworkers. One thing that is an effect of sexual harassment, even verbal harassment, in the workplace is that productivity is lost. Plans also need to be made to figure out how to deal with future comments. Engaging in these activities is sure to take time and concentration from work.

Drafting this passage, the writer seems to have built up to the idea about lost productivity (third sentence) after providing support for it in the first two sentences. The fourth sentence then adds more support. And sentences 2–4 all show a writer working out his ideas: Sentence subjects and verbs do not focus on the main actors and actions of the sentences, words repeat unnecessarily, and word groups run longer than needed for clarity.

These problems disappear from the edited version below, which moves the idea of the passage up front, uses subjects and verbs to state what the sentences are about (underlined), and cuts unneeded words.

> CONCISE AND CLEAR   Even verbal sexual <u>harassment</u> in the workplace <u>causes</u> a loss of productivity. Worrying about suggestive comments from others, discussing those comments with coworkers, planning how to deal with future comments — these <u>activities</u> <u>consume</u> time and concentration that a harassed employee could spend on work.

CHECKLIST FOR REVISING A CAUSE-AND-EFFECT ESSAY

✔ **Subject.** Have you been able to cover your subject adequately in the time and space available? Should you perhaps narrow the subject so that you can fairly address the important causes and/or effects?

✔ **Thesis.** For your readers' benefit, have you focused your analysis by stating your main idea succinctly in a thesis statement?

✔ **Completeness.** Have you included all relevant causes or effects? Does your analysis reach back to locate remote causes or forward to locate remote effects?

✔ **Causal relations.** Have you presented a clear pattern of causes or effects? Have you distinguished the remote from the immediate, the major from the minor?

✔ **Accuracy and fairness.** Have you avoided the *post hoc* fallacy, assuming that A caused B just because it preceded B? Have you also avoided oversimplifying and instead covered causes or effects in all their complexity?

✔ **Clarity and conciseness.** Have you edited your draft to foreground your main points and tighten your sentences?

CAUSE AND EFFECT IN ACADEMIC WRITING

A History Textbook

These paragraphs from Alan Brinkley's *American History: A Survey* explain the causes behind President Lyndon Johnson's decision in the 1960s to escalate the ongoing conflict in Vietnam into "a full-scale American war" — a decision that, as the author's text goes on to explain, had grave and far-reaching consequences for the United States.

Many factors played a role in Johnson's decision. But the most obvious explanation is that the new president faced many pressures to expand the American involvement and very few to limit it. As the untested successor to a revered and martyred president, he felt obliged to prove his worthiness for the office by continuing the policies of his predecessor. Aid to South Vietnam had been one of the most prominent of those policies. Johnson also felt it necessary to retain in his administration many of the important figures of the Kennedy years. In doing so, he surrounded himself with a group of foreign policy advisers — Secretary of State Dean Rusk, Secretary of Defense Robert McNamara, National Security Adviser McGeorge Bundy, and others — who firmly believed that the United States had an important obligation to resist Communism in Vietnam. A compliant Congress raised little protest to, and indeed at one point openly endorsed, Johnson's use of executive powers to lead the nation into war. And for several years at least, public opinion remained firmly behind him — in part because Barry Goldwater's bellicose remarks about the war during the 1964 campaign made Johnson seem by comparison to be a moderate on the issue.

Above all, intervention in South Vietnam was fully consistent with nearly twenty years of American foreign policy. An anti-Communist ally was appealing to the United States for assistance; all the assumptions of the containment doctrine, as it had come to be defined by the 1960s, seemed to require the nation to oblige. Vietnam, Johnson believed, was a test of American willingness to fight Communist aggression, a test he was determined not to fail.

Topic sentence: summary of causes to be discussed

Causes:
- *Need to prove worthiness*

- *Advisers urging involvement*

- *Congressional cooperation*

- *Support of public opinion*

- *Consistency with American foreign policy against Communism*

A Letter to the Editor

To encourage interaction between readers and writers, most newspapers, magazines, and journals, as well as some Web sites, solicit and publish letters to the editor. Unlike the anonymous comments readers may attach to news and opinion articles online, letters to the editor are signed by their authors and screened by editors. To be published, such letters generally must take a calm tone and express ideas rationally. In most cases, the writer refers to the original article or other piece that prompted the letter and responds by agreeing or disagreeing (or a little of both). The point is to add a new perspective and move a conversation forward.

An ardent supporter of her school's track team, Kate Krueger was a sophomore during the team's first winning season in many years. At the end of the season, the student newspaper published a sports column crediting the successes to a new coach. Krueger found this explanation inadequate and wrote her own cause-and-effect analysis in the following letter to the newspaper's editor. Notice that because Krueger actually agreed with the original writer that the coach had helped the team, she acknowledged the coach's contributions while also detailing the other causes she saw at work.

May 2, 2013

To the Editor:

I take issue with Tom Boatz's column that was printed in the April 30 *Weekly*. Boatz attributes the success of this year's track team solely to the new coach, John Barak. I have several close friends who are athletes on the track team, so as an interested observer and fan I believe that Boatz oversimplified the causes of the team's recent success.

> Reason for writing: Original author oversimplified a cause-and-effect relationship

To be sure, Coach Barak did improve the training regimen and overall morale, and these have certainly contributed to the winning season. Both Coach Barak and the team members themselves can share credit for an impressive work ethic and a sense of camaraderie unequaled in previous years. However, several factors outside Coach Barak's control were also influential.

> Point of agreement: The new coach was one cause of the team's success

> Thesis statement: Other causes played a role

This year's team gained several phenomenal freshman athletes, such as Kristin Hall, who anchored the 4x400 and 4x800 relays and played an integral part in setting several school records, and Eric Asper, who was undefeated in the shot put.

> Other causes:
> • Talented new team members

Even more important, and also unmentioned by Tom Boatz, is the college's increased funding for the track program. Last year the school allotted fifty percent more for equipment, and the results have been dramatic. For example, the new vaulting poles are now the correct length and correspond to the weights of the individual athletes, giving them more power and height. Some vaulters have been able to vault as much as a foot higher than their previous records. Similarly, new starting blocks have allowed the team's sprinters to drop valuable seconds off their times.

> • Financial support from the college

> Examples of positive effects:
> • Improved vaulting performance

> • Improved sprinting times

I agree with Tom Boatz that Coach Barak deserves much credit for the track team's successes. But the athletes do, too, and so does the college for at last supporting its track program.

> Conclusion summarizes Krueger's analysis

— Kate Krueger '15

CHITRA DIVAKARUNI

Born in 1956 in Calcutta, India, Chitra Banerjee Divakaruni spent nineteen years in her homeland before immigrating to the United States. She holds a BA from the University of Calcutta, an MA from Wright State University, and a PhD from the University of California, Berkeley. Her books, often addressing the immigrant experience in America, include the novels *The Mistress of Spice* (1997), which was named one of the hundred best books of the twentieth century by the *San Francisco Chronicle*, *Queen of Dreams* (2004), and *One Amazing Thing* (2009); the story collections *Arranged Marriage* (1995) and *The Unknown Errors of Our Lives* (2001); and the poetry collections *Leaving Yuba City* (1997) and *Black Candle* (1991, revised 2000). Divakaruni has received a number of awards for her work, including the Before Columbus Foundation's 1996 American Book Award and the Indian Culture Center's 2009 Cultural Jewel Award. She teaches creative writing at the University of Houston and serves on the boards of several organizations that help women and children.

Live Free and Starve

Many of the consumer goods sold in the United States — shoes, clothing, toys, rugs — are made in countries whose labor practices do not meet US standards for safety and fairness. Americans have been horrified at tales of children put to work by force or under contracts (called *indentures*) with the children's parents. Some in the US government have tried to stop or at least discourage such practices: For instance, the bill Divakaruni cites in her first paragraph, which was signed into law, requires the Customs Service to issue a detention order on goods that are suspected of having been produced by forced or indentured child labor; and the Department of Labor publishes an annual list of products made with child labor. In this essay from *Salon* magazine in 1997, Divakaruni argues that these efforts, however well intentioned they are, can mean dreadful consequences for the very people they are designed to protect.

For a different perspective on the effects of globalization, see the next essay, Marie Javdani's *"Plata o Plomo:* Silver or Lead."

Some days back, the House passed a bill that stated that the United States would no longer permit the import of goods from factories where forced or indentured child labor was used. My liberal friends applauded the bill. It was a triumphant advance in the field of human rights. Now children in Third World countries wouldn't have to spend their days chained to their posts in factories manufacturing goods for other people to enjoy while their childhoods slipped by them. They could be free and happy, like American children.

I am not so sure.   2

It is true that child labor is a terrible thing, especially for those children   3
who are sold to employers by their parents at the age of five or six and have no
way to protect themselves from abuse. In many cases it will be decades — perhaps a lifetime, due to the fines heaped upon them whenever they make mistakes — before they can buy back their freedom. Meanwhile these children,
mostly employed by rug-makers, spend their days in dark, ill-ventilated rooms
doing work that damages their eyes and lungs. They aren't even allowed to
stand up and stretch. Each time they go to the bathroom, they suffer a pay cut.

But is this bill, which, if it passes the Senate and is signed by President   4
Clinton, will lead to the unemployment of almost a million children, the
answer? If the children themselves were asked whether they would rather
work under such harsh conditions or enjoy a leisure that comes without the
benefit of food or clothing or shelter, I wonder what their response would be.

It is easy for us in America to make the error of evaluating situations   5
in the rest of the world as though they were happening in this country and
propose solutions that make excellent sense — in the context of our society.
Even we immigrants, who should know better, have wiped from our minds the
memory of what it is to live under the kind of desperate conditions that force
a parent to sell his or her child. Looking down from the heights of Maslow's
pyramid,[1] it seems inconceivable to us that someone could actually prefer
bread to freedom.

When I was growing up in Calcutta, there was a boy who used to work in   6
our house. His name was Nimai, and when he came to us, he must have been
about ten or so, just a little older than my brother and I. He'd been brought to
our home by his uncle, who lived in our ancestral village and was a field laborer
for my grandfather. The uncle explained to my mother that Nimai's parents
were too poor to feed their several children, and while his older brothers were
already working in the fields and earning their keep, Nimai was too frail to do
so. My mother was reluctant to take on a sickly child who might prove more
of a burden than a help, but finally she agreed, and Nimai lived and worked in
our home for six or seven years. My mother was a good employer — Nimai ate
the same food that we children did and was given new clothes during Indian
New Year, just as we were. In the time between his chores — dusting and
sweeping and pumping water from the tube-well and running to the market —
my mother encouraged him to learn to read and write. Still, I would not

---

[1] The psychologist Abraham Maslow (1908–70) proposed a "hierarchy of needs" in the
shape of a five-level pyramid with survival needs at the bottom and "self-actualization" and
"self-transcendence" at the top. According to Maslow, one must satisfy the needs at each level
before moving up to the next. — EDS.

disagree with anyone who says that it was hardly a desirable existence for a child.

But what would life have been like for Nimai if an anti–child-labor law   7 had prohibited my mother from hiring him? Every year, when we went to visit our grandfather in the village, we were struck by the many children we saw by the mud roads, their ribs sticking out through the rags they wore. They trailed after us, begging for a few paise.[2] When the hunger was too much to bear, they stole into the neighbors' fields and ate whatever they could find — raw potatoes, cauliflower, green sugar cane and corn torn from the stalk — even though they knew they'd be beaten for it. Whenever Nimai passed these children, he always walked a little taller. And when he handed the bulk of his earnings over to his father, there was a certain pride in his eye. Exploitation, you might be thinking. But he thought he was a responsible member of his family.

A bill like the one we've just passed is of no use unless it goes hand in   8 hand with programs that will offer a new life to these newly released children. But where are the schools in which they are to be educated? Where is the money to buy them food and clothing and medication, so that they don't return home to become the extra weight that capsizes the already shaky raft of their family's finances? Their own governments, mired in countless other problems, seem incapable of bringing these services to them. Are we in America who, with one blithe stroke of our congressional pen, rendered these children jobless, willing to shoulder that burden? And when many of these children turn to the streets, to survival through thievery and violence and begging and prostitution — as surely in the absence of other options they must — are we willing to shoulder that responsibility?

*For a reading quiz, visit **bedfordstmartins.com/thebedfordreader**.*

Journal Writing

Write a journal response to Divakaruni's argument against legislation that bans goods produced by forced or indentured child laborers. Do you basically agree or disagree with the author? Why? (To take your journal writing further, see "From Journal to Essay" on the facing page.)

[2] *Paise* (pronounced "pie-say") are the smallest unit of Indian currency, worth a fraction of an American penny. — Eds.

Questions on Meaning

1. What do you take to be Divakaruni's PURPOSE in this essay? When was it clear?
2. What is Divakaruni's THESIS? Where is it stated?
3. What are "Third World countries" (par. 1)?
4. From the further information given in the footnote on page 373, what does it mean to be "[l]ooking down from the heights of Maslow's pyramid" (par. 5)? What point is Divakaruni making here?
5. In paragraph 8 Divakaruni suggests some of the reasons that children in other countries may be forced or sold into labor. What are they?

Questions on Writing Strategy

1. In her last paragraph, Divakaruni asks a series of RHETORICAL QUESTIONS. What is the EFFECT of this strategy?
2. How does the structure of paragraph 3 clarify causes and effects?
3. **OTHER METHODS** What does the extended EXAMPLE of Nimai (pars. 6–7) contribute to Divakaruni's argument? What, if anything, does it add to Divakaruni's authority? What does it tell us about child labor abroad?

Questions on Language

1. Divakaruni says that laboring children could otherwise be "the extra weight that capsizes the already shaky raft of their family's finances" (par. 8). How does this metaphor capture the problem of children in poor families? (See FIGURES OF SPEECH in Useful Terms for a definition of *metaphor*.)
2. What do the words in paragraph 7 tell you about Divakaruni's attitude toward the village children? Is it disdain? pity? compassion? horror?
3. Consult a dictionary if you need help in defining the following: indentured (par. 1); inconceivable (5); exploitation (7); mired, blithe (8).

Suggestions for Writing

1. **FROM JOURNAL TO ESSAY** Starting from your journal entry, write a letter to your congressional representative or one of your senators who takes a position for or against laws such as that opposed by Divakaruni. You can use quotations from Divakaruni's essay if they serve your purpose, but the letter should center on your own views of the issue. When you've finished your letter, send it. (You can find your representative's and senators' names and addresses on the Web at *house.gov/ writerep* and *senate.gov*.)
2. David Parker, a photographer and doctor, has documented child laborers in a series of powerful photographs (*childlaborphotographs.com*). He asks viewers, "Under what circumstances and conditions should children work?" Look at Parker's photographs, and answer his question in an essay. What kind of paid work, for how many hours a week, is appropriate for, say, a ten- or twelve-year-old child? Consider: What about children working in their family's business? Where do you draw the line between occasional babysitting or lawn mowing and full-time factory work?

3. Research the history of child labor in the United States, including the development of child-labor laws. Then write an essay in which you explain how and why
   the laws evolved and what the current laws are.

4. **CRITICAL WRITING** Divakaruni's essay depends significantly on appeals to readers' emotions (see p. 443). Locate one emotional appeal that either helps to convince you of the author's point or, in your mind, weakens the argument. What
   does the appeal ASSUME about the reader's (your) feelings or values? Why are the
   assumptions correct or incorrect in your case? How, specifically, does the appeal
   strengthen or undermine Divakaruni's argument?

5. **CONNECTIONS** In the next essay, *"Plata o Plomo:* Silver or Lead," Marie Javdani
   examines another global relationship that can harm children: the international
   traffic in cocaine, heroin, and other drugs. To what extent do you think the
   people in one country are responsible for what happens in other countries as a
   result of their actions? Write a brief essay that answers this question, explaining
   clearly the beliefs and values that guide your answer.

Chitra Divakaruni on Writing

Chitra Divakaruni is both a writer and a community worker, reaching out to
immigrants and other groups through organizations such as Maitri, a refuge for
abused women that she helped to found. In a 1998 interview in the online
Atlantic Unbound, Katie Bolick asked Divakaruni how her activism and writing
affected each other. Here is Divakaruni's response.

Being helpful where I can has always been an important value for me. I did
community work in India, and I continue to do it in America, because being involved in my community is something I feel I need to do. Activism has given me
enormous satisfaction — not just as a person, but also as a writer. The lives of
people I would have only known from the outside, or had stereotyped notions
of, have been opened up to me. My hotline work with Maitri has certainly
influenced both my life and my writing immensely. Overall, I have a great
deal of sensitivity that I did not have before, and a lot of my preconceptions
have changed. I hope that translates into my writing and reaches my readers.

For Discussion

1. What evidence does "Live Free and Starve" give to support Divakaruni's statement about how her activist work has affected her writing?

2. What does Divakaruni mean by "lives . . . I would have only known from the
   outside"? Of what use is "insider's" knowledge to an activist? to a writer?

3. Do you have a project or an activity — comparable to Divakaruni's activism — that you believe positively affects your writing? What is it? How does it
   help you as you write?

MARIE JAVDANI

Marie Javdani was born in Albuquerque, New Mexico, and attended the University of Oregon, where she earned a BA and an MA in geography and was published in *Harvest*, the university's annual writing publication. As an undergraduate Javdani became interested in international development. She worked as a research assistant for Harvard's Center for International Development and traveled to Malawi to conduct research on the connection between fertilizer subsidies and food security. Currently involved with a nonprofit organization devoted to bringing clean water to communities in Kenya, Javdani is also a musician whose instrument of choice is the marimba, an African percussion device similar to the xylophone.

Plata o Plomo: Silver or Lead

Like Chitra Divakaruni in the previous selection, Javdani is concerned in this essay with how actions taken in the United States can affect people in other countries, often without our realizing it. To make her argument concrete, Javdani tells the stories of two boys, Eric, an American, and Miguel, a Colombian. (Colombia is a country in South America.) Reminding us that global problems start and end with people, the boys represent cause and effect at their most specific. Javdani wrote this paper for a freshman writing course and revised it for us in 2004. It is documented in MLA style, described on pages 70–83.

At 8:00 on a Friday night, Eric walks down the street in his American   1
hometown whistling. Tonight, for the first time in almost a week, Eric does not have to do homework or chores. Tonight Eric is a free spirit. Best of all, tonight Eric has scored some drugs. He and his friends will trade their bland, controlled existence for some action and a little bit of fun.

At 8:00 on a Friday night, Miguel creeps down the road in his Colombian   2
village praying. Tonight, for the last time in his life, Miguel will have to watch where he is going and listen anxiously for distant gunshots. Tonight Miguel will die. The guerillas who have been threatening him and his father will end his life for some coca and a lot of money.

Eric and Miguel represent opposite poles in what the United States gov-   3
ernment refers to as the "war on drugs." Miguel's home is where it starts. In his little village, drug production is the only possible way of life. Eric's home is where it ends. In his suburban paradise, the stress of homework and

ex-girlfriends requires weekend breaks for drugs. All but ignoring both youths, congresspeople, governors, and presidents talk about how their actions will combat the flow of drugs into our homeland. In an attempt to find the quickest route around a complicated problem, the United States sends billions in aid dollars every year to the governments of Latin American "drug-source" countries such as Colombia, Ecuador, Bolivia, and Peru (Carpenter 205). But the solution isn't working: Political turmoil and violence continue to plague the countries to which we are sending aid, and illegal drug use in the United States remains fairly constant (Vásquez 571–75). To begin to solve the problem, we need to understand what's happening in drug-source countries, how the United States can and can't help there, and what, instead, can be done at home.

Miguel's country, Colombia, is one of the top recipients of US money 4 and military weaponry and equipment. According to the US Department of State, Colombia produces nearly 80% of the world's cocaine as well as a significant amount of the US heroin supply. Drug production has become a way of life for Colombians. Some call it the *plata o plomo* mentality. As Gonzalo Sanchez explains it, *plata o plomo* is literally translated as "silver or lead" and means that one can either take the money — drug money, bribe money, and so on — or take a bullet (7). Since 1964, the country has been essentially run by drug lords and leftist extremists, mainly the FARC (the military wing of the Colombian Communist Party), whose guerilla presence is much stronger and more threatening than that of the actual government. In response, extreme right-wing paramilitary forces act in an equally deadly manner. Both of these groups raid villages continually, looking to root out "traitors" and executing whomever they please (Sanchez 12–15).

According to the humanitarian organization Human Rights Watch, US 5 aid money has helped fund, supply, and train Colombian military units that maintain close alliances with paramilitary groups. Although Colombia has recently taken a tougher stance toward the paramilitaries and peace negotiations are in progress, the US State Department, major human rights organizations, and the United Nations claim that the Colombian government is still linked to illicit paramilitary activities. For example, government forces have often invaded, emptied, and then left a guerilla-held area, clearing the way for paramilitary fighters to take control (Carpenter 162). Human rights groups also criticize what Adam Isacson calls a "forgive and forget" government policy toward paramilitary leaders accused of crimes, including promises of amnesty in return for gradual demobilization (251–52). Although the US has threatened to suspend aid if Colombia does not break such ties with paramilitary groups, the full amount of promised aid continues to be granted (Human Rights Watch).

For the past forty years, the people of Colombia have found themselves   6
between a rock and a hard place over the production of coca, the plant used
for making cocaine and heroin. Under threats from the rebel drug lords, who
now control many areas, civilians must either allow their land to be cultivated
for the growth of coca or put themselves and their families at deadly risk. At
the same time, however, the consequence of "cooperation" with the rebels
is execution by paramilitary groups or even by the Colombian government.
Some coca farmers, fearful of the government, willingly form alliances with
rebels who offer to protect their farms for a fee (Vásquez 572).

Entire villages get caught in the crossfire between paramilitaries and   7
rebels. In the past ten years, over 35,000 civilians have lost their lives in
the conflict and hundreds of thousands have been forced from their homes
(Carpenter 215). A terrible incident in the town of Bellavista was reported in
the *New York Times* in 2002 (Forero, "Colombian War"). Paramilitary forces
took over the town in an attempt to gain control of jungle smuggling routes.
When leftist rebels arrived ready to fight a battle, the paramilitaries fled, leaving the civilians trapped and defenseless. Most of the villagers huddled
together in their church, and 117 were killed when a stray rocket destroyed
the church.

What is to be done to prevent such atrocities? The United States rushes   8
aid to Colombia, hoping to stop the violence and the drugs. Unfortunately,
the solutions attempted so far have had their own bad results. For instance,
eradicating coca fields has alienated peasants, who then turn to the rebels
for support, and it has also escalated violence over the reduced coca supply
(Vásquez 575). Money intended to help peasants establish alternative crops
has ended up buying weapons for branches of the military that support paramilitary operations (Human Rights Watch). Not long ago $2 million intended
for the Colombian police just disappeared (Forero, "Two Million").

Obviously, the United States needs to monitor how its dollars are used in   9
Colombia. It can continue to discourage the Colombian government from supporting the paramilitaries and encourage it to seek peace among the warring
factions. But ultimately the United States is limited in what it can do by international law and by the tolerance of the US people for foreign intervention.

Instead, the United States should be looking to its home front and should   10
focus on cutting the demand for drugs. Any economist will affirm that where
there is demand, there will be supply. A report by the United Nations Office
on Drugs and Crime connects this basic economic principle to illegal drugs:

> Production of illicit drugs is market driven. In the United States alone, illicit
> drugs are an $80 billion market. More than $70 billion of that amount goes
> to traffickers, those who bring the drugs to market. Stopping the demand
> would stop their business. (26)

The United States should reduce demand by dramatically increasing both treatment and education. The first will help people stop using drugs. The second will make users aware of the consequences of their choices.

The war on drugs is not fought just in the jungles of some distant country.   11
It takes place daily at our schools, in our homes, and on our streets. People my age who justify their use of illegal drugs by saying "It's my life, and I can do with it what I please" should be made aware that they are funding drug lords and contributing to the suffering of people across the globe, including in Colombia. Eric's "little bit of fun" is costing Miguel his life.

Works Cited

Carpenter, Ted Galen. *Peace and Freedom: Foreign Policy for a Constitutional Republic*. Washington: Cato, 2002. Print.

Forero, Juan. "Colombian War Brings Carnage to Village Altar." *New York Times* 9 May 2002. *LexisNexis Academic*. Web. 18 Mar. 2004.

– – –. "Two Million in US Aid to Colombia Missing from Colombian Police Fund." *New York Times* 11 May 2002. *LexisNexis Academic*. Web. 18 Mar. 2004.

Human Rights Watch. *World Report 2003*. Human Rights Watch. 2004. Web. 9 Mar. 2004.

Isacson, Adam. "Optimism, Pessimism, and Terrorism: The United States and Colombia in 2003." *Brown Journal of World Affairs* 10.2 (2004): 245–55. Print.

Sanchez, Gonzalo. *Violence in Colombia*. Wilmington: Scholarly Resources, 1992. Print.

United Nations. Office on Drugs and Crime. *Drug Consumption Stimulates Cultivation and Trade*. UNODC, 3 Dec. 2003. Web. 18 Mar. 2004.

United States. Dept. of State. *International Narcotics Control Strategy Report, 2003*. US State Dept., 1 Mar. 2004. Web. 12 Mar. 2004.

Vásquez, Ian. "The International War on Drugs." *Cato Handbook for Congress: Policy Recommendations for the 108th Congress*. Ed. Edward H. Crane and David Boaz. Washington: Cato, 2003. 567–76. *Cato Institute*. 2003. Web. 18 Mar. 2004.

For a reading quiz, visit **bedfordstmartins.com/thebedfordreader**.

Journal Writing

What do you think about Javdani's solution to the twin problems of violence in drug-producing countries and drug use in the United States (pars. 10–11)? Do you think her solution would work? Why, or why not? (To take your journal writing further, see "From Journal to Essay" below.)

Questions on Meaning

1. Where does Javdani state her THESIS? How does she develop the thesis?
2. Why do the Colombian peasants often support the Communist rebels rather than the government?
3. What, according to Javdani, are the problems caused by the US government's sending "billions in aid dollars every year to the governments of Latin American 'drug-source' countries" (par. 3)? What does Javdani offer as a solution?

Questions on Writing Strategy

1. Who seems to be Javdani's intended AUDIENCE for this essay? How does she appeal to this audience?
2. With whom do Javdani's sympathies lie? What EVIDENCE in the essay supports your answer?
3. Javdani cites a variety of outside sources throughout the essay. What is the EFFECT of her use of these sources?
4. **OTHER METHODS** Why does Javdani use COMPARISON AND CONTRAST in her opening paragraphs? What is the effect of her returning to this comparison in her conclusion?

Questions on Language

1. In paragraph 6 Javdani describes the people of Colombia as "between a rock and a hard place over the production of coca." What does she mean?
2. How and why does Javdani use IRONY to describe Eric in paragraph 3?
3. Why does Javdani use quotation marks around *traitors* (par. 4) and *cooperation* (6)?
4. Consult a dictionary if you are unsure of the meanings of any of the following words: guerillas (par. 2); turmoil, plague (3); paramilitary (4); humanitarian, amnesty, demobilization (5); atrocities, eradicating, alienated (8).

Suggestions for Writing

1. **FROM JOURNAL TO ESSAY** Working from your journal writing and, like Javdani, drawing on research, develop an essay that lays out your view of the most effective ways to curtail either the production or the consumption of illegal drugs.

Which current US government efforts are successful, and which fall short? What more could be done?

2. Write a report on the use of illegal drugs by US adolescents, focusing on an aspect of the problem that interests you, such as how widespread it is, what groups it affects most and least, or what drugs are involved. An excellent starting place for your research is Monitoring the Future, a long-term study of "the behavior, attitudes, and values" of students and young adults. Its 2012 report, *National Results on Adolescent Drug Use,* is available at *monitoringthefuture.org/pubs/monographs/mtf-overview2012.pdf.*

3. **CRITICAL WRITING**   Is Javdani's essay an effective ARGUMENT? Consider the thesis development, the organization, the evidence, and the clarity of the presentation. What would you say are the strengths and weaknesses of this argument?

4. **CONNECTIONS**   Javdani's essay and Chitra Divakaruni's "Live Free and Starve" (p. 372) both look at effects of globalization, the increasing economic, cultural, and political connections among nations and their people. Write a brief essay discussing what you see as the main advantages and the main disadvantages of globalization. For instance, advantages might include the availability in this country of varied ethnic foods or of relatively inexpensive consumer goods that were produced elsewhere, while disadvantages might include the loss of American manufacturing jobs to foreign factories or the strong international drug trade.

Marie Javdani on Writing

In an interview for this book, we asked Marie Javdani to describe her writing process.

Depending on my writing topic, it can often take a while to get a good start. If it's a topic I chose myself and am interested in or am at least somewhat knowledgeable about, the first steps are usually much easier. I usually start by brainstorming an outline by just writing things as I think of them. What questions do I want to answer? How does this topic actually affect people? Once I get a start, the writing process usually goes fairly quickly. I try to write in a way that I would speak if I were, for instance, teaching on the subject. That tends to make my work more readable. As for the introduction, I try to stay away from prescribed formats. I try to think of what would make me want to read more about a topic or to put a spin on it that makes it stand out. Also, I tend to write my introduction last. I've found that if I write it first it typically doesn't match what I write once I get "on a roll." If I plan ahead properly, I don't usually have to do more than two drafts unless I come upon new research that makes me need to rearrange my arguments. I try to write early enough to leave it alone for a few days before I go back and proofread it.

Javdani also offered suggestions for college writers based on her own experiences as a student.

From a student's perspective, the best thing you can do to improve your writing is to be interested in your topic. On the same note, however, don't soapbox. Just say what you want to say, support it, and move on. If you're writing for an assignment for which you weren't able to choose the topic, try to take an angle that you think no one else will take. . . . Do take the time to spell-check and edit your writing. The spelling checker on the computer is not sufficient. You're (not *your*) in college and you know (not *no*) better. Try reading your writing out loud to yourself. If it doesn't sound good when you say it, it doesn't sound good on paper either.

For Discussion

1. Do you share Javdani's experience that it's usually easier to write when you're interested in your topic? How does your writing process differ when you're interested beforehand from when you're not?
2. Why do you think Javdani advises "don't soapbox"? (If you aren't sure what *soapbox* means, look it up in a dictionary.)

DAN ARIELY

Dan Ariely is an Israeli American behavioral economist known for his sense of humor and for conducting what one reviewer characterized as "rigorous but goofy-sounding experiments [that] lend themselves to a genial, gee-whiz style." He was born in 1968 in New York City and earned a BA from Tel Aviv University, an MA from the University of North Carolina at Chapel Hill, and two PhDs — in cognitive psychology and in business administration — from Duke University. In addition to publishing scores of papers in academic journals, Ariely writes a regular column for the *Wall Street Journal,* produces a weekly podcast of interviews with researchers, and has written two well-received books for general readers: *Predictably Irrational: The Hidden Forces That Shape Our Decisions* (2008) and *The (Honest) Truth about Dishonesty: How We Lie to Everyone — Especially Ourselves* (2012). He teaches at both Duke University and the Massachusetts Institute of Technology, where he is also a principal investigator at the MIT Media Lab, director of the Center for Advanced Hindsight, and director of the eRationality Research Group.

Why We Lie

Psychologists have claimed that most people lie at least once a day, and one study found that college students lied in half of their conversations with their mothers. In "Why We Lie," adapted for the *Wall Street Journal* from *The (Honest) Truth about Dishonesty*, Ariely details the results of psychological experiments that he and colleagues conducted on unwitting college students. Given an opportunity to cheat, they discovered, most people will do so — but only in small doses. Understanding why could be the key to curbing the "misbehavior that affects all of us, as both perpetrators and victims."

Not too long ago, one of my students, named Peter, told me a story that captures rather nicely our society's misguided efforts to deal with dishonesty. One day, Peter locked himself out of his house. After a spell, the locksmith pulled up in his truck and picked the lock in about a minute.

"I was amazed at how quickly and easily this guy was able to open the door," Peter said. The locksmith told him that locks are on doors only to keep honest people honest. One percent of people will always be honest and never steal. Another 1% will always be dishonest and always try to pick your lock and steal your television; locks won't do much to protect you from the hardened thieves, who can get into your house if they really want to. The purpose of locks, the locksmith said, is to protect you from the 98% of mostly honest people who might be tempted to try your door if it had no lock.

We tend to think that people are either honest or dishonest. In the age of   3
Bernie Madoff and Mark McGwire, James Frey and John Edwards,[1] we like to
believe that most people are virtuous, but a few bad apples spoil the bunch.
If this were true, society might easily remedy its problems with cheating and
dishonesty. Human-resources departments could screen for cheaters when
hiring. Dishonest financial advisers or building contractors could be flagged
quickly and shunned. Cheaters in sports and other arenas would be easy to
spot before they rose to the tops of their professions.

But that is not how dishonesty works. Over the past decade or so, my   4
colleagues and I have taken a close look at why people cheat, using a variety
of experiments and looking at a panoply of unique data sets — from insurance claims to employment histories to the treatment records of doctors and
dentists. What we have found, in a nutshell: Everybody has the capacity to
be dishonest, and almost everybody cheats — just by a little. Except for a few
outliers at the top and bottom, the behavior of almost everyone is driven by
two opposing motivations. On the one hand, we want to benefit from cheating
and get as much money and glory as possible; on the other hand, we want to
view ourselves as honest, honorable people. Sadly, it is this kind of small-scale
mass cheating, not the high-profile cases, that is most corrosive to society.

Much of what we have learned about the causes of dishonesty comes from   5
a simple little experiment that we call the "matrix task," which we have been
using in many variations. It has shown rather conclusively that cheating does
not correspond to the traditional, rational model of human behavior — that
is, the idea that people simply weigh the benefits (say, money) against the
costs (the possibility of getting caught and punished) and act accordingly.

The basic matrix task goes as follows: Test subjects (usually college stu-   6
dents) are given a sheet of paper containing a series of 20 different matrices
(structured like the example you can see on the next page) and are told to
find in each of the matrices two numbers that add up to 10. They have five
minutes to solve as many of the matrices as possible, and they get paid based
on how many they solve correctly. When we want to make it possible for
subjects to cheat on the matrix task, we introduce what we call the "shredder
condition." The subjects are told to count their correct answers on their own

---

[1] Bernie Madoff is a financial adviser serving a 150-year prison sentence for defrauding
thousands of investors out of billions of dollars. Mark McGwire admitted he was using steroids
when he broke professional baseball's record for home runs. Writer James Frey fabricated parts
of his supposedly factual memoir, *A Million Little Pieces*. Former US Senator and presidential
candidate John Edwards was indicted for (but not convicted of) breaking campaign contribution laws; he also had an extramarital affair while his wife was undergoing treatment for breast
cancer. — Eds.

1.69	1.82	2.91
4.67	4.81	3.05
5.82	5.06	4.28
6.36	5.19	4.57

Which two numbers in this matrix add up to 10? Asked to solve a batch of these problems, most people cheated (claiming to have solved more of them than they had) when given the chance.

and then put their work sheets through a paper shredder at the back of the room. They then tell us how many matrices they solved correctly and get paid accordingly.

What happens when we put people through the control condition and the shredder condition and then compare their scores? In the control condition, it turns out that most people can solve about four matrices in five minutes. But in the shredder condition, something funny happens: Everyone suddenly and miraculously gets a little smarter. Participants in the shredder condition claim to solve an average of six matrices — two more than in the control condition. This overall increase results not from a few individuals who claim to solve a lot more matrices but from lots of people who cheat just by a little.   7

Would putting more money on the line make people cheat more? We tried varying the amount that we paid for a solved matrix, from 50 cents to $10, but more money did not lead to more cheating. In fact, the amount of cheating was slightly lower when we promised our participants the highest amount for each correct answer. (Why? I suspect that at $10 per solved matrix, it was harder for participants to cheat and still feel good about their own sense of integrity.)   8

Would a higher probability of getting caught cause people to cheat less? We tried conditions for the experiment in which people shredded only half their answer sheet, in which they paid themselves money from a bowl in the hallway, even one in which a noticeably blind research assistant administered the experiment. Once again, lots of people cheated, though just by a bit. But the level of cheating was unaffected by the probability of getting caught.   9

Knowing that most people cheat — but just by a little — the next logical question is what makes us cheat more or less.   10

One thing that increased cheating in our experiments was making the   11
prospect of a monetary payoff more "distant," in psychological terms. In one
variation of the matrix task, we tempted students to cheat for tokens (which
would immediately be traded in for cash). Subjects in this token condition
cheated twice as much as those lying directly for money.

Another thing that boosted cheating: Having another student in the   12
room who was clearly cheating. In this version of the matrix task, we had
an acting student named David get up about a minute into the experiment
(the participants in the study didn't know he was an actor) and implausibly claim that he had solved all the matrices. Watching this mini-Madoff
clearly cheat — and waltz away with a wad of cash — the remaining students
claimed they had solved double the number of matrices as the control group.
Cheating, it seems, is infectious.

Other factors that increased the dishonesty of our test subjects included   13
knowingly wearing knockoff fashions, being drained from the demands of a
mentally difficult task and thinking that "teammates" would benefit from
one's cheating in a group version of the matrix task. These factors have little
to do with cost-benefit analysis and everything to do with the balancing act
that we are constantly performing in our heads. If I am already wearing fake
Gucci sunglasses, then maybe I am more comfortable pushing some other ethical limits (we call this the "What the hell" effect). If I am mentally depleted
from sticking to a tough diet, how can you expect me to be scrupulously honest? (It's a lot of effort!) If it is my teammates who benefit from my fudging the
numbers, surely that makes me a virtuous person!

The results of these experiments should leave you wondering about the   14
ways that we currently try to keep people honest. Does the prospect of heavy
fines or increased enforcement really make someone less likely to cheat on
their taxes, to fill out a fraudulent insurance claim, to recommend a bum
investment or to steal from his or her company? It may have a small effect
on our behavior, but it is probably going to be of little consequence when it
comes up against the brute psychological force of "I'm only fudging a little" or
"Everyone does it" or "It's for a greater good."

What, then — if anything — pushes people toward greater honesty?   15

There's a joke about a man who loses his bike outside his synagogue and   16
goes to his rabbi for advice. "Next week come to services, sit in the front row,"
the rabbi tells the man, "and when we recite the Ten Commandments, turn
around and look at the people behind you. When we get to 'Thou shalt not
steal,' see who can't look you in the eyes. That's your guy." After the next
service, the rabbi is curious to learn whether his advice panned out. "So, did it
work?" he asks the man. "Like a charm," the man answers. "The moment we
got to 'Thou shalt not commit adultery,' I remembered where I left my bike."

What this little joke suggests is that simply being reminded of moral codes   17
has a significant effect on how we view our own behavior.

Inspired by the thought, my colleagues and I ran an experiment at the Uni-   18
versity of California, Los Angeles. We took a group of 450 participants, split
them into two groups and set them loose on our usual matrix task. We asked
half of them to recall the Ten Commandments and the other half to recall
ten books that they had read in high school. Among the group who recalled
the ten books, we saw the typical widespread but moderate cheating. But in
the group that was asked to recall the Ten Commandments, we observed no
cheating whatsoever. We reran the experiment, reminding students of their
schools' honor codes instead of the Ten Commandments, and we got the same
result. We even reran the experiment on a group of self-declared atheists, asking them to swear on a Bible, and got the same no-cheating results yet again.

This experiment has obvious implications for the real world. While ethics   19
lectures and training seem to have little to no effect on people, reminders of
morality — right at the point where people are making a decision — appear
to have an outsized effect on behavior.

Another set of our experiments, conducted with mock tax forms, con-   20
vinced us that it would be better to have people put their signature at the top
of the forms (before they filled in false information) rather than at the bottom
(after the lying was done). Unable to get the IRS to give our theory a go in the
real world, we tested it out with automobile-insurance forms. An insurance
company gave us 20,000 forms with which to play. For half of them, we kept
the usual arrangement, with the signature line at the bottom of the page along
with the statement: "I promise that the information I am providing is true."
For the other half, we moved the statement and signature line to the top. We
mailed the forms to 20,000 customers, and when we got the forms back, we
compared the amount of driving reported on the two types of forms.

People filling out such forms have an incentive to underreport how many   21
miles they drive, so as to be charged a lower premium. What did we find?
Those who signed the form at the top said, on average, that they had driven
26,100 miles, while those who signed at the bottom said, on average, that
they had driven 23,700 miles — a difference of about 2,400 miles. We don't
know, of course, how much those who signed at the top really drove, so we
don't know if they were perfectly honest — but we do know that they cheated
a good deal less than our control group.

Such tricks aren't going to save us from the next big Ponzi scheme or   22
doping athlete or thieving politician. But they could rein in the vast majority of people who cheat "just by a little." Across all of our experiments, we
have tested thousands of people, and from time to time, we did see aggressive
cheaters who kept as much money as possible. In the matrix experiments,

The Forces That Shape Dishonesty

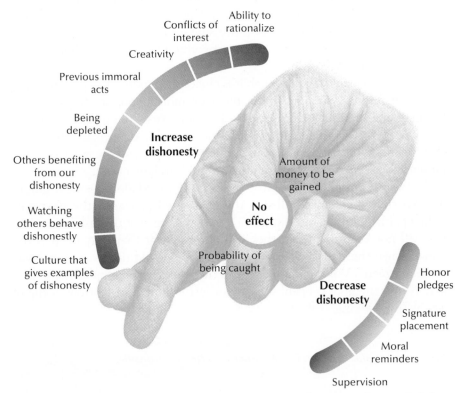

A variety of experiments have identified many factors that can make people behave in a more or less honest fashion.

for example, we have never seen anyone claim to solve 18 or 19 out of the 20 matrices. But once in a while, a participant claimed to have solved all 20. Fortunately, we did not encounter many of these people, and because they seemed to be the exception and not the rule, we lost only a few hundred dollars to these big cheaters. At the same time, we had thousands and thousands of participants who cheated by "just" a few matrices, but because there were so many of them, we lost thousands and thousands of dollars to them.

In short, very few people steal to a maximal degree, but many good people   23
cheat just a little here and there. We fib to round up our billable hours, claim higher losses on our insurance claims, recommend unnecessary treatments and so on.

Companies also find many ways to game the system just a little. Think   24
about credit-card companies that raise interest rates ever so slightly for no

apparent reason and invent all kinds of hidden fees and penalties (which are often referred to, within companies, as "revenue enhancements"). Think about banks that slow down check processing so that they can hold on to our money for an extra day or two or charge exorbitant fees for overdraft protection and for using ATMs.

All of this means that, although it is obviously important to pay attention   25
to flagrant misbehaviors, it is probably even more important to discourage the small and more ubiquitous forms of dishonesty — the misbehavior that affects all of us, as both perpetrators and victims. This is especially true given what we know about the contagious nature of cheating and the way that small transgressions can grease the psychological skids to larger ones.

We want to install locks to stop the next Bernie Madoff, the next Enron,   26
the next steroid-enhanced all-star, the next serial plagiarist, the next self-dealing political miscreant. But locking our doors against the dishonest monsters will not keep them out; they will always cheat their way in. It is the woman down the hallway — the sweet one who could not even carry away your flat-screen TV if she wanted to — who needs to be reminded constantly that, even if the door is open, she cannot just walk in and "borrow" a cup of sugar without asking.

For a reading quiz, visit **bedfordstmartins.com/thebedfordreader**.

Journal Writing

"Everybody has the capacity to be dishonest," Ariely writes in paragraph 4, "and almost everybody cheats." That must mean you, too. Think of some times you have cheated "just by a little." When is the last time you cheated? What circumstances have justified lying? Have you ever been ashamed of a lie or faced consequences for lying? (To take your journal writing further, see "From Journal to Essay" on the facing page.)

Questions on Meaning

1. What do you take to be Ariely's reason for writing this essay? Is he merely reporting the results of his research, or does he seem to have another PURPOSE in mind?
2. What does Ariely mean by "cost-benefit analysis" (par. 13)? Why is the concept significant to his explanation of why people lie?
3. Under what circumstances are people more likely to lie? List at least three of the factors Ariely cites.

4. What solution to cheating does Ariely propose? Is he optimistic or pessimistic that people can be encouraged to be more honest?
5. What is Ariely's THESIS? Does he state it anywhere, or is it implied?

Questions on Writing Strategy

1. For whom does Ariely seem to be writing? Cheaters and liars, their victims, other researchers, insurance administrators, bankers, the IRS, his study participants, another group? How can you tell?
2. The BODY of "Why We Lie" has three fairly distinct sections — paragraphs 4–9, 10–14, and 15–21. What is the focus of each section? How does Ariely ensure that his essay has UNITY and COHERENCE?
3. Why does Ariely relate a religious joke in paragraph 16? What function does it serve?
4. Take a close look at the two visual images that appear in this essay. Why does Ariely include them? What do the sample matrix and the infographic contribute to his meaning?
5. **OTHER METHODS**   Ariely introduces his essay with a short NARRATIVE recounting a student's conversation with a locksmith. What is the point of this ANECDOTE? Where in the essay does Ariely return to it?

Questions on Language

1. Find examples of COLLOQUIAL EXPRESSIONS and FIGURES OF SPEECH in Ariely's essay. What is the effect of such language? Does it strike you as appropriate for an academic analysis?
2. Consult a dictionary for definitions of the following words: virtuous (par. 3); panoply, outliers, corrosive (4); integrity (8); monetary (11); implausibly (12); factors, depleted, scrupulously (13); prospect, fraudulent (14); atheists (18); mock (20); incentive (21); Ponzi scheme, doping, rein (22); exorbitant (24); flagrant, ubiquitous, perpetrators, transgressions (25); serial, miscreant (26).
3. Ariely uses the words *cheat* and *lie* and the phrase "just by a little" several times in this essay. What are the CONNOTATIONS of these terms? How does the repetition of these key words emphasize the author's point?

Suggestions for Writing

1. **FROM JOURNAL TO ESSAY**   Develop one or more of the lies you recalled in your journal into an essay. You may choose to elaborate on your lies by examining their causes and effects, by narrating the circumstances surrounding a particular lie, or by CLASSIFYING your lies according to some principle. Give your reader a sense of your motivation for lying and the outcome you expected to achieve with it.
2. Do you agree with Ariely that most college students think cheating is acceptable, even virtuous in some circumstances? How common is cheating at your school? What are your classmates' attitudes toward it? Write an essay in which you ANALYZE the problem of student cheating on your campus. Who does it? Why? What

do others think about it? What does the school do about it? If cheating is uncommon at your school, analyze why.

3. Like other social scientists, Ariely and his colleagues work under a code of ethics that specifies how they may and may not treat the human subjects of their experiments. Read about this subject, perhaps starting with the Human Research Protections page of the American Psychological Association (*apa.org/ethics/code/index/aspx*) or with the psychology department or Institutional Review Board (IRB) at your school. Then write an essay in which you explain the ethical obligations of behavioral research.

4. **CRITICAL WRITING** In an essay, EVALUATE Ariely's cause-and-effect analysis. How truly does it resonate with your own experience? How persuasive do you find his EVIDENCE? How well does he convince you of the extent of small-scale cheating and of its consequences? How well do you think he develops his proposed solutions?

5. **CONNECTIONS** Jeff Wise, in "Deadly Mind Traps" (p. 353), also writes about cost-benefit analysis and the "what-the-hell effect." Based on what Ariely and Wise have to say, what parallels can you draw between cheating and self-destructive behavior? Do lies and mistakes stem from the same impulses? Do they risk similar consequences? How so? Write an essay that answers these questions and that points out any other similarities or differences you notice between lies and mental errors. Use evidence from the two essays and from your own experience to support your thesis.

CHRISTOPHER BEAM

Christopher Beam is a reporter for *Slate* magazine who specializes in politics and crime. His writing has also been published in *New York* magazine, *Business Week*, the *New Republic, Gentlemen's Quarterly,* and other magazines. The son of a *Boston Globe* columnist, Beam grew up in Newton, Massachusetts, attended the Roxbury Latin school, and in 2006 completed a degree in American history at Columbia University. With his friend Nick Summers he cofounded *IvyGate*, a popular college news and gossip blog. Beam currently lives in Beijing, China, where he is studying as a Luce Scholar with the Asia Foundation and, by his own account, performing miserably at table tennis.

Blood Loss

Television crime dramas regularly feature plots in which a series of murders are committed by the same person. But how common are such characters in real life? In this 2011 article for *Slate*, Beam reports a surprising trend: Serial killings occur much less often than they did a generation ago. He suggests that shifting cultural anxieties, not just police work, can explain the decline.

When it came to serial killing, Stephen Griffiths did everything by the book. He targeted prostitutes in the slums of Bradford, a city in Northern England. He chose a unique murder weapon: a crossbow. He claimed to have eaten parts of his victims — two of them cooked, one of them raw. "I'm misanthropic," he told police investigators when he was finally caught in 2010. "I don't have much time for the human race." When he appeared in court, he gave his name as the "crossbow cannibal." It was as if he'd studied up on the art of serial murder. (In fact, he had: Griffiths was a part-time PhD student at Bradford University, where he was studying criminology.) And yet, for all his efforts, he got only one short blurb in the *New York Times* when he was sentenced last month.

Serial killers just aren't the sensation they used to be. They haven't disappeared, of course. Last month, Suffolk County, New York, police found the bodies of four women dumped near a beach in Long Island. Philadelphia police have attributed the murders of three women in the city's Kensington neighborhood to one "Kensington Strangler." On Tuesday, an accused serial stabber in Flint, Michigan, filed an insanity plea.

But the number of serial murders seems to be dwindling, as does the public's fascination with them. "It does seem the golden age of serial murderers is probably past," says Harold Schechter, a professor at Queens College of the City University of New York who studies crime.

Statistics on serial murder are hard to come by — the FBI doesn't keep   4
numbers, according to a spokeswoman — but the data we do have suggests
serial murders peaked in the 1980s and have been declining ever since. James
Alan Fox, a criminology professor at Northeastern University and co-author
of *Extreme Killing: Understanding Serial and Mass Murder*, keeps a database of
confirmed serial murderers starting in 1900. According to his count, based on
newspaper clippings, books, and Web sources, there were only a dozen or so
serial killers before 1960 in the United States. Then serial killings took off:
There were 19 in the 1960s, 119 in the '70s, and 200 in the '80s. In the '90s,
the number of cases dropped to 141. And the 2000s saw only 61 serial murderers. (Definitions of *serial murder* vary, but Fox defines it as "a string of four or
more homicides committed by one or a few perpetrators that spans a period
of days, weeks, months, or even years." To avoid double-counting, he assigns
killers to the decade in which they reached the midpoint of their careers.)

There are plenty of structural explanations for the rise of reported serial   5
murders through the 1980s. Data collection and record-keeping improved,
making it easier to find cases of serial murder. Law enforcement developed
more sophisticated methods of investigation, enabling police to identify link-
ages between cases — especially across states — that they would have otherwise ignored. The media's growing obsession with serial killers in the 1970s
and '80s may have created a minor snowball effect, offering a short path to
celebrity.

Trends in Serial Killing

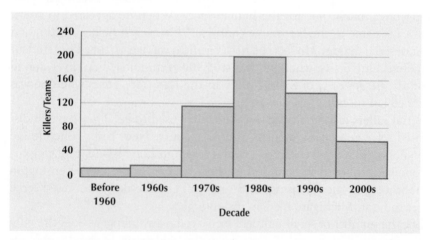

Source: James Alan Fox and Jack Levin, *Extreme Killing: Understanding Serial and Mass
Murder*, Sage Publications, 2011.

But those factors don't explain away the decline in serial murders since   6
1990. If anything, they make it more significant. Then why the downtrend?
It's hard to say. Better law enforcement could have played a role, as police
catch would-be serial killers after their first crime. So could the increased
incarceration rate, says Fox: "Maybe they're still behind bars." Whatever the
reason, the decline in serial murders tracks with a dramatic drop in overall
violent crime since the '80s. (One caveat: The numbers for the 2000s may
skew low, since some serial killers haven't been caught yet.)

As the raw numbers have declined, the media have paid less attention, too.   7
Sure, you've still got the occasional Beltway sniper or Grim Sleeper who ter-
rorizes a community. But nothing in the last decade has captured the popular
imagination like the sex-addled psychopaths of the '70s and '80s, such as Ted
Bundy (feigned injuries to win sympathy before killing women; about thirty
victims), John Wayne Gacy (stored bodies in his ceiling crawlspace; thirty-
three victims), or Jeffrey Dahmer (kept body parts in his closet and freezer;
seventeen victims). These crimes caused media frenzies in part because of the
way they tapped into the obsessions and fears of the time: Bundy, a golden
boy who worked on Nelson Rockefeller's presidential campaign in Seattle,
seemed to represent the evil lurking beneath America's cheery exterior.
Gacy, who dressed up as a clown and preyed on teenage boys, was every parent's nightmare. "Son of Sam" David Berkowitz milked — and, in so doing,
mocked — the media's obsession with serial killers by sending a letter to *New
York Daily News* reporter Jimmy Breslin.

The media returned the favor, inflating the perception that serial kill-   8
ers were everywhere and repeating the erroneous statistic that there were
five thousand serial murder victims every year. These horror stories were not
exactly discouraged by the FBI, one of whose agents coined the term "serial
killer" in 1981. (The phrase "serial murderer" first appeared in 1961, in a
review of Fritz Lang's M,[1] according to the *Oxford English Dictionary*.) The
perception of a serial murder epidemic also led to the creation of the FBI's
National Center for the Analysis of Violent Crime in 1981.

Infamous crimes almost always needle the anxieties of their periods. The   9
murder of a fourteen-year-old boy by University of Chicago students Nathan
Leopold and Richard Loeb in 1924 captured the growing obsession with modern psychiatry, as the pair considered themselves examples of Nietzsche's
Übermensch,[2] unbound by moral codes. A series of child abductions in the

---

[1] A 1931 movie about the hunt for a child killer in Germany. — EDS.

[2] Friedrich Nietzsche (1844–1900) was a German philosopher. The concept of *Übermensch*, loosely translated as "superhuman," embodies his idea that human beings should strive
for God-like perfection. — EDS.

1920s and '30s, from the Wineville Chicken Coop Murders to the killing of Charles Lindbergh's son, became a symbol of societal decay during the Depression. Charles Manson, who presided over the Tate murders in 1969, embodied a sexual revolution gone mad. The Columbine massacre preyed on parental fears of the effects of violent movies and video games.

Conversely, sensational crimes that *don't* play into a larger societal narrative fade away. In 1927, Andrew Kehoe detonated three bombs at a school in Bath Township, Michigan, killing thirty-eight children and seven adults, including Kehoe — one of the largest cases of domestic terrorism before the Oklahoma City bombing in 1995. The disaster made headlines, but was soon eclipsed by Charles Lindbergh's trans-Atlantic flight. "It was a crime that was ahead of its time," says Schechter.   10

Indeed, if something like the Bath School massacre happened today, it would probably resonate more deeply than it did in the 1920s. What child abductors were to the '20s and serial killers were to the '70s and '80s, terrorists are to the early twenty-first century. After 9/11, fear of social unraveling has been replaced by anxiety over airplanes, bombs, and instant mass annihilation. Stephen Griffiths isn't the new Jeffrey Dahmer. The Times Square bomber is.   11

*For a reading quiz, visit **bedfordstmartins.com/thebedfordreader**.*

Journal Writing

Since Beam wrote this essay, "something like the Bath School massacre" (par. 11) *did* occur. On December 14, 2012, a shooter forced his way into Sandy Hook Elementary School in Newtown, Connecticut, murdering twenty children and six adults before turning the gun on himself. And as Beam predicted, the slaughter of innocents touched a nerve in the national consciousness. How did you react to the news? In your journal, write down what you recall most vividly about your emotions in the wake of the shooting. (To take your journal writing further, see "From Journal to Essay" on the facing page.)

Questions on Meaning

1. What seems to be Beam's primary PURPOSE in this piece? Does he want to inform his readers about a trend? express relief that serial killings are on the decline? expose a new threat to public safety? propose a theory? How can you tell?

2. Although Beam gives details about some of the killers he discusses, he mentions others — such as the Beltway sniper, the Grim Sleeper, David Berkowitz, the Times Square bomber — without explaining who they are or what they did. Why? What ASSUMPTIONS does he make about his readers' interests and knowledge? Must one be familiar with the particulars of the crimes Beam cites to understand his point?

3. According to Beam, what role do the media play in the rise and fall of certain types of crime? Does he really mean to suggest that journalists are at least partly to blame for the spike in serial murders in the 1980s?

4. How would you summarize Beam's THESIS? Where in the essay does he state it most directly?

Questions on Writing Strategy

1. Why do you think Beam opens his essay as he does? What is the EFFECT of this opening?

2. What does Beam mean by "structural explanations" (par. 5)? What point is he making here?

3. How does Beam explain the drop in serial killings over the past two decades? What possible causes does he dismiss?

4. In paragraph 4 and the bar graph on page 394, Beam cites a number of statistics, or facts expressed numerically. How reliable are these statistics? What do they accomplish?

5. **OTHER METHODS**   Where in the essay does Beam use DEFINITION to clarify the meaning of *serial murder*?

Questions on Language

1. Find some examples of formal and informal DICTION in the essay. What is the effect of Beam's word choice?

2. What does Beam mean by "golden boy" in paragraph 7? What are the CONNOTATIONS of this term, especially as applied to Ted Bundy?

3. If any of the following words are new to you, look them up in a dictionary: crossbow, misanthropic, criminology (par. 1); incarceration, caveat (6); feigned (7); erroneous, epidemic (8); needle (9); conversely, eclipsed (10); annihilation (11).

Suggestions for Writing

1. **FROM JOURNAL TO ESSAY**   The horror at Newtown renewed a contentious national debate over gun control and the Second Amendment. Some people argue that gun ownership must be limited in some way for the protection of society; others argue that gun ownership is a constitutional right that must be protected. What do you think? Research the major ARGUMENTS that have taken shape on both sides of the issue since December 2012. Then build on the emotions you described in your journal entry to argue your position on some aspect of the debate. Should certain types of people be prohibited from owning guns? Should certain

types of guns (or ammunition) be banned? Should more people carry firearms? Should school guards or teachers be armed? Why do you think so? Make appropriate emotional APPEALS as you draft your essay, but be sure to keep your argument grounded in reason.

2. In his final paragraph Beam writes, "After 9/11, fear of social unraveling has been replaced by anxiety over airplanes, bombs, and instant mass annihilation." How has the continued threat of terrorist attacks affected your life and the lives of others you know? How has the threat affected the country more generally? Do you and other people feel safer now than in the months immediately following 9/11? Why, or why not? Write an essay in which you detail your view of the aftereffects of 9/11.

3. Choose a subject that has seen significant change in the past twenty years or so — for example, gender roles, communication technology, fashion, manners, a particular sport, ideals of beauty, or attitudes toward a particular group such as gays and lesbians, African Americans, or immigrants. Do some research on the topic, and then write an essay that examines the causes and effects of the change. Support your essay with specific EVIDENCE from your experience, observation, and research.

4. **CRITICAL WRITING**   Take a close look at Beam's use of SUMMARY, PARAPHRASE, and direct QUOTATION. In an essay, analyze the way he SYNTHESIZES information and ideas from SOURCES. Why does he quote directly where he does? How effective are his summaries and paraphrases? How does he combine source materials to develop a thesis of his own?

5. **CONNECTIONS**   Like Christopher Beam, Guillermo del Toro and Chuck Hogan, in "Vampires Never Die" (p. 291), and James Parker, in "Our Zombies, Ourselves" (p. 298), also examine cultural anxieties and mass media. What do news outlets have in common with popular culture productions such as movies and TV dramas? How are they different? Drawing on the ideas presented in all three essays as well as your own experience and observations, write an essay of your own that considers the ways in which the media both reflect and shape cultural anxieties, whether for good or bad.

ADDITIONAL WRITING TOPICS
Cause and Effect

1. In a short essay, explain *either* the causes *or* the effects of a situation that concerns you. Narrow your topic enough to treat it in some detail, and provide more than a mere list of causes or effects. If you focus on causes, you will have to decide carefully how far back to go in your search for remote causes. If stating effects, fill your essay with examples. Here are some topics to consider:

   Labor strikes in professional sports
   Minors encountering pornography on the Internet
   State laws mandating the use of seat belts in cars (or the wearing of helmets when riding motorcycles)
   Friction between two roommates, or two friends
   The pressure on students to get good grades
   Some quirk in your personality, or a friend's
   The increasing need for more than one breadwinner per family
   The temptation to do something dishonest to get ahead
   The popularity of a particular TV program, comic strip, or performer
   The steady increase in college costs
   The scarcity of people training for employment as skilled workers: plumbers, tool and die makers, electricians, masons, and carpenters, to name a few
   A decision to enter the ministry or a religious order
   The fact that cigarette advertising is banned from television
   The absence of a military draft
   The fact that more couples are choosing to have only one child, or none
   The growing popularity of private elementary and high schools
   Being "born again"
   The fact that women increasingly get jobs formerly regarded as being for men only
   The pressure on young people to conform to the standards of their peers
   The emphasis on competitive sports in high school and college

2. In *Blue Highways* (1982), an account of his rambles around the United States, William Least Heat-Moon explains why Americans, and not the British, settled the vast tract of northern land that lies between the Mississippi and the Rockies. He traces what he believes to be the major cause in this paragraph:

   > Were it not for a web-footed rodent and a haberdashery fad in eighteenth-century Europe, Minnesota might be a Canadian province today. The beaver, almost as much as the horse, helped shape the course of early American history. Some *Mayflower* colonists paid their passage with beaver pelts; and a good fur could bring an Indian three steel knives or a five-foot stack could bring a musket. But even more influential were the trappers and fur traders penetrating the great Northern wilderness between the Mississippi River and the Rocky Mountains, since it was their presence that helped hold the Near West against British expansion from the north; and it was their explorations that opened the heart of

the nation to white settlement. These men, by making pelts the currency of the wilds, laid the base for a new economy that quickly overwhelmed the old. And all because European men of mode simply had to wear a beaver hat.

In a Heat-Moon–like paragraph of your own, explain how a small cause produced a large effect. You might generate ideas by browsing in a history book — where you might find, for instance, that a cow belonging to Mrs. Patrick O'Leary is believed to have started the Great Chicago Fire of 1871 by kicking over a lighted lantern — or in a collection of *Ripley's Believe It or Not*. If some small event in your life has had large consequences, you might care to write instead from personal experience.

THERE'S STRONG.
THEN THERE'S
ARMY STRONG.

ARE YOU ARMY STRONG?

goarmy.com

U.S.ARMY

ARMY STRONG.℠

12

DEFINITION

Tracing Boundaries

◀ **Definition in an advertisement**

This army recruitment ad doesn't define *strong*. Instead, it invites
viewers to work military service into their own personal definitions of the word. The ad is part of a campaign, launched in
2006, that presents the slogan with images of diverse soldiers on
Web sites and in magazines read by young adults. Who seem to
be the intended viewers of such ads? What goals of the advertiser
is the campaign meant to address? What desires and concerns
in readers might the ad appeal to? Why is the ad image so stark,
and what does each of its few elements contribute to the appeal?
What does the text contribute? At the same time, what concerns
in viewers does the ad ignore or even reject?

THE METHOD

As a rule, when we hear the word DEFINITION, we immediately think of a dictionary. In that helpful storehouse — a writer's best friend — we find the literal and specific meaning (or meanings) of a word. The dictionary supplies this information concisely: in a sentence, in a phrase, or even in a *synonym* — a single word that means the same thing ("**narrative** [năr-e-tĭv] *n.* **1:** story . . .").

Stating such a definition is often a good way to begin an essay when basic terms may be in doubt. A short definition can clarify your subject to your reader, and perhaps help you limit what you have to say. If, for instance, you are writing a psychology paper about schizophrenia, you might offer a short definition at the outset, clarifying your subject and your key term.

In constructing a short definition, the usual procedure is to state the general class to which the subject belongs and then add any particular features that distinguish it. You could say: "Schizophrenia is a brain disease" — the general class — "whose symptoms include hallucinations, disorganized behavior, incoherence, and, often, withdrawal." Short definitions may be useful at *any* point in an essay, whenever you introduce a technical term that readers may not know.

When a term is central to your essay and likely to be misunderstood, a *stipulative definition* may be helpful. This fuller explanation stipulates, or specifies, the particular way you are using a term. The following paragraph, defining *TV addiction*, could be a stipulative definition in an essay about the causes and cures of the addiction.

> Who is addicted to television? According to Marie Winn, author of *The Plug-in Drug: Television, Children, and Family Life,* TV addicts are similar to drug or alcohol addicts: They seek a more pleasurable experience than they can get from normal life; they depend on the source of this pleasure; and their lives are damaged by their dependency. TV addicts, says Winn, use television to screen out the real world of feelings, worries, demands. They watch compulsively — four, five, even six hours on a work day. And they reject (usually passively, sometimes actively) interaction with family or friends, diverting or productive work at hobbies or chores, and chances for change and growth.

In this chapter we are mainly concerned with *extended definition*, a kind of expository writing that relies on a variety of other methods. Suppose you wanted to write an essay to make clear what *poetry* means. You would specify its elements — rhythm, IMAGES, and so on — by using DIVISION or ANALYSIS. You'd probably provide EXAMPLES of each element. You might COMPARE AND CONTRAST poetry with prose. You might discuss the EFFECT of poetry on the reader. (The poet Emily Dickinson once stated the effect that reading a poem had on her: "I feel as if the top of my head were taken off.") In fact, extended definition, unlike other methods of writing discussed in this book, is perhaps less a method in itself than the application of a variety of methods to achieve a purpose. Like DESCRIPTION, extended definition tries to *show* a reader its subject. It does so by establishing boundaries, as its writer tries to differentiate a subject from anything that might be confused with it.

An extended definition can define a word (like *poetry*), a thing (a laser beam), a condition (schizophrenia), a concept (TV addiction), or a general phenomenon (the popularity of *YouTube*). Unlike a sentence definition or any you would find in a standard dictionary, an extended definition takes room: at least a paragraph, often an entire essay. Also unlike a dictionary definition, which sets forth meaning in an unimpassioned manner, an extended definition often reflects or champions the author's bias. When Barbara Kingsolver, in her essay in this chapter, seeks to define the word *rural*, she examines her experiences of living in a farming community, specifying the meaning of her subject in a particular political context.

THE PROCESS

Discovery of Meanings

The purpose of almost any extended definition is to explore a topic in its full complexity, to explain its meaning or sometimes to argue for (or against) a particular meaning. To discover this complexity, you may find it useful to ask yourself the following questions. To illustrate how the questions might work, at least in one instance, let's say you plan to write a paper defining *sexism*.[1]

- **Is this subject unique, or are there others of its kind? If it resembles others, in what ways? How is it different?** As you can see, these last two questions invite you to compare and contrast. Applied to the concept of sexism, these questions might prompt you to compare sexism with one or two other -isms, such as racism or ageism. Or the questions might remind you that sexists can be both women and men, leading you to note the differences.

- **In what different forms does it occur, while keeping its own identity?** Specific examples might occur to you: a magazine story you read about a woman's experiences in the army and a girlfriend who is nastily suspicious of all men. Each form — the soldier and the girlfriend — might rate a description.

[1] The six questions that follow are freely adapted from those first stated by Richard E. Young, Alton L. Becker, and Kenneth L. Pike in *Rhetoric: Discovery and Change* (1970).

Definition

- **When and where do we find it? Under what circumstances and in what situations?** Well, where have you been lately? at any parties where sexism reared its ugly head? in any classroom discussions? Consider other areas of your experience: Did you encounter any sexists while holding a job?

- **What is it at the present moment?** Perhaps you might make the point that sexism was once considered an exclusively male preserve but is now an attribute of women as well. Or you could observe that many men have gone underground with their sexism, refraining from expressing it blatantly while still harboring negative attitudes about women. In either case you might care to draw examples from life.

- **What does it do? What are its functions and activities?** Sexists stereotype and sometimes act to exclude or oppress people of the opposite sex. These questions might also invite you to reply with a PROCESS ANALYSIS: You might show, for instance, how a sexist man you know, a personnel director who determines pay scales, systematically eliminates women from better-paying jobs.

- **How is it put together? What parts make it up? What holds these parts together?** You could apply analysis to the various beliefs and assumptions that, all together, make up sexism. This question might work well in writing about an organization: the personnel director's company, for instance, with its unfair hiring and promotion policies.

Not all these questions will fit every subject under the sun, and some may lead nowhere, but you will usually find them well worth asking. They can make you aware of points to notice, remind you of facts you already know. They can also suggest interesting aspects you need to find out more about.

Methods of Development

The preceding questions will give you a good start in using whatever method or methods of writing can best answer the overall question "What is the nature of this subject?" You will probably find yourself making use of much that you have learned earlier from this book. A short definition like the one for *schizophrenia* on page 404 may be a good start for your essay, especially if you think your readers need a quick grounding in the subject. (But feel no duty to place a dictionaryish definition in the INTRODUCTION of every essay you write: The device is overused.) In explaining schizophrenia, if your readers already have at least a vague idea of the meaning of the term and need no short, formal definition of it, you could open your extended definition with a description of the experiences of a person who has the disease:

On his twenty-fifth birthday, Michael sensed danger everywhere. The voices in his head argued loudly about whether he should step outside. He could see people walking by who he knew meant him harm — the trick would be to wait for a break in the traffic and make a run for it. But the arguing and another noise — a clanging like a streetcar bell — made it difficult to concentrate, and Michael paced restlessly most of the day.

You could proceed from this opening to explain how Michael's experiences illustrate some symptoms of schizophrenia. You could provide other examples of symptoms. You could, through process analysis, explain how the disease generally starts and progresses. You could use CAUSE AND EFFECT to explore the theories of why schizophrenia develops — from abnormalities in the part of the brain that controls sensation to incompatibilities in the blood types or antibodies of a mother and her infant.

Thesis

Opening up your subject with questions and developing it with various methods are good ways to see what it has to offer, but they can also leave you with a welter of ideas and a blurred focus. As in description, when all your details build to a DOMINANT IMPRESSION, so in definition you want to center all your ideas and evidence about the subject on a single controlling idea, a THESIS. It's not essential to state this idea in a THESIS STATEMENT, although doing so can serve your readers. It is essential that the idea govern.

Here, from the essays in this chapter, are two thesis statements. Notice how each makes an assertion about the subject, and how we can detect the author's bias toward the subject.

> The people in my grandmother's living room took a word [*nigger*] that whites used to signify worthlessness or degradation and rendered it impotent. . . . Meeting the word head-on, they proved it had absolutely nothing to do with the way they were determined to live their lives.
> — Gloria Naylor, "The Meanings of a Word"

> The word *chink* may have been created to harm, ridicule, and humiliate, but for us [Chinese Americans] it may have done the exact opposite.
> — Christine Leong, "Being a Chink"

Evidence

Writing an extended definition, you are like a mapmaker charting a territory, taking in some of what lies within the boundaries and ignoring what lies outside. The boundaries, of course, may be wide; and for this reason, the writing of an extended definition sometimes tempts a writer to sweep across a continent airily and to soar off into abstract clouds. Like any other method of expository writing, though, definition will work only for the writer who remembers the world of the senses and supports every generalization with concrete evidence.

Never lose sight of the reality you are attempting to enclose, even if its frontiers are as inclusive as those of *psychological burnout* or *human economic rights*. Give your reader examples, narrate an illustrative story, bring in specific description — whatever method you use, keep coming down to earth. Without your eyes on the world, you will define no reality. You might define *animal husbandry* till the cows come home and never make clear what it means.

FOCUS ON PARAGRAPH AND ESSAY UNITY

When drafting a definition, you may find yourself being pulled away from your subject by the narratives, descriptions, examples, comparisons, and other methods you use to specify meaning. Let yourself explore the byways of your subject — doing so will help you discover what you think. But in revising you'll need to make sure that all paragraphs focus on your thesis and, within paragraphs, that all sentences focus on the paragraph topic, generally expressed in a TOPIC SENTENCE. In other words, you'll need to ensure the UNITY of your essay and its paragraphs.

Gloria Naylor's "The Meanings of a Word" (p. 412) opens with several paragraphs of background to the definition of the freighted word *nigger* as it was used in Naylor's extended African American family at a certain moment in time. When Naylor focuses on defining, she proceeds methodically. As shown in the following outline, the paragraphs begin with topic sentences that state parts of the definition, which Naylor then illustrates with examples. (Some parts of the definition require more than a single paragraph, but Naylor keeps the groups of paragraphs focused on a single idea.)

PARAGRAPH 6	In the singular, the word was always applied to . . .
PARAGRAPH 9	When used with a possessive adjective by a woman — "my nigger" — it became a term of . . .
PARAGRAPH 10	In the plural, it became a description of . . .
PARAGRAPH 11	A woman could never be a "nigger" in the singular . . .
PARAGRAPH 13	But if the word was used in a third-person reference or shortened . . . , it always involved . . .

CHECKLIST FOR REVISING A DEFINITION

✔ **Meanings.** Have you explored your subject fully, turning up both its obvious and its not-so-obvious meanings?

✔ **Methods of development.** Have you used an appropriate range of other methods to develop your subject?

✔ **Thesis.** Have you focused your definition and kept within that focus, drawing clear boundaries around your subject?

✔ **Evidence.** Is your definition specific? Do examples, anecdotes, and concrete details both pin the subject down and make it vivid for readers?

✔ **Unity.** Do all paragraphs focus on your thesis, and do individual paragraphs or groups of paragraphs focus on parts of your definition?

DEFINITION IN ACADEMIC WRITING

A Biology Textbook

This paragraph from *Life: The Science of Biology*, by William K. Purves and Gordon H. Orians, defines a term, *homology*, that is useful in explaining the evolution of different species from a common ancestor (the topic at this point in the textbook). The paragraph provides a brief definition, a more extensive one, and finally examples of the concept.

When the character traits found in any two species owe their resemblance to a common ancestry, taxonomists say the states are *homologous*, or are *homologues* of each other. *Homology* is defined as correspondence between two structures due to inheritance from a common ancestor. Homologous structures can be identical in appearance and can even be based on identical genes. However, such structures can diverge until they become very different in both appearance and function. Nevertheless, homologous structures usually retain certain basic features that betray a common ancestry. Consider the forelimbs of vertebrates. It is easy to make a detailed, bone-by-bone, muscle-by-muscle comparison of the forearm of a person and a monkey and to conclude that the forearms, as well as the various parts of the forearm, are homologous. The forelimb of a dog, however, shows marked differences from those of primates in both appearance and function. The forelimb is used for locomotion by dogs but for grasping and manipulation by people and monkeys. Even so, all of the bones can still be matched. The wing of a bird and the flipper of a seal are even more different from each other or from the human forearm, yet they too are constructed around bones that can be matched on a nearly perfect one-to-one basis.

Margin notes:

Definition of *homology* and related words

Short definition

Refined definition

Examples:
- Similar appearance, function, and structure
- Dissimilar appearance and function, but similar structure

Definition

An Essay Exam

You might worry about essay exams — many students do — but take heart: Instructors who assign in-class timed essays don't expect prize-winning compositions. They do, however, expect students to demonstrate their knowledge and critical thinking about important concepts covered in lectures and assignments.

Often you'll need to interpret the wording of an exam question to figure out what kind of response is appropriate. Questions that ask *why*, for example, might call for CAUSE-AND-EFFECT analysis, while those that ask *how* might lead to a PROCESS ANALYSIS. Keep in mind that an essay you write for an in-class exam will necessarily be less polished than one you write at home. That's fine — as long as you draft an accurate, detailed, and reasonably coherent answer to the question asked.

The midterm exam for Martin Ward's introductory government class included multiple-choice questions, a short-answer section, and one short-essay question: "Explain the meaning of *civil liberties*, including an explanation of how civil liberties differ from civil rights." Ward quickly recognized that "explain the meaning of" called for a definition and that "differ" called for an element of COMPARISON AND CONTRAST. Following the advice of his teaching assistant in the exam review session, Ward quickly outlined the points he needed to cover before he started writing. Then he composed the following response.

Civil liberties are the freedoms that individuals have against state intrusion. Laws protecting civil liberties limit or prohibit government action. The Constitution's Bill of Rights guarantees many of these liberties, including freedom of expression, freedom of religion, and freedom from unreasonable searches and seizures. Historically, the protection of civil liberties was established before the US Constitution in documents such as the English Magna Carta (1215). Since that time, free countries have defined themselves against authoritarian countries by their respect for — and legal protections of — these freedoms.

Short definition of *civil liberties*

Examples

Brief history of the concept

While most people agree that civil liberties are essential to a free state, there is some controversy surrounding their meaning. People don't always agree which rights are civil liberties. For example, the debate over abortion reflects a dispute over whether the Constitution protects privacy rights that include the right to have an abortion. There is also disagreement about

Extended definition considers issues that complicate meaning:

• Which rights are civil liberties?

what constitutes a violation of civil liberties. As the federal government has taken measures to protect the country from terrorism, many have questioned whether practices such as warrantless wiretapping violate privacy rights, speech rights, or the prohibition of unreasonable searches and seizures.

• What violates civil liberties?

People often confuse civil liberties with civil rights. Civil liberties are freedoms from government intrusion protected primarily by the Bill of Rights. Civil rights, however, concern the equal treatment of individuals in society and are established mainly by the Equal Protection Clause of the Fourteenth Amendment. An example is the right of citizens to attend public schools regardless of their color or gender. Civil liberties and civil rights differ in another important way as well: While protections of civil liberties prohibit government action, the government must often act to protect civil rights, as in the creation of antidiscrimination laws.

Point-by-point contrast with civil rights

GLORIA NAYLOR

Gloria Naylor describes herself as "just a girl from Queens who can turn a sentence," but she is well known for bringing African American women vividly within the fold of American literature. She was born in 1950 in New York City and served for some years as a missionary for the Jehovah's Witnesses, working "for better world conditions." While in college, she made her living as a telephone operator. She graduated from Brooklyn College in 1981 and received an MA in African American literature from Yale University in 1983. While teaching at several universities and publishing numerous stories and essays, Naylor has written five interconnected novels: *The Women of Brewster Place* (1982), *Linden Hills* (1985), *Mama Day* (1988), *Bailey's Cafe* (1992), and *The Men of Brewster Place* (1998). *The Women of Brewster Place* won the American Book Award for best first novel. In 2004 she published *Conversations with Gloria Naylor*, a collection of interviews. A fictionalized memoir, *1996*, followed in 2005. Naylor is also the founder and president of One Way Productions, an independent film and multimedia company in Brooklyn, New York.

The Meanings of a Word

When she was in third grade, Naylor was stung by a word that seemed new. Only later did she realize that she'd been hearing the word all her life, but in an entirely different context. In "The Meanings of a Word" she uses definition to explore the varying meanings that context creates. The essay first appeared in the *New York Times* in 1986.

The essay following this one, Christine Leong's "Being a Chink," responds directly to Naylor and extends her point about context and meaning.

Language is the subject. It is the written form with which I've managed to keep the wolf away from the door and, in diaries, to keep my sanity. In spite of this, I consider the written word inferior to the spoken, and much of the frustration experienced by novelists is the awareness that whatever we manage to capture in even the most transcendent passages falls far short of the richness of life. Dialogue achieves its power in the dynamics of a fleeting moment of sight, sound, smell, and touch.

I'm not going to enter the debate here about whether it is language that shapes reality or vice versa. That battle is doomed to be waged whenever we seek intermittent reprieve from the chicken and egg dispute. I will simply take the position that the spoken word, like the written word, amounts to a nonsensical arrangement of sounds or letters without a consensus that assigns "meaning." And building from the meanings of what we hear, we order reality. Words themselves are innocuous; it is the consensus that gives them true power.

I remember the first time I heard the word *nigger*. In my third-grade class, our math tests were being passed down the rows, and as I handed the papers to a little boy in back of me, I remarked that once again he had received a much lower mark than I did. He snatched his test from me and spit out that word. Had he called me a nymphomaniac or a necrophiliac, I couldn't have been more puzzled. I didn't know what a nigger was, but I knew that whatever it meant, it was something he shouldn't have called me. This was verified when I raised my hand, and in a loud voice repeated what he had said and watched the teacher scold him for using a "bad" word. I was later to go home and ask the inevitable question that every black parent must face — "Mommy, what does *nigger* mean?"

And what exactly did it mean? Thinking back, I realize that this could not have been the first time the word was used in my presence. I was part of a large extended family that had migrated from the rural South after World War II and formed a close-knit network that gravitated around my maternal grandparents. Their ground-floor apartment in one of the buildings they owned in Harlem was a weekend mecca for my immediate family, along with countless aunts, uncles, and cousins who brought along assorted friends. It was a bustling and open house with assorted neighbors and tenants popping in and out to exchange bits of gossip, pick up an old quarrel, or referee the ongoing checkers game in which my grandmother cheated shamelessly. They were all there to let down their hair and put up their feet after a week of labor in the factories, laundries, and shipyards of New York.

Amid the clamor, which could reach deafening proportions — two or three conversations going on simultaneously, punctuated by the sound of a baby's crying somewhere in the back rooms or out on the street — there was still a rigid set of rules about what was said and how. Older children were sent out of the living room when it was time to get into the juicy details about "you-know-who" up on the third floor who had gone and gotten herself "p-r-e-g-n-a-n-t!" But my parents, knowing that I could spell well beyond my years, always demanded that I follow the others out to play. Beyond sexual misconduct and death, everything else was considered harmless for our young ears. And so among the anecdotes of the triumphs and disappointments in the various workings of their lives, the word *nigger* was used in my presence, but it was set within contexts and inflections that caused it to register in my mind as something else.[1]

In the singular, the word was always applied to a man who had distinguished himself in some situation that brought their approval for his strength, intelligence, or drive: 6

"Did Johnny *really* do that?"   7

"I'm telling you, that nigger pulled in $6,000 of overtime last year. Said he got enough for a down payment on a house."   8

When used with a possessive adjective by a woman — "my nigger" — it became a term of endearment for her husband or boyfriend. But it could be more than just a term applied to a man. In their mouths it became the pure essence of manhood — a disembodied force that channeled their past history of struggle and present survival against the odds into a victorious statement of being: "Yeah, that old foreman found out quick enough — you don't mess with a nigger."   9

In the plural, it became a description of some group within the community that had overstepped the bounds of decency as my family defined it. Parents who neglected their children, a drunken couple who fought in public, people who simply refused to look for work, those with excessively dirty mouths or unkempt households were all "trifling niggers." This particular circle could forgive hard times, unemployment, the occasional bout of depression — they had gone through all of that themselves — but the unforgivable sin was a lack of self-respect.   10

A woman could never be a "nigger" in the singular, with its connotation of confirming worth. The noun *girl* was its closest equivalent in that sense, but only when used in direct address and regardless of the gender doing the addressing. *Girl* was a token of respect for a woman. The one-syllable word was drawn out to sound like three in recognition of the extra ounce of wit, nerve, or daring that the woman had shown in the situation under discussion.   11

"G-i-r-l, stop. You mean you said that to his face?"   12

But if the word was used in a third-person reference or shortened so that it almost snapped out of the mouth, it always involved some element of communal disapproval. And age became an important factor in these exchanges. It was only between individuals of the same generation, or from any older person to a younger (but never the other way around), that *girl* would be considered a compliment.   13

---

[1] The author wants it understood that the use of the word *nigger* is reprehensible in today's society. This essay speaks to a specific time and place when that word was utilized to empower African Americans; today it is used to degrade them even if spoken from their own mouths. — Gloria Naylor

I don't agree with the argument that use of the word *nigger* at this social   14
stratum of the black community was an internalization of racism. The dynamics were the exact opposite: The people in my grandmother's living room took a word that whites used to signify worthlessness or degradation and rendered it impotent. Gathering there together, they transformed *nigger* to signify the varied and complex human beings they knew themselves to be. If the word was to disappear totally from the mouths of even the most liberal of white society, no one in that room was naive enough to believe it would disappear from white minds. Meeting the word head-on, they proved it had absolutely nothing to do with the way they were determined to live their lives.

So there must have been dozens of times that *nigger* was spoken in front of   15
me before I reached the third grade. But I didn't "hear" it until it was said by a small pair of lips that had already learned it could be a way to humiliate me. That was the word I went home and asked my mother about. And since she knew that I had to grow up in America, she took me in her lap and explained.

*For a reading quiz, visit **bedfordstmartins.com/thebedfordreader**.*

Journal Writing

As Naylor shows, the language of stereotypes can be powerful and painful to encounter. In your journal, recall when you have experienced or witnessed this kind of labeling. What were your reactions? Keep in mind that race is but one object of stereotypes. Consider income, education, body type or other physical attributes, sexual preference, activities, or neighborhood, for just a few other characteristics. (To take your journal writing further, see "From Journal to Essay" on the next page.)

Questions on Meaning

1. Why does Naylor think that written language is inferior to spoken language (par. 1)?
2. In paragraph 15, Naylor says that although the word *nigger* had been used in her presence many times, she didn't really "hear" the word until a mean little boy said it. How do you explain this contradiction?
3. Naylor says that "[t]he people in my grandmother's living room . . . transformed *nigger*" (par. 14). How?
4. What is Naylor's primary PURPOSE in this essay?

Questions on Writing Strategy

1. In her first two paragraphs, Naylor discusses language in the ABSTRACT. How are these paragraphs connected to her stories about the word *nigger*? Why do you think she begins the essay this way? Is this INTRODUCTION effective or not? Why?
2. Go through Naylor's essay and note which paragraphs discuss the racist uses of *nigger* and which discuss the nonracist uses. How do Naylor's organization and the space she devotes to each use help her make her point? How does Naylor integrate the two definitions to achieve UNITY?
3. Look back at the last two sentences of Naylor's essay. What is the EFFECT of ending on this idea?
4. **OTHER METHODS** After each definition of the words *nigger* and *girl*, Naylor gives an EXAMPLE in the form of a quotation. These examples are in paragraphs 7–10 (for instance, "Yeah, that old foreman found out quick enough — you don't mess with a nigger" [9]) and paragraph 12 ("G-i-r-l, stop. You mean you said that to his face?"). What do such examples add to Naylor's definitions?

Questions on Language

1. What is "the chicken and egg dispute" (par. 2)? What does this dispute say about the relationship between language and reality?
2. What do the words *nymphomaniac* and *necrophiliac* CONNOTE in paragraph 3?
3. If you don't know the meanings of the following words, look them up in a dictionary: transcendent, dynamics (par. 1); intermittent, reprieve, consensus, innocuous (2); verified (3); gravitated, mecca (4); clamor, inflections (5); endearment, disembodied (9); unkempt, trifling (10); communal (13); stratum, internalization, degradation, rendered, impotent, naive (14).

Suggestions for Writing

1. **FROM JOURNAL TO ESSAY** Using as examples the experiences you wrote about in your journal entry, write an essay modeled on Naylor's in which you define "the meanings of a word" (or words). Do you find, too, that meaning varies with context? If so, make the variations clear.
2. Can you think of other labels that may be defined in more than one way? (These might include *smart, childish, old-fashioned, artistic, proud, attractive, heroic*, and so on.) Choose one such label, and write one paragraph for each possible definition. Be sure to explain the contexts for each definition and to give enough examples so that the meanings are clear.
3. Americans continually debate the use of the word *nigger*. Some have proposed banning the word entirely, while others argue that eliminating the word would erase its role in US history and its painful legacy. Even Naylor has changed her position, as her author's note on page 414 explains. Two books explore the theoretical and practical issues of the word: Randall Kennedy, *Nigger: The Strange Career of a Troublesome Word* (2002), and Jabari Asim, *The N-Word: Who Can Say It, Who Shouldn't, and Why* (2007). Consult one or both of these books, and

form your own opinion about how the word should be treated. Explain your position in an essay.

4. **CRITICAL WRITING**   Naylor claims that words are "nonsensical . . . without a consensus that assigns 'meaning' " (par. 2). If so, how do we understand the meaning
of a word like *nigger*, when Naylor has shown us that there is more than one
consensus about its meaning? Does Naylor contradict herself? Write an essay that
either supports or refutes Naylor's claim about meaning and context. You will
need to consider how she and you define *consensus*.

5. **CONNECTIONS**   The next essay, Christine Leong's "Being a Chink," identifies a
moment when Leong was first struck by the negative power of racist language.
Write an essay that COMPARES AND CONTRASTS Naylor's and Leong's reactions to
a derogatory label. How did the context help shape their reactions?

Gloria Naylor on Writing

Studying literature in college was somewhat disappointing for Gloria
Naylor. "What I wanted to see," she told William Goldstein of *Publishers
Weekly*, "were reflections of me and my existence and experience." Then,
reading African American literature in graduate school, she discovered that
"blacks have been writing in this country since this country has been writing
and have a literary heritage of their own. Unfortunately, they haven't had
encouragement or recognition for their efforts. . . . What had happened was
that when black people wrote, it wasn't quite [considered] serious work — it
was race work or protest work."

For Naylor this discovery was a turning point. "I wanted to become a
writer because I felt that my presence as a black woman and my perspective as
a woman in general had been underrepresented." Her work tries to "articulate
experiences that want articulating — for those readers who reflect the subject
matter, black readers, and for those who don't, basically white middle-class
readers."

For Discussion

1. What does Naylor mean when she says that she tries to "articulate experiences
that want articulating"?

2. Naylor is motivated to write by a consciousness of herself as an African American
and a woman. How do you see this motivation driving her essay "The Meanings
of a Word"?

CHRISTINE LEONG

Christine Leong was born in New York City in 1976 and attended Stuyvesant High School there, graduating in 1994. At the Stern School of Business at New York University, she majored in finance and information systems and interned at an investment firm. She graduated with a BS in 1998 and began a career in financial services. In her free time, Leong enjoys a good doughnut and cheering on the New York Yankees. "The one thing I couldn't live without," she says, "is music."

Being a Chink

Leong wrote this essay for a freshman composition class at NYU, and it was published in *Mercer Street,* a collection of NYU students' essays. As you'll see, Leong was inspired by Gloria Naylor's "The Meanings of a Word" (p. 412) to report her own experiences and to define a word that can be either hurtful or warm, depending on the speaker.

The power of language is something that people often underestimate. It is the one thing that allows people to communicate with each other, to be understood, to be heard. It gives us identity, personality, social status, and it also creates communities, defining both insiders and outsiders. Language has the ability to heal or to harm, to praise or belittle, to promote peace or even to glorify hate. But perhaps most important, language is the tool used to define us and differentiate us from the next person. Names and labels are what separate us from each other. Sometimes these things are innocuous, depending on the particular word and the context in which it is used. Often they serve to ridicule and humiliate.

I remember the first time I saw the word *chink*. I used to work over the summers at my father's Chinese restaurant, the Oriental, to earn a few extra dollars of spending money. It was a warm, sunny Friday morning, and I was busy performing my weekly task of cleaning out the storage area under the cash register at the front of the store. Armed with a large can of Pledge furniture polish and an old cloth, I started attacking the old oak shelves, sorting through junk mail that had accumulated over the last week, separating the bills and other important things that had to be set aside for later, before wiping each wooden panel clean. It was a pretty uneventful chore, that is, until I got to the bottom shelf, the last of three. I always hated cleaning this particular shelf because it required me to get down on my hands and knees behind the counter and reach all the way back into the compartment to dig out all the stuff that managed to get wedged against the wall.

After bending to scoop all the papers out of that third cubicle, I began   3
to sort through them haphazardly. A few old menus, a gum wrapper (I always wondered how little things like that got stuffed in there), some promotional flyers, two capless pens, a dusty scratch pad, and something that appeared to be a little white envelope. Nothing seemed unusual until I examined that last item more closely. It was an old MidLantic envelope from the bank across the street. I was just about to crumple it up and throw it into the trash can when I decided to check if there was any money left in it. Too lazy to deal with the actual "chore" of opening the envelope, I held it up to the light.

As the faint yellow glow from the antique light fixture above me shone   4
through the envelope, turning it transparent, my suspicion that it was empty was confirmed. However, what I found was more shocking than anything I could have imagined. There, outlined by the light, was the word *chink* written backwards. I quickly lowered my arm onto the cool, smooth surface of the counter and flipped the envelope onto its other side, refusing to believe what I had just read. On the back, in dark blue ink with a large circle drawn around it, was the word *CHINK* written in my father's handwriting.

Up until that moment, I hadn't known that my father knew such words,   5
and thinking again, perhaps he didn't know this one either. After all, it was a habit of his to write down English words he did not know when he heard them and look them up in the dictionary later that day, learning them and adding them to his vocabulary. My mind began spinning with all the possible reasons he had written this particular word down. I wondered if an angry patron who had come in earlier had called him that.

I was shocked at that possibility, but I was not surprised. Being one of only   6
two Asian families living and running a business in a small suburban town predominately inhabited by old Caucasian people was bound to breed some kind of discrimination, if not hatred. I know that my father might not have known exactly what the word *chink* meant, but he must have had a good idea, because he never came to ask me about it as he did with all the other slang words that couldn't be found in the dictionary. It's funny, though, I do not remember the first time I was called a *chink*. I only remember the pain and outrage I felt the first time I saw it in writing, perhaps the first time I discovered that someone had used that hateful word to degrade my father.

In her essay "The Meanings of a Word," Gloria Naylor examines the various   7
meanings of the word *nigger*, definitions that have consensual meanings throughout society and others that vary according to how and when the word

is used. In this piece, Naylor uses personal examples to describe how "[t]he people in [her] grandmother's living room took a word that whites used to signify worthlessness or degradation and rendered it impotent," by transforming *nigger* into a word signifying "the varied and complex human beings that they knew themselves to be" (415). Naylor goes on to add that although none of these people were foolish enough to believe that the word *nigger* would magically be erased from the minds of all humankind, they were convinced that their "head-on" approach of dealing with the label that society had put on them "proved [that] it had absolutely nothing to do with the way they were determined to live their lives" (415).

It has been nearly eight years since that day I stumbled across the bank   8
envelope. Since then we have moved from that suburb in New Jersey to New York City, where the Asian population is much larger, and the word *chink,* although still heard, is either heard less frequently or in a rather "harmless" manner between myself and fellow Chinese (Asian) teenage friends. I do not remember how it happened exactly. I just know that we have been calling each other *chink* for quite a long while now. The word has never been used to belittle or degrade, but rather as a term of endearment, a loving insult between friends, almost but not quite exactly the way *nigger* is sometimes used among black people. It is a practice that we still engage in today, and although we know that there are times when the use of the word *chink* is very inappropriate, it is an accepted term within our circle.

Do not misunderstand us, we are all intelligent Asian youths, all graduat-   9
ing from New York City's top high school, all college students, and we know what the word *chink* truly means. We know, because over the years we have heard it countless times, from strangers on the streets and in stores, from fellow students and peers, and in some instances even from teachers, although it might not have been meant for us to hear.

So you see, even though we may use the term *chink* rather casually, it is   10
only used that way amongst ourselves because we know that when we say it to each other it is truly without malice or harmful intent. I do not think that any of us knows exactly why we do it, but perhaps it is our own way, like the characters in Naylor's piece, of dealing with a label that can never be removed. It is not determined by who we are on the inside, or what we are capable of accomplishing, but instead by what we look like — the shape of our eyes, the color of our skin, the texture of our hair, and our delicate features. Perhaps we intentionally misuse the word as a symbol of our overcoming the stereotypes that American society has imposed upon us, a way of showing that although others have tried to make us feel small, weak, and insignificant, we are the opposite. We are strong, we are determined, we are the voices of the future, and we refuse to let a simple word paralyze us, belittle us, or control us.

The word *chink* may have been created to harm, ridicule, and humiliate, 11 but for us it may have done the exact opposite. In some ways it has helped us find a certain comfort in each other, each of us knowing what the other has gone through, a common thread of racism binding us all together, a strange union born from the word *chink* that was used against us, and a shared goal of perseverance.

Work Cited

Naylor, Gloria. "The Meanings of a Word." Kennedy, X. J., et al., eds. *The Bedford Reader*. 12th ed. Boston: Bedford, 2014. 412–15. Print.

*For a reading quiz, visit **bedfordstmartins.com/thebedfordreader**.*

Journal Writing

Although children often assume they will be protected by their parents, Leong presents a situation in which she felt the need to protect her father. Can you identify with Leong's feelings? Have you ever felt particularly angry or defensive on behalf of a parent? In your journal, explore why and what happened as a result. (To take your journal writing further, see "From Journal to Essay" on the next page.)

Questions on Meaning

1. In paragraph 9 Leong says that she and her friends "know what the word *chink* truly means." Where in her essay does she explain this "true" meaning?
2. What has the word *chink* come to mean when Leong and her friends use it? Where in the essay does Leong explain this?
3. One might argue that the THESIS of Leong's essay is that language is not absolute. Is her PURPOSE, then, to propose a new DEFINITION for a word, to teach the reader something about how labels work, or to explain how adapting a racist term can be a form of gaining power? How do you know?

Questions on Writing Strategy

1. Look carefully at Gloria Naylor's essay "The Meanings of a Word" (p. 412). What structural similarities do you notice between it and Leong's? Why do you think Leong adapts these features of Naylor's essay?
2. In paragraph 3 Leong details all the forgotten items she finds under the counter.

What is the EFFECT of ending with the "old MidLantic envelope from the bank across the street"?

3. What is the main purpose of the extended example from Naylor's essay in paragraph 7?

4. Why is Leong so careful to explain that she and her friends are all intelligent and educated (par. 9)?

5. **OTHER METHODS**   Leong suggests CAUSE AND EFFECT when she expresses shock and disbelief at seeing the word *chink* in writing (par. 4). Why does Leong react so strongly to the writing on the envelope?

Questions on Language

1. In paragraph 10 Leong explains that she and her friends are "dealing with a label that can never be removed." What other words does she use in this paragraph to suggest the potential helplessness of being permanently labeled?

2. What do the CONNOTATIONS of "term of endearment" (par. 8) indicate about the way Leong and her friends have redefined *chink*?

3. Make sure you know the meanings of the following words: status, belittle, innocuous (par. 1); cubicle, haphazardly (3); Caucasian, degrade (6); consensual (7); malice (10); perseverance (11).

Suggestions for Writing

1. **FROM JOURNAL TO ESSAY**   Write an essay that explores why and how children might feel compelled to act like parents toward their own parents. Is this a shift that comes with age? with specific circumstances? out of the blue? Make some GENERALIZATIONS about this process, using as EVIDENCE the personal recollections from your journal entry.

2. As Leong explains in her INTRODUCTION, not all labels are intended to be hurtful. Often they are shorthand ways for our families and friends to identify us, perhaps reflecting something about our appearance ("Red," "Slim") or our interests ("Sport," "Chef "). What do your family or friends call you? Write several paragraphs giving a careful definition of this label. Where did it come from? Why is it appropriate (or not)?

3. Research the history of Chinese Americans. When and why did the initial wave of immigration occur? What forces have led to other patterns of immigration over the years? Have Chinese Americans faced different kinds of discrimination than other immigrants have? In an essay, answer these or other questions that occur to you.

4. **CRITICAL WRITING**   In her opening paragraph Leong says that "language is the tool used to define us." But she goes on to explain how she and her friends *refuse* to be defined by racist language. Does this apparent contradiction weaken her essay? Why, or why not? (To answer this question, consider the purpose of Leong's essay; see question 3 of "Questions on Meaning.")

5. **CONNECTIONS**   Both Christine Leong and Gloria Naylor, in "The Meanings of a Word" (p. 412), show that racist language can be taken over by those against whom it is directed. They also show that for groups or communities to redefine,

and thus to own, these racist slurs can be empowering. Do you find their ARGU-MENTS convincing, or do these redefinitions reveal what Naylor denies — namely, "an internalization of racism" (par. 14)? In an essay, explain your opinion on this issue, using as evidence passages from Naylor's and Leong's essays as well as insights and EXAMPLES from your own observations and experience.

Christine Leong on Writing

Christine Leong commented for this book on the difficulties of writing and the rewards that can ensue.

Writing is something that comes easily for many people, but unfortunately I am not one of them. For me the writing process is one of the hardest and quite possibly is *the* most nerve-wracking thing that I have ever experienced. I can't even begin to count all the hours I have spent throughout the course of my life staring at a blank computer screen, trying desperately to come up with the right combination of words to express my thoughts and feelings, and although after many hours of frustration I eventually end up with something, I am never happy with it because I am undoubtedly my own worst critic. Perhaps my mentality of "it's not good enough yet" stems from my belief that writing can never really be completed; to me it has no beginning and no end but is rather a small representation of who I am at a given moment in time, and I believe that the more things I experience in life, the more I am able to contribute to my writing. Thus, whatever I write always has the potential of being better; there's always room for improvement via more revisions, greater insight, and about a hundred more drafts.

I used to believe that writing always had to make sense, but since then I have learned that there are many things in this life that do not adhere to this "rule." I now realize that writing doesn't necessarily have to be grammatically correct or even sensible, and the only thing that really matters is that whatever is written is truly inspired. Passion comes through very clearly in a writer's words, and the more emotion that goes into a piece, the more impact it will ultimately have on the reader. In recent years I have learned that there are no real writing guidelines, and that writing is much like any other art form: It can be abstract or it can follow more traditional "themes." However, in order for a piece of writing to be effective, in the sense that it can differentiate itself from any other writing sample and hopefully have some significance to the reader, I believe that it has to come from within.

The majority of what I write about, and that which I feel is worth reading, is inspired by actual experiences that I have had. For example, "Being a Chink" began as an assignment in a freshman writing workshop class in college. When first presented with the task of writing it, I was at a complete loss for words and had absolutely no clue where to start. However, after reading Gloria Naylor's "The Meanings of a Word," I was reminded of one of the most traumatic and memorable events in my life. The piece triggered a very strong memory, and before long I found myself writing down anything that came into my head, letting my thoughts and emotions flow freely in the form of words without thinking about whether or not they made any kind of sense. Many hours later I discovered that I had written the basic structure of what would eventually be my final product. I must honestly say that I can't really recall the actual process of writing "Being a Chink"; it was just an essay that seemed to take on a life and form of its own. Perhaps that, along with its universal theme, is what makes it such a strong piece. It not only is a recollection from my adolescence but is something that defines the very essence of the person that I have become since then.

In retrospect, I now realize that writing "Being a Chink" was not only about completing an essay and fulfilling a writing requirement; it was also about the acknowledgment of my own growth as a person. In many ways, without my initially being aware of it, the piece has helped me come to terms with one of the most controversial issues that I have ever been faced with.

For Discussion

1. Does Leong's characterization of writing as "nerve-wracking" ring a bell for you? How do you overcome writer's block?
2. What do you think about Leong's statement that "writing doesn't necessarily have to be grammatically correct or even sensible, and the only thing that really matters is that whatever is written is truly inspired"? In your experience with writing, what are the roles of correctness, sense, and inspiration? What matters most to you? What matters most to readers?

MEGHAN DAUM

Born in 1970 in Palo Alto, California, Meghan Daum is a writer known for provocative, witty essays on American life. Daum graduated from Vassar College with a BA in English in 1992 and earned an MA in writing from Columbia University in 1996. A former contributing editor for *Harper's Bazaar* and since 2005 a syndicated columnist for the *Los Angeles Times*, Daum has published her work in a variety of newspapers and magazines, including *The New Yorker*, *Gentlemen's Quarterly*, *Vogue,* and the *New York Times Book Review.* She is the author of four books: *The Quality of Life Report* (2003), a novel; *Let the Trinkets Do the Talking* (2001) and *My Misspent Youth* (2001), essay collections; and *Life Would Be Perfect If I Lived in That House* (2011), a humorous memoir about the author's unhealthy obsession with real estate. Daum is also an occasional guest on National Public Radio and has contributed to *Marketplace, Morning Edition,* and *This American Life.* She lives in Los Angeles.

Narcissist — Give It a Rest

In this column first published in the *Los Angeles Times* in 2011, Daum takes issue with the current usage of one particular word. We might be a nation of narcissists, she concedes, except we're not. As far as Daum is concerned, Americans are something else entirely.

At any given moment a whole lot of people are accusing a whole lot 1
of other people of being narcissists. In recent years, the term for a self-destructive "personality disorder" has become the insult of choice for almost anyone doing almost anything.

The concept of narcissism as a broad cultural condition, and the word's 2
use as an everyday term, goes back several decades. Christopher Lasch published *The Culture of Narcissism* in 1979, three years after Tom Wolfe[1] declared the era the "me decade." The 1980s turned out to be even more "me" than the '70s had been, and by the 1990s, the rise of identity politics, the birth of reality television and the proliferation of the language of self-help (remember Wendy Kaminer's *I'm Dysfunctional, You're Dysfunctional?*) effectively elevated self-absorption from a passing (if protracted) trend to, well, pretty much just the way things were. To accuse someone of being a narcissist was kind of like accusing them of breathing. In other words, what was the point?

---

[1] American journalist (born 1931) best known for *The Electric Kool-Aid Acid Test* (1968) and *The Right Stuff* (1979). — Eds.

But lately the word seems to be enjoying a resurgence, often among   3
people who give the impression that they just discovered it. Professional
pundits love it, as do bloggers, politicians, religious leaders, celebrity shrinks,
cultural critics, Internet commenters and blowhards at parties. And why
shouldn't we? (Yes, I include myself in this mix; I am, after all, a you-know-
what.) It's the handiest weapon in our arsenal: a derogatory *apercu*[2] that's one-
size-fits-all.

Democrats, Republicans, red state folks, blue state folks, baby boomers,   4
Gen Xers, millennials: all narcissists! Parents, nonparents, vegans, meat eaters, city dwellers, rural dwellers, people who travel a lot, people who refuse to
travel, writers who use the first person: all vectors in the national scourge of
self-involvement. In practice, any behavior you don't like can be dismissed
as abrasively, idiotically, dangerously self-centered, with a $10, three-syllable
word that has a way of making even a nincompoop feel like he's saying something intellectual. . . .

Here's the problem with the charge of narcissism. The term has been   5
misused and overused so flagrantly that it's now all but meaningless when it
comes to labeling truly destructive tendencies. These days, you can be called
a narcissist merely by having self-esteem and showing a little ambition — in
other words, for trying to survive in the world. In fact, so fluid has the definition become that narcissism's true home for the last forty-four years, the
Diagnostic and Statistical Manual of Mental Disorders, has dropped the diagnosis
from its roster.

As for anyone still itching to attribute our collective addiction to *Face-*   6
book and e-mail and other self-referential forms of communication to a narcissism epidemic, I beg to differ. That stuff hasn't made us into egomaniacs; it's
made us into boring, semi-verbal zombies who bang into each other when we
exit movie theaters because we're buried in our iPhones.

So perhaps it's time to declare a moratorium on the indiscriminate use   7
of this particular n-word. After all, we're not a nation of narcissists. We're a
nation of jerks. Which also happens to be a lot easier to spell.

For a reading quiz, visit **bedfordstmartins.com/thebedfordreader**.

---

[2] French, "perception" or "insight." Daum uses the word in its colloquial sense of linguistic
shorthand. — Eds.

Journal Writing

Daum writes that "baby boomers, Gen Xers, [and] millennials" (par. 4) have all been characterized as narcissists. To what generation do you belong? How do you and your peers tend to be described in the media? Do you agree that people in your age group are "dangerously self-centered" (4) or otherwise unpleasant to others? In your journal, write down your own characterization of members of your generation. (To take your journal writing further, see "From Journal to Essay" below.)

Questions on Meaning

1. When, according to Daum, did people start misusing the word *narcissist?* Why is the timing significant to her?
2. What would you say is Daum's PURPOSE in this essay?
3. Does Daum have a THESIS? In which sentence or sentences does she state her main idea most directly?

Questions on Writing Strategy

1. What AUDIENCE probably would not like this essay? Why would they not like it?
2. Daum defines mostly by negation. In your own words, SUMMARIZE her implied definition of *narcissist.* How does it differ from the meanings commonly attached to the word?
3. Analyze the organization of this essay. What does Daum discuss in each of her paragraphs? How does she create UNITY among them?
4. **OTHER METHODS**   Where in the essay does Daum list some of the people and attitudes that have been called narcissistic? What seems to be the intended EFFECT of these EXAMPLES?

Questions on Language

1. How would you describe the TONE of this essay?
2. Be sure you know the meanings of the following words, checking a dictionary if necessary: proliferation, protracted (par. 2); resurgence (3); vegans, vectors, scourge (4); flagrantly, roster (5); moratorium, indiscriminate (7).
3. What is the effect of "you-know-what" in paragraph 3 and "this particular n-word" in paragraph 7? Why doesn't Daum just say "narcissist" in these instances?

Suggestions for Writing

1. **FROM JOURNAL TO ESSAY**   Write an essay that gives an extended definition of the age group of which you consider yourself a member, drawing on your journal entry, Daum's essay, and any other sources that offer ideas. You might use one of the labels Daum cites (baby boomers, Gen Xers, millennials) or come up with

a name of your own. Keep in mind that characterizing such a large and diverse group requires GENERALIZATION. How does your definition compare with other definitions you have heard in the media? Does any attempt to characterize an age group necessarily oversimplify? Do you find value or interest in the exercise?

2. Think of another word or phrase that is commonly misused or overused (or both). Examples might include *literally, amazing, hero, like, LOL, I could care less,* or *beg the question*. Following Daum's essay as a model, write an essay of your own explaining your objections and imploring people to stop using the word or phrase.

3. Daum suggests that, thanks to "self-referential forms of communication" (par. 6) such as social media and smartphones, Americans have become increasingly self-absorbed and rude. Write an essay in which you offer your own viewpoint on this idea. Are we, in fact, "a nation of jerks" (7)? If you generally agree, offer specific examples and speculate about the causes of this change. If you generally disagree, challenge Daum's assumptions with examples that counter her claim.

4. **CRITICAL WRITING**   The decision to remove narcissistic personality disorder from the *Diagnostic and Statistical Manual of Mental Disorders* raised some controversy when it was announced in late 2010 — just a few weeks before Daum wrote her essay. Research the controversy so that you understand the views for and against retaining narcissism as a psychiatric diagnosis. In an essay, briefly summarize the controversy, and then analyze Daum's essay as a contribution to the conversation. On which side of the debate does her position seem to fall? Does she agree with the decision to drop the disorder from the psychiatrists' manual? Or does she seem to think it should have stayed? Use PARAPHRASES and QUOTATIONS from the essay to support your conclusions.

5. **CONNECTIONS**   In the cartoon "Dr. Carmella's Guide to Understanding the Introverted" (*bedfordstmartins.com/thebedfordreader*), Schroeder Jones portrays another type of personality that seems often misunderstood. How does Jones define *introversion*? Does he see it as a "personality disorder" on a par with Daum's narcissism, or as a mostly positive trait? Write an essay that COMPARES AND CONTRASTS introversion and narcissism as Jones and Daum define them. Why might some people consider introverts self-centered, for instance? Is it possible that people accused of narcissism are just loners drained by social interaction? Should either personality trait be classified as a disorder? Why, or why not?

Meghan Daum on Writing

At least once a week, Daum claims, she hears from a "student who's been assigned a paper about my writing and wants me to tell her what to say." In this excerpt from a 2011 *LA Times* column, she explains why those students should not expect a response.

I know, I know. I should be flattered. I should be heartened that the youth of America are reading newspapers (albeit under duress) and, for that matter, that anyone's reading my column at all. . . . Still, I find myself consistently irked over this whole phenomenon, and not just because I feel guilty when I don't answer these e-mails and resentful when I do. It's because in a world of hyper-accessibility, writers are expected not only to write things but then engage with readers via e-mail or comment boards or book festival Q&As about why they wrote it and what they meant. Nothing is ever considered enough. Readers don't want to simply read stuff and mull it over on their own; they want a personal dialog with the writer about what they were supposed to get out of it.

Students, especially, should be figuring out the how and why of a piece of writing based not on what the author explains to them in an Internet chat room but by tapping into the pure recesses of their own minds. That kind of approach is the highest compliment a reader can give a writer. It's also, by definition, the one we just can't offer any help on.

For Discussion

1. What does Daum mean when she says that students should be "tapping into the pure recesses of their own minds"?
2. Have you ever contacted (or been tempted to contact) a writer to ask about something she or he has written? How do you respond to Daum's suggestion that such requests miss the point?

BARBARA KINGSOLVER

A writer of fiction, poetry, and nonfiction and a self-described "human rights activist," Barbara Kingsolver was born in Annapolis, Maryland, in 1955 and grew up in eastern Kentucky. She studied biology at DePauw University (BA, 1977) and the University of Arizona (MS, 1981) and worked in the field as a researcher and technical writer. A full-time writer since 1985, Kingsolver has published a variety of well-received books including the novels *The Bean Trees* (1988), *The Poisonwood Bible* (1998), and *Flight Behavior* (2012); the essay collections *High Tide in Tucson* (1995) and *Small Wonder* (2002); a poetry collection in English and Spanish, *Another America/Otra America* (1990); and the observational memoir *Animal, Vegetable, Miracle: A Year of Food Life* (2007). In 2000, Kingsolver won the National Humanities Medal for service through the arts.

Rural Delivery

In *Animal, Vegetable, Miracle,* Kingsolver records and reflects on a year-long project to eat nothing but locally produced organic food. Having uprooted themselves from Tucson, Arizona, she and her family settled on a small farm in Appalachia and began raising poultry and planting, harvesting, and preserving their own fruits and vegetables, calling on nearby farmers and merchants for beef, pork, and sundries. In this excerpt from the book, Kingsolver explores the labels and assumptions too often used to define a small yet significant group of Americans.

I grew up among farmers. In my school system we were all born to 1 our rank, as inescapably as Hindus, the castes[1] being only two: "farm" and "town." Though my father worked in town, we did not live there, and so by the numinous but unyielding rules of high school, I was "farmer." It might seem astonishing that a rural-urban distinction like this could be made in a county that boasted, in its entirety, exactly two stoplights, one hardware store, no beer joints (the county was dry), and fewer residents than an average Caribbean cruise ship. After I went away to school, I remained in more or less constant marvel over the fact that my so-called small liberal arts college, with an enrollment of about 2,000, was 25% larger than my hometown.

And yet, even in a community as rural as that, we still had our self- 2 identified bourgeoisie, categorically distinguished from our rustics. We of the

[1] Traditional Indian Hindu society groups people into five social classes, or castes: intellectuals, rulers, merchants, laborers, and "untouchables." The classes are assigned at birth and, because they are based on heredity, can never be changed. —Eds.

latter tribe could be identified by our shoes (sometimes muddy, if we had to cover rough country to get to the school bus), our clothes (less frequently updated), or just the bare fact of a Rural Free Delivery mailing address. I spent my childhood in awe of the storybook addresses of some of my classmates, like "14 Locust Street." In retrospect I'm unsure of how fact-based the distinction really was: Most of us "farm" kids were well-scrubbed and occasionally even stylish. Nevertheless, the line of apartheid was unimpeachably drawn. Little socializing across this line was allowed except during special events forced on us by adults, such as the French Club Dinner, and mixed-caste dating was unthinkable except to the tragic romantics.

Why should this have been? How did the leafy, sidewalked blocks behind   3 the newspaper office confer on their residents a different sense of self than did the homes couched among cow pastures and tobacco fields? The townie shine would have dimmed quickly (I now realize) if the merchants' confident offspring were catapulted suddenly into Philadelphia or Louisville. "Urban" is relative. But the bottom line is that it matters. The antipathy in our culture between the urban and nonurban is so durable, it has its own vocabulary: (A) city slicker, tenderfoot; (B) hick, redneck, hayseed, bumpkin, rube, yokel, clodhopper, hoecake, hillbilly, Dogpatch, Daisy Mae, farmer's daughter, from the provinces, something out of *Deliverance*.[2] Maybe you see where I'm going with this. The list is lopsided. I don't think there's much doubt, on either side, as to which class is winning the culture wars.

Most rural people of my acquaintance would not gladly give up their sta-   4 tus. Like other minorities, we've managed to turn several of the aforementioned slurs into celebrated cultural identifiers (for use by insiders only). In my own life I've had ample opportunity to reinvent myself as a city person—to *pass*, as it were—but I've remained tacitly rural-identified in my psyche, even while living in some of the world's major cities. It's probably this dual citizenship that has sensitized me to my nation's urban-rural antipathy, and how it affects people in both camps. Rural concerns are less covered by the mainstream media, and often considered intrinsically comic. Corruption in city governments is reported as grim news everywhere; from small towns (or Tennessee) it is fodder for talk-show jokes. Thomas Hardy[3] wrote about the sort of people who milked cows, but writers who do so in the modern era will be dismissed as marginal. The policy of our nation is made in cities, controlled largely by urban voters who aren't well informed about the changes on the face of our land, and the men and women who work it.

---

[2] James Dickey's 1970 novel, made into a film in 1972, in which city residents taking a river-rafting trip in backcountry Georgia are hunted and tortured by locals.—EDS.
[3] English novelist (1840–1928).—EDS.

Those changes can be mapped on worry lines: As the years have gone ⁵
by, as farms have gone out of business, America has given an ever-smaller cut
of each food dollar (now less than 19%) to its farmers. The psychic divide
between rural and urban people is surely a part of the problem. "Eaters must
understand," Wendell Berry⁴ writes, "that eating takes place inescapably in the
world, that it is inescapably an agricultural act, and that how we eat determines,
to a considerable extent, how the world is used." Eaters *must*, he claims, but it
sure looks like most eaters *don't*. If they did, how would we frame the sentence
suggested by today's food-buying habits, directed toward today's farmers? "Let
them eat dirt" is hardly overstating it. The urban US middle class appears
more specifically concerned about exploited Asian factory workers.

Symptomatic of this rural-urban identity crisis is our eager embrace of a ⁶
recently imposed divide: the Red States and the Blue States. That color map
comes to us with the suggestion that both coasts are populated by educated
civil libertarians, while the vast middle and south are crisscrossed with the
studded tracks of ATVs leaving a trail of flying beer cans and rebel yells. Okay,
I'm exaggerating a little. But I certainly sense a bit of that when urban friends
ask me how I can stand living here, "*so far from everything?*" (When I hear this
question over the phone, I'm usually looking out the window at a forest, a running creek, and a vegetable garden, thinking: Define *everything*.) Otherwise
sensitive coastal-dwelling folk may refer to the whole chunk of our continent
lying between the Cascades and the Hudson River as "the Interior." I gather
this is now a common designation. It's hard for me to see the usefulness of
lumping Minneapolis, Atlanta, my little hometown in Kentucky, Yellowstone
Park, and so forth, into a single category that does not include New York
and California. "Going into the Interior" sounds like an endeavor that might
require machetes to hack through the tangled vines.

In fact, the politics of rural regions are no more predictable than those ⁷
in cities. "Conservative" is a reasonable position for a farmer who can lose
home and livelihood all in one year by taking a risk on a new crop. But that's
conservative as in, "eager to conserve what we have, reluctant to change the
rules overnight," and unrelated to how the term is currently (often incompre-
hensibly) applied in party politics. The farm county where I grew up had so
few Republicans, they all registered Democrat so they could vote in the only
local primary. My earliest understanding of radical, class-conscious politics
came from miners' strikes in one of the most rural parts of my state, and of our
nation.

The only useful generalization I'd hazard about rural politics is that they ⁸
tend to break on the line of "insider" vs. "outsider." When my country neigh-

---

⁴ American farmer and writer, born in 1934. — Eds.

bors sit down with a new social group, the first question they ask one another is not "What do you do?" but rather, "Who are your people?" Commonly we will spend more than the first ten minutes of a new acquaintance tracing how our families might be related. If not by blood, then by marriage. Failing that, by identifying someone significant we have known in common. Only after this ritual of familial placing does the conversation comfortably move on to other subjects. I am blessed with an ancestor who was the physician in this county from about 1910 into the 1940s. From older people I'll often hear of some memorably dire birth or farm accident to which my great-uncle was called; lucky for me he was skilled and Hippocratic.[5] But even a criminal ancestor will get you insider status, among the forgiving. Not so lucky are those who move here with no identifiable family ties. Such a dark horse is likely to remain "the new fellow" for the rest of his natural life, even if he arrived in his prime and lives to be a hundred.

The country tradition of mistrusting outsiders may be unfairly applied, but it's not hard to understand. For much of US history, rural regions have been treated essentially as colonial property of the cities. The carpetbaggers of the reconstruction era[6] were not the first or the last opportunists to capitalize on an extractive economy. When urban-headquartered companies come to the country with a big plan—whether their game is coal, timber, or industrial agriculture—the plan is to take out the good stuff, ship it to the population centers, make a fortune, and leave behind a mess.

Given this history, one might expect the so-called Red States to vote consistently for candidates supporting working-class values. In fact, our nation in almost every region is divided in a near dead heat between two parties that apparently don't distinguish themselves clearly along class lines. If every state were visually represented with the exact blend of red and blue it earned in recent elections, we'd have ourselves a big purple country. The tidy divide is a media just-so story.

Our uneasy relationship between heartland and coasts, farm and factory, country and town, is certainly real. But it is both more rudimentary and more subtle than most political analysts make it out to be. It's about loyalties, perceived communities, and the things each side understands to be important because of the ground, literally, upon which we stand. Wendell Berry summed it up much better than "blue and red" in one line of dialogue from his novel *Jayber Crow*, which is peopled by farmers struggling to survive on what the

9

10

11

[5] A reference to the Hippocratic Oath of doctors to practice ethically. The oath is generally attributed to the ancient Greek doctor Hippocrates. —Eds.

[6] After the Civil War many northern politicians and businessmen went to the South in search of opportunity. Some had luggage made of heavy tapestry—hence the derisive name *carpetbaggers*. —Eds.

modern, mostly urban market will pay for food. After watching nearly all the farms in the county go bankrupt, one of these men comments: "I've wished sometimes that the sons of bitches would starve. And now I'm getting afraid they actually will."

For a reading quiz, visit **bedfordstmartins.com/thebedfordreader**.

Journal Writing

Where did you grow up? Is the area considered rural, urban, or something in between? Take a few minutes to characterize your hometown in your journal. Consider its physical attributes (landscape, buildings, roads, and such) as well as its culture and politics. (To take your journal writing further, see "From Journal to Essay" on the facing page.)

Questions on Meaning

1. In your own words, SUMMARIZE Kingsolver's definition of *rural*.
2. Kingsolver writes in her introduction (par. 1) that "by the numinous but unyielding rules of high school, I was 'farmer.'" What does she mean? Does she, in fact, consider herself a farmer? Explain your answer.
3. How do paragraphs 9–11 contribute to Kingsolver's definition?
4. What would you say is Kingsolver's PURPOSE in this essay?

Questions on Writing Strategy

1. Why do you suppose Kingsolver opens the essay as she does? What point does she make by discussing her childhood identity?
2. How does Kingsolver maintain UNITY in her essay?
3. "Rural Delivery" is a model of an *extended* definition, yet the essay also includes several *stipulative* definitions. Locate at least two of these. What do they contribute to Kingsolver's meaning?
4. **OTHER METHODS** Paragraphs 6–10 develop a binary, or two-part, CLASSIFICATION. Why do you think Kingsolver considers "Red States" and "Blue States" at such length? To what is she ALLUDING?

Questions on Language

1. Kingsolver twice quotes Wendell Berry in her essay. Why? What is the EFFECT of these quotations?
2. Find some examples of both formal and informal DICTION in the essay. What is the effect of Kingsolver's word choices?

3. Be sure you know the meanings of the following words, checking a dictionary if necessary: numinous (par. 1); bourgeoisie, categorically, latter, apartheid, unimpeachably (2); confer, catapulted, antipathy (3); tacitly, psyche, intrinsically (4); symptomatic, civil libertarians, endeavor (6); colonial, capitalize, extractive (9); rudimentary (11).

Suggestions for Writing

1. **FROM JOURNAL TO ESSAY**   How do outsiders view the place where you grew up? Building on your journal entry and using Kingsolver's essay as a model, write an essay of your own that COMPARES AND CONTRASTS your perception of your hometown with the perception of it by people who don't live there. What ASSUMPTIONS do others make, and how accurate are they? Are there any misconceptions you would like to correct, or do you share outsiders' assessment of the area? Why?

2. According to the National Institute of Food and Agriculture, 17% of Americans live in rural areas and fewer than 2% farm for a living. Research a current issue with family farms in the United States: Timely topics include competition with agribusiness, federal regulations and subsidies, financial stability, and opportunities. Then write an essay that presents your findings.

3. **CRITICAL WRITING**   Based on this essay, ANALYZE Kingsolver's view of the state of national politics. In what ways has the political climate changed in recent years, according to the writer? How meaningful does she find the distinction between "red" and "blue" states? How does she portray conservative and liberal philosophies, as well as disagreements among political parties? Which groups does Kingsolver consider most powerful and which most disadvantaged? Why? What problems does she identify, and what solutions, if any, does she propose?

4. **CONNECTIONS**   Kingsolver writes in paragraph 4 that "[l]ike other minorities," rural people have "managed to turn several . . . slurs into celebrated cultural identifiers (for use by insiders only)"—an effort similar to those discussed in detail by Gloria Naylor in "The Meanings of a Word" (p. 412) and by Christine Leong in "Being a Chink" (p. 418). Where those two writers tackle issues of race, however, Kingsolver bases her idea of what constitutes a *minority* on culture and geography. How might Naylor and Leong respond to Kingsolver's use of the word *minority* to characterize herself? Are slurs aimed at cultural or geographic identity of the same caliber as those aimed at race? In an essay, bring these three writers together, considering what they have in common as well as what they do not.

ADDITIONAL WRITING TOPICS
Definition

1. Write an essay in which you define an institution, trend, phenomenon, or abstraction as specifically and concretely as possible. Following are some suggestions designed to stimulate ideas. Before you begin, limit your subject.

Responsibility	Sportsmanship
Fun	Leadership
Sorrow	Leisure
Unethical behavior	Originality
The environment	Character
Education	Imagination
Progress	Democracy
Advertising	A smile
Happiness	A classic (of music, literature, art, or film)
Fads	Dieting
Feminism	Meditation
Marriage	Friendship

2. In a brief essay, define one of the following. In each instance, you have a choice of something good or something bad to talk about.

   A good or bad boss
   A good or bad parent
   A good or bad host
   A good or bad newscaster
   A good or bad physician
   A good or bad nurse
   A good or bad minister, priest, rabbi, or imam
   A good or bad roommate
   A good or bad driver
   A good or bad DJ

3. In a paragraph, define a slang expression or specialized term for someone who has never heard it. Possible expressions include *bling, sick, hook up, truthiness, tweet, wicked, poser, app, swag, chill, sweet.*

13

ARGUMENT AND PERSUASION

Stating Opinions and Proposals

◀ **Argument and persuasion in an image**

Adbusters Media Foundation, an activist group "concerned about the erosion of our physical and cultural environments by commercial forces," launched its Corporate America flag in 1999. This version appeared in a full-page advertisement in the *New York Times*. Showing the American flag's stars replaced by well-known corporate logos, the image adapts a symbol that many Americans revere to make a strong argument about the United States. What is the argument? How do you respond to the image: Are you offended? persuaded? amused? Why? Whatever your view, do you understand why others might think differently?

THE METHOD

Practically every day, we try to persuade ourselves or someone else. We usually attempt such persuasion without being aware that we follow any special method at all. Often, we'll state an *opinion*: We'll tell someone our own way of viewing things. We say to a friend, "I'm starting to like Senator Clark. Look at all she's done to help people with disabilities. Look at her voting record on toxic waste." And, having stated these opinions, we might go on to make a *proposal*, to recommend that some action be taken. Addressing our friend, we might suggest, "Hey, Senator Clark is talking on campus at four-thirty. Want to come with me and listen to her?"

Many professions involve persuading people in writing. Before arguing a case in court, a lawyer prepares a brief setting forth all the points in favor of his or her side. Businesspeople regularly put in writing their ideas for new products and ventures, for improvements in cost control and job efficiency. Researchers write proposals for grants to obtain money to support their work. Scientists write and publish papers to persuade the scientific community that their findings are valid, often stating hypotheses, or tentative opinions.

Even if you never produce a single persuasive work (which is very unlikely), you will certainly encounter such works directed at you. We live our lives under a steady rain of opinions and proposals. Organizations that work for causes campaign with social media and direct mail, all hoping that we will see things their way. Moreover, we are bombarded with proposals from people who wish us to act. Religious leaders urge us to lead more virtuous lives. Advertisers urge us to rush right out and buy the large economy size.

Small wonder, then, that argument and persuasion — and CRITICAL THINKING about argument and persuasion — may be among the most useful skills a college student can acquire. Time and again, your instructors will ask you to criticize or to state opinions, either in class or in writing. You may be asked to state your view of anything from the electoral college to animal rights. You may be asked to judge the desirability or undesirability of compulsory testing for drugs or revision of the existing immigration laws. Critically reading other people's arguments and composing your own, you will find, helps you discover what you think, refine it, and share what you believe.

The terms *argument* and *persuasion* have somewhat different meanings: PERSUASION aims to influence readers' actions, or their support for an action, by engaging their beliefs and feelings, while ARGUMENT aims to win readers' agreement with an assertion or claim by engaging their powers of reasoning. However, most effective argument or persuasion contains elements of both methods. In this book we tend to use the terms interchangeably.

One other point: We tend to talk here about *writing* argument and persuasion, but most of what we say has to do with *reading* them as well. When we discuss your need, as a writer, to support your claims, we are also discussing your need, as a reader, to question the support other authors provide for their claims. In reading arguments critically, you apply the critical-thinking skills we discussed in Chapter 1 — ANALYSIS, INFERENCE, SYNTHESIS, and EVALUATION — to a particular kind of writing.

Audience and Common Ground

Unlike some advertisers, responsible writers of argument and persuasion do not try to storm people's minds. In writing a paper for a course, you persuade by gentler means: by sharing your view with an AUDIENCE willing to consider it. You'll want to learn how to express your view clearly and vigorously. But to be fair and persuasive, it is important to understand your readers' views as well.

In stating your opinion, you present the truth as you see it: "The immigration laws discourage employers from hiring nonnative workers" or "The immigration laws protect legal aliens." To persuade your readers that your view makes sense, you need not begin by proclaiming that your view is absolutely right and should prevail. Instead, you might begin by trying to state what your readers probably think, as best you can infer it. You don't consider views that differ from your own merely to flatter your readers. You do so to balance your own view and make it more accurate. Writer and reader become two sensible people trying to find COMMON GROUND, or points on which both can agree. This approach will relieve you, whenever you have to state your opinions in writing, of the terrible obligation to be one hundred percent right at all times.

Elements of Argument

The British philosopher Stephen Toulmin has proposed a useful division of argument into three parts. Adapted to the terminology of this book, they are *claims*, *evidence*, and *assumptions*.

Claims and Thesis Statements

A CLAIM is an assertion that requires support. It is what an argument tries to convince readers to accept. The central claim — the main point — is almost always stated explicitly in a THESIS STATEMENT like one of the following:

A CLAIM ABOUT REALITY   The war on drugs is not winnable because it cannot eradicate demand or the supply to meet it.

A CLAIM OF VALUE   Drug abuse is a personal matter that should not be subject to law.

A CLAIM FOR A COURSE OF ACTION   The United States must intensify its efforts to reduce production of heroin in Afghanistan.

Usually, but not always, you'll state your thesis at the beginning of your essay, making a play for readers' attention and clueing them in to your purpose. But if you think readers may have difficulty accepting your thesis until they've heard some or all of your argument, then you might save the thesis statement for the middle or end.

The essays in this chapter provide a variety of thesis statements as models. Here are three examples:

> The fact that so many illegal immigrants are intertwined with American citizens or legal residents, either as spouses or parents, should give pause to those who'd like to see all illegal immigrants rounded up and deported or their lives made so miserable they leave on their own.
>
>   — Linda Chavez, "Supporting Family Values"

> People may think *marriage* is a word wholly owned by religion, but actually it's wholly owned by the state. . . . [T]wo men or two women should be able to marry, even if religions oppose it and it makes some heterosexuals, raised in those religions, uncomfortable.
>
>   — Katha Pollitt, "What's Wrong with Gay Marriage?"

> Tragically, the sexual revolution led to the decoupling of marriage and procreation; same-sex "marriage" would pull them completely apart, leading to an explosive increase in family collapse, out-of-wedlock births — and crime.
>
>   — Charles Colson, "Gay 'Marriage': Societal Suicide"

Evidence and Appeals

Claims are nothing without the EVIDENCE to make them believable and convincing. Toulmin calls evidence *data* or *grounds,* using terms that convey how specific and fundamental it is. Depending on your subject, your evidence may include facts, statistics (facts expressed in numbers), expert opinions, examples, and reported experiences. These kinds of evidence should meet certain criteria.

- **Accuracy:** Facts, examples, and opinions are taken from reliable sources and presented without error or distortion.

- **Representation:** Evidence reflects reality, neither slanting nor exaggerating it.

- **Relevance:** Evidence is directly applicable to the claims, reflecting current thinking by recognized experts.

- **Adequacy:** Evidence is sufficient to support the claims entirely, not just in part.

To strengthen the support for your claims, you can also make APPEALS to readers either directly or indirectly, in the way you present your argument.

- **Rational appeals** rely on sound reasoning and marshal evidence that meets the criteria above. See pages 444–47 for more on reasoning.

- **Ethical appeals** show readers that you are a well-informed person of goodwill, good sense, and good moral character — and, therefore, to be believed. Strengthen your ethical appeal by collecting ample evidence, reasoning carefully, demonstrating respect for opposing views, using an appropriate emotional appeal (see below), and minding your TONE (see pp. 449–50).

- **Emotional appeals** acknowledge what you know of readers' sympathies and beliefs and show how your argument relates to them. An example in this chapter appears in Linda Chavez's "Supporting Family Values": The author argues for immigration reform by appealing to readers' respect for intact families and fear of cultural disintegration. Carefully used, an emotional appeal can stir readers to constructive belief and action by engaging their feelings as well as their minds, as long as the appeal is appropriate for the audience and the argument.

Assumptions

The third element of argument, the ASSUMPTION, is in Toulmin's conception the connective tissue between grounds, or evidence, and claims: An assumption explains why the evidence leads to and justifies a claim. Called a *warrant* by Toulmin, an assumption is usually a belief, a principle, or an inference whose truth the writer takes for granted. Here is how an assumption might figure in an argument for one of the claims given earlier:

CLAIM   The United States must intensify its efforts to reduce the production of heroin in Afghanistan.

EVIDENCE   Afghanistan is the world's largest heroin producer and a major supplier to the United States.

ASSUMPTION   The United States can and should reduce the production of heroin in other countries when its own citizens are affected.

As important as they are, the assumptions underlying an argument are not always stated. As we will see in the discussion of deductive reasoning, which begins on this page, unstated assumptions can sometimes pitch an argument into trouble.

Reasoning

When we argue rationally, we reason — that is, we make statements that lead to a conclusion. Two reliable methods of rational argument date back to the Greek philosopher Aristotle, who identified the complementary processes of inductive and deductive reasoning.

Inductive Reasoning

In INDUCTIVE REASONING, the method of the sciences, we collect bits of evidence on which to base a GENERALIZATION, the claim of the argument. The assumption linking evidence and claim is that what is true for some circumstances is true for others as well. For instance, you might interview a hundred representative students about their attitudes toward changing your school's honor code. You find that 65% of the interviewees believe that the code should remain as it is, 15% believe that the code should be toughened, 10% believe that it should be loosened, and 10% have no opinion. You then assume that these statistics can be applied to the student body as a whole and make a claim against changing the code because 65% of students don't want change.

The more evidence you have, the more trustworthy your claim will be, but it would never be airtight unless you interviewed every student on campus. Since such thoroughness is almost always impractical if not impossible, you assume in an *inductive leap* that the results can be generalized. The smaller the leap — the more evidence you have — the better.

Deductive Reasoning

DEDUCTIVE REASONING works the opposite of inductive reasoning: It moves from a general statement to particular cases. The basis of deduction is the SYL-LOGISM, a three-step form of reasoning practiced by Aristotle:

All men are mortal.

Socrates is a man.

Therefore, Socrates is mortal.

The first statement, called a *major premise*, is an assumption: a fact, principle, or inference that you believe to be true. The second statement, or *minor premise*, is the evidence — the new information about a particular member of the larger group named in the major premise. The third statement, or *conclusion*, is the claim that follows inevitably from the premises. If the premises are true, then the conclusion must be true. Following is another example of a syllogism. You may recognize it from the discussion of assumptions on pages 443–44, only here the statements are simplified and arranged differently:

MAJOR PREMISE (ASSUMPTION)   The United States can and should reduce heroin production when its own citizens are affected.

MINOR PREMISE (EVIDENCE)   A major producer of heroin for the US market is Afghanistan.

CONCLUSION (THESIS)   The United States can and should reduce heroin production in Afghanistan.

Problems with deductive reasoning start in the premises. Consider this untrustworthy syllogism: "To do well in school, students must cheat a little. Jolene wants to do well in school. Therefore, she must cheat." This is bad deductive reasoning, and its flaw is in its major premise, which is demonstrably untrue: Plenty of students do well without cheating. Because the premise is false, the conclusion is necessarily false as well.

When they're spelled out neatly, bad syllogisms are pretty easy to spot. But many deductive arguments are not spelled out. Instead, one of the premises goes unstated, as in this statement: "Mayor Perkins was humiliated in his recent bid for reelection, winning only 2,000 out of 5,000 votes." The unstated assumption here, the major premise, is "Winning only two-fifths of the votes humiliates a candidate." (The rest of the syllogism: "Mayor Perkins received only two-fifths of the votes. Thus, Mayor Perkins was humiliated.")

The unstated premise isn't necessarily a problem in argument — in fact, it's quite common. But it *is* a problem when it's wrong or unfounded. For instance, in the statement "She shouldn't be elected mayor because her husband has bad ideas on how to run the city," the unstated assumption is that the candidate cannot form ideas independently of her husband. This is a possibility, perhaps, but it requires its own discussion and proof, not concealment behind other assertions.

Logical Fallacies

In arguments we read and hear, we often meet logical FALLACIES: errors in reasoning that lead to wrong conclusions. From the time you start thinking about your thesis and claims and begin planning your paper, you'll need to watch out for them. To help you recognize logical fallacies when you see them or hear them, and so guard against them when you write, here is a list of the most common.

- **Non sequitur** (from the Latin, "it does not follow"): stating a conclusion that doesn't follow from one or both premises.

  I've lived in this town a long time — why, my grandfather was the first mayor — so I'm against putting fluoride in the drinking water.

- **Oversimplification:** supplying neat and easy explanations for large and complicated phenomena.

  No wonder drug abuse is out of control. Look at how the courts have hob-bled police officers.

  Oversimplified solutions are also popular:

  All these teenage kids that get in trouble with the law — why, they ought to put them in work camps. That would straighten them out!

  (See also p. 367.)

- **Hasty generalization:** leaping to a generalization from inadequate or faulty evidence. The most familiar hasty generalization is the stereotype.

  Men aren't sensitive enough to be day-care providers.
  Women are too emotional to fight in combat.

- **Either/or reasoning:** assuming that a reality may be divided into only two parts or extremes or assuming that a given problem has only one of two possible solutions.

  What's to be done about the trade imbalance with Asia? Either we ban all Asian imports, or American industry will collapse.

  Obviously, either/or reasoning is a kind of extreme oversimplification.

- **Argument from doubtful or unidentified authority:**

  Uncle Oswald says that we ought to imprison all sex offenders for life.
  According to reliable sources, my opponent is lying.

- **Argument ad hominem** (from the Latin, "to the man"): attacking a person's views by attacking his or her character.

  Mayor Burns is divorced and estranged from his family. How can we listen to his pleas for a city nursing home?

- **Begging the question:** taking for granted from the start what you set out to demonstrate. When you reason in a *logical* way, you state that because something is true, then, as a result, some other truth follows. When you beg the question, however, you repeat that what is true is true.

Dogs are a menace to people because they are dangerous.

This statement proves nothing, because the idea that dogs are dangerous is already assumed in the statement that they are a menace. Beggars of questions often just repeat what they already believe, only in different words. This fallacy sometimes takes the form of arguing in a circle, or demonstrating a premise by a conclusion and a conclusion by a premise.

I am in college because that is the right thing to do. Going to college is the right thing to do because it is expected of me.

- **Post hoc, ergo propter hoc** (from the Latin, "after this, therefore because of this"), or *post hoc* for short: assuming that because B follows A, B was caused by A.

Ever since the city suspended height restrictions on skyscrapers, the city budget has been balanced.

(See also pp. 366–67.)

- **False analogy:** the claim of persuasive likeness when no significant likeness exists. An ANALOGY asserts that because two things are comparable in some respects, they are comparable in other respects as well. Analogies cannot serve as evidence in rational arguments because the differences always outweigh the similarities; but analogies can reinforce such arguments *if* the subjects are indeed similar in some ways. If they aren't, the analogy is false. Many observers see the "war on drugs" as a false and damaging analogy because warfare aims for clear victory over a specific, organized enemy, whereas the complete eradication of illegal drugs is probably unrealistic and, in any event, the "enemy" isn't well defined: the drugs themselves? users? sellers? producers? the producing nations? (These critics urge approaching drugs as a social problem to be skillfully managed and reduced.)

THE PROCESS

Finding a Subject

Your way into a subject will probably vary depending on whether you're writing an argument that supports an opinion or one that proposes. In stating an opinion, you set forth and support a claim — a truth you believe. You may find such a truth by thinking and feeling, by reading, by talking to your instructors or fellow students, by listening to a discussion of some problem or controversy. Before you run with a subject, take a minute to weigh it: Is this something about which reasonable people disagree? Arguments go nowhere when they start with ideas that are generally accepted (pets should not have to endure physical abuse from their owners) or are beyond the pale (pet own-ers should be able to hurt their animals if they want).

In stating a proposal, you already have an opinion in mind, and from there, you go on to urge an action or a solution to a problem. Usually, these two statements will take place within the same piece of writing: You will first set forth a view ("The campus honor code is unfair to first offenders"), provide the evidence to support it, and then present your proposal as a remedy ("The campus honor code should be revised to give more latitude to first offenders").

Whatever your subject, resist the temptation to make it big. If you have two weeks to prepare, an argument about the litter problem in your town is probably manageable: In that time you could conduct your own visual research and talk to town officials. But an argument about the litter problem in your town compared with that in similar-sized towns across the state would surely demand more time than you have.

Organizing

There's no one right way to organize an argument because so much depends on how your readers will greet your claim and your evidence. Below we give some ideas for different situations.

Introduction

In your opening paragraph or two, draw readers in by connecting them to your subject if possible, showing its significance, and providing any needed background. End the INTRODUCTION with your thesis statement if you think readers will entertain it before they've seen the evidence. Put the thesis state-ment later, in the middle or even at the end of the essay, if you think readers need to see some or all of the evidence in order to be open to the idea.

Body

The BODY of the essay develops and defends the points that support your thesis. Generally, start with your least important point and build in a cre-scendo to your strongest point. However, if you think readers may resist your ideas, consider starting strong and then offering the more minor points as reinforcement.

For every point you make, give the evidence that supports it. The methods of development can help here, providing many options for injecting evidence.

Say you were arguing for or against further reductions in welfare funding. You might give EXAMPLES of wasteful spending, or of neighborhoods where welfare funds are still needed. You might spell out the CAUSES of social problems that call for welfare funds, or foresee the likely EFFECTS of cutting welfare programs or of keeping them. You could use NARRATION to tell a pointed story; you could use DESCRIPTION to portray certain welfare recipients and their neighborhoods.

Response to Objections

Part of the body of the essay, but separated here for emphasis, a response to probable objections is crucial to effective argument. If you are arguing fairly, you should be able to face potential criticisms fairly and give your critics due credit, reasoning with them, not dismissing them. This is the strategy Linda Chavez uses later in this chapter in "Supporting Family Values" (p. 454) by conceding, more than once, that arguments against immigration have some merit ("But the greater concern for some opponents," "It is true that," and so on) before she points out what she sees as their logical flaws. As Chavez does, you can tackle possible objections throughout your essay, as they pertain to your points. You can also field objections near the end of the essay, an approach that allows you to draw on all of your evidence. But if you think that readers' own opposing views may stiffen their resistance to your argument, you may want to address those views very early, before developing your own points.

Conclusion

The CONCLUSION gives you a chance to gather your points, restate your thesis in a fresh way, and leave readers with a compelling final idea. In an essay with a strong emotional component, you may want to end with an appeal to readers' feelings. But even in a mostly rational argument, try to involve readers in some way, showing why they should care or what they can do.

FOCUS ON TONE

Readers are most likely to be persuaded by an argument when they sense that the writer is reasonable, trustworthy, and sincere. Sound reasoning, strong evidence, and acknowledgment of opposing views do much to convey these attributes, but so does TONE, the attitude implied by choice of words and sentence structures.

(continued)

Generally, you should try for a tone of moderation in your view of your subject and a tone of respectfulness and goodwill toward readers and opponents.

- **State opinions and facts calmly:**

  OVEREXCITED   One clueless administrator was quoted in the newspaper as saying she thought many students who claim learning disabilities are faking their difficulties to obtain special treatment! Has she never heard of dyslexia, attention-deficit disorders, and other well-established disabilities?

  CALM   Particularly worrisome was one administrator's statement, quoted in the newspaper, that many students who claim learning disabilities may be "faking" their difficulties to obtain special treatment.

- **Replace arrogance with deference and sarcasm with plain speaking:**

  ARROGANT   I happen to know that many students would rather party or just bury their heads in the sand than get involved in a serious, worthy campaign against the school's unjust learning-disabled policies.

  DEFERENTIAL   Time pressures and lack of information about the issues may be what prevent students from joining the campaign against the school's unjust learning-disabled policies.

  SARCASTIC   Of course, the administration knows even without meeting students what is best for every one of them.

  PLAIN   The administration should agree to meet with each learning-disabled student to learn about his or her needs.

- **Choose words whose CONNOTATIONS convey reasonableness** rather than anger, hostility, or another negative emotion:

  HOSTILE   The administration coerced some students into dropping their lawsuits. [*Coerced* implies the use of threats or even violence.]

  REASONABLE   The administration convinced some students to drop their lawsuits. [*Convinced* implies the use of reason.]

CHECKLIST FOR REVISING ARGUMENT AND PERSUASION

✔ **Audience.** Have you taken account of your readers' probable views? Have you reasoned with readers, not attacked them? Are your emotional appeals appropriate to readers' likely feelings? Do you acknowledge opposing views?

✔ **Thesis.** Does your argument have a thesis, a claim about how your subject is or should be? Is the thesis narrow enough to argue convincingly in the space and time available? Is it stated clearly? Is it reasonable?

✔ **Evidence.** Is your thesis well supported with facts, statistics, expert opinions, and examples? Is your evidence accurate, representative, relevant, and adequate?

✔ **Assumptions.** Have you made sound connections between your evidence and your thesis and other claims?

✔ **Logical fallacies.** Have you avoided common errors in reasoning, such as oversimplifying or begging the question? (See pp. 446–47 for a list of fallacies.)

✔ **Structure.** Does your organization lead readers through your argument step by step, building to your strongest ideas and frequently connecting your evidence to your central claim?

✔ **Tone.** Is the tone of your argument reasonable and respectful?

ARGUMENT AND PERSUASION IN ACADEMIC WRITING

A Public Relations Textbook

Taken from *Public Relations: Strategies and Tactics*, by Dennis L. Wilcox, Phillip H. Ault, and Warren K. Agee, the following paragraph argues that lobbyists (who work to persuade public officials on behalf of a cause) are not slick manipulators but something else. The paragraph falls in the textbook's section on lobbying as a form of public relations, and its purpose is to correct a mistaken definition.

Although the public stereotypes a lobbyist as a fast-talking person twisting an elected official's arm to get special concessions, the reality is quite different. Today's lobbyist, who may be fully employed by one industry or represent a variety of clients, is often a quiet-spoken, well-educated man or woman armed with statistics and research reports. Robert Gray, former head of Hill and Knowlton's Washington office and a public affairs expert for thirty years, adds, "Lobbying is no longer a booze and buddies business. It's presenting honest facts and convincing Congress that your side has more merit than the other." He rejects lobbying as being simply "influence peddling and button-holing" top administration officials. Although the public has the perception that lobbying is done only by big business, Gray correctly points out that a variety of special interests also do it. These may include such groups as the Sierra Club, Mothers Against Drunk Driving, the National Association of Social Workers, the American Civil Liberties Union, and the American Federation of Labor. Even the American Society of Plastic and Reconstructive Surgeons hired a Washington public relations firm in their battle

Topic sentence: the claim

Evidence:
• Expert opinion

• Facts and examples

against restrictions on breast implants. Lobbying, quite literally, is an activity in which widely diverse groups and organizations engage as an exercise of free speech and representation in the marketplace of ideas. Lobbyists often balance each other and work toward legislative compromises that benefit not only their self-interests but society as a whole.

A Proposal

In many courses and occupations, you'll be expected to write proposals that identify specific problems or related sets of problems and argue for reasonable solutions. A proposal addresses clearly defined readers who are in a position to take action or approve an action. It addresses those readers' unique needs and concerns, anticipating objections and offering evidence to demonstrate the benefits of the solution.

As a member of Corden University's Green Student Group, Amelia Jones knew that some nearby schools had recently instituted green policies and programs. Eager to see her own campus improve its environmental standing, she researched possible changes and also the attitudes toward change on the part of students, faculty, and administrators. The following paragraphs come from her longer proposal that the university adopt an environmental initiative similar to those that had proven successful elsewhere. Before this section, Jones opened with an overview of environmental problems on campus. After this section, she explained the potential solutions in greater detail, suggested steps for implementing them, and outlined the anticipated costs.

These problems of waste, costliness, and irresponsibility need not dominate the university's environmental profile. By adopting an environmental initiative like that at other schools, the university can achieve practical benefits for itself and its students while behaving ethically in its community and on earth. Such an initiative calls for simple changes in energy use, food procurement and disposal, and educational programs.

> Transition from discussion of problems
>
> Solution: environmental initiative
>
> Elements of the solution:

Reducing energy use would not only reduce carbon emissions but also save money. Based on the Accounting Office's most recent report on campus utility costs, lowering the average temperature in all campus buildings from 72 to 68 degrees and installing more efficient light bulbs and water lines could save the university almost $2 million per year. Other measures, such as campuswide recycling and composting and switching to

> • Reducing energy use to lower carbon emissions and costs

hybrid fleet vehicles, all have potential to cut costs significantly by reducing money spent on waste disposal and on fuel.

Of course, the practical benefits of a greener campus go beyond merely saving money. If Dining Services could obtain even thirty percent of its produce, dairy, and meat from local farmers, it would reduce the carbon emissions caused by shipping such products while it also strengthened ties with the local community. In addition, Dining Services could coordinate with the newly established Campus Food Bank and the Green Student Group to donate excess food and to compost unused produce, thereby reducing the amount of waste generated by the student dining halls.

Many prospective students would find the greening of our campus appealing both ethically and academically. An interdisciplinary environmental initiative would allow the environmental studies and engineering programs to offer hands-on practice as students design new green roofs for dorms or install solar-powered recycling bins. Students could have the option to devote their senior projects to implementing new parts of the environmental initiative. At the same time, the initiative could earn the school additional funding by attracting sustainability grants from public agencies and private foundations.

Some administrators and alumni who oppose environmental actions argue that our campus accounts for a barely measurable percentage of the country's greenhouse emissions. They also claim that such actions are outside the traditional mission of the school and that diverting funds to them from other programs would be unacceptable. But cost would be an issue only for the first years of an environmental initiative, because many of the projects will pay for themselves over time by reducing operational costs, attracting more students, and attracting more funding. Moreover, higher education has a higher calling: In the face of the projected large-scale effects of global warming, what "mission" is more important than conservation and moderation? These actions go beyond any simple costs-and-benefits analysis. They are the responsible course — and the right course.

- Shopping locally to reduce carbon emissions and improve community ties

- Food donation and composting to reduce waste

- Integrating academic programs to attract students, provide practical student projects, and possibly increase funding

Acknowledgment of objections

Response to objections

Argument and Persuasion

LINDA CHAVEZ

An outspoken commentator on issues of civil rights and affirmative action, Linda Chavez was born in 1947 in Albuquerque, New Mexico, to a Spanish American family long established in the Southwest. She graduated from the University of Colorado (BA, 1970) and did graduate work at the University of California at Los Angeles and at the University of Maryland. She has held a number of government positions, including director of the White House Office of Public Liaison under President Ronald Reagan and chair of the National Commission on Migrant Education under President George H. W. Bush. She has published three books: *Out of the Barrio: Toward a New Politics of Hispanic Assimilation* (1991), which argues against affirmative action and bilingual education; *An Unlikely Conservative: The Transformation of an Ex-Liberal (Or How I Became the Most Hated Hispanic in America)* (2002); and *Betrayal: How Union Bosses Shake Down Their Members and Corrupt American Politics* (with Daniel Gray, 2004). Chavez currently chairs the Center for Equal Opportunity, a public-policy research organization. She also writes a syndicated newspaper column and is a political analyst for Fox News. She lives in Purcellville, Virginia.

Supporting Family Values

In this piece written in 2009 for *townhall.com*, a conservative news and information Web site, Chavez makes an unusual case in favor of immigration, legal or not. Presenting evidence that challenges the stereotype of immigrants as unstable and unable to adapt to life in the United States, she argues that established American citizens should be taking life lessons from their newest neighbors.

A new report out this week from the Pew Hispanic Center confirms what many observers already suspected about the illegal immigrant population in the United States: It is made up increasingly of intact families and their American-born children. Nearly half of illegal immigrant households consist of two-parent families with children, and 73% of these children were born here and are therefore US citizens.

The hard-line immigration restrictionists will, no doubt, find more cause for alarm in these numbers. But they should represent hope to the rest of us. One of the chief social problems afflicting this country is the breakdown in the traditional family. But among immigrants, the two-parent household is alive and well.

"Supporting Family Values" from *townhall.com*, Friday, April 17, 2009. Reprinted by permission of Linda Chavez and Creators Syndicate, Inc.

Only 21% of native households are made up of two parents living with 3 their own children. Among legal immigrants, the percentage of such households jumps to 35%. But among the illegal population, 47% of households consist of a mother, a father and their children.

Age accounts for the major difference in household composition between 4 the native and foreign-born populations: Immigrants, especially illegal immigrants, tend to be younger, while the native population includes large numbers of older Americans whose children have already left home. But out-of-wedlock births and divorce, which are more common among the native born — especially blacks, but also Hispanics and whites — also mean that even young native households with children are more likely to be headed by single women than immigrant households are.

But the greater concern for some opponents of immigration — legal and 5 illegal — is the fear that these newcomers will never fully adapt, won't learn English, will remain poor and uneducated, and transform the United States into a replica of Mexico or some other Latin American country. The same fears led Americans of the mid-nineteenth century to fear German and Irish immigrants, and in the early twentieth century to fear Italians, Jews, Poles, and others from Eastern and Southern Europe.

Such worries are no more rational today — or born out of actual evi- 6 dence — than they were a hundred years ago. It is true that Hispanic immigrants today take a while to catch up with the native born just as their European predecessors did, and illegal immigrants never fully do so in terms of education or earnings. But there is still some room for optimism in the Pew Hispanic report. Nearly half of illegal immigrants between the ages of 18 and 24 who have graduated from high school attend college. A surprising 25% of illegal immigrant adults have at least some college, with 15% having completed college.

And although earnings among illegal immigrants are lower than among 7 either the native population or legal immigrants, they are far from destitute. The median household income for illegal immigrants was $36,000 in 2007 compared with $50,000 for native-born households. And illegal immigrant males have much higher labor force participation rates than the native born, 94% compared with 83% for US-born males.

The inflow of illegal immigrants has slowed substantially since the peak, 8 which occurred during the economic boom of the late 1990s, not in recent years, contrary to popular but uninformed opinion. The Pew Hispanic Center estimates there are nearly 12 million illegal immigrants living in the United States now, a number that has stabilized over the last few years as a result both of better border enforcement and the declining job market. As a result, there might never be a better time to grapple with what to do about this population than right now.

The fact that so many illegal immigrants are intertwined with American   9
citizens or legal residents, either as spouses or parents, should give pause to those who'd like to see all illegal immigrants rounded up and deported or their lives made so miserable they leave on their own. A better approach would allow those who have made their lives here, established families, bought homes, worked continuously and paid taxes to remain after paying fines, demonstrating English fluency and proving they have no criminal record. Such an approach is as much about supporting family values as it is granting amnesty.

For a reading quiz, visit **bedfordstmartins.com/thebedfordreader**.

Journal Writing

How do you feel about illegal immigrants? Are they criminals who should be punished? victims of circumstance who should be helped? something in between? In your journal, explore your thoughts on illegal immigration. Why do you feel as you do? (To take your journal writing further, see "From Journal to Essay" on the facing page.)

Questions on Meaning

1. What seems to have prompted Chavez's essay? How can you tell?
2. What distinctions, if any, does Chavez make between legal and illegal immigrants? Are such distinctions important to her?
3. What is Chavez's point in paragraphs 5 and 6, and how does this point fit into her larger argument?
4. At what point does Chavez reveal her PURPOSE in writing? Why do you suppose she chose not to state her THESIS in the introduction?

Questions on Writing Strategy

1. How does Chavez characterize those who hold opposing views? What does this characterization suggest about how she imagines her AUDIENCE?
2. On what underlying ASSUMPTION does Chavez base her argument? Is that assumption reasonable?
3. As a whole, is Chavez's essay an appeal to emotion or a reasoned argument, or both? Give EVIDENCE to support your answer.
4. **OTHER METHODS**   Where and how does Chavez use CLASSIFICATION to support her argument?

Questions on Language

1. Consult a dictionary if you are unsure of the meaning of any of the following: restrictionists (par. 2); wedlock (4); replica (5); predecessors (6); destitute, median (7); stabilized, grapple (8); intertwined, amnesty (9).
2. What does Chavez mean by "native" households and populations? Do you detect any IRONY in her use of the word?
3. How would you describe Chavez's TONE in this essay?

Suggestions for Writing

1. **FROM JOURNAL TO ESSAY**   Based on your journal entry, draft an essay in which you respond directly to Chavez, explaining why you agree or disagree with her position. If you wish, write your essay as a letter to the editor of *townhall.com*, the online journal in which Chavez's essay was published. (See p. 371 for an example of a letter to the editor.)
2. Write an essay in which you present your view on an aspect of US immigration policy or practice that you have strong opinions about — for example, amnesty for illegal immigrants, treatment of asylum seekers, border control, or restrictions on immigration. Before beginning your draft, do some research to support your position and also to explore opposing views so that you answer them squarely and fairly.
3. Identify a current controversy over national policy — Social Security benefits for the wealthy, the right to carry a concealed weapon, government funding for private schools, and so on. Read newspaper and weekly magazine editorials, letters to the editor, and other statements on the subject of the controversy. You could also discuss the issue with your friends and family. Based on your research, write a classification essay in which you group people according to their stand on the issue. Try to be as objective as possible.
4. **CRITICAL WRITING**   Write an essay in which you ANALYZE the main CLAIMS of Chavez's argument. What evidence does she provide to back up these claims? Do you find the evidence adequate? (You may wish to track down and examine the source Chavez cites in her introduction: Published by the Pew Hispanic Center on April 14, 2009, its title is *A Portrait of Unauthorized Immigrants in the United States*.)
5. **CONNECTIONS**   While defending the status of some illegal immigrants, Chavez stresses the need for all immigrants to "fully adapt," or assimilate, to American culture. Take a look at the US Census Bureau's "America's Foreign Born in the Last 50 Years" (*bedfordstmartins.com/thebedfordreader*), which classifies newcomers to the United States by country of origin and other criteria. What does it mean to be "American" in a country as diverse as the United States? In an essay, define, defend, or dispute the concept of assimilation. To what extent should recent immigrants be expected to trade ethnic or national identity for a new American identity? What might such an identity encompass, and how could it be obtained? What is gained, or lost, when immigrants become "Americanized"?

Linda Chavez on Writing

To Linda Chavez, telling writers they don't need to know the rules of grammar is like "telling aerospace engineers they don't need to learn the laws of physics." In a 2002 article for *The Enterprise*, Chavez writes about her affection for the lost art of diagramming sentences — using a branching structure to identify sentence parts and map their relationships. She fondly recalls her years in elementary school, then called "grammar school," when learning "where to place a modifier and whether to use an adverb or adjective" was an essential part of the curriculum. Abandoning grammar instruction, she writes, is leaving students scrambled.

Chavez criticizes recent classroom practices of emphasizing creativity over accuracy in composition: "For years now, schools have been teaching students to 'express' themselves, without worrying about transmitting the finer points of grammar and syntax. . . . But effective communication always entails understanding the rules. There are no short-cuts to good writing." According to Chavez, self-expression and grammar are not at odds with each other at all. As she sees it, a solid grasp of grammar is what allows a writer to clearly communicate meaning. In her own writing, Chavez follows the adage of her childhood teacher: "If you can't diagram it, don't write it."

For Discussion

1. Why do you think grammar may not be taught the same way it once was? Are there advantages to writing freely without worrying about form?
2. Why does Chavez draw the comparison between a writer without knowledge of grammar and an aerospace engineer without knowledge of physics?

KATHA POLLITT

Katha Pollitt is a poet and an essayist. Her poetry has been praised for its "serious charm" and "spare delicacy" in capturing thought and feeling. Her essays have contained strong and convincing commentary on such topics as surrogate motherhood and women in the media. Pollitt was born in New York City in 1949 and earned a BA from Radcliffe College and an MFA from Columbia University. Her verse has been collected in *Antarctic Traveler* (1982), which won a National Book Critics Circle award, and *The Mind-Body Problem* (2009). Pollitt has received other notable awards, including a grant from the National Endowment for the Arts and a Guggenheim fellowship. Her essays and criticism have appeared in *Mother Jones,* the *New York Times, The New Yorker,* and *The Nation,* where she currently writes a regular column. Her books include *Reasonable Creatures: Essays on Women and Feminism* (1994), *Subject to Debate: Sense and Dissent on Women, Politics, and Culture* (2001), and *Learning to Drive and Other Life Stories* (2007). In addition to writing, Pollitt has taught at many universities, including Harvard, Princeton, and Barnard. She lives in New York City.

What's Wrong with Gay Marriage?

In her *Nation* column Pollitt regularly takes on controversial topics from a fresh, unabashedly liberal perspective. In this 2003 essay she counters arguments against marriage between homosexuals, including those posed by Charles Colson in the next essay, "Gay 'Marriage': Societal Suicide" (p. 464).

Both Pollitt and Colson refer to the 2003 decision of the Massachusetts Supreme Judicial Court that gays and lesbians cannot be denied the right to marry under the state constitution. As of late 2013 the District of Columbia and fourteen more states have legalized gay marriage, while twenty-nine states have banned it. The US Supreme Court struck down as unconstitutional a federal statute that had defined marriage as a heterosexual union, but the issue of same-sex marriage continues to play out in the states and will not likely be resolved on the national level any time soon.

Will someone please explain to me how permitting gays and lesbians to marry threatens the institution of marriage? Now that the Massachusetts Supreme Court has declared gay marriage a constitutional right, opponents really have to get their arguments in line. The most popular theory, advanced by David Blankenhorn, Jean Bethke Elshtain and other social conservatives, is that under the tulle and orange blossom, marriage is all about procreation. There's some truth to this as a practical matter — couples often live together and tie the knot only when baby's on the way. But whether or not marriage is the best framework for child rearing, having children isn't a marital requirement. As many have pointed out, the law permits marriage to the infertile, the elderly, the impotent and those with no wish to procreate; it allows married couples to use birth control, to get sterilized, to be celibate. There's something creepily authoritarian and insulting about reducing marriage to procreation, as if intimacy mattered less than biological fitness. It's not a view that anyone outside a right-wing think tank, a Catholic marriage tribunal or an ultra-Orthodox rabbi's court is likely to find persuasive.

So scratch procreation. How about: Marriage is the way women domesticate men. This theory, a favorite of right-wing writer George Gilder, has some statistical support — married men are much less likely than singles to kill people, crash the car, take drugs, commit suicide — although it overlooks such husbandly failings as domestic violence, child abuse, infidelity and abandonment. If a man rapes his wife instead of his date, it probably won't show up on a police blotter, but has civilization moved forward? Of course, this view of marriage as a barbarian-adoption program doesn't explain why women should undertake it — as is obvious from the state of the world, they haven't been too successful at it anyway. Nor does it explain why marriage should be restricted to heterosexual couples. The gay men and lesbians who want to marry don't impinge on the male-improvement project one way or the other. Surely not even Gilder believes that a heterosexual pothead with plans for murder and suicide would be reformed by marrying a lesbian? 2

What about the argument from history? According to this, marriage has been around forever and has stood the test of time. Actually, though, marriage as we understand it — voluntary, monogamous, legally egalitarian, based on love, involving adults only — is a pretty recent phenomenon. For much of human history, polygyny was the rule — read your Old Testament — and in much of Africa and the Muslim world, it still is. Arranged marriages, forced marriages, child marriages, marriages predicated on the subjugation of women — gay marriage is like a fairy-tale romance compared with most chapters of the history of wedlock. 3

The trouble with these and other arguments against gay marriage is that they overlook how loose, flexible, individualized and easily dissolved the bonds of marriage already are. Virtually any man and woman can marry, no matter how ill assorted or little acquainted. An eighty-year-old can marry an eighteen-year-old; a john can marry a prostitute; two terminally ill patients 4 can marry each other from their hospital beds. You can get married by proxy, like medieval royalty, and not see each other in the flesh for years. Whatever may have been the case in the past, what undergirds marriage in most people's minds today is not some sociobiological theory about reproduction or male socialization. Nor is it the enormous bundle of privileges society awards to married people. It's love, commitment, stability.

Speaking just for myself, I don't like marriage. I prefer the old-fashioned 5 ideal of monogamous free love, not that it worked out particularly well in my case. As a social mechanism, moreover, marriage seems to me a deeply unfair way of distributing social goods like health insurance and retirement checks, things everyone needs. Why should one's marital status determine how much you pay the doctor, or whether you eat cat food in old age, or whether a child gets a government check if a parent dies? It's outrageous that, for example, a working wife who pays Social Security all her life gets no more back from the system than if she had married a male worker earning the same amount and stayed home. Still, as long as marriage is here, how can it be right to deny it to those who want it? In fact, you would think that, given how many hetero-sexuals are happy to live in sin, social conservatives would welcome maritally minded gays with open arms. Gays already have the baby — they can adopt in many states, and lesbians can give birth in all of them — so why deprive them of the marital bathwater?

At bottom, the objections to gay marriage are based on religious preju- 6 dice: The marriage of man and woman is "sacred," and opening it to same-sexers violates its sacral nature. That is why so many people can live with civil unions but draw the line at marriage — spiritual union. In fact, polls show a striking correlation of religiosity, especially evangelical Protestantism, with opposition to gay marriage and with belief in homosexuality as a choice, the famous "gay lifestyle." For these people gay marriage is wrong because it lets gays and lesbians avoid turning themselves into the straights God wants them to be. As a matter of law, however, marriage is not about Adam and Eve versus Adam and Steve. It's not about what God blesses; it's about what the govern-ment permits. People may think *marriage* is a word wholly owned by religion, but actually it's wholly owned by the state. No matter how big your church wedding, you still have to get a marriage license from city hall. And just as divorced people can marry even if the Catholic Church considers it bigamy, and Muslim and Mormon men can marry only one woman even if their holy books tell them they can wed all the girls in Apartment 3G, two men or two women should be able to marry, even if religions oppose it and it makes some heterosexuals, raised in those religions, uncomfortable.

Gay marriage — it's not about sex, it's about separation of church and 7 state.

For a reading quiz, visit **bedfordstmartins.com/thebedfordreader**.

Journal Writing

Write in your journal about your thoughts on marriage — not necessarily who should be allowed to marry or what you see as the ideal marriage, but rather why you think people marry. What do they hope to gain? What do they give up? How is being married different from simply living together as a couple? Base your entry on your observations and experiences. (To take your journal writing further, see "From Journal to Essay" on the facing page.)

Questions on Meaning

1. What three arguments against same-sex marriage does Pollitt summarize in her first three paragraphs, and how does she refute each argument?
2. What, according to Pollitt, is the common understanding of what marriage is? What is Pollitt's own attitude toward marriage?
3. What does Pollitt believe to be the most basic reason why people object to same-sex marriage?
4. What is Pollitt's THESIS, and where does she state it directly?

Questions on Writing Strategy

1. What is the EFFECT of Pollitt's opening her essay with the question that she does? of her asking several questions in paragraphs 2 and 5?
2. Why, in paragraphs 1 and 2, does Pollitt admit "some truth" to the point that "marriage is all about procreation" and admit "some statistical support" for the point that "[m]arriage is the way women domesticate men"? How do these concessions affect her argument?
3. ANALYZE Pollitt's TRANSITIONS between paragraphs 1 and 2, 2 and 3, 3 and 4, and 5 and 6. How do they work?
4. Why do you think Pollitt spends a paragraph on her own negative views of marriage? Does this paragraph strengthen or weaken her argument?
5. **OTHER METHODS**   How does Pollitt use DIVISION or ANALYSIS to structure her argument?

Questions on Language

1. Some of the language in paragraph 2 is deliberately humorous. Point to EXAMPLES of humor in the paragraph. Why do you think Pollitt chose to use such language at this point in the essay?

2. In the second-to-last sentence of paragraph 5, why does Pollitt use the phrase "live in sin" rather than, say, "live together without being married"? Does she believe such living situations are sinful?
3. What is Pollitt's point in putting some words in paragraph 6 in quotation marks?
4. Notice the PARALLELISM and repetition in the passage beginning "As a matter of law" in the middle of paragraph 6. What is the effect of the writing here?
5. Consult a dictionary if you are unsure of the meaning of any of the following: tulle, procreation, celibate, authoritarian (par. 1); impinge (2); monogamous, egalitarian, polygyny, subjugation (3); proxy, undergirds (4).

Suggestions for Writing

1. **FROM JOURNAL TO ESSAY**   Using your journal writing as a starting point, write an essay that presents a detailed view of the function of marriage in contemporary society. Refer to specific examples from your experience as appropriate. If you wish, use your observations and reflections to make a point about same-sex marriage.
2. Pollitt writes in paragraph 3 that "marriage as we understand it . . . is a pretty recent phenomenon." Research the history of marriage, beginning with its earliest forms and including marriage in non-Western cultures. Use your research in an essay to amplify or dispute Pollitt's CLAIM.
3. **CRITICAL WRITING**   Write an essay in which you analyze Pollitt's TONE in the essay. How does she present herself and her attitudes toward others (gays, women, men, opponents of gay marriage)? How do you respond to her tone?
4. **CONNECTIONS**   The next essay, by Charles Colson, argues against same-sex marriage. Write an essay in which you evaluate both Pollitt's and Colson's arguments for their EVIDENCE, reasonableness, fairness, response to opposing views, tone, and overall success. Be as OBJECTIVE as possible: Imagine yourself (if you aren't in fact) undecided on the issue of same-sex marriage.

CHARLES COLSON

Born in Boston in 1931, Charles Colson graduated from Brown University and earned a law degree from George Washington University. He served in the US Marine Corps and was a partner in a law firm before rising to national prominence — and notoriety — as special counsel to President Richard Nixon during the Watergate scandal that caused Nixon to resign. Colson ended up serving seven months in prison for his involvement in the scandal. After his release in 1974, he founded Prison Fellowship, an outreach ministry that provides support both for prisoners and for victims of crime; he donated all of his book royalties to the organization. Colson's many books include the autobiographies *Born Again* (1976) and *Life Sentence* (1979), *Why America Doesn't Work* (1991), *God and Government: An Insider's View on the Boundaries between Faith and Politics* (2007), and *The Sky Is Not Falling: Living Fearlessly in These Turbulent Times* (2011). Colson was also a contributing editor of *Christianity Today* magazine and a radio commentator. He died in 2012.

Gay "Marriage": Societal Suicide

Written with Anne Morse for *Christianity Today* in 2004, this essay presents a case against same-sex marriage and thus counters the preceding essay, Katha Pollitt's "What's Wrong with Gay Marriage?" For a summary of the legal status of gay marriage as of this writing, see the headnote to Pollitt's essay on page 459.

Is America witnessing the end of marriage? The Supreme Judicial Court 1 of Massachusetts has ordered that the state issue marriage licenses to same-sex couples. (By late March, the Massachusetts legislature voted to recognize same-sex civil unions instead.) An unprecedented period of municipal lawlessness has followed, with officials in California, New York, Oregon, and New Mexico gleefully mocking their state constitutions and laws. The result: Thousands of gays rushed to these municipalities to "marry," while much of the news media egged them on.

In the midst of the chaos, President Bush announced his support for a 2 Federal Marriage Amendment, which assures that this contentious issue will be debated in every quarter of American life. It should be, because the consequences of having "gay marriage" forced on us by judicial (or mayoral) fiat will fall on all Americans — not just those who embrace it.

As a supporter of the amendment, I'm well aware of the critical argu- 3
ments. As the president noted, "After more than two centuries of American
jurisprudence, and millennia of human experience, a few judges and local
authorities are presuming to change the most fundamental institution of civilization. Their action has created confusion on an issue that requires clarity."

He's right. Here's the clarity: Marriage is the traditional building block 4
of human society, intended both to unite couples and bring children into the
world. Tragically, the sexual revolution led to the decoupling of marriage and
procreation; same-sex "marriage" would pull them completely apart, leading to
an explosive increase in family collapse, out-of-wedlock births — and crime.

How do we know this? In nearly thirty years of prison ministry, I've wit- 5
nessed the disastrous consequences of family breakdown — in the lives of
thousands of delinquents. Dozens of studies now confirm the evidence I've
seen with my own eyes. Boys who grow up without fathers are at least twice
as likely as other boys to end up in prison. Sixty percent of rapists and 72%
of adolescent murderers never knew or lived with their fathers. Even in the
toughest inner-city neighborhoods, just 10% of kids from intact families get
into trouble, but 90% of those from broken families do. Girls raised without
a father in the home are five times more likely to become mothers while still
adolescents. Children from broken homes have more academic and behavioral
problems at school and are nearly twice as likely to drop out of high school.

Critics agree with this but claim gay "marriage" will not weaken hetero- 6
sexual marriage. The evidence says they're wrong. Stanley Kurtz of the Hoover
Institution writes: "It follows that once marriage is redefined to accommodate same-sex couples, that change cannot help but lock in and reinforce the
very cultural separation between marriage and parenthood that makes gay
marriage conceivable to begin with." He cites Norway, where courts imposed
same-sex "marriage" in 1993 — a time when Norwegians enjoyed a low out-
of-wedlock birth rate. After the imposition of same-sex "marriage," Norway's
out-of-wedlock birth rate shot up as the link between marriage and childbear-
ing was broken and cohabitation became the norm.

Gay "marriage" supporters argue that most family tragedies occur because 7
of broken *heterosexual* marriages — including those of many Christians. They
are right. We ought to accept our share of the blame, repent, and clean up our
own house. But the fact that we have badly served the institution of marriage
is not a reflection on the institution itself; it is a reflection on us.

As we debate the wisdom of legalizing gay "marriage," we must remember 8
that, like it or not, there is a natural moral order for the family. History and
tradition — and the teachings of Jews, Muslims, and Christians — support
the overwhelming empirical evidence: The family, led by a married mother
and father, is the best available structure for both child rearing and cultural

health. This is why, although some people will always pair off in unorthodox ways, society as a whole must never legitimize any form of marriage other than that of one man and one woman, united with the intention of permanency and the nurturing of children.

Marriage is not a private institution designed solely for the individual   9 gratification of its participants. If we fail to enact a Federal Marriage Amendment, we can expect, not just more family breakdown, but also more criminals behind bars and more chaos in our streets.

For a reading quiz, visit **bedfordstmartins.com/thebedfordreader**.

Journal Writing

In paragraph 5 Colson makes a number of claims about the effect on children of being raised by single parents, particularly single mothers. Write in your journal about friends and family members — or the children of friends and family members — who have been raised by a single parent. (If you were raised by a single parent, consider yourself as well.) What have been the effects? (To take your journal writing further, see "From Journal to Essay" on the facing page.)

Questions on Meaning

1. What is Colson's THESIS? Where does he state it directly?
2. What EVIDENCE does Colson present to link same-sex marriage to an increase in out-of-wedlock births? to link single-parent households to increases in crime, early parenthood, and other problems of young people? How effective do you find this evidence?
3. What other argument does Colson make against same-sex marriage?

Questions on Writing Strategy

1. ANALYZE the DEDUCTIVE REASONING in Colson's argument. What are its CLAIM and ASSUMPTION? What is the SYLLOGISM?
2. Why does Colson use quotation marks around *marriage* when referring to same-sex unions?
3. What is the EFFECT of the question with which Colson opens his essay?
4. What is the purpose of paragraph 7? Why do you think Colson includes it?
5. **OTHER METHODS**   What role does CAUSE AND EFFECT play in the essay?

Questions on Language

1. How do the words Colson uses in paragraphs 1 and 2 reinforce his opinion of recent moves to legitimate same-sex marriage?
2. Why do you think Colson uses the words *imposed* and *imposition* in the last two sentences of paragraph 6?
3. Consult a dictionary if you are unsure of the meaning of any of the following: unprecedented, gleefully (par. 1); millennia (3); decoupling, procreation (4); intact (5); unorthodox (8).

Suggestions for Writing

1. **FROM JOURNAL TO ESSAY**   Using your journal entry as a starting point, write an essay in which you explain what you think are the effects on children of being raised in single-parent households. From what you have seen, do such children fit the patterns described by Colson? If your observations do not coincide with Colson's, how do you account for the differences?
2. Research the current status of same-sex marriage in the United States, including both state laws and constitutional amendments and any cases pending with the US Supreme Court. Then write an essay in which you discuss your findings and predict what you believe will be the future of legally recognized unions between same-sex partners.
3. **CRITICAL WRITING**   Write an essay in which you examine the TONE of Colson's essay. How does the author present himself, his issue, and his opponents? How reasonable do you find his language?
4. **CONNECTIONS**   In the previous essay, Katha Pollitt addresses many of the arguments raised by opponents of same-sex marriage, including those of Colson. Draw on Pollitt's and Colson's essays as you see fit to argue your own views on same-sex marriage.

BILL McKIBBEN

Hailed by *Time* magazine as "the planet's best green journalist," Bill McKibben is an environmental activist with global influence. As the founder of the grassroots organizations Step It Up and *350.org*, he has organized thousands of rallies in nearly two hundred countries and launched large-scale demonstrations to educate people about climate issues and to demand political change. He was born in 1960 in Palo Alto, California, grew up in Lexington, Massachusetts, and graduated from Harvard University in 1982. A former staff writer for *The New Yorker*, McKibben has long made a career as a freelance writer; his work frequently appears in *The Atlantic Monthly, Orion, Grist, Outside*, the *New York Times*, and many other magazines and newspapers. He has also authored more than a dozen books, among them *The End of Nature* (1989), *Enough: Staying Human in an Engineered Age* (2003), and *Eaarth: Making a Life on a Tough New Planet* (2010). A 2011 inductee to the American Academy of Arts and Sciences, McKibben is the Schumann Distinguished Scholar at Middlebury College. He lives in Ripton, Vermont.

Waste Not, Want Not

In this essay first published in *Mother Jones* in 2009, McKibben rues the excesses of consumerism and argues for a shift in priorities. One way to slow climate change, he proposes, is to return to the frugality of simpler times.

For other views of the effects of individuals' actions on the environment, see the next two essays, Derrick Jensen's "Forget Shorter Showers" (p. 475) and Margaret Lundberg's "Eating Green" (p. 481).

Once a year or so, it's my turn to run recycling day for our tiny town. 1
Saturday morning, nine to twelve, a steady stream of people show up to sort out their plastics (No. 1, No. 2, etc.), their corrugated cardboard (flattened, please), their glass (and their returnable glass, which goes to benefit the elementary school), their Styrofoam peanuts, their paper, their cans. It's quite satisfying — everything in its place.

But it's also kind of disturbing, this waste stream. For one, a town of 550 2
sure generates a lot — a trailer load every couple of weeks. Sometimes you have to put a kid into the bin and tell her to jump up and down so the lid can close.

More than that, though, so much of it seems utterly unnecessary. Not just 3
waste, but wasteful. Plastic water bottles, one after another — 80 million of

them get tossed every day. The ones I'm stomping down are being "recycled," but so what? In a country where almost everyone has access to clean drinking water, they define waste to begin with. I mean, you don't have a mug? In fact, once you start thinking about it, the category of "waste" begins to expand, until it includes an alarming percentage of our economy. Let's do some intellectual sorting:

There's old-fashioned waste, the dangerous, sooty kind. You're making   4
something useful, but you're not using the latest technology, and so you're spewing: particulates into the air, or maybe sewage into the water. You wish to keep doing it, because it's cheap, and you block any regulation that might interfere with your right to spew. This is the kind of waste that's easy to attack; it's obvious and obnoxious and a lot of it falls under the Clean Air Act and Clean Water Act and so on. There's actually less of this kind of waste than there used to be — that's why we can swim in most of our rivers again.

There's waste that comes from everything operating as it should, only too   5
much so. If carbon monoxide (carbon with one oxygen atom) exemplifies pollution of the first type, then carbon dioxide (carbon with two oxygen atoms) typifies the second. Carbon monoxide poisons you in your garage and turns Beijing's air brown, but if you put a catalytic converter on your tailpipe it all but disappears. Carbon dioxide doesn't do anything to you directly — a clean-burning engine used to be defined as one that released only CO_2 and water vapor — but in sufficient quantity it melts the ice caps, converts grassland into desert, and turns every coastal city into New Orleans.

There's waste that comes from doing something that manifestly doesn't   6
need doing. A hundred million trees are cut every year just to satisfy the junk-mail industry. You can argue about cutting trees for newspapers, or magazines, or Bibles, or symphony scores — but the cascade of stuffporn that arrives daily in our mailboxes? It wastes forests, and also our time. Which, actually, is precious — we each get about 30,000 days, and it makes one a little sick to calculate how many of them have been spent opening credit card offers.

Or think about what we've done with cars. From 1975 to 1985, fuel effi-   7
ciency for the average new car improved from 14 to 28 miles per gallon. Then we stopped worrying about oil and put all that engineering talent to work on torque. In the mid-1980s, the typical car accelerated from 0 to 60 mph in 14.5 seconds. Today's average (even though vehicles are much heavier) is 9.5 seconds. But it's barely legal to accelerate like that, and it makes you look like an idiot, or a teenager.

Then there's the waste that comes with doing something maybe perhaps   8
vaguely useful when you could be doing something actually useful instead. For instance: Congress is being lobbied really, really hard to fork over billions of dollars to the nuclear industry, on the premise that it will fight global

warming. There is, of course, that little matter of nuclear waste — but lay that aside (in Nevada or someplace). The greater problem is the wasted opportunity: That money could go to improving efficiency, which can produce the same carbon reductions for about a fifth of the price.

Our wasteful habits wouldn't matter much if there were just a few of us — a Neanderthal hunting band could have discarded six plastic water bottles apiece every day with no real effect except someday puzzling anthropologists. But the volumes we manage are something else. Chris Jordan is the photographer laureate of waste — his most recent project, "Running the Numbers," uses exquisite images to show the 106,000 aluminum cans Americans toss every 30 seconds, or the 1 million plastic cups distributed on US airline flights every 6 hours, or the 2 million plastic beverage bottles we run through every 5 minutes, or the 426,000 cell phones we discard every day, or the 1.14 million brown paper supermarket bags we use each hour, or the 60,000 plastic bags we use every 5 seconds, or the 15 million sheets of office paper we use every 5 minutes, or the 170,000 Energizer batteries produced every 15 minutes. The simple amount of stuff it takes — energy especially — to manage this kind of throughput makes it daunting to even think about our waste problem. (Meanwhile, the next time someone tells you that population is at the root of our troubles, remind them that the average American uses more energy between the stroke of midnight on New Year's Eve and dinner on January 2 than the average, say, Tanzanian consumes in a year. Population matters, but it *really* matters when you multiply it by proximity to Costco.)

Would you like me to go on? Americans discard enough aluminum to rebuild our entire commercial air fleet every three months — and aluminum represents less than 1% of our solid waste stream. We toss 14% of the food we buy at the store. More than 46,000 pieces of plastic debris float on each square mile of ocean. And — oh, forget it.

These kinds of numbers get in the way of figuring out how much we really waste. In recent years, for instance, 40% of Harvard graduates have gone into finance, consulting, and business. They had just spent four years with the world's greatest library, some of its finest museum collections, an unparalleled assemblage of Nobel-quality scholars, and all they wanted to do was go to lower Manhattan and stare into computer screens. What a waste! And when they got to Wall Street, of course, they figured out extravagant ways to waste the life savings of millions of Americans, which in turn required the waste of taxpayer dollars to bail them out, money that could have been spent on completely useful things: trains to get us where we want to go — say, new national parks.

Perhaps the only kind of waste we've gotten good at cutting is the kind we least needed to eliminate: An entire industry of consultants survives on telling companies how to get rid of inefficiencies — which generally means people. And an entire class of politicians survives by railing about government waste, which also ends up meaning programs for people: Health care for poor children, what a boondoggle. . . .

We've gotten away with all of this for a long time because we had margin, all kinds of margin. Money, for sure — we were the richest nation on Earth, and when we wanted more we just borrowed it from China. But margin in other ways as well: We landed on a continent with topsoil more than a foot thick across its vast interior, so the fact that we immediately started to waste it with inefficient plowing hardly mattered. We inherited an atmosphere that could buffer our emissions for the first 150 years of the Industrial Revolution. We somehow got away with wasting the talents of black people and women and gay folks. 13

But our margin is gone. We're out of cash, we're out of atmosphere, we're out of luck. The current economic carnage is what happens when you waste — when the CEO of Merrill Lynch thinks he needs a $35,000 commode, when the CEO of Tyco thinks it would be fun to spend a million dollars on his wife's birthday party, complete with an ice sculpture of Michelangelo's *David* peeing vodka. The melted Arctic ice cap is what you get when everyone in America thinks he requires the kind of vehicle that might make sense for a forest ranger. 14

Getting out of the fix we're in — if it's still possible — requires in part that we relearn some very old lessons. We were once famously thrifty: Yankee frugality, straightening bent nails, saving string. We used to have a holiday, Thrift Week, which began on Ben Franklin's birthday: "Beware of little expenses; a small leak will sink a great ship," said he. We disapproved of frippery, couldn't imagine wasting money on ourselves, made do or did without. It took a mighty effort to make us what we are today — in fact, it took a mighty industry, advertising, which soaks up plenty more of those Harvard grads and represents an almost total waste. 15

In the end, we built an economy that depended on waste, and boundless waste is what it has produced. And the really sad part is, it felt that way, too. Making enough money to build houses with rooms we never used, and cars with engines we had no need of, meant wasting endless hours at work. Which meant that we had, on average, one-third fewer friends than our parents' generation. What waste that! "Getting and spending, we lay waste our powers," wrote Wordsworth.[1] We can't say we weren't warned. 16

---

[1] William Wordsworth (1770–1850) was an English poet. The line is from his 1807 sonnet "The World Is Too Much with Us." — EDS.

The economic mess now transfixing us will mean some kind of change. 17 We can try to hang on to the status quo — living a Walmart life so we can buy cheaply enough to keep the stream of stuff coming. Or we can say uncle. There are all kinds of experiments in postwaste living springing up: Freecycling, and Craigslisting, and Dumpster diving, and car sharing (those unoccupied seats in your vehicle — what a waste!), and open sourcing. We're sharing buses, and going to the library in greater numbers. Economists keep hoping we'll figure out a way to revert — that we'll waste a little more, and pull us out of the economic doldrums. But the psychological tide suddenly runs the other way.

We may have waited too long — we may have wasted our last good 18 chance. It's possible the planet will keep warming and the economy keep sinking no matter what. But perhaps not — and we seem ready to shoot for something nobler than the hyperconsumerism that's wasted so much of the last few decades. Barack Obama said he would "call out" the nation's mayors if they wasted their stimulus money. That's the mood we're in, and it's about time.

For a reading quiz, visit **bedfordstmartins.com/thebedfordreader**.

Journal Writing

McKibben makes the point that the United States is more wasteful than other countries are, saying "the average American uses more energy between the stroke of midnight on New Year's Eve and dinner on January 2 than the average, say, Tanzanian consumes in a year" (par. 9). How do you feel about this discrepancy? Are Americans really as wasteful as McKibben claims, or do you feel he's exaggerating his case? Why might residents of the United States use more energy or consume more goods than people in other parts of the world? Do geography, cultural ideas, product output, or other characteristics somehow make the United States more needful or deserving of resources than other nations? Consider these questions in your journal. (To take your journal writing further, see "From Journal to Essay" on the facing page.)

Questions on Meaning

1. McKibben focuses on two issues related to waste: the environment and the economy. Which of his arguments deal with the first issue, and which the second? How is each issue related to his THESIS?
2. What reasons does McKibben give for our wastefulness? What EXAMPLES does he provide of this kind of behavior?

3. McKibben doesn't get to his proposed solution until the end of the essay. What solution does he propose? What action does he ask readers to take?

Questions on Writing Strategy

1. Does McKibben seem to expect his AUDIENCE to agree or disagree with his position? In answering this question, consider his use of pronouns (*we* and *you* especially): What audience reaction does he seem to be seeking in his presentation of examples?
2. Locate examples of emotional, ethical, and rational APPEALS in McKibben's argument. Which appeals do you consider most effective? least effective? Why?
3. McKibben's overall argument is based on a SYLLOGISM. Express his major premise, minor premise, and conclusion in your own words. Is his reasoning valid, in your opinion?
4. Where and how does McKibben address objections or opposing arguments? Do you find his strategy of counterargument effective? Why, or why not?
5. **OTHER METHODS**   How does McKibben use CLASSIFICATION to sort out the different kinds of waste he sees in the contemporary world? What categories of waste does he identify? Why do the distinctions matter?

Questions on Language

1. Notice McKibben's frequent use of informal language and COLLOQUIAL EXPRESSIONS, such as "oh, forget it" (par. 10). What does he achieve with this attitude? Do you find his TONE appropriate, given the seriousness of the subject?
2. What does "stuffporn" (par. 6) mean? What about "throughput" (9)? Locate other examples of business JARGON in the essay and explain their effect. Why does McKibben use these words?
3. Be sure you are familiar with the following words, checking a dictionary if necessary: particulates (par. 4); manifestly, scores, cascade (6); torque (7); Neanderthal, laureate, exquisite, daunting (9); debris (10); railing, boondoggle (12); buffer (13); carnage, commode (14); frugality, frippery (15); transfixing, status quo, revert, doldrums (17).

Suggestions for Writing

1. **FROM JOURNAL TO ESSAY**   Expand your journal entry into a full argumentative essay that defends or argues against the current levels of resource consumption in the United States. In formulating your argument, consider also how a person from another country might respond — a resident of, say, Tanzania or Italy or China.
2. Chris Jordan's photography exhibit, "Running the Numbers," which McKibben mentions in paragraph 9, is available for viewing at *chrisjordan.com/gallery/rtn/ #unsinkable*. Look through the gallery and select a photograph that you find especially striking. Then write an essay in which you ANALYZE the image. Why do you find it so compelling? What message does Jordan attempt to get across? What elements contribute to the effectiveness of the image? How does the artist's

caption complicate the meaning of his picture? Be sure your finished essay centers on a thesis that reassembles the parts of your analysis into a new coherent whole.

3. **CRITICAL WRITING** McKibben suggests that consumer culture leads to unhappiness: "Making enough money to build houses with rooms we never used, and cars with engines we had no need of, meant wasting endless hours at work. Which meant that we had, on average, one-third fewer friends than our parents' generation. What waste that!" (par. 16). And yet for many Americans those hours at work could be said to improve the quality of life — by paying for a vacation, or a new sofa, or even bare necessities such as food and health care. Write an essay arguing for or against McKibben's statement, based on your own experiences and observations.

4. **CONNECTIONS** Like McKibben, Derrick Jensen (next essay) objects to the levels of personal consumption encouraged by industrial economy. Similarly, Margaret Lundberg (p. 481) asserts that industrialized meat consumption is destructive to the planet. Write an essay that defends or argues against consumption for its own sake, making a point of explaining what, in your mind, constitutes a necessity and what a luxury. Do we have a right — even an obligation — to buy or eat things we don't truly need? Why, or why not?

DERRICK JENSEN

Born in 1960 and raised amid chaos in a violent household, Derrick Jensen is an environmental writer and activist known for biting political criticism and an insistence that modern civilization is "destroying the planet." He graduated from the Colorado School of Mines with a degree in mineral engineering and physics and briefly ran a beekeeping operation and a small chicken farm before receiving an MFA in creative writing from Eastern Washington University in 1991. Jensen writes a regular column for *Orion* magazine and has contributed to many other periodicals, among them the *New York Times Magazine, Audubon, Earth Island Journal*, the *Ecologist*, and the *Sun*. He has published more than twenty books, including *Listening to the Land* (1995), *A Language Older than Words* (2000), *The Culture of Make Believe* (2002), and *Resistance against Empire* (2010). The recipient of numerous awards, Jensen has also taught writing at Pelican Bay State Prison and Eastern Washington University.

Forget Shorter Showers

Why bother with personal change? In this 2009 essay for *Orion*, Jensen challenges the notion that individual behaviors have any real effect on the environment. Mocking solutions like Bill McKibben's in "Waste Not, Want Not" (p. 468), Jensen lays out his own radical proposal for saving the earth. The essay following this one, by student writer Margaret Lundberg (p. 481), offers another suggestion.

Would any sane person think Dumpster diving would have stopped Hitler, or that composting would have ended slavery or brought about the eight-hour workday, or that chopping wood and carrying water would have gotten people out of Tsarist prisons, or that dancing naked around a fire would have helped put in place the Voting Rights Act of 1957 or the Civil Rights Act of 1964? Then why now, with all the world at stake, do so many people retreat into these entirely personal "solutions"?

Part of the problem is that we've been victims of a campaign of systematic misdirection. Consumer culture and the capitalist mindset have taught us to substitute acts of personal consumption (or enlightenment) for organized political resistance. *An Inconvenient Truth*[1] helped raise consciousness about global warming. But did you notice that all of the solutions presented had to

[1] A 2006 film based on the book by former US Vice President Al Gore. — EDS.

do with personal consumption — changing light bulbs, inflating tires, driving half as much — and had nothing to do with shifting power away from corporations, or stopping the growth economy that is destroying the planet? Even if every person in the United States did everything the movie suggested, US carbon emissions would fall by only 22%. Scientific consensus is that emissions must be reduced by at least 75% worldwide.

Or let's talk water. We so often hear that the world is running out of water. 3 People are dying from lack of water. Rivers are dewatered from lack of water. Because of this we need to take shorter showers. See the disconnect? *Because I take showers, I'm responsible for drawing down aquifers?* Well, no. More than 90% of the water used by humans is used by agriculture and industry. The remaining 10% is split between municipalities and actual living breathing individual humans. Collectively, municipal golf courses use as much water as municipal human beings. People (both human people and fish people) aren't dying because the world is running out of water. They're dying because the water is being stolen.

Or let's talk energy. Kirkpatrick Sale[2] summarized it well: "For the past 4 fifteen years the story has been the same every year: individual consumption — residential, by private car, and so on — is never more than about a quarter of all consumption; the vast majority is commercial, industrial, corporate, by agribusiness and government [he forgot military]. So, even if we all took up cycling and wood stoves it would have a negligible impact on energy use, global warming, and atmospheric pollution."

Or let's talk waste. In 2005, per-capita municipal waste production (basi- 5 cally everything that's put out at the curb) in the US was about 1,660 pounds. Let's say you're a die-hard simple-living activist, and you reduce this to zero. You recycle everything. You bring cloth bags shopping. You fix your toaster. Your toes poke out of old tennis shoes. You're not done yet, though. Since municipal waste includes not just residential waste, but also waste from government offices and businesses, you march to those offices, waste reduction pamphlets in hand, and convince them to cut down on their waste enough to eliminate your share of it. Uh, I've got some bad news. Municipal waste accounts for only 3% of total waste production in the United States.

I want to be clear. I'm not saying we shouldn't live simply. I live reason- 6 ably simply myself, but I don't pretend that not buying much (or not driving much, or not having kids) is a powerful political act, or that it's deeply revolutionary. It's not. Personal change doesn't equal social change.

So how, then, and especially with all the world at stake, have we come 7 to accept these utterly insufficient responses? I think part of it is that we're in

[2] An American journalist who often writes about environmental issues, economics, and politics. — EDS.

a double bind. A double bind is where you're given multiple options, but no matter what option you choose, you lose, and withdrawal is not an option. At this point, it should be pretty easy to recognize that every action involving the industrial economy is destructive (and we shouldn't pretend that solar photovoltaics,[3] for example, exempt us from this: they still require mining and transportation infrastructures at every point in the production processes; the same can be said for every other so-called green technology). So if we choose option one — if we avidly participate in the industrial economy — we may in the short term think we win because we may accumulate wealth, the marker of "success" in this culture. But we lose, because in doing so we give up our empathy, our animal humanity. And we really lose because industrial civilization is killing the planet, which means everyone loses. If we choose the "alternative" option of living more simply, thus causing less harm, but still not stopping the industrial economy from killing the planet, we may in the short term think we win because we get to feel pure, and we didn't even have to give up all of our empathy (just enough to justify not stopping the horrors), but once again we really lose because industrial civilization is still killing the planet, which means everyone still loses. The third option, acting decisively to stop the industrial economy, is very scary for a number of reasons, including but not restricted to the fact that we'd lose some of the luxuries (like electricity) to which we've grown accustomed, and the fact that those in power might try to kill us if we seriously impede their ability to exploit the world — none of which alters the fact that it's a better option than a dead planet. Any option is a better option than a dead planet.

Besides being ineffective at causing the sorts of changes necessary to stop   8
this culture from killing the planet, there are at least four other problems with perceiving simple living as a political act (as opposed to living simply because that's what you want to do). The first is that it's predicated on the flawed notion that humans inevitably harm their landbase. Simple living as a political act consists solely of harm reduction, ignoring the fact that humans can help the Earth as well as harm it. We can rehabilitate streams, we can get rid of noxious invasives, we can remove dams, we can disrupt a political system tilted toward the rich as well as an extractive economic system, we can destroy the industrial economy that is destroying the real, physical world.

The second problem — and this is another big one — is that it incor-   9
rectly assigns blame to the individual (and most especially to individuals who are particularly powerless) instead of to those who actually wield power in this system and to the system itself. Kirkpatrick Sale again: "The whole

---

[3] Film-coated panels that absorb sunlight and use its energy to generate electricity. — EDS.

individualist what-you-can-do-to-save-the-Earth guilt trip is a myth. We, as individuals, are not creating the crises, and we can't solve them."

The third problem is that it accepts capitalism's redefinition of us from citizens to consumers. By accepting this redefinition, we reduce our potential forms of resistance to consuming and not consuming. Citizens have a much wider range of available resistance tactics, including voting, not voting, running for office, pamphleting, boycotting, organizing, lobbying, protesting, and, when a government becomes destructive of life, liberty, and the pursuit of happiness, we have the right to alter or abolish it.   10

The fourth problem is that the endpoint of the logic behind simple living as a political act is suicide. If every act within an industrial economy is destructive, and if we want to stop this destruction, and if we are unwilling (or unable) to question (much less destroy) the intellectual, moral, economic, and physical infrastructures that cause every act within an industrial economy to be destructive, then we can easily come to believe that we will cause the least destruction possible if we are dead.   11

The good news is that there are other options. We can follow the examples of brave activists who lived through the difficult times I mentioned — Nazi Germany, Tsarist Russia, antebellum United States — who did far more than manifest a form of moral purity; they actively opposed the injustices that surrounded them. We can follow the example of those who remembered that the role of an activist is not to navigate systems of oppressive power with as much integrity as possible, but rather to confront and take down those systems.   12

For a reading quiz, visit **bedfordstmartins.com/thebedfordreader**.

Journal Writing

Jensen notes that acquiring money is "the marker of 'success' in this culture" (par. 7). Do you agree? In your journal, consider the meaning of *success*, focusing on these questions: Whom do you consider to be successful, and why? Where do your ideas of success come from — your parents? your friends? your schooling? the media? (To take your journal writing further, see "From Journal to Essay" on the facing page.)

Questions on Meaning

1. What is the THESIS of Jensen's argument? Where is this thesis stated most clearly? What does it reveal about Jensen's PURPOSE for writing?

2. On what points does Jensen seem to agree with fellow *Orion* writer Bill McKibben (p. 468)? On what points does he disagree? To what extent do the two writers' perspectives explain their difference of opinion?
3. What does Jensen mean by a "double bind" (par. 7)? Why does he believe that the industrial economy creates an impossible situation? What is his preferred solution to the problem?
4. Given his effort to convince readers that simple living is not a solution to environmental problems, why does Jensen make a point of explaining that he's "not saying we shouldn't live simply" (par. 6)?

Questions on Writing Strategy

1. To what extent does Jensen use rational, emotional, and ethical APPEALS in his argument? Identify examples of each kind of appeal in your answer.
2. Why, in an essay about the environment, does Jensen open and close with examples involving Hitler, American slaves, Russian prison camps, and civil rights movements? What point is he making with these EXAMPLES?
3. Whom does Jensen seem to be addressing in this essay: general readers? politicians? business leaders? some other group? (Hint: Look up *Orion* magazine's mission and history.) What influence does he apparently hope to have on his readers' behavior? To what extent did he influence your opinion of simple living?
4. Jensen suggests that some of his opponents' arguments are based on faulty reasoning. What logical FALLACIES does he implicitly or explicitly identify? Does Jensen lapse into any logical fallacies himself? If so, where?
5. **OTHER METHODS** Much of Jensen's argument is developed by CAUSE-AND-EFFECT analysis. Why is this method particularly effective for countering simple-living advocates, given Jensen's main point?

Questions on Language

1. Check a dictionary if you are unfamiliar with the meanings of any of the following words: composting (par. 1); systematic (2); aquifers, municipalities (3); agribusiness, negligible (4); per-capita (5); infrastructures, avidly, empathy, impede, exploit (7); predicated, rehabilitate, noxious, extractive (8); antebellum, manifest, integrity (12).
2. How would you characterize Jensen's TONE in this essay — for instance, worried, condescending, frustrated, dismissive, eager, angry, militant, reassuring, serious, irritated? Is it consistent throughout? Give examples to support your analysis.
3. Take a close look at the first sentences of paragraphs 3–5. What is distinctive about them? What EFFECT do they produce?
4. Why do you suppose Jensen quotes Kirkpatrick Sale twice? What does he achieve by using another writer's words to explain his points?

Suggestions for Writing

1. **FROM JOURNAL TO ESSAY** Write an extended DEFINITION of *success* that includes an examination of the sources of your definition, as you explored them in your journal. (The sources could be negative as well as positive — that is, your ideas of

success may have formed in reaction *against* others' ideas as well as in agreement *with* them.) Be sure your essay has a clear thesis and provides plenty of examples to make your definition precise.

2. Using the Internet, research an environmental organization such as Greenpeace or *350.org*. In an essay, summarize the global vision the organization outlines in its mission statement, which may include goals met to date as well as plans for the future. Then discuss whether you agree with the organization's assessment of the current environmental situation, its proposed solutions, and its methods for achieving those solutions. (You may need to narrow this discussion to a particular environmental problem.)

3. **CRITICAL WRITING**   Jensen's proposal to "stop the industrial economy" is radical and, as he says, "very scary for a number of reasons" (par. 7). How do you react to his argument, particularly to his view that revolution is necessary to save the planet? Write an essay of your own responding to Jensen's essay. Be sure to include evidence to support your view.

4. **CONNECTIONS**   Like Bill McKibben in the previous essay, Margaret Lundberg in the next essay expresses concern that Western countries use more than their fair share of natural resources and proposes cutting back — in her case, by adopting a vegetarian diet. But Jensen suggests that advocates of simple living like McKibben and Lundberg miss the point: "Consumer culture and the capitalist mindset have taught us to substitute acts of personal consumption (or enlightenment) for organized political resistance" (par. 2). Do McKibben's and Lundberg's purposes in their essays seem entirely focused on the personal? Do they ignore culture and politics, as Jensen implies? How do you think they might respond to Jensen's criticism?

Derrick Jensen on Writing

In *Walking on Water: Reading, Writing, and Revolution* (2003), Jensen reflects on his experiences as a writing teacher. Here we share his first five rules for writing, as he recounts them in a classroom dialog:

"The first rule of writing is . . ."
A chorus: "Don't bore the reader."
"Good. The second rule of writing is: Don't bore the reader."
Someone says, "But that's . . ."
"Exactly. And the third rule of writing is: Don't bore the reader. Now, can anyone guess the fourth and fifth rules?"

For Discussion

Why is consideration of AUDIENCE so important in writing? What does a writer need to know and do to avoid boring readers?

MARGARET LUNDBERG

Margaret Lundberg grew up in Fremont, California, and moved to Washington state as a newlywed in 1976. A former art teacher, she made her living as a free-lance muralist and decorator for nearly two decades before deciding to return to college. After graduating from Tacoma Community College in 2011 with an associate's degree in politics, philosophy, and economics, she transferred to the University of Washington, Tacoma. She completed a BA in arts, media, and culture, with a minor in education, in 2013 and obtained a curatorial position at the Museum of Glass in Tacoma.

Eating Green

Why go vegan? Lundberg explores several answers to the question, finding one especially compelling. In arguing the environmental benefits of a restricted diet, she expands on both Bill McKibben's and Derrick Jensen's proposals in the previous two essays. "Eating Green" was published in the 2010 edition of *Una Voce,* a collection of work by students in the first-year writing course at Tacoma Community College. Lundberg revised her essay for this book in 2013.

Lundberg's researched essay follows MLA style for documenting sources, discussed on pages 70–83.

When I was a child, our family's diet was important to my mother. We had two vegetables with every meal, ate plain yogurt for breakfast, and exercised with Jack LaLanne. Later, as a young mom myself, I learned to cook meals from scratch, froze and canned fresh produce, and did aerobics with Jane Fonda. I was concerned with my sons' nutrition, having learned early that good health didn't just happen — you had to work for it. Now that my family circle has widened to include grandchildren, I find that my concerns go beyond just the health of my own family, to the health of the planet we live on. I believe that our personal and global health is tightly interconnected, and what benefits one will benefit the other.

I became a vegetarian about three years ago, and "went vegan" last spring. I could tout all sorts of reasons, but suffice it to say that I look and feel better at fifty-two than I did five years ago. For my health and well-being, becoming a vegetarian was the best thing I could have done. Which got me thinking — what if we could establish that a vegetarian diet would benefit not only our personal health, but the health of the planet as well? Between pollution, greenhouse gases, and dependence on a dwindling supply of fossil fuels, our little blue planet isn't feeling too well. If all of us adopting a vegetarian diet could slow or stop all of these ills, shouldn't we consider it? The idea is not as far-fetched as it might sound: a vegetarian diet could be "just what the doctor ordered" for our global health.

In March of 1984, I was on a bus headed to the airport in Jerusalem, trav-   3
eling with a group of American tourists on our way home from a two-week trip to Israel. We had been exposed to incredible sights, smells, and experiences during our trip, yet on that last evening we were all feeling a bit homesick. And each of us was asking the same question: "Where's the beef?"[1] We had just come from an amazing dinner at an Arab restaurant in East Jerusalem, yet we were all longing for a hamburger — Golden Arches, here we come! Eating meat is such a big part of the American way of life that it almost feels unpatriotic to spurn it. Would it still be Thanksgiving without the turkey, the Fourth of July without the hamburgers, a baseball game without the hotdogs? All of these things seem to be permanently interwoven into our culture. We just like meat.

But the great American love affair with burgers and fries also has a dark   4
side. Just as the standard American diet is killing us individually — with sky-rocketing rates of obesity, diabetes, heart disease, and a host of other ills — it is also having devastating effects on our planet. Pollution, global warming, and an alarming dependence on fossil fuels can all be traced back, in large part, to the agricultural practices that are required to feed our ever-growing craving for meat. Dietician Kate Geagan compares the environmental impact of the American diet with that of "our love affair with SUVs," warning that the energy use involved in the "production, transport, processing, packaging, storing, and preparation [of food] is now the single largest contributor to global warming" (x).

Livestock production in this country and throughout the Western world   5
has come a long way from the era of the American cowboy. The days of cattle grazing serenely on huge expanses of prairie pasture land are pretty much over. As Michael Pollan points out, raising cattle and other livestock is a multi-billion dollar operation that is now more manufacturing plant than traditional ranching. Cows no longer spend their lives grazing the hillsides until they are ready for slaughter. They are warehoused and fed a diet that is contrary to their very physiology — intended to eat grass, they are now fattened on corn, in as short a time as possible. In the early 1900s it took four to five years to ready a steer for slaughter; it now takes fourteen to sixteen months. The

---

[1] Advertising slogan for the hamburger chain Wendy's (1984–85). — Eds.

corn-based diet they are fed leads to a variety of health issues for the cattle (77, 82–83). In his article "The Ecology of Eating: The Power of the Fork," Mark Hyman states, "Of the 24 million pounds of antibiotics produced each year in this country, 19 million are put in the factory-farmed animals' feed to prevent infection, which results from overcrowding, and to prevent the cow's stomach from exploding with gas from the fermentation of the corn" (15). As a result of what is basically indigestion, he explains, cattle belch vast amounts of methane, which is twenty-three times more potent at trapping heat than carbon dioxide. Livestock manure is the source of two-thirds of the man-made nitrous oxide now circulating in our atmosphere — a greenhouse gas that is three hundred times more potent than carbon dioxide (14).

Other statistics are equally grim. Kate Geagan reports that livestock   6 raised for meat production are responsible for 18% of greenhouse gas emissions — more than the cars we drive. The average household could make a bigger impact on greenhouse gas emissions by cutting their meat consumption in half than by cutting their driving in half! The food sector is responsible for 20% of the total energy use in the United States every year, and most of that comes from the raising and packaging of livestock animals (30).

A nonvegetarian diet requires 2.9 times more water, 2.5 times more   7 energy, 13 times more fertilizer (also made from petroleum products), and 1.4 times more pesticides than does a vegetarian diet — and the greatest difference comes from beef consumption (Marlow et al. 1699S). Less than half of the harvested acreage in the United States is used to grow food for people, and it takes sixteen pounds of grain and soybeans fed to cattle to get one pound of meat ready for us to eat. Ten times as much land is required for meat-protein production than is required for plant-protein production, and producing one pound of animal protein uses almost a hundred times more water than it takes to produce one pound of plant protein (Vegan Society). Already, says journalist Pat Joseph, more than 20% of the Amazon rainforest in Brazil has been cleared to meet global demand for beef; it is now home to cattle ranches and the soybean farms needed to feed the livestock (128). We have yet to understand what the continuing loss of rainforest will cost us in the long run, but at the very least tropical deforestation contributes 70% of Brazil's release of carbon dioxide levels into the atmosphere (Joseph 109).

As a population's income rises, its people have traditionally eaten more   8 meat and dairy foods, replacing wheat and rice in their diets — exactly what we have been experiencing over the last fifty years (Bittman). Nevertheless, between global warming and decreased natural resources such as farmable land and water, the earth simply can't support any greater increase in meat production. In my lifetime, the world population has doubled, and it is still growing exponentially. Yet, with finite resources, how will we continue to feed us all? Factory farming is simply unsustainable. Even Dennis Avery, director of the Centre for Global Food Issues (a very pro-livestock organization), has commented that "[t]he world must create 5 billion vegans in the next several decades, or triple its total farm output without using more land" (qtd. in Vegan Society). If *he* thinks so, it *must* be time to rethink our diet!

But what about our burgers? For far too many of us, giving up meat seems like an unreasonable thing to ask. Meat is good for us, isn't it? "Meat has tremendous nutritional value and is very good for you," argues Randall Huffman, vice president of scientific affairs for the American Meat Institute. Huffman says that "even the fat in meat is — in some respects — healthy. Fully one third of the saturated fat found in meat is stearic acid, which actually helps lower blood cholesterol levels" (qtd. in Masci 132). Maybe. But the average American consumes nearly 200 pounds of meat a year — 33% more than five decades ago. We eat about 110 grams of protein a day (more than three-quarters of which is animal protein), while the USDA's Food Pyramid recommends less than half that — an amount still nearly twice the 30 grams most other experts say we actually *need* (Bittman). Since the advent of products like McDonald's Quarter Pounder with Cheese (30 grams of protein all by itself!), it has become entirely too easy to eat much more meat than any of us could ever need. Our expanding waistlines and rising levels of diabetes and heart disease prove that any benefit we might gain from a modest amount of meat in our diet is being overcome by the sheer amount we are eating on a daily basis.

With growing evidence that human activities in general — and livestock production in particular — are causing large-scale environmental effects, many major corporations are attempting to make changes and "do their part" for the environment. A group of dairy farmers in New York state, for example, is teaming with General Electric to produce renewable energy from cow manure. Apparently manure from 2,500 cows can generate enough electricity for 200 homes. In a state with over 600,000 dairy cows, that's a lot of potential kilowatts. "We've estimated that this could generate $38 million in new revenue for dairy farmers around the country and offset 2 million tons of carbon dioxide equivalents annually by 2020," says Rick Naczi, executive vice president at Dairy Management Inc., in a press release ("GE, US Dairy"). Naczi reports that the dairy industry has committed to reducing greenhouse gas emissions by 25% by 2020 — the equivalent of getting "1.25 million passenger cars off the road every year." That's a lot of gas.

But even if we *can* make electricity from "cow pies," does that make up for the fact that we in the Western world are using far more than our fair share of the earth's limited resources? We use substantial amounts of fossil fuels and other nonrenewable resources to grow a "crop" that many in our global population cannot access; one that pollutes and sickens the planet — and its inhabitants — in ways we are only beginning to comprehend. In the face of a looming worldwide crisis where food prices are rising and nearly 3 billion people earn less than two dollars a day, two of every three people in the world already subsist on a vegetarian diet (Clemmit 1). Yet in the industrialized world over 50% of the grain that we grow is used to fatten livestock (Hyman 14). Peter Timmer, a fellow at the Washington-based Center for Global Development, states, "There's still plenty of food for everyone, but only if everyone eats a grain and legume-based diet. If the diet includes large . . . amounts of animal protein . . . , food demand is running ahead of global production" (qtd. in Clemmit 3).

With finite resources already being stretched thin by a growing global   12
population, is it rational for us to continue on as we are? Our food systems are not sustainable, and today's livestock production methods make potential food crises more likely every day. If greenhouse gases continue to build as they have over the last fifty years, the effects on today's farmlands may be irreversible. As global temperatures continue to rise, Alaska may become the new "Corn Belt" and the Midwest could become a desert. How much of the land we now depend on to feed us could be lost to agriculture? A vegetarian diet would enable us to healthfully feed many more people, and make much better use of the resources we have. Do we really want to wait until it's too late to change our way of eating?

Works Cited

Bittman, Mark. "Rethinking the Meat-Guzzler." *New York Times*. New York Times, 27 Jan. 2008. Web. 14 Jan. 2013.

Clemmit, Marcia. "Global Food Crisis: What's Causing the Rising Prices?" *Social Problems: Selections from CQ Researcher*. Ed. Sage Publications Editors. Thousand Oaks: Pine Forge, 2010. 1–24. Print.

Geagan, Kate. *Go Green Get Lean: Trim Your Waistline with the Ultimate Low-Carbon Footprint Diet*. New York: Rodale, 2009. Print.

"GE, US Dairy Industry Shine Light on Potential of 'Cow Power' in New York." *Business Wire*. Business Wire, 29 Oct. 2009. Web. 14 Jan. 2013.

Hyman, Mark. "The Ecology of Eating: The Power of the Fork." *Alternative Therapies in Health and Medicine* 15.4 (2009): 14–15. *ProQuest*. Web. 25 Jan. 2013.

Joseph, Pat. "Soy in the Amazon." *Virginia Quarterly Review* 83.4 (2007): 106–29. *ProQuest*. Web. 25 Jan. 2013.

Marlow, Harold J., et al. "Diet and the Environment: Does What You Eat Matter?" *American Journal of Clinical Nutrition* 89 (2009): 1699S–1703S. Print.

Masci, David. "Diet and Health: Can Certain Foods Fight Disease?" *CQ Researcher* 11.7 (2001): 129–60. Print.

McDonald's. "USA Nutrition Facts for Popular Menu Items." *McDonald's.com*. McDonald's, n.d. Web. 14 Jan. 2013.

Pollan, Michael. *The Omnivore's Dilemma: A Natural History of Four Meals*. New York: Penguin, 2006. Nook file.

Vegan Society. "Land." *Information Resources*. Vegan Society, n.d. Web. 14 Jan. 2013.

For a reading quiz, visit **bedfordstmartins.com/thebedfordreader.**

Journal Writing

In your journal, respond to Lundberg's contention that we should all become vegetarians because of the "large-scale environmental effects" (par. 10) of the industrialized raising of livestock. How persuaded are you by her argument? Do you agree that giving up meat would help to slow global warming and ensure that everyone on the planet can continue to be fed, or can you think of alternative solutions? What are they? (To take your journal writing further, see "From Journal to Essay" on the facing page.)

Questions on Meaning

1. What is Lundberg's THESIS, and where does she state it?
2. How, according to Lundberg, does "the standard American diet" (par. 4) damage the environment? SUMMARIZE the main points she uses to support her claim.
3. Why does Lundberg note that the nitrous oxide released by cow manure is "a greenhouse gas that is three hundred times more potent than carbon dioxide" (par. 5)? What point is she making here?
4. What does Lundberg ASSUME about her AUDIENCE? To what extent do you fit her assumptions?
5. What would you say is Lundberg's PURPOSE in this argument? Does she really expect readers to give up meat entirely? What evidence in the essay supports your answer?

Questions on Writing Strategy

1. Why do you suppose Lundberg opens the essay as she does? What does she accomplish by discussing her personal health and diet? What is the EFFECT of her

admission that she once craved a hamburger almost immediately after eating a vegetarian meal?

2. Where does Lundberg acknowledge opposing arguments? Do her concessions seem adequate to you? Why, or why not?

3. Lundberg ends her essay with several questions. What is the purpose of these questions, and what is their effect?

4. **OTHER METHODS** Lundberg's argument is based largely on CAUSE-AND-EFFECT analysis. Does her analysis seem sound to you? Do you think she overemphasizes some causes or effects or overlooks others? Explain.

Questions on Language

1. Look for places where Lundberg puts words in quotation marks though not actually quoting anyone in particular. What do the quotation marks signify?

2. What are the implications of Lundberg's ALLUSIONS to Wendy's and McDonald's (pars. 3, 9)?

3. Explain the double meaning of the word *green* in Lundberg's title.

4. Use a dictionary if necessary to help you define any of the following words: vegetarian, vegan, tout, suffice (par. 2); interwoven (3); serenely, physiology, ecology, fermentation, methane (5); sector (6); deforestation (7); exponentially, finite (8); advent (9); kilowatts, offset (10); subsist, industrialized, legume (11); sustainable (12).

Suggestions for Writing

1. **FROM JOURNAL TO ESSAY** Expand your journal writing into an essay in which you respond personally to Lundberg's argument that "all of us adopting a vegetarian diet could slow or stop" environmental destruction (par. 2). If you generally agree with Lundberg, what can you add to convince others who do not? If you generally disagree, how do you answer Lundberg's concerns?

2. As Lundberg suggests at several points in her essay, scientists believe that rising global temperatures are caused in large part by carbon dioxide emissions. Use a carbon calculator on the Internet, such as the one provided by the Nature Conservancy at *nature.org/initiatives/climatechange/calculator*, to measure your impact on climate change. What can you do in your daily life to reduce carbon emissions? Do further research, if necessary, and then write a PROCESS ANALYSIS laying out the steps by which you personally might help stem global warming.

3. **CRITICAL WRITING** Lundberg's argument relies mainly on statistics and other EVIDENCE from published SOURCES. Write an essay in which you discuss how effective, or ineffective, you find her use of sources to be and explore what else, if anything, she might have brought in to support her claims.

4. **CONNECTIONS** Margaret Lundberg, Bill McKibben (p. 468), and Derrick Jensen (p. 475) all take global warming as a given, but some observers dispute the notion that the planet is in trouble. Write a brief essay about your view of one aspect of the state of the environment. Do you regard waste, climate change, or dwindling natural resources as critical problems? Do you believe that the government is taking adequate steps to protect the environment? Do you believe that the actions

of individuals can make a difference? Your essay may but need not be an argument: That is, you could explain your answer to any of these questions or argue a specific point. Either way, choose a narrow focus and use examples and details to support your ideas.

Margaret Lundberg on Writing

Margaret Lundberg decided to research the environmental effects of diet because, she says, the topic "is pretty close to my heart." At the time she wrote she had "been a vegetarian for almost four years and a vegan for about a year," a choice made "not so much for ethical reasons (at least not involving animals anyway!) but for health reasons." She was concerned, she explains, not "just for my personal health, but for the health of the planet." Writing about the subject helped Lundberg to clarify her position and reinforce the value of her decisions. Her advice to other writers is straightforward: "Keep a notebook handy at all times. You never know when that 'perfect' idea will show up."

For Discussion

1. Besides recording inspirations for writing, what are some other benefits of keeping a notebook on hand?
2. Discuss a time when a writing project helped you learn more about a topic you cared about.

ADDITIONAL WRITING TOPICS

Argument and Persuasion

1. Write a persuasive essay in which you express a deeply felt opinion. In it, address a particular person or audience. For instance, you might direct your essay to any of the following readers:

   A friend unwilling to attend a ballet performance (or a wrestling match) with you on the grounds that such an event is a waste of time

   A teacher who asserts that more term papers, and longer ones, are necessary for students to master academic writing

   A developer who plans to tear down a historic house

   Someone who sees no purpose in studying a foreign language

   A high-school class whose members don't want to go to college

   An older generation skeptical of the value of current popular music

   An atheist who asserts that religion just distracts us from the here and now

   The members of a library board who want to ban a book you love

2. Write a letter to your campus newspaper or a city newspaper in which you argue for or against a certain cause or view. You may wish to object to a particular feature or editorial in the paper. Send your letter and see if it is published.

3. Write a short letter to your congressional or state representative, arguing in favor of (or against) the passage of some pending legislation. Look in a news magazine or a newspaper for a worthwhile bill to write about. Or else write in favor of some continuing cause: for instance, requiring (or not requiring) cars to reduce exhaust emissions, reducing (or increasing) military spending, providing (or reducing) aid to the arts, expanding (or reducing) government loans to college students.

4. Write an essay arguing that something you feel strongly about should be changed, removed, abolished, enforced, repealed, revised, reinstated, or reconsidered. Be sure to propose some plan for carrying out whatever suggestions you make. Possible topics, listed to start you thinking, are these:

   Gun laws

   Graduation requirements

   ROTC programs in schools and colleges

   Movie ratings (G, PG, PG-13, R, NC-17, X)

   School prayer

   Fraternities and sororities

   Dress codes in primary and secondary schools

PART THREE

MIXING THE METHODS

Everywhere in this book, we have tried to prove how flexible the methods of development are. All the preceding essays offer superb examples of DESCRIPTION or CLASSIFICATION or DEFINITION or ARGUMENT, but every one also illustrates other methods, too — description in PROCESS ANALYSIS, ANALYSIS and NARRATION in COMPARISON, EXAMPLES and CAUSE AND EFFECT in argument.

In this part of the book, we take this point even further by abandoning the individual methods. Instead, we offer a collection of eight essays, most of them considered classics, all of them by well-known writers. The selections range widely in their subjects and approaches, but they share a significant feature: All the authors draw on whatever methods of development, at whatever length, will help them achieve their PURPOSES with readers. To show how the writers combine methods, we have highlighted the most significant ones in the notes preceding each essay.

You have already begun to command the methods by focusing on them individually, making each a part of your kit of writing tools. Now, when you face a writing assignment, you can consider whether and how each method may help you sharpen your focus, develop your ideas, and achieve your aim. Indeed, as we noted in Chapter 2, one way to approach a subject is to apply each method to it, one by one. The following list distills the discussion on pages 31–32 to a set of questions that you can ask about any subject.

- **Narration:** Can you tell a story about the subject?

- **Description:** Can you use your senses to illuminate the subject?

- **Example:** Can you point to instances that will make the subject concrete and specific?

- **Comparison and contrast:** Will setting the subject alongside another generate useful information?

- **Process analysis:** Will a step-by-step explanation of how the subject works add to the reader's understanding?

- **Division or analysis:** Can slicing the subject into its parts produce a clearer vision of it?

- **Classification:** Is it worthwhile to sort the subject into kinds or groups?

- **Cause and effect:** Does it add to the subject to ask why it happened or what its results are?

- **Definition:** Can you trace boundaries that will clarify the meaning of the subject?

- **Argument and persuasion:** Can you back up an opinion or make a proposal about the subject?

Rarely will every one of these questions produce fruit for a given essay, but inevitably two or three or four will. Try the whole list when you're stuck at the beginning of an assignment or when you're snagged in the middle of a draft. You'll find the questions are as good at removing obstacles as they are at generating ideas.

SHERMAN ALEXIE

Sherman Alexie is an award-winning poet, fiction writer, and filmmaker known for witty and frank explorations of the lives of contemporary American Indians. A member of the Spokane/Coeur d'Alene tribe, Alexie was born in 1966 and grew up on the Spokane reservation in Wellpinit, Washington. An unusually intelligent child, he attended the tribal school on the reservation through the seventh grade, then decided to seek a better education at an off-reservation school thirty-five miles away. He spent two years at Gonzaga University before transferring to Washington State University in Pullman. In the same year he graduated, 1991, Alexie published *The Business of Fancydancing*, a book of poetry that led the *New York Times Book Review* to call him "one of the major lyric voices of our time." Since then Alexie has published many more books, including the poetry collections *I Would Steal Horses* (1993) and *One Stick Song* (2000); the novels *Reservation Blues* (1995), *Indian Killer* (1996), and *The Absolutely True Diary of a Part-Time Indian* (2007); and the story collections *The Lone Ranger and Tonto Fistfight in Heaven* (1993), *War Dances* (2009), and *Blasphemy* (2012). Alexie also wrote and produced *Smoke Signals*, a film that won awards at the 1998 Sundance Film Festival. Living in Seattle, Alexie occasionally performs as a stand-up comic and directs projects at Longhouse Media, a filmmaking studio for teens.

Superman and Me

Alexie has made it his mission to subvert stereotypes of American Indians as an impoverished, alcoholic, stoic people. In this essay, commissioned for *The Most Wonderful Books: Writers on Discovering the Pleasures of Reading* (1997), Alexie explains how books saved his life when he was a child and expresses hope that he can return the favor.

Primarily a narrative (Chap. 4), "Superman and Me" mixes several methods of development to show the difficult yet fruitful efforts of one writer's self-designed education:

Description (Chap. 5): paragraphs 2, 4–5
Example (Chap. 6): paragraphs 2, 7
Comparison and contrast (Chap. 7): paragraphs 3, 6, 8
Process analysis (Chap. 8): paragraphs 4, 7
Division or analysis (Chap. 9): paragraphs 1, 3
Classification (Chap. 10): paragraphs 2, 6–7
Cause and effect (Chap. 11): paragraphs 7–8

I learned to read with a Superman comic book. Simple enough, I suppose. I cannot recall which particular Superman comic book I read, nor can I

1

remember which villain he fought in that issue. I cannot remember the plot, nor the means by which I obtained the comic book. What I can remember is this: I was 3 years old, a Spokane Indian boy living with his family on the Spokane Indian Reservation in eastern Washington state. We were poor by most standards, but one of my parents usually managed to find some minimum-wage job or another, which made us middle-class by reservation standards. I had a brother and three sisters. We lived on a combination of irregular paychecks, hope, fear and government surplus food.

My father, who is one of the few Indians who went to Catholic school on   2
purpose, was an avid reader of westerns, spy thrillers, murder mysteries, gangster epics, basketball player biographies and anything else he could find. He bought his books by the pound at Dutch's Pawn Shop, Goodwill, Salvation Army and Value Village. When he had extra money, he bought new novels at supermarkets, convenience stores and hospital gift shops. Our house was filled with books. They were stacked in crazy piles in the bathroom, bedrooms and living room. In a fit of unemployment-inspired creative energy, my father built a set of bookshelves and soon filled them with a random assortment of books about the Kennedy assassination, Watergate, the Vietnam War and the entire 23-book series of the Apache westerns. My father loved books, and since I loved my father with an aching devotion, I decided to love books as well.

I can remember picking up my father's books before I could read. The   3
words themselves were mostly foreign, but I still remember the exact moment when I first understood, with a sudden clarity, the purpose of a paragraph. I didn't have the vocabulary to say "paragraph," but I realized that a paragraph was a fence that held words. The words inside a paragraph worked together for a common purpose. They had some specific reason for being inside the same fence. This knowledge delighted me. I began to think of everything in terms of paragraphs. Our reservation was a small paragraph within the United States. My family's house was a paragraph, distinct from the other paragraphs of the LeBrets to the north, the Fords to our south and the Tribal School to the west. Inside our house, each family member existed as a separate paragraph but still had genetics and common experiences to link us. Now, using this logic, I can see my changed family as an essay of seven paragraphs: mother, father, older brother, the deceased sister, my younger twin sisters and our adopted little brother.

At the same time I was seeing the world in paragraphs, I also picked up   4
that Superman comic book. Each panel, complete with picture, dialogue and narrative was a three-dimensional paragraph. In one panel, Superman breaks through a door. His suit is red, blue and yellow. The brown door shatters into many pieces. I look at the narrative above the picture. I cannot read the words, but I assume it tells me that "Superman is breaking down the door." Aloud,

I pretend to read the words and say, "Superman is breaking down the door." Words, dialogue, also float out of Superman's mouth. Because he is breaking down the door, I assume he says, "I am breaking down the door." Once again, I pretend to read the words and say aloud, "I am breaking down the door." In this way, I learned to read.

This might be an interesting story all by itself. A little Indian boy teaches himself to read at an early age and advances quickly. He reads *Grapes of Wrath* in kindergarten when other children are struggling through *Dick and Jane*. If he'd been anything but an Indian boy living on the reservation, he might have been called a prodigy. But he is an Indian boy living on the reservation and is simply an oddity. He grows into a man who often speaks of his childhood in the third-person, as if it will somehow dull the pain and make him sound more modest about his talents.

A smart Indian is a dangerous person, widely feared and ridiculed by Indians and non-Indians alike. I fought with my classmates on a daily basis. They wanted me to stay quiet when the non-Indian teacher asked for answers, for volunteers, for help. We were Indian children who were expected to be stupid. Most lived up to those expectations inside the classroom but subverted them on the outside. They struggled with basic reading in school but could remember how to sing a few dozen powwow songs. They were monosyllabic in front of their non-Indian teachers but could tell complicated stories and jokes at the dinner table. They submissively ducked their heads when confronted by a non-Indian adult but would slug it out with the Indian bully who was 10 years older. As Indian children, we were expected to fail in the non-Indian world. Those who failed were ceremonially accepted by other Indians and appropriately pitied by non-Indians.

I refused to fail. I was smart. I was arrogant. I was lucky. I read books late into the night, until I could barely keep my eyes open. I read books at recess, then during lunch, and in the few minutes left after I had finished my classroom assignments. I read books in the car when my family traveled to powwows or basketball games. In shopping malls, I ran to the bookstores and read bits and pieces of as many books as I could. I read the books my father brought home from the pawnshops and secondhand. I read the books I borrowed from the library. I read the backs of cereal boxes. I read the newspaper. I read the bulletins posted on the walls of the school, the clinic, the tribal offices, the post office. I read junk mail. I read auto-repair manuals. I read magazines. I read anything that had words and paragraphs. I read with equal parts joy and desperation. I loved those books, but I also knew that love had only one purpose. I was trying to save my life.

Despite all the books I read, I am still surprised I became a writer. I was   8
going to be a pediatrician. These days, I write novels, short stories and poems.
I visit schools and teach creative writing to Indian kids. In all my years in the
reservation school system, I was never taught how to write poetry, short stories
or novels. I was certainly never taught that Indians wrote poetry, short stories
and novels. Writing was something beyond Indians. I cannot recall a single
time that a guest teacher visited the reservation. There must have been visiting teachers. Who were they? Where are they now? Do they exist? I visit the
schools as often as possible. The Indian kids crowd the classroom. Many are
writing their own poems, short stories and novels. They have read my books.
They have read many other books. They look at me with bright eyes and arrogant wonder. They are trying to save their lives. Then there are the sullen and
already defeated Indian kids who sit in the back rows and ignore me with theatrical precision. The pages of their notebooks are empty. They carry neither
pencil nor pen. They stare out the window. They refuse and resist. "Books," I
say to them. "Books," I say. I throw my weight against their locked doors. The
door holds. I am smart. I am arrogant. I am lucky. I am trying to save our lives.

*For a reading quiz, visit **bedfordstmartins.com/thebedfordreader**.*

Journal Writing

Alexie believes that learning to read, which he did on his own, saved his life. Write
down some of your own memorable learning experiences, whether with reading and
writing or some other skill that's important to you, such as math, science, or technology. Was learning difficult or easy? Did you teach yourself, or did you have help? How
has the skill affected your life? (To take your journal writing further, see "From Journal
to Essay" on the next page.)

Questions on Meaning

1. What do you take to be Alexie's main PURPOSE in writing?
2. Alexie says that he "often speaks of his childhood in the third-person" (par. 5).
   (If necessary, see Useful Terms for a definition of *person*.) Why? What is the point
   of this statement, and what is the EFFECT?
3. "A smart Indian is a dangerous person," Alexie writes in paragraph 6. What does
   he mean? Dangerous how, and to whom?

4. What action of Superman's does Alexie stress in paragraph 4? How does he return to this IMAGE in his CONCLUSION? What point does Alexie seem to be making about how he sees himself?

Questions on Writing Strategy

1. Does Alexie seem to be writing mainly for other American Indians or for a wider AUDIENCE? Cite passages from the essay to support your answer.
2. Notice the repetition of "I read" (thirteen times) in paragraph 7. Where else does Alexie repeat himself, and why? What is the effect of these repetitions?
3. What can you INFER about Alexie's "novels, short stories and poems" (par. 8) from the information about his education (6–7), the details about his father's reading (2), and his attempts to reach out to student writers (8)?
4. **OTHER METHODS**   What device does Alexie use to clarify his COMPARISON of Indian children in school and outside in paragraph 6? What point is he making here?
5. **OTHER METHODS**   What portrait of life on an Indian reservation emerges from Alexie's DESCRIPTIONS?

Questions on Language

1. Alexie uses very short, simple sentences through most of this essay. Why?
2. Explain the extended metaphor in paragraph 3. (For a definition of *metaphor*, see FIGURES OF SPEECH in Useful Terms.) Why do you suppose Alexie "began to think of everything in terms of paragraphs"? What do PARAGRAPHS represent to him?
3. Consult a dictionary if you need help in defining the following: genetics, deceased (par. 3); prodigy (5); subverted, monosyllabic, submissively, ceremonially (6).

Suggestions for Writing

1. **FROM JOURNAL TO ESSAY**   Write an essay that explores how you learned a particular skill. You might focus on a single event, a series of events over a number of years, or perhaps one significant year, but focus on a challenge or a struggle or an achievement that is important to you. As you relate your story, try to give your personal experience meaning for your readers.
2. One of Alexie's underlying themes in this essay is the difficulties American Indians often face on reservations. Do some research about the conditions of reservation life. Then write an essay in which you report your findings.
3. **CRITICAL WRITING**   Alexie is known for injecting humor, sometimes very dark humor, into tales that might otherwise be unrelievedly bleak. Where do you see humor in "Superman and Me"? How effective is the humor? Write an essay analyzing Alexie's use of humor, focusing your analysis on a single central idea of your own and supporting it with examples from Alexie's essay.
4. **CONNECTIONS**   Luis Alberto Urrea, in "Life on the Mississippi" (*bedfordstmartins .com/thebedfordreader*), also examines the impact of reading, explaining how Mark Twain's *The Adventures of Tom Sawyer* altered his perception of the world

around him. Listen to his audio essay, then write an essay that considers how Urrea's memory compares with Alexie's. What do the two writers have in common? Where do their experiences diverge? If a particular book has ever had a strong influence on *you*, include your own experiences in your considerations.

5. **CONNECTIONS** Like Alexie's "Superman and Me," Maya Angelou's "Champion of the World" (p. 104) and Amy Tan's "Fish Cheeks" (p. 110) report experiences of being culturally and racially different from mainstream white America. Earlier "Connections" topics asked you to compare and contrast Angelou's and Tan's perceptions of what sets them apart from the dominant culture (p. 108) or their uses of narration to convey their differing POINTS OF VIEW (p. 113). Now bring Alexie into one of those comparisons of Angelou and Tan, or both. Be sure to use examples from the essays to support your main idea.

Sherman Alexie on Writing

The humor woven into his work sometimes surprises first-time readers of Sherman Alexie. "One of the biggest misconceptions about Indians is that we're stoic," Alexie told Pam Lambert of *People Weekly*. "But humor is an essential part of our culture." The humor in Alexie's writing reflects its role in the lives of contemporary American Indians for whom, Alexie told Doug Marx of *Publishers Weekly*, "laughter is a ceremony. It's the way people cope."

Alexie does not avoid depicting the poverty, alcoholism, and despair experienced by many Indians. Sometimes criticized by other Indians for portraying reservation life as hopeless, Alexie responded to Doug Marx: "I write what I know and don't try to mythologize myself, which is what some seem to want, and which some Indian women and men writers are doing, this Earth Mother and Shaman Man thing, trying to create these 'authentic, traditional' Indians. We don't live our lives that way."

Alexie believes that as an American Indian writer he has a special responsibility "to tell the truth," as he put it to E. K. Caldwell in another interview. But, he continued, "Part of the danger in being an artist of whatever color is that you fall in love with your wrinkles. The danger is that if you fall in love with your wrinkles then you don't want to get rid of them. You start to glorify them and perpetuate them. If you write about pain, you can end up searching for more pain to write about, that kind of thing, that self-destructive route. We need to get away from that. We can write about pain and anger without having it consume us."

Alexie doesn't mind being typecast as an Indian writer. Speaking to Joel McNally of *The Writer* magazine, Alexie said, "If you object to being defined by your race and culture, you are saying there is something wrong with writing about your race and your culture. I'm not going to let others define me. . . . If I write it, it's an Indian novel. If I wrote about Martians, it would be an Indian novel. If I wrote about the Amish, it would be an Indian novel. That's who I am."

For Discussion

1. What do you think Alexie means by the "Earth Mother and Shaman Man thing" that he disparages in the work of some Indian writers? Why does he disapprove of it?
2. Judging from his essay "Superman and Me," how well would you say Alexie follows his own advice to "write about the pain and anger without having it consume us"?

JUDY BRADY

Judy Brady was born in 1937 in San Francisco, where she now lives, and earned a BFA in painting from the University of Iowa in 1962. Drawn into political action by her work in the feminist movement, she went to Cuba in 1973, where she studied class relationships as a way of understanding change in a society. When she was diagnosed with cancer in 1980, Brady became an activist against what she calls "the cancer establishment." ("Cancer is, after all, a multibillion-dollar business," she says.) In 1991 she published *1 in 3: Women with Cancer Confront an Epidemic,* an anthology of writings by women. She is a board member of Greenaction, an environmental justice organization, and a founding member of the Toxic Links Coalition, which seeks to educate people about the links between environmental toxins and public health. She provided a chapter for the book *Sweeping the Earth: Women Taking Action for a Healthy Planet* (1999), and she writes articles for Breast Cancer Action in San Francisco. Brady is also featured in the 2011 movie *Pink Ribbons, Inc.*, a documentary critiquing corporate breast cancer philanthropy.

I Want a Wife

After reading "I Want a Wife" aloud at a 1970 women's meeting in San Francisco, Brady submitted the essay for the Spring 1972 issue of *Ms.* magazine, which had started the year before as a vehicle for the modern feminist movement, then in its first decade. "I Want a Wife" became one of the best-known manifestos in popular feminist writing. In the essay Brady trenchantly examines the multiple duties and functions expected of a wife, leading to an inescapable conclusion.

On the whole a definition (Chap. 12) of *wife* that relies on division or analysis (Chap. 9) to identify the parts of the role, "I Want a Wife" uses several other methods of development to show both how Brady sees her expected duties in marriage and why she resents them:

Example (Chap. 6): paragraphs 2–4
Comparison and contrast (Chap. 7): paragraphs 5, 7
Process analysis (Chap. 8): paragraphs 4, 6
Classification (Chap. 10): paragraphs 3–7
Cause and effect (Chap. 11): paragraph 3

I belong to that classification of people known as wives. I am A Wife. 1
And, not altogether incidentally, I am a mother.

Not too long ago a male friend of mine appeared on the scene fresh from 2
a recent divorce. He had one child, who is, of course, with his ex-wife. He

is looking for another wife. As I thought about him while I was ironing one evening, it suddenly occurred to me that I, too, would like to have a wife. Why do I want a wife?

I would like to go back to school so that I can become economically inde- 3 pendent, support myself, and, if need be, support those dependent upon me. I want a wife who will work and send me to school. And while I am going to school I want a wife to take care of my children. I want a wife to keep track of the children's doctor and dentist appointments. And to keep track of mine, too. I want a wife to make sure my children eat properly and are kept clean. I want a wife who will wash the children's clothes and keep them mended. I want a wife who is a good nurturant attendant to my children, who arranges for their schooling, makes sure that they have an adequate social life with their peers, takes them to the park, the zoo, etc. I want a wife who takes care of the children when they are sick, a wife who arranges to be around when the children need special care, because, of course, I cannot miss classes at school. My wife must arrange to lose time at work and not lose the job. It may mean a small cut in my wife's income from time to time, but I guess I can tolerate that. Needless to say, my wife will arrange and pay for the care of the children while my wife is working.

I want a wife who will take care of my physical needs. I want a wife who 4 will keep my house clean. A wife who will pick up after my children, a wife who will pick up after me. I want a wife who will keep my clothes clean, ironed, mended, replaced when need be, and who will see to it that my personal things are kept in their proper place so that I can find what I need the minute I need it. I want a wife who cooks the meals, a wife who is a *good* cook. I want a wife who will plan the menus, do the necessary grocery shopping, prepare the meals, serve them pleasantly, and then do the cleaning up while I do my studying. I want a wife who will care for me when I am sick and sympathize with my pain and loss of time from school. I want a wife to go along when our family takes vacation so that someone can continue to care for me and my children when I need a rest and change of scene.

I want a wife who will not bother me with rambling complaints about a 5 wife's duties. But I want a wife who will listen to me when I feel the need to explain a rather difficult point I have come across in my course of studies. And I want a wife who will type my papers for me when I have written them.

I want a wife who will take care of the details of my social life. When my 6 wife and I are invited out by my friends, I want a wife who will take care of the babysitting arrangements. When I meet people at school that I like and want to entertain, I want a wife who will have the house clean, will prepare a special meal, serve it to me and my friends, and not interrupt when I talk about things that interest me and my friends. I want a wife who will have arranged that the children are fed and ready for bed before my guests arrive so that the children do not bother us. I want a wife who takes care of the needs of my guests so that they feel comfortable, who makes sure that they have an ashtray, that they are passed the hors d'oeuvres, that they are offered a second helping of the food, that their wine glasses are replenished when necessary, that their coffee is served to them as they like it. And I want a wife who knows that sometimes I need a night out by myself.

I want a wife who is sensitive to my sexual needs, a wife who makes love   7
passionately and eagerly when I feel like it, a wife who makes sure that I am satisfied. And, of course, I want a wife who will not demand sexual attention when I am not in the mood for it. I want a wife who assumes the complete responsibility for birth control, because I do not want more children. I want a wife who will remain sexually faithful to me so that I do not have to clutter up my intellectual life with jealousies. And I want a wife who understands that *my* sexual needs may entail more than strict adherence to monogamy. I must, after all, be able to relate to people as fully as possible.

If, by chance, I find another person more suitable as a wife than the wife I   8
already have, I want the liberty to replace my present wife with another one. Naturally, I will expect a fresh, new life; my wife will take the children and be solely responsible for them so that I am left free.

When I am through with school and have a job, I want my wife to quit   9
working and remain at home so that my wife can more fully and completely take care of a wife's duties.

My God, who *wouldn't* want a wife?   10

For a reading quiz, visit **bedfordstmartins.com/thebedfordreader**.

Journal Writing

Brady addresses the traditional obligations of a wife and mother. In your journal, jot down parallel obligations of a husband and father. (To take your journal writing further, see "From Journal to Essay" on the next page.)

Questions on Meaning

1. Sum up the duties of a wife as Brady sees them.
2. To what inequities in the roles traditionally assigned to men and to women does "I Want a Wife" call attention?

3. What is the THESIS of this essay? Is it stated or implied?
4. Is Brady unfair to men?

Questions on Writing Strategy

1. What EFFECT does Brady obtain with the title "I Want a Wife"?
2. What do the first two paragraphs accomplish?
3. What is the TONE of this essay?
4. How do you explain the fact that Brady never uses the pronoun *she* to refer to a wife? Does this make her prose unnecessarily awkward?
5. Knowing that this essay was first published in *Ms.* magazine in 1972, what can you guess about its intended readers? Does "I Want a Wife" strike a college AUDIENCE today as revolutionary?
6. **OTHER METHODS** What principle of ANALYSIS does Brady use to analyze the role of wife? Can you think of some other principle for analyzing the role?
7. **OTHER METHODS** Although she mainly divides or analyzes the role of wife, Brady also creates a DEFINITION by using CLASSIFICATION to sort the many duties and responsibilities into manageable groups. What are the groups?

Questions on Language

1. What is achieved by the author's frequent repetition of the phrase "I want a wife"?
2. Be sure you know how to define the following words as Brady uses them: nurturant (par. 3); replenished (6); adherence, monogamy (7).
3. In general, how would you describe the DICTION of this essay? How well does it suit the essay's intended audience?

Suggestions for Writing

1. **FROM JOURNAL TO ESSAY** Working from your journal entry, write an essay titled "I Want a Husband" in which, using examples as Brady does, you enumerate the roles traditionally assigned to men in our society.
2. Imagining that you want to employ someone to do a specific job, divide the task into its duties and functions. Then, guided by your analysis, write an accurate job description in essay form.
3. **CRITICAL WRITING** As indicated in the note introducing it, Brady's essay was first published in 1972 in *Ms.*, a feminist magazine. Do some research about the women's movement of the 1960s and '70s. Where did women stand in higher education (studying and teaching), in medicine and other professions, in the workforce, as wives and mothers, as homemakers, and so on? What kinds of change did feminists seek, and how did they go about demanding those changes? How did society as a whole seem to respond? Based on your research, write an essay in which you SUMMARIZE Brady's view as you understand it and then EVALUATE her essay. Consider: Is Brady fair? If not, is unfairness justified? Provide specific EVIDENCE from your experience, observation, and research.

4. **CONNECTIONS**   At *bedfordstmartins.com/thebedfordreader*, Anne-Marie Slaughter and Andrew Cohen both examine gender roles in marriage and parenting in the early twenty-first century. Read "Why Women Still Can't Have It All" and "'Having It All'? How about 'Doing the Best I Can'?" and assess how much has changed since Brady wrote in 1970. What duties and tasks are expected of wives and husbands today? Are mothers better or worse off than they were four decades ago? How about fathers? Do you imagine Brady is pleased or disturbed by married women's roles as they stand today? Why?

5. **CONNECTIONS**   Judy Brady's "I Want a Wife" and Martin Luther King's "I Have a Dream" (p. 507) were both written around the same time as persuasive speeches, yet they take very different approaches to influencing their listeners. COMPARE AND CONTRAST the authors' strategies, considering especially their effectiveness for the situation each spoke in and the audience each addressed. Consider as well how successfully each speech translates into a text for reading. What is lost (or gained) when an address that was intended to be heard is instead read in silence?

Judy Brady on Writing

Before Judy Brady penned "I Want a Wife" in 1970, she had never considered being a writer. In a 2007 interview with Dick Gordon on American Public Media, Brady recalled that the idea of writing the essay was planted at a women's movement gathering at Glide Memorial Church in San Francisco: "Well, I was complaining at one of the consciousness-raising group meetings and somebody just said, 'Why don't you write it?' Which hadn't occurred to me. And I went home and did."

Brady says that although writing the essay took her only a couple of hours, its inspiration had been brewing for the decade of marriage and motherhood that preceded it. Brady remembers feeling spitefully awakened when she began to speak with other women about their position in the home and in society: "There was tremendous anger when I began to understand how I had been . . . how can I say this? . . . how I had been *molded* by forces about which I was totally unconscious."

At a rally celebrating the fiftieth anniversary of American women's right to vote, Brady read "I Want a Wife" aloud (and "totally terrified") to a gathering of both supporters and hecklers. Her now ex-husband bought her flowers after the event, a gesture that Brady describes as "bizarre." "He meant it well, but he sort of didn't get it," she says.

Inspired by the response to her essay, Brady became an active supporter of social and political causes, volunteering in Cuba, advocating for cancer

patients, and getting involved in the environmental movement while continuing to work for women's rights. Reflecting on the impact of "I Want a
Wife" forty years later, Brady is still frustrated by what she sees as a lack of
meaningful change for women and for underprivileged people in general.
Writing the essay did, however, affect her personally: "I've had a much more
interesting life than I would have had had I not found the women's movement
and not . . . done this essay."

For Discussion

1. What sparked Brady to write "I Want a Wife"? Why does she say that it was the
   work of ten years rather than just a couple of hours?
2. What did Brady's husband not "get" about her essay? Why do you think he may
   have failed to grasp its point?

MARTIN LUTHER KING, JR.

Martin Luther King, Jr. (1929–68), was born in Atlanta, the son of a Baptist minister, and was himself ordained in the same denomination. He received a BA from Morehouse College in 1948, a BD from Crozer Theological Seminary in 1951, and a PhD from Boston University in 1955. Stepping to the forefront of the civil rights movement in 1955, King led African Americans in a boycott of segregated city buses in Montgomery, Alabama; became the first president of the Southern Christian Leadership Conference; and staged sit-ins and mass marches that helped bring about the Civil Rights Act passed by Congress in 1964 and the Voting Rights Act of 1965. He received the Nobel Peace Prize in 1964. While King preached "nonviolent resistance," he was himself the target of violence. He was stabbed in New York and pelted with stones in Chicago; his home in Montgomery was bombed; and ultimately he was assassinated in Memphis by a sniper. On his tombstone near Atlanta's Ebenezer Baptist Church are these words from the spiritual he quotes at the conclusion of "I Have a Dream": "Free at last, free at last, thank God almighty, I'm free at last." Martin Luther King's birthday, January 15, is now a national holiday.

I Have a Dream

In Washington, DC, on August 28, 1963, King's campaign of nonviolent resistance reached its historic climax. On that date, commemorating the centennial of Lincoln's Emancipation Proclamation freeing the slaves, King led a march of 200,000 persons, black and white, from the Washington Monument to the Lincoln Memorial. Before this throng, and to millions who watched on television, he delivered an unforgettable speech. (We reprint a version that King prepared for print publication.)

Intended to inspire and motivate its audience, King's speech is a model of a certain kind of persuasion. To make his point, King draws on a number of methods:

Narration (Chap. 4): paragraphs 1–2
Description (Chap. 5): paragraphs 2, 4
Example (Chap. 6): paragraphs 6–9, 12–16, 21–22
Comparison and contrast (Chap. 7): paragraphs 3–4, 6
Cause and effect (Chap. 11): paragraphs 5, 7, 19
Argument and persuasion (Chap. 13): throughout

Five score years ago, a great American, in whose symbolic shadow we 1 stand, signed the Emancipation Proclamation. This momentous decree came as a great beacon light of hope to millions of Negro slaves who had been seared in the flames of withering injustice. It came as a joyous daybreak to end the long night of captivity.

But one hundred years later, we must face the tragic fact that the Negro is still not free. One hundred years later, the life of the Negro is still sadly crippled by the manacles of segregation and the chains of discrimination. One hundred years later, the Negro lives on a lonely island of poverty in the midst of a vast ocean of material prosperity. One hundred years later, the Negro is still languishing in the corners of American society and finds himself in exile in his own land. So we have come here today to dramatize an appalling condition. 2

In a sense we have come to our nation's capital to cash a check. When the architects of our republic wrote the magnificent words of the Constitution and the Declaration of Independence, they were signing a promissory note to which every American was to fall heir. This note was a promise that all men would be guaranteed the unalienable rights of life, liberty, and the pursuit of happiness. 3

It is obvious today that America has defaulted on this promissory note insofar as her citizens of color are concerned. Instead of honoring this sacred obligation, America has given the Negro people a bad check; a check which has come back marked "insufficient funds." But we refuse to believe that the bank of justice is bankrupt. We refuse to believe that there are insufficient funds in the great vaults of opportunity of this nation. So we have come to cash this check — a check that will give us upon demand the riches of freedom and the security of justice. We have also come to this hallowed spot to remind America of the fierce urgency of *now*. This is no time to engage in the luxury of cooling off or to take the tranquilizing drugs of gradualism. *Now* is the time to make real the promises of Democracy. *Now* is the time to rise from the dark and desolate valley of segregation to the sunlit path of racial justice. *Now* is the time to open the doors of opportunity to all of God's children. *Now* is the time to lift our nation from the quicksands of racial injustice to the solid rock of brotherhood. 4

It would be fatal for the nation to overlook the urgency of the moment and to underestimate the determination of the Negro. This sweltering summer of the Negro's legitimate discontent will not pass until there is an invigorating autumn of freedom and equality; 1963 is not an end, but a beginning. Those who hope that the Negro needed to blow off steam and will now be content will have a rude awakening if the nation returns to business as usual. There will be neither rest nor tranquillity in America until the Negro is granted his citizenship rights. The whirlwinds of revolt will continue to shake the foundations of our nation until the bright day of justice emerges. 5

But there is something that I must say to my people who stand on the warm threshold which leads into the palace of justice. In the process of gaining our rightful place we must not be guilty of wrongful deeds. Let us not seek to satisfy our thirst for freedom by drinking from the cup of bitterness and hatred. We must forever conduct our struggle on the high plane of dignity and discipline. We must not allow our creative protest to degenerate into physical violence. Again and again we must rise to the majestic heights of meeting physical force with soul force. The marvelous new militancy which has engulfed the Negro community must not lead us to a distrust of all white people, for many of our white brothers, as evidenced by their presence here today, have come to realize that their destiny is tied up with our destiny and their freedom is inextricably bound to our freedom. We cannot walk alone. 6

And as we walk, we must make the pledge that we shall march ahead. We cannot turn back. There are those who are asking the devotees of civil rights, "When will you be satisfied?" We can never be satisfied as long as the Negro is the victim of the unspeakable horrors of police brutality. We can never be satisfied as long as our bodies, heavy with the fatigue of travel, cannot gain lodging in the motels of the highways and the hotels of the cities. We cannot be satisfied as long as the Negro's basic mobility is from a smaller ghetto to a larger one. We can never be satisfied as long as a Negro in Mississippi cannot vote and a Negro in New York believes he has nothing for which to vote. No, no, we are not satisfied, and we will not be satisfied until justice rolls down like waters and righteousness like a mighty stream. 7

I am not unmindful that some of you have come here out of great trials and tribulations. Some of you have come fresh from narrow jail cells. Some of you have come from areas where your quest for freedom left you battered by the storms of persecution and staggered by the winds of police brutality. You have been the veterans of creative suffering. Continue to work with the faith that unearned suffering is redemptive. 8

Go back to Mississippi, go back to Alabama, go back to South Carolina, go back to Georgia, go back to Louisiana, go back to the slums and ghettos of our northern cities, knowing that somehow this situation can and will be changed. Let us not wallow in the valley of despair. 9

I say to you today, my friends, that in spite of the difficulties and frustrations of the moment I still have a dream. It is a dream deeply rooted in the American dream. 10

I have a dream that one day this nation will rise up and live out the true meaning of its creed: "We hold these truths to be self-evident; that all men are created equal." 11

I have a dream that one day on the red hills of Georgia the sons of former [12] slaves and the sons of former slaveowners will be able to sit down together at the table of brotherhood.

I have a dream that one day even the state of Mississippi, a desert state [13] sweltering with the heat of injustice and oppression, will be transformed into an oasis of freedom and justice.

I have a dream that my four little children will one day live in a nation [14] where they will not be judged by the color of their skin but by the content of their character.

I have a dream today. [15]

I have a dream that one day the state of Alabama, whose governor's lips [16] are presently dripping with the words of interposition and nullification, will be transformed into a situation where little black boys and black girls will be able to join hands with little white boys and white girls and walk together as sisters and brothers.

I have a dream today. [17]

I have a dream that one day every valley shall be exalted, every hill [18] and mountain shall be made low, the rough places will be made plain, and the crooked places will be made straight, and the glory of the Lord shall be revealed, and all flesh shall see it together.

This is our hope. This is the faith with which I return to the South. With [19] this faith we will be able to hew out of the mountain of despair a stone of hope. With this faith we will be able to transform the jangling discords of our nation into a beautiful symphony of brotherhood. With this faith we will be able to work together, to pray together, to struggle together, to go to jail together, to stand up for freedom together, knowing that we will be free one day.

This will be the day when all of God's children will be able to sing with [20] new meaning

> My country, 'tis of thee,
> Sweet land of liberty,
>   Of thee I sing:
> Land where my fathers died,
> Land of the pilgrims' pride,
> From every mountainside
>   Let freedom ring.

And if America is to be a great nation this must become true. So let free- [21] dom ring from the prodigious hilltops of New Hampshire. Let freedom ring from the mighty mountains of New York. Let freedom ring from the heightening Alleghenies of Pennsylvania!

Let freedom ring from the snowcapped Rockies of Colorado! [22]

Let freedom ring from the curvaceous peaks of California!   23

But not only that; let freedom ring from Stone Mountain of Georgia!   24

Let freedom ring from Lookout Mountain of Tennessee!   25

Let freedom ring from every hill and molehill of Mississippi. From every   26
mountainside, let freedom ring.

When we let freedom ring, when we let it ring from every village and   27
every hamlet, from every state and every city, we will be able to speed up that
day when all of God's children, black men and white men, Jews and Gentiles,
Protestants and Catholics, will be able to join hands and sing in the words of
the old Negro spiritual, "Free at last! free at last! thank God almighty, we are
free at last!"

---

*For a reading quiz, visit **bedfordstmartins.com/thebedfordreader**.*

Journal Writing

Do you think we have moved closer to fulfilling King's dream in the decades since
he gave this famous speech? In your journal, explore why or why not. (To take your
journal writing further, see "From Journal to Essay" on the next page.)

Questions on Meaning

1. What is the apparent PURPOSE of this speech?
2. What THESIS does King develop in his first four paragraphs?
3. What does King mean by the "marvelous new militancy which has engulfed the
   Negro community" (par. 6)? Does this contradict King's nonviolent philosophy?
4. In what passages of his speech does King notice events of history? Where does he
   acknowledge the historic occasion on which he is speaking?

Questions on Writing Strategy

1. What indicates that King's words were meant primarily for an AUDIENCE of listeners, and only secondarily for a reading audience? To hear these indications, try
   reading the speech aloud. What uses of PARALLELISM do you notice?
2. Where in the speech does King acknowledge that not all of his listeners are African American?
3. How much EMPHASIS does King place on the past? How much does he place on
   the future?

4. **MIXED METHODS**   Analyze the ETHICAL APPEAL of King's ARGUMENT (see p. 443). Where in the speech, for instance, does he present himself as reasonable despite his passion? To what extent does his personal authority lend power to his words?
5. **MIXED METHODS**   The DESCRIPTION in paragraphs 2 and 4 depends on metaphor, a FIGURE OF SPEECH in which one thing is said to be another thing. How do the metaphors in these paragraphs work for King's purpose?

Questions on Language

1. In general, is the language of King's speech ABSTRACT or CONCRETE? How is this level appropriate to his message and to the span of history with which he deals?
2. Point to memorable figures of speech besides those examined in the "Mixed Methods" question above.
3. Define momentous (par. 1); manacles, languishing (2); promissory note, unalienable (3); defaulted, hallowed, gradualism (4); inextricably (6); mobility, ghetto (7); tribulations, redemptive (8); interposition, nullification (16); prodigious (21); curvaceous (23); hamlet (27).

Suggestions for Writing

1. **FROM JOURNAL TO ESSAY**   Use your journal entry to write an essay that explains your sense of how well the United States has progressed toward realizing King's dream. You may choose to focus on the country as a whole or on your particular community, but you should use specific EVIDENCE to support your opinion.
2. Propose some course of action in a situation that you consider an injustice. Racial injustice is one possible area, or unfairness to any minority, or to women, children, the elderly, ex-convicts, the disabled, the poor. If possible, narrow your subject to a particular incident or a local situation on which you can write knowledgeably.
3. **CRITICAL WRITING**   What can you INFER from this speech about King's own attitudes toward oppression and injustice? Does he follow his own injunction not "to satisfy our thirst for freedom by drinking from the cup of bitterness and hatred" (par. 6)? Explain your answer, using evidence from the speech.
4. **CONNECTIONS**   King's "I Have a Dream" and Linda Chavez's "Supporting Family Values" (p. 454) both seek to influence readers, either to cause them to act or to change their views. Yet the two authors take very different approaches to achieve their purposes. COMPARE AND CONTRAST the authors' persuasive strategies, considering especially their effectiveness for the situation each writes about and the audience each addresses.
5. **CONNECTIONS**   King's speech was delivered in 1963. Brent Staples's essay "Black Men and Public Space" (p. 195) was first published in 1986. In an essay, explore the changes, if any, that are evident in the ASSUMPTIONS the authors make about their audiences' attitudes, about race in general, and about racism.

MAXINE HONG KINGSTON

Maxine Hong Kingston grew up caught between two complex and very different cultures: the China of her parents and the America of her surroundings. In her first two books, *The Woman Warrior: Memoirs of a Girlhood among Ghosts* (1976) and *China Men* (1980), Kingston combines Chinese myth and history with family tales to create a dreamlike world that shifts between reality and fantasy. Born in 1940 in Stockton, California, Kingston was the first American-born child of a scholar and a medical practitioner who became laundry workers in this country. After graduating from the University of California at Berkeley (BA, 1962), Kingston taught English at California and Hawaii high schools, at the University of Hawaii, and for many years at UC Berkeley. She has contributed essays, poems, and stories to many periodicals, including *The New Yorker,* the *New York Times Magazine,* and *Ms.* Other books by Kingston include a collection of essays, *Hawaii One Summer* (1987); a novel, *Tripmaster Monkey: His Fake Book* (1989); a collection of lectures and verse, *To Be the Poet* (2002); a blend of fiction and nonfiction, *The Fifth Book of Peace* (2003); and a memoir in verse, *I Love a Broad Margin to My Life* (2011). She also edited *Veterans of War, Veterans of Peace* (2006), a collection of essays written in workshops she holds for military veterans.

No Name Woman

"No Name Woman" is part of *The Woman Warrior.* Like much of Kingston's writing, it blends the "talk-stories" of Kingston's elders, her own vivid imaginings, and the reality of her experience — this time to discover why her Chinese aunt drowned herself in the family well.

Kingston develops "No Name Woman" with four main methods, all intertwined: In the context of narrating her own experiences, she seeks the causes of her aunt's suicide by comparing various narratives of it, and she employs description to make the narratives concrete and vivid. The main uses of these methods appear below:

Narration (Chap. 4): paragraphs 1–8, 14, 16–20, 23, 28–30, 34–35, 37–46
Description (Chap. 5): paragraphs 4–8, 21, 23–27, 31, 37, 40–46
Comparison and contrast (Chap. 7): paragraphs 15–18, 20–24, 27–28, 31
Cause and effect (Chap. 11): paragraphs 10–11, 15–18, 21–25, 29–31, 33–39, 44–48

"You must not tell anyone," my mother said, "what I am about to tell you. In China your father had a sister who killed herself. She jumped into the family well. We say that your father has all brothers because it is as if she had never been born.

"In 1924 just a few days after our village celebrated seventeen hurry-up weddings — to make sure that every young man who went 'out on the road' would responsibly come home — your father and his brothers and your grandfather and his brothers and your aunt's new husband sailed for America, the Gold Mountain. It was your grandfather's last trip. Those lucky enough to get contracts waved good-bye from the decks. They fed and guarded the stowaways and helped them off in Cuba, New York, Bali, Hawaii. 'We'll meet in California next year,' they said. All of them sent money home.

"I remember looking at your aunt one day when she and I were dressing; I had not noticed before that she had such a protruding melon of a stomach. But I did not think, 'She's pregnant,' until she began to look like other pregnant women, her shirt pulling and the white tops of her black pants showing. She could not have been pregnant, you see, because her husband had been gone for years. No one said anything. We did not discuss it. In early summer she was ready to have the child, long after the time when it could have been possible.

"The village had also been counting. On the night the baby was to be born the villagers raided our house. Some were crying. Like a great saw, teeth strung with lights, files of people walked zigzag across our land, tearing the rice. Their lanterns doubled in the disturbed black water, which drained away through the broken bunds. As the villagers closed in, we could see that some of them, probably men and women we knew well, wore white masks. The people with long hair hung it over their faces. Women with short hair made it stand up on end. Some had tied white bands around their foreheads, arms, and legs.

"At first they threw mud and rocks at the house. Then they threw eggs and began slaughtering our stock. We could hear the animals scream their deaths — the roosters, the pigs, a last great roar from the ox. Familiar wild heads flared in our night windows; the villagers encircled us. Some of the faces stopped to peer at us, their eyes rushing like searchlights. The hands flattened against the panes, framed heads, and left red prints.

"The villagers broke in the front and the back doors at the same time, even though we had not locked the doors against them. Their knives dripped with the blood of our animals. They smeared blood on the doors and walls. One woman swung a chicken, whose throat she had slit, splattering blood in red arcs about her. We stood together in the middle of our house, in the family hall with the pictures and tables of the ancestors around us, and looked straight ahead.

"At that time the house had only two wings. When the men came back, we would build two more to enclose our courtyard and a third one to begin a second courtyard. The villagers pushed through both wings, even your grandparents' rooms, to find your aunt's, which was also mine until the men returned. From this room a new wing for one of the younger families would grow. They ripped up her clothes and shoes and broke her combs, grinding them underfoot. They tore her work from the loom. They scattered the cooking fire and rolled the new weaving in it. We could hear them in the kitchen breaking our bowls and banging the pots. They overturned the great waist-high earthenware jugs; duck eggs, pickled fruits, vegetables burst out and mixed in acrid torrents. The old woman from the next field swept a broom through the air and loosed the spirits-of-the-broom over our heads. 'Pig.' 'Ghost.' 'Pig,' they sobbed and scolded while they ruined our house.

"When they left, they took sugar and oranges to bless themselves. They   8
cut pieces from the dead animals. Some of them took bowls that were not broken and clothes that were not torn. Afterward we swept up the rice and sewed it back up into sacks. But the smells from the spilled preserves lasted. Your aunt gave birth in the pigsty that night. The next morning when I went up for the water, I found her and the baby plugging up the family well.

"Don't let your father know that I told you. He denies her. Now that you   9
have started to menstruate, what happened to her could happen to you. Don't humiliate us. You wouldn't like to be forgotten as if you had never been born. The villagers are watchful."

Whenever she had to warn us about life, my mother told stories that ran   10
like this one, a story to grow up on. She tested our strength to establish realities. Those in the emigrant generations who could not reassert brute survival died young and far from home. Those of us in the first American generations have had to figure out how the invisible world the emigrants built around our childhoods fit in solid America.

The emigrants confused the gods by diverting their curses, misleading   11
them with crooked streets and false names. They must try to confuse their offspring as well, who, I suppose, threaten them in similar ways — always trying to get things straight, always trying to name the unspeakable. The Chinese I know hide their names; sojourners take new names when their lives change and guard their real names with silence.

Chinese-Americans, when you try to understand what things in you are   12
Chinese, how do you separate what is peculiar to childhood, to poverty, insanities, one family, your mother who marked your growing with stories, from what is Chinese? What is Chinese tradition and what is the movies?

If I want to learn what clothes my aunt wore, whether flashy or ordinary,   13
I would have to begin, "Remember Father's drowned-in-the-well sister?" I cannot ask that. My mother has told me once and for all the useful parts. She will add nothing unless powered by Necessity, a riverbank that guides her life.

She plants vegetable gardens rather than lawns; she carries the odd-shaped tomatoes home from the fields and eats food left for the gods.

Whenever we did frivolous things, we used up energy; we flew high kites. We children came up off the ground over the melting cones our parents brought home from work and the American movie on New Year's Day — *Oh, You Beautiful Doll* with Betty Grable one year, and *She Wore a Yellow Ribbon* with John Wayne another year. After the one carnival ride each, we paid in guilt; our tired father counted his change on the dark walk home.   14

Adultery is extravagance. Could people who hatch their own chicks and eat the embryos and the heads for delicacies and boil the feet in vinegar for party food, leaving only the gravel, eating even the gizzard lining — could such people engender a prodigal aunt? To be a woman, to have a daughter in starvation time was a waste enough. My aunt could not have been the lone romantic who gave up everything for sex. Women in the old China did not choose. Some man had commanded her to lie with him and be his secret evil. I wonder whether he masked himself when he joined the raid on her family.   15

Perhaps she encountered him in the fields or on the mountain where the daughters-in-law collected fuel. Or perhaps he first noticed her in the market-place. He was not a stranger because the village housed no strangers. She had to have dealings with him other than sex. Perhaps he worked an adjoining field, or he sold her the cloth for the dress she sewed and wore. His demand must have surprised, then terrified her. She obeyed him; she always did as she was told.   16

When the family found a young man in the next village to be her husband, she stood tractably beside the best rooster, his proxy, and promised before they met that she would be his forever. She was lucky that he was her age and she would be the first wife, an advantage secure now. The night she first saw him, he had sex with her. Then he left for America. She had almost forgotten what he looked like. When she tried to envision him, she only saw the black and white face in the group photograph the men had had taken before leaving.   17

The other man was not, after all, much different from her husband. They both gave orders: she followed. "If you tell your family, I'll beat you. I'll kill you. Be here again next week." No one talked sex, ever. And she might have separated the rapes from the rest of living if only she did not have to buy her oil from him or gather wood in the same forest. I want her fear to have lasted just as long as rape lasted so that the fear could have been contained. No drawn-out fear. But women at sex hazarded birth and hence lifetimes. The fear did not stop but permeated everywhere. She told the man, "I think I'm pregnant." He organized the raid against her.   18

On nights when my mother and father talked about their life back home, sometimes they mentioned an "outcast table" whose business they still seemed to be settling, their voices tight. In a commensal tradition, where food is pre-   19 cious, the powerful older people made wrongdoers eat alone. Instead of letting them start separate new lives like the Japanese, who could become samurais and geishas, the Chinese family, faces averted but eyes glowering sideways, hung on to the offenders and fed them leftovers. My aunt must have lived in the same house as my parents and eaten at an outcast table. My mother spoke about the raid as if she had seen it, when she and my aunt, a daughter-in-law to a different household, should not have been living together at all. Daughters-in-law lived with their husbands' parents, not their own; a synonym for marriage in Chinese is "taking a daughter-in-law." Her husband's parents could have sold her, mortgaged her, stoned her. But they had sent her back to her own mother and father, a mysterious act hinting at disgraces not told me. Perhaps they had thrown her out to deflect the avengers.

She was the only daughter; her four brothers went with her father, hus- 20 band, and uncles "out on the road" and for some years became western men. When the goods were divided among the family, three of the brothers took land, and the youngest, my father, chose an education. After my grandparents gave their daughter away to her husband's family, they had dispensed all the adventure and all the property. They expected her alone to keep the traditional ways, which her brothers, now among the barbarians, could fumble without detection. The heavy, deep-rooted women were to maintain the past against the flood, safe for returning. But the rare urge west had fixed upon our family, and so my aunt crossed boundaries not delineated in space.

The work of preservation demands that the feelings playing about in one's 21 guts not be turned into action. Just watch their passing like cherry blossoms. But perhaps my aunt, my forerunner, caught in a slow life, let dreams grow and fade and after some months or years went toward what persisted. Fear at the enormities of the forbidden kept her desires delicate, wire and bone. She looked at a man because she liked the way the hair was tucked behind his ears, or she liked the question-mark line of a long torso curving at the shoulder and straight at the hip. For warm eyes or a soft voice or a slow walk — that's all — a few hairs, a line, a brightness, a sound, a pace, she gave up family. She offered us up for a charm that vanished with tiredness, a pigtail that didn't toss when the wind died. Why, the wrong lighting could erase the dearest thing about him.

It could very well have been, however, that my aunt did not take subtle 22 enjoyment of her friend, but, a wild woman, kept rollicking company. Imagining her free with sex doesn't fit, though. I don't know any women like that, or men either. Unless I see her life branching into mine, she gives me no ancestral help.

To sustain her being in love, she often worked at herself in the mirror, 23 guessing at the colors and shapes that would interest him, changing them frequently in order to hit on the right combination. She wanted him to look back.

On a farm near the sea, a woman who tended her appearance reaped a   24
reputation for eccentricity. All the married women blunt-cut their hair in flaps about their ears or pulled it back in tight buns. No nonsense. Neither style blew easily into heart-catching tangles. And at their weddings they displayed themselves in their long hair for the last time. "It brushed the backs of my knees," my mother tells me. "It was braided, and even so, it brushed the backs of my knees."

At the mirror my aunt combed individuality into her bob. A bun could   25
have been contrived to escape into black streamers blowing in the wind or in quiet wisps about her face, but only the older women in our picture album wear buns. She brushed her hair back from her forehead, tucking the flaps behind her ears. She looped a piece of thread, knotted into a circle between her index fingers and thumbs, and ran the double strand across her forehead. When she closed her fingers as if she were making a pair of shadow geese bite, the string twisted together catching the little hairs. Then she pulled the thread away from her skin, ripping the hairs out neatly, her eyes watering from the needles of pain. Opening her fingers, she cleaned the thread, then rolled it along her hairline and the tops of her eyebrows. My mother did the same to me and my sisters and herself. I used to believe that the expression "caught by the short hairs" meant a captive held with a depilatory string. It especially hurt at the temples, but my mother said we were lucky we didn't have to have our feet bound when we were seven. Sisters used to sit on their beds and cry together, she said, as their mothers or their slaves removed the bandages for a few minutes each night and let the blood gush back into their veins. I hope that the man my aunt loved appreciated a smooth brow, that he wasn't just a tits-and-ass man.

Once my aunt found a freckle on her chin, at a spot that the almanac said   26
predestined her for unhappiness. She dug it out with a hot needle and washed the wound with peroxide.

More attention to her looks than these pullings of hairs and pickings at   27
spots would have caused gossip among the villagers. They owned work clothes and good clothes, and they wore good clothes for feasting the new seasons. But since a woman combing her hair hexes beginnings, my aunt rarely found an occasion to look her best. Women looked like great sea snails — the corded wood, babies, and laundry they carried were the whorls on their backs. The Chinese did not admire a bent back; goddesses and warriors stood straight. Still there must have been a marvelous freeing of beauty when a worker laid down her burden and stretched and arched.

Such commonplace loveliness, however, was not enough for my aunt. She 28
dreamed of a lover for the fifteen days of New Year's, the time for families
to exchange visits, money, and food. She plied her secret comb. And sure
enough she cursed the year, the family, the village, and herself.

Even as her hair lured her imminent lover, many other men looked at her. 29
Uncles, cousins, nephews, brothers would have looked, too, had they been
home between journeys. Perhaps they had already been restraining their curiosity, and they left, fearful that their glances, like a field of nesting birds, might
be startled and caught. Poverty hurt, and that was their first reason for leaving.
But another, final reason for leaving the crowded house was the never-said.

She may have been unusually beloved, the precious only daughter, spoiled 30
and mirror gazing because of the affection the family lavished on her. When
her husband left, they welcomed the chance to take her back from the in-
laws; she could live like the little daughter for just a while longer. There are
stories that my grandfather was different from other people, "crazy ever since
the little Jap bayoneted him in the head." He used to put his naked penis on
the dinner table, laughing. And one day he brought home a baby girl, wrapped
up inside his brown western-style greatcoat. He had traded one of his sons,
probably my father, the youngest, for her. My grandmother made him trade
back. When he finally got a daughter of his own, he doted on her. They must
have all loved her, except perhaps my father, the only brother who never went
back to China, having once been traded for a girl.

Brothers and sisters, newly men and women, had to efface their sexual 31
color and present plain miens. Disturbing hair and eyes, a smile like no other,
threatened the ideal of five generations living under one roof. To focus blurs,
people shouted face to face and yelled from room to room. The immigrants
I know have loud voices, unmodulated to American tones even after years
away from the village where they called their friendships out across the
fields. I have not been able to stop my mother's screams in public libraries or over telephones. Walking erect (knees straight, toes pointed forward,
not pigeontoed, which is Chinese-feminine) and speaking in an inaudible
voice, I have tried to turn myself American-feminine. Chinese communication was loud, public. Only sick people had to whisper. But at the dinner
table, where the family members came nearest one another, no one could
talk, not the outcasts nor any eaters. Every word that falls from the mouth
is a coin lost. Silently they gave and accepted food with both hands. A preoccupied child who took his bowl with one hand got a sideways glare. A
complete moment of total attention is due everyone alike. Children and
lovers have no singularity here, but my aunt used a secret voice, a separate
attentiveness.

She kept the man's name to herself throughout her labor and dying; she   32
did not accuse him that he be punished with her. To save her inseminator's
name she gave silent birth.

He may have been somebody in her own household, but intercourse with   33
a man outside the family would have been no less abhorrent. All the village
were kinsmen, and the titles shouted in loud country voices never let kinship
be forgotten. Any man within visiting distance would have been neutralized
as a lover — "brother," "younger brother," "older brother" — one hundred
and fifteen relationship titles. Parents researched birth charts probably not so
much to assure good fortune as to circumvent incest in a population that has
but one hundred surnames. Everybody has eight million relatives. How useless
then sexual mannerisms, how dangerous.

As if it came from an atavism deeper than fear, I used to add "brother"   34
silently to boys' names. It hexed the boys, who would or would not ask me to
dance, and made them less scary and as familiar and deserving of benevolence
as girls.

But, of course, I hexed myself also — no dates. I should have stood up,   35
both arms waving, and shouted out across libraries, "Hey, you! Love me back."
I had no idea, though, how to make attraction selective, how to control its
direction and magnitude. If I made myself American-pretty so that the five
or six Chinese boys in the class fell in love with me, everyone else — the
Caucasian, Negro, and Japanese boys — would too. Sisterliness, dignified and
honorable, made much more sense.

Attraction eludes control so stubbornly that whole societies designed to   36
organize relationships among people cannot keep order, not even when they
bind people to one another from childhood and raise them together. Among
the very poor and the wealthy, brothers married their adopted sisters, like
doves. Our family allowed some romance, paying adult brides' prices and providing dowries so that their sons and daughters could marry strangers. Marriage promises to turn strangers into friendly relatives — a nation of siblings.

In the village structure, spirits shimmered among the live creatures, bal-   37
anced and held in equilibrium by time and land. But one human being flaring
up into violence could open up a black hole, a maelstrom that pulled in the
sky. The frightened villagers, who depended on one another to maintain the
real, went to my aunt to show her a personal, physical representation of
the break she made in the "roundness." Misallying couples snapped off the
future, which was to be embodied in true offspring. The villagers punished her
for acting as if she could have a private life, secret and apart from them.

If my aunt had betrayed the family at a time of large grain yields and peace,   38
when many boys were born, and wings were being built on many houses, per-

haps she might have escaped such severe punishment. But the men — hungry, greedy, tired of planting in dry soil, cuckolded — had been forced to leave the village in order to send food-money home. There were ghost plagues, bandit plagues, wars with the Japanese, floods. My Chinese brother and sister had died of an unknown sickness. Adultery, perhaps only a mistake during good times, became a crime when the village needed food.

The round moon cakes and round doorways, the round tables of grad- 39 uated size that fit one roundness inside another, round windows and rice bowls — these talismans had lost their power to warn this family of the law: A family must be whole, faithfully keeping the descent line by having sons to feed the old and the dead who in turn look after the family. The villagers came to show my aunt and lover-in-hiding a broken house. The villagers were speeding up the circling of events because she was too shortsighted to see that her infidelity had already harmed the village, that waves of consequences would return unpredictably, sometimes in disguise, as now, to hurt her. This roundness had to be made coin-sized so that she would see its circumference: punish her at the birth of her baby. Awaken her to the inexorable. People who refused fatalism because they could invent small resources insisted on culpa-bility. Deny accidents and wrest fault from the stars.

After the villagers left, their lanterns now scattering in various directions 40 toward home, the family broke their silence and cursed her. "Aiaa, we're going to die. Death is coming. Death is coming. Look what you've done. You've killed us. Ghost! Dead Ghost! Ghost! You've never been born." She ran out into the fields, far enough from the house so that she could no longer hear their voices, and pressed herself against the earth, her own land no more. When she felt the birth coming, she thought that she had been hurt. Her body seized together. "They've hurt me too much," she thought. "This is gall, and it will kill me." With forehead and knees against the earth, her body convulsed and then relaxed. She turned on her back, lay on the ground. The black well of sky and stars went out and out and out forever; her body and her complexity seemed to disappear. She was one of the stars, a bright dot in blackness, with-out home, without a companion, in eternal cold and silence. An agoraphobia rose in her, speeding higher and higher, bigger and bigger; she would not be able to contain it; there would be no end to fear.

Flayed, unprotected against space, she felt pain return, focusing her body. 41 This pain chilled her — a cold, steady kind of surface pain. Inside, spasmodi-cally, the other pain, the pain of the child, heated her. For hours she lay on the ground, alternately body and space. Sometimes a vision of normal com-fort obliterated reality: She saw the family in the evening gambling at the dinner table, the young people massaging their elders' backs. She saw them congratulating one another, high joy on the mornings the rice shoots came up. When these pictures burst, the stars drew out further apart. Black space opened.

She got to her feet to fight better and remembered that old-fashioned   42
women gave birth in their pigsties to fool the jealous, pain-dealing gods, who do not snatch piglets. Before the next spasms could stop her, she ran to the pigsty, each step a rushing out into emptiness. She climbed over the fence and knelt in the dirt. It was good to have a fence enclosing her, a tribal person alone.

Laboring, this woman who had carried her child as a foreign growth that   43
sickened her every day, expelled it at last. She reached down to touch the hot, wet, moving mass, surely smaller than anything human, and could feel that it was human after all — fingers, toes, nails, nose. She pulled it up on to her belly, and it lay curled there, butt in the air, feet precisely tucked one under the other. She opened her loose shirt and buttoned the child inside. After resting, it squirmed and thrashed and she pushed it up to her breast. It turned its head this way and that until it found her nipple. There, it made little snuffling noises. She clenched her teeth at its preciousness, lovely as a young calf, a piglet, a little dog.

She may have gone to the pigsty as a last act of responsibility: She would   44
protect this child as she had protected its father. It would look after her soul, leaving supplies on her grave. But how would this tiny child without family find her grave when there would be no marker for her anywhere, neither in the earth nor the family hall? No one would give her a family hall name. She had taken the child with her into the wastes. At its birth the two of them had felt the same raw pain of separation, a wound that only the family pressing tight could close. A child with no descent line would not soften her life but only trail after her, ghostlike, begging her to give it purpose. At dawn the villagers on their way to the fields would stand around the fence and look.

Full of milk, the little ghost slept. When it awoke, she hardened her   45
breasts against the milk that crying loosens. Toward morning she picked up the baby and walked to the well.

Carrying the baby to the well shows loving. Otherwise abandon it. Turn   46
its face into the mud. Mothers who love their children take them along. It was probably a girl; there is some hope of forgiveness for boys.

"Don't tell anyone you had an aunt. Your father does not want to hear her   47
name. She has never been born." I have believed that sex was unspeakable and words so strong and fathers so frail that "aunt" would do my father mysterious harm. I have thought that my family, having settled among immigrants who had also been their neighbors in the ancestral land, needed to clean their name, and a wrong word would incite the kinspeople even here. But there is

more to this silence: They want me to participate in her punishment. And I have.

In the twenty years since I heard this story I have not asked for details nor 48 said my aunt's name; I do not know it. People who comfort the dead can also chase after them to hurt them further — a reverse ancestor worship. The real punishment was not the raid swiftly inflicted by the villagers, but the family's deliberately forgetting her. Her betrayal so maddened them, they saw to it that she would suffer forever, even after death. Always hungry, always needing, she would have to beg food from other ghosts, snatch and steal it from those whose living descendants give them gifts. She would have to fight the ghosts massed at crossroads for the buns a few thoughtful citizens leave to decoy her away from village and home so that the ancestral spirits could feast unharassed. At peace, they could act like gods, not ghosts, their descent lines providing them with paper suits and dresses, spirit money, paper houses, paper automobiles, chicken, meat, and rice into eternity — essences delivered up in smoke and flames, steam and incense rising from each rice bowl. In an attempt to make the Chinese care for people outside the family, Chairman Mao encourages us now to give our paper replicas to the spirits of outstanding soldiers and workers, no matter whose ancestors they may be. My aunt remains forever hungry. Goods are not distributed evenly among the dead.

My aunt haunts me — her ghost drawn to me because now, after fifty 49 years of neglect, I alone devote pages of paper to her, though not origamied into houses and clothes. I do not think she always means me well. I am telling on her, and she was a spite suicide, drowning herself in the drinking water. The Chinese are always very frightened of the drowned one, whose weeping ghost, wet hair hanging and skin bloated, waits silently by the water to pull down a substitute.

For a reading quiz, visit **bedfordstmartins.com/thebedfordreader**.

Journal Writing

Most of us have heard family stories that left lasting impressions — ghost stories like Kingston's, biographies of ancestors, explanations for traditions, family superstitions, and so on. Write in your journal about a family story you remember vividly from your childhood. (To take your journal writing further, see "From Journal to Essay" on page 525.)

Questions on Meaning

1. What PURPOSE does Kingston have in telling her aunt's story? How does this differ from her mother's purpose in relating the tale?
2. According to Kingston, who could have been the father of her aunt's child? Who could not?
3. Kingston says that her mother told stories "to warn us about life" (par. 10). What warning does this story provide?
4. Why is Kingston so fascinated by her aunt's life and death?

Questions on Writing Strategy

1. Whom does Kingston seem to include in her AUDIENCE: her family and other older Chinese? second-generation Chinese Americans like herself? other Americans? How might she expect each of these groups to respond to her essay?
2. Why is Kingston's opening line — her mother's "You must not tell anyone" — especially fitting for this essay? What secrets are being told? Why does Kingston divulge them?
3. As Kingston tells her tale of her aunt, some events are based on her mother's story or her knowledge of Chinese customs, while others are wholly imaginary. What is the EFFECT of blending these several threads of reality, perception, and imagination?
4. **MIXED METHODS**   Examine the details in the two contrasting NARRATIVES of how Kingston's aunt became pregnant: one in paragraphs 15–18 and the other in paragraphs 21–28. How do the details create different realities? Which version does Kingston seem more committed to? Why?
5. **MIXED METHODS**   Kingston COMPARES AND CONTRASTS various versions of her aunt's story, trying to find the CAUSES that led her aunt to drown in the well. In the end, what causes does Kingston seem to accept?

Questions on Language

1. How does Kingston's language — lyrical, poetic, full of FIGURES OF SPEECH and other IMAGES — reveal her relationship to her Chinese heritage? Find phrases that are especially striking.
2. Look up any of these words you do not know: bunds (par. 4); acrid (7); frivolous (14); tractably, proxy (17); hazarded (18); commensal (19); delineated (20); depilatory (25); plied (28); miens (31); abhorrent, circumvent (33); atavism (34); maelstrom (37); talismans, inexorable, fatalism, culpability (39); gall, agoraphobia (40); spasmodically (41).
3. Sometimes Kingston indicates that she is reconstructing or imagining events through verbs like "would have" and words like "maybe" and "perhaps" ("Perhaps she encountered him in the fields," par. 16). Other times she presents obviously imaginary events as if they actually happened ("Once my aunt found a freckle on her chin," 26). What effect does Kingston achieve with these apparent inconsistencies?

Suggestions for Writing

1. **FROM JOURNAL TO ESSAY**   Develop the family story from your journal into a narrative essay. Build in the context of the story as well: Who told it to you? What purpose did he or she have in telling it to you? How does it illustrate your family's beliefs and values?

2. Write an essay explaining the role of ancestors in Chinese family and religious life, supplementing what Kingston says with research in the library or on the Web or (if you are Chinese American) drawing on your own experiences.

3. **CRITICAL WRITING**   ANALYZE the ideas about gender roles revealed in "No Name Woman," both in China and in the Chinese American culture Kingston grew up in. How have these ideas affected Kingston? Do you perceive any semblance of them in contemporary American culture?

4. **CONNECTIONS**   Both Maxine Hong Kingston and Brad Manning, in "Arm Wrestling with My Father" (p. 138), examine communication within their families. Relate an incident or incidents from your own childhood that portray something about communication within your family. You might want to focus on the language of communication, such as the words used to discuss (or not discuss) a taboo topic, the special family meanings for familiar words, a misunderstanding between you and an adult about something the adult said. Use dialog and as much CONCRETE detail as you can to clarify your experience and its significance.

5. **CONNECTIONS**   Like Kingston, several other authors in this book write about relationships between immigrant parents and their American-raised children. These include Amy Tan in "Fish Cheeks" (p. 110), Junot Díaz in "The Dreamer" (p. 120), Kellie Young in "The Undercurrent" (p. 178), Andrea Roman in "We're Not . . ." (p. 226), Firoozeh Dumas in "Sweet, Sour, and Resentful" (p. 252), and Christine Leong in "Being a Chink" (p. 418). Select two or three of these essays and read or re-read them. Then, in an essay of your own, analyze what your chosen set of authors suggest about the experiences of the children of immigrants to the United States. Do any expectations, supports, or conflicts strike you as common, even universal? How do your own experiences with your parents (or grandparents) compare? Do particular cultures seem to influence family relationships in particular ways? Why do you think so?

Maxine Hong Kingston on Writing

In an interview with Jean W. Ross published in *Contemporary Authors* in 1984, Maxine Hong Kingston discusses the writing and revising of *The Woman Warrior*. Ross asks Kingston to clarify an earlier statement that she had "no idea how people who don't write endure their lives." Kingston replies: "When I said that, I was thinking about how words and stories create order. Some of the things that happen to us in life seem to have no meaning, but when you write them down you find the meanings for them; or, as you translate life into words, you force a meaning. Meaning is intrinsic in words and stories."

Ross then asks if Kingston used an outline and planned to blend fact with legend in *The Woman Warrior*. "Oh no, no," Kingston answers. "What I have at the beginning of a book is not an outline. I have no idea of how stories will end or where the beginning will lead. Sometimes I draw pictures. I draw a blob and then I have a little arrow and it goes to this other blob, if you want to call that an outline. It's hardly even words; it's like a doodle. Then when it turns into words, I find the words lead me to various scenes and stories which I don't know about until I get there. I don't see the order until very late in the writing and sometimes the ending just comes. I just run up against it. All of a sudden the book's over and I didn't know it would be over."

A question from Ross about whether her emotions enter her writing leads Kingston to talk about revision. "Well, when I first set something down I feel the emotions I write about. But when I do a second draft, third draft, ninth draft, then I don't feel very emotional. The rewriting is very intellectual; all my education and reading and intellect are involved. The mechanics of sentences, how one phrase or word goes with another one — all that happens in later drafts. There's a very emotional first draft and a very technical last draft."

For Discussion

1. Do you agree with Kingston that when you write things down you find their meaning? Give examples of when the writing process has or hasn't clarified an experience for you.

2. Kingston doodles as a way to discover her material. How do you discover what you have to say?

3. What does Kingston mean by "[t]he mechanics of sentences"? Do you consider this element as you revise?

GEORGE ORWELL

George Orwell was the pen name of Eric Blair (1903–50), born in Bengal, India, the son of an English civil servant. After attending Eton on a scholarship, he joined the British police in Burma, where he acquired a distrust for the methods of the empire. Then followed years of tramping, odd jobs, and near-starvation — recalled in *Down and Out in Paris and London* (1933). Severely wounded while fighting in the Spanish civil war, he wrote a memoir, *Homage to Catalonia* (1938), voicing disillusionment with Loyalists who, he claimed, sought not to free Spain but to exterminate their political enemies. A socialist by conviction, Orwell kept pointing to the dangers of a collective state run by totalitarians. In *Animal Farm* (1945), he satirized Soviet bureaucracy; and in his famous novel *Nineteen Eighty-Four* (1949), he foresaw a regimented England whose government perverts truth and spies on citizens. (The motto of the state and its leader: Big Brother Is Watching You.) The late journalist Christopher Hitchens captured why so many hold Orwell in high esteem: "By declining to lie, even as far as possible to himself, and by his determination to seek elusive but verifiable truth, he showed how much can be accomplished by an individual who unites the qualities of intellectual honesty and moral courage." The *Times* of London placed Orwell at number two on a list of the greatest British writers of the twentieth century.

Shooting an Elephant

Orwell wrote compellingly of his five years as a police officer in Burma, a southeast Asian country (now known as Myanmar) that the British began colonizing in the early 1800s and ruled until 1947. In this selection from *Shooting an Elephant and Other Essays* (1950), Orwell combines personal experience and piercing insight to expose both an oppressive government and himself as the government's hireling.

"Shooting an Elephant" is foremost a narrative, but Orwell uses description, example, and cause and effect as well to develop and give significance to his tale.

Narration (Chap. 4): throughout
Description (Chap. 5): paragraphs 2, 4–12
Example (Chap. 6): paragraphs 1–2, 4, 14
Cause and effect (Chap. 11): paragraphs 1–2, 6–7

In Moulmein, in Lower Burma, I was hated by large numbers of people — the only time in my life that I have been important enough for this to happen to me. I was subdivisional police officer of the town, and in an aimless, petty kind of way anti-European feeling was very bitter. No one had the guts to raise a riot, but if a European woman went through the bazaars alone somebody would probably spit betel juice over her dress. As a police officer I was an obvious target and was baited whenever it seemed safe to do so. When a nimble Burman tripped me up on the football field and the referee (another Burman) looked the other way, the crowd yelled with hideous laughter. This happened more than once. In the end the sneering yellow faces of young men that met me everywhere, the insults hooted after me when I was at a safe distance, got badly on my nerves. The young Buddhist priests were the worst of all. There were several thousands of them in the town and none of them seemed to have anything to do except stand on street corners and jeer at Europeans.

All this was perplexing and upsetting. For at that time I had already made up my mind that imperialism was an evil thing and the sooner I chucked up my job and got out of it the better. Theoretically — and secretly, of course — I was all for the Burmese and all against the oppressors, the British. As for the job I was doing, I hated it more bitterly than I can perhaps make clear. In a job like that you see the dirty work of Empire at close quarters. The wretched prisoners huddling in the stinking cages of the lockups, the grey, cowed faces of the long-term convicts, the scarred buttocks of the men who had been flogged with bamboos — all these oppressed me with an intolerable sense of guilt. But I could get nothing into perspective. I was young and ill-educated and I had had to think out my problems in the utter silence that is imposed on every Englishman in the East. I did not even know that the British Empire is dying, still less did I know that it is a great deal better than the younger empires that are going to supplant it. All I knew was that I was stuck between my hatred of the empire I served and my rage against the evil-spirited little beasts who tried to make my job impossible. With one part of my mind I thought of the British Raj[1] as an unbreakable tyranny, as something clamped down, in *saecula saeculorum,*[2] upon the will of prostrate peoples; with another part I thought that the greatest joy in the world would be to drive a bayonet into a Buddhist priest's guts. Feelings like these are the normal by-products of imperialism; ask any Anglo-Indian official, if you can catch him off duty.

One day something happened which in a roundabout way was enlightening. It was a tiny incident in itself, but it gave me a better glimpse than I had had before of the real nature of imperialism — the real motives for which despotic governments act. Early one morning the subinspector at a police station the other end of town rang me up on the phone and said that an elephant was ravaging the bazaar. Would I please come and do something about it? I

---

[1] British imperial government. *Raj* in Hindi means "reign," a word similar to *rajah,* "ruler." — Eds.

[2] Latin, "world without end." — Eds.

did not know what I could do, but I wanted to see what was happening and I got on to a pony and started out. I took my rifle, an old .44 Winchester and much too small to kill an elephant, but I thought the noise might be useful *in terrorem*.[3] Various Burmans stopped me on the way and told me about the elephant's doings. It was not, of course, a wild elephant, but a tame one which had gone "must." It had been chained up, as tame elephants always are when their attack of "must" is due, but on the previous night it had broken its chain and escaped. Its mahout,[4] the only person who could manage it when it was in that state, had set out in pursuit, but had taken the wrong direction and was now twelve hours' journey away, and in the morning the elephant had suddenly reappeared in the town. The Burmese population had no weapons and were quite helpless against it. It had already destroyed somebody's bamboo hut, killed a cow and raided some fruit stalls and devoured the stock; also it had met the municipal rubbish van and, when the driver jumped out and took to his heels, had turned the van over and inflicted violences upon it.

The Burmese subinspector and some Indian constables were waiting for me in the quarter where the elephant had been seen. It was a very poor quarter, a labyrinth of squalid bamboo huts, thatched with palmleaf, winding all over a steep hillside. I remember that it was a cloudy, stuffy morning at the beginning of the rains. We began questioning the people as to where the elephant had gone and, as usual, failed to get any definite information. That is invariably the case in the East; a story always sounds clear enough at a distance, but the nearer you get to the scene of events the vaguer it becomes. Some of the people said that the elephant had gone in one direction, some said that he had gone in another, some professed not even to have heard of any elephant. I had almost made up my mind that the whole story was a pack of lies, when we heard yells a little distance away. There was a loud, scandalized cry of "Go away, child! Go away this instant!" and an old woman with a switch in her hand came round the corner of a hut, violently shooing away a crowd of naked children. Some more women followed, clicking their tongues and exclaiming; evidently there was something that the children ought not to have seen. I rounded the hut and saw a man's dead body sprawling in the mud. He was an Indian, a black Dravidian coolie, almost naked, and he could not have been dead many minutes. The people said that the elephant had come suddenly upon him round the corner of the hut, caught him with its trunk, put its foot on his back and ground him into the earth. This was the rainy season and the ground was soft, and his face had scored a trench a foot deep and a couple of yards long. He was lying on his belly with arms crucified and

---

[3] Latin, "to give warning." — Eds.
[4] Keeper or groom, a servant of the elephant's owner. — Eds.

head sharply twisted to one side. His face was coated with mud, the eyes wide open, the teeth bared and grinning with an expression of unendurable agony. (Never tell me, by the way, that the dead look peaceful. Most of the corpses I have seen looked devilish.) The friction of the great beast's foot had stripped the skin from his back as neatly as one skins a rabbit. As soon as I saw the dead man I sent an orderly to a friend's house nearby to borrow an elephant rifle. I had already sent back the pony, not wanting it to go mad with fright and throw me if it smelled the elephant.

The orderly came back in a few minutes with a rifle and five cartridges,   5 and meanwhile some Burmans had arrived and told us that the elephant was in the paddy fields below, only a few hundred yards away. As I started forward practically the whole population of the quarter flocked out of the houses and followed me. They had seen the rifle and were all shouting excitedly that I was going to shoot the elephant. They had not shown much interest in the elephant when he was merely ravaging their homes, but it was different now that he was going to be shot. It was a bit of fun to them, as it would be to an English crowd; besides they wanted the meat. It made me vaguely uneasy. I had no intention of shooting the elephant — I had merely sent for the rifle to defend myself if necessary — and it is always unnerving to have a crowd following you. I marched down the hill, looking and feeling a fool, with the rifle over my shoulder and an ever-growing army of people jostling at my heels. At the bottom, when you got away from the huts, there was a metalled road and beyond that a miry waste of paddy fields a thousand yards across, not yet ploughed but soggy from the first rains and dotted with coarse grass. The elephant was standing eight yards from the road, his left side towards us. He took not the slightest notice of the crowd's approach. He was tearing up bunches of grass, beating them against his knees to clean them and stuffing them into his mouth.

I had halted on the road. As soon as I saw the elephant I knew with per-   6 fect certainty that I ought not to shoot him. It is a serious matter to shoot a working elephant — it is comparable to destroying a huge and costly piece of machinery — and obviously one ought not to do it if it can possibly be avoided. And at that distance, peacefully eating, the elephant looked no more dangerous than a cow. I thought then and I think now that his attack of "must" was already passing off; in which case he would merely wander harmlessly about until the mahout came back and caught him. Moreover, I did not in the least want to shoot him. I decided that I would watch him for a little while to make sure that he did not turn savage again, and then go home.

But at that moment, I glanced round at the crowd that had followed me. It   7 was an immense crowd, two thousand at the least and growing every minute.

It blocked the road for a long distance on either side. I looked at the sea of yellow faces above the garish clothes — faces all happy and excited over this bit of fun, all certain that the elephant was going to be shot. They were watching me as they would watch a conjuror about to perform a trick. They did not like me, but with the magical rifle in my hands I was momentarily worth watching. And suddenly I realized that I should have to shoot the elephant after all. The people expected it of me and I had got to do it; I could feel their two thousand wills pressing me forward, irresistibly. And it was at this moment, as I stood there with the rifle in my hands, that I first grasped the hollowness, the futility of the white man's dominion in the East. Here was I, the white man with his gun, standing in front of the unarmed native crowd — seemingly the leading actor of the piece; but in reality I was only an absurd puppet pushed to and fro by the will of those yellow faces behind. I perceived in this moment that when the white man turns tyrant it is his own freedom that he destroys. He becomes a sort of hollow, posing dummy, the conventionalized figure of a sahib. For it is the condition of his rule that he shall spend his life in trying to impress the "natives," and so in every crisis he has got to do what the "natives" expect of him. He wears a mask, and his face grows to fit it. I had got to shoot the elephant. I had committed myself to doing it when I sent for the rifle. A sahib has got to act like a sahib; he has got to appear resolute, to know his own mind and do definite things. To come all that way, rifle in hand, with two thousand people marching at my heels, and then to trail feebly away, having done nothing — no, that was impossible. The crowd would laugh at me. And my whole life, every white man's life in the East, was one long struggle not to be laughed at.

But I did not want to shoot the elephant. I watched him beating his 8 bunch of grass against his knees, with that preoccupied grandmotherly air that elephants have. It seemed to me that it would be murder to shoot him. At that age I was not squeamish about killing animals, but I had never shot an elephant and never wanted to. (Somehow it always seems worse to kill a *large* animal.) Besides, there was the beast's owner to be considered. Alive, the elephant was worth at least a hundred pounds; dead, he would only be worth the value of his tusks, five pounds, possibly. But I had got to act quickly. I turned to some experienced-looking Burmans who had been there when we arrived, and asked them how the elephant had been behaving. They all said the same thing: He took no notice of you if you left him alone, but he might charge if you went too close to him.

It was perfectly clear to me what I ought to do. I ought to walk up to 9 within, say, twenty-five yards of the elephant and test his behavior. If he charged, I could shoot; if he took no notice of me, it would be safe to leave him until the mahout came back. But also I knew that I was going to do no such thing. I was a poor shot with a rifle and the ground was soft mud into which one would sink at every step. If the elephant charged and I missed him, I should have about as much chance as a toad under a steamroller. But even then I was not thinking particularly of my own skin, only of the watchful yellow faces behind. For at that moment, with the crowd watching me, I was not afraid in the ordinary sense, as I would have been if I had been alone. A white man mustn't be frightened in front of "natives"; and so, in general, he isn't frightened. The sole thought in my mind was that if anything went wrong those two thousand Burmans would see me pursued, caught, trampled on, and reduced to a grinning corpse like that Indian up the hill. And if that happened it was quite probable that some of them would laugh. That would never do. There was only one alternative. I shoved the cartridges into the magazine and lay down on the road to get a better aim.

The crowd grew very still, and a deep, low, happy sigh, as of people who 10
see the theater curtain go up at last, breathed from innumerable throats. They were going to have their bit of fun after all. The rifle was a beautiful German thing with cross-hair sights. I did not then know that in shooting an elephant one would shoot to cut an imaginary bar running from ear-hole to ear-hole. I ought, therefore, as the elephant was sideways on, to have aimed straight at his ear-hole; actually I aimed several inches in front of this, thinking the brain would be further forward.

When I pulled the trigger I did not hear the bang or feel the kick — one 11
never does when a shot goes home — but I heard the devilish roar of glee that went up from the crowd. In that instant, in too short a time, one would have thought, even for the bullet to get there, a mysterious, terrible change had come over the elephant. He neither stirred nor fell, but every line of his body had altered. He looked suddenly stricken, shrunken, immensely old, as though the frightful impact of the bullet had paralyzed him without knocking him down. At last, after what seemed a long time — it might have been five seconds, I dare say — he sagged flabbily to his knees. His mouth slobbered. An enormous senility seemed to have settled upon him. One could have imagined him thousands of years old. I fired again into the same spot. At the second shot he did not collapse but climbed with desperate slowness to his feet and stood weakly upright, with legs sagging and head drooping. I fired a third time. That was the shot that did for him. You could see the agony of it jolt his whole body and knock the last remnant of strength from his legs. But in falling he seemed for a moment to rise, for as his hind legs collapsed beneath him he seemed to tower upward like a huge rock toppling, his trunk reaching skywards like a tree. He trumpeted, for the first and only time. And then down

he came, his belly towards me, with a crash that seemed to shake the ground even where I lay.

I got up. The Burmans were already racing past me across the mud. It was obvious that the elephant would never rise again, but he was not dead. He was breathing very rhythmically with long rattling gasps, his great mound of a side painfully rising and falling. His mouth was wide open. I could see far down into caverns of pale pink throat. I waited a long time for him to die, but his breathing did not weaken. Finally I fired my two remaining shots into the spot where I thought his heart must be. The thick blood welled out of him like red velvet, but still he did not die. His body did not even jerk when the shots hit him, the tortured breathing continued without a pause. He was dying, very slowly and in great agony, but in some world remote from me where not even a bullet could damage him further. I felt I had got to put an end to that dreadful noise. It seemed dreadful to see the great beast lying there, powerless to move and yet powerless to die, and not even to be able to finish him. I sent back for my small rifle and poured shot after shot into his heart and down his throat. They seemed to make no impression. The tortured gasps continued as steadily as the ticking of a clock.

In the end I could not stand it any longer and went away. I heard later that it took him half an hour to die. Burmans were bringing dahs and baskets even before I left, and I was told they had stripped his body almost to the bones by the afternoon.

Afterwards, of course, there were endless discussions about the shooting of the elephant. The owner was furious, but he was only an Indian and could do nothing. Besides, legally I had done the right thing, for a mad elephant has to be killed, like a mad dog, if its owner fails to control it. Among the Europeans opinion was divided. The older men said I was right, the younger men said it was a damn shame to shoot an elephant for killing a coolie, because the elephant was worth more than any damn Coringhee coolie. And afterwards I was very glad that the coolie had been killed; it put me legally in the right and it gave me sufficient pretext for shooting the elephant. I often wondered whether any of the others grasped that I had done it solely to avoid looking a fool.

12

13

14

For a reading quiz, visit **bedfordstmartins.com/thebedfordreader**.

Journal Writing

How do you respond to Orwell's decision to shoot the elephant even though he believed it unnecessary to do so? Do you have any sympathy for his action? Recall a time when you acted against your better judgment in order to save face in front of others. Write as honestly as you can about what motivated you and what mistakes you made. (To take your journal writing further, see "From Journal to Essay" below.)

Questions on Meaning

1. How would you answer the exasperated student who, after reading this essay, exploded, "Why didn't Orwell just leave his gun at home?"
2. Why did Orwell shoot the elephant?
3. Describe the epiphany that Orwell experiences in the course of the event he writes about. (An *epiphany* is a sudden realization of a truth.)
4. In the last paragraph of his essay, Orwell says he was "glad that the coolie had been killed." How do you account for this remark?
5. What is the PURPOSE of this essay?

Questions on Writing Strategy

1. In addition to serving as an INTRODUCTION to Orwell's essay, what function is performed by paragraphs 1 and 2?
2. From what circumstances does the IRONY of Orwell's essay spring?
3. What does "Shooting an Elephant" gain from having been written years after the events it recounts?
4. **MIXED METHODS**   What does the blend of NARRATION and DESCRIPTION in paragraphs 11–12 contribute to the story? How does it further Orwell's purpose?
5. **MIXED METHODS**   How do the EXAMPLES in paragraphs 1 and 2 illustrate Orwell's conflict about his work as a police officer in Burma?

Questions on Language

1. What do you understand by Orwell's statement that the elephant had "gone 'must'" (par. 3)? Look up *must* or its variant *musth* in your dictionary.
2. What examples of English (as opposed to American) usage do you find in Orwell's essay?
3. Define, if necessary, bazaars, betel (par. 1); intolerable, supplant, prostrate (2); despotic (3); labyrinth, squalid, invariably (4); dominion, sahib (7); magazine (9); innumerable (10); senility (11).

Suggestions for Writing

1. **FROM JOURNAL TO ESSAY**   Write a narrative essay that expands on your journal entry. Tell the story of your action, and consider what the results were, what you might have done differently, and what you learned from the experience.

2. With what examples of governmental face-saving are you familiar? If none leaps to mind, read a newspaper or watch the news on television to catch public officials in the act of covering themselves. (Not only national government but also local or student government may provide examples.) In an essay, ANALYZE two or three examples: What do you think was really going on that needed covering? Did the officials succeed in saving face, or did their efforts fail? Were the efforts harmful in any way?

3. **CRITICAL WRITING**   Orwell is honest with himself and his readers in acknowledging his mistakes as a government official. Write an essay that examines the degree to which confession may, or may not, erase blameworthiness for misdeeds. Does Orwell remain just as guilty as he would have been if he had not taken responsibility for his actions? Why, or why not? Feel free to supplement your analysis of Orwell's case with examples from your own life or from the news.

4. **CONNECTIONS**   Read William Lutz's "The World of Doublespeak" (p. 337), which classifies language that deliberately conceals or misleads. In an essay, examine which of Lutz's categories of doublespeak seem to arise from the motives Orwell describes in paragraph 7: the need "to impress," to do what is expected of one, "to appear resolute," "not to be laughed at." Use specific examples from Lutz's essay — or from your own experience — to support your ideas.

5. **CONNECTIONS**   Like "Shooting an Elephant," Maya Angelou's "Champion of the World" (p. 104) also blends narration and description. COMPARE AND CONTRAST the two essays, not on their purposes, which are vastly different, but on this blending. What senses do the authors rely on? How do they keep their narratives moving? How much of themselves do they inject into their essays?

George Orwell on Writing

George Orwell explains the motives for his own writing in the essay "Why I Write" (1946), from which we reprint the following excerpts.

What I have most wanted to do throughout the past ten years is to make political writing into an art. My starting point is always a feeling of partisanship, a sense of injustice. When I sit down to write a book, I do not say to myself, "I am going to produce a work of art." I write it because there is some lie that I want to expose, some fact to which I want to draw attention, and my initial concern is to get a hearing. But I could not do the work of writing a book, or even a long magazine article, if it were not also an esthetic experience. Anyone who cares to examine my work will see that even when it is downright propaganda it contains much that a full-time politician would consider irrelevant. I am not able, and I do not want, completely to abandon the worldview that I acquired in childhood. So long as I remain alive and well

I shall continue to feel strongly about prose style, to love the surface of the earth, and to take a pleasure in solid objects and scraps of useless information. It is no use trying to suppress that side of myself. The job is to reconcile my ingrained likes and dislikes with the essentially public, nonindividual activities that this age forces on all of us.

It is not easy. It raises problems of construction and of language, and it raises in a new way the problem of truthfulness. Let me give just one example of the cruder kind of difficulty that arises. My book about the Spanish civil war, *Homage to Catalonia,* is, of course, a frankly political book, but in the main it is written with a certain detachment and regard for form. I did try very hard in it to tell the whole truth without violating my literary instincts. But among other things it contains a long chapter, full of newspaper quotations and the like, defending the Trotskyists who were accused of plotting with Franco. Clearly such a chapter, which after a year or two would lose its interest for any ordinary reader, must ruin the book. A critic whom I respect read me a lecture about it. "Why did you put in all that stuff?" he said. "You've turned what might have been a good book into journalism." What he said was true, but I could not have done otherwise. I happened to know, what very few people in England had been allowed to know, that innocent men were being falsely accused. If I had not been angry about that I should never have written the book.

In one form or another this problem comes up again. The problem of language is subtler and would take too long to discuss. I will only say that of late years I have tried to write less picturesquely and more exactly. In any case I find that by the time you have perfected any style of writing, you have always outgrown it. *Animal Farm* was the first book in which I tried, with full consciousness of what I was doing, to fuse political purpose and artistic purpose into the whole. . . .

Looking back through the last page or two, I see that I have made it appear as though my motives in writing were wholly public-spirited. I don't want to leave that as the final impression. All writers are vain, selfish, and lazy, and at the very bottom of their motives there lies a mystery. Writing a book is a horrible, exhausting struggle, like a long bout of some painful illness. One would never undertake such a thing if one were not driven on by some demon whom one can neither resist nor understand. For all one knows that demon is simply the same instinct that makes a baby squall for attention. And yet it is also true that one can write nothing readable unless one constantly struggles to efface one's own personality. Good prose is like a windowpane. I cannot say with certainty which of my motives are the strongest, but I know which of them deserve to be followed. And looking back through my work, I see that it is invariably where I lacked a *political* purpose that I wrote lifeless books and was betrayed into purple passages, sentences without meaning, decorative adjectives, and humbug generally.

For Discussion

1. What does Orwell mean by his "political purpose" in writing? by his "artistic purpose"? How did he sometimes find it hard to fulfill both purposes?
2. Think about Orwell's remark that "one can write nothing readable unless one constantly struggles to efface one's own personality." From your own experience, have you found any truth in this observation, or any reason to think otherwise?

E. B. WHITE

For half a century Elwyn Brooks White (1899–1985) was a regular contributor to *The New Yorker,* and his essays, editorials, anonymous features for "The Talk of the Town," and fillers helped build the magazine a reputation for wit and good writing. If as a child you read *Charlotte's Web* (1952), you have met E. B. White before. The book reflects some of his own life on a farm in North Brooklin, Maine. White wrote other children's books, including *Stuart Little* (1945), and in 1970 he received the Laura Ingalls Wilder Award for his "substantial and last-ing contribution to literature for children." He is also widely known for revising and expanding *The Elements of Style* (50th anniversary edition, 2008), a writer's guide by his college professor William Strunk, Jr. White's *Letters* were collected in 1976, his *Essays* in 1977, and his *Poems and Sketches* in 1981. On July 4, 1963, President Kennedy named White in the first group of Americans to receive the Presidential Medal of Freedom, with a citation that called him "an essayist whose concise comment . . . has revealed to yet another age the vigor of the English sentence."

Once More to the Lake

"Once More to the Lake" first appeared in *Harper's* magazine in 1941. Per-haps if a duller writer had written the essay, or an essay with the same title, we wouldn't much care about it, for at first its subject seems as personal and ordi-nary as a letter home. White's loving and exact portrayal, however, brings this lakeside camp to life for us. In the end, the writer arrives at an awareness that shocks him — shocks us, too, with a familiar sensory detail.

"Once More to the Lake" is a stunning mixture of description and narration, but it is also more. To make his observations and emotions clear and immediate, White relies extensively on several other methods of development as well.

Narration (Chap. 4): throughout
Description (Chap. 5): throughout
Example (Chap. 6): paragraphs 2, 7–8, 11, 12
Comparison and contrast (Chap. 7): paragraphs 4–7, 9–10, 11–12
Process analysis (Chap. 8): paragraphs 9, 10, 12

August 1941

One summer, along about 1904, my father rented a camp on a lake in Maine and took us all there for the month of August. We all got ringworm from some kittens and had to rub Pond's Extract on our arms and legs night and morning, and my father rolled over in a canoe with all his clothes on; but outside of that the vacation was a success and from then on none of us ever thought there was any place in the world like that lake in Maine. We returned summer after summer — always on August 1 for one month. I have since become a salt-water man, but sometimes in summer there are days when the restlessness of the tides and the fearful cold of the sea water and the incessant wind that blows across the afternoon and into the evening make me wish for the placidity of a lake in the woods. A few weeks ago this feeling got so strong I bought myself a couple of bass hooks and a spinner and returned to the lake where we used to go, for a week's fishing and to revisit old haunts.

I took along my son, who had never had any fresh water up his nose and who had seen lily pads only from train windows. On the journey over to the lake I began to wonder what it would be like. I wondered how time would have marred this unique, this holy spot — the coves and streams, the hills that the sun set behind, the camps and the paths behind the camps. I was sure that the tarred road would have found it out, and I wondered in what other ways it would be desolated. It is strange how much you can remember about places like that once you allow your mind to return into the grooves that lead back. You remember one thing, and that suddenly reminds you of another thing. I guess I remembered clearest of all the early mornings, when the lake was cool and motionless, remembered how the bedroom smelled of the lumber it was made of and of the wet woods whose scent entered through the screen. The partitions in the camp were thin and did not extend clear to the top of the rooms, and as I was always the first up I would dress softly so as not to wake the others, and sneak out into the sweet outdoors and start out in the canoe, keeping close along the shore in the long shadows of the pines. I remembered being very careful never to rub my paddle against the gunwale for fear of disturbing the stillness of the cathedral.

The lake had never been what you would call a wild lake. There were cottages sprinkled around the shores, and it was in farming country although the shores of the lake were quite heavily wooded. Some of the cottages were owned by nearby farmers, and you would live at the shore and eat your meals at the farmhouse. That's what our family did. But although it wasn't wild, it was a fairly large and undisturbed lake and there were places in it that, to a child at least, seemed infinitely remote and primeval.

I was right about the tar: It led to within half a mile of the shore. But when I got back there, with my boy, and we settled into a camp near a farmhouse and into the kind of summertime I had known, I could tell that it was going to be pretty much the same as it had been before — I knew it, lying in bed the first morning smelling the bedroom and hearing the boy sneak quietly out and go off along the shore in a boat. I began to sustain the illusion that he was I, and therefore, by simple transposition, that I was my father. This sensation persisted, kept cropping up all the time we were there. It was not an entirely new feeling, but in this setting it grew much stronger. I seemed to be living a dual existence. I would be in the middle of some simple act, I would be picking up a bait box or laying down a table fork, or I would be saying something and suddenly it would be not I but my father who was saying the words or making the gesture. It gave me a creepy sensation.

We went fishing the first morning. I felt the same damp moss covering the worms in the bait can, and saw the dragonfly alight on the tip of my rod as it hovered a few inches from the surface of the water. It was the arrival of this fly that convinced me beyond any doubt that everything was as it always had been, that the years were a mirage and that there had been no years. The small waves were the same, chucking the rowboat under the chin as we fished at anchor, and the boat was the same boat, the same color green and the ribs broken in the same places, and under the floorboards the same fresh water leavings and debris — the dead hellgrammite, the wisps of moss, the rusty discarded fishhook, the dried blood from yesterday's catch. We stared silently at the tips of our rods, at the dragonflies that came and went. I lowered the tip of mine into the water, tentatively, pensively dislodging the fly, which darted two feet away, poised, darted two feet back, and came to rest again a little farther up the rod. There had been no years between the ducking of this dragonfly and the other one — the one that was part of memory. I looked at the boy, who was silently watching his fly, and it was my hands that held his rod, my eyes watching. I felt dizzy and didn't know which rod I was at the end of. 5

We caught two bass, hauling them in briskly as though they were mackerel, pulling them over the side of the boat in a businesslike manner without any landing net, and stunning them with a blow on the back of the head. When we got back for a swim before lunch, the lake was exactly where we had left it, the same number of inches from the dock, and there was only the merest suggestion of a breeze. This seemed an utterly enchanted sea, this lake you could leave to its own devices for a few hours and come back to, and find that it had not stirred, this constant and trustworthy body of water. In the shallows, the dark, water-soaked sticks and twigs, smooth and old, were undulating in clusters on the bottom against the clean ribbed sand, and the track of the mussel was plain. A school of minnows swam by, each minnow with its small individual shadow, doubling the attendance, so clear and sharp in the sunlight. Some of the other campers were in swimming, along the shore, one of them with a cake of soap, and the water felt thin and clear and unsubstantial. Over the years there had been this person with the cake of soap, this cultist, and here he was. There had been no years. 6

Up to the farmhouse to dinner through the teeming dusty field, the road under our sneakers was only a two-track road. The middle track was missing, the one with the marks of the hooves and the splotches of dried, flaky manure. 7

There had always been three tracks to choose from in choosing which track to walk in; now the choice was narrowed down to two. For a moment I missed terribly the middle alternative. But the way led past the tennis court, and something about the way it lay there in the sun reassured me; the tape had loosened along the backline, the alleys were green with plantains and other weeds, and the net (installed in June and removed in September) sagged in the dry noon, and the whole place steamed with midday heat and hunger and emptiness. There was a choice of pie for dessert, and one was blueberry and one was apple, and the waitresses were the same country girls, there having been no passage of time, only the illusion of it as in a dropped curtain — the waitresses were still fifteen; their hair had been washed, that was the only difference — they had been to the movies and seen the pretty girls with the clean hair.

Summertime, oh, summertime, pattern of life indelible, the fade-proof 8 lake, the woods unshatterable, the pasture with the sweetfern and the juniper forever and ever, summer without end; this was the background, and the life along the shore was the design, the cottages with their innocent and tranquil design, their tiny docks with the flagpole and the American flag floating against the white clouds in the blue sky, the little paths over the roots of the trees leading from camp to camp and the paths leading back to the outhouses and the can of lime for sprinkling, and at the souvenir counters at the store the miniature birchbark canoes and the postcards that showed things looking a little better than they looked. This was the American family at play, escaping the city heat, wondering whether the newcomers in the camp at the head of the cove were "common" or "nice," wondering whether it was true that the people who drove up for Sunday dinner at the farmhouse were turned away because there wasn't enough chicken.

It seemed to me, as I kept remembering all this, that those times and 9 those summers had been infinitely precious and worth saving. There had been jollity and peace and goodness. The arriving (at the beginning of August) had been so big a business in itself, at the railway station the farm wagon drawn up, the first smell of the pine-laden air, the first glimpse of the smiling farmer, and the great importance of the trunks and your father's enormous authority in such matters, and the feel of the wagon under you for the long ten-mile haul, and at the top of the last long hill catching the first view of the lake after eleven months of not seeing this cherished body of water. The shouts and cries of the other campers when they saw you, and the trunks to be unpacked, to give up their rich burden. (Arriving was less exciting nowadays, when you sneaked up in your car and parked it under a tree near the camp and took out the bags and in five minutes it was all over, no fuss, no loud wonderful fuss about trunks.)

Peace and goodness and jollity. The only thing that was wrong now, really,   10
was the sound of the place, an unfamiliar nervous sound of the outboard
motors. This was the note that jarred, the one thing that would sometimes
break the illusion and set the years moving. In those other summertimes all
motors were inboard; and when they were at a little distance, the noise they
made was a sedative, an ingredient of summer sleep. They were one-cylinder
and two-cylinder engines, and some were make-and-break and some were
jump-spark, but they all made a sleepy sound across the lake. The one-lungers
throbbed and fluttered, and the twin-cylinder ones purred and purred, and
that was a quiet sound, too. But now the campers all had outboards. In the
daytime, in the hot mornings, these motors made a petulant irritable sound;
at night in the still evening when the afterglow lit the water, they whined
about one's ears like mosquitoes. My boy loved our rented outboard, and his
great desire was to achieve single-handed mastery over it, and authority, and
he soon learned the trick of choking it a little (but not too much), and the
adjustment of the needle valve. Watching him I would remember the things
you could do with the old one-cylinder engine with the heavy flywheel, how
you could have it eating out of your hand if you got really close to it spiritually.
Motorboats in those days didn't have clutches, and you would make a landing
by shutting off the motor at the proper time and coasting in with a dead rud-
der. But there was a way of reversing them, if you learned the trick, by cutting
the switch and putting it on again exactly on the final dying revolution of the
flywheel, so that it would kick back against compression and begin reversing.
Approaching a dock in a strong following breeze, it was difficult to slow up
sufficiently by the ordinary coasting method, and if a boy felt he had complete
mastery over his motor, he was tempted to keep it running beyond its time and
then reverse it a few feet from the dock. It took a cool nerve, because if you
threw the switch a twentieth of a second too soon you would catch the flywheel when it still had speed enough to go up past center, and the boat would
leap ahead, charging bull-fashion at the dock.

We had a good week at the camp. The bass were biting well and the sun   11
shone endlessly, day after day. We would be tired at night and lie down in the
accumulated heat of the little bedrooms after the long hot day and the breeze
would stir almost imperceptibly outside and the smell of the swamp drift in
through the rusty screens. Sleep would come easily and in the morning the
red squirrel would be on the roof, tapping out his gay routine. I kept remembering everything, lying in bed in the mornings — the small steamboat that
had a long rounded stern like the lip of a Ubangi, and how quietly she ran on
the moonlight sails, when the older boys played their mandolins and the girls
sang and we ate doughnuts dipped in sugar, and how sweet the music was on
the water in the shining night, and what it had felt like to think about girls

then. After breakfast we would go up to the store and the things were in the same place — the minnows in a bottle, the plugs and spinners disarranged and pawed over by the youngsters from the boys' camp, the Fig Newtons and the Beeman's gum. Outside, the road was tarred and cars stood in front of the store. Inside, all was just as it had always been, except there was more Coca-Cola and not so much Moxie and root beer and birch beer and sarsaparilla. We would walk out with a bottle of pop apiece and sometimes the pop would backfire up our noses and hurt. We explored the streams, quietly, where the turtles slid off the sunny logs and dug their way into the soft bottom; and we lay on the town wharf and fed worms to the tame bass. Everywhere we went I had trouble making out which was I, the one walking at my side, the one walking in my pants.

One afternoon while we were at the lake a thunderstorm came up. It was   12
like the revival of an old melodrama that I had seen long ago with childish awe. The second-act climax of the drama of the electrical disturbance over a lake in America had not changed in any important respect. This was the big scene, still the big scene. The whole thing was so familiar, the first feeling of oppression and heat and a general air around camp of not wanting to go very far away. In midafternoon (it was all the same) a curious darkening of the sky, and a lull in everything that had made life tick; and then the way the boats suddenly swung the other way at their moorings with the coming of a breeze out of the new quarter, and the premonitory rumble. Then the kettle drum, then the snare, then the bass drum and cymbals, then crackling light against the dark, and the gods grinning and licking their chops in the hills. Afterward the calm, the rain steadily rustling in the calm lake, the return of light and hope and spirits, and the campers running out in joy and relief to go swimming in the rain, their bright cries perpetuating the deathless joke about how they were getting simply drenched, and the children screaming with delight at the new sensation of bathing in the rain, and the joke about getting drenched linking the generations in a strong indestructible chain. And the comedian who waded in carrying an umbrella.

When the others went swimming my son said he was going in, too. He   13
pulled his dripping trunks from the line where they had hung all through the shower and wrung them out. Languidly, and with no thought of going in, I watched him, his hard little body, skinny and bare, saw him wince slightly as he pulled up around his vitals the small, soggy, icy garment. As he buckled the swollen belt, suddenly my groin felt the chill of death.

*For a reading quiz, visit **bedfordstmartins.com/thebedfordreader**.*

Journal Writing

White strongly evokes the lake camp as a place that was important to him as a child. What place or places were most important to you as a child? In your journal, jot down some memories. (To take your journal writing further, see "From Journal to Essay" on the facing page.)

Questions on Meaning

1. How do you account for the distortions that creep into the author's sense of time?
2. What does the discussion of inboard and outboard motors (par. 10) have to do with the author's divided sense of time?
3. To what degree does White make us aware of his son's impression of this trip to the lake?
4. What do you take to be White's main PURPOSE in the essay? At what point do you become aware of it?

Questions on Writing Strategy

1. In paragraph 4 the author first introduces his confused feeling that he has gone back in time to his own childhood, an idea that he repeats and expands throughout his account. What is the function of these repetitions?
2. Try to describe the impact of the essay's final paragraph. By what means is it achieved?
3. To what extent is this essay written to appeal to any but middle-aged readers? Is it comprehensible to anyone whose vacations were never spent at a Maine summer cottage?
4. What is the TONE of White's essay?
5. **MIXED METHODS**   White's DESCRIPTION depends on many IMAGES that are not FIGURES OF SPEECH but literal translations of sensory impressions. Locate four such images.
6. **MIXED METHODS**   Within White's description and NARRATION of his visit to the lake, what purpose is served by the COMPARISON AND CONTRAST between the lake now and when he was a boy?

Questions on Language

1. Be sure you know the meanings of the following words: incessant, placidity (par. 1); gunwale (2); primeval (3); transposition (4); hellgrammite (5); undulating, cultist (6); indelible, tranquil (8); petulant (10); imperceptibly (11); premonitory (12); languidly (13).
2. Comment on White's DICTION in his reference to the lake as "this unique, this holy spot" (par. 2).
3. Explain what White is describing in the sentence that begins, "Then the kettle drum . . ." (par. 12). Where else does the author use figures of speech?

Suggestions for Writing

1. **FROM JOURNAL TO ESSAY**   Choose one of the places suggested by your journal entry, and write an essay describing the place now, revisiting it as an adult. (If you haven't visited the place since childhood, you can imagine what seeing it now would be like.) Your description should draw on your childhood memories, making them as vivid as possible for the reader, but you should also consider how your POINT OF VIEW toward the place differs now.

2. In a descriptive paragraph about a real or imagined place, try to appeal to each of your reader's five senses.

3. **CRITICAL WRITING**   While on the vacation he describes, White wrote to his wife, "This place is as American as a drink of Coca-Cola. The white collar family having its annual liberty." Obviously, not everyone has a chance at the lakeside summers White enjoyed. To what extent, if at all, does White's privileged point of view deprive his essay of universal meaning and significance? Write an essay answering this question. Back up your ideas with EVIDENCE from White's essay.

4. **CONNECTIONS**   In White's "Once More to the Lake" and Brad Manning's "Arm Wrestling with My Father" (p. 138), the writers reveal a changing sense of what it means to be a father. Write an essay that examines the similarities and differences in their definitions of fatherhood. How does a changing idea of what it means to be a son connect with this redefinition of fatherhood?

5. **CONNECTIONS**   White's essay is full of images that place readers in an important setting of his childhood. David Sedaris, in "Remembering My Childhood on the Continent of Africa" (p. 232), also uses vivid images to evoke childhood, both his own and that of his partner. After reading these two essays, write an essay of your own ANALYZING four or five images from each that strike you as especially evocative. What sense impression does each image draw on? What does each one tell you about the author's feelings?

E. B. White on Writing

"You asked me about writing — how I did it," E. B. White replied to a seventeen-year-old who had written to him, wanting to become a professional writer but feeling discouraged. "There is no trick to it. If you like to write and want to write, you write, no matter where you are or what else you are doing or whether anyone pays any heed. I must have written half a million words (mostly in my journal) before I had anything published, save for a couple of short items in *St. Nicholas*.[1] If you want to write about feelings, about the end of the summer, about growing, write about it. A great deal of writing is not 'plotted' — most of my essays have no plot structure, they are a ramble in the

---

[1] A magazine for children, popular early in the twentieth century. — EDS.

woods, or a ramble in the basement of my mind. You ask, 'Who cares?' Everybody cares. You say, 'It's been written before.' Everything has been written before. . . . Henry Thoreau, who wrote *Walden*, said, 'I learned this at least by my experiment: that if one advances confidently in the direction of his dreams and endeavors to live the life which he has imagined, he will meet with a success unexpected in common hours.' The sentence, after more than a hundred years, is still alive. So, advance confidently."

In trying to characterize his own writing, White was modest in his claims. To his brother Stanley Hart White, he once remarked, "I discovered a long time ago that writing of the small things of the day, the trivial matters of the heart, the inconsequential but near things of this living, was the only kind of creative work which I could accomplish with any sincerity or grace. As a reporter, I was a flop, because I always came back laden not with facts about the case, but with a mind full of the little difficulties and amusements I had encountered in my travels. Not till *The New Yorker* came along did I ever find any means of expressing those impertinences and irrelevancies. Thus yesterday, setting out to get a story on how police horses are trained, I ended by writing a story entitled 'How Police Horses Are Trained' which never even mentions a police horse, but has to do entirely with my own absurd adventures at police headquarters. The rewards of such endeavor are not that I have acquired an audience or a following, as you suggest (fame of any kind being a Pyrrhic victory[2]), but that sometimes in writing of myself — which is the only subject anyone knows intimately — I have occasionally had the exquisite thrill of putting my finger on a little capsule of truth, and heard it give the faint squeak of mortality under my pressure, an antic sound."

For Discussion

1. Sometimes young writers are counseled to study the market and then try to write something that will sell. How would you expect E. B. White to have reacted to such advice?
2. What, exactly, does White mean when he says, "Everything has been written before"? How might an aspiring writer take this remark as encouragement?
3. What interesting distinction does White make between reporting and essay writing?

---

[2] A victory won at great cost. The Greek king Pyrrhus defeated the Romans in 279 BC but exclaimed afterward, "One more such victory and I am lost." — EDS.

APPENDIX

APA DOCUMENTATION

On the following pages we explain the documentation style of the American Psychological Association, as described in the *Publication Manual of the American Psychological Association*, 6th edition (2010). APA style is used in psychology, sociology, business, education, economics, political science, and other social sciences.

This appendix concludes with sample pages adapted to APA style from Rosie Anaya's researched essay "The Best Kept Secret on Campus," an MLA version of which appears in Chapter 3 on academic writing (pp. 84–88).

SOURCE CITATION USING APA STYLE

APA documentation involves a citation within the text that identifies the author and date of a source, as well as the page number(s) for a quotation or paraphrase (page numbers are not required for a summary). The author's name may appear in a SIGNAL PHRASE in your text, or it may appear in parentheses along with the date and any page numbers. Together, the citation information directs readers to the source's full publication information in a list of references at the end of the text:

TEXT CITATION, AUTHOR NAMED IN SIGNAL PHRASE

As Quindlen (2014) has suggested, people's dwellings seem to have lost their emotional hold and to have become just investments (p. 191).

TEXT CITATION, AUTHOR NAMED IN PARENTHESES

One observer has suggested that people's dwellings seem to have lost their emotional hold and to have become just investments (Quindlen, 2014, p. 191).

ENTRY IN REFERENCE LIST

Quindlen, A. Homeless. (2014). In X. J. Kennedy, D. M. Kennedy, J. E. Aaron, & E. K. Repetto (Eds.), *The Bedford Reader* (12th ed., pp. 190-192). Boston: Bedford.

APA Parenthetical Citations

The following examples of APA text citations show the author named in a signal phrase or named in parentheses.

A work with two authors

Addison and McGee (2010) reported that a mere 18% of high school teachers had their students visit a writing center, presumably because only a small number of schools offered such centralized tutoring (p. 157).

A work with three to five authors

With more than two but fewer than six authors, list all of the authors in the first parenthetical citation. Separate the names with commas, and precede the final name with &.

APA Parenthetical Citations

Young boys are almost five times more likely to be diagnosed with autism than are girls (Shelton, Hertz-Picciotto, & Pessah, 2012, p. 944).

In later references to the same source, shorten the citation to the first author's name followed by et al. (*et alii*, "and others").

Shelton et al. (2012) have suggested that increased exposure to pesticides might explain increased levels of autism in the general population (p. 945).

A work with six or more authors

Name only the first author followed by et al. (*et alii*, "and others").

Despite the global economic downturn of recent years, household spending in the United States has actually increased (Thiel et al., 2010, p. 26).

A work with a group author

For a work published under the name of an organization, such as a government agency or a corporation, use the name of the group as the author.

The United States Conference of Mayors (2010) reported that most cities do not have enough emergency shelter beds to accommodate the needs of homeless residents (p. 2).

A work with no identified author

Cite an unsigned work by using the first one or two main words of the title (excluding any initial "A," "An," or "The").

A growing number of national chain hotels allow guests to bring dogs and cats with them ("Rooming," 2012, p. 10)—a welcome relief for travelers whose pets require specialized care.

Two or more works by exactly the same author(s)

If you cite more than one work by the same author or authors, in most cases the year of publication will indicate which work you're referring to. If two or more works were published in the same year, assign lowercase letters to the years in your list of references (see pp. 553–54) and include the same letters in your parenthetical citations.

Gladwell (2011a) has claimed that although popular wisdom held that Apple founder "[Steve] Jobs stole the personal computer from Xerox," the reality was that he refined ideas that Xerox showed little interest in pursuing (p. 48).

According to Gladwell (2011b), Jobs's most significant personality trait—more so than his perfectionism, his aggressiveness, or his resilience—was his preference to "tweak" other people's inventions instead of innovate from scratch.

An electronic source

Cite a nonprint source, such as a Web document or a DVD, just as you would a print source: by author's name or, if there is no author, by title. If a source numbers paragraphs instead of pages, give the appropriate number(s) as in the following model, after para. (one paragraph) or paras. (more than one paragraph).

For six years in the 1970s, folk singer Joni Mitchell occasionally appeared on stage disguised as a black man, a deviant practice that Grier (2012) has claimed gave her "legitimacy and authority" among rock musicians (para. 1).

For a source with no page or paragraph numbers, provide a heading for the section in which the cited material appears (abbreviated if it is long), followed by the paragraph number within the section, as determined by your own count.

One patient developed a painful, swollen rash that dermatologists attributed to an exclusive diet of fast food; in the months he abstained from such meals, his condition improved (Sundhar et al., 2012, Case section, para. 1).

An indirect source

Use as cited in to indicate that you found the source you quote within another source.

Martha Ballard's complaint that Hannah Sewall and her husband "were intimidated" by their doctor (as cited in Ulrich, 1990, p. 177) hinted at midwives' resentment of the medical intrusions into childbirth that were becoming standard practice in the late eighteenth century.

More than one work in the same citation

List the names in alphabetical order and separate the entries with a semicolon.

Moving welfare recipients out of blighted neighborhoods has been shown to increase their happiness, if not their earning potential (Johnson, 2012; Tavernese, 2012).

Personal communications

Interviews you conduct and letters, e-mails, and messages you receive should be cited in your text with the correspondent's initials and last name, the words personal communication, and the full date. Because readers cannot retrieve such materials, they are not included in the list of references.

> A county health inspector explained that meat must be shelved at the bottom of refrigeration units to reduce the risk of contaminating vegetables and dairy products with bacteria (M. K. Edwards, personal communication, August 30, 2012).

APA Reference List

Your reference list is a complete record of your sources. Follow these guidelines for the list:

- **Title the list References.**
- **Double-space the entire list.**
- **Arrange the sources alphabetically** by the last name of the first author or by the first main word of the title if the source has no named author.
- **Begin the first line of each entry at the left margin.** Indent the subsequent lines of the entry one-half inch or five spaces.

Following are the essentials of a reference-list entry:

- **Reverse the names of the authors,** last name first, followed by a comma and initials for first and middle names (even if the names are given in full on the source), with another comma after the initials.
- **Provide a publication date** in parentheses after the name or names.
- **Give the full title of the work.** For titles of books, use italics and capitalize only the first word of the title and subtitle and any proper nouns. Use the same capitalization style for titles of articles, but don't italicize them or enclose them in quotation marks. For titles of periodicals, capitalize all major words and italicize the title.
- **Give publication information.** For books, include the city and state of publication and the publisher's name. For periodicals, include the volume number and sometimes the issue number along with the page numbers for the article you cite. For print periodical articles, also include a digital object identifier (DOI) if one is available. Always include the DOI or a URL for online periodical articles. (See p. 555 for more on DOIs and URLs.)

APA Reference List

- **Use periods between parts of each entry,** but do not include a period at the end of a DOI or URL.

You may need to combine some of the following models to document a particular source — for instance, combine "Eight or more authors" and "A periodical article in an online database" for a database article with twelve authors.

Authors

One author

Boo, K. (2012). *Behind the beautiful forevers: Life, death, and hope in a Mumbai undercity.* New York, NY: Random House.

Two to seven authors

Amabile, T., & Kramer, S. (2011). *The progress principle: Using small wins to ignite joy, engagement, and creativity at work.* Boston, MA: Harvard Business Review Press.

Clark, R. L., Burkhauser, R. V., Moon, M., Quinn, J. F., & Smeeding, T. M.
(2004). *The economics of an aging society.* Boston, MA: Blackwell.

Eight or more authors

Name the first six authors, insert ellipses, and end with the name of the
last listed author.

Judge, L. W., Bellar, D., Blom, L. C., Don, L., Harris, B., Turk, M., . . .
Johnson, J. (2012). Perceived social support from strength and
conditioning coaches among injured student athletes. *Journal of
Strength & Conditioning Research, 26,* 1154-1161.

A group author

U.S. Department of Education, National Center for Education Evaluation and
Regional Assistance. (2010). *The effectiveness of mandatory-random
student drug testing* (NCEE Publication No. 2010–4025). Retrieved from
http://ies.ed.gov/ncee/pubs/20104025/pdf/20104025.pdf

No identified author

Start the entry with the title of the work, followed by the date and publication information.

The flight from marriage. (2011, August 20). *The Economist, 400*(8707),
21-24.

More than one work by exactly the same author(s)

When you cite two or more works by the same author that were published
in *different* years, include the author's name in each entry and list the entries
in chronological order by publication date.

Turkle, S. (1995). *Life on the screen: Identity in the age of the Internet.* New
York, NY: Touchstone.
Turkle, S. (2011). *Alone together: Why we expect more from technology and
less from each other.* New York, NY: Basic Books.

When you cite two or more works by the same author that were published
in the *same* year, list the works in alphabetical order by title and add lowercase
letters (a, b, c, etc.) to the date. Use the same letters with the date in the corresponding parenthetical citations (see pp. 549–50).

Gladwell, M. (2011a, May 16). Creation myth: Xerox PARC, Apple, and the truth about innovation. *The New Yorker, 87*(13), 44-53.

Gladwell, M. (2011b, November 14). The tweaker: The real genius of Steve Jobs. *The New Yorker, 87*(36), 32-35.

Print Periodicals: Journals, Magazines, and Newspapers

When a digital object identifier (DOI) is assigned to a print periodical article, add it at the end of the entry. (See pp. 555–56 for more on DOIs and an example.)

An article in a journal

Most journals number issues consecutively throughout the year, so that the first page of issue 3, for instance, might begin on page 407. In such cases, follow the journal title with the volume number (italicized), a comma, the inclusive page numbers of the article, and a period.

Smith, A. (2010). Decolonization in unexpected places: Native evangelicalism and the rearticulation of mission. *American Quarterly, 62,* 569-570.

If a journal starts each issue with page 1, include the issue number in parentheses (not italicized) after the volume number.

Collier, L. (2012). Capitalizing on social media to find professional community. *Council Chronicle, 21*(3), 6, 26-27.

An article in a magazine

Include the full date in parentheses and provide volume and issue numbers.

Helgoe, L. (2010, October). Revenge of the introvert. *Psychology Today, 43*(5), 54-61.

Thompson, M. (2010, November 22). Bringing dogs to heal. *Time, 176*(21), 54-57.

An article in a newspaper

Include the year, month, and day in the date. List all page numbers, preceded by p. (for one page) or pp. (for multiple pages).

Burge, K. (2012, March 25). For homeless families, hotel is a life in limbo. *Boston Sunday Globe,* pp. A1, A14-A15.

Print Books

A book with an author

Sacks, O. (2012). *Hallucinations*. New York, NY: Knopf.

A book with an editor

Allison, J., & Gediman, D. (Eds.). (2007). *This I believe: The personal philosophies of remarkable men and women*. New York, NY: Holt.

Bowles, D. J. (Ed.). (2011). *Gerontology nursing case studies: 100 narratives for learning*. New York, NY: Springer.

A later edition

Ehrenreich, B., & English, D. (2005). *For her own good: Two centuries of the experts' advice to women* (Rev. ed.). New York, NY: Random House.

A selection from an anthology

Use the anthology's publication year after the author's name, even if the selection was originally published earlier. In the page numbers in parentheses, give the location of the cited selection within the anthology.

Barnet, R. (2010). Why didn't the boat sink? How a kindertransportee kept afloat. In S. Kriger (Ed.), *Marking humanity: Stories, poems, and essays by Holocaust survivors* (pp. 64-67). Toronto, Canada: Soul Inscriptions Press.

Online and Other Electronic Sources

Electronic sources vary greatly, and they may be and often are updated. Your aim in citing such a source should be to tell what version you used and how readers can find it for themselves. APA strongly recommends listing the digital object identifier (DOI) for any source that has one assigned to it; if no DOI is provided, give the URL of the source. (If you must break a DOI or URL, do it after the two slashes following http:// or before a single slash, a period, or another punctuation mark. Do not add a hyphen.) Include the date on which you accessed the source only if the source is likely to change or if it lacks a publication date or version number (see p. 558 for an example). Substitute n.d. (for "no date") in parentheses if a source is undated.

If you don't see a model for the type of source you used, follow a model that comes close. If you can't find all the information shown in a model, give what you can find.

A journal article on the Web

Base an entry for an online journal article on one of the models on page 554 for a print journal article. Add the DOI if one is provided.

Yu, Z., Day, D. A., Connal-Nicolaou, A., & Enders, F. T. (2011). Early food allergen exposure may be protective against food allergies: An extension of the hygiene hypothesis. *Internet Journal of Epidemiology, 10*(1). doi:10.5580/243a

If no DOI is provided, give the URL of the journal's home page after Retrieved from.

Rylat, P. (2012). The benefits of creative therapy for patients with dementia. *Nursing Standard, 26*(33), 42-47. Retrieved from http://nursingstandard .rcnpublishing.co.uk

A newspaper or magazine article on the Web

Bernstein, E. (2012, September 19). When it never gets easier to say goodbye. *The Wall Street Journal.* Retrieved from http://online .wsj.com

Christian, B. (2011, March). Mind vs. machine. *The Atlantic, 307*(2). Retrieved from http://www.theatlantic.com

A periodical article in an online database

For an article that you obtain from a library or other database, provide print publication information using the models for journals, magazines, and newspapers on page 554. Add the DOI or, if there is none, the URL of the periodical's home page. Do not include the name of the database.

Reed, M. G., & George, C. (2011). Where in the world is environmental justice? *Progress in Human Geography, 35*, 835-842. doi:10.1177 /0309132510388384

Walsh, B. (2012, August 6). When the rains stop. *Time, 180*(6), 34-37. Retrieved from http://www.time.com

A book on the Web

Instead of print publication information, provide the URL you used to retrieve the book. In this example, the final parenthesis provides the date of the book's original publication:

Barker, C. H. (2004). *Wanted, a young woman to do housework: Business principles applied to housework.* Retrieved from http://www.gutenberg .org/files/14117/14117-h/14117-h.htm (Original work published 1915)

A book on an e-reader

For an electronic book on an e-reader such as a Kindle, Nook, or iPad, add the type of file in brackets after the title, followed by the URL where you retrieved the book.

Urrea, L. A. (1996). *By the lake of sleeping children: The secret life of the Mexican border* [Nook version]. Retrieved from http://www .barnesandnoble.com

A video or audio recording on the Web

Include a description of the medium or file type in brackets after the title of the work.

Fraser, S. (2012, May). Why eyewitnesses get it wrong [Video file]. Retrieved from http://www.ted.com/talks/scott_fraser_the_problem _with_eyewitness_testimony.html

Tevis, J. (2009, January 6). Fairy tales of the atomic age [Audio file]. Retrieved from http://www.orionmagazine.org/index.php /audio-video/categories/C296/P30

A podcast on the Web

Levitt, S. D., & Dubner, S. J. (Hosts). (2011, April 13). Does college still matter? [Audio podcast]. *Freakonomics radio podcast.* Retrieved from http://www.npr.org/rss/podcast/podcast_directory.php

A posting to a blog or discussion group

Moran, C. (2012, September 19). This is why people hate health insurance companies. Retrieved from http://consumerist.com

A document from a Web site

Include as much of the following information as you can find: author's name, date of publication or last update, title, and URL.

Rigoglioso, M. (2012, April 17). *The psychology around voter turnout.*
    Retrieved from http://csi.gsb.stanford.edu/getting-out-vote

If no author is listed, begin the entry with the title followed by the date in
parentheses. The following example also includes the date of retrieval because
the source has no publication date.

Asperger's syndrome. (n.d.). Retrieved September 18, 2012, from http://
    www.webmd.com/brain/autism/mental-health-aspergers-syndrome

SAMPLE PAGES IN APA STYLE

The following paragraphs excerpted and adapted from Rosie Anaya's
"The Best Kept Secret on Campus" (p. 84) show APA documentation style in
a sample of student writing.

Despite the prevalence of depression and related disorders
on campus, most students avoid seeking help when they need it.
The American Psychiatric Association (2011) has maintained that
most mental-health issues can be managed or overcome with
treatment by therapy and/or medication ("Do Psychiatrists Do
More," para. 1). But among students with a history of depression, according to the American College Health Association
(2012), a mere 10% received any kind of treatment (p. 35). One
reason for such low numbers can be found in a study published
in *Journal of Mental Health Counseling:* Four in five American
college students were unwilling to ask for help even when they
were certain they needed it, because they perceived mental illness as embarrassing or shameful (Aegisdóttir, O'Heron, Hartong,
Haynes, & Linville, 2011, pp. 327-328). Thus students who need
help suffer additional pain—and no treatment—because they
fear the stigma of mental illness.

> Citation of a source with a group author named in the text.

> Abbreviated section heading and paragraph number for paraphrase from an unpaged Web document.

> First citation of a source with five authors not named in the text.

Friedman (2008) has explained that journalists tend to
emphasize mental illness in reports of violent crime even though
the connection is rare—accounting for less than 5% of all inci-

> Citation of a source with one author named in the text.

dents of violence (Second section, para. 2). He also warned that this tendency feeds harmful stereotypes:

> Popular media affect not just how the public views people with psychiatric illness but how the public thinks about the disorders themselves. . . . Major mental disorders are quite treatable and have response rates to psychosocial and biological treatments that are on par with, if not better than, common nonpsychiatric medical illnesses. But the public has little sense from stories in the popular media that mentally ill people can get better with treatment, recover, and go on to lead productive lives. (Third section, para. 6)

Although there is little reason to fear people with mental disorders, we are bombarded with the message that they are dangerous and incurable.

————————

Even at schools that do offer mental-health services, legal restrictions can make psychiatric intervention difficult or impossible. Reiss (2011) has pointed out that the Americans with Disabilities Act protects people with mental illness from discrimination, so schools cannot screen for psychological disorders or force students to obtain treatment unless a court or "threat assessment team" declares them to be dangerous. And because nearly all college students are adults, confidentiality rules prevent schools from notifying parents or teachers of potential problems without the student's consent (p. A76). This combination of social stigma and legal obstacle creates an awkward dilemma: Students suffering from mental illness are reluctant to ask for help, yet the very people who can help are prevented from reaching out.

————————

Students themselves can also take the lead in addressing mental-health issues. At the University of Pennsylvania, junior Alison Malmon responded to her schizophrenic brother's suicide by starting the 350-chapter support group Active Minds, which

Section identification and paragraph number for paraphrase from an unpaged online article.

Name and date here and date later in the paragraph frame the material borrowed from Reiss.

advocates for students with psychological disorders and stresses that "people with mental illness are no more violent than people without mental illness" (as cited in Reiss, 2010, p. 31). At a smaller college, a freshman who was successfully treated for depression told her story in the school paper and helped dozens of other students to recognize and seek help for their illnesses (Kadison & DiGeronimo, 2004). As these examples show, students everywhere can make an enormous difference simply by sharing their feelings.

Citation of an indirect quotation.

Citation of a source with two authors not named in the text.

References

Aegisdóttir, S., O'Heron, M. P., Hartong, J. M., Haynes, S. A., & Linville, M. K. (2011). Enhancing attitudes and reducing fears about mental health counseling: An analogue study. *Journal of Mental Health Counseling, 33*, 327-346.

American College Health Association. (2012). *National college health assessment: Fall 2011 reference group data report.* Retrieved from http://www.achancha.org/docs/ACHA -NCHA-II_ReferenceGroup_DataReport_Fall2011.pdf

American Psychiatric Association. (2011). *Mental illness.* Retrieved from http://www.healthyminds.org/Main-Topic /Mental-Illness.aspx

Friedman, R. A. (2008, July-August). Media and madness. *The American Prospect.* Retrieved from http://prospect.org

Kadison, R., & DiGeronimo, T. F. (2004). *College of the overwhelmed: The campus mental health crisis and what to do about it.* San Francisco, CA: Jossey-Bass.

Reiss, B. (2010, April 4). Madness after Virginia Tech: From psychiatric risk to institutional vulnerability. *Social Text, 28*(4), 25-44. doi:10.1215/01642472-2010-009

Reiss, B. (2011, February 4). Campus security and the specter of mental-health profiling. *Chronicle of Higher Education.* Retrieved from http://chronicle.com

Reference list begins on a new page.

An article with five authors from a print journal.

A report with a group author posted on the Web.

A document from a Web site.

An article in the online version of a magazine.

A book with two authors.

A journal article with a DOI from an online database.

A newspaper article without a DOI from an online database.

USEFUL TERMS

Abstract and concrete Two kinds of language. *Abstract* words refer to ideas, conditions, and qualities we cannot directly perceive: *truth, love, happiness, courage, evil, poverty, progressive*. *Concrete* words indicate things we can know with our senses: *tree, chair, bird, pen, courthouse, motorcycle, perfume, thunderclap*. Concrete words lend vigor and clarity to writing, for they help a reader to picture things. See IMAGE.

Writers of expository and argumentative essays tend to shift back and forth from one kind of language to the other. They often begin a paragraph with a general statement full of abstract words ("There is *hope* for the *future* of *motoring*"). Then they usually go on to give examples and present evidence in sentences full of concrete words ("Inventor *Jones* claims his *car* will go from *Fresno* to *Los Angeles* on a *gallon* of *peanut oil*"). Inexperienced writers often use too many abstract words and not enough concrete ones. See also pages 42 and 134.

Academic writing The kind of writing generally undertaken by scholars and students, in which a writer responds to another's work or uses multiple SOURCES to develop and support an original idea. Typically based on one or more TEXTS, all academic writing calls on a writer's CRITICAL THINKING, READING, AND WRITING and shares the common goal of using reading and writing to build and exchange knowledge. See Chapter 3.

Active voice   The form of the verb when the sentence subject is the actor: *Trees* [subject] *shed* [active verb] *their leaves in autumn.* Contrast PASSIVE VOICE.

Allude, allusion   To refer to a person, place, or thing believed to be common knowledge (*allude*), or the act or result of doing so (*allusion*). An allusion may point to a famous event, a familiar saying, a noted personality, a well-known story or song. Usually brief, an allusion is a space-saving way to convey much meaning. For example, the statement "The game was Coach Johnson's Waterloo" informs the reader that, like Napoleon meeting defeat in a celebrated battle, the coach led a confrontation resulting in his downfall and that of his team. If the writer is also showing Johnson's character, the allusion might further tell us that the coach is a man of Napoleonic ambition and pride. To make an effective allusion, you have to ensure that it will be clear to your audience. Not every reader, for example, would understand an allusion to a neighbor, to a seventeenth-century Russian harpsichordist, or to a little-known stock-car driver.

Analogy   An extended comparison based on the like features of two unlike things: one familiar or easily understood, the other unfamiliar, abstract, or complicated. For instance, most people know at least vaguely how the human eye works: The pupil adjusts to admit light, which registers as an image on the retina at the back of the eye. You might use this familiar information to explain something less familiar to many people, such as how a camera works: The aperture (like the pupil) adjusts to admit light, which registers as an image on the film (like the retina) at the back of the camera. Analogies are especially helpful for explaining technical information in a way that is nontechnical, more easily grasped. For example, the spacecraft *Voyager 2* transmitted spectacular pictures of Saturn to Earth. To explain the difficulty of their achievement, NASA scientists compared their feat to a golfer sinking a putt from five hundred miles away. Because it can make abstract ideas vivid and memorable, analogy is also a favorite device of philosophers, politicians, and preachers. In his celebrated speech "I Have a Dream" (p. 507), Martin Luther King, Jr., draws a remarkable analogy to express the anger and disappointment of African Americans that, one hundred years after Lincoln's Emancipation Proclamation, their full freedom has yet to be achieved. "It is obvious today," declares King, "that America has defaulted on this promissory note"; and he compares the Founding Fathers' written guarantee — of the rights of life, liberty, and the pursuit of happiness — to a bad check returned for insufficient funds.

Analogy is similar to the method of COMPARISON AND CONTRAST. Both identify the distinctive features of two things and then set the features side by side. But a comparison explains two obviously similar things — two responses to a mess — and considers both their differences and their similarities. An analogy yokes two apparently unlike things (eye and camera, spaceflight and golf, guaranteed human rights and bad checks) and focuses only on their major similarities. Analogy is thus an extended *metaphor,* the FIGURE OF SPEECH that declares one thing to be another — even though it isn't, in a strictly literal sense — for the purpose of making us aware of similarity: "Hope," writes the poet Emily Dickinson, "is the thing with feathers / That perches in the soul."

In an ARGUMENT, analogy can make readers more receptive to a point or inspire them, but it can't prove anything because in the end the subjects are dissimilar. A false analogy is a logical FALLACY that claims a fundamental likeness when none exists. See page 447.

Analyze, analysis   To separate a subject into its parts (*analyze*), or the act or result of doing so (*analysis*, also called *division*). Analysis is a key skill in CRITICAL THINK-ING, READING, AND WRITING; see pages 16, 18–22, and 24–25. It is also considered a method of development; see Chapter 9.

Anecdote   A brief NARRATIVE, or retelling of a story or event. Anecdotes have many uses: as essay openers or closers, as examples, as sheer entertainment. See Chapter 4.

Appeals   Resources writers draw on to connect with and persuade readers:

- A **rational appeal** asks readers to use their intellects and their powers of rea-soning. It relies on established conventions of logic and evidence.
- An **emotional appeal** asks readers to respond out of their beliefs, values, or feelings. It inspires, affirms, frightens, angers.
- An **ethical appeal** asks readers to look favorably on the writer. It stresses the writer's intelligence, competence, fairness, morality, and other qualities desir-able in a trustworthy debater or teacher.

See also page 443.

Argument   A mode of writing intended to win readers' agreement with an assertion by engaging their powers of reasoning. Argument often overlaps PERSUASION. See Chapter 13.

Assume, assumption   To take something for granted (*assume*), or a belief or opinion taken for granted (*assumption*). Whether stated or unstated, assumptions influ-ence a writer's choices of subject, viewpoint, EVIDENCE, and even language. See also pages 17 and 443–44.

Audience   A writer's readers. Having in mind a particular audience helps the writer in choosing strategies. Imagine, for instance, that you are writing two reviews of a new movie, one for students who read the campus newspaper, the other for ama-teur and professional filmmakers who read *Millimeter*. For the first audience, you might write about the actors, the plot, and especially dramatic scenes. You might judge the film and urge your readers to see it — or to avoid it. Writing for *Mil-limeter*, you might discuss special effects, shooting techniques, problems in editing and in mixing picture and sound. In this review, you might use more specialized and technical terms. Obviously, an awareness of the interests and knowledge of your readers, in each case, would help you decide how to write. If you told readers of the campus paper too much about filming techniques, you would lose most of them. If you told *Millimeter*'s readers the film's plot in detail, probably you would put them to sleep.

   You can increase your awareness of your audience by asking yourself a few questions before you begin to write. Who are to be your readers? What is their age level? background? education? Where do they live? What are their beliefs and attitudes? What interests them? What, if anything, sets them apart from most people? How familiar are they with your subject? Knowing your audience can help you write so that your readers will not only understand you better but care more deeply about what you say.

Body   The part of an essay, usually several PARAGRAPHS, that develops the writer's main idea. See pages 35–36.

Cause and effect   A method of development in which a writer ANALYZES reasons for an action, event, or decision, or analyzes its consequences. See Chapter 11. See also EFFECT.

Chronological order   The arrangement of events as they occurred or occur in time, first to last. Most NARRATIVES and PROCESS ANALYSES use chronological order.

Claim   The proposition that an ARGUMENT demonstrates, generally expressed in a THESIS STATEMENT. See pages 441–42.

Classification   A method of development in which a writer sorts out multiple things (contact sports, college students, kinds of music) into categories. See Chapter 10.

Cliché   A worn-out, trite expression that a writer employs thoughtlessly. Although at one time the expression may have been colorful, from heavy use it has lost its luster. It is now "old as the hills." In conversation, most of us sometimes use clichés, but in writing they "stick out like sore thumbs." Alert writers, when they revise, replace a cliché with a fresh, CONCRETE expression. Writers who have trouble recognizing clichés should be suspicious of any phrase they've heard before and should try to read more widely. Their problem is that, because so many expressions are new to them, they do not know which ones are full of moths.

Coherence   The clear connection of the parts in effective writing so that the reader can easily follow the flow of ideas between sentences, paragraphs, and larger divisions, and can see how they relate successively to one another.

In making your essay coherent, you may find certain devices useful. TRANSITIONS, for instance, can bridge ideas. Reminders of points you have stated earlier are helpful to a reader who may have forgotten them — as readers tend to do sometimes, particularly if your essay is long. However, a coherent essay is not one merely pasted together with transitions and reminders. It derives its coherence from the clear relationship between its THESIS (or central idea) and all its parts. See also pages 40–41 and 287–88.

Colloquial expressions   Words and phrases occurring primarily in speech and in informal writing that seeks a relaxed, conversational tone. "My favorite chow is a burger and a shake" or "This math exam has me wired" may be acceptable in talking to a roommate, in corresponding with a friend, or in writing a humorous essay for general readers. Such choices of words, however, would be out of place in formal writing — in, say, a laboratory report or a letter to your senator. Contractions (*let's, don't, we'll*) and abbreviated words (*photo, sales rep, ad*) are the shorthand of spoken language. Good writers use such expressions with an awareness that they produce an effect of casualness.

Common ground   One or more aspects of an ARGUMENT on which both writer and reader can agree. A writer arguing in favor of raising highway speed limits might, for example, start by acknowledging the importance of safe driving before citing evidence showing that higher average speeds would have little effect on accident rates. By conceding the validity of opposing points or identifying ASSUMPTIONS shared by people on both sides of an issue, the writer establishes the fairness of his or her position and helps to win over readers who may otherwise be inclined to reject the argument outright. See page 441.

Comparison and contrast   Two methods of development usually found together. Using them, a writer examines the similarities and differences between two things to reveal their natures. See Chapter 7.

Conclusion   The sentences or paragraphs that bring an essay to a satisfying and logical end. See page 38.

Concrete   See ABSTRACT AND CONCRETE.

Connotation and denotation   Two types of meanings most words have. *Denotation* is the explicit, literal, dictionary definition of a word. *Connotation* refers to a word's implied meaning, resonant with associations. The denotation of *blood* is "the fluid that circulates in the vascular system." The connotations of *blood* range from *life force* to *gore* to *family bond*. A doctor might use the word *blood* for its denotation, and a mystery writer might rely on the word's connotations to heighten a scene.

Because people have different experiences, they bring to the same word different associations. A conservative's emotional response to the word *welfare* is not likely to be the same as a liberal's. And referring to your senator as a *diplomat* evokes a different response, from the senator and from others, than would *baby-kisser, political hack,* or even *politician*. The effective use of words involves knowing both what they mean literally and what they are likely to suggest.

Critical thinking, reading, and writing   A group of interlocking skills that are essential for college work and beyond. Each seeks the meaning beneath the surface of a statement, poem, editorial, picture, advertisement, Web site, or other TEXT. Using ANALYSIS, INFERENCE, SYNTHESIS, and often EVALUATION, the critical thinker, reader, and writer separates this text into its elements in order to see and judge meanings, relations, and ASSUMPTIONS that might otherwise remain buried. See also pages 9–12, 15–26, 285, and 440–41.

Data   A name for EVIDENCE favored by philosopher Stephen Toulmin in his conception of ARGUMENT. See pages 442–43.

Deductive reasoning, deduction   The method of reasoning from the general to the particular: From information about what we already know, we deduce what we need or want to know. See Chapter 13, pages 444–45.

Definition   A statement of the literal and specific meaning or meanings of a word or a method of developing an essay. In the latter, the writer usually explains the nature of a word, a thing, a concept, or a phenomenon. Such a definition may employ NARRATION, DESCRIPTION, or any other method. See Chapter 12.

Denotation   See CONNOTATION AND DENOTATION.

Description   A mode of writing that conveys the evidence of the senses: sight, hearing, touch, taste, smell. See Chapter 5.

Diction   The choice of words. Every written or spoken statement uses diction of some kind. To describe certain aspects of diction, the following terms may be useful:

- **Standard English:** the common American language, words, and grammatical forms that are used and expected in schools, businesses, and other sites.
- **Nonstandard English:** words and grammatical forms such as *theirselves* and *ain't* that are used mainly by people who speak a dialect other than standard English.
- **Dialect:** a variety of English based on differences in geography, education, or social background. Dialect is usually spoken but may be written. Maya Angelou's essay in Chapter 4 transcribes the words of dialect speakers ("'He gone whip him till that white boy call him Momma'").
- **Slang:** certain words in highly informal speech or writing, or in the speech of a particular group — for example, *blow off, dis, dweeb.*
- **Colloquial expressions:** words and phrases from conversation. See COLLOQUIAL EXPRESSIONS for examples.

- **Regional terms:** words heard in a certain locality, such as *spritzing* for "raining" in Pennsylvania Dutch country.
- **Technical terms:** words and phrases that form the vocabulary of a particular discipline (*monocotyledon* from botany), occupation (*drawplate* from die-making), or avocation (*interval training* from running). See also JARGON.
- **Archaisms:** old-fashioned expressions, once common but now used to suggest an earlier style, such as *ere* and *forsooth*.
- **Obsolete diction:** words that have passed out of use (such as the verb *werien*, "to protect or defend," and the noun *isetnesses*, "agreements"). *Obsolete* may also refer to certain meanings of words no longer current (*fond* for foolish, *clipping* for hugging or embracing).
- **Pretentious diction:** use of words more numerous and elaborate than necessary, such as *institution of higher learning* for "college," and *partake of solid nourishment* for "eat."

Archaic, obsolete, and pretentious diction usually has no place in good writing unless for ironic or humorous effect: The journalist and critic H. L. Mencken delighted in the hifalutin use of *tonsorial studio* instead of barber shop. Still, any diction may be the right diction for a certain occasion: The choice of words depends on a writer's PURPOSE and AUDIENCE.

Discovery The stage of the writing process before the first draft. It may include deciding on a topic, narrowing the topic, creating or finding ideas, doing reading and other research, defining PURPOSE and AUDIENCE, planning and arranging material. Discovery may follow from daydreaming or meditation, reading, or perhaps carefully ransacking memory. In practice, though, it usually involves considerable writing and is aided by the act of writing. The operations of discovery — reading, research, further idea creation, and refinement of subject, purpose, and audience — may all continue well into drafting as well. See also pages 30–32.

Division See ANALYZE, ANALYSIS.

Dominant impression The main idea a writer conveys about a subject through DESCRIPTION — that an elephant is gigantic, for example, or an experience scary. See Chapter 5.

Drafting The stage of the writing process during which a writer expresses ideas in complete sentences, links them, and arranges them in a sequence. See also pages 34–35 and 47–49.

Editing The final stage of the writing process, during which a writer corrects errors and improves stylistic matters by, for example, using the ACTIVE VOICE and reworking sentences to achieve PARALLEL STRUCTURE. Contrast with REVISION. And see pages 41–47 and 52–53.

Effect The result of an event or action, usually considered together with CAUSE as a method of development. See the discussion of cause and effect in Chapter 11. In discussing writing, the term *effect* also refers to the impression a word, a sentence, a paragraph, or an entire work makes on the reader: how convincing it is, whether it elicits an emotional response, what associations it conjures up, and so on.

Emotional appeal See APPEALS.

Emphasis The stress or special importance given to a certain point or element to make it stand out. A skillful writer draws attention to what is most important in a sentence, a paragraph, or an essay by controlling emphasis in any of the following ways:

- **Proportion:** Important ideas are given greater coverage than minor points.
- **Position:** The beginnings and ends of sentences, paragraphs, and larger divisions are the strongest positions. Placing key ideas in these spots helps draw attention to their importance. The end is the stronger position, for what stands last stands out. A sentence in which less important details precede the main point is called a **periodic sentence:** "Having disguised himself as a guard and walked through the courtyard to the side gate, the prisoner made his escape." A sentence in which the main point precedes less important details is a **loose sentence:** "Autumn is orange: gourds in baskets at roadside stands, the harvest moon hanging like a pumpkin, and oak leaves flashing like goldfish."
- **Repetition:** Careful repetition of key words or phrases can give them greater importance. (Careless repetition, however, can cause boredom.)
- **Mechanical devices:** Italics (underlining), capital letters, and exclamation points can make words or sentences stand out. Writers sometimes fall back on these devices, however, after failing to show significance by other means. Italics and exclamation points can be useful in reporting speech, but excessive use makes writing sound exaggerated or bombastic.

For additional ways to emphasize ideas at the sentence level, see pages 43–44.

Essay   A short nonfiction composition on one central theme or subject in which the writer may offer personal views. Essays are sometimes classified as either formal or informal. In general, a **formal essay** is one whose DICTION is that of the written language (not colloquial speech), whose TONE is serious, and whose focus is on a subject the writer believes is important. (For example, see Dan Ariely's "Why We Lie.") An **informal essay**, in contrast, is more likely to admit COLLOQUIAL EXPRESSIONS; the writer's tone tends to be lighter, perhaps humorous, and the subject is likely to be personal, sometimes even trivial. (See Dave Barry's "Batting Clean-Up and Striking Out.") These distinctions, however, are rough ones: An essay such as Judy Brady's "I Want a Wife" uses colloquial language and speaks of personal experience, but its tone is serious and its subject important. See also EXPOSITION.

Ethical appeal   See APPEALS.

Euphemism   The use of inoffensive language in place of language that readers or listeners may find hurtful, distasteful, frightening, or otherwise objectionable — for instance, a police officer's announcing that someone *passed on* rather than *died,* or a politician's calling for *revenue enhancement* rather than *taxation.* Writers sometimes use euphemism out of consideration for readers' feelings, but just as often they use it to deceive readers or shirk responsibility. (For more on euphemism, see William Lutz's "The World of Doublespeak" in Chap. 10.)

Evaluate, evaluation   To judge the merits of something (*evaluate*) or the act or result of doing so (*evaluation*). Evaluation is often part of CRITICAL THINKING, READING, AND WRITING. In evaluating a work of writing, you base your judgment on your ANALYSIS of it and your sense of its quality or value. See also pages 17, 23, 26, and 66–69.

Evidence   The details that support an argument or an explanation, including facts, examples, and expert opinions. A writer's opinions and GENERALIZATIONS must rest upon evidence. See pages 442–43.

Example   Also called **exemplification** or **illustration**, a method of development in which the writer provides instances of a general idea. See Chapter 6. An *example* is a verbal illustration.

Exposition   The mode of prose writing that explains (or exposes) its subject. Its function is to inform, to instruct, or to set forth ideas: the major trade routes in the Middle East, how to make a dulcimer, why the United States consumes more energy than it needs. Exposition may call various methods to its service: EXAMPLE, COMPARISON AND CONTRAST, PROCESS ANALYSIS, and so on. Most college writing is at least partly exposition, and so are most of the ESSAYS in this book.

Fallacies   Errors in reasoning. See pages 445–47 for a list and examples.

Figures of speech   Expressions that depart from the literal meanings of words for the sake of emphasis or vividness. To say "She's a jewel" doesn't mean that the subject of praise is literally a kind of shining stone; the statement makes sense because the CONNOTATIONS of *jewel* come to mind: rare, priceless, worth cherishing. Some figures of speech involve comparisons of two objects apparently unlike:

- A **simile** (from the Latin, "likeness") states the comparison directly, usually connecting the two things using *like, as,* or *than:* "The moon is like a snowball," "He's as lazy as a cat full of cream," "My feet are flatter than flyswatters."
- A **metaphor** (from the Greek, "transfer") declares one thing to *be* another: "A mighty fortress is our God," "The sheep were bolls of cotton on the hill." (A **dead metaphor** is a word or phrase that, originally a figure of speech, has come to be literal through common usage: "the *hands* of a clock.")
- **Personification** is a simile or metaphor that assigns human traits to inanimate objects or abstractions: "A stoop-shouldered refrigerator hummed quietly to itself," "The solution to the math problem sat there winking at me."

Other figures of speech consist of deliberate misrepresentations:

- **Hyperbole** (from the Greek, "throwing beyond") is a conscious exaggeration: "I'm so hungry I could eat a saddle," "I'd wait for you a thousand years."
- The opposite of hyperbole, **understatement**, creates an ironic or humorous effect: "I accepted the ride. At the moment, I didn't feel like walking across the Mojave Desert."
- A **paradox** (from the Greek, "conflicting with expectation") is a seemingly self-contradictory statement that, on reflection, makes sense: "Children are the poor person's wealth" (wealth can be monetary, or it can be spiritual). *Paradox* may also refer to a situation that is inexplicable or contradictory, such as the restriction of one group's rights in order to secure the rights of another group.

Flashback   A technique of NARRATION in which the sequence of events is interrupted to recall an earlier period.

Focus   The narrowing of a subject to make it manageable. Beginning with a general subject, you concentrate on a certain aspect of it. For instance, you may select crafts as a general subject, then decide your main interest lies in weaving. You could focus your essay still further by narrowing it to operating a hand loom. You also focus your writing according to who will read it (AUDIENCE) or what you want it to achieve (PURPOSE).

General and specific   Terms that describe the relative number of instances or objects included in the group signified by a word. *General* words name a group or class (*flowers*); *specific* words limit the class by naming its individual members (*rose, violet, dahlia, marigold*). Words may be arranged in a series from more general to more specific: *clothes, pants, jeans, Levis*. The word *cat* is more specific than *animal*, but less specific than *tiger cat*, or *Garfield*. See also ABSTRACT AND CONCRETE and pages 42 and 152–53.

Generalization   A statement about a class based on an examination of some of its members: "Lions are fierce." The more members examined and the more representative they are of the class, the sturdier the generalization. The statement "Solar heat saves home owners money" would be challenged by home owners who have yet to recover their installation costs. "Solar heat can save home owners money in the long run" would be a sounder generalization. Insufficient or nonrepresentative EVIDENCE often leads to a hasty generalization, such as "All freshmen hate their roommates" or "Men never express their feelings." Words such as *all, every, only, never,* and *always* have to be used with care: "Some men don't express their feelings" is more credible. Making a trustworthy generalization involves the use of INDUCTIVE REASONING (discussed on p. 444).

Genre   The category into which a piece of writing fits. Shaped by PURPOSE, AUDIENCE, and context, genres range from broad types (such as fiction and nonfiction) to general groups (novel, essay) to narrower groups (science fiction novel, personal narrative) to specific document formats (steampunk graphic novel, post on a retail workers' forum) — and they tend to overlap. The genres of college writing vary widely. Examples appear on pages 101 (case study), 136 (field observation), 176 (job-application letter), 212 (review), 250 (lab report), 289 (annotated bibliography), 324 (résumé), 370 (letter to the editor), 410 (essay exam), and 452 (proposal).

   Most readers are instinctively aware of individual genres and the characteristics that distinguish them, and they expect writers to follow the genre's conventions for POINT OF VIEW, structure and organization, types of EVIDENCE, language, TONE, length, appearance, and so forth. Consider, for instance, your daily newspaper: As a reader, you expect the news articles to be objective statements of fact, with none of the reporters' personal thoughts and little rhetorical flourish; but when you turn to the op-ed page or your favorite columnist, such opinions and clever turns of phrase are precisely what you're looking for. Similar expectations exist for every kind of writing, and good writers make a point of knowing what they are. See also pages 10, 29–30, and 39 and the individual chapter introductions in Part Two.

Grounds   A name for EVIDENCE favored by philosopher Stephen Toulmin in his conception of ARGUMENT. See page 442.

Hyperbole   See FIGURES OF SPEECH.

Illustration   Another name for EXAMPLE. See Chapter 6.

Image   A word or word sequence that evokes a sensory experience. Whether literal ("We picked two red apples") or figurative ("His cheeks looked like two red apples, buffed and shining"), an image appeals to the reader's memory of seeing, hearing, smelling, touching, or tasting. Images add concreteness to fiction — "The farm looked as tiny and still as a seashell, with the little knob of a house surrounded by its curved furrows of tomato plants" (Eudora Welty in a short story, "The Whistle")—and are an important element in poetry. But writers of essays, too, use images to bring ideas down to earth. See also FIGURES OF SPEECH.

Inductive reasoning, induction   The process of reasoning to a conclusion about an entire class by examining some of its members. See page 444.

Infer, inference   To draw a conclusion (*infer*), or the act or result of doing so (*inference*). In CRITICAL THINKING, READING, AND WRITING, inference is the means to understanding a writer's meaning, ASSUMPTIONS, PURPOSE, fairness, and other attributes. See also pages 16–17, 23, and 25–26.

Introduction   The opening of a written work. Often it states the writer's subject, narrows it, and communicates the writer's main idea (THESIS). See page 37.

Irony   A manner of speaking or writing that does not directly state a discrepancy, but implies one. **Verbal irony** is the intentional use of words to suggest a meaning other than literal: "What a mansion!" (said of a shack); "There's nothing like sunshine" (said on a foggy morning). (For more examples, see the essays by Jessica Mitford and Judy Brady.) If irony is delivered contemptuously with an intent to hurt, we call it **sarcasm:** "Oh, you're a real friend!" (said to someone who refuses to lend the speaker the coins to operate a clothes dryer). With **situational irony,** the circumstances themselves are incongruous, run contrary to expectations, or twist fate: Juliet regains consciousness only to find that Romeo, believing her dead, has stabbed himself. See also SATIRE.

Jargon   Strictly speaking, the special vocabulary of a trade or profession. The term has also come to mean inflated, vague, meaningless language of any kind. It is characterized by wordiness, ABSTRACTIONS galore, pretentious DICTION, and needlessly complicated word order. Whenever you meet a sentence that obviously could express its idea in fewer words and shorter ones, chances are that it is jargon. For instance: "The motivating force compelling her to opt continually for the most labor-intensive mode of operation in performing her functions was consistently observed to be the single constant and regular factor in her behavior patterns." Translation: "She did everything the hard way." (For more on such jargon, see William Lutz's "The World of Doublespeak" in Chap. 10.)

Journal   A record of one's thoughts, kept daily or at least regularly. Keeping a journal faithfully can help a writer gain confidence and develop ideas. See also pages 30–31.

Metaphor   See FIGURES OF SPEECH.

Narration, narrative   The mode of writing (*narration*) that tells a story (*narrative*). See Chapter 4.

Narrator   The teller of a story, usually either in the first PERSON (*I*) or in the third (*he, she, it, they*). See pages 95–96.

Nonstandard English   See DICTION.

Objective and subjective   Kinds of writing that differ in emphasis. In *objective* writing the emphasis falls on the topic; in *subjective* writing it falls on the writer's view of the topic. Objective writing occurs in factual journalism, science reports, certain PROCESS ANALYSES (such as recipes, directions, and instructions), and logical arguments in which the writer attempts to downplay personal feelings and opinions. Subjective writing sets forth the writer's feelings, opinions, and interpretations. It occurs in friendly letters, journals, bylined feature stories and columns in newspapers, personal essays, and ARGUMENTS that appeal to emotion. Few essays, however, contain one kind of writing exclusive of the other.

Organization   The way ideas and supporting evidence are structured in the BODY of an essay. The methods of development typically lend themselves to different approaches, discussed in the introductions to Chapters 4–13. Independent of the methods, a successful writer orders subpoints and details in whatever way will best get the main idea across. While a NARRATIVE or a PROCESS ANALYSIS typically follows a CHRONOLOGICAL ORDER, for instance, the writer may need to step back to relate previous or concurrent events. And the writer of an essay that presents EXAMPLES or an ARGUMENT may choose to move from most compelling points to least, or vice versa, depending on the desired EFFECT. See pages 20–21, 36, 98–99 (narration), 132–33 (DESCRIPTION), 208–09 (COMPARISON AND CONTRAST), 246 (process analysis), 287 (DIVISION OR ANALYSIS), 322–23 (CLASSIFICATION), and 448–49 (argument or persuasion).

Paradox   See FIGURES OF SPEECH.

Paragraph   A group of closely related sentences that develop a central idea. In an essay, a paragraph is the most important unit of thought because it is both self-contained and part of the larger whole. Paragraphs separate long and involved ideas into smaller parts that are more manageable for the writer and easier for the reader to take in. Good paragraphs, like good essays, possess UNITY and COHERENCE. The central idea is usually stated in a TOPIC SENTENCE, often found at the beginning of the paragraph and related directly to the essay's THESIS. All other sentences in the paragraph relate to this topic sentence, defining it, explaining it, illustrating it, providing it with evidence and support. If you meet a unified and coherent paragraph that has no topic sentence, it will contain a central idea that no sentence in it explicitly states, but that every sentence in it clearly implies. See also pages 40–41, 287–88 (paragraph coherence); 40, 323 (paragraph development); and 40, 408 (paragraph unity).

Parallelism, parallel structure   A habit of good writers: keeping ideas of equal importance in similar grammatical form. A writer may place nouns side by side ("*Trees* and *streams* are my weekend tonic") or in a series ("Give me *wind, sea, and stars*"). Phrases, too, may be arranged in parallel structure ("*Out of my bed, into my shoes, up to my classroom*—that's my life"), as may clauses ("Ask not what your country can do for you; ask what you can do for your country").

Parallelism may be found not only in single sentences but in larger units as well. A paragraph might read: "Rhythm is everywhere. It throbs in the rain forests of Brazil. It vibrates ballroom floors in Vienna. It snaps its fingers on street corners in Chicago." In a whole essay, parallelism may be the principle used to arrange ideas in a balanced or harmonious structure. See the famous speech given by Martin Luther King, Jr. (p. 507), in which paragraphs 11–18 all begin with the words "I have a dream" and describe an imagined future. Not only does such a parallel structure organize ideas, but it also lends them force. See also pages 44–45 and 210–11.

Paraphrase   Putting another writer's thoughts into your own words. In writing a research paper or an essay containing EVIDENCE gathered from your reading, you will find it necessary to paraphrase—unless you are using another writer's very words with quotation marks around them—and to acknowledge your sources. Contrast SUMMARY. And see pages 62–63.

Passive voice   The form of the verb when the sentence subject is acted upon: *The report* [subject] *was published* [passive verb] *anonymously*. Contrast ACTIVE VOICE.

Person   A grammatical distinction made between the speaker, the one spoken to, and the one spoken about. In the first person (*I, we*), the subject is speaking. In the second person (*you*), the subject is being spoken to. In the third person (*he, she, it*), the subject is being spoken about. The point of view of an essay or work of fiction is often specified according to person: "This short story is told from a first-person point of view." See POINT OF VIEW.

Personification   See FIGURES OF SPEECH.

Persuasion   A mode of writing intended to influence people's actions by engaging their beliefs and feelings. Persuasion often overlaps ARGUMENT. See Chapter 13.

Plagiarism   The use of someone else's ideas or words as if they were your own, without acknowledging the original author. See pages 60–64.

Point of view   In an essay, the physical position or the mental angle from which a writer beholds a subject. On the subject of starlings, the following three writers would likely have different points of view: An ornithologist might write OBJEC-TIVELY about the introduction of these birds into North America, a farmer might advise other farmers how to prevent the birds from eating seed, and a bird watcher might SUBJECTIVELY describe a first glad sighting of the species. Whether objective or subjective, point of view also encompasses a writer's biases and ASSUMPTIONS about a subject. For instance, the scientist, farmer, and bird watcher would likely all have different perspectives on starlings' reputation as nuisances: Although such perspectives may or may not be expressed directly, they would likely influence each writer's approach to the subject. See also PERSON.

Premise   A proposition or ASSUMPTION that leads to a conclusion. See pages 443–44 for examples.

Process analysis   A method of development that most often explains step by step how something is done or how to do something. See Chapter 8.

Purpose   A writer's reason for trying to convey a particular idea (THESIS) about a particular subject to a particular AUDIENCE of readers. Though it may emerge gradually during the writing process, in the end, purpose should govern every element of a piece of writing.

   In trying to define the purpose of an essay you read, ask yourself, "Why did the writer write this?" or "What was this writer trying to achieve?" Even though you cannot know the writer's intentions with absolute certainty, an effective essay will make some purpose clear. See also pages 18–19, 29, and 39.

Rational appeal   See APPEALS.

Revision   The stage of the writing process during which a writer "re-sees" a draft from the viewpoint of a reader. Revision usually involves rethinking fundamental matters such as PURPOSE and organization as well as rewriting to ensure COHER-ENCE and UNITY. See pages 38–41 and 49–52. See also EDITING.

Rhetoric   The study (and the art) of using language effectively. *Rhetoric* also has a negative CONNOTATION of empty or pretentious language meant to waffle, stall, or even deceive. This is the meaning in "The president had nothing substantial to say about taxes, just the usual rhetoric."

Rhetorical question   A question posed for effect, one that requires no answer. Instead, it often provokes thought, lends emphasis to a point, asserts or denies something without making a direct statement, launches further discussion, introduces an opinion, or leads the reader where the writer intends. Sometimes a writer throws one in to introduce variety in a paragraph full of declarative sentences. The following questions are rhetorical: "When will the United States learn that sending people into space does not feed them on the earth?" "Shall I compare thee to a summer's day?" "What is the point of making money if you've no one but yourself to spend it on?" Both reader and writer know what the answers are supposed to be. (1) Someday, if the United States ever wises up. (2) Yes. (3) None.

Sarcasm See IRONY.

Satire A form of writing that employs wit to attack folly. Unlike most comedy, the purpose of satire is not merely to entertain, but to bring about enlightenment — even reform. See also IRONY.

Scene In a NARRATION, an event retold in detail to re-create an experience. See Chapter 4.

Sentimentality A quality sometimes found in writing that fails to communicate. Such writing calls for an extreme emotional response on the part of an AUDIENCE, although its writer fails to supply adequate reason for any such reaction. A sentimental writer delights in waxing teary over certain objects: great-grandmother's portrait, the first stick of chewing gum baby chewed (now a shapeless wad), an empty popcorn box saved from the World Series of 1996. Sentimental writing usually results when writers shut their eyes to the actual world, preferring to snuffle the sweet scents of remembrance.

Signal phrase Words used to introduce a quotation, PARAPHRASE, or SUMMARY, often including the source author's name and generally telling readers how the source material should be interpreted: "Nelson argues that the legislation will backfire." See also pages 64–65.

Simile See FIGURES OF SPEECH.

Slang See DICTION.

Source Any outside TEXT or material that a writer uses to develop and support ideas. Often found through the process of researching a subject, a single source might be the focus of an essay (as when you write about a selection in this book), or a writer might SYNTHESIZE multiple sources as EVIDENCE for one or more points. Any source referred to in an essay must be documented with an in-text citation and an entry in a works-cited or references list. See Chapter 3 on academic writing, especially pages 70–83, and the Appendix on APA documentation.

Specific See GENERAL AND SPECIFIC.

Standard English See DICTION.

Strategy Whatever means a writer employs to write effectively. The methods set forth in this book are strategies; but so are narrowing a subject, organizing ideas clearly, using TRANSITIONS, writing with an awareness of your reader, and other effective writing practices.

Style The distinctive manner in which a writer writes. Style may be seen especially in the writer's choice of words and sentence structures. Two writers may write on the same subject, even express similar ideas, but it is style that gives each writer's work a personality.

Subjective See OBJECTIVE AND SUBJECTIVE.

Summarize, summary To condense a work (essay, movie, news story) to its essence (*summarize*), or the act or result of doing so (*summary*). Summarizing a piece of writing in one's own words is an effective way to understand it. (See pp. 15–16.)

Summarizing (and acknowledging) others' writing in your own text is a good way to support your ideas. (See pp. 59 and 61–62.) Contrast PARAPHRASE.

Suspense   Often an element in NARRATION: the pleasurable expectation or anxiety we feel that keeps us reading a story. In an exciting mystery story, suspense is constant: How will it all turn out? Will the detective get to the scene in time to prevent another murder? But there can be suspense in less melodramatic accounts as well.

Syllogism   A three-step form of reasoning that employs DEDUCTION. See page 445 for an illustration.

Symbol   A visible object or action that suggests further meaning. The flag suggests country; the crown suggests royalty—these are conventional symbols familiar to us. Life abounds in such clear-cut symbols. Football teams use dolphins and rams for easy identification; married couples symbolize their union with a ring.

In writing, symbols usually do not have such a one-to-one correspondence, but evoke a whole constellation of associations. In Herman Melville's *Moby-Dick*, the whale suggests more than the large mammal it is. It hints at evil, obsession, and the untamable forces of nature. Such a symbol carries meanings too complex or elusive to be neatly defined.

Although more common in fiction and poetry, symbols can be used to good purpose in nonfiction because they often communicate an idea in a compact and concrete way.

Synthesize, synthesis   To link elements into a whole (*synthesize*), or the act or result of doing so (*synthesis*). In CRITICAL THINKING, READING, AND WRITING, synthesis is the key step during which you use your own perspective to reassemble a work you have ANALYZED or to connect the work with others. (See pp. 17 and 26.) Synthesis is a hallmark of ACADEMIC WRITING in which you respond to others' work or use multiple sources to support your ideas. (See pp. 58–59 and 69–70.)

Text   Any creation—written, visual, auditory, physical, or experiential—that can be interpreted or used as a SOURCE for writing. The starting point for most ACADEMIC WRITING, texts include written documents such as essays, articles, and books, of course, but also photographs, paintings, advertisements, Web sites, performances, musical scores, experiments, conversations, lectures, field observations, interviews, dreams, jokes—anything that invites a response, sparks an idea, or lends itself to CRITICAL THINKING, READING, AND WRITING. See pages 57–59.

Thesis, thesis statement   The central idea in a work of writing (*thesis*), to which everything else in the work refers; one or more sentences that express that central idea (*thesis statement*). In some way, each sentence and PARAGRAPH in an effective essay serves to support the thesis and to make it clear and explicit to readers. Good writers, while writing, often set down a thesis statement to help them define their purpose. They also often include this statement in their essay as a promise and a guide to readers. See pages 18, 32–34, 39–40 and the introductions to Chapters 4–13.

Tone   The way a writer expresses his or her regard for subject, AUDIENCE, or self. Through word choice, sentence structures, and what is actually said, the writer conveys an attitude and sets a prevailing spirit. Tone in writing varies as greatly as tone of voice varies in conversation. It can be serious, distant, flippant, angry, enthusiastic, sincere, sympathetic. Whatever tone a writer chooses, usually it informs an entire essay and helps a reader decide how to respond. For works of strong tone, see the essays by Maya Angelou, Jessica Mitford, David Sedaris, Russell Baker, Chitra Divakaruni, Derrick Jensen, Judy Brady, and Martin Luther King, Jr. See also pages 449–50.

Topic sentence   The statement of the central idea in a PARAGRAPH, usually asserting one aspect of an essay's THESIS. Often the topic sentence will appear at (or near) the beginning of the paragraph, announcing the idea and beginning its development. Because all other sentences in the paragraph explain and support this central idea, the topic sentence is a way to create UNITY.

Transitions   Words, phrases, sentences, or even paragraphs that relate ideas. In moving from one topic to the next, a writer has to bring the reader along by showing how the ideas are developing, what bearing a new thought or detail has on an earlier discussion, or why a new topic is being introduced. A clear purpose, strong ideas, and logical development certainly aid COHERENCE, but to ensure that the reader is following along, good writers provide signals, or transitions.

To bridge sentences or paragraphs and to point out relationships within them, you can use some of the following devices of transition:

- Repeat or restate words or phrases to produce an echo in the reader's mind.
- Use PARALLEL STRUCTURES to produce a rhythm that moves the reader forward.
- Use pronouns to refer back to nouns in earlier passages.
- Use transitional words and phrases. These may indicate a relationship of time (*right away, later, soon, meanwhile, in a few minutes, that night*), proximity (*beside, close to, distant from, nearby, facing*), effect (*therefore, for this reason, as a result, consequently*), comparison (*similarly, in the same way, likewise*), or contrast (*yet, but, nevertheless, however, despite*). Some words and phrases of transition simply add on: *besides, too, also, moreover, in addition to, second, last, in the end.*

Understatement   See FIGURES OF SPEECH.

Unity   The quality of good writing in which all parts relate to the THESIS. In a unified essay, all words, sentences, and PARAGRAPHS support the single central idea. Your first step in achieving unity is to state your thesis; your next step is to organize your thoughts so that they make your thesis clear. See also pages 40 and 408.

Voice   In writing, the sense of the author's character, personality, and attitude that comes through the words. See TONE.

Warrant   The name for ASSUMPTION favored by philosopher Stephen Toulmin in his conception of ARGUMENT. See pages 443–44.

Acknowledgments

Sherman Alexie, "Superman and Me," copyright © 1997 by Sherman Alexie. All rights reserved. Used by permission of Nancy Stauffer Associates.

Maya Angelou, "Champion of the World" (editors' title), copyright © 1969 and renewed 1997 by Maya Angelou, from *I Know Why The Caged Bird Sings* by Maya Angelou. Used by permission of Random House, Inc. Any third party use of this material, outside of this publication, is prohibited. Interested parties must apply directly to Random House, Inc. for permission.

Dan Ariely, "Why We Lie" adapted in *The Wall Street Journal*, May 26, 2012 from *The Honest Truth about Dishonesty*. Copyright © 2012 by Dan Ariely. Reprinted by permission of HarperCollins Publishers.

Russell Baker, "The Plot against People" from *The New York Times*, June 18, 1968. Copyright © 1968 by The New York Times. All rights reserved. Used by permission and protected by the Copyright Laws of the United States. The printing, copying, redistribution, or retransmission of the Material without express written permission is prohibited. "Russell Baker on Writing" from "Computer Fallout" from *The New York Times Magazine*, October 11, 1987. Reprinted by permission of Don Congdon Associates, Inc. Copyright © 1987 by Russell Baker.

Dave Barry, "Batting Clean-Up and Striking Out," copyright © 1988 by Dave Barry, from *Dave Barry's Greatest Hits*. Used by permission of Crown Publishers, a division of Random House, Inc. Any third party use of this material, outside of this publication, is prohibited. Interested parties must apply directly to Random House, Inc. for permission. "Dave Barry on Writing" from Gale Group. Contemporary Authors Online. © Gale, a part of Cengage Learning, Inc. Reproduced by permission. *www.cengage.com/permissions*.

Christopher Beam, "Blood Loss" from *Slate*, Jan. 5, 2011, copyright © 2011 by The Slate Group. All rights reserved. Used by permission and protected by the Copyright Laws of the United States. The printing, copying, redistribution, or retransmission of the Material without express written permission is prohibited.

Sven Birkerts, "Ladder" from *The Other Walk: Essays*. Copyright © 2011 by Sven Birkerts. Reprinted with the permission of The Permissions Company, Inc. on behalf of Graywolf Press, Minneapolis, Minnesota, *www.graywolfpress.org*.

Judy Brady. "I Want a Wife." Copyright © 1970 by Judy Brady. Reprinted with the permission of the author.

Suzanne Britt. "Neat People vs. Sloppy People" from *Show and Tell* (1982). Reprinted by permission of the author. "Suzanne Britt on Writing" reprinted by permission of the author.

Michael Chabon, "XO9" from *Manhood for Amateurs*, copyright © 2009 by Michael Chabon. Reprinted by permission of HarperCollins Publishers and HarperCollins Publishers Ltd. All rights reserved. From an interview by Carolyn Kellogg published as "Michael Chabon Q&A: Fatherhood and Writing at Midnight" by Carolyn Kellogg, from the *Los Angeles Times*, Oct. 13, 2009, copyright © 2009 Los Angeles Times. Reprinted with permission.

Linda Chavez. "Supporting Family Values" *townhall.com*, Friday, April 17, 2009. By permission of Linda Chavez and Creators Syndicate, Inc.

Charles Colson with Anne Morse. "Gay 'Marriage': Societal Suicide" from *Breakpoint*, copyright © 2013. Reprinted with permission of Prison Fellowship, *www.breakpoint.org*.

Meghan Daum, "Narcissist—Give It a Rest" from the *Los Angeles Times*, Jan. 6, 2011, and from "Kids, Do Your Own Homework" from the *Los Angeles Times*, April 21, 2011. Reprinted by permission of the author.

Guillermo del Toro and Chuck Hogan. "Why Vampires Never Die" from *The New York Times*, copyright © July 13, 2009 by The New York Times. All rights reserved. Used by permission and protected by the Copyright Laws of the United States. The printing, copying, redistribution, or retransmission of the Material without express written permission is prohibited.

Junot Díaz, "The Dreamer," first published in *More* magazine, copyright © 2011 by Junot Díaz. "Becoming a Writer" first published in *O, The Oprah Magazine*. Reprinted by permission of the author c/o Nicole Aragi.

Gloria Naylor. "The Meanings of a Word" (editors' title; originally titled "A Word's Meaning Can Often Depend on Who Says It") from *The New York Times Magazine* (February 20, 1986). Reprinted by permission of SLL/Sterling Lord Literistic, Inc. Copyright by Gloria Naylor.

George Orwell. "Shooting an Elephant" from *A Collection of Essays* by George Orwell. Copyright 1950 by Sonia Brownell Orwell and renewed © 1978 by Sonia Pitt-Rivers. Reprinted by permission of Houghton Mifflin Harcourt. All rights reserved. George Orwell, "George Orwell on Writing" excerpted from "Why I Write" from *Such, Such Were the Joys* by George Orwell. Copyright 1953 by Sonia Brownell Orwell and renewed 1981 by Mrs. George K. Perutz, Mrs. Miriam Gross, and Dr. Michael Dickson, executors of the Estate of Sonia Brownell Orwell, reprinted by permission of Houghton Mifflin Harcourt Publishing Company. All rights reserved.

Robert Parker, "Our Zombies, Ourselves" first published in *The Atlantic* magazine, Feb. 24, 2011. Copyright © 2011 by The Atlantic Media Co. All rights reserved. Distributed by Tribune Media Services.

Katha Pollitt. "What's Wrong with Gay Marriage?" (editors' title; originally titled "Adam and Steve—Together at Last"), *The Nation*, December 15, 2003. Copyright © 2003 by Katha Pollitt. Reprinted with the permission of the author.

Francine Prose, "What Words Can Tell" (editors' title) from pages 15–19 of *Reading Like a Writer* by Francine Prose. Copyright © 2006 by Francine Prose. Reprinted by permission of HarperCollins Publishers.

Anna Quindlen. "Homeless" and from "In the Beginning," from *Living Out Loud* by Anna Quindlen, copyright © 1988 by Anna Quindlen. Used by permission of Random House, Inc. Any third party use of this material, outside of this publication, is prohibited. Interested parties must apply directly to Random House, Inc. for permission. Electronic rights by permission of International Creative Management.

David Sedaris. "Remembering My Childhood in Africa" and "Nutcracker.com" from *Me Talk Pretty One Day* by David Sedaris. Copyright © 2000 by David Sedaris. By permission of Little, Brown and Company. All rights reserved. Electronic use by permission of Don Congdon Associates, Inc.

Brent Staples. "Black Man and Public Spaces" published in *Harper's* magazine, December 1986. Used by permission of the author.

Amy Tan. "Fish Cheeks." Copyright © 1987 by Amy Tan. First appeared in *Seventeen Magazine*. Reprinted by permission of the author and the Sandra Dijkstra Literary Agency.

Deborah Tannen. "But What Do You Mean?" text (as adapted in the October 1994 issue of *Redbook* magazine) from *Talking from 9 to 5* by Deborah Tannen. Copyright © 1994 by Deborah Tannen. Reprinted by permission of HarperCollins. Electronic use by permission of International Creative Management. Deborah Tannen, from "Forum: The Inevitability of the Personal," *PMLA*, (1996): 1151–52. Reprinted by permission of the Modern Language Association of America.

Sarah Vowell. "Shooting Dad" reprinted with the permission of Simon & Schuster Inc. from *Take the Canoli* by Sarah Vowell. Copyright © 2000 by Sarah Vowell. All rights reserved. Electronic rights by permission of Bresnick Weil Literary Agency, LLC.

Sheila Weller, "Maya Angelou on Writing" excerpted from Sheila Weller, "Work in Progress/Maya Angelou," from *Intellectual Digest*, June 1973. Reprinted with the permission of Sheila Weller.

E. B. White. "Once More to the Lake" from *One Man's Meat*, text copyright © 1941 by E. B. White. Copyright renewed. Reprinted by permission of Tilbury House, Publishers, Gardiner, Maine. Electronic rights by permission of International Creative Management. All rights reserved. Excerpts from pp. 84–85, 649–650 from *Letters of E. B. White*, Revised Edition, Originally edited by Dorothy Lobrano Guth. Revised and updated by Martha White. Copyright © 2006 by White Literary LLC. Reprinted by permission of HarperCollins Publishers.

Jeff Wise, "Deadly Mind Traps" by Jeff Wise from *Reader's Digest*, July/August 2012, pp. 102–07, 180–81. Originally published in different form in *Psychology Today*, Jan./Feb. 2012 issue. Reprinted with permission from *Reader's Digest* by Jeff Wise.

Visual Images

Page 24: Robin Rayne Nelson.

Page 92: From *Point Your Face at This* by Demetri Martin. Copyright © 2013 by Demitri Martin. By permission of Grand Central Publishing. All rights reserved.

Page 128: Photograph © Margaret Morton © OmbraLuce LLC.

Page 170: © Glen Le Lievre/The New Yorker Collection/www.cartoonbank.com.

Page 204: Grant Wood, American, 1891–1942, *American Gothic*, 1930, Oil on Beaver Board, 78 × 65.3 cm (30 3/4 × 25 3/4 in.), Friends of American Art Collection, 1930.934, The Art Institute of Chicago. Photography © The Art Institute of Chicago. Art © Figge Art Museum, successors to the Estate of Nan Wood Graham/Licensed by VAGA, New York, NY.

Page 204: © CORBIS.

Page 242: © Wally McNamee/CORBIS

Page 282: © Roz Chast/The New Yorker Collection/www.cartoonbank.com.

Page 318: © 2012 National Public Radio, Inc. Graphic from NPR news report titled "How the Poor, the Middle Class, and the Rich Spend Their Money" was originally published on *NPR.org* on August 1, 2012, and is used with permission of NPR. Any unauthorized duplication is strictly prohibited.

Page 362: © Mike Luckovich. Used with permission of Mike Luckovich and Creators Syndicate. All rights reserved.

Page 402: United States Army.

Page 438: Courtesy of Adbusters Media Foundation.

INDEX

Page numbers in bold type refer to definitions in the glossary, Useful Terms.

Advertisement
  argument and persuasion in an, 438
  "Corporate America Flag" (Adbusters Media Foundation), 438
  definition in an, 402
  "Evolution" (Dove), 🄴
  in MLA list of works cited, 82
  "There's Strong . . . " (US Army), 402
Agreement
  pronoun-antecedent, 46–47, 248
  subject-verb, 46
Alexie, Sherman, 494
  Sherman Alexie on Writing, 499–500
  "Superman and Me," 494–97
Allude, allusion, 562
"America's Foreign Born in the Last 50 Years" (US Census Bureau), 🄴
American Gothic (painting by Grant Wood), 134, 204
Analogy, 562
  argument and persuasion and, 447
  comparison and contrast and, 207
Analyze, analysis, 16, 32, 563. *See also* Division or analysis; Process analysis
  argument and persuasion and, 441
  comparison and contrast and, 212
  critical reading and, 16
  critical thinking with, 285
  of essay, 18–22
  mixing other methods with, 492
  of visual image, 25
Anaya, Rosie, 4, 6, 12, 13–15, 30–31, 47, 57, 58, 62, 83
  "Best Kept Secret on Campus, The," 69, 84–88, 558–60
  "Mental Illness on Television," 47–55, 59, 62
  Rosie Anaya on Writing, 88–90
Anecdote, 37, 563
  example and, 174
  in narration, 94
  Staples on, 200
Angelou, Maya, 96, 97, 104
  "Champion of the World," 104–07
  Maya Angelou on Writing, 108–09
Annotated bibliography, 289–90
APA (American Psychological Association) style, 547–58
  case study in (Thibodeau), 101–03
  guides to models, 548, 552
  parenthetical citations, 548–51
  reference list, 551–58

sample pages from research paper in (Anaya), 558–60
Appeals, 563
  emotional, 443, 563
  ethical, 443, 563
  rational, 443, 563
Archaisms, 566
Argument and persuasion, 439–89, 563
  in academic writing, 451–53
  additional writing topics for, 489
  in an advertisement, 438
  analogy in, 447
  analysis in, 441
  appeals in, 443
  assumptions in, 443–44, 451
  audience and, 441, 450
  authority and, 446
  checklist for revising, 450–51
  claims and, 441–42
  conclusion and, 449
  critical thinking about, 440
  data or grounds in, 442
  deductive reasoning in, 444–45
  description and, 131
  elements of, 441–44
  emotional appeal in, 443
  ethical appeal in, 443
  evaluation and, 441
  evidence in, 442–43, 451
  generalization in, 444
  in an image, 439
  inductive reasoning in, 444
  inference and, 441
  logical fallacies and, 445–47, 451
  major premise and, 444
  method of, 440–47
  minor premise and, 444
  mixing other methods with, 493
  narration and, 94
  objections, responses to, 449
  organization of, 448–49
  process of, 447–49
  in a proposal, 452–53
  purpose in, 440, 447–48
  rational appeal in, 443
  reasoning and, 444–47, 451
  subject and, 447–48
  syllogism in, 444–45
  synthesis and, 441
  in a textbook, 451–52
  thesis and, 441–42, 450
  tone and, 443, 449–50, 451
  Toulmin and, 441–44

Missing something? To access the online material that accompanies this text, visit **bedfordstmartins.com/ thebedfordreader**. Students who do not buy a new book can purchase access at this site.

Inside the Bedford Integrated Media for *The Brief Bedford Reader*

National Geographic, from *The Pine Ridge Community Storytelling Project* [oral histories]

Joan Didion, *The Santa Ana* [audio essay]

Luis Alberto Urrea, *Life on the Mississippi* [audio essay]

Fatawesome, *Cat-Friend vs. Dog-Friend* [video]

Dove, *Evolution* [video]

Jamaica Kincaid, *Girl* [audio short story]

US Census Bureau, *America's Foreign Born in the Last 50 Years* [infographic]

Bonnie Berkowitz and Laura Stanton, *Roller Coasters: Feeling Loopy* [interactive graphic]

Schroeder Jones, *Dr. Carmella's Guide to Understanding the Introverted* [cartoon]

Anne-Marie Slaughter, *Why Women Still Can't Have It All* [magazine feature]

Reader's Digest, *The Essay That Rocked the Internet* [quotations]

Andrew Cohen, *"Having It All"? How about "Doing the Best I Can"?* [blog entry]